POYNINGS' LAW
AND THE MAKING OF LAW IN IRELAND, 1660–1800

IN THIS SERIES*

ALSO AVAILABLE

The Irish Legal History Society (1989)

* Volumes 1–7 are published by Irish Academic Press.

Poynings' Law
and the making of law in Ireland, 1660–1800

JAMES KELLY

FOUR COURTS PRESS

in association with

THE IRISH LEGAL HISTORY SOCIETY

Typeset in 10.5pt on 12.5pt EhrhardtMt by
Carrigboy Typesetting Services for
FOUR COURTS PRESS LTD
7 Malpas Street, Dublin 8, Ireland
e-mail: info@fourcourtspress.ie
and in North America for
FOUR COURTS PRESS
c/o ISBS, 920 N.E. 58th Avenue, Suite 300, Portland, OR 97213.

A catalogue record for this title is available
from the British Library.

ISBN 978–1–84682–078–6

Printed by MPG Books Ltd, Bodmin, Cornwall.

Contents

Illustrations

appearing between pages 244 and 245

Tables

Acknowledgements

IT IS A PLEASURE FORMALLY to acknowledge the friends, colleagues, archivists, librarians, institutions and publishers without whose support, counsel and assistance this study might not have been completed. First among those to whom acknowledgement is due is the Royal Irish Academy, since it was the award by this body of a 'small grant' in aid of research that permitted the initial exploration of the records of the English/British Privy Council. This convinced me that an extended study of the impact of Poynings' Law would provide a valuable perspective on the operation of the Irish parliament in the eighteenth century. Having arrived at this conclusion, the challenge was to find the time and resources necessary to explore the large corpus of material generated by the Council, to locate the surviving traces of its Irish equivalent and to examine the records of the Irish parliament. This endeavour was funded initially from personal resources. More recently, welcome support has been provided by a number of grants in aid of research from the Research Committee of St Patrick's College.

I am grateful for helpful guidance and advice from the staffs of the archives and libraries, which have assisted with this project – particularly the Cregan Library, St Patrick's College; the National Archives, Public Record Office; the Gilbert Library, Dublin Public Libraries; the Departments of Manuscripts and Early Printed Books, Trinity College Dublin; the National Library of Ireland; the British Library, and the Beinecke Library, Yale University. I wish also to thank the owners, custodians, trustees and keepers of manuscripts consulted in the care of the National Archives, Public Record Office; the British Library; the Library of Congress; the National Archives of Ireland; the National Library of Ireland; the National Library of Scotland; the Public Record Office of Northern Ireland; Suffolk Record Office; the Manuscript Department, Trinity College Dublin; the Beinecke and Sterling libraries of Yale University; and the other libraries and repositories cited in the bibliography for facilitating and permitting access to the collections upon which this study is grounded.

The final stages in the preparation of this manuscript have taken place while the author is embarked with Professor David Hayton, Dr John Bergin and Dr Andrew Sneddon in preparing a database of Irish legislation, 1692–1800 funded by the Leverhulme Trust; this study antedates the latter project, but it should be seen as complementary, and I wish to express my gratitude to my colleagues in this undertaking. Assistance in respect of specific queries or references were provided by Mr James McGuire, Dr John Bergin, Professor David Hayton, Dr Marie-Louise Legg, Dr A.P.W. Malcomson, Professor Nial Osborough, Dr Neal Garnham, Dr Ivar McGrath and Dr Desmond McCabe. My grateful thanks also to Dr Bergin, Dr McGrath and Mr McGuire for reading the text in whole or in part and for suggestions for improvement. Thanks are due also to Paul Murphy for his photographical expertise, to Professor Raymond Gillespie, Dr Bernadette Cunningham and Dr Toby Barnard for their counsel and encouragement, and to my departmental colleagues, Diarmaid Ferriter, Dáire Keogh, Carla King, Marian Lyons and Matthew Stout for their fellowship and congeniality. Most of all, I must, once again, avow my personal indebtedness to Judith Brady, and Eva and James Kelly for the unconscious generosity with which they have allowed me to pursue this subject when they had stronger calls to my time and attention.

Abbreviations

Add. MS	Additional Manuscript
BL	British Library
Cal. HO papers	*Calendar of Home Office papers, 1760–75* (4 vols, London, 1878–99)
Cal. SP (Dom.)	*Calendar of state papers, Domestic series*
Cal. SP (Irl.)	*Calendar of state Papers, Ireland series*
Commons Jn. (Irl.)	*Journal of the House of Commons of the Kingdom of Ireland, 1613–1800* (21 vols, Dublin, 1796–1802)
DNB	*Dictionary of National Biography*
EHR	*English Historical Review*
HMC	Historical Manuscripts Commission
Lords Jn. (Irl.)	*Journal of the House of Lords of the Kingdom of Ireland* (8 vols, Dublin, 1782–1800)
IHS	*Irish Historical Studies*
MS(S)	Manuscript(s)
NA	The National Archives, Public Record Office
NAI	National Archives of Ireland
NLI	National Library of Ireland
PC	Privy Council
PRONI	Public Record Office of Northern Ireland
QUB	Queen's University, Belfast
RIA proc.	*Royal Irish Academy, Proceedings*
TCD	Trinity College, Dublin
UCD	University College, Dublin

Introduction

'AN ACT THAT NO PARLIAMENT BE holden in this land until the acts be certified into England' or Poynings' Law, to accord it its more familiar title, remained a live measure on the Irish statute book for just over three centuries from its enactment in 1494.[1] Though the subject of significant amendment in the sixteenth century and profoundly altered in 1782, it became legislatively redundant only when the Irish parliament passed out of existence on 1 January 1801. Prior to that date, Poynings' Law served, during its earlier 'executive' phase, which spanned the sixteenth and early seventeenth centuries, to restrict the legislative authority of the Irish executive and, during its subsequent 'parliamentary' phase, spanning the remainder of the seventeenth and the eighteenth centuries, to confine the freedom of the Irish legislature to make law. In keeping with a law of such obvious importance, Poynings' Law has figured prominently in the attempts by historians to describe the operations of the Irish parliament and to analyse Anglo-Irish relations. As a result, we possess a good understanding of the operation of the Law during its so-called 'executive' phase. By comparison, its 'parliamentary' phase has been explored only episodically. The purpose of this study is to redress this imbalance by examining the operation and impact of Poynings' Law on the legislative endeavour of the Irish parliament between the restoration of the monarchy in 1660 and the ratification in 1800 of the Anglo-Irish union.

THE HISTORIOGRAPHICAL AND EVIDENTIAL CONTEXT

The historiographical consensus that Poynings' Law operated unchanged between its enactment in December 1494 and the concession of 'legislative independence' in 1782 was exploded in the 1940s. In a number of articles published in the early issues of *Irish Historical Studies*, D.B. Quinn, T.W. Moody and R. Dudley Edwards established, in the words of the former, that the 'Law ... passed through various stages of interpretation and significance which require to be studied separately'.[2] Edwards and Moody were more explicit. They observed that

> the primary dividing-line in the history of the law falls between the parliaments of 1613–15 and 1634–5. Prior to 1634, parliament defended the law as a safeguard of its own interests, and it was the Irish executive that

---

1. 10 Henry VII, chap 4
2. D.B. Quinn, 'The early interpretation of Poynings' Law, 1494–1534', *IHS*, 2 (1940–1), pp 241–54, especially p. 241; R. Dudley Edwards and T.W. Moody, 'The history of Poynings' Law: part 1, 1494–1615', *IHS*, 2 (1940–1), pp 415–24.

found it an embarrassment. In 1634–5 the law was first used ... as a weapon
against parliamentary self-assertion ...[3]

There were, Edwards and Moody observed, further 'dividing-lines' within the
major 'stages' they established. Following Quinn, they identified 'the fall of the
House of Kildare in 1534, the permanent establishment of an English administration in Dublin, subject to constant supervision from London, and the
introduction of the English reformation into Ireland, with its profoundly
disturbing effects on the old English colony' as crucial influences on the operation
of the law. On these grounds, they divided their 'earlier period' – spanning the
years 1494–1615 – into 'two main phases: (i) 1494–1534, (ii) 1534–1615'.[4] And,
building on Quinn's pioneering reconstruction of the operation of the law during
the first of these phases, Edwards and Moody prepared 'a magisterial study' of the
operation of Poynings' Law to 1615.[5] Conceived of as the first of a two–part
assessment, the purpose of which was to trace the history of the Law from its
inception to the concession of legislative independence in 1782, the promised
exploration of the operation of the Law during the later period never materialised.
As a result, the history of Poynings' Law after 1615 lay uncharted until 1972 when
Aidan Clarke produced his forensic dissection of the application of the law during
the early seventeenth century in which he revealed how it was reinterpreted in the
1630s to confine the legislative initiative of parliament.[6]

Though Clarke's article implicitly invited others to pursue the history of
Poynings' Law beyond 1641, no work along these lines was produced during the
two decades that followed. Yet, the centrality of the act to an understanding of the
operation of the post-Restoration Irish parliament ensured that Poynings' Law
was not ignored, and most historians of government and administration in the
eighteenth century have engaged, sometimes at length, with the Law and the
heads of bill process that evolved in the late seventeenth century to allow the Irish
parliament some legislative initiative in the course of an assessment of the
restrictions under which the Irish parliament operated.[7] Similarly, every account
of the politics of patriotism has analysed how the law was perceived by its critics.[8]

---

3. Edwards and Moody, 'The history of Poynings' Law', p. 415.   4. Ibid., p. 416.
5. The phrase is Aidan Clarke's: see his 'The history of Poynings' Law, 1615–41', *IHS*, 18 (1972–3),
    p. 207.
6. Clarke, 'Poynings' Law, 1615–41', pp 207–22.
7. E.M. Johnston, *Great Britain and Ireland 1760–1800: a study in political administration* (Edinburgh,
    1963), pp 98–103; idem, *Ireland in the eighteenth century* (Dublin, 1974), pp 54–6; David Dickson,
    Ireland: new foundations, 1660–1800 (2nd ed., Dublin, 2000); F.G. James, *Ireland in the empire,
    1688–1770* (Cambridge, MA, 1973), pp 11–13, 262–3, 282–3; Gerard O'Brien, *Anglo-Irish politics in
    the age of Grattan and Pitt* (Dublin, 1987), pp 20–1, 28–31; R.E. Burns, *Irish parliamentary politics in
    the eighteenth century* (2 vols, Washington, 1989–90), i, 5–6; F.G. James, *Lords of the ascendancy: the
    Irish House of Lords and its members 1600–1800* (Dublin, 1995), pp 77–8; James Kelly, *Prelude to
    Union: Anglo-Irish politics in the 1780s* (Cork, 1992), pp 157–8, 235–6.
8. See, for example, O'Brien, *Anglo-Irish parties*, pp 32–44.

This has amplified understanding of the operation of Poynings' Law in many respects, but it has also meant that its constitutional and administrative dimensions have elicited less attention than its political implications, with the result that the evolution of the heads of bills process in the seventeenth century, and the precise impact of Poynings' Law on legislative practice in the eighteenth century have yet to be reconstructed.[9] It is noteworthy in this context that J.G. Simms's accounts of the making of the Bishops' Banishment act (1697) and the act to prevent the further growth of popery (1704) have produced few imitations,[10] and that both J.C. Beckett's analysis of the impact of the amendment of Poynings' Law in 1782, and Gerard O'Brien's briefer exploration of the response of the British Privy Council to legislation transmitted from Ireland in the 1760s and 1770s do not emulate the broad perspective that is one of the major strengths of writing on Poynings' Law in the sixteenth and seventeenth centuries.[11] Paradoxically, Poynings' Law has fared badly by comparison with the less consequential Declaratory Act, enacted at Westminster in 1720, which empowered the British parliament to make law for Ireland.[12]

9. The sole exception is the unsuccessful attempt by M.T. Hayden, 'The origin and development of heads of bills in the Irish parliament', *Journal of the Royal Society of Antiquaries of Ireland*, 55 (1925), pp 112–25. It is also noteworthy that the National Library of Ireland did not copy the relevant Irish material in the registers and unbound Privy Council papers when, in the 1950s and 1960s, it was engaged actively in assembling a microfilm record of manuscript material of Irish interest in foreign archives. The publication in the late 1960s by the List and Index Society of a photocopy of the rudimentary, hand-written catalogue of the unbound papers, then the main guide to their content, also animated little interest (The List and Index Society, *Privy Council Office: list of unbound papers preserved in the Public Record Office*: 3 vols, London, 1967–8).

10. J.G. Simms, 'The making of a penal law (2 Anne, c. 6), 1703–04', *IHS*, 12 (1960), pp 105–18; idem, 'The Bishops' Banishment act of 1697 (9 Will. III, c. 1)', *IHS*, 17 (1970), pp 185–99. A.P.W. Malcomson's exemplary article, 'The Newtown act of 1748: revision and reconstruction', *IHS*, 18 (1972–3), pp 313–44, adopts a different approach.

11. O'Brien, *Anglo-Irish politics*, pp 29–31; J.C. Beckett, 'Anglo-Irish constitutional relations in the later eighteenth century', *IHS*, 14 (1964), pp 20–38 reprinted in idem, *Confrontations* (London, 1972), pp 123–42. This criticism can also be made of the present author's essay on Poynings' Law on the 1760s in D.W. Hayton (ed.), *The Irish parliament in the eighteenth century: the long apprenticeship* (Edinburgh, 2001), pp 87–106.

12. J.C. Beckett, 'The Irish parliament in the eighteenth century', *Proceedings of the Belfast Natural History and Philosophical Society*, 2nd series, 4 (1951) pp 17–37; A.G. Donaldson, 'The application in Ireland of English and British legislation made before 1801 (PhD, QUB, 1952); A.G. Donaldson, *Some comparative aspects of Irish law* (London, 1957), pp 48–51; see also idem, 'Methods of applying English legislation in Ireland', *Bulletin of the Irish Committee of Historical Sciences*, no. 67 (1953), pp 4–5; Isolde Victory, 'The Declaratory Act of 1720' in Gerard O'Brien (ed.), *Parliament, politics and people: essays in eighteenth-century Irish history* (Dublin, 1989), pp 9–29; David Hayton, 'The Stanhope-Sunderland ministry and the repudiation of Irish independence', *EHR*, 93 (1999), pp 610–36. As well as the legislative initiatives that reached the statute book, Julian Hoppit has provided another dimension by tabulating those failed legislative initiatives at Westminster appertaining to Ireland: *Failed legislation, 1660–1800: extracted from the Commons and Lords journal* (London, 1997).

Recently, there have been signs of a renewed interest in the subject of parliament, its structures, membership and deliberations, symbolised by the devoting in 2001 of a special number of the journal *Parliamentary History* to the subject of the Irish parliament in the eighteenth century and by the publication in 2002 of a multi-volume *History of the Irish parliament, 1692–1800*.[13] The work of Patrick McNally on the structure of government and administration during the reign of George I, and by Ivar McGrath on the constitutional, administrative and political dimensions of the raising of revenue between 1692 and 1714 are equally indicative. Because both projects were pursued independently, it should be noted that McGrath's identification of the centrality of the 'compromise' of 1695 in defining the pattern of parliamentary government that operated in respect of the crucial function of raising revenue during the eighteenth century both anticipates and confirms the interpretation advanced here in respect of the generality of legislation.[14] In a more explicitly historiographical sense, McGrath's painstaking work on the revenue has encouraged others working on the law-making function of the Irish legislature. John Bergin's ongoing forensic exploration of the implications for Poynings' Law on legislative practice during the 1690s and 1700s is the most direct parallel to McGrath's study, while this author has pursued an attempt to assess the impact of Poynings' Law over a longer time frame.[15]

In any attempt to explain this historiographical pattern with respect to Poynings' Law in the late seventeenth and early eighteenth centuries, the doleful experience of the records of the Irish Privy Council is indisputably of significance. The fire that engulfed the Council Chamber in April 1711 and the destruction of the bulk of the records housed by the Public Record Office of Ireland in 1922 have ensured the near total loss of a potentially major archive.[16] An index of the heads

13. E.M. Johnston-Liik, *History of the Irish parliament, 1692–1800* (6 vols, Belfast, 2002); Hayton (ed.), *The Irish parliament in the eighteenth century*.

14. Patrick McNally, *Parties, patriots and undertakers: parliamentary politics in early Hanoverian Ireland* (Dublin, 1997), pp 29–30; Charles Ivar McGrath, *The making of the eighteenth-century Irish constitution: government, parliament and the revenue, 1692–1714* (Dublin, 2000).

15. John Bergin, 'Poynings' Law in the eighteenth century', *Pages: postgraduate research in progress* 1 (1994), pp 9–18; idem, 'The Quaker lobby and its influence on Irish legislation, 1692–1705', *Eighteenth-Century Ireland*, 19 (2004), pp 9–36; James Kelly, 'Monitoring the constitution: the operation of Poynings' Law in the 1760s' in Hayton (ed.), *The Irish parliament in the eighteenth century*, pp 87–106; idem, 'The making of law in eighteenth-century Ireland: the significance and import of Poynings' Law' in N.M. Dawson (ed.), *Reflections on law and history* (Dublin, 2006), pp 259–77. See also David Hayton, 'Patriots and legislators: Irishmen and their parliaments, *c.*1689–*c.*1740' in Julian Hoppit (ed.), *Parliaments, nations and identities in Britain and Ireland, 1660–1850* (Manchester, 2003), pp 83–102.

16. Compared with the conflagration of 1922, that of 1711 is little known, but as well as 'many of the papers' of the Privy Council that were consumed, the Surveyor's Office, and with it among other categories of manuscripts, the original Civil Surveys and much church matter were also incinerated ('Diary of Elizabeth Freke', *Journal of the Cork Historical and Archaeological Society*, 2nd series (1912), p. 153; Curtis to Bonnell, 17 Apr. 1711 (NLI, Smythe of Barbaville Papers, MS 41580/29); Bolton to King, 17 July 1712, King to Maule, 8 May 1722 (TCD, King Papers, MSS 1995–2008 f. 1433, MS 750/7 f. 106); Waite to Wilmot, 17 Dec. 1767 (PRONI, Wilmot Papers, T3019/5641).

of bills, 1711–82, and transmisses, 1753–80, communicated from the Irish Council to its British equivalent escaped the second inferno, but it has passed all but unnoticed, and, at any event, is no substitute for the original bills and allied supporting materials.[17] The letters accompanying bills transmitted from the Irish to the English/British Council have fared better; nothing close to a complete series exists, but broken sequences can be constructed from those that survive in the state papers, the unbound papers of the British Council and, more erratically, in the surviving papers of British solicitors and attorneys general.[18]

In sharp contrast, the English (from 1707 British) Privy Council is well served archivally. Its main component is the formal minutes of the Council and its committees, spanning the years 1661 to 1800, which are preserved in one hundred large registers. When this bureaucratic regime operated efficiently, as it did from the 1690s, these imposing volumes provide a dependable guide to the experience at the Council Board of virtually every measure received from Ireland; they indicate whether a bill was respited, postponed, laid aside or passed unaltered; and they list the amendments sanctioned at the Council board for incorporation in those measures deemed appropriate to become law.[19] Unfortunately, because of the manner in which amendments are cited, they are not always amenable to easy interpretation.

Ideally, in order to achieve maximum understanding of the history of Irish legislation at the English/British Council Board, the evidential record would embrace the engrossed bill and the accompanying letter prepared at the Irish Privy Council and, when they were written, the letters written by lords justices and lords lieutenant; the minute of the bill's receipt and referral by the Council or Irish bills' committee to the Crown law officers or, when this option was chosen, to other bodies; a copy of any petition or protest offered against the measure and a record of any hearings held as a result; the report or reports of the law officers and, where applicable, of other bodies; the report of the Irish bills' committee; the minute of the decision of the full Council; and, in the case of those bills it was adjudged were appropriate to receive the royal assent, the order-in-council directing the attorney general to cause the bill to be delivered to the clerk of the crown who was 'required to engross the same with [the authorised] alterations and amendments in order to pass the great seal of England'; and the commission or warrant prepared subject to the supervision of the lord chancellor empowering 'the lord lieutenant of Ireland to give the royal assent to [the] said bill in case the same should be agreed upon in the parliament of Ireland'.[20] However, there is no instance in which all of these records are extant, and the category to have suffered most is the original parchment bills transmitted from Ireland. According to the Record Commission report for 1800, pre–1782 bills were then kept with the

17. NAI, Index to heads of bills, 1711–82, and transmisses, 1753–80 (Location, IA.52.155).
18. NA, SP63, SP67; PC1; BL, Hardwicke Papers, Add. MS 36136 ff 200–7, MS 36138 ff 219–20.
19. The Privy Council Registers are in The National Archives: Public Record Office, PC2/55–155.
20. The quotation is taken from orders in council issued in 1703, 1704 and 1760 (NA, C183/2).

records of the clerk of the Crown in the Crown Office. Since they were seldom required, they were not readily accessible, and it is to be assumed that this had some bearing on the fact that they were allowed to fall into decay or were destroyed sometime thereafter. The net result is that, other than a smattering of survivals, or paper copies, only those for the 1634–5 session exist.[21]

The fate of the other categories of records generated at the English/British Council Board is less bleak. A complete run of the orders in council authorising the royal assent for bills between 1703 and 1800 survive in the chancery records in the National Archives,[22] and a smaller selection spanning the years 1738 to 1755 is to be found in the papers of Philip Yorke, first earl of Hardwicke, who was successively solicitor general (1720–4), attorney general (1724–34) and lord chancellor (1737–64).[23] Copies of the commissions issued by the clerk of the Crown empowering the lord lieutenant of Ireland to give the royal assent to those bills that were returned also survive enrolled on the dorse of patent rolls.[24] The notes of the clerks of the council that provide the basis for the formal minutes now contained in the registers also exist; dating from 1670, they are bound in four bulky volumes, whose rude format does not facilitate easy use.[25] There are, in addition, stray copies of the reports made by the law officers and minutes of the Irish bills committee in the surviving private papers of individual officers and in significant numbers in the unbound Privy Council papers.[26] They are not commonplace before 1760, but taken together with the extensive formal minutes preserved in the registers, which constitute a full and dependable guide to the decisions of the Council, and the accounts and proceedings to be found on occasions in the private and official correspondence of members of the Dublin and London executives, it is possible to construct a detailed analysis of the fate of Irish legislation at the British Council.

This is an important element of this study. But it aspires also to establish the implications of Poynings' Law for legislative practice in general and, more specifically, to identify its impact on the law-making activity of both houses of the Irish parliament. This has involved reconstructing the legislative activities of the Irish parliament from the printed journals of the Commons and Lords, and

---

21. The bills of the 1634–5 session can be found in NA, C86. Copies of the acts for this session were enrolled on the parliamentary rolls (C65/191C, 193) but this practice was not continued. The information presented here about the fate of the Irish bills is taken from the introduction to this document class. Information on surviving bills will be included on the Irish Legislation database currently in preparation, but copies of five bills exist in parchment in NA, SP66, Case B. I am thankful to John Bergin for drawing these to my notice.

22. NA, C183/1–2. These two bundles deal respectively with the years 1760–1800 and 1703–60. It is not apparent why they do not follow the more obvious and logical sequence. The orders in council list the amendments approved at the English/British Council Board.

23. BL, Hardwicke Papers, Add. MSS 35872–4.

24. NA, C66. These are largely formulaic, and do not include the text of the bills.

25. Minutes [*sic*] of the clerks of the Council, 1670–1776, 1764–95 (NA, PC4/1–4).

26. NA, PC1 passim.

amplifying this evidential trail with the manuscript record. As this corresponds with a number of phases in the history of the Irish parliament and in the application of Poynings' Law, it has encouraged the employment of a variety of approaches. The study opens with a reconstruction of the legislative histories of the parliaments held in the period 1660–99, when the Irish legislature established its entitlement to initiate legislation. Such an approach is appropriate for this phase, despite the substantial number of bills and heads of bills that were prepared, since the procedures of both the English and Irish Privy Councils were still at a formative stage, and the pattern of law making identifiable then does not lend itself to systematic statistical analysis. However, once it became normative for the Irish parliament to meet regularly, and to initiate legislation in the form of heads of bills, and the English/British Council streamlined its administrative practices, the process of law making is more amenable to a quantitative analysis that permits a statistical examination of the impact of the English/British Council and, indirectly, of the Irish Council on the pattern of law-making in eighteenth-century Ireland. This informs the approach taken with respect of the period 1703–82, and the era of legislative independence, 1782–1800.

The gaps in the documentation, notwithstanding, a quantitative analysis of the operation of Poynings' Law *post* 1703 without a complementary detailed engagement with the application of the act, as well as of the motives and aspirations of those responsible for its administration, must be unsatisfactory. By identifying and following the course of each legislative initiative, it is possible to offer a general perspective on the problems encountered by legislation, to establish the concerns of privy councillors and representatives, and to identify trends and patterns in both kingdoms. While this is useful in and of itself, it is also highly revealing of the operation of the Irish parliament as a legislature, of the meaning of 'legislative dependence' *ante* 1782, and of 'legislative independence' thereafter. No less pertinently, though the task is more problematical, it is possible to reconstruct the role performed by the Irish Council and, by comparing the number of heads of bills forwarded from the Irish Lords and Commons with those received by the British Privy Council, to calculate the proportion of bills that failed at the Irish Council. The identification of the response of the Irish legislature to amendments introduced at the British Council requires less ingenuity, but it is no less critical to an understanding the legislative significance of Poynings' Law. Ironically, contrary to the strongly held perception in eighteenth-century Ireland, and since, the practice of submitting petitions to the British Council Board indicates that the procedures provided for by Poynings' Law were not universally regarded in a negative light; it has been claimed that they were perceived by some, and by the Irish Catholic lobby in particular, in the words of Patrick Fagan, as 'a blessing in disguise'.[27] This is hardly a rounded assessment of Catholic attitudes, and others

---

27. Patrick Fagan, *Catholics in a Protestant country: the papist constituency in eighteenth-century Dublin* (Dublin, 1998), p. 73; Jacqueline Hill, 'Convergence and conflict in eighteenth-century Ireland', *Historical Journal*, 44 (2001), p. 1041.

were distinctly more ambivalent. Yet the acceptance by the Irish parliament during the eighteenth century that a high proportion of its legislation would be amended or respited at the English/British and Irish Councils underlines, what Quinn, Moody and Edwards have identified for the sixteenth century, that Poynings' Law generated opportunities as well as difficulties, and that it did not always operate as anticipated or have the expected effects.

POYNINGS' LAW, 1494–1641

While it is a legal (and historical) commonplace that the interpretation of law is seldom static, the potential for interpretation and reinterpretation of a crucial statute such as Poynings' Law was enhanced by the haste with which it was drafted. The precise circumstances are elusive, but the suggestion of Steven Ellis that 'the act was simply abstracted from the instructions given' to Sir Edward Poynings may explain the infelicitous wording and awkward syntax that are a feature of the measure.[28] It runs as follows:

> That at the next parliament that there shall be holden by the king's command-ment and licence (wherein, amongst other, the king's grace intendeth to have a general resumption of his whole revenues since the last day of the reign of King Edward the Second[29]) no parliament be holden hereafter in the said land but at such season as the king's lieutenant and council there first do certify the king, under the great seal of that land, the causes and consider-ations and all such acts as them seemeth should pass in the said parliament; and such causes, considerations and acts affirmed by the king and his council to be good and expedient for that land and his licence thereupon (as well in affirmation of the said causes and acts, as to summon the said parliament) under his great seal of England had and obtained, that done, a parliament to be had and holden after the form and effect afore rehearsed; and if any parliament be holden in that land hereafter contrary to the form and provision aforesaid, it be deemed void and of none effect in law.[30]

Its inelegance, notwithstanding, this enactment was pregnant with implication for the government of Ireland. For whether one favours Ellis's assessment that it was 'part of a reforming legislative programme of political and constitutional import' or Richardson's and Sayles's asseveration that it was 'an opportunist and transient expedient', it is indisputable that it was 'designed to strengthen royal control over the Irish parliament as a legislature'.[31]

---

28. S.G. Ellis, *Ireland in the age of the Tudors, 1447–1603: English expansion and the end of Gaelic rule* (London, 1998), p. 93.
29. Edward II died in 1327.   30. 10 Henry VII, chap 4.
31. S.G. Ellis, *Reform and revival: English government in Ireland, 1470–1534* (Woodbridge and New

This was necessary because the Anglo-Irish feudal magnates, who administered the Lordship of Ireland on behalf of the Crown, demonstrated an unwelcome readiness to comfort enemies of the ruling Tudor dynasty and to give priority to the pursuit of their own strategic objectives over those of the Crown. The most alarming episode of this kind occurred in 1487, when Lambert Simnel, a pretender to the throne, was crowned Edward VI in Dublin with the support of, among others, Gearóid Mór, the eighth earl of Kildare, who was acting deputy for Henry VII's son. Kildare was more circumspect when Perkin Warbeck sought to press a similar claim in the early 1490s, but it was insufficient to deflect suspicion. Determined to protect his Irish flank, Henry VII instructed Sir Edward Poynings to take Kildare's place in Ireland in September 1494. Poynings arrived in Ireland some time later, accompanied by a sizeable number of civilian administrators and soldiers, to pursue his dual strategy of reducing the country to obedience and introducing a series of constitutional and administrative reforms.[32] He was less successful than anticipated, but the parliament he convened at Drogheda late in 1494 has been described as a 'watershed' between medieval and early modern Ireland for a variety of reasons of which the measure known as 'Poynings' Law' is one of the most important.[33]

An act that no parliament be holden in this land until the acts be certified into England was the fourth of forty-nine items of legislation approved by the busy parliament of 1494–5.[34] Prompted by the Crown's determination to prevent a repeat of the situation that had arisen in 1487, the bill sought to ensure that a parliament could not be convened in Ireland for the purpose of recognising a pretender to the throne, or for any other purpose, by restricting the capacity both of the king's deputy to call a parliament and the parliament's authority to make law. Specifically, the act ordained firstly that no parliament could legally be convened without the prior communication from the king's lieutenant and Council in Ireland of 'the causes and considerations' requiring such an assembly, and the certification under the great seal of England by the King in Council that the reasons proffered were acceptable. And secondly, Poynings' Law directed that 'acts' communicated from the Council in Ireland could only become law if they were deemed 'good and expedient' by the King in Council.[35] These restrictions on the freedom of action of the king's lieutenant or his deputy in Ireland and on the legislative authority of the Irish parliament were augmented by complementary

York, 1986), p. 149; H.G. Richardson and G.O. Sayles, *The Irish parliament in the Middle Ages* (Philadelphia, 1964), p. 279.

32. This account draws on Ellis, *Ireland in the age of the Tudors*, pp 90–3; Richardson and Sayles, *The Irish parliament*, pp 269–75.

33. Jocelyn Otway-Ruthven, *A history of medieval Ireland* (London, 1968), p. 408; Ellis, *Reform and revival*, p. 209; Richardson and Sayles, *The Irish parliament*, p. 280.

34. For the best guide see Edmund Curtis, 'The acts of the Drogheda parliament, 1494–5, or "Poynings' Laws"' in Agnes Conway, *Henry VII's relations with Scotland and Ireland, 1485–1498* (Cambridge, 1932), pp 118–43.

35. 10 Henry VII, chap 4; Ellis, *Ireland in the age of the Tudors*, pp 92–3.

regulations that provided that major offices could be held during pleasure only, and not for life as was previously the practice.[36]

While these regulations achieved their aim of strengthening royal influence in the Lordship of Ireland by limiting that of the king's lieutenant, it was soon apparent that Poynings' Law was administratively inflexible as well as politically confining. It did not, for instance, provide for the transmission of additional bills from Ireland, or from the English Council to Ireland, after a licence to hold a parliament in Ireland had been issued or a parliament was convened. This problem was alleviated by separating the request for a commission to hold parliament from the transmission of bills, but this was not always appropriate.[37] As a result, it may be that a number of measures were enrolled between 1498 and 1516 that 'had not been formally transmitted from England'.[38] This was not consistent with the Law, but even when the practice of relying on Anglo-Irish magnates was abandoned following the Kildare Rebellion of 1534 and the reins of power in Ireland were vested thereafter in English appointees, neither careful management nor refinements to administrative procedures could surmount all the problems attributable to the restrictive requirements of Poynings' Law. Delays proved especially frustrating in the 1530s and 1560s, when the Catholic interest insisted on the precise application of the statute to frustrate the advancement of unwelcome religious and other legislation. To counter this, the Irish administration sought repeatedly to modify or to suspend Poynings' Law, and temporary suspensions were sanctioned on two occasions (1536, 1569). On other occasions the letter of the Law was infringed; so it was appropriate that it was determined in 1557 to legalise the practice whereby bills, communicated by the viceroy and Council after the licence to convene parliament had been issued, could on their return from the English Council become law in the usual way.[39] This amending act also served to clarify the operation of the 1494 act in several additional respects by establishing that the monarch was not obliged, as his deputy in Ireland was, to consult his Council; by asserting the crown's right to amend bills received from Ireland; and by explicitly restricting 'the legislative competence of the Irish parliament to such bills as had been approved by the King in the prescribed form'. This did not preclude the Irish parliament from amending bills submitted to it, or initiating new bills, but the latter only acquired legal status when they were transmitted by the Irish Council to England in due form.[40]

While such statutory refinements assisted in the process of law making for Ireland, and affirmed the subordination of the Irish parliament and Council to the King in Council in England – a point underlined by the fact that the latter could

36. Ellis, *Ireland in the age of the Tudors*, p. 93.
37. Quinn, 'The early interpretation', pp 245–8; Edwards and Moody, 'Poynings' Law', p. 417; Aidan Clarke, 'Colonial constitutional attitudes in Ireland 1640–60', *RIA proc.*, 90C (1990), p. 365.
38. Quinn, 'The early interpretation', p. 252.
39. Edwards and Moody, 'The history of Poynings' Law', pp 418–19; Ellis, *Ireland in the age of the Tudors*, pp 144, 294; Clarke, 'Colonial constitutional attitudes', p. 365.
40. Edwards and Moody, 'The history of Poynings' Law', pp 420–1; 3 & 4 Philip and Mary, chap 4.

add to as well as veto legislation transmitted from Ireland – the Irish parliament was unwilling to become a mere cipher of either the Irish executive or the Crown.[41] The practice whereby legislation was generated in response to a request by the Irish Commons, employed fictively as early as 1498, acquired more substantive reality during the sixteenth century. MPs were prepared to shelter behind Poynings' Law, as in 1585, when it was their primary protection against the efforts of an assertive executive to advance unpalatable legislation.[42] However, their determination to secure an active role in law making was equally strong, and members asserted their right to amend and to initiate bills 'within the framework of the Poynings' Law system' in the 1613–15 parliament. In so far as can be established, private bills 'seem generally to have originated with parliament' at this time. There were suggestions also that public bills might also take their rise there, but peers and MPs only hesitantly offered 'drafts' rather than titles, which was the established practice, and the early dissolution of the parliament inhibited the development at this point of the later practice of initiating legislation in the form of heads of bills.[43]

The changes in the manner in which Poynings' Law was applied and interpreted between its enactment and the 1613–15 parliament are revealing of the operation of the early modern Irish parliament, but such variations in practice as took place were within a framework whose purpose was to curb the Irish executive. Hints offered in the run up to the 1613–15 parliament that this was no longer adequate, and that the law might have to be amended to reflect this fact were reflexively resisted in England, and the prospect of significant change was not assisted when Lord Deputy Falkland's failure to interpret Poynings' Law correctly ensured that it was not possible to convene an Irish parliament to ratify the Graces in 1629. The insistence at this time that the correct 'forms for calling a parliament' in Ireland should be adhered to reinforced James I's refusal to accede to the request of the Lord Deputy, Arthur Chichester, to suspend Poynings' Law in respect of private bills in 1612, and underlined the Crown's reliance upon this Law to control the law-making process in Ireland. If this was advisable in the case of Lord Deputy Falkland, whose inability to negotiate the procedural requirements preparatory to convening a parliament did not promote confidence in his political skill or judgement, it was manifestly unnecessary in the case of his successor, Thomas Wentworth, who was a zealous proponent of strong monarchical government. He turned Poynings' Law on its head in 1634–5 by demonstrating that 'a measure originally intended to limit the power of the Irish government to manipulate the Irish parliament [could] be used to empower the government to regulate the proceedings of parliament in minute detail'.[44]

41. Clarke, 'Colonial constitutional attitudes', p. 365.
42. Quinn, 'The early interpretation', pp 249–50; Edwards and Moody, 'The history of Poynings' Law', pp 420–1.
43. Edwards and Moody, 'The history of Poynings' Law', pp 422–3; Clarke, 'Colonial constitutional attitudes', p. 365, n 55.
44. Clarke, 'Poynings' Law 1615–41', pp 207–9, 211.

Wentworth did this by extending to all nobility Arthur Chichester's denial of the request by Catholic noblemen in the run-in to the 1613–15 parliament to be consulted on the legislation that was to be sent from the Irish Council to England, and by asserting the sole authority of the 'lord deputy and council' in Ireland 'for the framing and drawing up any acts to pass in parliament'. He acknowledged in a statement to the House of Lords that peers had the authority 'to represent to the lord deputy and council … such public considerations as they shall think fit and good for the commonwealth, and so to submit them to be drawn into acts and transmitted into England', but his observation that they might also be 'altered or rejected according as the lord deputy and council in their wisdom shall judge and hold expedient', and that any bill amended by the Irish parliament had to be retransmitted to England meant there was no ambiguity as to his determination to increase the power of the executive at the expense of the legislature.[45] Indeed, the manner in which Wentworth interpreted and applied Poynings's Law deprived the Irish parliament of an active role in the making of law. His unwillingness to accept that it even had the right of veto diminished its authority further, and reduced it, in Aidan Clarke's words, 'to the subordinate status of a legislative agency obediently giving statutory effect to executive policy'.[46]

This was not acceptable to the members of the Irish parliament, but they were out-manoeuvred by Wentworth during the 1634–5 session. However, they refused to accept that this established a pattern for the future, and when a new parliament was convened in 1640–1, they sought systematically to 'restore the authority of government to its former proportions'. Wentworth's presence did not allow them press their position during the first sitting, but his recall to England to respond to a charge of high treason provided them with an opportunity to affirm their 'right to initiate legislation by drafting bills to present to the Council's legislative committee, and their entitlement to "become suitors for the transmission of the same, that they may be further passed as shall be thought fit"'. They also asserted their 'sole competence … to determine the manner in which subsidies should be assessed'. Christopher Wandesford, who (as Wentworth's deputy) was charged with overseeing the administration of Ireland, was disposed to resist these demands, but while he awaited instructions on the precise course of action he should pursue, the Commons signalled their determination to press this point to a favourable resolution on 10 November 1640 by establishing 'a committee to know whether the bills presented to the committee of the Council Board have been transmitted into England'.[47] Wandesford responded by proroguing parliament but, with the initiative in their grasp, MPs were intent on holding out until they secured official recognition of their position. To this end, when

45. Edwards and Moody, 'The history of Poynings' Law', pp 423–4; *Lords Jn. (Irl.)*, i, 20–5; Clarke, 'Poynings' Law 1615–41', p. 212; Conrad Russell, 'The British background to the Irish rebellion of 1641', *Bulletin of the Institute of Historical Research*, 61 (1988), p. 168.
46. Clarke, 'Poynings' Law 1615–41', p. 214; Clarke, 'Colonial constitutional attitudes', p. 367.
47. *Commons Jn. (Irl.)*, i, 164.

parliament reassembled in January 1641, the Commons sought to advance a bill 'for the further explanation of Poynings' Act' that would clarify the procedure for the certification of bills, and secure to them the right 'to draw up bills by their own committee and [to] transmit them' for which they believed no modification of Poynings' Law was necessary.[48]

In support of their endeavour to obtain an active role in the making of law in Ireland, MPs rejected every measure presented to them originating with the Irish executive in the spring of 1641. Parallel with this, they appointed new and directed existing committees to press their demands.[49] Persuaded, in the words of Charles, Lord Lambart, that 'if Poynings' Law be so understood as that parliament can do nothing but pass bills, that is scarce a parliament', and encouraged by news from England that concessions were possible, the Commons and Lords jointly presented the Irish Privy Council in April with draft bills for transmission to England. The Council's acquiescence seemed to suggest that parliament had taken a major step towards realising their wish that 'bills prepared in advance of meetings of parliament should be drawn up "with the privity and advice of some of the lords and principal gentlemen of every province"', as was the practice before Wentworth, and that 'the Irish government should have no authority to prevent the transmission of bills prepared by the Irish parliament, but should be reserved the right to advise upon them'.[50] The expectation was that the necessary statutory clarification of Poynings' Law would be soon forthcoming and, when it was not, MPs manifested their disapproval by rejecting a sequence of bills during the summer of 1641. Significantly, this latest disruption of parliamentary business created little stir, and it was apparent that the prospect of parliament securing formal recognition of its claim to possess an active role in the making of law had disappeared for the moment when Charles I rejected its 'key demand ... to transmit its own draft bills'.[51]

The outbreak of rebellion in Ireland in October 1641 and the commencement in the following year of Civil War in England meant Poynings' Law was pushed from the top of the political agenda for much of the next two decades though the magnitude of the political and constitutional implications of the Law, allied to the Westminster parliament's determination to assert its authority to legislate for

---

48. Except where otherwise indicated, this account of the events of 1640–41 is taken from Clarke, 'Poynings' Law 1615–41', pp 214–18; see also Russell, 'The British background', pp 170–1; Clarke, 'Colonial constitutional attitudes', pp 367–8. It must be noted, as Aidan Clarke has pointed out, that, important as it was, this demand was 'secondary' to the Irish parliament's wish to roll back the increased authority and power of the executive in Ireland in order to reopen 'the constitutional lines of communication with the King' that had been cut off by the Wentworth's 'replac[ing] the King in the government of Ireland'.

49. *Commons Jn. (Irl.)*, i, 183; Clarke, 'Poynings' Law 1615–41', p. 218.

50. Clarke, 'Poynings' Law 1615–41', pp 219–20.

51. Ibid., pp 220–1; Micheál Ó Siochrú, 'Catholic Confederates and the constitutional relationship between Ireland and England, 1641–49' in Ciaran Brady and Jane Ohlmeyer (eds), *British interventions in early modern Ireland* (Cambridge, 2005), pp 210–12.

Ireland, ensured that it featured prominently in the negotiations pursued by the Confederates with the Crown during the 1640s. These negotiations proved complex and prolonged, because of the Confederates' insistence on the repeal or suspension of Poynings' Law in order to secure for the kingdom an independent parliament collided with the preference of the monarchy to maintain the *status quo*. A 'compromise agreement' was eventually agreed in 1649, but by then it was too late to make any real difference as the King had lost the military struggle with parliament.[52] Despite this, the conviction that sustained the claim that an Irish parliament was entitled to an active role in the making of law for the kingdom of Ireland did not disappear, though Ireland was formally joined during the 1650s with England in a legislative union. When the next Irish parliament assembled in 1661, this exclusively Protestant body was to demonstrate a commitment to advance this point similar to that of its predecessor. Significantly, the Crown and its representatives in Ireland were to be more accommodating than Wentworth and Charles I. The emergence of an acceptable legislative arrangement proved prolonged, but it was apparent by 1666 that an interpretation of Poynings' Law that satisfied the requirements of both the English and Irish interests was possible. The formal elaboration of such an arrangement was delayed until the 1690s by the failure to convene an Irish parliament during the remainder of Charles II's reign, but the heads of bills arrangement that emerged during the 1660s constituted an important step towards the compromise the Irish parliament, the Irish executive and the English ministers finally agreed in the 1690s that set the pattern for the making of law for Ireland for most of the eighteenth century.

52. Ó Sióchrú, 'Catholic Confederates and the constitutional relationship between Ireland and England, 1641–49', pp 212–29; idem, *Confederate Ireland, 1642–49: a constitutional and political analysis* (Dublin, 1999), pp 61, 71–2, 77–9, 92–3, 110–12, 116.

Part One

Heads of Bills, 1661–99

CHAPTER ONE

The Restoration parliament, 1661–6

DESPITE THEIR EXPERIENCES in the war-torn 1640s, the New English – their number augmented by a substantial influx of New Protestants in the 1650s – emulated the Old English in seeking to assert the right of the Irish parliament to make law for Ireland. They were assisted to reach this conclusion as much by their dissatisfaction with the Anglo-Irish union of the 1650s as by the argument, once attributed to the Old English lawyer, Patrick Darcy, 'that acts passed by the English parliament, other than those that were declaratory of the common law, had no force in Ireland unless they were confirmed by the Irish parliament'.[1] Significantly, this accorded with the position of the participants in the influential General Convention of Protestants assembled in Dublin in the spring of 1660, which promoted the restoration of the Stuart monarchy. Anxious to put an end to the unsatisfactory arrangement that had obtained for most of the 1650s when law for Ireland was made at Westminster, they appealed in their submission to Charles II on 20 June 1660 not only that 'a parliament may be called in Ireland with all convenient speed' but also offered a number of suggestions for bills. No mention was made of Poynings' Law by the commissioners appointed by the General Convention to present the 'humble desires' of Irish Protestants to Charles II, but the affirmation by the Convention that 'no tax, imposition or other charges whatsoever be laid upon your Majesty's subjects of Ireland but by common consent in parliament there' indicated that they would not accede to the interpretation of Poynings' Law advanced by Thomas Wentworth.[2] They were not disposed to be entirely unaccommodating, however, and the request to the King to 'direct' the chief governor and Privy Council of Ireland to transmit bills to the King and Privy Council of England to expedite their admission to law is

1. 'A declaration how, and by what means, the laws and statutes of England, from time to time, came to be in force in Ireland' in Walter Harris (ed.), *Hibernia* (Dublin, 1747–50), part II, 1–21. It is discussed by Aidan Clarke, 'Colonial constitutional attitudes in Ireland, 1640–60', *RIA proc.*, 90C (1990), pp 357–8 from where the quotation is taken and in idem, 'Patrick Darcy and the constitutional relationship between Ireland and Britain' in Jane Ohlmeyer (ed.), *Political thought in seventeenth-century Ireland* (Cambridge, 2000), pp 35–55.

2. The humble desires presented to his majesty by commissioners appointed by the General Convention of Ireland, June 1660 (TCD, MS 808 ff 155–8) (I wish to thank James McGuire for this reference); Clarke, 'Colonial constitutional attitudes', pp 372–3; Aidan Clarke, *Prelude to restoration in Ireland: the end of the commonwealth, 1659–60* (Cambridge, 1999), passim; Sean Connolly, *Religion, law and power: the making of Protestant Ireland, 1660–1760* (Oxford, 1992), pp 8–9.

suggestive of their willingness at this point to work within the broad parameters of Poynings' Law so long as they were allowed a reasonable degree of control over the law that was passed.

In obvious contrast, officials in England were anxious that Poynings' Law should be observed strictly deriving from their determination to maintain Ireland's dependent relationship in the aftermath of the disappointing Anglo-Irish union of the 1650s.[3] Eager to put the government of Ireland on solid foundations and to resolve the myriad difficulties generated over the preceding twenty years – particularly the fiscal problems of the crown, land ownership and religion – they accepted that a meeting of parliament was necessary, but they were determined that the Irish parliament should not be at liberty to devise or to implement legislative solutions without reference to England. This was attested by the memorandum 'Some doubts touching Poynings' Act in Ireland' prepared for the English lord chancellor. Accordingly, officials were content to accept that 'such acts as [the lord lieutenant and Council in Ireland] shall think fitt to pass ... ought to begin' in Ireland and that bills could be transmitted '*pendente* parliaments', but they were categorical that 'they must be affirmed, altered or changed or returned under the great seal of England' and 'enrolled in the Chancery of England'.[4]

THE 1661–2 SESSIONS

Acutely conscious of the fact that it was assembled without prior royal authorisation, the Dublin Convention did not hesitate to appeal to Charles II to convene an Irish parliament once the King was restored to the throne in May 1660. This was consistent with the commitment of the Protestant interest in Ireland to a domestic legislature, but it was given added authority by the conclusion, informed by opposition to government from Westminster, that an Irish parliament was the appropriate body to raise the revenue required to pay for the running of the country. Since the depressed state of the revenue required the Convention to authorise a poll tax, parliamentary approval for new taxes was a priority, and it was one of the main incentives for an early meeting of parliament.[5] Another still more compelling influence was the desire to give statutory effect to the agreement arrived at between the King and the General Convention.

The restoration of monarchical government was sufficiently advanced before the end of 1660 for the Crown to instruct the lords justices 'appointed for the

---

3. James Kelly, 'The origins of the Act of Union: an examination of Unionist opinion in Britain and Ireland 1650–1800', *IHS*, 25 (1987), pp 237–8; Patrick Little, 'The first unionists?: Irish Protestant attitudes to union with England, 1653–9', *IHS*, 32 (2000), pp 44–58; T.C. Barnard, 'Planters and policies in Cromwellian Ireland', *Past and Present*, 61 (1973), pp 61–5.
4. 'Some doubts touching Poynings' Act in Ireland, touching transmitting of bills there', [mid-17th century] (BL, Privy Council Papers, Add. MS 30190 f. 173).
5. Clarke, 'Colonial constitutional attitudes', p. 273; Clarke, *Prelude to restoration*, pp 249, 257, 268–9, 285–6, 300, 301; James, 'Illustrious or notorious', pp 317–18.

government of Ireland', to prepare bills in accordance with the terms of Poynings' Law encompassing the concessions made to the General Convention so that a parliament could be convened:

> Draft such bills as you, with the advice of the Council, think are for the good of our subjects there, and submit them for our consideration according to the text of Poyning's law, in order to the calling of a Parliament there with all convenient speed.
>
> You shall reduce to the form of bills the concessions made by us to what is commonly [named] the General Convention of Ireland and transmit them to us that these may be passed in the Parliament intended to be called there.[6]

Pursuant to instructions, the lords justices (Lord Orrery, the earl of Mountrath and Sir Maurice Eustace) and their Council colleagues set about drafting legislation. In the absence of a formal record, information on the process is scant, but Lord Orrery's observation in 1661 that 'a bill for the full indemnity of my Lord Clancarty' was 'twice read at the council' before it was 'ordered to be engrossed, and ... speedily remitted' to London indicates that the Irish Privy Council conducted its affairs in an orderly fashion.[7] The preparation of bills is elusive, but it can be inferred from the correspondence of Lord Orrery that the lords justices were the primary instigators of legislation in Ireland. Thus, the conclusion registered by Orrery in November 1661 that a bill 'to prohibit all sale of gunpowder' was preferable to the existing proclamation prompted a suggestion that a measure based on the proclamation should be prepared. Evidently, this was not a priority as it featured some months later on a list of 'bills to be prepared'. But the fact that the list was transmitted by Orrery to the duke of Ormonde, who was appointed lord lieutenant in 1662, is indicative of the centrality of the role played by the lords justices, and is consistent with the fact that the five bills, which were transmitted in the winter of 1660–61 to provide the 'causes and considerations' for calling a parliament were certified in accordance with Poynings' Law.[8]

Though the certification of bills conferred a crucial role on the Irish Privy Council in the preparation of legislation, the fact that it was legally obliged to convey them to the English Council emphasised its subordinate status. This was highlighted in February 1661 when, in what was to become a familiar refrain, the lords justices of Ireland advised the secretary of state, Sir Edward Nicholas, of the fact that 'we are waiting for the return of bills transmitted to England in order to the calling of a parliament'.[9] Since the English Council had been reconstituted for

6. Draft of instructions for the lords justices, [Dec. 1660] in *Cal. SP (Irl.), 1660–62*, pp 678–9.
7. Orrery to Ormonde, [1661] in Thomas Morrice (ed.), *A collection of the state letters of Roger Boyle, the first earl of Orrery* (2 vols, Dublin, 1743), i, 38–9.
8. Orrery to Ormonde, 20 Nov., 28 Dec. 1661, Bills to be prepared during the prorogation, 1662, Some particulars ... , 1662 in *Orrery letters*, i, 43, 49, 123–4, 114–15.
9. Lords justices to Nicholas, Feb. 1661 in *Cal. SP (Irl.), 1660–62*, p. 224.

less than a year at this point, the lack of urgency can be attributed to uncertainty as to how best to deal with such matters as well as to more obvious administrative limitations. This situation was not to endure, however, for 'though less important than it had been, and constantly though slowly getting to be still less important, the Privy Council continued to be a body, great and august, more important for a while in ordinary government business than any other organ of the government'. The frequency with which it met, and the regular attendance of between 11 and 30 councillors (whose number increased from 28 to 29 in 1660 to 47 in 1679 when Charles II famously capped membership at 30) is evidence of its administrative centrality.[10] Ireland featured large among its concerns, and to assist in their management a committee for Irish affairs was established in June 1660, with the marquis of Ormonde, Lord Robartes and Arthur Annesley, each of whom had particular experience interest in Ireland, among its members.[11] This was obviously an advantage when it came to Irish business, for when the committee was reconstituted in April 1661 with a reduced membership of eight (subsequently increased to ten), the nomination of the duke of Albemarle, briefly lord lieutenant in 1660, and Viscount Valentia strengthened it as a body.[12] Though no explanation was offered for the change, the committee clearly had work to do, as one of its first decisions was to agree to meet each Saturday 'to prepare and dispatch business'. The Council's determination on 15 February 1661 'that the parliament intended to be called in the Kingdom of Ireland do begin on 8th May next' certainly ensured Irish business more, if not always decisive, attention. If the Committee for Irish Affairs had been so authorised, it would, as it made clear on 26 April, happily have taken responsibility for all matters (legislation included) relating to Ireland, but the Council was unwilling to authorise this though it might have been administratively advantageous.[13]

The lack of procedural refinement certainly contributed to the want of order and uniformity in the manner in which Irish bills were addressed and records maintained at the English Council board in the 1660s. As a result, it is not always possible to identify exactly when a bill was received and, if ordered for amendment, precisely what amendments were authorised. What is indisputable is that the five bills received from the Irish Council in the winter of 1660–1 were referred for consideration to the Crown's law officers – the attorney and solicitor generals. It is not apparent how long it was anticipated this would take them, but, following the enquiry from Dublin in February, the law officers were invited to present their

---

10. Edward Raymond Turner, *The Privy Council of England in the seventeenth and eighteenth centuries, 1603–1784* (2 vols, Baltimore, 1927), i, 371–2, 378–9, 382, 389.
11. NA, PC2/55 p. II; Robartes was appointed deputy to Albemarle, when he was lord lieutenant.
12. NA, PC2/55 f. 101.
13. NA, PC2/55 ff 70, 101. Significantly, the full Council determined on 15 May 1661 that no Irish peer who was outlawed during the 1640s and 1650s would be allowed sit in the Irish House of Lords unless the outlawry was reversed according to law (PC2/55 f. 112). Previously, on 6 February, a letter dated 26 January from the lords justices of Ireland concerning money was considered by the full Council (PC2/55 f. 66).

report 'with their exceptions and amendments' to a meeting of the Council on 6 March. As a result, four of the five bills were approved and ordered to be 'delivered to Mr Attorney generall in order to be engrosst … for passing the great seal of England' so they could receive the royal assent and become law if approved by the Irish parliament.[14] Since this was a legal requirement, it may explain the amplification of the authorisation directing bills to be engrossed from the brief instruction given to the attorney general in March 1661 to the fuller order made five years later:

> It was ordered that the said bills be sent to the Clerke of the Crowne, who is required to cause the same forthwith to be ingrossed, and presented to the Lord High Chancellor of England, to be passed under His Majesties great Seale of this Kingdome into Acts of Parliament to be transmitted into Ireland. And it was further ordered, that the Clerk of the Crown do likewise, and commissions for His Majestys signature to passe the Great Seale of England, authorizing the Lord Lieutenant of Ireland to give His Majesty's Royall assent in the Parliament of Ireland onto the said acts for which this shall be sufficient warrant.[15]

Initially, it appeared that two bills – one recognising Charles II's title to the kingdom of Ireland, the other a bill for administering the oath of supremacy to the House of Commons – might not be returned, but following further 'consider[ation]', the English Council underlined its authority in respect of Irish legislation by judging that the oath of supremacy bill should be 'suspend[ed] for the present'. Of the remainder, 'that concerning the Court of Justice' was returned to Ireland with unspecified modifications, whilst two advanced without alteration.[16]

With four approved bills, the way was clear for the Irish parliament to assemble and, to the satisfaction of the Irish executive, each bill enjoyed a trouble-free passage and received the royal assent on 12 June 1661.[17] This positive outcome seemed to demonstrate the capacity of the English and Irish Privy Councils to identify and to draft legislation that the kingdom of Ireland required and the Irish parliament was willing to approve within the restrictive legal and procedural parameters laid down by Poynings' Law. The problem was that while peers and MPs were content to sanction legislation that provided the 'causes and consider-ations' required permitting parliament to be convened, they also aspired to possess a direct say in the making of law by actively initiating legislation. This was not without precedent, of course, and it received the endorsement of William

14. NA, PC2/55 ff 80, 84; Turner, *The Privy Council of England*, ii, 149–50.
15. NA, PC2/59 f. 23.
16. *Cal. SP (Irl.), 1660–62*, pp 224, 269, 272.
17. 13 Chas II, chaps 1–4; *Commons Jn. (Irl.)*, i, 387, 388, 389, 394, 395, 397, 403; Fergus O'Donoghue, 'Parliament in Ireland in the reign of Charles II' (MA thesis, UCD, 1970), pp 48–51; Bramhall to Nicholas, 1 June 1661 in *Cal. SP (Irl.), 1660–62*, p. 345.

Domville, the attorney general of Ireland, who maintained that they had the right to contribute 'in the enacting of all such laws as were at any time of force among them'.[18] However, there was a palpable sense of concern in parliament and Privy Council that they should do nothing inconsistent with Poynings' Law and, with this in view, the Commons determined on 8 June to establish a 'grand committee to consider the manner and method of preparing and drawing of bills in order to [facilitate] the transmission of them into England according to Poynings' Law'.[19]

If the failure of this committee to report suggests that the Commons was more intent on throwing shapes than in asserting their claim to an active legislative role, then it is misleading. There was, to be sure, no established mode of proceeding, but one method employed by MPs to alert the Privy Council to their wishes was to prepare declarations on matters of concern that were given three readings in both houses before they were sent to be published.[20] Though this device enabled both houses of parliament to highlight matters of concern, it was not unproblematic. Objections from the Lords to the employment of the term 'ordinance' rather than 'declaration' in a Commons' statement on the collection of the customs and excise, on the grounds that it savoured of legislation and was therefore an infringement of Poynings' Law, were illustrative of how tender sensitivities were on this point. These differences were not unbridgeable, though the fact that agreement was accompanied by an assertion by the lower house on 31 May 1661 that it alone possessed 'the right of raising money' indicated that the Commons were more energetic in asserting the rights of parliament.[21] This was further manifested shortly afterwards when it came to the crucial matter of drafting a bill for the settlement of Ireland. Then, the Lords' conclusion that parliament, to be consistent with Poynings' Law, could not proceed beyond 'humbly thanking the King for his gracious declaration' of 30 November 1660 precipitated a row with MPs, who were unwilling to accept that they could merely express their hope that the 'declaration may be enacted and executed'. Significantly, the Lords' stance was officially commended in England as well as Ireland: it would, the secretary of state, Sir Edward Nicholas, averred, prove 'of unimaginable inconvenience' if anything real or 'imagined' was 'done ... against Poynings' Law'.[22]

Considering the sparring that occurred on this point, it is more than a little ironic that the suggestion, formally made on 10 June, that the Commons should prepare a draft bill for the settlement of Ireland based on the declaration of 30

18. James, 'Illustrious or notorious', pp 317–18; Clarke, 'Colonial constitutional attitudes', p. 363; William Domville, 'An act in England binding Ireland' (TCD, Molyneux Papers, MS 890).
19. *Commons Jn. (Irl.)*, i, 401.
20. O'Donoghue, 'Parliament ... Charles II', p. 57; Coleman A. Dennehy, 'Parliament in Ireland, 1661–6' (M Litt, UCD, 2002), p. 24; Bramhall to Nicholas, 1 June 1661 in *Cal. SP (Irl.), 1660–62*, p. 345.
21. O'Donoghue, 'Parliament ... Charles II', pp 57–9; Dennehy, 'Parliament in Ireland, 1661–6', p. 15.
22. Orrery to Ormonde, [mid-June 1661] in *Orrery letters*, i, 36–7; *Commons Jn. (Irl.)*, i, 401, 402, 403; Eustace to Nicholas, ante 3 June, Nicholas to Eustace, 4, 11, 29 June 1661 in *Cal. SP (Irl.), 1660–62*, pp 345, 347, 353, 369.

November 1660 originated with the King. It was an invitation well calculated to win favour in Ireland because it accorded with the Commons' aspiration to be allowed to prepare legislation. Yet, because this was not established practice, even the terminology employed lacked certitude and definition. Confusingly, legislative proposals arising in the Commons were routinely termed 'bills' though they only became law if, following scrutiny by the Irish and English Privy Councils, they were approved by the King in Council, and were returned to Ireland to be approved unaltered by both houses of the Irish parliament *en route* to receive the royal assent. For obvious reasons, it was necessary to develop a nomenclature that distinguished between 'bills' originating in the Irish parliament yet to be considered at Council and 'bills' presented for parliament's attention with the great seal of England attached. Since the former were inconsistent with the prevailing view of the spirit, if not of the letter of Poynings' Law, it was logical that whatever terminological innovation took place applied to them, and they became known as 'heads of bills' to distinguish them from measures admitted having come through the Irish and English Privy Councils, which retained the designation 'bills'. It was a distinction that did not just make sense, it mirrored the commitment of peers and MPs to best practice; significantly, the Commons' journals were scrutinised for precedents and procedural guidance at a number of points during the session.[23] This notwithstanding, it took time for the term 'heads of bills' to achieve common currency, but both the concept and the practice of parliament preparing 'heads of bills' were sufficiently well established by the summer of 1662 for the lords justices, Lord Chancellor Eustace and Lord Orrery, to employ the term in correspondence with the lord lieutenant, the duke of Ormonde.[24]

While it is understandable, given its centrality to the consolidation of the 'Protestant interest' that the 'Bill for the settlement of Ireland' should attract especial notice when the emergence of the 'heads of bills' process is being considered, it was only one of a number of 'heads' to arise in the Commons during the first session of the 1661–6 parliament.[25] Several, notably those seeking to institute public commemorations on 30 January, 29 May and 23 October, did not even go into committee, though this was by agreement since they were later taken up by the Privy Council.[26] Others deemed more urgent, completed all stages in the Commons, following which their progress was closely monitored by MPs who, on 5 July, established a 'committee to view such bills as are ready or

23. *Commons Jn. (Irl.)*, i, 401, 521, 726.
24. Eustace and Orrery to Ormonde, 20 June 1662 in *Orrery letters*, i, 123; O'Donoghue, 'Parliament ... Charles II', pp 99–100.
25. Orrery to Ormonde, [mid-June 1661] in *Orrery letters*, i, 36–7.
26. *Commons Jn. (Irl.)*, i, 396, 397, 399, 405, 420. These dates commemorated the anniversary of the execution of Charles I (30 January), the restoration of the monarchy (29 May), and the outbreak of the 1641 rebellion: see James Kelly, 'The glorious and immortal memory: commemoration and Protestant identity in Ireland, 1660–1800', *RIA proc.*, 94C (1994), pp 27–8.

preparing for transmission into England'. And in those instances when matters of particular importance was at stake – money and religion notably – a Commons' committee was appointed to attend the lords justices 'to desire the said bill may be prepared and transmitted by them'.[27]

Such actions did not ensure a bill priority when it reached the English Privy Council. For instance, though the earl of Orrery wrote to Secretary Nicholas on 19 August 1661 to express his 'hope' that a bill for 'the abolition of the Court of Wards', the idea for which 'took its rise from some in England, ... [would] receive the royal sanction' without delay, no identifiable early action was taken. Suggestions that Charles II was less than happy with the proposal ensured that when it was finally read at the Council Board on 21 April 1662 it was 'ordered to be suspended until further consideration'. This prompted the introduction of a clause 'that there should be no retrospect to ye Court of Wards there, beyond ye Act of Oblivion', following which the bill was forwarded to Ireland finally to receive the royal assent on 20 December 1662.[28] By contrast, in a number of instances, heads of bills (though they were not always so termed) arising with the Commons, such as the measure for raising £15,000, were returned in time to be considered fully by the Irish parliament, when others arising with or suggested by the Irish Council were not proceeded with. A notable case in point was a proposal to prepare a measure 'to leave Protestants in land in Connaught and Clare', which was overtaken by plans for an act or acts of settlement.[29]

The lack of regularity in the manner in which bills arose, were transmitted to and, particularly, were considered at the English Council board complicated the efforts of the Irish executive to manage both its legislative agenda and the Irish parliament. This can be illustrated by the [heads of a] bill for the continuance of the customs and excise to 25 March 1662 that was requested by the Irish Commons in July 1661. Anxious that it should be returned and made law to avoid the 'ill precedent that money should be raised by a parliament without the royal assent', a formal request was issued for its return on 26 December 1661. The eventual reception of the measure in Ireland in time to become law was welcomed by Orrery, who observed that it would allow the recovery of '£10,000 due to his majesty from the merchant importers who, without a law, would not pay one penny of those duties', but its late return had left the Irish administration with little room for manoeuvre had the measure met with opposition. Moreover, the fact that Orrery recommended in the same letter that parliament could only be adjourned for fifteen days (to 21 March) at that point, that 'if the bills are not remitted by that time, we must have the houses assemble, that again by their invitatory declaration we may have some rise to levy the excise', is revealing of the

---

27. *Commons Jn. (Irl.)*, i, 403, 419, 441, 460–63; O'Donoghue, 'Parliament ... Charles II', p. 100.
28. Orrery to Nicholas, 19 Aug. 1661 in *Cal. SP (Irl.), 1660–62*, p. 402; Orrery to Ormonde, 28 Dec. 1661 in *Orrery letters*, i, 56–9; NA, PC2/55 f. 311, 2/56 f. 18; *Commons Jn. (Irl.)*, i, 601, 602, 603, 612.
29. *Commons Jn. (Irl.)*, i, 475; NA, PC2/55 ff 129, 256.

political and organisational problems caused by the lack of administrative concert.[30]

This was all the more galling as there was more than enough legislation in the system, if properly managed, to ensure that parliamentary business was conducted in a more structured fashion. Significantly, a month prior to the communication to London in December 1661 of a request for the return of the customs and excise bill, five bills were transmitted from Ireland to the English Council. Referred to the solicitor general with the instruction that he 'take especial care that no expression in the said acts do attend to the weakening of the authority of any act of parliament made in England', and that they conform 'to His Majesty's declaration and the act of settlement', the bills received no further consideration.[31] If this was due to the fact that four of the five were private bills, a further seven bills of a public character received over the winter (one in December and six in February) of 1661–2 (one of which was sent to the solicitor general with a request 'to report his opinions thereon with all convenient speed') were also not returned.[32] Assuming (though there is no minute to this effect) that these bills did not progress because they were objectionable, the English Council was within its rights, according to Poynings' Law, to respite them. However, as will be seen, the fitful manner in which Irish bills were considered means that one cannot exclude the possibility that they did not progress because of administrative inefficiency.

The complex procedures applied to fulfil the requirements of Poynings' Law not alone determined the pattern of law making in Ireland during the first (8 May–31 July 1661), second and third sessions (6 September 1661–22 March 1662) of the parliament of Charles II, they played no small part also in ensuring that little law was made. Four acts (all originating with the Irish Privy Council) reached the statute book during the first session; two (with similar origins) were approved during the second, and only one (which also took its rise in the Irish Council) during the third.[33] If this seems a very modest total, it must be recalled that this was consistent with the pattern established in the sixteenth century when one of the observed consequences of Poynings' Law was that 'it limited the total amount of legislation considered and passed'.[34] It was certainly the case that no bill reached the statute book that had not been thoroughly scrutinised and, if required, reshaped by the English Privy Council. By this criterion alone, Poynings' Law can be said to have achieved the purpose of enabling the English

30. Orrery to Ormonde, 26 Dec. 1661, 5 Mar. 1662 in *Orrery letters*, i, 47, 101; 14 Charles II, session 3, chap 1; *Commons Jn. (Irl.)*, i, 441, 479.
31. NA, PC2/55 ff 233–4.
32. NA, PC2/55 ff 247, 283; PC2/56 f. 243.
33. 13 Chas II, session 1, chaps 1–4; session 2, chaps 1–2; session 3, chap 1; NA, PC2/55 ff. 165; Lords Justices to Nicholas, 16 Sept. 1661 in *Cal. SP (Irl.), 1660–2*, p. 424; *Commons Jn. (Irl.)*, i, 449, 450, 451.
34. Quinn, 'The early interpretation', p. 253.

Council to confine the legislative authority of the Irish parliament. However, the number of heads of bills arising with the Irish House of Commons and the number of suggestions for measures from other quarters indicated that this was no longer sufficient to meet Irish needs. As yet, the preparedness of all participants to accept Poynings' Law, as currently interpreted and applied, helped to deflect ill feeling.[35] There was no concerted resistance in Ireland to the fact that its parliament was so utterly legislatively subordinate to two privy councils it had failed to put a single piece of legislation of its own devising on the statute book over two sessions. It was unlikely the membership of the Irish parliament would continue to behave so passively if steps were not taken to meet their legislative aspirations, not least by developing mechanisms to make the operation of Poynings' Law more efficient as well as accommodating. It cannot be said that this is what makes the fourth session of the Irish parliament of Charles II noteworthy, but it did prove to be more legislatively productive.

THE FOURTH SESSION, 1662–3

Preparation of legislation in the run-up to the fourth session (17 April 1662–16 April 1663) of the 1661–6 parliament proceeded in the same manner as it had for the three previous sessions. Since much of what the Irish administration hoped to progress was already in the system, this was an appropriate course of action, not least because it was sufficiently elastic to accommodate such refinements as were deemed necessary without either disrupting established practice or requiring a major administrative rethink. Thus, for example, the practice occasionally employed in the early 1660s of referring bills to both English law officers was abandoned. Instead, when bills from Ireland were *formally* referred (and this was not invariably the case), the solicitor general alone was requested to 'peruse' and 'to prepare the state of each of them severally and [to report] what objections shall occur to him in every [one] of them respectively'.[36] In the case of financial legislation, which was usually bound to a tight schedule, this request could be accompanied by an instruction to report back to the full Council board 'with all convenient speed'.[37] In other instances, when the fate of a bill or bills was not a matter of urgency, the solicitor general had on occasion to be reminded to render 'his report to all such bills as remain in his hands relating to … Ireland'. Even then, reports were not always forthcoming.[38]

This is not to suggest, of course, that the procedures of the English Council were entirely fluid. Rather, there were a number of options, of which referral by

---

35. For example, it was agreed on 16 Sept. 1661 that the Lords Commissioners from Ireland should be allowed examine bills transmitted out of Ireland currently in the hands of the solicitor general and the clerk of the council (NA, PC2/55 f. 192).
36. NA, PC2/55 ff 196, 283, 311, 442; PC2/56 ff 9, 56, 76, 95.
37. NA, PC2/55 ff 196. See also NA PC2/55 f. 442.   38. NA, PC2/56 ff 14, 291.

full Council to the solicitor general was most commonly availed of. It was not a wholly efficient means of operation, but despite the occasional error and omission, it worked satisfactorily. The limitations of the Privy Council's record does not permit one to identify many mistakes, but they are suggested by the advice of the earl of Orrery in the spring of 1662 to the duke of Ormonde that two bills concerning the clergy should be 'returned' to London to be recast because they contained serious 'faults' that could not be corrected in Ireland.[39] 'Faults' are intrinsic to any system, but they were more likely in this instance because of the evolving and, in some respects, *ad hoc* character of existing arrangements. None the less, precedents established and procedures employed facilitated the emergence of a pattern of bill management by the English Privy Council that contributed to the creation of a better-structured system. One noteworthy innovation was the inauguration of the practice whereby reports on commercial and financial legislation were solicited from interests other than the usual legal and council bodies within whose ranks the circulation of a majority of Irish bills was confined.

The practice of appealing to experts in the commercial and financial realms for opinion on pertinent Irish bills commenced with measures 'for the setting of the excize of the kingdom of Ireland', and 'for settling the subsidie of poundage and granting a subsidie of tunnage'. Received at the English Council board in the late autumn–early winter of 1661, it was ordered that the accompanying book of rates should be 'transmitted to the chief officers and commissioners of customs' for a 'full' report on 'the rates of excise' envisioned. The absence of the relevant report means it is not possible to establish if the amendments made to the bills derived from recommendations contained therein, but they did not prevent either measure becoming law.[40] Other than these measures, the task of scrutinising and, where necessary, amending legislation was performed during the fourth session by the Privy Council, assisted by the solicitor general. Significantly, other than the bill of settlement, which will be considered below, the Committee for Irish affairs was not routinely involved.

There is much about the working relationship of the Council and the solicitor general at this time that remains opaque, but in contrast to the eighteenth century when the Privy Council was content in the overwhelming majority of cases to delegate the task of scrutinising Irish bills to the law officers and to accept their recommendation, the Council did not hesitate to indicate the sort of amendments it required. It is noteworthy, for example, that in several instances the Council referred bills to the solicitor general with the recommendation that he should incorporate a specific amendment. A case in point is provided by the measure 'for securing Sir Maurice Eustace ... in his lands of inheritance'; in this instance, as well as an instruction to the clerk of the crown to replace a reference to 'Oliver the

39. Orrery to Ormonde, 16 Apr. 1662 in *Orrery letters*, i, 108.
40. NA, PC2/55 ff 187, 214, 233–4, 248, 260, 442 513; *Commons Jn. (Irl.)*, i, 514, 519, 522, 525, 526, 528, 530, 531, 532, 533, 553; 14 and 15 Chas. II, session 4, chaps 8, 9.

tyrant' with 'Oliver Cromwell', the solicitor general was authorised to 'add a clause to keep his majesties grant subject to the new rents'.[41] On 21 April 1662, when bills appertaining to the licensing and retailing of wine and the sale of tobacco were at issue, the solicitor general was advised to replace clauses in both restricting the leasing of licences after seven years with a 'proviso' safeguarding the rights of the existing licence holders.[42] A more general instruction given on 25 November 1661 with respect to five bills was to 'take especial care that no expression in the said acts do attend to the weakening of the authority of any act of parliament made in England' or, in the case of the tunnage and poundage bill, 'that the words of the enacting part should be the same as are present in all bills that are passed in the parliament of England'.[43] In a similar vein, directions were also offered to ensure that all references to the 'Lords spirituall and temporall' were appropriately phrased.[44] The effect of this was to bring a degree of coherence and uniformity to the structure and content of legislation across the two kingdoms.

This was a crucial matter for the English Privy Council, which was intent not just on ensuring the Irish legislature adhered to the form already familiar in England, but conformed in substance and content to what the English parliament adjudged appropriate. As a result, when it was perceived at the English Council that bills from Ireland were well drafted and legislatively unexceptionable, the Council determined to send them directly for engrossment and the attachment of the great seal without the requirement of a report from the solicitor general. This was not commonplace, but the fact that it happened at all illustrates the closeness of the engagement by the full Council with Irish legislation at this time. Among the measures received from Ireland that were ordered for immediate engrossment were bills ordaining 29 May and 23 October as days of 'perpetual anniversary'.[45] Bills 'for the granting four subsidies' and 'for the enlargement of the periods of time limited in an act for the better execution of his majesties … declaration' invited closer consideration, but the necessity of their becoming law was a matter of such importance that they too were fast tracked.[46] There was less urgency with private bills, but once again there were instances when the full Privy Council deemed it appropriate to forward measures directly. Thus on 21 April 1662, at the same meeting that the solicitor general was instructed to amend the bill for securing the estates of Sir Maurice Eustace so it could be sent to be engrossed without delay, it was simply ordered that the measure to secure Sir Edward Massey the 'mannor and abby of Leix' should receive a clause affirming that he held the property by letters patent.[47]

41. NA, PC2/55 f. 311; *Commons Jn. (Irl.)*, i, 514, 522, 553; 14 and 15 Chas. II, session 4, chap 4.
42. NA, PC2/55 f. 610, PC2/56 f. 18. 43. NA, PC2/55 ff 233–4, 187, 513. 44. NA, PC2/55 f. 513.
45. 14 and 15 Chas. II, session 4, chaps 1, 23; NA, PC2/55 f. 311; *Commons Jn. (Irl.)*, i, 508, 533, 602, 603, 612.
46. 14 and 15 Chas. II, session 4, chaps 6, 12; NA, PC2/55 ff 311, 319, PC2/56 f. 60; *Commons Jn. (Irl.)*, i, 533, 538, 539, 541, 542, 553, 575, 576, 577, 589.
47. NA, PC2/55 f. 311, 2/56 f. 18; *Commons Jn. (Irl.)*, i, 570, 571, 573, 589; 14 and 15 Chas. II, session 4, chap 14.

Though the Privy Council was prepared to act decisively, on occasion, a large majority of the bills received from Ireland were not alone scrutinised by the solicitor general, it was his recommendation that determined in 1661–2 if they were sent for engrossment unaltered, with amendments or set aside. Because the solicitor general's reports, if they were ever formally presented, do not survive, it is difficult to establish why certain bills advanced unchanged when others were subject to severe alteration. What is clear is that a significant proportion of the total, some of which (like the bill to raise £30,000 for the duke of Ormonde) had arisen with the Irish Commons, were forwarded unchanged by the Council on receipt of the solicitor general's report.[48] A small number progressed with only modest amendment. One may place in this category the measure for 'the real union and division of parishes', in which instance 'a blank in the bill relating to the number of years wherein such divisions or exchanges shall be made' was 'filled in Council in the King's presence', and the measure 'for establishing an additional revenue upon his majesty, his heirs and successors' in which the date of commencement was altered from 10 to 20 December.[49]

Significantly, the number of measures to reach the statute book that underwent material amendment at the English Council was small. The case of the Court of Wards bill has already been considered.[50] The augmentation, from £1500 to £2000, of the allowance for Sir Robert Stewart provided in the act for raising £23,500 is also noteworthy.[51] Logically, bills requiring extensive amendment were less likely to become law, though it was unusual, as happened in the case of the bill to prohibit purveyors and others from taking provisions, for an amended bill not to be engrossed.[52] Of more common occurrence was the phenomenon of bills being received and 'read at the board' and, in some cases, being ordered for amendment of which there is no further formal record. The most likely explanation is that they were deemed inappropriate but, in the absence of any minute that this was the case, some doubt must remain.[53]

Based on the fleeting references they are afforded in the Council record for 1662, it is apparent that most Irish bills were processed with reasonable promptness. One measure – a bill for the settlement of Ireland – whose purpose was to give legislative effect to Charles II's 1660 declaration for settling the

---

48. Among those that later became law were 14 and 15 Chas II, session 4, chaps 3, 5, 7, 13, 15, 16, 18, 20, 21 and 24. See NA, PC2/55 ff 311, 442, PC2/56 ff 9, 56, 76, 84. For the Ormonde bill (14 and 15 Chas. II, session 4 chap 16) see Orrery to Ormonde, 29 Jan. 1662 in *Orrery letters*, i, 78–9, 100–01; O'Donoghue, 'Parliament ... Charles II', pp 96, 103–04; *Commons Jn. (Irl.)*, i, 494, 499.
49. 14 and 15 Chas II, session 4, chaps 10, 17; NA, PC2/55 ff 283, 296; PC2/56 f. 100; *Commons Jn. (Irl.)*, i, 495, 512, 531, 553, 602, 603, 612. 50. Above, p. 24.
51. 14 and 15 Chas II, session 4, chap 22; NA, PC2/56 ff 95, 100; *Commons Jn. (Irl.)*, 597, 601, 603, 612.
52. NA, PC2/55 f. 610; PC2/56 f. 18.
53. Among the measures to which this was the outcome were bills for freeing the College of Dublin from paying excise for ale or beer (NA, PC2/56 ff 9, 18); concerning the city of Dublin (PC2/56 f. 95); for enrolling of letters patent in the kingdom of Ireland (PC2/56 f. 95); for Mr Howard's invention for tanning of leather (PC2/56 f. 18).

kingdom of Ireland – could not be hurried because it encompassed the hopes and fears of both the Protestant and Catholic interests in Ireland. It was, for this reason, subject to a longer and more sustained examination than any other measure. It also generated challenges and problems – none of them unique – the response to which helped to shape the future management of Irish legislation at the English Council board. Specifically, the involvement of the Committee for Irish affairs, the reception of petitions and the taking of oral evidence established precedents that were to be followed when other controversial legislation, particularly that appertaining to Irish Catholics, was at issue.

Though complex gestations were not unusual in the 1660s, 'the bill for the settlement of Ireland' was exceptional by any standards. As already described, (pp 22–3), the measure was initiated in the Irish House of Commons in June 1661 on the instruction of Charles II. Significantly, the heads emanating from the Irish Commons, to which the Lords added several clauses, were not entirely to the satisfaction of the Irish Council. Having revised the text to reflect their concerns, the measure was dispatched in the late summer of 1661 to the English Council by which it was referred on 4 September to the solicitor general. In anticipation of that day, representatives of the Roman Catholics of Ireland had already requested and been granted permission to 'have a sight' of the bill and to present 'papers ... in answer to any parts of the declaration'.[54] There is no listing of these, but a reference, in the minute of 4 September, 'to the papers of exceptions given in by the Roman Catholiques of Ireland against the preamble' as well as 'other papers ... against the body of the same bill and such other papers as they shall hereafter deliver in ag[ain]st the said act' is a guide to their nature and extent. More importantly, the solicitor general was instructed to consider these submissions to establish 'whether in point of law there be anything conteyned in the said act contrary to his Majesties declaration', and to take on board 'such answers as the Committee from the Council and parliament of Ireland shall make unto them'. This was a more demanding task than that normally presented the solicitor general, and it was compounded by the instruction of Charles II, in response to the lobbying of Lord Massareene 'on behalf of the Adventurers on the double ordinance', that 'nothing be contained in the said act that may extend or be construed to extend to the confirmation of the said doubling ordinance'.[55]

While the solicitor general set about fulfilling these detailed instructions, arrangements were set in train for the full Council to commence considering the bill on 16 October. Fully aware of the magnitude of the task, it was adjudged that the so-called 'commissioners' deputed by both houses of the Irish parliament, the lords justices and the convocation of the Church of Ireland should assist and that the representatives of the Roman Catholics of Ireland should be permitted to

54. O'Donoghue, 'Parliament ... Charles II', pp 64, 67; NA, PC2/55 ff 174, 185, 186.
55. NA, PC2/55 f. 188. The 'doubling ordinance' of July 1643 provided that any adventurer who paid an additional fourth to his original subscription would receive double the measure of Irish land: see K.S. Bottigheimer, *English money and Irish land* (Oxford, 1971), p. 85.

attend. It was determined also that the Committee to oversee Irish affairs should meet as regularly as need be to receive petitions and to 'consider [the] papers offered by both sides', and that it should be attended by the solicitor general.[56] Given the range of concerns of these interests, it was hardly surprising that progress was slow. Part of the reason was the steady flow of petitions and other partisan statements of position.[57] However, having reaffirmed in November that 'his majesty's declaration be the grounds' of the measure, and that those who 'have lands in Ireland be obliged under great penalties to plant those lands with English and other Protestants', and in late January 1662 embraced a number of clarifications from the Committee for the affairs of Ireland the pace accelerated. The Council formally accepted the report of the solicitor general on 5 February and ordered that the bill, with a number of amendments, should be conveyed to the clerk of the crown for engrossment.[58] Before this could be completed, a number of Irish Catholics (Colonel Garrett Moore and Sir Richard Talbot), petitioning on their own behalf and on behalf of their 'fellow-sufferers', sought permission to peruse the measure. They were permitted to make their case on 14 February, but their request was rejected. Undaunted, and in spite of the fact that the bill was sent to be engrossed on 19 February, Moore, Talbot and Sir Nicholas Plunkett sought a further hearing. Plunkett was heard on 14 March, but he was not deemed to have proved his case and it was determined formally to hear no more petitions from Catholics. A number of late petitions were submitted, but once the engrossed bill received a final checking on 8 April it was carried to the lord chancellor so it could be passed under the great seal of England.[59]

While the attention that the Privy Council lavished on the bill for the settlement of Ireland was particular to this measure, it proved time well spent as this far-reaching legislation received the royal assent in Ireland before the end of July.[60] Significantly, it was not afforded an easy passage, but the realisation that this was the best they were likely to get tempered attitudes. However, as in 1661, MPs demonstrated that they were not prepared to be cowed into acquiescence since, as well as acceding to the bill, they prepared the heads of an 'explanatory' bill clarifying and redressing deficiencies in what was now the Act of Settlement. The resultant document – 'Collections of explanations humbly desired of several particulars in the act ... ' – was transmitted to the Irish Council. The duke of Ormonde and a majority of the Council were less than pleased with what they received; they deemed it 'very unreasonable' on the grounds that it sought rather to 'alter' than to 'explain'. None the less, it informed their drafting of a measure

56. NA, PC2/55 ff 206, 207.
57. Notably, in November, the answers of the Protestant commissioners of Ireland to the objections of the Roman Catholics (PC2/55 f. 230); and the Instructions from the Lords and Commons to their delegation to England (PC2/55 ff 249–55): J.I. McGuire, 'Bishop Michael Boyle' (unpublished paper, 2004).
58. NA, PC2/55 ff 218, 269, 270.   59. NA, PC2/55 ff 275, 279, 290, 293, 297, 303, 306.
60. *Commons Jn. (Irl.)*, i, 553.

entitled 'An explanation of an act ... for the settlement ... of Ireland', which incorporated some of the Commons' ideas into a bill. Other than amending the title to recite accurately that of the Act of Settlement, the bill passed unaltered through the English Council. However, the Irish parliament was unwilling to accede to the intervention of the Irish Council on this crucial matter, for when this bill was presented to them for approval, MPs once more demonstrated that they would not be dictated to on this issue by rejecting the bill in February 1663.[61]

Given the strong feelings the Act of Settlement generated, the negative response to the amended explanatory bill was predictable. The fact that the bill conveyed to London was the work of the Irish Council rather than the Irish parliament was crucial, though few MPs objected openly to the Privy Council's legislative endeavour. Indeed, in the same month that the 'Collections of explanations' was presented to the lords justices, the Commons requested the Irish Council to prepare a bill on the related matter of 'settling five hundred pounds per annum, beyond reprizers' on the primate.[62] This was not taken up, but rather than protest at the snub, MPs further demonstrated their unwillingness to play a passive role. In addition to rejecting the bill of explanation, they declined in 1662 to approve a number of measures that had negotiated the English Council. Among these were 'act[s] concerning tithing, oblations and mortuaries' and 'against grey merchants or pedlars' that were lost in committee.[63] This was the fate also of 'act[s] for retayling tobacco' and 'for lycencing and retayling of wine and strong waters', presumably because of the presence of a proviso inserted on the instruction of the English Council protecting the interest of patentee licence holders; and of a measure 'for setting up Erasmus Smith schools' amended to incorporate the names of thirty-five eminent Irish Protestants who were 'dissentients'.[64] More unusually, the House of Lords rejected a bill to enable 'ecclesiastical persons make leases for three score years' that negotiated the Commons.[65]

The rejection by the Lords of the ecclesiastical leases bill stands out because it was the quieter of the two houses of the Irish legislature. It was the Commons, for instance, that continued to seek precedents for such matters as 'making addresses for transmitting bills'.[66] More materially, they persisted with their efforts to carve

61. O'Donoghue, 'Parliament ... Charles II', pp 83–5, 162; NA, PC2/56 f. 123; *Commons Jn. (Irl.)*, i, 613–4; L.J. Arnold, *The Restoration land settlement in County Dublin, 1660–1688*, (Dublin, 1993), pp 86–7.

62. *Commons Jn. (Irl.)*, i, 520.

63. NA, PC2/55 ff 383, PC2/56 ff 9, 18; *Commons Jn. (Irl.)*, i, 581, 591, 592, 603, 604, 608, 609, 643, 644.

64. Above, p. 28 ; NA, PC2/55 ff 320, 323; *Commons Jn. (Irl.)*, i, 534, 536, 571, 577, 578, 592, 595, 597, 602, 603, 608, 610.

65. NA, PC2/55, f. 283, PC2/56 ff 9, 18; *Commons Jn. (Irl.)*, i, 576, 578, 579, 582, 583, 590, 591, 593, 604, 631, 637, 638, 642; *Lords Jn. (Irl.)*, i, 370, 371; O'Donoghue, ' Parliament ... Charles II', pp 173–4.

66. *Commons Jn. (Irl.)*, i, 521.

out an active legislative role by continuing to advance suggestions for heads of bills during the long fourth session. Little came of their initiatives in most instances. Indeed, in five cases, the only official record that legislation was attempted is the formal order requesting the preparation of a bill. A committee was appointed in five other cases 'to prepare' a named measure, but no bill was admitted.[67] In a further four instances, heads of bills reached the committee stage never to emerge; while two controversial measures – bills for the suppression of the popish hierarchy and for disabling members to serve in parliament that shall not take the oaths of allegiance or supremacy – were dropped following exchanges with the lord lieutenant because of their contentious character.[68] In addition, the heads of five bills that completed their Commons' passage were formally conveyed to the lord lieutenant for communication to the Irish Privy Council, but councillors evidently did not approve as no corresponding bills were forwarded to London.[69]

The House of Commons also engaged actively in promoting private legislation, though the distinction between public and private bills cannot always be clearly sustained. Numerically, private bills constituted a modest proportion of the total, but the fact that MPs afforded them the same scrutiny they gave public bills, and that estate bills for Arthur Hill, the earl of Anglesey and the duke of Albemarle that had been remitted from the English Council did not become law is an earnest of their determination to act as a proper legislature.[70] This conclusion is reinforced by the deferral in April 1663 of a bill whose purpose was to restore Theobald, Viscount Mayo to his estates, and by the request, conveyed some months earlier to the lord lieutenant, that a bill should be prepared for settling on Connaght MacGwyre land previously held by his grandfather.[71]

Twenty-four acts received the royal assent during the fourth session of the Irish parliament of Charles II. This was a striking improvement on the modest legislative achievement of the previous three sessions, but what was of greater import was the fact that among their number were bills that had taken their rise

---

67. *Commons Jn. (Irl.)*, i, 565 (bill concerning the taking of distresses); 559 (bill that the four first subsidies be levied in a moderate parliamentary way); 563 (bill against forgery and subornation of witnesses); 632 (bill against swearing); 563 (bill for the better prevention of perjury); 595 (bill for securing all such persons as shall pay the value due by the Act of Settlement); 602 (bill for repealing part of hearth money act); 560 (supplemental bill for regulating the subsidies); 539 (bill for destroying wolves and foxes); 549 (bill for repealing statute of distresses).

68. *Commons Jn. (Irl.)*, i, 568 (bill concerning the potting of butter); 519, 559, 563 (bill for punishing the sins of profanation of the sabbath, swearing and drunkenness); 650 (bill concerning public registers); 643 (heads of a bill for preventing frauds in the packing of butter); 638, 643, 649, 651, 652 (bill for suppression of popish hierarchy); 638, 649, 651, 652 (oaths bill); O'Donoghue, 'Parliament ... Charles II', pp 170–1.

69. *Commons Jn. (Irl.)*, i, 650, 652 (bill for ease to the sheriffs); 649, 651 (bill enjoining the oath of allegiance and supremacy for ministers of justice); 557, 564, 569, 570, 575, 577 (bill for two shilling hearth tax); 569, 570 (bill for levying twenty thousand pounds).

70. Orrery to Ormonde, 24 May 1661 in *Orrery letters*, i, 111–12; NA, PC2/55 f. 311, PC2/56 ff 9, 18, 53; *Commons Jn. (Irl.)*, i, 533, 534, 574, 578, 579, 583.

71. *Commons Jn. (Irl.)*, i, 656, 573, 584.

the Irish parliament. This was the logical outcome of the acknowledgement that the Commons could initiate legislation. Moreover, it did not contravene Poynings' Law because these measures, increasingly known as 'heads of bills', were referred to the Irish and English Privy Councils, after which they were presented as bills to the Irish parliament for ratification or rejection. While the Commons might claim that all legislation should conform to this pattern, in fact, other than asserting that they alone (and not the House of Lords) could initiate financial legislation, they contrived to avoid making exclusive or confrontational assertions along these lines. Significantly, rather than transmit a stream of already formed measures to the Irish Council, MPs continued to invite the Council to prepare legislation. Taken together with the procedural flexibility in the processing of Irish legislation at the English Council board, the long delays and high attrition rate, it is apparent that though Poynings' Law was effective at curbing the legislative initiative of the Irish parliament, it was less satisfactory in allowing law to be made. As a result, Lord Orrery was prompted to suggest in March 1663 that the Law might be suspended temporarily to facilitate the enactment of revenue legislation, but this was a step too far.[72] The protection Poynings' Law afforded royal authority in the making of law for Ireland was too valuable, even to suspend temporarily, particularly given the assertiveness of MPs in the spring of 1663, the emergence of the Commons 'as the mouthpiece of Protestant opinion', and Ormonde's limitations as a manager of men and legislation.[73]

Moreover, the legislative outcome of the fourth session was sufficiently encouraging for the Crown, Irish executive and Irish parliament to conclude that the Irish parliament could function well enough with Poynings' Law. It is significant in this context that the Irish parliament did not make an issue of the large number of bills transmitted from Ireland that were not returned. Indeed, the absence of protest suggests that MPs were reconciled to operating within the parameters ordained by Poynings' Law. This was contingent on the fact that the Irish parliament was treated as an active rather than a passive partner in the process of making law. In asserting this claim, MPs were behaving no differently than the other parties – the Irish and English Councils – that were joined in this complex legislative symphony, in that each was determined to exercise the powers they were allowed. At the same time, none of these bodies wielded the power they were permitted carelessly or, when the matter at issue was important or controversial, without a willingness to take cognisance of the views of others. This was crucial if the convoluted process of law making provided for by Poynings' Law was to function efficiently.

72. Orrery to Ormonde, 8 Mar. 1663 in *Orrery letters*, i, 174–5; O'Donoghue, 'Parliament … Charles II', p. 188.
73. O'Donoghue, 'Parliament … Charles II', pp 189–90, 161, 106–7, 273.

THE FIFTH SESSION, 1665–6

Though the final session of the Irish parliament of Charles II was not convened for two and a half years after the conclusion of the fourth session on 16 April 1663, the scrutiny of bills at the Irish Privy Council continued. This was in keeping with the pattern established in 1661–2, and it was appropriate if, as anticipated, a further session was to be convened before long. The lord lieutenant and Council in Ireland certainly operated in that expectation as, even before the conclusion of the fourth session, two bills were conveyed to the Council board in London in anticipation of the next. A further eleven, comprising a sizeable number of public acts and four for building bridges, were transmitted on 8 May; six were communicated in September, and still others were conveyed late in the year.[74] In keeping with existing practice, a number were promptly sent for engrossment (one with an amendment).[75] A majority were referred to the solicitor general for a report; two – bills appertaining to the tonnage and poundage and excise legislation approved in 1663[76] and a new customs bill – were referred to the lord high treasurer of England and to the chancellor of the exchequer, who were instructed 'to call onto them the farmers of H[is] M[ajecty]'s Customs'; while a number, including the bridge bills and a bill for disappropriating several rectories, were deferred until February 1666, thereby negating them since their proposed fund-raising mechanisms were invalid by that date.[77]

Because the Irish parliament was not in session, the instruction to the solicitor general on 10 July 1663 to report on seven public bills in a week, may seem to imply that the English Council had finally determined to deal with Irish legislation expeditiously and efficiently, when it just reflected the perception that a bill of explanation must be proceeded with at an early date. Nonetheless, the decision on 31 July to bolster the membership of the Committee for the Affairs of Ireland and to refer letters received from Ireland was significant,[78] for though it is unclear at this point if it was anticipated that bills from Ireland would also be referred to the Committee, this soon became the practice. Moreover, though this was a minor detail, the setting of a quorum at three not only facilitated the Committee's work, it also established the normative quorum that was to be applied to committees on Irish issues from this point onwards.[79]

It was certainly not anticipated that the redefining of the role of the Committee on the Affairs of Ireland would make the scrutiny of Irish legislation at the

---

74. NA, PC2/56 f. 197; Lord Lieutenant and Council to Bennett, 8 May 1663 in *Cal. SP (Irl.)*, *1663–65*, pp 81–2; O'Donoghue, 'Parliament ... Charles II', p. 186.
75. NA, PC2/56 f. 197.   76. 14 and 15 Chas II, session 4, chaps 8 and 9.
77. NA, PC2/56 ff 211, 243, 250, 265, PC2/58 f. 184; Lord Lieutenant and Council to Bennett, 8 May 1663 in *Cal. SP (Irl.)*, *1663–5*, pp 81–2.
78. Despite the fact that it had played an important role in the preparation of the Act for the Settlement of Ireland, the Committee for the Affairs of Ireland was described as 'formerly' active on 31 July 1663 (NA, PC2/56 f. 249).   79. NA, PC2/56 ff 249, 313.

English Council board more open or transparent. The English Council guarded its authority jealously, so when the Irish Council enquired towards the end of 1663 why some bills were deemed suitable and others not, the request was firmly denied:

> The Council here [England] neither by reason of State nor directed by any precedent do hold themselves obliged to give account of the reasons which may move their Lordships to alter, or suspend the sending back any bills sent hither ... [80]

Though this response was in keeping with custom, it also offered a convenient shield against requests for explanation. Queries might certainly have been posed as to why bills that had taken their rise in 1663 were forwarded only to become law in 1665–6,[81] while others, such as the gunpowder bill, that had also been on the political agenda for several years, were destined never to be presented to the Irish parliament because of decisions taken at the English Council.[82] Other bills, originally drafted in 1663, to fall by the wayside in 1666 for less than obvious reasons include measures to amend acts appertaining to the excise and tonnage and poundage, and the controversial bill for punishing offences in the Court of Castle Chamber, which was rejected by the Irish House of Commons in March 1666.[83]

Given the fitful embrace of greater regularity in the management of Irish legislation at the English Council to date, the involvement of the Committee for the Affairs of Ireland in the scrutiny of Irish bills from the early winter of 1663 not only represented an administrative change of consequence, it coincided with, and may therefore be connected with the maintenance of a fuller record of the amendments made to bills.[84] To illustrate: the minute recording a change recommended in November 1663 to a measure 'for the better ordering of the selling of wines' cites the parchment and line number at which the amendment required was to be introduced.[85] Few minutes were so precise, but the fact that before the end of November, amendments were recommended by the Committee for the affairs of Ireland not alone suggests its involvement had a bearing on the practice of making fuller minutes of decisions, it is indicative also of the enhanced role afforded this committee in the process. Indeed, in the case of a measure 'enabling ecclesiastical persons to make leases for 60 years', it was the Committee for the affairs of Ireland that instructed the solicitor general to delete all of the bill

---

80. Arlington to Privy Council, [post 17 Dec. 1663] in *Cal. SP (Irl.), 1669–70*, p. 478.
81. Notably, bills for the confirmation of marriages (17 & 18 Chas. II, chap 3), and for provision of ministers in cities and corporate towns and making the church of St Andrew's presentative forever (17 & 18 Chas. II, chap 7).
82. NA, PC2/56 ff 243, 265.
83. *Commons Jn (Irl.)*, i, 702, 710, 711, 712, 713, 714, 717, 728, 730; Ormonde to Arlington, 8 Mar. 1666 in *Cal. SP (Irl.), 1666–9*, p. 54.
84. NA, PC2/56 ff 291, 310, 314.   85. NA, PC2/56 ff 310, 314.

'save only the clause permitting incumbents building houses on the glebes of their parsonages' and to redraft it as appropriate.[86] The fact that it was also noted now which bills should be 'laid aside' is a further pointer to the more efficient management of business at the Council Board; previously bills that were deemed objectionable or undesirable were simply passed over and no record of the decision was made.[87]

But it was the legislation to explain the Act of Settlement that most vividly demonstrates how the power vested in the English Privy Council could be used to mould legislation received from Ireland. Following the rejection by the House of Commons of the explanatory bill returned to them in 1662,[88] MPs had set about preparing new heads to address their discontent with respect to the Act of Settlement and, in particular, with the powers vested in the commissioners nominated to give effect to its provisions. Comprising twenty-four clauses and a preamble justifying the measure on the grounds that it was essential to the security of the Protestant religion in Ireland, the bill's prospect of becoming law seemed slim since the King did not conceal his annoyance that the 1662 explanatory bill, which had been returned without amendment from the English Privy Council, had been rejected. The duke of Ormonde was more hopeful, and the bill's prospects of making it to the statute book improved dramatically when it was discovered in March 1663 that there was a plot afoot to seize Dublin Castle.

The adjournment of parliament in April afforded the Irish Privy Council an opportunity to prepare a measure that answered the determination of MPs to safeguard the security of Irish Protestants in possession of Irish lands, and the duke of Ormonde's wish 'to mitigate the vigour' of the Act of Settlement.[89] This was a challenging undertaking, but the Irish Council was in a position by 9 September to communicate a bill that, it observed deferentially, remedied the unanticipated defects of the Act of Settlement:

> How prudent soever the endeavours and consultations have been of His Majesty and the Lords of his most honourable Privy Council in order to that settlement, yet it is not possible any human wisdom could so forsee all particulars that must necessarily occur in so great and universal a work, but that some things must be needful to be added when the resolutions first taken came to be put in execution.[90]

If, as this implied, the Irish Council was aware of the deficiencies of the bill as forwarded, it was confirmed seven weeks later when Sir William Domville

---

86. NA, PC2/56 ff 310, 314
87. NA, PC2/56 ff 310. The bills were 'for the prevention of the frequent censure of excommunication' and 'for building a bridge over the river Shannon at Ballylogue'.
88. Above, pp 31–2; O'Donoghue, 'Parliament ... Charles II', pp 162–4.
89. O'Donoghue, 'Parliament ... Charles II', pp 164–8; Arnold, *Restoration land settlement*, p. 87.
90. Lord Lieutenant and Council to Bennet, 9 Sept. 1663 in *Cal. SP (Irl.), 1663–5*, pp 234–5.

communicated 'some amendments … to be transmitted as from the Board' to Secretary Bennet. Numbering seven in all, Domville's careful wording reflected the fact that a majority of the law officers in Ireland 'were of opinion that the [Irish] Board cannot transmit amendments or additions (by Poynings' Act) no more than the House of Commons can offer an amendment to any Bill after they had sent it up to the Lords. There is no precedent for sending a rider under the great seal to be added to any Bill.'[91] Irish officials contrived to minimise the novelty of what they were proposing by transcribing the bill 'with those amendments'; and they had reason to feel relieved when the bill and the 'additional proposals' were referred in the normal way to the solicitor general on 9 November. Since the solicitor general was only allowed a week to prepare his report, and the commissioners of the Court of Claims sent over from Ireland were requested to be present to hear it, councillors anticipated that the bill could be dealt with expeditiously. However, this calculation received the first of many reverses when, instead of proceeding, the full Council responded to the intervention of 'the adventurers', who were eager to put a permanent end to the investigations of the Court of Claims established under the Act of Settlement, by ordering that a copy of the bill should be communicated to them and that they should be present 'with all others concerned in the bill' on 23 November when the matter would finally be addressed.[92] A delay in making a copy of the bill, and other problems, prompted another postponement, and worse was to follow. Alerted by the submission on 30 November by the Irish Commissioners of Claims of a report 'about amending the bill', which revealed the complexity and sensitivity of the matters at issue, Charles II concluded that the bill could not be put into proper form with the expected speed, and he 'named a numerous committee to advise on the method to be pursued to that effect'.[93]

Informed by the King's direction that the committee should 'make his Declaration and Instructions the ground upon which they are to proceed', its members examined the bill received from Ireland and, deeming it unsatisfactory, advised that a new one should be prepared:

> Finding the matter was intricate and perplexed, [the Committee] resolved [on 11 December] to ask the King to direct the Attorney and Solicitor-General and the Commissioners to draft a new bill or to amend the old, going upon the lines of the new bill, the bill rejected last year, the heads of a bill presented by the Commissioners, and various papers sent in by the different interests, and taking as a basis the Declaration and Instructions.

The attorney and solicitor general were unhappy that they were charged with this task. They claimed that it was their function 'rather to criticise than to frame a

91. Domville to Bennet, 29 Oct. 1663 in *Cal. SP (Irl.), 1663–5*, p. 272.
92. NA, PC2/56 ff 309, 315.
93. NA, PC2/56 ff 322, 326; Bennet to Ormonde, 1 Dec. 1663 in *Cal. SP (Irl.), 1663–5*, p. 304.

bill'. As a result, the task of preparing a new text passed to the Council and the Commissioners, though this created still more serious procedural difficulties, as was pointed out in Ireland.[94]

News that, in the words of the earl of Orrery, 'the bill transmitted is rejected' came as a surprise to 'many' in Ireland. Acutely aware that whatever emerged would 'be liable to question', the lords justices, in the absence of the duke of Ormonde who was in England, advised against proceeding in this manner because Poynings' Law did not permit the drafting of Irish legislation at the English Council board:

> Many here fear – let the bill in the forge be never so good, it will still be liable to question, since it originally is made in England, Poynings' Act requiring all laws of this kingdom to be first transmitted hence. They may be altered at the English Council board, but never were originally and wholly sent thence to the Parliament of Ireland.[95]

This was a compelling objection. Unwilling to infringe Poynings' Law, the English Council chose not to proceed with its plan to draft a new bill, and the issue was dropped from the Council's agenda for some months.

Obliged to rethink their strategy, the English Privy Council determined when it re-engaged with the issue to focus once more on amending the 'Irish Explanatory bill' to accommodate its varied critics rather than on preparing a new bill. It was the only appropriate course of action, though the Council minutes are barely helpful in explaining how it came about. Meetings of the Committee for the Affairs of Ireland attended by the Commissioners for Claims on 19 February and 4 March may have been instrumental, but a decision was only finally made on 10 March when, 'after debate on the business of Ireland and consideration had which way to proceed upon an additional bill for setling the affairs of that kingdom, the Irish Explanatory bill was read and Mr Solicitor ordered to take notice of the amendments'. No information is provided as to the content of the amendments that were authorised, other than that an instruction was given 'to prepare a proviso for insertion ... for restoring Oliver Fitzwilliam, Earl of Tyrconnell, to the possession' of some of his family lands.[96] This was highly significant, as became clear four days later when it was agreed that a further 'proviso' should be admitted for restoring Sir Henry O'Neill to his Irish estates, because it indicated that Charles II had concluded that the bill of explanation offered him an opportunity to provide for a number of his most committed Irish supporters whose lands had been confiscated and redistributed by the Cromwellians.[97] Beneficiaries of the Cromwellian plantation were understandably less than content, and the Committee assembled to represent the Adventurers

94. Bennet to Ormonde, 1 Dec. 1663 in *Cal. SP (Irl.), 1663–5*, p. 315.
95. Orrery to Bennet, 1 Dec. 1663 in *Cal. SP (Irl.), 1663–5*, p. 348.
96. NA, PC2/57 ff 14, 20, 24.   97. NA, PC2/57 f. 25.

immediately requested, and were accorded, the opportunity on 30 March 'to be heard when matters of concern to them in Ireland are being considered and debated'.[98] The first fruit of this was a commitment to introduce a complex amendment dispelling 'doubts' that had arisen 'in the execution of the Act of Settlement' as to the ownership of 'lands, tenements and hereditaments' in possession of 'officers and soldiers' on 7 May 1659.[99]

These 'doubts' assuaged, the Council approved the introduction of further 'provisos' restoring, among others, Colonel Daniel O'Brien and Viscount Netterville, and authorising that 'those Irish officers' who had served Charles II abroad should be 'compensated out of the first moiety of the one sixth part assigned for reprisals'.[100] A brake was applied to the introduction of such amendments for a time thereafter as complaints from adventurers and soldiers against the decisions of the Commissioners for Claims increased. A question was also posed as to 'whether it was [legally] correct to restore Irish Roman Catholics and Protestants according to the Act of Settlement after July 1663'.[101] Reviews and hearings were held on both these matters without any particular decisions being reached. Several months then elapsed before the Council determined on 18 November 1664, in response to a petition by Sir George Lane protesting that he had been 'disinherited' of lands awarded by act of parliament by the Commissioners for Claims, to introduce an amendment permitting redress through the courts. At the same time, Charles II also secured the insertion of a clause to the effect that the measure should not take precedence over the law that deemed all properties forfeit in cases of treason.[102] This was not contentious; the issue of including provisos restoring named Catholic royalists to their properties was but, by the end of March 1665, as the wish finally to conclude discussion of the bill grew, the anxiety of the King to provide for more of his friends and allies necessitated the introduction of still more amendments. Some – those appertaining to the marquis of Antrim notably – were particularly troublesome, but though amendments of a comparable character continued to be admitted into the fourth week of July, the final preparations of the bill were already well under way by that date.[103] These commenced on 10 May when the Committee for Irish affairs was authorised 'to resolve and reconcile' the many amendments made to the bill. Two months later, on 8 July, a committee that included the duke of Ormonde, Lord Orrery and the solicitor general was established 'to peruse' the measure further. It was this group effectively that brought the process to a conclusion. After several days of deliberation at Salisbury, where the King had gone for the summer, during which still further amendments were agreed, the Privy Council forwarded the bill on 14

---

98. NA, PC2/57 f. 30.   99. NA, PC2/57 f. 30r.   100. NA, PC2/57 ff 32, 41, 43.
101. NA, PC2/57 ff 77, 80, 83, 86, 89, 91.   102. NA, PC2/57 ff 140, 152, 154.
103. NA, PC2/58 ff 47, 50–1, 93, 109, 110, 111, 112, 113. For an example of a proviso see *Cal. SP (Irl.)*, *1663–5*, pp 708–9. Significantly, individual members of the English Council were lobbied in respect of having provisos admitted (James Grahame to Earl of Lauderdale, 5 Apr. 1665: Tollemache Papers, Buckminster, Grantham, Lincs, listed in HMC Report, 1979, no. 1534).

August to the clerk of the Crown for engrossment and the attachment of the great seal.[104]

The detailed attention accorded the Irish explanatory bill over a period of nine months provides the best-documented illustration of the extent of the powers Poynings' Law allowed the English Privy Council to shape Irish legislation. These were not unlimited, as the decisive objections raised against the decision of December 1663 to prepare a 'new bill' demonstrate, but the measure returned to Ireland was palpably different to that originally transmitted. If this made the subordinate status of the Irish legislature *vis-à-vis* the English Privy Council explicit, it was underlined when a delay in the return of the measure prevented the convening of an Irish parliament before 26 October 1665. By that date, however, the Irish executive was the grateful recipient of eleven bills from among the larger number (a total of fifteen were communicated between August 1664 and September 1665) transmitted from Ireland. Only a proportion of these were returned, but taken together with those that had previously been forwarded, there was sufficient legislation to justify reconvening an Irish parliament.[105]

Appropriately, given the amount of time and effort allocated to its preparation, the explanatory bill dominated the early part of the 1665–6 session. The measure excited such exceptional interest that MPs were provided with printed copies, and the Commons assembled in grand committee when the bill reached committee stage. Attention focussed in particular on the vesting clause, whose deficiencies caused Richard Jones, the MP for County Roscommon, 'to arraign the whole bill very fiercely'. Persuaded that the measure was both defective 'as to the general settlement [and] to particular interests', MPs supported his call for the 'suspension of Poynings' Act so that the House could propose a bill that would secure to all men their estates', and a petition to that effect was presented to the lord lieutenant.[106] Lord Orrery did not believe this was either appropriate or necessary because the Irish Privy Council was empowered 'to explain or amend any part of the said bill which may lye as an obstruction or impediment'. He was also determined that Poynings' Law should not be infringed, though this meant, he noted starkly, that the Commons' only options were 'to pass, or not to pass' the bill. Ormonde was less blunt, but his warning that a new bill was unlikely to 'meet with full consent and return from the King and Council in England' made it clear that MPs would not be allowed to circumvent Poynings' Law. Realising that they were unlikely to secure a more agreeable measure, the explanatory bill was voted through on the way to receive the royal assent.[107]

104. NA, PC2/58 ff 66, 103, 121–2.
105. NA, PC2/57 f. 96, PC2/58 f. 127; Ormonde to Arlington, Oct. 1665 in *Cal. SP (Irl.), 1663–5*, p. 648; O'Donoghue, 'Parliament … Charles II', p. 195.
106. Orrery to Arlington, 16 Dec., Ormonde to Arlington, 21 Dec. 1665 in *Cal. SP (Irl.), 1663–5*, pp 682, 690–1; O'Donoghue, 'Parliament … Charles II', pp 193–5, 197–8.
107. Orrery to Ormonde, 14 Dec. 1665 and draft of answer, 11 Dec. 1664 in *Orrery letters*, i, 196–201; Lord Lieutenant and Council's answer to House of Commons, 15 Dec. 1665 in *Cal. SP (Irl.), 1663–5*, p. 686; *Commons Jn. (Irl.)*, i, 665–94 passim.

As well as defining the parameters of the English Council's authority to shape Irish legislation, the prolonged engagement of the English Council with the Acts of Settlement and Explanation hastened the development of a series of procedures that shaped the management of Irish bills at the English Council for a long time to come. Since both these acts were unusually weighty and complex, generalisations grounded on their particular histories may seem intrinsically problematic, but the acceptance of petitions, the hearing of oral testimony, the involvement of the Committee for Irish Affairs, and, most notably, the acceptance of extensive amendments set the pattern for later practice. Moreover, the response to the Committee of Adventurers and sundry royalists indicated also that lobbying at the English Council board could pay handsome dividends, since it provided a means whereby parties as well as individuals could circumvent both the Irish parliament and the Irish Privy Council.

Given this context, it is remarkable that the Irish parliament – the protests against the bill of explanation apart – demonstrated such a readiness to operate within the parameters of Poynings' law. Indeed, it not alone approved financial legislation in 1665–6 providing the Crown with a permanent revenue supply – the so-called hereditary revenue – that freed Charles II from having to convene another parliament in Ireland during his lifetime, it did so on its own initiative. In April 1666, for example, the lord lieutenant was invited by the House of Commons 'to frame and send over, according to Poynings' Law, a bill' for carrying a resolution to provide subsidies.[108] Out of this concern to provide for the finances of the Crown emerged an Act for the grant of four entire subsidies by the temporality, an Act for graunting foure entire subsidies by the temporalitie, for the defence of his majesties kingdome, and an additional Act for the better ordering and collecting the revenue arising by hearth-money.[109] No less pertinently, the Act of Explanation obviously excepted, most of the private and public bills returned from the English Council, were ushered into law without difficulty. These included an Act for the confirmation of marriages and an Act for the securing several lands, tenements and hereditaments unto George, duke of Albemarle, both of which had arisen in the Lords and which, in the case of the latter, had failed to reach the statute book in 1663.[110] This was the case also with an Act concerning tythings, oblations and mortuaries.[111] Indeed, while it has been fairly said of an Act for the relief of poor prisoners that it was a measure that 'few noticed', this observation is equally applicable to other measures on a legislative list that, finance

---

108. Ormonde and Council to Arlington, 4 Apr. 1666 in *Cal. SP (Irl.), 1666–9*, p. 81
109. 17 and 18 Chas. II, chaps 1, 17, 18; NA, PC2/58 f. 127, PC2/59 f. 23; O'Donoghue, 'Parliament ... Charles II', pp 196, 237–8; *Commons Jn. (Irl.)*, i, 683, 685, 694, 747, 748, 749, 772, 773.
110. 17 and 18 Chas. II, chaps 3, 5; O'Donoghue, 'Parliament ... Charles II', pp 171, 174, 197, 212–3, 218; *Lords Jn. (Irl.)*, i, 392; *Commons Jn. (Irl.)*, i, 688, 689, 694.
111. 17 and 18 Chas. II, chap 13; NA, PC2/58 f. 104; O'Donoghue, 'Parliament ... Charles II', pp 236–7; *Commons Jn. (Irl.)*, i, 741, 742, 746.

and two acts to promote the production and sale of linen and old and new draperies apart, was dominated by minor measures.[112]

The other striking exception to this pattern was the bill to provide 'for the uniformity of public prayers and administration of sacraments'. Modelled on the 1662 English Act of Uniformity, and transmitted originally to London in 1664, the version offered to the Irish parliament in January 1666 was unacceptable to the Commons because the time allowed for compliance was too short. As a result, it had to be redrafted and retransmitted. Returned unamended, it was expeditiously pushed through all stages on the way to become law.[113] This conformed to what became general practice when the 'heads of bill' process operated at its most effective during the eighteenth century, except that in this instance the term was not employed with reference to this measure. This is not of especial significance since the term was still not part of the accepted political lexicon. Yet, it is noteworthy as well as significant that measures arising in the Commons were more routinely described as 'heads of bills' in the official record of the 1665–6 session than was the case in earlier sessions.[114] This step towards the terminological regularisation of what was now practice is borne out by the fact that in other respects the granting of leave to prepare 'bills' in the 1660s, and the presentation of 'bills' and heads of bills in 1666 by the House of Commons to the lord lieutenant described measures with similar origins. It has been claimed that the bills originating in the House of Commons in 1665–6 attested to 'a new sophistication' in terms of what 'parliament wanted', but this is hardly corroborated by the heads of bills themselves. A number – notably a measure to farm the collections of the hearth tax – were ambitious as well as controversial but, otherwise, their most striking feature is that, including those communicated to the lord lieutenant for transmission to London, they were fewer in number than in 1662–3.[115]

The measures just referred to failed to become law because they did not negotiate the Irish parliament. Others forwarded from the Irish Council during the course of the session were lost at the English Council because of perceived

---

112. 17 and 18 Chas. II, chaps 8, 9, 15; NA, PC2/57 f. 96; PC2/58 ff 64, 127, 177, 184; O'Donoghue, 'Parliament ... Charles II', pp 239–40, 241–2; *Commons Jn. (Irl.)*, i, 697, 698, 702, 703, 740, 741, 745.

113. 17 and 18 Chas. II, chap 6; NA, PC2/57 f. 60, PC2/58 f. 205; *Commons Jn. (Irl.)*, i, 696, 700, 701, 702, 703, 704, 705, 708, 709, 710, 712. 741, 742, 745; Rawdon to Conway, 3 Mar. 1666 in *Cal. SP (Irl.), 1666–9*, p. 52; O'Donoghue, 'Parliament ... Charles II', p. 245.

114. See, for examples, *Commons Jn. (Irl.)*, i, 736 (where a Commons' committee was appointed 'to prepare heads'), 750 (where a committee was instructed 'to consider on heads of said bill'), 740 (where a committee was instructed to 'report heads' in one case and in another 'to present said heads to Lord Lieutenant').

115. O'Donoghue, 'Parliament ... Charles II', pp 248–52; *Commons Jn. (Irl.)*, i, 697, 701, 714, 716, 719, 740; Rawdon to Conway, 3 Mar. 1666 in *Cal. SP (Irl.), 1666–9*, p. 52. Three bills sent to the lord lieutenant were a 'Bill whereby debts may be assigned', the 'Heads of a bill for regulating the fees of the sheriffs' and a 'bill whereby persons indicted and acquitted may be discharged without paying fees' (*Commons Jn. (Irl.)*, i, 740, 745, 758).

deficiencies or the belief that a particular law was unnecessary.[116] There was also a small number, deemed sufficiently acceptable to be sent for engrossment and the attachment of the Great Seal, which failed to become law because they were not presented to the Irish parliament on their return.[117] The reasons for this are not readily identifiable, but it is reasonable to attribute this outcome to objectionable amendments approved at the English Council. This may account also for the loss of the 'Star Chamber bill' in May 1666, of the Court of Wards bill in June, and of the Boyne river bridge bill in July 1666 all of which were rejected by the Commons; the privileges of parliament bill (which was 'absolutely rejected') and a city of Dublin bill were both lost in the Lords.[118] The attempt by the Irish parliament in a number of instances to amend bills returned from England ensured that they too were lost since none of those received at the Irish Council were recertified and transmitted to England.[119]

CONCLUSION

Despite the many obstacles in the way of a bill making it to the Irish statute book in the 1660s, 54 acts (46 public and 8 private) were approved over the five sessions held between 8 May 1661 and 7 August 1666. Because of the fitful nature of the surviving record, it is difficult to establish with any precision what proportion of the total number of legislative initiatives this represents, but it may have been as little as one-third. While this is low, it would be surprising if it were otherwise given the convoluted course legislation had to complete, and the absence of pro-cedural clarity at the English and, one assumes, the Irish Council. Furthermore, the evolving nature of the 'heads of bills' process, and the fluctuating mood of Irish Protestants ensured that this was not an environment calculated to foster either the expeditious or efficient making of law. The most obvious index of this is the varying legislative output of the five sessions, which was as follows: session one – 4 acts; session two – 2 acts; session three – 1 act; session four – 24 acts; and session five – 23 acts. This pattern was intensified by the pattern of law making that occurred within sessions; in 1662–3, 10 of that session's 24 statutes were given the royal assent in July 1662 and 7 in December; in 1665–6, 5 acts received

116. NA, PC2/58 f. 184.
117. NA, PC2/57 f. 76, PC2/58 ff 184, 195. The measures were entitled: 'An act for disappropriating the rectory of Baltinglass', 'An act for disappropriating the several rectories of Narroghmore'; 'An act for the settling of certain lands of Erasmus Smith', and 'A bill for the piouse uses of Erasmus Smith'.
118. O'Donoghue, 'Parliament ... Charles II', p. 243; NA, PC2/57 f 130, PC2/58 ff 109, 127 184. PC2/59 f 23; *Commons Jn. (Irl.)*, i, 719, 720, 731, 744, 745, 749, 750, 751, 756; *Lords Jn. (Irl.)*, i, 417, 434; Rawdon to Conway, 3 Mar., Leigh to Williamson, 10 July, Lane to Arlington, 11 July, Warburton to Arlington, 12 July 1666 in *Cal. SP (Irl.), 1666–9*, pp 52, 151, 152, 153.
119. As was the case with measure 'for the better securing of his majesty in his forfeitures' (NA, PC2/58 f. 39; *Commons Jn. (Irl.)*, i, 764); 'the bill of free and general pardon, indemnity and oblivion' (NA, PC2/57 f. 97, PC2/58 f. 127; *Commons Jn. (Irl.)*, i, 772).

the royal assent in December 1665, and the remainder, in two batches, in June and August 1666.[120]

Despite this irregularity, the five sessions of parliament held during the reign of Charles II were sufficiently successful to suggest, had parliament met again during the lifetime of the King, that it could have continued to perform a productive legislative function. This conclusion is strengthened by the efficient manner in which the Irish Privy Council prepared 18 bills in 1678 and 26 bills in 1680 for planned parliaments that never took place, as well as by the efficient manner in which the Committee on Irish affairs engaged with them, obtained expert advice and input and availed of the legal expertise of the law officers to determine which should be amended, vetoed or laid aside.[121] As a consequence, the Irish parliament of Charles II was unique in respect of some of the practices it permitted and procedures it employed. None the less, in the comparatively short time that it sat, it established some important principles that had a direct influence on the operation of the Irish parliament during the eighteenth century, on the manner in which the Anglo-Irish nexus functioned, and, not least, on the application of Poynings' Law. It is particularly striking that the Irish Privy Council's relations with the Irish parliament in the 1660s and its interpretation of Poynings' Law were so different from the model of executive control applied in the 1630s by Thomas Wentworth, when parliament was forced to accept a passive role, and content itself with approving and rejecting legislation that took its rise in the Privy Council. Charles II and his ministers, by contrast, were prepared to allow parliament an active say in the preparation of legislation, and MPs (for it was emphatically the lower house that took the lead in initiating legislation) were content for the most part to work with rather than against the Irish Council. Thus, they regularly approved requests inviting the Council to prepare bills and they transmitted declarations and heads of bills to the lord lieutenant in anticipation that he would convey them to the Council for scrutiny and certification prior to transmission to London.[122] More generally, their failure openly to criticise its employment indicated that MPs were content to work within the parameters defined by Poynings' Law, though, saliently, their interest in the details of bill transmission was more conspicuous in 1665–6 than it had been earlier in the decade.[123]

The willingness shown at executive and Council during the 1660s to recognise the right of MPs to initiate legislation was in keeping with this. It is particularly noteworthy in this context that though none of the statutes approved during the first session of the Irish parliament originated in the Irish parliament, within five years the Commons had not only established the right to initiate legislation, it had

120. The dates upon which bills received the assent are cited in O'Donoghue, 'Parliament ... Charles II', appendix A; see also idem, pp 231, 232.
121. James Aydelotte, 'The duke of Ormonde and English government in Ireland, 1677–85' (PhD, University of Iowa, 1975), i, 30–194 passim.
122. Above, p. 42; O'Donoghue, 'Parliament ... Charles II', p. 214.
123. O'Donoghue, 'Parliament ... Charles II', pp 247–8.

in 'heads of bills' identified a means by which it could do so and given the procedure a distinct nomenclature. The fact that the Commons deemed it necessary on 27 March 1666 to appoint a committee 'to peruse the journals of parliament ... , and to make [a] report whether they find bills or only heads of bills most frequently prepared in parliaments within this kingdom since the time of passing Poyning's Law' suggests that the terminology was not universally acknowledged.[124] However, it was also apparent by that date that the Commons had established its entitlement to initiate legislation. To be sure, in theory heads of bills were merely requests for legislation, not formal legislative initiatives, as evidenced by the presence of the supplicatory opening phrase 'we pray it be enacted' instead of the command 'be it enacted' in legislation proper. However, they were treated in the House in which they arose as if they were full and proper bills, and whilst heads that had completed all stages were sent for transmission to the Irish Privy Council to commence their Council scrutiny and only to the other house 'for information',[125] the increasing frequency with which dispatches from Dublin cited what the Commons would accept attests to their prominent legislative role as well as to the acknowledgement of this reality. In particular, MPs asserted in March 1666 that additional financial legislation could not be introduced without their approval, which was an important further step in defining a legislative role for the Commons.[126]

This occurred, of course, within a framework that explicitly and affirmatively acknowledged the legislative roles of both the English and Irish Privy Councils. Their roles complemented each other, but they also differed in fundamental ways. The most striking difference was that the Irish Council could initiate legislation. The English Council asserted the right to draft bills in the winter of 1665–6, but its inability to press this claim in the face of criticism from Ireland that to do so would be to infringe Poynings' Law indicated that it was not a right it could sustain. It was obliged instead to rely on its undisputed entitlement to respite, veto and amend prospective legislation referred to it from Ireland. A precise calculation of the percentage of bills so affected is impossible because of inadequate minuting of decisions, but perhaps as much as 30 per cent of the bills received at the English Council were not returned to Ireland. Many others were extensively amended. Significantly, the 1660s did witness some distinct procedural improvement in the way in which bills received from Ireland were managed at the English Council board, notably in establishing that the solicitor general had a key role in their scrutiny, in the acceptance of petitions from those whose interests were affected by particular items of legislation, and in the increasing practice of involving the Committee for Irish Affairs. However, the Council as a whole continued to engage directly with Irish bills and manifested no willingness to delegate that responsibility.

124. *Commons Jn. (Irl.)*, i, 726
125. The phrasing is Patrick Fagan's (*Catholics in a Protestant country*, p. 53).
126. As well as the contents of this chapter, see McNally, *Parties, patriots and undertakers*, p. 42; O'Donoghue. 'Parliament ... Charles II', pp 193, 243–7.

CHAPTER TWO

The heads of bills process
established, 1692–9

THE DENIAL OF Ormonde's initiatives to convene a meeting of parliament in Ireland in the late 1670s was possible because the hereditary revenue voted in the 1660s provided funds sufficient to pay for the ongoing administration of the kingdom. This was a source of comfort to Charles II, who preferred to govern without recourse to parliament, and who was enabled to do so in respect of the kingdom of Ireland for the remainder of his reign. It was the preference also of his brother, James II, who succeeded him in 1685, and whose briefer, more eventful reign, witnessed only one parliamentary gathering – the extraordinary 'Jacobite parliament' convened in Dublin in 1689. Since James was in Ireland at this time seeking to regain the throne from which he had been deposed by William of Orange, it was not possible to prepare legislation strictly according to the terms of Poynings' Law. None the less, James firmly resisted Irish calls for its repeal. His successors, William and Mary, were no less intent, as they demonstrated in the run up to the meeting of the Irish parliament held in 1692, of availing of the powers it provided to secure a direct and active say in the making of Irish law.[1] The problem they encountered was that there was a strong current of opinion within the Protestant interest in Ireland that was unwilling to acquiesce in the application of Poynings' Law in a manner than confined their entitlement to initiate legislation. This right had been acknowledged in the 1660s, but whereas parliamentary opinion was content then to allow the Privy Council the upper hand so long as MPs and peers could suggest measures and present heads of bills, it was more assertive in the 1690s. As a consequence, the meeting of parliament convened in 1692 proved politically dramatic and legislatively unsuccessful. Unwilling, for fiscal and other reasons, to contemplate governing Ireland without a domestic legislature, the King and his ministers were obliged to accommodate the determination of Irish Protestants to possess the leading role in the making of Irish law by accepting, beginning in 1695, that the heads of bills constituted the primary means whereby legislation was initiated. As a result, the role of the Irish Privy Council in the Irish legislative process was attenuated in the sessions that followed; that of parliament, particularly the Commons, elevated; and, assisted by

1. J.G. Simms, *The Jacobite parliament of 1689* (Dundalk, 1974), pp 7–9; Connolly, *Religion, law and power*, pp 34–5.

47

procedural refinements at the English Council board, Poynings' Law embarked
fitfully on a new phase in its complex history.

PREPARING FOR PARLIAMENT, 1690–2

When James II's Irish supporters assembled in parliament in Dublin in 1689,
Poynings' Law figured prominently among the 'constitutional questions' that the
overwhelmingly Catholic membership of the assembly wanted addressed. Like
their confederate predecessors in the 1640s, their preference was that it should be
repealed, and a bill to this end was presented to the Commons. However, James II
was unwilling to agree to any diminution in the royal prerogative, and his
insistence that approval should be forthcoming from the King in council before
any bill became law ensured the measure did not progress. This was in keeping
with the position James had adopted prior to the opening of the session when the
legislative programme was scrutinised by the King in council.[2]

While it can be argued that it was not within the letter of Poynings' Law that
the legislation for a session of parliament in Ireland should be considered by the
King in council *in* Ireland, it was, Simms has suggested, consistent with the spirit
of the measure.[3] However, it was not the spirit but the political and constitutional
implications of the Law that English officials were most anxious to perpetuate.
They had indicated as much in the late 1670s when the Lords of the Privy
Council Committee on Trade with responsibility for the colonies sought to apply
the provisions of Poynings' Law to confine the legislative liberties of the
Caribbean island of Jamaica and the North American colony of Virginia.[4] They
were unsuccessful, but the fact that Charles II replicated his 1679 decision in
respect of the English Privy Council with a directive to reduce the Irish Council
to thirty indicated that the Crown was eager that the Privy Council would
continue to play a key role in government and administration on both sides of the
Irish Sea. This was underlined in February 1689 by the establishment by the
English Privy Council of a committee for the affairs of Ireland.[5]

Though the primary purpose of this committee was to oversee the conduct of
the war in Ireland,[6] the restoration of a stable system of government became its

---

2. J.G. Simms, 'The Jacobite parliament of 1689' in D.W. Hayton and G. O'Brien (eds), *War and
    politics in Ireland, 1649–1730* (London, 1986), pp 70–1; Connolly, *Religion, law and power*, pp 34–5.
3. Simms, 'The Jacobite parliament', p. 70.
4. Jack P. Greene, *Peripheries and centre: constitutional development in the extended polities of the
    British empire and the United States, 1607–1788* (New York and London, 1990), pp 13–14; Neil
    Longley York, *Neither kingdom nor nation: the Irish quest for constitutional rights* (Washington,
    DC, 1994), p. 247; below, pp 361–2.
5. Turner, *The Privy Council of England*, i, 448–50; Minute and entry book of the Committee for
    Ireland, 1689–91 (NA, PC6/2).
6. For some perspective on its activities see John Miller, 'William III: the English view' in
    Bernadette Whelan (ed.), *Essays on the war of the three kings in Ireland* (Limerick, 1995), pp 25–6;

priority once William of Orange had put James II to flight.[7] This took longer than anticipated, but well before it was complete thoughts had turned to the future structures of government that would apply. One of the options canvassed was a legislative union.[8] This was recommended on a variety of grounds, one of which was informed by the conviction that since the Irish were possessed of 'an irreconcileable antipathy … to the English' it was 'not possible to secure England' from the threat of 'despotic and arbitrary power' being introduced through Ireland other than 'by bringing that kingdom under the same laws with England'.[9] Of course, Poynings' Law provided a recognised mechanism whereby the English Privy Council could control the legislation of the Irish parliament, but this did not ease the concerns of those who believed responsibility should be vested in the Westminster parliament:

> [N]or is Poynings' Law, which is not understood in England, any way in favour of the laws of England, but, just the contrary, for it places, in a manner, the legislative power in the King and Council; and it seems the government and judges of Ireland believe it so, when they deny the Commons so much as proposing the most easy way for the country to raise money demanded of them, though they readily submitted to the sum demanded. The meaning is easily understood – Ireland was to be under absolute government.[10]

A legislative union, such as the author of this observation favoured, was too radical a proposition for most English politicians. Taking their cue from William of Orange, who had given undertakings to this effect on a number of occasions, they recommended that a parliament should be convened in Ireland as soon as practicable.[11] They were content, meanwhile, that 'a great part of that work [the settlement of Ireland] will be done by our parliament here'.[12] The ratification at Westminster in 1689 and 1691 of acts nullifying the decisions of the Jacobite

Henry Horowitz, *Parliament, policy and politics in the reign of William III* (Manchester, 1977), pp 34, 38.

7. The standard account is J.G. Simms, *Jacobite Ireland, 1685–91* (London, 1969); see also Piers Wauchope, *Patrick Sarsfield and the Williamite war* (Dublin, 1992).

8. For a brief discussion see James Kelly, 'The origins of the Act of Union: an examination of unionist opinion in Britain and Ireland, 1660–1800', *IHS*, 25 (1987), pp 240–2; idem, 'Public and political opinion in Ireland and the idea of an Anglo-Irish union' and David Hayton, 'Ideas of Union in Anglo-Irish political discourse, 1692–1720: meaning and use' in D.G. Boyce, R. Eccleshall and Vincent Geoghegan (eds), *Political discourse in seventeenth and eighteenth-century Ireland* (Basingstoke, 2001), pp 113–21, 142–68.

9. *Cal. SP (Dom.), 1690*, pp 201–2.

10. Ibid.

11. James McGuire, 'The Irish parliament of 1692' in Thomas Bartlett and D.W. Hayton (eds), *Penal era and golden age* (Belfast, 1979), p. 2.

12. The quotation, from John Pulteney, clerk of the Irish council, is taken from McGuire, 'The Irish parliament of 1692', p. 3.

parliament and instituting new oaths hinted at the shape they wished the settlement to take, but while this approach to the government of Ireland was not
without influential (or self-interested) advocates, the convening of an Irish
parliament was always more likely.[13]

In this event, the composition of the Irish Privy Council was a matter of some
import as the author of a memorandum to the King on the grievances of Ireland
pointed out.[14] Convinced (like Charles II) that a large Council was unwieldy,
William and Mary admitted only 23 to its ranks in November 1690, though their
number was to rise to 50 within seven years. Since it was widely credited that
when the Council numbered 'above four score', notables sought membership for
the sole reason that 'they might have place and precedence before all other persons
of their own rank and quality', the expectation in the early 1690s was that a slimmed-
down Council would be more businesslike. It was anticipated particularly that it
should set promptly to preparing bills for transmission to England in readiness for
a meeting of the Irish parliament.[15]

As it happened, the Irish Council was reluctant to embark on this task. While
councillors could cite the absence of an explicit instruction from London as a
justification for their inactivity, the realisation that it must prove troublesome also
weighed heavily. As a result, few if any preparations had been made when Robert
Southwell, the principal secretary for Ireland, observed in December 1691 that it
would not be possible to convene a meeting of the Irish parliament before April
1692.[16] Even this proved wildly optimistic, as the English Council did not
formally instruct the lords justices of Ireland to prepare 'the proper heads and
materials ... to be formed into laws' for scrutiny at the English Council board
until 9 March. Significantly, this instruction included 'the titles of [ten] bills,
which the Lords of the Committee think may be necessary to be passed into acts
of parliament'. A further list, this time with twelve titles, was conveyed three
weeks later, which (allowing for overlap) provided the Irish executive with a total
of fourteen material legislative ideas.[17] No detailed explanation was forthcoming
as to ministerial thinking in respect either of individual 'titles' or of the rationale
for communicating these lists, but even if it is accepted that the decision was
prompted by a wish to assist the Irish executive, it is apparent that it was not
without wider implications. It was certainly in keeping with contemporary
English assumptions as to Ireland's dependent status symbolised by the absence

13. McGuire, 'The parliament of 1692', pp 3–5; Wooter Troost, 'William III and religious tolerance' in
    Whelan (ed.), *Essays on the war of the three kings*, p. 48; Horwitz, *Parliament, policy and politics*, p. 74.
14. Memorandum on the grievances of Ireland, [1690] in *Cal. SP (Dom.), 1691–2*, pp 69–70.
15. Warrant to admit to Privy Council, 6 Nov. 1690 in ibid., p. 158; James, *Lords of the ascendancy*,
    pp 55–6; Lords of the Council, 6 Dec. 1691 (BL, Ellis Papers, Add. MS 28941 f. 369).
16. Southwell to King, 17 Dec. 1691 (TCD, King Papers, MSS 1995–2008 f. 195).
17. Lords Justices to Nottingham, 1 Feb. 1692 in *Cal. SP (Dom.), 1695*, p. 179; Nottingham to
    Lords Justices, 9 Mar. 1692 in *Cal. SP (Dom.), 1691–2*, p. 174; Nottingham to Lords Justices, 2
    Apr. 1692 (NA, SP67/1 ff 159–60).

of major constitutional legislation of the kind approved at Westminster, from the list.[18] More pertinently in respect of Poynings' Law, it suggested that ministers were intent on taking advantage of the lack of certitude in Ireland, attributable to the breakdown in government and communication during the late 1680s and early 1690s, the wholesale changes in personnel, and the lack of recent experience in applying Poynings' Law, to assume an entitlement to instruct the Irish Privy Council as to the legislation it should prepare. Significantly, this contrasted with the procedure followed in 1677–8 and 1679–80, when the Irish Council took the lead in initiating legislation.[19]

This was a development of potentially critical significance for the future pattern of Anglo-Irish relations as well as for the operation of the Irish parliament and the application of Poynings' Law. But if officeholders in the Irish administration were disquieted, they kept their own counsel. Perhaps they did not deem it judicious to articulate reservations, as anxiety lest a meeting of parliament should expose differences over the Treaty of Limerick and create problems for a number of the highest officers of state who, with good reason, feared that parliament would 'be … clamorous against them', further delayed the preparation of bills.[20] London was unimpressed, and when no bills were received by the secretary of state by early July, Lord Nottingham wrote in the name of Queen Mary to inform the lords justices that she was 'extremely displeased with this delay' and to instruct them to ensure that 'the bills …, w[hi]ch were directed to be first drawn, be forthwith transmitted hither in paper that no more time be lost'.[21] Given the severity of this rebuke, it was understandable that the lords justices should seek to lay the blame on the legal officials (the attorney and solicitor generals and chief justice) to whom the task had been delegated. This was correct in so far as it went, but it was also blatantly self-serving, for though two bills – one appertaining to the establishment of a militia and the other to encourage the linen manufacture – were in a state of near readiness, it was not the law officers who decided that there was no need for revenue legislation and that consideration of a bill for attainder should be postponed until the arrival of the lord lieutenant, Lord Sydney.[22] Moreover, the failure of the lords justices to provide decisive leadership in this respect had the further unintended consequence of providing the English executive with an opportunity to prepare bills for consideration at the Irish Council. Three draft bills, one of which bore the title 'an act declaring all attainders made in the late pretended parliament to be void', were communicated

18. Ireland's status as a dependent kingdom, stated in 1541, was confirmed at this time (Johnston-Liik, *History of the Irish parliament*, i, 213–14).
19. Aydelotte, 'The duke of Ormonde and the English government of Ireland', chapter 1.
20. McGuire, 'The parliament of 1692', pp 3–4; J.G. Simms, *The Williamite confiscation in Ireland, 1690–1703* (London, 1956), passim.
21. Nottingham to Lords Justices, 5 July 1692 (NA, SP 67/1 f. 169).
22. Lords Justices to Nottingham, 16 July 1692 in *Cal. SP (Dom.), 1695*, pp 189–90. The lords justices reiterated the criticism of the law officers and judges on 25 July (*Cal. SP (Dom.), 1695*, pp 194–5).

by Nottingham on 9 July and five more were in a state of sufficient readiness eleven days later to be conveyed to the (English) attorney general for comment.[23]

The receipt from England of three draft bills had a galvanic impact on the Irish executive. Choosing, for obvious reasons, to accord these measures priority, they were in a state of sufficient readiness by 21 July for the lords justices to direct that they should be sent for transmission 'in the usual form under the great seal of this kingdom'. Of the three, only one – recognising their majesties' undoubted right to the throne of Ireland – was transmitted in the form in which it had been received from England. The others – the attainder bill and 'an act confirming the acts of settlement and explanation' – were subject to amendment on a number of points, though the apologetic justification advanced by the lords justices is indicative of their eagerness to accede to the wishes of the English Privy Council:

> We have made these several alterations in our transmission of the bills sent over to us, though we had no directions from you to alter anything therein, because we are sure there can be no inconvenience thereby to their Majesties' affairs, for if her Majesty shall not be satisfied with the reasons given by us for our altering the said bills they may be altered again in England, and made to agree in all things with those bills sent over to us before they are sent back to us under the great seal of England; for though no change can be made here in any bill sent over hither under the said seal, yet the Lords of the Council in England may make any such alterations as they shall think fit in any bill sent over from here under the said seal of this kingdom.[24]

In point of fact, such deference was unnecessary. On their reception, the bills were sent for scrutiny to the attorney and solicitor general and, pursuant to their report that they were appropriate to advance subject only to 'some [unspecified] amendments and provisions', an order in council was duly issued.[25]

With the certification of these bills and the issuing of a commission to Lord Sydney, the way was clear finally for parliament to meet in Ireland. Lord Nottingham did not conceal his eagerness that the lords justices should have everything 'in as great readiness as is possible ... [to] prevent any delay' when Sydney reached Dublin. The lords justices were so disposed to comply, they transmitted what were described tellingly as *draft* bills, seven in number, to the English Privy Council in late August.[26] The communication of these bills 'in

---

23. Nottingham to Lords Justices, 9 July 1692 (NA, SP67/1 ff 169–70); Nottingham to Attorney General, 20 July 1692 in *Cal. SP (Dom.), 1691–2*, pp 375–6.
24. Lords Justices to Nottingham, 21 July 1692 in *Cal. SP (Dom.), 1695*, pp 190–2.
25. Nottingham to Attorney General, 25 July 1692 in *Cal. SP (Dom.), 1691–2*, p. 382; NA, PC2/74 ff 228–9.
26. Lords Justices to Nottingham, 21, 25 July in *Cal. SP (Dom.), 1695*, pp. 192, pp 194–5; Nottingham to Lords Justices, 23 July, 6, 25 Aug. 1692 (NA, SP67/1 ff 170–3). Four of these bills had previously been relayed to Sydney, who had referred them to Nottingham.

paper' rather than in an engrossed form, on parchment, was not consistent with Poynings' Law, but the broadly positive response of the Committee on Irish Affairs to five of these measures and to two more contentious proposals (militia and indemnity bills) 'sent in paper' suggested that these would encounter few difficulties when they were revised and communicated in proper form.[27] The challenge was to get these draft bills put in a proper form in the time available. This was not as straightforward as it sounded, since even simple errors could cause complications. Sometimes, these derived from bureaucratic misunderstanding. Shortly after his arrival in Ireland in late August, Lord Sydney wrote to Nottingham to enquire as to the whereabouts of the three measures that had passed under the great seal of England on 1 August. It so happened that the bills had been annexed to Sydney's patent without his knowledge, but the exchange of letters that ensued between Dublin Castle and Whitehall is revealing of the deficiencies of current administrative practice.[28]

Lord Sydney's arrival prompted a visible acceleration in the pace of preparations for the meeting of parliament. This was assisted by the fact that the Irish Council was more actively engaged in drafting bills at this point than earlier in the year when the lords justices had delegated the task to its lawyers. Legal assistance was crucial as Sydney had determined on the risky strategy of asking the Irish parliament to agree 'a supply towards the charge of this government'. This meant drafting financial legislation. The method adopted was to request a 'committee of the Privy Council' to report on 'the best ways and means of raising' a supply, and for their report to constitute the basis for a discussion by 'the committee of the whole board' at which a bill was 'went through and agreed'.[29] Three money bills in all were prepared in this manner. Communicated to London towards the end of September with the request that they be returned 'with all speed', Sydney's urgency contrasted with his inability earlier in the month to expedite the transmission of militia and indemnity bills; these took a number of weeks to negotiate the Irish Council, perhaps because that body adhered to its practice of meeting once a week (on Fridays).[30]

The English Council's participation in drafting bills for transmission to Ireland, albeit in response to the failure of the Irish executive to produce bills promptly, suggested that councillors as well as ministers were willing to interpret Poynings' Law somewhat loosely in 1692. The transmission from Ireland of draft bills was consistent with this. And a further indication was provided on 13 September, when Sydney was apprised by Nottingham that any militia bill emanating from Ireland stood a better chance if it was 'perpetuall'. Conscious that

27. Nottingham to Sydney, 23 Aug. 1692 (NA, SP67/1 ff 172–3, *Cal. SP (Dom.), 1691–2*, pp 420–1).
28. Sydney to Nottingham, 27, 30 Aug. in *Cal. SP (Dom.), 1692*, p. 196; Nottingham to Sydney, 3 Sept. 1692 (NA, SP67/1 f. 215).
29. Sydney to Nottingham, 24, 28 Sept. in *Cal. SP (Dom.), 1692*, pp 204–5; Nottingham to Sydney, 27 Sept. 1692 (NA, SP67/1 f. 217).
30. Sydney to Nottingham, 9, 13 Sept. 1692 in *Cal. SP (Dom.), 1692*, pp 198–9, 202.

this was unlikely to be warmly received in Ireland, ministers expressed the pietistic hope that such a measure might be carried 'while the late misfortunes of ye kingdom are fresh ... in memory', but, unwilling to be proscriptive they advised Sydney to adopt the problematic expedient of transmitting two bills – 'one temporary, ye other perpetuall' – so they could choose between them.[31] The counsel offered on the matter of an indemnity bill was less specific, yet the observation that such a measure was 'necessary to the peace' of Ireland, as it alone would 'extinguish all occasions of feuds and animosities', was indicative of the commitment to prevail over entrenched 'contrary interests' in Ireland should this be necessary.[32] This was underscored by the decision that a bill received from Ireland 'about the lawyers of Galway' could not be returned to be put in due and proper order 'because it ... would have been of ill consequence', and that difficulties over a private bill for the relief of Colonel John Browne's creditors would be better accommodated by means of a clause inserted in another act.[33] Guided by such considerations, the eleven bills transmitted under the seal of Ireland on 29 September included a bill of indemnity, two militia bills (one for three and one for five years), and three money bills. However, the inclusion of a bill for securing the Protestant creditors of John Browne and a mining bill indicates that the Irish Council, for its part, did not conceive of itself as the passive recipient of instruction from its English counterpart.[34] That said, the fact that many of the engrossed measures transmitted from the Irish Council at the end of September had previously crossed the Irish Sea in 'paper' form illustrates that the English Council was exerting a degree of influence over prospective Irish legislation in the run-up to the 1692 parliament greater than a strict reading of Poynings' Law allowed.

The eleven bills received from Dublin were promptly referred to the attorney general, Sir John Somers, for 'consideration'. In an attempt to facilitate the Irish executive in its dealings with the Irish parliament, which assembled on 5 October, Nottingham suggested that the Lords of the Committee for Irish Affairs should determine at its meeting on the same day which of the bills should 'be quickly returned to Ireland'.[35] This suggestion was not taken up, however, because of legal uncertainty as to the propriety of returning bills received 'under one great seal of Ireland' under 'several great seals from England'.[36] Such doubts were set at rest after only a short delay, and the report of the attorney general was heard on six of the eleven bills on 7 October, when it was agreed that five should be

---

31. Nottingham to Sydney, 13 Sept. 1692 (NA, SP67/1 f. 216).
32. Ibid.; Sydney to Nottingham, 28 Sept. 1692 in *Cal. SP (Dom.)*, *1692*, p. 205.
33. Nottingham to Sydney, 13 Sept. 1692 (NA, SP67/1 f. 216).
34. Sydney to Nottingham, 28, 29 Sept. 1692 in *Cal. SP (Dom.)*, *1692*, pp 205–8; McGuire, 'The parliament of 1692', p. 5.
35. NA, PC2/75 f. 3; Nottingham to Sydney, 4 Oct. 1692 (NA, SP67/1 f. 217).
36. Nottingham to Temple and reply, 7, 8 Oct. 1692 in *Cal. SP (Dom.)*, *1691–2*, p. 474, and *Cal. SP (Dom.)*, *1698*, p. 212.

returned to Ireland. Among their number was an 'act for punishing officers or souldiers who shall mutiny or desert their majesties service', which was forwarded without alteration.[37] Between one and six amendments were authorised with respect to four bills, but in no instance can they be defined as significant. They were primarily syntactical and technical clarifications – 'some few literall amendments', Nottingham described them – introduced to eradicate interpretative ambiguity, syntactical error and verbal infelicity. Thus in the measure 'for settling the militia of this kingdom', it was determined at two points to introduce a reference to 'insurrection' after 'invasion', while in other instances the point at issue involved changing the tense of a verb.[38] A similar pattern is observable in respect of the larger number of amendments that were authorised to two (out of three) revenue bills approved on 10 October.[39] Significantly, a full record of the changes recommended in these instances by Attorney General Somers, and approved by the Queen in Council, was included in the minute of proceedings. This was not the first instance of such a minute; equivalent records were made on a number of occasions in 1665–6, but it represented an improvement in administrative practice at the English Council, and it inaugurated a pattern of systematic record-keeping that was to endure.

The greater regularity in the management of Irish bills at the English Council board identifiable from 1692 also facilitated the provision of more information as to the particular fate of bills. Thus when Lord Nottingham informed Viscount Sydney on 8 October that he was returning five bills with some 'not very materiall' alterations, he also made it known that seven bills that had been received previously were deemed 'very irregular'. Significantly, in a further illustration of the somewhat loose interpretation of Poynings' Law being applied, it was decided in the case of two of these – bills to punish mutiny and desertion and to encourage Protestant strangers – that they should be returned to Ireland so they could be revised and retransmitted in a more acceptable form. And, it was advised in respect of three other 'useful' bills that they should also be 'sent hither in form under the great seal of Ireland'.[40]

Of the eleven bills received from the Irish Council in late September, the measure that best illustrates the lengths to which the English Privy Council was

37. NA, PC2/75 ff 6–7; Yard to Williamson, 8 Oct. 1692 in *Cal. SP (Dom.), 1691–2*, pp 475–6.
38. NA, PC2/75 ff 6–7; Nottingham to the Clerk of the Crown, 7 Oct. 1692 in *Cal. SP (Dom.), 1691–92*, p. 473; Nottingham to Sydney, 8 Oct. 1692 (NA, SP 67/1 f. 218). As well as those cited in the text, the bills reported as appropriate to succeed were An act for encouragement of Protestant strangers to settle in the kingdome of Ireland; An act for the prevention of vexatious suits that may be brought against any person who acted in this kingdome for their majesties service, and An act for the taking of affidavits in the courts to be made use of in the Courts of Kings Bench, Common Pleas and Exchequer.   39. NA, PC2/75 ff 9–10.
40. Nottingham to Sydney, 8 Oct. 1692 (NA, SP 67/1 f 218). The 'useful' bills to which Nottingham referred were measures to settle intestate estates, to exempt Protestant dissenters from the penalty of certain laws, and to prevent frauds and perjuries. He also invited him to return a mines bill that had encountered stern opposition at the English Council.

prepared to go to bring bills drafted in Ireland into line was the indemnity bill.
Prompted by William of Orange's wish to provide some statutory recognition for
the treaties of Galway and Limerick, it was made clear to the Irish administration
in late August that

> Her Majesty would have such clauses added as shall be necessary for
> pardoning all such persons as are comprehended in any of the articles
> granted to the places that surrendered which should be recited, and also all
> such as have submitted pursuant to His Majesty's proclamations and
> declarations or any others issued by His Majesty's directions or have taken
> protections ... according to the intent and meaning of such proclamations
> and declarations [provided they] lived peaceably and quietly and with all
> due obedience to their majesties ever since the time of their submission.[41]

The strong opposition of Irish Protestants to any initiative that was 'to the favour
of the popish party' made the formulation of a measure that stood a chance of
becoming law a delicate task, but the government was unyielding. It was made
clear to Sydney in mid-September that ministers believed such legislation was
'necessary to the peace of th[e] country, which can never be established without
an Act of Indemnity to extinguish all occasions of feuds and animosities'.[42]
Obliged to address the question, the Irish Council had a draft bill in sufficient
readiness by the end of the month for the lord lieutenant to opine confidently that
they had fulfilled their instructions in this respect. This was not strictly true since,
in an attempt to allay the unease of 'the contending interests and different ...
parties' in Ireland, councillors 'went beyond her Majesty's directions' by
introducing clauses to penalise Jacobites who were abroad by excluding them from
any 'benefit' from the proposed indemnity, and by providing that they could be
attainted for disloyalty. The effect of this, Sydney explained, was to 'join ... in one
what might otherwise have been proper for two bills'.[43]

Sydney's expectation was that what was now described as the 'attainder and
indemnity bill' would encounter resistance at the English Council board. He
anticipated that the main objections would arise with councillors, who perceived
that the bill contravened the instruction to prepare an indemnity measure only,
whereas it was quickly apparent that the bill's sharpest critics were Irish Catholics.
Indeed, the measure was no sooner referred to the attorney general than a petition
was received from 'the Roman Catholics of Ireland' requesting a copy of this bill,
and of the bill for securing the Protestant creditors of John Browne, and seeking
the right to present their objections before either was ratified. Since the

---

41. Nottingham to Sydney, 25 Aug. 1692 (NA, SP67/1 ff 172–3). The letter is calendared in *Cal.
    SP (Dom.), 1691–2*, pp 420–1.
42. Nottingham to Sydney, 13 Sept. 1692 (NA, SP67/1 f. 216).
43. Sydney to Nottingham, 9 Sept., Sydney and Irish Council to Nottingham, 28 Sept., Sydney to
    Nottingham, 29 Sept. 1692 in *Cal. SP (Dom.), 1691–2*, pp 198–9, 205–7.

entitlement of interested parties to scrutinise bills and to petition for the admission of amendments had been established in the 1660s, the Council was eager not to add to the grievances of Irish Catholics on this point. Their request was promptly conveyed to the attorney general with the direction that he should 'permit [Irish Catholics] to have a sight of and [to] peruse the said bill[s], and having heard and received what objections they shall make unto them, to report the same with his opinion thereupon'.[44] The expectation was that this would not cause more than a few days' delay. This remained the official view, though it was conceded at the Council on 10 October, in response to further Catholic requests, that they should be allowed 'reasonable time … to make their necessary observations'. Delays were inevitable by this date, since the Privy Council had by then received requests from some twenty Catholics urging amendments to the bill to permit 'indemnities, reversal of outlawries, restoration of estates or … free and general pardons'. Having concluded that Catholic concerns on these points could best be allayed by introducing 'general rules', the attorney general was directed to address this matter 'with the assistance' of his Irish counterpart, Sir John Temple.[45] The advice and support of the chief justices of the courts of King's Bench and Common Pleas were also made available, but even these were insufficient to surmount the 'many difficulties' the law officers encountered, and within a few days the secretary of state admitted that he could not honestly say when the bill might be returned.[46] This was the first real hint of the seriousness of the problems facing officials as they contrived to come to terms with the 'many objections' they encountered. Unwilling to let the issue drop, yet aware that the 'objections' could not be 'determined in time' to allow the bill to 'be past this parliament', it was proposed not just to amend, but to engage in a total rewrite of the measure.[47]

This decision was taken on 27 October when the solicitor general, Sir Thomas Trevor, was instructed to assist the attorney general to recast the bill 'so as to make it a confirmation of the capitulations of Limerick and Galway, and a discharge of all actions and suits comenced, or to be comenced or brought by, or against any person or persons comprized within these articles upon occasion of their being concerned or engaged on either side'.[48] Put more pithily by Nottingham, the attorney general was instructed 'to prepare a confirmation of the Articles of Limerick', 'in lieu' of the existing indemnity bill. This was consistent with the commitment William of Orange had entered into to 'recommend [the treaty] to a parliament'. It was anticipated further that it would 'goe a great way towards the extinguishing of private suits, tho' not fully effect all that seems necessary for …

---

44. NA, PC2/75 ff 6–7; Yard to Williamson, 11 Oct. 1692 in *Cal. SP (Dom.), 1691–2*, p. 478. It is noteworthy that on the same day a petition from Thomas Tilson requesting the introduction of a proviso 'in the bill … touching forfeited estates' that would secure his interest in the office of usher of the Court of Chancery was also referred to the attorney general for a 'report'.
45. NA, PC2/75 ff 8, 10–12.   46. Nottingham to Sydney, 11, 14 Oct. 1692 (NA, SP67/1 f. 219).
47. Nottingham to Sydney, 2 Nov. 1692 (NA, SP67/1 ff 219–20).   48. NA, PC2/75 f. 22.

quieting [the] kingdom of Ireland'. It was not surprising, therefore, when the full Council, in the presence of William III, received what was in effect a new indemnity bill from the attorney general on 3 November that approval was forthcoming. As a result, the extant long bill received from Ireland was replaced by a 'very short one' offering those 'comprized within' the Treaty immunity against 'all actions and suits of what nature soever from which by the true intent and meaning of the said articles they were to be discharged'.[49]

Though its experience was exceptional, the crucial point with respect to the indemnity bill was that the version transmitted to Ireland reflected what the King in Council believed should become law. The Council was also decisive in determining to return the bill for the relief of the Protestant creditors of John Browne. This represented a dramatic change in fortune for this measure. From being in a situation in mid-September in which it appeared that the best Browne's creditors could anticipate was a clause tacked onto another measure, it was enabled with Sydney's combative support to negotiate all hurdles, including an attempt to have it laid aside and the opposition of Catholics, at the Council Board on 10 October.[50] The outcome in this instance was unexpected, but the decision to respite a bill for the relief of Dissenters, transmitted in response to Lord Nottingham's request on 8 October, indicated that the Council was quite prepared to be guided in its actions in respect of certain measures by Lord Sydney. In this case, Sydney made it clear that the bill would, if returned, meet with resistance in the House of Lords because it did not include a sacramental test.[51] The rationale for rejecting a mining bill, against Sydney's advice, was not political; but in this instance the obstacle arose from the fact that the proposed bill conflicted with the grant by James II to James Hamilton 'of all gold and silver mines within the kingdom'. Consideration was given to challenging the patent of which Hamilton was the beneficiary, but pending the resolution of that problem, it was determined not to proceed with the measure.[52]

A total of thirteen bills from the substantially larger number of legislative suggestions, 'paper' drafts and engrossed bills that were considered by the English

---

49. NA, PC2/75 f. 23; Nottingham to Sydney, 9 Nov. 1692 (NA, SP67/1 f. 220, calendared in *Cal. SP (Dom.), 1691–2*, p. 497.

50. Above p. 54; NA, PC2/75 ff 6–7, 8, 21; Yard to Williamson, 11 Oct. 1692 in *Cal. SP (Dom.), 1691–2*, p. 478; Nottingham to Sydney, 2 Nov. 1692 (NA, SP67/1 ff 219–20).

51. Sydney to Nottingham, 18 Oct., Nottingham to Sydney, 22 Oct. 1692 in *Cal. SP (Dom.), 1692*, pp 214, 487; NA, PC2/75 ff 20, 21. Two of the four bills communicated on 18 September were returned with few amendments; these were An act for the prevention of frauds and injuries which was returned with two amendments, and An act for the better settling intestate estates, which was returned with five. In respect of the Dissenter bill, the perception that the measure was unlikely to find favour with the Dissenters prompted the Council to 'reject' it for the present (Sydney to Nottingham, 18 Oct. in *Cal. SP (Dom.), 1692*, p. 214; Nottingham to Sydney, 2 Nov. 1692 (NA, SP67/1 ff 219–20)).

52. Sydney to Nottingham, 28 Sept. in *Cal. SP (Dom.), 1695*, pp 205–7; NA, PC2/75 ff 20, 22; Nottingham to Sydney, 2 Nov. 1692 (NA, SP67/1 ff 219–20, calendared in *Cal. SP (Dom.), 1691–2*, pp 492–3).

and Irish Privy Councils during the prolonged, and less than entirely regular preparations for the 1692 session were deemed suitable for presentation to the Irish parliament. It was neither an impressive nor a disappointing total, but the way in which they emerged, and were certified suggested that both English ministers and councillors were intent on interpreting Poynings' Law in a manner that afforded it a major role in the initiation of Irish law. The most pregnant manifestation of this was the suggestion emanating from the English Council that Irish legislation should be transmitted in the first instance in draft form. The ostensible rationale for this was that the engrossed bills received from Ireland were error-prone and poorly constructed, but since bills were frequently drafted in a hurry, this was only to be anticipated. It would be surprising if bills prepared within the space of eight or fourteen days were exemplary illustrations of the art of draughtsmanship. The fact that a high proportion of bills that were commu-nicated in 1692 reflected what English ministers believed were the issues requiring legislative attention in Ireland was also a consideration. This appealed to ministers, of course, because it implied that they would be in a position to apply the powers conferred on the English Council by Poynings' Law expansively, which meant in turn, if it became normative practice, that the legislative activity of the Irish parliament would not just be subordinate but secondary to that of the English Council, and potentially confined to vetoing or approving Privy Council bills. This did not augur well for the Irish Council either, since it was no less likely if the examples of the indemnity and mining bills set the standard that the Irish Council's subordination to its English equivalent would mean that the Irish Council's role in shaping legislation would also be greatly qualified.

In more energetic hands than those of the lords justices and more adroit political hands than those of Viscount Sydney, it may be that the Irish Council might have shown greater initiative in 1692, but there is little reason to believe it would have made a material difference. Sydney was sent to Ireland to serve as the Crown's representative and, as his initiation at the Irish Privy Council of money bills indicates, his priority was to protect the royal prerogative. Moreover, it must be borne in mind that because the Irish parliament had not assembled in twenty-six years (the 'Jacobite parliament' excepted) that ministers, officials and privy councillors in London were unlikely to possess a better opportunity both to interpret and to apply the powers granted to them under Poynings' Law in a manner consistent with their conviction that they were entitled, morally if not legally and politically if not constitutionally, to exercise a determining influence on the legislation of the Irish parliament. Significantly, they were unable to sustain this because of opposition in Ireland that Sydney did not anticipate, and was unable to overcome. Thus his failure to canvass the views of MPs prior to the meeting of parliament was to prove costly. In common with others at the pinnacle of the administrative apparatus in Ireland, he seems to have assumed that the personnel of the Irish parliament would not object strenuously to being presented with a full legislative agenda. Given that the Irish parliament convened in the

1660s had accepted this role it was not an unreasonable assumption, but Irish Protestants were disposed to be more assertive in the early 1690s. And their decisive intervention in 1692 set in train a sequence of events that was to ensure, before the end of the decade, that the practice of law-making for Ireland was to take a form that ensured neither the English nor the Irish Councils possessed the dominant role in the shaping and initiating of legislation they exercised in the unique circumstances of the lead-up to the 1692 session.

FAILURE IN 1692

The jurists, politicians and privy councillors who were occupied on both sides of the Irish Sea during the months of September and October shaping the legislation to be offered to the Irish parliament did so in anticipation that the political representatives of Protestant Ireland would conduct themselves after an essentially passive fashion. However, MPs were unwilling to acquiesce in an arrangement that meant, as one of Bishop William King of Derry's correspondents put it: 'We either entirely receive ... or entirely reject ... we not having the liberty to add or subtract any the least word or so much as alter a false spelling.'[53] Evidential lacunae mean that their preparations for the opening of the session are obscure, but they were encouraged to behave assertively by the example of MPs at Westminster, who had manifested their determination to possess a central role in the political process by affirming their entitlement to vote the Crown the money it needed to prosecute the ongoing war with France and to pay for current expenditure. As a result, parliament became firmly established during the 1690s as a key locus of power in the emerging constitutional monarchy in Britain.[54] Irish Protestants believed they were entitled to a parliament with similar powers. They did not specify how they would use these powers, but their dislike of the Treaty of Limerick and their identification of corruption at the highest levels of government combined to ensure that MPs approached the session in a determined frame of mind.[55] The mood was not lightened, certainly, by rumours to the effect that, as well as bills recognising the new monarchs and invalidating the actions of the Jacobite parliament, they would be presented with a bill 'to confirm the Treaty of Limerick'. Described by one sympathetic to their position as the equivalent of making 'popery an established religion' and of depriving 'all Protestants of their actions against the Papists by whom they were plundered', it ensured that the session that commenced on 5 October would be eventful.[56]

53. [ ] to King, 19 Dec. 1695 (TCD, King Papers, MSS 1995–2008 f. 482).
54. Clayton Roberts, 'The constitutional significance of the financial settlement of 1690', *Historical Journal*, 20 (1977), pp 59–76; McNally, *Parties, patriots and undertakers*, pp 38–9.
55. Dickson, *New foundations*, p. 43; Connolly, *Religion, law and power*, p. 75; McGuire, 'The parliament of 1692', pp 3–4, 10–11.
56. *An account of the sessions of parliament in Ireland, 1692* (London, 1693), pp 2–3.

This was not apparent during the opening days when parliamentary time was largely taken up with non-contentious procedural matters, and approval was readily forthcoming for a Privy Council bill recognising 'their majesties undoubted right to the crown of Ireland'.[57] Yet, Sydney's observation on 12 October that MPs were of 'a mind to be angry' was ominous, since it indicated that the implicit assumption at the English and Irish Council Boards that the Irish parliament would accede to a subordinate role was untenable. None of the anger was targeted at Sydney at this point, but the fact that some MPs 'talk[ed] of freeing themselves from the yoke of England [and] of taking away Poynings' law' was evidence of deep-seated constitutional restlessness.[58] This was certainly visible in the House of Commons on 21 October when MPs signalled their determination to loosen the restraints of Poynings' Law by rejecting the Privy Council bill 'confirming the acts of settlement and explanation', though the justification offered for this action was that the measure would, if ratified, 'unsettle … the greatest part of the estates of this kingdom'.[59] If this was an isolated event, it could have been overlooked, but their approval of a resolution on 27 October asserting their 'sole right' to raise money bills and, on 28 October, to reject one of the two money bills drafted at the Irish Council and returned 'from England under the Great Seal there' was quite a different matter. Significantly, they justified this action on explicitly constitutional grounds, summarised by a contemporary as follows:

> It has always been conceived the original right of the Commons that mony [*sic*] bills should take their rise in their house, and that as well as the *quantum*, as the method of raising it should be determined by them; the House lookt upon this to be their inherent fundamental right, and that the same was not taken away by any act of parliament in this kingdom; as in reason they thought none cou'd be so good judges of the properest and easiest way of taxing the subject as they, and even since *Poyning's* [*sic*] *Act* those rights of the House are found asserted in the Journals on the bringing in of Mony Bills, whereof they did not prepare the heads.[60]

The suggestion, explicit in this account, that the Commons' action was both consonant with Poynings' Law and consistent with long-established practice – though sincerely made – was based on foundations that were less secure than its advocates assumed. The claim, in the main account of proceedings, that the Commons' action was consistent with 'a standing order' that 'no bill to tax the

---

57. For the Act of recognition (4 William and Mary, chap 1), see *Commons Jn. (Irl.)*, ii, 14, 15; *Lords Jn. (Irl.)*, i, 452.

58. Sydney to Nottingham, 12, 17 Oct. 1692 in *Cal. SP (Dom.)*, *1695*, pp 212, 213–14.

59. *An account of the sessions … , 1692*, p. 12; *Commons Jn. (Irl.)*, ii, 21; Sydney to Nottingham, 22 Oct. 1692 in *Cal. SP (Dom.)*, *1695* pp 214–15; D.W. Hayton, *Ruling Ireland, 1685–1742: politics, politicians and parties* (Woodbridge, 2004), p. 44.

60. *An account of the sessions … , 1692*, pp 14–15.

subject be brought into the House without leave of the House first obtained' was doubtful, though it was the basis for the assertion on 27 October 'that it was, and is the sole and undoubted right of the Commons to prepare heads of bills for raising money'.[61] Granted, the House had asserted this right in 1661 and in 1666, but it was not uncontested though few, other than the Irish attorney general, Sir John Temple, queried whether the so-called 'standing order' justified their contention. Temple maintained, with some reason, that the assertion by the House of Commons in the 1660s that they possessed the sole right to initiate financial legislation was nothing more than an affectation seized upon by MPs as an affirmation of their consequence.[62]

Ostensibly untroubled by claims to the contrary, the Commons intensified its demand to possess an active role in the making of law. Thus, as well as rejecting a money bill because it did not 'rise in this house', they negatived the measure 'declaring all attainders, and all other acts made in the late pretended parliament to be void'; they refused to agree to the proposal 'for settling the militia in this kingdom'; and they allowed bills 'for the prevention of vexatious suits' and for punishing mutiny and desertion, which were forwarded having negotiated the House of Lords, to fall.[63] Their adherence to the principle of the 'sole right' of MPs to initiate money bills was not inflexible, however; they acknowledged that in 'the present exigencies of affairs, ... the public necessity of speedily raising a supply for their majesties' was such that it was financially desirable to sanction 'an additional duty of excise upon beer, ale and other liquors'. Significantly, the amount of money raised thereby was insufficient to sustain the Irish adminis-tration for long; but, as an additional precaution, it was approved with the explicit caveat that it would not be 'drawn into precedent hereafter'.[64] And, in a further assertion of their entitlement to initiate law, they prepared the heads of a bill 'for settling the militia' in lieu of the official measure they had rejected.[65]

Other than the utterly non-contentious 'act of recognition' and the act providing an additional duty of excise on beer, the House of Commons approved only two bills before Viscount Sydney determined in a show of authority to suspend the session.[66] This was a drastic action, but the administration was left with no alternative because the House of Commons was, Sir William Temple

61. Ibid., p. 15; *Commons Jn. (Irl.)*, ii, 28.
62. Above, pp 22, 34, 46; Sir William Temple, Discourse on Ireland, 1695 (BL, Add. MS 27382 ff 3–6).
63. *Commons Jn. (Irl.)*, ii, 24, 30, 32, 34; *Lords Jn. (Irl.)*, i, 465–6; *An account of the sessions ... , 1692*, pp 22–4.
64. McGuire, 'The parliament of 1692', pp 19–20; *An account of the sessions ... , 1692*, pp 15–16; *Commons Jn. (Irl.)*, ii, 28; Sydney to Nottingham, 28 Oct. 1692 in *Cal. SP (Dom.), 1692*, p. 215.
65. *Commons Jn. (Irl.)*, ii, 30, 32, 34. This had reached the committee stage before it was over taken by events, but this was not acknowledged either by the Lord Lieutenant or by his officials.
66. As well as the Act of Recognition and the Act for an additional duty of excise on beer, ale and other liquors, they were an Act for the encouragement of Protestant strangers; and an Act for taking affidavits in the country.

concluded, asserting an 'entirely new' and threatening doctrine.[67] Sydney concurred; he observed that if the Commons' claim to possess the 'sole right' to raise money bills was conceded 'the effects it will have by lessening the dependency of this kingdom upon the crown of England ... will be very prejudicial'.[68] Determined this should not come to pass, the lord lieutenant adjudged that he could best uphold 'their majesties' prerogative and the undoubted right of the Crown of England' by suspending the session. And, he did not mince his words when he pointed out to MPs on 3 November that they had not only 'not answered the ends for which they were called together', but also had 'behaved ... undutifully and ungratefully, in invading their majesties prerogative'. Understandably, given the active part they had played in the preparations for the session, ministers and officials in London endorsed Sydney's stand; they shared his assessment that the Irish parliament must accept what was 'the constant practice and usage' and work within the parameters of Poynings' Law as currently understood and implemented.[69]

* * *

The short, eventful, and legislatively unproductive 1692 session offered a stark demonstration of how quickly a political *impasse* could be generated if the English and Irish executives insisted on applying Poynings' Law in a manner that did not allow the Irish parliament, as the representative body of the Protestant interest in Ireland, an active role in the making of law. One might have thought for this reason that the priority of the Irish administration would be to reach an early accommodation with its critics, but Sydney devoted more effort to proving that he was legally and constitutionally justified in acting as he did. To this end, the Irish judiciary was invited to examine the claim of the Commons to possess the 'sole right' to initiate supply legislation, and to report without delay. Formally requested by the lord lieutenant and Council on 6 February 1693 and submitted eight days later, their report provided the administration with welcome legal backing.[70] Moreover, it was warmly received in London, and eager 'to strengthen and add weight to it', as well as to eradicate all doubt about the impartiality of the Irish judges' verdict, which had been impugned in some quarters, the Queen in Council instructed the English judiciary to undertake a similar investigation.[71]

67. Sir William Temple, Discourse on Ireland, 1695 (BL, Add. MS 27382 ff 3–6).
68. Sydney to Nottingham, 6 Nov. 1692 in *Cal. SP (Dom.), 1695*, pp 217–18.
69. *An account of the sessions ... 1692*, pp 24–5; *A collection of the protests of the Lords of Ireland from the first upon record to the end of the session in March 1770* (London, 1771), pp 18–23; Nottingham to Temple, 7 Nov. 1692 in *Cal. SP (Dom.), 1691–2*, pp 494–5.
70. *Cal. SP (Dom.), 1693*, pp 28, 35; Opinion of Irish judges on sole right, 14 Feb. 1693 (BL, Harleian MS 6274 ff 123–38, Add. MS 9715 ff 8–14).
71. Nottingham to Sydney, 18 Mar., 29 Apr. 1693 (NA, SP67/1 ff 226, 228); Burns, *Irish parliamentary politics*, i, 8–9.

Difficulties attributable to the absence of the judges on circuit delayed the presentation of their findings until 23 June, but this was less important than the content, which offered a ringing endorsement of the official position:

> We ... are of opinion that it is not the sole and undoubted right of the Commons of Ireland assembled in parliament to prepare heads of bills for raising money. ... The Lord Lieutenant and Council [of Ireland] may prepare and certify bills for raising money to your majesties and the council of England ... to be returned under the great seal of England and afterwards sent to the Commons, albeit the heads of bills have not first their rise in that house.[72]

The opinion of the judiciary in both kingdoms provided ministers and officials with legal support for their position, but there was a risk – obscured by the current preoccupation with the legal basis for the Irish Commons' claim of 'sole right' – that the foundations of parliamentary government in Ireland would be permanently undermined if a settlement was not forthcoming. Nobody in government on either side of the Irish Sea showed any willingness to contemplate concession at this moment, and they were affirmed in this conviction by rumours, circulating in London during the spring of 1693, to the effect 'that most of the members of the last [1692] parliament were sensible of their mistake in the late vote of the sole right'. These hopes were dashed by better-informed noises emanating from Dublin Castle that not only indicated the opposite, but also convinced Sydney that his ambition to reconvene the Irish parliament at an early date was unrealisable.[73] An important pointer was provided by Alan Brodrick, the MP for Cork and one of the leaders of Irish Protestantism, who was to the fore asserting the Commons' 'sole right' in respect of money bills in 1692; he observed in June 1693 that the insistence on reserving the exclusive right to initiate law to the Privy Council was comparable to Wentworth's attempt in the 1630s to make parliament subordinate to the Council. Citing the opinion of an unnamed councillor that 'we should be governed by the council board and ... they would give us the law', he concluded decisively that MPs could not back down if they aspired (as he certainly did) to an active role in the making of law for the kingdom of Ireland.[74] Since, as Brodrick averred and Sydney was compelled to acknowledge, this was the majority view among Irish Protestants, it was soon apparent that such preparations as the Irish and English Privy Councils had embarked upon in

72. Opinion of the judges in England about money bills in Ireland, 23 June 1693 in *Cal. SP (Dom.)*, *1693*, p. 191.
73. C.I. McGrath, 'Securing the Protestant interest: policy, politics and parliament in Ireland in the aftermath of the Glorious Revolution 1690–95' (MA thesis, UCD, 1991), p. 124.
74. Alan to Thomas Brodrick, 23 June 1693 (Guildford Muniment Room, Midleton papers, cited in Burns, *Irish parliamentary politics*, i, 6–8). See also McGrath, 'Securing the Protestant interest', pp 125–6.

respect of reconvening the Irish parliament in the autumn of 1693 were futile.[75] Sydney's assessment in May that the Irish parliament 'will never yield the point about the sole right', and that it might seek even to impeach the judiciary who denied its legality also suggested that his continued presence in Ireland was no longer beneficial, and he was replaced in June by lords justices.[76]

The assumption by Lord Capell, Sir Cyril Wyche and William Duncombe of the reins of power in Ireland brought about a perceptible softening in attitude within the Irish executive on the thorny matter of 'sole right'. Parallel with this, the Irish administration recognised that it was in its interest to ensure that the manner in which bills were prepared conformed to the letter of Poynings' Law. To this end, as they readied a number of bills, prepared 'according to the commands sent us', for transmission to England in September, the lords justices pointed out to Nottingham that 'there can be but one transmission before a parliament be called'.[77] Predictably, Nottingham was intent on interpreting the Law in a manner that allowed the Councils in both kingdoms maximum influence. He conceded that the lords justices were correct to assert that 'there can be but one transmission before the calling of parliament', but his observation that 'there may be many more after the issuing of writs' expressed London's preference that the Irish Privy Council would continue actively to initiate legislation and to do so while parliament was in session as well as prior to its assembly. Since this was permitted by Poynings' Law, it was not contentious. However, Nottingham's pronouncement that the English Council was eager to continue the practice implemented in 1692 of receiving bills, including money bills, in draft (i.e. on paper) as well as in engrossed form was more problematic:

> Her Majesty commands me to acquaint you that she would have you prepare as many bills for money or other matters relating to the good of that kingdom as you shall judge proper, and not in forme under the Great Seale that they may be sent back with the amendments which shall be thought fitt.[78]

Nottingham justified this instruction on the obvious grounds that it ensured when bills were 'transmitted in forme, there will be less trouble in the returne of them'. Since this was the arrangement the Irish Council and lords justices had acceded to prior to the 1692 session, their successors were hardly well positioned to disagree, but having reconsidered the implications of transmitting 'paper bills', they concluded early in October 1693 that it was inadvisable, since it was 'contrary to Poynings' Law' to transmit any bill that had not been formally passed at the

---

75. Nottingham to Somers, 24 May in *Cal. SP (Dom.), 1693*, p. 152; Nottingham to Sydney, 21 June 1693 (NA, SP67/1 f. 235, calendared in *Cal. SP (Dom.), 1693*, pp 188–9).
76. McGrath, 'Securing the Protestant interest', p. 127; *Cal. SP (Dom.), 1693*, p. 186.
77. Lords Justices to Nottingham, 9 Sept. 1693 in *Cal. SP (Dom.), 1693*, pp 319–20.
78. Nottingham to Lords Justices, 19 Sept. 1693 (NA, SP67/1 f. 237, calendared in *Cal. SP (Dom.), 1693*, p. 332).

Irish Council, sent for engrossment, and transmitted under the great seal of Ireland. In support of this position, they cited the arrangement that 'bills should begin here and be first transmitted under the great seal from hence', and observed pertinently that 'a bill will not be thought to have begun here in construction of law, which shall be brought to council as it has been framed in England, and pass here only for form's sake without any liberty of alteration'.[79]

These were weighty considerations upon which English officials would have liked to have prevailed, but the combination of legal requirements and the practical objection that the mode of proceeding London favoured must prolong the process of preparing legislation were not easily countered. Unwilling simply to yield, Nottingham contended on 17 October that draft bills could be sent from Ireland as 'private papers' rather than as 'the publick acts of the lords justices and Councill of Ireland', since this did not in any way

> preclude your lords of Councill from altering any part of those paper draughts when they should be returned ... , nor from considering any other matters which might occure to your Lordships or the Councill as proper for bills; but on the contrary that any such things might be proposed at Councill, as also that the paper draughts should be offer'd as other things of that nature are used to be and not as the directions of the Queene, and therefore might freely be debated and altered and so transmitted hither in forme so that her Majesty does think this method can be no ways contradictory to Poynings' Law etc., but having been usefully practic'd in King Charles the 2nds time and lately in her own reigne her majesty thinks it may be for her service now.[80]

Obliged to yield, the lords justices undertook for the moment to communicate 'paper bills' on the understanding that it was accepted that they were 'crude and indigested things'.[81] It was hardly an ideal arrangement, but the significant fact was that, by pursuing this exchange, the lord justices had not just clarified the procedural implications of transferring draft legislation between the two kingdoms, they had effectively stemmed the transfer of the initiative in the making of law for Ireland to London, and from the Irish to the English Privy Council.

This established, the realisation that it was simply not possible to complete the preparations required to allow parliament to assemble either in late 1693 or early 1694 pushed the issue of Ireland down the political agenda in England for a time. Paradoxically, this served to underline the urgency of a parliament being

---

79. Lords Justices to Nottingham, 7 Oct. 1693 in *Cal. SP (Dom.), 1693*, pp 356–7. The lords justices sustained this argument by maintaining that a bill promoted by Lord Massereene in the 1692 parliament 'did not arise here but came out of England to the Board'.
80. Nottingham to Lords Justices, 17 Oct. 1693 (NA, SP67/1 f. 240, calendared in *Cal. SP (Dom.), 1693*, p. 367).
81. Lords Justices to Nottingham, 24 Oct. 1693 (*Cal. SP (Dom.), 1693*, p. 378).

convened, as the appreciating arrears on the civil and military list and other 'debts owing from the crown' became a cause of mounting concern. In addition, 'some temporary laws' required renewal, while the necessity of regulation in a variety of other areas including the politically sensitive matter of 'securing the English and Protestant interest' was also pressing.[82] Acutely conscious of the importance of each of these points, as well as of allowing William III to honour his 'word' to secure parliamentary protection for the Treaty of Limerick, preparations were renewed in the late spring of 1694. Inevitably, queries were raised at the English Council as to 'whether the parliament will insist upon the right of beginning money bills as they did the last sessions'.[83] Unwilling to cede what was now deemed an important principle,[84] but anxious for some way out of the *impasse* on the matter, ministers took heart from reports from Ireland, which indicated an amelioration in attitudes. The most significant pointer was provided by the growing flexibility of the Brodrick faction.

While he adhered to his conviction that it was the 'just right of the Commons to prepare heads of money bills', Alan Brodrick was increasingly willing to contemplate a compromise if ministers permitted the Irish parliament to consider a body of legislation that provided for the settlement of Ireland along the lines desired by the 'Protestant interest'.[85] Lord Capell, who was the senior and most ambitious of the three lords justices, was quick to seize on this, and writing in July 1694 to John Trenchard, who had succeeded the earl of Nottingham as secretary of state, he expressed optimism that if a parliament was convened 'all heats will be laid aside', and that members would 'do their majesties, and their country, all the service than can be expected from good English men and Protestants'. He fully anticipated that some MPs would 'stand to their former vote of having the sole power of money bills', but he was quietly confident, having 'discoursed with all sorts of people', that the mood was palpably different to what it was in 1692.[86]

This was encouraging. What remained unclear was the precise mechanism that would be employed to accommodate the Crown's insistence, reiterated once more in July 1694, 'that their Majesties will by no means part from their right of sending money bills as well as others', with the resolve of Irish Protestants to affirm their right to initiate financial legislation.[87] The fact that it would take

82. Capell to Trenchard, 14 July 1694 in HMC, *Buccleuch and Queensbury*, ii, 99–101.
83. Privy Council minute, 22, 29 Apr., Shrewsbury to Capell, 14 June 1694 in HMC, *Buccleuch and Queensbury*, ii, 63, 81; Trenchard to Lords Justices, 28 Apr. 1694 (NA, SP67/1 f. 196).
84. In an 'opinion' dating from 1694, the judges of England affirmed their view that the Irish parliament did not have the right to prepare heads of bills for raising money but accepted that the Irish Council was entitled 'to prepare and certify bills' to this end that did not 'first ... rise in' the Irish Commons: *Cal. SP (Dom.), 1694–5*, p. 371.
85. McGrath, 'Securing the Protestant interest', pp 134–5, 148–51; McGrath, *Making the constitution*, p. 94.
86. [Capell to Trenchard], 14 July in HMC, *Buccleuch and Queensbury*, ii, 100–1; Capell to William III, 27 July [1694] in *Cal. SP (Dom.), 1693*, p. 237; Hayton, *Ruling Ireland*, p. 52.
87. Trenchard to Lords Justices, 28 July 1694 (NA, SP67/1 f. 203).

'several months' at the least to prepare for parliament meant there was still time to settle this point, and it helped that specific proposals were being contemplated.[88] One suggestion emanating from England was

> that the speech in opening the parliament [in Ireland] shall mention nothing concerning money, but the House of Commons shall no sooner meet, but immediately they shall resolute themselves into a Committee of the whole House, and, before all other things, shall vote heads for bills of money to be presented for the Government.[89]

This seemed hopeful, since it offered the possibility of financial legislation arising with MPs, but Capell anticipated problems, and his conclusion that it did not possess 'much credit' and must negatively 'embroil the King's affairs here' ensured it fell by the wayside. Capell remained upbeat, none the less, that a 'lasting settlement and good laws' was possible, so when rumours at the end of the year of changes to the personnel of government threatened to undermine the commitment of 'many gentlemen ... to waive the *sole right*' unless Capell made good his part of the bargain to allow the Irish parliament prepare legislation, he reiterated his conviction there was a real probability of agreement if he was given the opportunity to put his plan into effect:

> My ambition to settle this poor kingdom, and to confirm the people thereof in their duty to the King, together with my fear of being disappointed, if joined with any other, and almost certainty of success if left alone ... make[s] me persuade myself they will not by an unreasonable obstinacy (after having given me their words) disoblige the King, which may deprive them of that settlement so essential to their own present and future happiness'.[90]

Capell was assured of the opportunity he craved when William III made him lord deputy in May 1695. A few weeks later, after two and a half years of skirmishing and uncertainty as to the future of the Irish parliament's legislative role, the English lords justices invited Dublin Castle to demonstrate there were due 'causes and considerations' to convene an Irish parliament, and preparations began for what was to become a landmark session in the indivisible histories of the Irish parliament and Poynings' Law.[91]

88. Capell to Shrewsbury, 19 Oct. 1694 in HMC, *Buccleuch and Queensbury*, ii, 150.
89. Capell to Shrewsbury, 1 Nov. 1694 in HMC, *Buccleuch and Queensbury*, ii, 156.
90. Capell to Shrewsbury, [Dec. 1694] in HMC, *Buccleuch and Queensbury*, ii, 168–9.
91. HMC, *Buccleuch and Queensbury*, ii, 182–3; Minutes of Lords Justices, 20 May 1695 in *Cal. SP (Dom.), 1694–5*, pp 473–4.

THE 1695 COMPROMISE

In stark contrast to the situation in 1692, the drafting of bills for presentation to the Irish parliament in 1695 proceeded smoothly. This was due in no small part to Capell's efficient management, but the continuing reverberations of the sole right controversy allied to changes to the personnel of the Irish Privy Council, which made it more efficient and amenable, was also significant.[92] A crucial development was the relaxation by ministers of their previous demand that prospective legislation was first transmitted on 'paper' and, in another noteworthy change from 1692, the suspension of the practice of communicating lists of bills to the Irish Council for drafting and transmission was also helpful. These latter changes did not mean that the English Council ceded its entitlement to identify issues requiring legislative attention, but such 'instructions' as were transmitted in 1695 appertained to private rather than to public matters, and they were presented as authorisations rather than directions.[93]

The preparation of bills at the Irish Privy Council, which occurred over a few weeks between the end of May and mid-June is sparsely documented, but Capell's observation that 'most of the bills are transcripts of English Acts', and his commitment to communicate only those that were well drawn ensured that fourteen bills were ready by 18 June.[94] Since there was to be only one transmiss prior to the meeting of parliament, Capell was understandably eager that it should be sizeable, but he was anxious also to minimise the grounds for controversy by ensuring that only three bills engaged with contentious subjects. Inevitably, finance featured among them, but Capell's decision that 'for asserting the King's prerogative, 'twere fit that one money-bill should be tendered to the [Irish] House' of Commons, and that this should [only] be an excise measure for raising the modest sum of £20,000, was well calculated to minimise opposition in Ireland. Determined to uphold the Crown's 'prerogative', but to do so in a manner that did not discommode the advocates of the 'sole right', Capell was hopeful that upon 'his Majesty's right being asserted, as all agree it will, by their passing that bill, it would be gracious in his majesty to leave the preparing the heads of the other money bills to the House' of Commons.[95] Support for this strategy was forthcoming from the tory lord chancellor, Sir Charles Porter, who reminded the new secretary of state, Sir William Trumbull, that the Irish

---

92. See McGrath, 'Securing the Protestant interest', pp 157, 160–4 passim.
93. Shrewsbury to Capell, 8 May 1695 (NA, SP67/2 f. 19); Shrewsbury to Athlone, 12 July 1695 in *Cal. SP (Dom.), 1695*, p. 15; Capell to Shrewsbury, 4 June 1695 in HMC, *Buccleuch and Queensbury*, ii, 187. The measures proposed were for 'confirming the outlawries and attainders of William Dongan, late earl of Limerick, and Christopher Fleming, late Baron of Slane and for the confirming of severall grants and letters patent made to Godart, Earl of Athlone' and 'for confirming the private estate of Mrs Villiers'.
94. Capell to Lords Justices, 28 May 1695 in *Cal. SP (Dom.), 1694–5*, p. 480; Capell to Vernon, 18 June 1695 in *Cal. SP (Dom.), 1695*, p. 500.
95. Capell to Shrewsbury, 18 June 1695 in HMC, *Buccleuch and Queensbury*, ii, 193–4.

parliament was possessed of the same 'right' to 'reject' as the King was 'to transmit bills for money', and that the Irish Commons was also possessed the 'liberty to prepare heads of bills'. Members of the Irish executive were not normally so direct, but it was Porter's contentious assessment that, since the Irish parliament was obligated to communicate such 'heads' as they agreed to 'the Chief Governor and Council to be framed if they approve of them', the crucial question was 'whether the Commons have the sole right [to initiate legislation] exclusive of the King'.[96] Since the answer to this was they did not, Capell was hopeful that his strategy would be acceptable to London though the contention of the former lords justices, Cyril Wyche and William Duncombe, from whom Capell was now estranged, that the excise bill was an insufficient assertion of the King's rights cautioned against over-confidence.

Capell had reason to be anxious certainly for the 'two new bills' – 'one for disarming the Papists and the other for restraining foreign education' – that were present in the transmiss of 18 June. Deemed necessary to 'secure the Protestant interest, and … the Protestant religion', their progress was as material as that of the excise bill to the outcome of the session since they were essential to the 'settlement' desired by a majority of Irish Protestant opinion. Little opposition was expected from that quarter to the bills as drafted, but there were clear indications that the Catholic lobby was determined to press hard for amendments at the English Council board. The problem was that the more successful they were in securing changes the more likely it was that the bills would encounter problems with the Irish legislature on their return.[97]

The fourteen bills received from Ireland were referred to the attorney general at the English Council. Attention focussed initially on the excise bill. Given the troubled history of recent money bills, the reservation conveyed by Wyche and Duncombe that the bill did not constitute 'a sufficient assertion of the King's right in sending over money bills, the value of it being small', was potentially crucial. However, Capell had prepared the ground well, and such was the eagerness to draw a line under the 'sole right' issue that even those who harboured reservations refused to stand in the way of the measure proceeding. Happy to accept the report of the attorney general that the bill before them was 'sufficient to assert the right of sending money bills', and in accordance with 'Poynings' Act [which] does not exclude the [Irish] parliament from proposing the methods of laying taxes, provided it is not pretended to as a sole right, and thereby to exclude the King', it was forwarded with five minor amendments.[98] This was such an anti-climax that some, including the secretary of state, could not conceal their delight

96. Porter to Trumbull, 22 June, 8 July 1695 in HMC, *Downshire*, i, 482–3, 496–7.
97. Capell to Vernon, 18 June 1695 in *Cal. SP (Dom.)*, *1695*, p. 500; Trumbull to Capell, 29 June 1695 in HMC, *Downshire*, i, 488–9
98. Minutes of the proceedings of the Lords Justices, 28 June, 4 July in *Cal. SP (Dom.)*, *1695*, pp, 4–5, 513; Trumbull to Capell, 29 June 1695 in HMC, *Downshire*, i, 488–9; NA, PC2/76 f. 101.

at the outcome.[99] In truth, Trumbull had little reason to feel surprised, since he was in an unrivalled position to observe the mood of co-operative earnestness that characterised relations between the two executives at this moment. This was further manifest on 28 June when, as well as the excise bill, the attorney general reported favourably on five other bills. Significantly, in four cases the recommendation was that the bills should progress without amendment, while only one clarification was made in the fifth.[100] On 2 and 3 July, the attorney general delivered similar reports on six more bills, arising out of which four were recommended to pass in an amended form. The changes agreed in some instances were more material than the usual run-of-the-mill verbal clarifications, but no attempt was made to alter the thrust or purpose of any measure in a substantial way.[101]

More problems were anticipated with respect of the measure 'for the better settling intestates estates', which was the subject of a petition from the earl of Antrim and others 'on behalf of the Roman Catholicks of Ireland'. However, doubts about the representative status of Antrim and his co-petitioners, combined with the vagueness of their contention that the bill 'may intrench upon the articles of Lymerick or Galway' to ensure their objections were given short shrift, and the bill progressed with three amendments on 2 July.[102] Clearly, petitions had to be well conceived if they were to have the desired effect, as the rules and procedures employed at the Council Board were applied with greater consistency.[103] The petition of Viscount Fitzwilliam of Merrion, Colonel Nicholas Purcell and John Seagrave was more precise and, as Capell had anticipated, caused the 'new bills' for disarming Catholics and prohibiting them going abroad to be educated considerable difficulties.[104] Significantly, this arose less from complaints that the bills 'contained matters injurious to the petitioners rights, and contrary to several articles etc. granted by his majesty for security of his Roman Catholic subjects', than from the eagerness of the English Council to ensure that the terms of the Treaty of Limerick were upheld.[105] Thus, in respect of the arms bill, concern that

99. Trumbull to Porter, 29 June 1695 in HMC, *Downshire*, i, 488–9.

100. As note 96. The bills were An act declaring all attainders, and all other acts of the late pretended parliament to be void; An act to take away the benefit of clergy; An act for the more effectually suppressing cursing; An act to take away the writ *de heretico comburendo*; An act to take away damage clere.

101. NA, PC2/76 ff 101–2. The bills were An act for the better settlement of intestate estates; An act for the more easy discharging of sheriffs; An act for preventing frauds; An act for the redress of inconvenciencys; An act for reviving two statutes, and An act for declaring which days in the year … holidays.

102. NA, PC2/76 f. 101; PC4/1 f. 217; Shrewsbury to Capell, 2 July 1695 in HMC, *Buccleuch and Queensbury*, ii, 197–8.

103. A point that can be illustrated by the search for precedents on the subject of 'whether it be necessary to make but one return of all bills transmitted from Ireland at one time' (Minutes of the proceedings of the Lords Justices, 25 June 1795 in *Cal. SP (Dom.), 1695*, p. 506).

104. Minutes of the proceedings of the Lords Justices, 28 June in *Cal. SP (Dom.), 1695*, p. 513; Trumbull to Capell, 29 June 1695 in HMC, *Downshire*, i, 488–9.

105. Trumbull to Capell, 29 June 1695 in HMC, *Downshire*, i, 488–9.

'the general clause disarming all papists seemed to take away the benefit of the Art[icles] of Lim[erick]' elicited an instruction for the attorney general 'to bring in a clause ... describing and exempting the ... persons mentioned there, but not naming the Art[icles] either of Lim[erick] or Gall[way]'. There was unease also with 'the clause for taking away ... horses above the value of £5', which some concluded should embrace an exemption for Catholic gentry. These issues were not amenable to easy resolution, but the inclusion of a long and complex amendment prepared by Attorney General Trevor exempting those who came under the terms of the treaties of Limerick and Galway, and allowing Catholic 'noblemen' and 'gentlemen' to possess 'a sword, ... a case of pistols and a gun' for self-defence under licence, was deemed sufficient and the bill was forwarded for engrossment on 5 July. Councillors also considered incorporating a provision to allow wealthy Catholics to keep 'coach horses or better horses to ride on', but Capell's resistance ensured the bill was not altered to meet this objection.[106]

Capell's active lobbying on behalf of the disarming bill was critical to his commitment to present the Irish Commons with a corpus of legislation they desired. He promoted the bill 'to restrain forrain education' on similar grounds. The English Council was not easily convinced, and they subjected the measure to meticulous scrutiny following which they approved a number of substantial amendments that increased the burden of proof when prosecutions were brought; they refused to allow the bill to be applied retrospectively; and they permitted Catholics education at home.[107] Capell did not object. Indeed, since its approval on 6 July meant that all of the fourteen Privy Council bills conveyed in June had negotiated the English Council, it would have been surprising if he had. It was, by any standards, a remarkable turnaround from the situation that had prevailed during the early 1660s and in 1692, when bills communicated from Ireland were routinely laid aside, and it provided a clear index of the determination of officials in Britain and Ireland to ensure the parliamentary session was a legislative success. In this context, Capell's preparedness to accommodate the wish of the Irish parliament for legislation that would secure Irish Protestants against Catholic *revanche* and allow MPs an active role in initiating legislation was critical, but the pattern of concession was not all one-way. Irish Protestants also took a step back from the confrontational position they had adopted in October 1692, to allow the Irish executive to maintain that 'the King's prerogative in the matter of the sole right is fully vindicated'.[108]

Despite the essentially trouble free preparations, there was some unease in government circles as peers and MPs gathered in advance of the opening of the

---

106. Porter to Trumbull, 8 July in HMC, *Downshire*, i, 496–7; C.I. McGrath, 'Securing the Protestant interest: the origins and purpose of the penal laws of 1695', *IHS* (1996), pp 36–8, 41–2; Minutes of the proceedings of the Lords Justices, 12 July 1695 in *Cal. SP (Dom.), 1695*, p. 15; NA, PC2/76 f. 103; PC4/1 ff 217–18, 223.

107. Porter to Trumbull, 8 July in HMC, *Downshire*, i, 496–7; McGrath, 'Securing the Protestant interest, 1695', pp 44–5; NA, PC2/76 ff 104–05; PC4/1 f. 224.

108. Rochfort to Somers, 24 Oct. 1695 in HMC, *Downshire*, i, 568.

1695 session on 10 August. The lord chancellor, Sir Charles Porter, who did not enjoy Capell's confidence and who was to become the 'focus of resistance' to the lord deputy's policies, apprehended 'great opposition in the contested point of the sole right of money bills'.[109] Capell was more positive, and he made it clear to MPs that he was willing to compromise with them on the matter of making law and the sole right by observing in his speech opening parliament that members had been given the 'opportunity' they had long awaited to 'provide ... for your future security'.[110] The 'security' measures the lord deputy had in mind were the bills for disarming Catholics and limiting their access to education, but the main focus of attention at the beginning of the session was the excise bill and, to the administration's immense satisfaction, enough MPs were drawn to Capell's 'compromise' to ensure it was approved easily. The 'sole men', as the most resolute advocates of the rights of the Irish parliament were now called, did offer resistance but they performed feebly in the division lobbies.[111] Indeed, the observation of Thomas Brodrick that the Commons had gone 'beyond even the King's demand' on the matter of the 'sole right' by voting more money than demanded, because 'this was the most likely way his Excellency [Capell] could propose for obtaining so great a sum as seems absolutely necessary for defraying the charge of the Government' indicated the extent to which the opposition had yielded.[112] Yet Capell had also compromised on this point by acceding to the Commons' wish to initiate financial legislation, and while MPs pondered what they might propose in addition to heads of bills granting a supply, the co-operative mood ensured the fourteen Privy Council bills passed all stages and received the royal assent before the end of October.[113]

Though most of this legislation made it onto the statute book with ease, the two 'security' bills were not without their critics. Described by some as 'ill drawn and of no great consequence', opposition was targeted at the authority vested in the lord lieutenant and council to permit Catholics bear arms under licence and to provide for the education of their children. Since these regulations were the handiwork of the English Council, they might have provided a focus for critics of Poynings' Law, but this did not transpire. Rather, when they were faced with the choice of rejecting or accepting the bills, a majority of MPs opted, an observer noted waspishly, to 'swallow ... them with their faults'.[114] This disposition to avoid confrontation was also evident in the approval forthcoming for the heads of

109. Porter to Trumbull, 15 July 1695 in HMC, *Downshire*, i, 507; Hayton, *Ruling Ireland*, p. 54.
110. *Commons Jn. (Irl.)*, ii, 644; C.I. McGrath, 'English ministers and Ireland in 1690s', *EHR*, 119 (2004), pp 603, 605–7, 611–12.
111. Capell to Shrewsbury, 6, 7 Sept. in HMC, *Buccleuch and Queensbury*, ii, 223; Capell to Shrewsbury, 6 Sept. 1695 in A.P.W. Malcomson (ed.), *Eighteenth century Irish official papers, vol. i* (Belfast, [1973]), p. 14; McGrath, *Making the constitution*, pp 100–6.
112. Brodrick to Shrewsbury, 10 Sept. 1695 in HMC, *Buccleuch and Queensbury*, ii, 224–5.
113. 7 William III, chaps 1–14; *Commons Jn. (Irl.)*, ii, 49–105 passim.
114. McGrath, 'Securing the Protestant interest', pp 185–6.

three money bills providing for a poll tax, an 'additional custom on several goods and merchandises', and for continuing the statute providing 'an additional excise on beer, ale and other liquors', which went a long way to meet the Irish administration's financial needs.[115] The ratification of these, and their communication to the lord deputy for referral to the Privy Council demonstrated better than any other action how the Irish legislature could employ the 'heads of bill' process to make law that assisted with the government of Ireland.

It was not the wish of the House of Commons or of the House of Lords only to manifest their capacity to work with the administration in the making of law. They also possessed a legislative agenda that did not dovetail in all respects with that of the administration. Their desire to promote a *habeas corpus* bill is one indication; another centred on the effort to obtain a bill of rights similar to that on the statue book in England.[116] In addition, a variety of legislative schemes and ideas promoted in the Commons for which leave was given did not result in the presentation of heads of bills.[117] In other instances, heads that were presented did not find favour,[118] or were sent to the lord deputy but did not emerge out of the Irish Privy Council.[119] Heads of bills that arose in the Lords generally stood a better chance of progressing,[120] though several that found favour with the

---

115. McGrath, *Making the constitution*, pp 108–10 passim; 7 William III, chaps 14, 15, 23; Capell to Shrewsbury, 28 Sept. 1695 in HMC, *Buccleuch and Queensbury*, ii, 229; *Commons Jn. (Irl.)*, ii, 128, 129, 130, 134, 137, 138, 141, 142, 145. The revenue impact of the poll bill was calculated at £100,000, of the extended additional excise bill at £40,000, and of the additional duty import excise at £23,000.

116. McGrath, 'Securing the Protestant interest', pp 189–90, 213–14; Philip O'Regan, *Archbishop William King*, p. 80; *Commons Jn. (Irl.)*, ii, 83, 85, 87, 95, 105, 107, 109.

117. *Commons Jn. (Irl.)*, ii, 95 (the value of brass money), 125 (for the better making and regulating of the woollen manufacture), 129 (to prevent the illegal raising of money by grand juries).

118. *Commons Jn. (Irl.)*, ii, 73 (heads of a bill for regulating the Privy Council); 86 (heads of a bill for the preservation of house doves and tame pigeons); 92, 96, 116 (heads of a bill for attainting such as died or were killed in the late rebellion); 143 (heads of a bill to secure Protestants who purchased houses or lands in corporations from papists); 145 (heads of a bill to settle the rights of tenants in common).

119. Among those recorded as 'sent to the Lord Deputy', but of which there is no further reference are the heads of bills 'for preventing abuses in the false packing and uncertain tare of butter casks'; 'for punishing unlawful cutting, stealing, striping or spoiling of wood'; 'for the building and repairing of churches, … and provision of the poor'; 'for redress of certain abuses in making of pewter and brass'; 'for the punishment of the mother and reputed father of a bastard'; 'for the improvement of the breed of horses and destruction of vermin'; 'for prohibiting importation of foreign wool, cards and card wire': *Commons Jn. (Irl.)*, ii, 118, 126, 145; P.D. Fitzgerald, 'Poverty and vagrancy in early modern Ireland 1540–1770 (unpublished PhD, QUB, 1994), pp 234–5). In this category, one may also include a number of heads sent to the lord deputy that were animated in 1697/98 when they became law ('heads of a bill to take away the benefit of clergy' and 'to make the collector's receipts for quit and crown rents legal discharges' (*Commons Jn. (Irl.)*, ii, 145, 142). The 'heads of a bill for promoting the linen, sail, canvas cordage and other manufactures … ' was deferred until reanimated in 1697 (*Commons Jn. (Irl.)*, ii, 125, 126, 205).

120. One that did not advance is the heads of a bill that the judges may hold their places *quamdiu se bene gesserint* (*Lords Jn. (Irl.)*, i, 505).

Commons did not negotiate the Irish Privy Council. In this category belongs the 'heads of a bill of rights', which was presented to Capell by a joint deputation from both houses in late October, a bill 'for securing the honours and estates of Protestants', and a number of other measures.[121] It is apparent from this that the Irish parliament was determined to be legislatively active, and it achieved a palpable breakthrough when it emerged that a large proportion of the measures included in the inter-sessional transmiss that, it was anticipated, would provide the Irish parliament with its legislative agenda for the second part of the busy 1695 session had taken their rise as heads of bills.

Meanwhile, the Irish Council was also active, and the communication from Dublin on 6 September, less than a month after the opening of the session, of a transmiss of eight Privy Council bills vindicated Capell's perception that the co-operative environment he had generated would allow Council and parliament to work in tandem in originating legislation.[122] Six of the eight were private bills, of which three (those for 'confirming several grants to the Earl of Athlone', for 'confirming certain letters patent' to Elizabeth Villiers and the earl of Romney) were prepared in response to suggestions from England that they were fit matters for legislation.[123] Whatever the circumstances of their origins, all were subject to the usual scrutiny at the English Council. In the case of the two public bills – 'for the better observation of the Lords day' and 'for taking special bails' – only one minor amendment appertaining to the date when the former would take effect was required.[124] The private bill for 'vesting certain manors, lands and tenements belonging to the duke of Ormond in trustees' likewise enjoyed a trouble-free scrutiny. The experience of the remainder was more chequered.[125] The most complex and troublesome was that for confirming several grants and letters patent to Godard, earl of Athlone. The subject of a petition from a number of Catholic parties 'humbly praying that a saving of their rights may be inserted', the bill was subject to a substantial amendment to safeguard the entitlement of Colonel Thomas Dongan to pursue a claim that the lands awarded to the earl of Athlone were rightfully his.[126] A hearing was also required to adjudicate between the father and son, Francis and Edward Stafford, following the receipt of a petition presented by the former against the Stafford bill. On the basis of amendments recommended by the attorney general, the bill was not without defects, but none of the twelve amendments that were introduced were designed to aid the elder Stafford.[127]

121. *Lords Jn. (Irl.)*, i, 517–39 passim; *Commons Jn. (Irl.)*, ii, 107; the other bills include the heads 'to regulate the manner of allowing the benefit of clergy to persons convicted of felony' and 'for securing the honours and estates of protestants' (*Lords Jn. (Irl.)*, i, 520–21, 585).

122. Shrewsbury to Capell, 12 Sept. 1695 in *Cal. SP (Dom.)*, *1695*, pp 64–5.

123. Capell to Somers, 6 Oct. 1695 in [Malcomson] (ed.), *Irish official papers*, i, 15.

124. NA, PC2/76 ff 117, 120. 125. Ibid.

126. NA, PC2/76 ff 117, 125, 134–5; Trumbull's notes on Privy Council meeting, 24 Oct. 1695 (BL, Trumbull Papers, Add. MS 72566); Notes and minutes of evidence on behalf of Col. Dongan, 31 Oct. 1695 (BL, Privy Council memoranda 1660–1708, Add. MS 35707 ff 21–4).

127. NA, PC2/76 ff 117, 120, 123, 135.

The Stafford bill was not finally reported until 28 November, some eleven weeks after it was received, but this was still preferable than a decision not to report, which was the fate of the remaining three private bills (Rawdon, Villiers and Romney). There is no obvious explanation for this, but it may have something to do with the fact that following the receipt in late October of thirty-one bills in the third, and main, transmiss of the 1695 session and a further three measures on 5 November, the attention of the English Council shifted from bills originating at the Irish Council to bills that had taken their rise as heads in parliament, and from public to private bills.[128] This is not improbable, since councillors were so anxious to be seen to conduct themselves in a manner that was above reproach, they even alleged that the Irish parliament had taken an 'unusual privilege' in 'preparing bills and addressing ... the [Irish] Privy Council to pass them'. An investigation at the Council Board in mid-November cleared up this misunderstanding (deriving from 'the misrepresentation [that] bills instead of heads of bills [were] delivered to the chief governor'), and it had no negative impact on the manner in which this most recent transmiss of Irish bills were dealt with.[129] Referred to the attorney general, many were subject to brisk scrutiny, and sixteen were 'passed here' and ready to return before the end of November, one of Bishop William King's London correspondents reported.[130]

Though reports such as this fostered a contrary impression, the reality was that a strikingly smaller proportion of the forty-two bills transmitted from Ireland between 6 September and 5 November were certified at the English Privy Council in 1695 than was the case of the fourteen transmitted prior to the opening of the session. Since the earlier bills had all originated with the Irish Council, it may be tempting to conclude that its English counterpart was more demanding in its scrutiny of bills that arose with the Irish parliament when the reality was more prosaic, and many bills were simply not processed at this point for want of time. This is not to deny that councillors were aware of the place of origin of bills, but the crucial factor in determining whether or not they would proceed was content not origins. The proposed 'act for suppressing all friaries, monasteries, nunneries and other popish convents and for banishing all regulars of the popish clergy out

128. NA, PC2/76 ff 126–7, 128. As a result, a substantial number of private bills were left unprocessed – three from the September transmiss (Rawdon, Villiers and Romney bills) and six from the October transmiss – Domville, Parsons, Morres, Jephson, Fitzgerald, Burt (NA, PC2/76 ff 126–7). Among those transmitted later, that were also unreported, were the Jervis, Ormsby and Jones bills (NA, PC2/76 ff 131, 134), and the private bill for the relief of the earl of Cavan, received on 19 December, which was subject to a petition (NA, PC2/76 ff 138, 144).

129. Capell to Shrewsbury, 24 Oct., 23 Nov., Shrewsbury to Trumbull, 30, 31 Oct., Trumbull to Shrewsbury, 1, 5 Nov., Privy Council Minutes, 13, 14 Nov. in HMC, *Buccleuch and Queensbury*, ii, 244, 251, 252, 253, 255, 256, 266; Shrewsbury to Trumbull, 30 Oct. in HMC, *Downshire*, i, 573; Trumbull to Shrewsbury, 1 Nov. in *Cal. SP (Dom.), 1695*, p. 94.

130. Shrewsbury to Capell, 21 Nov. (NA, SP67/2 f. 44); Privy Council minutes, 24 Nov. in HMC, *Buccleuch and Queensbury*, ii, 267; Tollet to King, 26 Nov. 1695 (TCD, King Papers, MS 1995–2008 f. 477).

of this kingdom' is a case in point: the result of the consolidation of separate 'heads' that were initiated in the Commons and the Lords, the measure was assured of particular scrutiny even before it was received on 29 October because of embarrassing questions posed by diplomatic representatives of Emperor Leopold of Austria on behalf of 'the Roman Catholics of Ireland' to the effect that it infringed the Treaty of Limerick. William III denied that this was so, but the representations achieved their purpose as the measure was silently passed over.[131] This was the fate also of four bills – 'for abrogating the Court of Castle Chamber', for 'the recovery of tithes', 'for the relief of the subject against old dormant judgements' and 'concerning mines' – that took their rise in the Lords, and of the 'act to prevent Protestants intermarrying with papists', which was a Commons' measure.[132] In obvious contrast, William of Orange's tart observation, when it was reported at Council that Capell disapproved of the proposal 'for the better securing the liberty of the subject', that 'he s[houl]d not have sent it over' offers a clear indication as to why this bill was put aside.[133] The objections of petitioners also contributed to the loss of a number of measures, such as the bills for 'the better recovery of small debts', which was seen to infract 'the articles of Galway', and 'for the relief of poor prisoners', which was opposed by the 'marshal of the four courts in Dublin'.[134]

The pattern observable in respect of these bills is replicated in the case of the eleven public bills returned from London in November 1695 to become law in Ireland. Two took their rise as heads of bills, but all were dealt with in the same way though they included important measures such as the poll tax bill and the additional customs bill, which prompted high-level lobbying by individual and chartered interests, as well as quotidian efforts to deter gaming and to suppress tories. Saliently, the same can be said of the number and import of the amendments that were ordered at the English Council board at this time; they were introduced with specific syntactical or legal purpose. Furthermore, where no amendment was required none was made. On 28 November, for instance, nine bills (eight public and one private) were ordered to pass unchanged under the Great Seal of England.[135]

---

131. J.G. Simms, 'The bishops' banishment act of 1697', pp 237–8; Trumbull to Shrewsbury, 26 Oct. in HMC, *Buccleuch and Queensbury*, ii, 246; Shrewsbury to Trumbull, 31 Oct. in HMC, *Downshire*, i, 573–4; *Lords Jn. (Irl.)*, i, 522, 523; NA, PC2/76 ff 126–7; Dickson, *New Foundations*, p. 45; C. Giblin (ed.), 'Nunziatura di Fiandra, part 9' in *Collectanea Hibernica*, 13 (1970), pp 63, 64.

132. *Lords Jn. (Irl.)*, i, 491, 521, 522, 584; NA, PC2/76 ff 126–7, 131. Another bill that belongs in this category was that permitting the distraint of 'corn and hay for rent (PC2/76 ff 126–7).

133. NA, PC2/76 ff 126–7; Privy Council note, 13 Nov. 1695 (BL, Trumbull Papers, Add. MS 72566).   134. NA, PC2/76 ff 126–7, 130, 131.

135. NA, PC2/76 ff 126–7, 128, 134–6; Minutes of the Clerks of Council, 1670–1776, 5 Nov. 1695 (NA, PC4/1 ff 239–40); Privy Council, 12 Nov. 1695 (BL, Trumbull Papers, Add. MS 72566); Privy Council minutes, 12 Nov. 1695 in HMC, *Buccleuch and Queensbury*, ii, 255.

Twenty-six (62 per cent) of the forty-two bills received at the English Council between early September and early November were returned to Ireland. These had of course to be approved by the Irish parliament before they could receive the royal assent. This could not be assumed, moreover, since this was the only opportunity available to the Irish parliament to make plain its resentment at the restrictions imposed by Poynings' Law by rejecting bills that had not arisen in that assembly or that were amended at the Irish or English Council Boards. Addressing this subject, Bishop William King stoutly averred:

> I think that Magna Charta established the liberty of the subject and that it fundamentally consists in the choosing our own representatives and to be governed by laws of our own choosing … all that we desire is a negative to such laws as the [Privy] Council here and in England offers us, and if our making use of that negative sometimes be looked on as design of independence, it is the same that has always been used … [136]

In 1695, two bills – against gaming and for reviving a statute for the real union and division of parishes – that enjoyed uncomplicated journeys through the English Council were unexpectedly ambushed in the Lords.[137] A bill exempting Quakers from the penalties in the bill for disarming papists approved by the Commons was not taken up in the Lords, while a measure for building houses and making improvements on church lands was not presented for consideration.[138] Furthermore, a number of private bills were mislaid. In the case of the Eustace bill, which had been heavily amended at the English Council board, and the Ponsonby bill, this was quite accidental, and both went on to become law in 1697. However, the bill to 'enable James Barry to charge his estate with the payment of his debts' was not heard of again.[139]

Despite these and other notable legislative casualties, thirty-one acts were added to the Irish statute book in the course of the 1695 session. It would have been more had it not been decided to suspend the sitting in December, which meant that many of the sixteen bills outstanding from those transmitted from Ireland between early September and early November, and all of the bills conveyed subsequently were overtaken by events. This greatly complicates any statistical analysis of the legislative output of the session, but it can be established that seventy-six public and private bills were transmitted from the Irish to the English Council in 1695 and, when one takes into account measures that became

---

136. King to Clifford, 4 Dec. 1697 cited in O'Regan, *Archbishop William King*, p. 91.
137. NA, PC2/76 ff 126–7, 128, 134, 136; *Lords Jn. (Irl.)*, i, 565, 567; [ ] to King, 19 Dec. 1695 (TCD, King Papers, MS 1995–2008 f. 482). There does not seem to be any basis for F.G. James's claim that the Lords insisted successfully on the restoration of the wording of a bill annulling the attainder of the 1689 parliament (7 William III, chap 3), since it arose with the Privy Council (James, *Lords of the ascendancy*, p. 78).
138. NA, PC2/76 ff 126–7, 131, 136; *Lords Jn. (Irl.)*, i, 530; *Commons Jn. (Irl.)*, ii, 86, 143.
139. NA, PC2/76 ff 126–7, 130, 135–6; PC4/1 f. 253; *Commons Jn. (Irl.)*, ii, 210; below p. 83.

law in 1697, that the overall legislative success rate of bills to acts was in the realm of 50 per cent. This rate disimproves considerably if one includes the number of heads of bills initiated in the Irish houses of parliament that did not progress, but this must not occlude the main significance of the 1695 session – that it dispelled the spectre of failure that was the main legacy of 1692 by demonstrating that it was possible for the Irish parliament to operate as an effective law-making body within the restrictive parameters of Poynings' Law. Moreover, it did so, in a manner that reconciled the determination of the Protestant interest in Ireland to be more than just the passive recipient of the legislative ideas of the Irish and English Privy Councils. This was symbolised in December 1695 when, having given the royal assent to twelve bills, Baron Capell observed contentedly that there was 'not the least unquiet temper in the House'.[140] Indeed, rather than make an issue of the many heads of bills – notably the *habeas corpus*, bill of rights and others – that had been transmitted from Ireland and whose fate was unclear, the House of Commons agreed an address to William III on 13 December thanking him for 'those inestimable laws given us by your majesty in this session of parliament ... whereby not only our religion and legal rights are confirmed to us, but this your majesty's kingdom of Ireland is firmly secured to the Crown of England'.[141] The contrast with the acrimonious conclusion to the 1692 session could not have been sharper, and Capell's pleasure at the outcome was well deserved. The parliament of 1695 was not only the most legislatively productive in the history of the Irish parliament to date, it was a defining session for the future. In the course of approximately ten weeks it had established that parliament and Privy Council could work together to make law for Ireland and, arising from the skilful manner in which Capell involved Irish politicians, put in place a system of parliamentary management that was to endure, *mutatis mutandis*, for more than three-quarters of a century. This was only possible because it had established the principle that the Irish parliament could initiate legislation and, in particular, financial legislation in the form of heads of bills.[142] This was not an unconditional concession, however; in return, the House of Commons effectively accepted not only that it did not possess the 'sole right' to initiate financial legislation, it implicitly acknowledged, for the time being at least, that the Irish Privy Council possessed an equivalent entitlement to prepare legislation. It was a considerable achievement.

THE ENGLISH AND IRISH PRIVY COUNCILS AND THE 1697 PARLIAMENT

When the Irish parliament adjourned in December 1695, it was widely anticipated that it would resume in the spring of 1696 to address the outstanding bills at the

140. Capell to Shrewsbury, 10 Dec. 1695 in HMC, *Buccleuch and Queensbury*, ii, 276.
141. *Commons Jn. (Irl.)*, ii, 815.
142. McGrath, *Making the constitution*, pp 116–17.

English Council board and any new legislative suggestions that arose with either the Irish Council or parliament.[143] Had this occurred, it must have facilitated the early embedding of the arrangements effected in 1695. This ultimately was what was to happen, but the foreshortening of the session meant that some twenty bills were left in a state of suspended animation. This did not mean that they were lost; a bill for 'securing the debts owed the Protestant creditors of John Browne', which encountered problems in 1692, was ushered on to the statute book in 1695.[144] However, the fact that so many bills were left in the system, combined with a lack of procedural efficiency and an identifiable disinclination at the English Council in 1697 to accept the implications of Capell's system in *toto*, ensured that the manner in which law was made and Poynings' Law applied in the late 1690s was less smooth and palpably less regular than it might have been. As a result, it took longer than may have been anticipated at the end of 1695 to establish an efficient, orderly and mutually agreed set of procedures for the making of Irish law.

One obvious reason for this was the long interval between the 1695 and 1697 sessions, but the death of Capell in office on 30 May 1696 was still more crucial since it deprived the Anglo-Irish nexus of the architect of the 'compromise' of 1695.[145] This brought a destabilising measure of uncertainty to the political environment, symbolised by the appointment of a succession of lords justices in the twelve months from May 1696 to May 1697.[146] Inevitably, legislative matters did not disappear off the political agenda during this time, but discussion was dominated by a comparatively small number of issues that were addressed in isolation rather than in the structured manner pioneered by Capell. The most persistent, and difficult, was what to do with respect of the Treaty of Limerick, for though this had been a live issue for several years, Capell's recognition that Irish Protestants were strongly opposed to any attempt to confirm 'the articles of Limerick' ensured it did not feature in any transmiss conveyed from Ireland while he was in office. The fact that Capell possessed the support of a majority on the Irish Privy Council, who advised in October 1695 that 'it was not a proper time to prepare a bill for that purpose', was important in enabling him to overcome the efforts of Lord Chancellor Porter who shared the King's view that it must receive legislative endorsement.[147] Porter's appointment as a lord justice in June 1696 meant he was better positioned then to advance the matter, but the circumstances were still not right. Saliently, it was not until 23 April 1697, some four months

143. Shrewsbury to Capell, 30 Nov. 1695 (BL, Vernon Papers, Add. MS 40771); Trumbull to Capell, 28 Dec. 1695 in HMC, *Downshire*, i, 603.
144. NA, PC2/76 ff 126, 128, 134–5; 7 William III, chap 1.
145. McGrath, *Making the constitution*, chapter 3.
146. The lords justices appointed between 16 May 1696 and 14 May 1697 are conveniently listed in *New History of Ireland*, ix (Oxford, 1984), pp 490–1.
147. Wouter Troost, *William III and the Treaty of Limerick, 1691–97* (Leiden, 1983), p. 151; Capell to Shrewsbury, 15 Aug., 17 Nov. in HMC, *Buccleuch and Queensbury*, ii, 215–16, 257–8; Trumbull to Porter, 12 Sept. 1695 in HMC, *Downshire*, i, 548.

after Porter's death, that the lords justices received an instruction to prepare a bill 'for confirming so much of the Articles of Limerick, as we have promised to use our utmost endeavours to have ratified and confirmed in parliament'.[148]

This instruction, which was accompanied by directions to prepare and transmit bills 'for vesting all the forfeited estates in Ireland', 'for confirming ... attainders and outlawries' as well as 'for encouraging the linnen manufacture in Ireland' provided a clear signal that ministers had concluded it was time to convene another meeting of parliament and, the events of 1695 notwithstanding, that they were intent on exerting a direct influence on the legislation that would be proffered.[149] The implication that ministers were intent on acting as they had done in 1692, rather than in 1695, was reinforced by the decision to consider the Irish bills received in 1695 but not processed at that time. Had the Council determined that these bills had fallen with the adjournment of the session in December 1695, and left it to the Irish Council to present bills, it would have permitted closer adherence to the procedures promoted by Capell in 1695, and accelerated the administrative impact of the system he had applied to such effect.

Passing references during 1696 to outstanding measures received from Ireland, such as the bill of rights and *habeas corpus*, ensured that consideration of Irish legislative measures at the English Privy Council did not cease completely following the adjournment of the 1695 session, but this was not prosecuted with any vigour until April 1697 when it was determined that the Irish parliament should reassemble before the end of the calendar year.[150] Indicatively, the report of the attorney general on the Ormsby private bill, originally communicated from Ireland in November 1695, was accepted by the English Council on 8 April 1697, and the bill was sent to pass under the great seal in preparation for transmission to Ireland.[151] But the clearest pointer to the fact that ministers were not only intent on preparing the way for a new session of parliament, but also disposed to exert decisive influence on its deliberations was provided at Council a fortnight later by the instruction that 'all bills' received from Ireland 'and now depending' should be considered at the Board 'as soon as convenient', and that the report of the attorney general on the private bill concerning the estate of William Domville, which had been received at the Council on 29 October 1695, should be presented.[152] It is not apparent why this measure was singled out, but when the

---

148. Vernon to Shrewsbury, 28/29 Sept. 1696 in G.P.R. James (ed.), *Letters illustrative of the reign of William III from 1696 to 1708 addressed to the duke of Shrewsbury by James Vernon* (3 vols, London, 1841), i, 8–9; James, *Lords of the ascendancy*, p. 60; Instructions of Lords Justices, 23 Apr. 1697 (NA, SP67/2 f. 81).

149. Instructions of Lords Justices, 23 Apr. 1697 (NA, SP67/2 f. 81). The reference to a linen bill reflects the eagerness of English opinion to foster flax and linen production in Ireland; see the Representation of the Commissioners of trade and plantations, Dec. 1697 in HMC, *House of Lords MSS*, n.s, x, 153, 157, 159–60.

150. Minutes of proceedings of Lords Justices, 20 Aug. 1696 in *Cal. SP (Dom.), 1696*, p. 354.

151. NA, PC2/76 ff 134, 323.   152. NA, PC2/76 ff 329–30, PC2/77 f. 3.

Council returned to the matter of 'depending' bills, having reiterated the instruction that 'all the bills transmitted from Ireland which remain undispatched' should be brought to the Board, Domville's bill was approved with two minor amendments and ordered to be returned to Ireland 'on the next transmission of bills'.[153] More materially, the Council was informed on the same day that there were eighteen 'undispatched' bills still pending. Comprising eight public and ten private bills passed over in 1695, the public bills embraced potentially controversial measures 'for better securing the liberty of the subject', 'for suppressing all fryaries, monasteries and nunneries' and banishing regulars, and for preventing 'Protestants intermarrying with papists'. The remaining, less obviously contentious measures, appertained to 'the better payment of tythes', 'the relief of the subject against old dormant judgements', the abrogation of the Court of Castle Chamber, the distraint of corn and hay for rent and 'the more easy recovery of small debts'. The private bills were less diverse; concerned largely with empowering individuals to sell land to pay debts, they appertained to the affairs of Sir Arthur Rawdon, Sir Humphrey Jervis, Sir Laurence and William Parsons, Richard Burt, James Fitzgerald, Richard Delamer, Samuel Morres, William Jephson, Oliver Jones and the earl of Cavan.[154]

Because the English Council chose to animate these bills rather than to commence preparations for the meeting of parliament anew, the lead-up to the meeting of parliament in 1697 took a strikingly different form than it had in 1695. This was made still more likely by the fact that, in the absence of William of Orange on the continent, the Council chose not to deal with the bills in the expeditious fashion they had employed in 1695. Choosing in the first instance to focus on private bills it was agreed on 17 May that the Morres and Parsons bills should be sent for engrossment.[155] The receipt three days later of a petition against the Jephson bill served curiously to animate a measure that was about to be 'laid aside' because it was believed that Jephson was dead; it also ensured the inclusion of an important amendment safeguarding the interest of family members, following which the bill was forwarded.[156] The situation was comparable with respect of the Delamer bill; in this instance, William Delamer petitioned to have the bill 'stopt or so amended as that ... [his son] Richard ... may have no more than an estate for life in the petitioner's estate'. The Privy Council concurred, though this necessitated the introduction of an extensive amendment, amounting in effect to the rewriting of the bill, in order to safeguard the interests both of William Delamer and Richard Delamer's male heirs.[157]

Having certified these four measures, private bills were pushed down the priority list, though the number in the system ensured they continued to feature

153. NA, PC2/77 ff 3, 7.   154. NA, PC2/77 f. 6.

155. NA, PC2/77 ff 7, 8–9; Vernon to Blathwayt, 18 May 1697 (Beinecke Library, Blathwayt Papers, Box 19).

156. NA, PC2/77 ff 15–16.   157. NA, PC2/77 ff 6, 21–2, 22–3.

on the Council's agenda throughout the summer.[158] Inevitably, those requiring no amendments or only minor clarification proceeded effortlessly through the system.[159] Among their number were the Ponsonby and Eustace bills, both of which had previously been approved in 1695. The Eustace bill was heavily amended at that time to secure educational provision for 'poor children', and Ponsonby's forwarded without alteration, but because both were 'lost' (i.e. mislaid) at the secretary's office in Dublin, the bills were required to pass once more under the great seal of England.[160] This was highly unusual and, though it did not prevent either making it into law, it was indicative of the procedural flexibility and administrative laxity that still pertained, and the problems this could cause. Indeed, the Irish lord chancellor, John Methuen, observed, in respect of the missing bills, that it might have happened more often since 'everything here is in the same manner'.[161]

Though the procedures applied by both Councils were not without deficiency, such allegations of administrative slackness as were made flowed primarily in a westwards direction across the Irish Sea, and the English Council contrived to take advantage of this to attempt to affirm their role in the making of Irish law. One point that registered strongly was the failure of those seeking legislative solutions to private difficulties to observe 'the ancient custom ... to first petition the King in Council for leave to offer such a bill'. The merits of applying such a procedure, the secretary of state for the southern department, Lord Shrewsbury, advised, was that 'by this means time is given to all parties to apply, and not to be too surprised by too hasty proceedings'. Shrewsbury conceded that there was little to be gained thereby when private bills were not proceeded with at the Irish Council 'without first hearing all the parties concerned', but this was not regular practice. The Irish Council was at fault in this respect, but it mattered little since the English Council was in error in seeking to resuscitate the 'ancient custom' that those seeking private acts of parliament should petition the King in council because this 'custom' never operated in Ireland. A search conducted by the deputy clerk of the Irish Council 'among the books and papers belonging to the Council Chamber' failed to reveal 'any direction ... for the parties concerned in any private bill ... to first petition

---

158. Vernon to Shrewsbury, 29 June, 1 July in James (ed.), *Vernon-Shrewsbury Corres.*, i, 300, 305; Vernon to Blathwayt, 6 July (Beinecke Library, Blathwayt Papers, Box 19); Shrewsbury to Methuen, 9 July in HMC, *Buccleuch and Queensbury*, ii, 489; Vernon to Williamson, 9 July 1697 in *Cal. SP (Dom.), 1697*, p. 237.

159. As well as those already noted, this characterisation can be applied to the Folliott bill (NA, PC2/77 ff 35, 36; 9 William III, chap 1); Jones bill (PC2/77 ff 35, 36; 9 William III, chap 7); Stopford bill (PC2/77 ff 27, 32); Barton and Usher bill (PC2/77 ff 10, 27, 32) and Barry bill (PC2/77 ff 27, 32; 9 William III, chap 13). The Folliott, Jones and Barry bills were transmitted for the first time in 1697. See Lords Justices of Ireland to Lords Justices of England, 2 Aug. in *Cal. SP (Dom.), 1697*, p. 279; Galway to Shrewsbury, 3 Aug. 1697 in HMC, *Buccleuch and Queensbury*, ii, 517.

160. NA, PC2/76 ff 126–7, 135–6; 2/77 ff 37–8; PC4/1 f. 253.

161. Methuen to Vernon, 3 Aug. 1697 in *Cal. SP (Dom.), 1697*, p. 283.

the King and Council in England for leave to have such bills drawn'. None the less, an instruction was issued that parties 'desiring a private bill here must first make application in England', but though this would, if pursued, have increased the power of the English Council, it did not become normative practice.[162]

Despite the general willingness of ministers and officials to avow their explicit confidence in the Irish Council in respect of their processing private bills and, on occasions, to return private bills concerning which they entertained reservations, eight private bills (five 'depending' and three new) were not reported in 1697.[163] One cannot assume all of these were objectionable since, in a further manifestation of administrative laxity, the Privy Council was disinclined formally to 'remit' bills at this point. However, the fact that a number of contested private bills did not progress is hardly coincidental. The Cavan and Irwin bills fit this definition; others, such as the Dillon and Inchiquin bills, failed for no identifiable reason.[164]

In all, 27 Irish private bills were considered at the English Privy Council board in the summer and autumn of 1697. Of this number, 19 passed under the great seal of England, and 13 made it onto the Irish statute book. Significantly, this was, by a substantial margin, the largest number of private bills approved in one session between 1660 and 1720. If one adds to this the private bills that were pursued in 1695, of the 36 items of private legislation that were initiated in 1695 and 1697, 28 (78 per cent) negotiated the English Privy Council and nineteen became law. The route to the statute book was prolonged in many instances, but the fact that the legislative dividend was so high compared with 1692 when the one private bill that was initiated failed to receive parliamentary sanction, meant not just that the procedures whereby a private individual could seek legislative redress were clearly established, but that the private bill emerged as a distinct legislative category during these years.

Inevitably, private bills featured less prominently than public bills in the exchanges that passed between officials in Dublin and London in the run-up to and during the 1697 meeting of parliament. The eight 'depending' public bills presented at the English Council board on 11 May were an obvious focus of attention, though few were regarded with particular favour in Ireland. Indeed, of the eight, the only one that the Irish lords justices requested should be returned was

162. Shrewsbury to Lords Justices of Ireland, 3 Aug. 1697 (NA, SP67/2 ff 88–9, calendared in *Cal. SP (Dom.), 1697*, p. 283 and HMC, *Buccleuch and Queensbury*, ii, 515–16); Minutes of proceedings of the Lords Justices, 17 Aug. 1697 in *Cal. SP (Dom.), 1697*, p. 315.

163. The five private bills transmitted in 1695 were the Sir Humphrey Jervis bill (NA, PC2/76 f. 131; PC2/77 f. 6); Oliver Jones bill (PC2/76 f. 134; PC2/77 f. 6); Sir Arthur Rawdon bill (PC2/76 f. 117; PC2/77 f. 6); James Fitzgerald bill (PC2/76 ff 126–7; PC2/77 f. 6) and earl of Cavan bill (PC2/76 ff 134, 138; PC2/77 f. 6). Those transmitted in 1697 were the Irwin bill (PC2/77 ff 53, 56, 61); Dillon bill (PC2/77 f. 46); and Inchiquin bill (PC2/77 f. 27).

164. It is noteworthy that the Dillon bill was strongly recommended by the lords justices of Ireland (Lords Justices of Ireland to Lords Justices of England, 23 Sept, Lord Galway to Vernon, 6 Oct. 1697 in *Cal. SP (Dom.), 1697*, pp 393, 416).

the bill 'to prevent Protestants intermarrying with papists', which was deemed 'very reasonable and ... much desired by the Protestants of this kingdom'. Ministers were happy to comply with this request, for though 'great exceptions to it, as it was drawn' were expressed at the Council Board, the introduction of more than twenty amendments, several of which appertained to the provision of certificates to protect against abuse, ensured the bill was ordered to proceed.[165] The English Council was content also to return the bill to enable landlords distrain corn and hay with two technical amendments to its dating provisions; and, more controversially, 'for the better payment of tythes', which required fundamental amendments to accommodate the removal of a clause that allowed for the imprisonment of Quakers.[166] These changes did not make the bills palatable in Ireland, and neither was presented to parliament for ratification. The fate of the bills for 'suppressing' Catholic religious houses and for banishing regular clergy was still different. Approved at the English Council board on 15 July with a panoply of minor amendments and one substantive addition 'vesting in his Majesty, his heirs etc., [the concealed lands of] all guilds, chantries, fraternities or religious societies which still remain and are employed for supporting Popish superstition', the bill was deemed to infringe 'the settlement of Ireland by breaking into the Act of Settlement and Explanation'. Fears that it would endanger the title of many 'adventurers and soldiers' ensured the bill encountered strong resistance, and it was lost in the Lords.[167]

* * *

Four of the eight 'depending' public bills were returned to Ireland to join the larger number of private bills that were also approved in the summer of 1697 for presentation to the Irish parliament. This was perceived as an achievement by ministers, who were palpably uneasy with some of the public bills they considered, as indicated by Shrewsbury's observation that the bill for the relief of subjects against dormant judgements was potentially of a 'very dangerous'

165. Vernon to Blathwayt, 11 June, 13 July (Beinecke Library, Osborn Collection, Blathwayt Papers, Box 19); Lords Justices to Shrewsbury, 12 July (NAI, MS 2447 ff 2–3); Vernon to Williamson, 2, 6 July, Minutes of the proceedings of the Lords Justices, 6 July 1697 in *Cal. SP (Dom.)*, *1697*, pp 231, 228, 234; NA, PC2/77 ff 22–3.

166. NA, PC2/77 ff 6, 22–3, 35; Shrewsbury to Lords Justices, 3 Aug. (NA, SP67/2 ff 88–9 calendared in *Cal. SP (Dom.)*, *1697*, p. 283); Minutes of proceedings of Lords Justices, 10 Aug., Vernon to Williamson, 3 Aug. 1697 in *Cal. SP (Dom.)*, 1697, pp 200, 297–8; Shrewsbury to Methuen, 9 July, Shrewsbury to Lords justices, 12 July 1697 in HMC, *Buccleuch and Queensbury*, ii, 489, 530.

167. NA, PC2/77 ff 6, 22–3; *Lords Jn. (Irl.)*, i, 617; Shrewsbury to Lords Justices, 13 July (NA, SP67/2 ff 85–6, calendared in *Cal. SP (Dom.)*, *1697*, p. 250); Vernon to Blathwayt, 13 July (Beinecke Library, Osborn Collection, Blathwayt Papers, Box 19); Shrewsbury to Blathwayt, 13 July, Methuen to Shrewsbury, 30 July 1697 in HMC, *Buccleuch and Queensbury*, ii, 493, 513; below, p. 90.

consequence.[168] The expectation, at any event, was that the Irish Privy Council would fulfil its constitutional role by adding substantially to their number and, with this in mind, the lords justices advanced five possibilities at a meeting of the Irish Council in June. These embraced measures 'for confirming the attainders and outlawries, and for vesting in his majesty all forfeited estates'; for 'confirming so much of the Articles of Limerick as the King had promised'; for encouraging the manufacture of linen; for preventing the Irish in France from returning to Ireland; and for encouraging the education of the Irish in the Protestant religion. They 'were received with great approbation' and 'a committee was appointed to prepare the bills accordingly'.[169] Given the continuing preoccupation of Irish Protestants with the Catholic/Jacobite threat, these proposals were well calculated to win favour in Ireland, and the lords justices were optimistic that their preparation would not be protracted. Their general confidence was augmented still further by the assumption that since the 1695 session had never formally concluded, they were under no obligation to assert the King's prerogative in respect of raising revenue. Quite the opposite; they could 'leave it to the Commons to propose the heads of the money bills, without giving them the opportunity of claiming a "sole right", which was allowed at the beginning of this session'.[170] It was for this reason that the lord chancellor, John Methuen, objected when officials in London recommended the omission of any reference to the adjournment in the speech traditionally delivered at the opening of every session. 'The mentioning of the adjournment' represented 'a full assertion of the King's prerogative against the "sole right"', he pointed out.[171]

Though the exchanges on this point were essentially tactical, since both parties were in agreement on the desirability of protecting the royal prerogative, they accurately reflected the prevailing lack of unanimity on a number of key constitutional and procedural points, and the disinclination in England to be guided by the experience of 1695. This was underlined by the instruction communicated to the lords justices of Ireland on 13 July that they should refrain from sending large transmisses to avoid 'delay', when the practice employed successfully in 1695 had been to do precisely that. More importantly, it was inconsistent

168. NA, PC2/77 f. 6; Shrewsbury to Lords Justices, 3 Aug. 1697 (NA, SP67/2 f. 89 calendared in *Cal. SP (Dom.), 1697*, p. 283 and HMC, *Buccleuch and Queensbury*, ii, 516); Vernon to Shrewsbury, 1 July 1697 in James (ed.), *Vernon letters*, i, 305. Also lost were measures for 'abrogating the ... Court of Castle Chamber' and for 'the more easy recovery of small debts' (PC2/77 f. 6).

169. Vernon to Williamson, 15 June 1697 in *Cal. SP (Dom.), 1697*, pp 197–8.

170. HMC, *Buccleuch and Queensbury*, ii, 483; Lords Justices of Ireland to Shrewsbury, 15 June 1697 in *Cal. SP (Dom.), 1697*, pp 196–7. This is what was done. In the speech opening the session, Galway and Winchester expressed confidence that parliament would vote 'unto his majesty such supplies as are wanting' (cited in O'Regan, *Archbishop William King*, p. 85).

171. Methuen to Vernon, 12 July in *Cal. SP (Dom.), 1697*, pp 243; Methuen to Shrewsbury, 12 July in HMC, *Buccleuch and Queensbury*, ii, 490–1; Vernon to Shrewsbury, 19 June 1697 in James (ed.), *Vernon letters*, i, 298; McGrath, *Making the constitution*, pp 122–3.

with the strict reading of Poynings' Law agreed in 1695 that only one transmiss should be communicated from Ireland prior to the commencement of a session. This affirms McGrath's conclusion that 'the governments on both sides of the water remained confused on the whole question of the 1695 compromise'.[172]

In the absence of a strong guiding hand such as was provided by Capell in 1695, it was only to be anticipated that the confidence registered in Ireland in June 1697 that five Privy Council bills would be ready for transmission in short order was misplaced. By the end of June, three was seen as more realistic.[173] Councillors remained confident, none the less, that parliament would behave 'cheerfully' when it assembled on 27 July and 'do all the King's business' despite the difficulties they encountered in agreeing the content of the bills they intended to present. Disagreement was sharpest on the bill for confirming the articles of Limerick, which was approved only 'with ... difficulty' owing to the lack of consensus on the incorporation of the sixth article of the treaty because of the insistence of 'severall of the Councill' that the measure should not preclude prosecutions 'for goods taken or rents detained during the war'. An unsatisfactory compromise was reached whereby the lords justices undertook to invite the King to amend the relevant clause to reflect the concerns of the Protestants of Ireland, though their affirmation that 'the bill will pass in the parliament here without it' made it clear where they stood on the point.[174]

Drafting a bill 'for confirming outlawries and attainders' also caused problems as a result of the decision to incorporate — what was conceived of initially as a separate measure — a prohibition on 'the returne of such natives of this kingdome as are in the service of His Majesty's enemys abroad'. It so happened that the failure to incorporate a clause 'vesting the forfeitures in His Majesty' proved no less problematical, though it attracted less notice because of intense lobbying by and on behalf of a variety of individuals who sought exempting 'provisoes'.[175] The Irish Privy Council engaged with such lobbyists as a matter of course and, when there were grounds, amended legislation appropriately. It was able to do so, moreover, consistently with its own procedural processes, which meant that bills were referred to committees and read 'twice in Council'.[176] This could be time-

---

172. Above p. 69; Shrewsbury to Lords Justices, 13 July in HMC, *Buccleuch and Queensbury*, ii, 494; Methuen to Vernon, 20 July 1697 in *Cal. SP (Dom.), 1697*, p 259; McGrath, *Making the constitution*, p. 123.

173. Methuen to Somers, 26 June 1697 in [Malcomson (ed.)], *Irish official papers*, i, 17–18.

174. Ibid.; Winchester to Shrewsbury, 26 June, Galway to Shrewsbury, 29 June in HMC, *Buccleuch and Queensbury*, ii, 484, 485; Lords Justices to Shrewsbury, 12 July, Lords Justices to Blathwayt, 12 July 1697 (NAI, Irish Correspondence, 1697–1798, MS 2447 ff 2–5).

175. Lords Justices to Shrewsbury, 12 July, Lords Justices to Blathwayt, 12 July (NAI, Irish Correspondence, 1697–1798, MS 2447 ff 2–5); Methuen to Shrewsbury, 12 July in HMC, *Buccleuch and Queensbury*, ii, 490–1. For evidence of lobbying in respect of provisoes see Shrewsbury to Blathwayt, 9 July, Shrewsbury to Galway, 9 July, Winchester to Shrewsbury, 12 July, Blathwayt to Shrewsbury, [15]–25 July in HMC, *Buccleuch and Queensbury*, ii, 488, 490, 495.

176. Vernon to Williamson, 9 July 1697 in *Cal. SP (Dom.), 1697*, p. 237; May to Blathwayt, 5 Oct. 1697 (NAI, May-Blathwayt Correspondence, 1697–8, MS 3070).

consuming, but it worked well enough in the summer of 1697 to allow the Irish Council to transmit three public and five private bills to the English Council board on 12 July.[177]

The arrival of these bills and the accompanying elucidatory missives at the English Council constituted a further test of the administrative and political arrangements put in place to give effect to Poynings' Law. They were, as it happened, up to the test, but the process exposed certain limitations both in the administrative procedures that were employed, and differences in the legislative priorities of both kingdoms that were only overcome by the understanding and good will displayed in both jurisdictions. The effect of this was to enhance mutual awareness that contributed in no small way to the defusing of tensions that could otherwise have been divisive, and to assist in the development of procedures that facilitated the smooth application of Poynings' Law.

Ironically, the stage seemed set fair at the outset for the prompt return of the key measures – the Treaty of Limerick and outlawries bills – received from the Irish Council.[178] At a meeting of the English Council of 20 July at which the latter was discussed, it was agreed to admit six provisoes communicated from Ireland plus a number of additional names, and 'a clause to preserve the King's power of pardoning the lives of such of these persons outlawed, or who shall … be outlawed'.[179] Two days later, bills for confirming the articles of Limerick and for barring remainders and reversions were approved with, in Lord Shrewsbury's terms, 'no alterations … worth his Majesty's knowledge'.[180] However, shortly afterwards when the three bills were being prepared to be engrossed so they could be returned to Ireland, the secretary of state James Vernon detected an inconsistency in the Treaty of Limerick bill between the Articles of Limerick that were cited and the Articles agreed in 1690. Though he attributed it to 'carelessness' rather than to intention, councillors adjudged that they had no option but to suspend the return of the measure, because the point at issue appertained to 'all

---

177. Lords Justices of Ireland to Lords Justices of England, 12 July 1697 in *Cal. SP (Dom.), 1697*, pp 243–6. The five private bills were the archiepiscopal see of Tuam, Barton and Usher, Inchiquin, Stopford and Barry bills. As well as the two noted, the third public bill was for 'barring the remainders or reversions on estates tail forfeited to the Crown'.

178. For the lethargy with respect of Irish matters in the summer of 1697, as well as notes 179 and 180, see Shrewsbury to Lords Justices, 17 July (NA, SP67/2 f. 87); Methuen to Shrewsbury, 12 July, Shrewsbury to Galway, Shrewsbury to Methuen, 17 July in HMC, *Buccleuch and Queensbury*, ii, 490, 498–9; Methuen to Vernon, 12 July, Vernon to Williamson, 16 July, Yard to Williamson, 16 July in *Cal. SP (Dom.), 1697*, pp 243, 251.

179. Lords Justices of Ireland to Lords Justices of England, 12 July 1697 in *Cal. SP (Dom.), 1697*, pp 244–6; Shrewsbury to Lords Justices, 20 July (NA, SP67/2 f. 87); Shrewsbury to Blathwayt, 20 July in HMC, *Buccleuch and Queensbury*, ii, 501; Vernon to Williamson, 20 July 1697 in *Cal. SP (Dom.), 1697*, pp 255–6. Significantly, despite the failure (on the grounds that it was too late (*Cal. SP (Dom.), 1697*, pp 263, 281–2)) of the Lords Justices of Ireland efforts to have another name added, cases continued to be made (HMC, *Buccleuch and Queensbury*, ii, 509).

180. NA, PC2/77 ff 25–6; Shrewsbury to Blathwayt, 23 July in HMC, *Buccleuch and Queensbury*, ii, 505–06; Vernon to [ ], 23 July 1697 in *Cal. SP (Dom.), 1697*, p. 264.

such as were under protection in the five counties of Limerick, Clare, Kerry, Cork and Mayo ... till they hear from Ireland'. Shrewsbury too accepted that the omission was due to oversight, but he was determined it would not proceed without the offending clause, 'which the King had specially ordered to be inserted'.[181]

Despite the obvious eagerness of ministers to prevent this matter becoming a source of disagreement between Ireland and England, neither the return of the outlawries and remainders bills, nor the rapid processing of the private bills received from Ireland on 12 July could conceal the embarrassment felt all round.[182] The fact that it coincided with the uneventful opening weeks of the Irish parliament was helpful, but William III's determination 'to respite the signification of his pleasure until' an explanation was received from Ireland hardened attitudes in London.[183] Their firm stand seemed entirely justified when Lord Chancellor Methuen confessed that the omission was not an accident, and that the bill was 'much more acceptable without those words'. He was confident, despite this, that the revised bill would pass, which was not his considered opinion of the bill for banishing regular clergy; this would fail, he observed, because of the insistence of the English Council that 'concealed lands' of Catholic guilds and chantries should be vested in the Crown.[184]

These problems are revealing of the procedural as well as political difficulties that the more flexible application of Poynings' Law employed in 1697 generated. Moreover, the differences they highlighted might have become acute had the interest of officials on both sides of the Irish Sea in identifying solutions not curbed their reflexive instinct to fix upon points of principle. Indicatively, the Irish Council did not hesitate at this moment to implement the instructions of the English Council that it should 'prepare and transmit a bill ... for the better security of His Majestys Royall person and government' even though it greatly alarmed 'our great churchmen'.[185] They responded with comparable alacrity to a suggestion from Lord Shrewsbury in August that they should prepare 'some bill

181. Vernon to [ ], 27 July, Minutes of the proceedings of the Lords Justices, 27 July in *Cal. SP (Dom.), 1697*, p. 268; Shrewsbury to Lords Justices, 27 July (NA, SP67/2 f. 88 calendared in *Cal. SP (Dom.), 1697*, p. 272 and HMC, *Buccleuch and Queensbury*, ii, 509); Shrewsbury to Blathwayt, 27 July, Shrewsbury to Methuen, 27 July 1697 in HMC, *Buccleuch and Queensbury*, ii, 508–10.

182. For progress on bills, notably the archiepiscopal see of Tuam bill (see *Cal. SP (Dom.), 1697*, p. 276; NA, PC2/77 ff 27, 28, 31), and private bills see Shrewsbury to Lords Justices, 3 Aug. 1697 (NA, SP67/2 ff 88–9). For a sense of the embarrassment see Shrewsbury to Winchester, 5 Aug., Shrewsbury to Galway, 5 Aug. in HMC, *Buccleuch and Queensbury*, ii, 520–1.

183. May to Blathwayt, 19 Aug. (NAI, May-Blathwayt Corres., 1697–8, MS 3070); Lords justices to Blathwayt, 10 Aug., 4, 7, 9 Sept. 1697 (NAI, Lords Justices' letterbooks, 1697, MS 2454); Winchester to Shrewsbury, 27 July, Blathwayt to Shrewsbury, 2–12 Aug. in HMC, *Buccleuch and Queensbury*, ii, 510–11, 515.

184. Methuen to Shrewsbury, 30 July, 3 Aug., Winchester to Shrewsbury, 3 Aug. 1697 in HMC, *Buccleuch and Queensbury*, ii, 510–11, 517–18.

185. NA, PC2/77 f. 25; Shrewsbury to Lords Justices, 20 July, Methuen to Vernon, 12 Aug. in *Cal. SP (Dom.), 1697*, pp 258–9, 306–7; Shrewsbury to Lords Justices, 7 Aug. 1697 (NA, SP67/2 f. 90).

that would effectually encourage the linen manufacture'. Shrewsbury maintained that a measure of this kind must 'be of great advantage to England as well as to Ireland', but his real motive was pre-emptive; he apprehended that 'unless something be now done to show the Parliament here that the Irish will turn their industry to what may divert them from the woollen trade ... the next session the Irish will certainly receive a mortification'.[186]

While this advice was hardly calculated to raise spirits in Ireland, the fact that the Irish Council set about preparing a bill for the encouragement of linen and hempen manufacture demonstrated its readiness to take such advice when it was perceived to be advantageous. They were not the passive recipients of direction, however, and their defence of their position on the Treaty of Limerick bill, the banishment of the regular clergy bill, and the outlawries bill provide a clear demonstration of their growing confidence. The primary source of difference with respect of the bill for suppressing friaries and expelling regular clergy was the clause introduced at the English Council board for dissolving chantries and other religious bodies and for vesting their assets in the Crown. Persuaded that 'no one person of either House [of parliament] would give his consent to the passing of the bill' so long as the clause remained, the lords justices of Ireland were vindicated when the House of Lords declined to give the measure a second reading on 3 August. However, rather than let the matter drop, they promptly approved 'the same bill in due form, without the said clause and with some small change in the title, as an act for banishing all papists exercising ecclesiastical jurisdiction, and all regulars of the popish clergy out of the kingdom'.[187] Encouraged by noises from Ireland that 'the whole parliament is very desirous of the bill', and by the realisation that 'the nature of the matter was not understood here' because the lands at issue 'are already most of them in the hands of Protestants', ministers and officials backed down. There remained the not unimportant matter of lobbying on behalf of the Catholics of Ireland by the imperial envoy to William III, but on this occasion the strength of anti-Catholicism in England as well as Ireland deterred William from taking the representations on board.[188] The 'new made' bill was referred to the attorney general, Sir Thomas Trevor, for a report on 13 August, considered at a meeting of

186. Shrewsbury to Galway, 30 Aug. in HMC, *Buccleuch and Queensbury*, ii, 543; Lords Justices to Shrewsbury, 11 Sept. 1697 in *Cal. SP (Dom.), 1697*, p. 364.

187. Lords Justices and Council of Ireland to the Lords Justices of England, 3 Aug. 1697 in *Cal. SP (Dom.), 1697*, pp 283–4; Simms, 'Bishops' Banishment Act of 1697', pp 239–40.

188. For evidence of the strength of anti-Catholicism in England in the mid-1690s, notably the prosecution of Catholic printers and the seizure of horses owned by Catholics out of fear that they might be used by invaders see NA, PC2/76, 77; for imperial lobbying on behalf of Irish Catholics see Fagan, *Divided loyalties*, pp 22–3; Simms, 'Bishops' Banishment Act', pp 187–8; Hugh Fenning, *The Irish Dominican province, 1698–1797* (Dublin, 1990); Cathaldus Giblin (ed.), 'Catalogue of *Nunziatura di Fiandra*', part 2, *Collectanea Hibernica*, 4 (1961), pp 56–67; idem, 'Catalogue of *Nunziatura di Fiandra*', part 9, *Collectanea Hibernica*, 13 (1970), pp 66–72; Vernon to Shrewsbury, 7 Sept. 1697 in James (ed.), *Vernon letters*, i, 346.

the full English Council four days later, approved without amendment and sent to pass under the great seal.[189] This should have spelled the end of their involvement with the bill excepting unforeseen problems in Ireland, but for some unaccountable reason the bill returned to Ireland was 'not engrossed'. The delays incurred in securing a proper copy meant the bill was not available for presentation to the Irish parliament until September when it finally became law.[190]

If the ratification of what became known as the Bishops' Banishment Act owed much to the persistence of the Irish Council, the stand it made on the matter of the 'missing clause' in the bill ratifying the Treaty of Limerick was equally important in ensuring that the Irish Council did not become a subordinate body that acted upon the instructions of its English equivalent. Having made it known that the preference in Ireland was that the bill should be returned without the offending missing clause, since this alone was acceptable to 'the Protestant and English interest there', ministers appealed to William of Orange for guidance. The King was not amused, but he was unwilling to generate further difficulties in Ireland by continuing to press the point. As a result, when it came to deciding the matter in late August, the lords justices of England adjudged that it was 'the King's pleasure that the bill for the ratification of the Articles of Limerick be passed without the additional clause that was inserted in England'. This decision was welcomed by the lords justices of Ireland, and their stand was vindicated when the bill negotiated the Commons with little difficulty. However, it encountered severe resistance in the Lords where, among other criticisms, peers objected to 'breaking the Articles of Lymerick under colour of confirming them'. And in an action that could have had major implications for Poynings' Law, the peers requested an explanation from the Irish lords justices of the 'reasons given by the Lords Justices and Council of the Lords Justices of England for transmitting the bill without the additional words'. Conscious that the request was 'without precedent' and that any effort to meet it must trespass upon the confidentiality of the English Council's deliberations and expose Poynings' Law to potentially damaging scrutiny, the Lords Justices of Ireland protested that it was not in their 'power to comply':

> We can only inform them that the bill was detained by the Lords Justices of England till they had laid before the King all the difficulties concerning it, and received his pleasure that it should pass in its present form.[191]

189. Vernon to Williamson, 6, 13 Aug., Minutes of proceedings of the Lords Justices, 13 Aug. in *Cal. SP (Dom.), 1697*, pp 286, 307, 309; Shrewsbury to Methuen, 14 Aug. 1697 in HMC, *Buccleuch and Queensbury*, ii, 533; NA, PC2/77 f. 36.

190. Winchester to Vernon, 24 Aug. 1697, Methuen to Vernon, 24 Aug. 1697 in *Cal. SP (Dom.), 1697*, pp 324, 328; May to Blathwayt, 31 Aug. 1697 (NAI, May-Blathwayt Corres., 1697–8, MS 3070); *Lords Jn. (Irl.)*, i, 620; *Commons Jn. (Irl.)*, ii, 184, 186, 187, 188, 191, 193, 210.

191. Lords Justices of Ireland to Shrewsbury, 22 Sept. in *Cal. SP (Dom.), 1697*, p. 390. See also Vernon to Williamson, 26 Sept. in *Cal. SP (Dom.), 1697*, p. 398; May to Blathwayt, 14 Sept.

This response achieved its purpose, and the administration was enabled, with the support of 'the temporal lords', to ensure the measure progressed to receive the royal assent on 25 September.[192]

Emboldened by its success in respect of both of these measures, the Irish Council was equally assertive when the outlawries and attainders bill encountered difficulties. The first hint of this was provided on 13 August when, in response to expressions of unease that 'many Protestants may be affected and injured' if the Crown invoked the powers provided for in the bill, leave was given in the Commons to prepare the heads of a supplemental bill 'for saving the estates, rights, titles and possessions of Protestants from being prejudiced'. However, when comparable reservations were articulated in the Lords, and concern was expressed lest the ratification of the bill should provide a parliamentary seal of approval for William III's controversial land grant to the countess of Orkney, the administration declined 'to venture the third reading'.[193] This was less an admission of defeat than a strategic retreat as the lords justices adjudged that they could best allay the concerns of 'both Lords and Commons' with respect of the bill by deciding 'that a new one shall be prepared, embodying the necessary alterations' at the Irish Council. Having contemplated preparing 'a bill for confirming the outlawries etc. (with another title), to comply with what the Lords would have left out' while leaving it to the Commons to meet their own concerns, this idea was soon abandoned in favour of a single measure 'to hinder the reversal of severall outlawries and attainders and to prevent the return of the subjects of this kingdom who have gone to the dominions of the French king in Europe'.[194] Received at the English Council board on 16 September, the admission of a

(NAI, May-Blathwayt Corres., 1697–8, MS 3070); Lords Justices to Blathwayt, 18 Sept. 1697 (NAI, Lords Justices letterbooks, 1697, MS 2454).

192. As well as the sources indicated, this paragraph draws on Minutes of proceedings of Lords Justices, 13, 24, 26 Aug., Winchester to Vernon, 31 Aug., Lords Justices to Shrewsbury, 31 Aug., 22, 23 Sept., Vernon to Williamson, 26 Sept., 1 Oct. in *Cal. SP (Dom.), 1697*, pp 311, 327, 331, 341–2, 390, 393, 398, 407; Shrewsbury to Blathwayt, 13 Aug. (Beinecke Library, Osborn Collection, Blathwayt Papers, calendared in HMC, *Buccleuch and Queensbury*, ii, 531); Shrewsbury to Winchester, 14 Aug., Shrewsbury to Methuen, 14 Aug., Winchester to Shrewsbury, 9 Sept. in HMC, *Buccleuch and Queensbury*, ii, 531–2, 533, 553; Connolly, *Religion, law and power*, pp 268–9; King to Bishop of Waterford, 5 Oct., King to Bishop of Kildare, 9 Oct. 1697 (TCD, King Papers, MS 750/1 ff 97–8, 103); *Commons Jn. (Irl.)*, ii, 186, 193, 195, 196, 208, 210.

193. James, *Lords of the ascendancy*, pp 62–3; Lords Justices of Ireland to Shrewsbury, 14 Aug. (NAI, Irish Correspondence, MS 2447 ff 6–7 calendared in *Cal. SP (Dom.), 1697*, p. 312); Winchester to Shrewsbury, 15, 19 Aug., Galway to Shrewsbury, 17, 19 Aug., in HMC, *Buccleuch and Queensbury*, ii, 534, 537, 535, 536; Lords Justices to Shrewsbury, 21 Aug., Vernon to Williamson, 24 Aug., Methuen to Vernon, 24 Aug. in *Cal. SP (Dom.), 1697*, pp 323, 324–5, 328–9; Vernon to Blathwayt, 24 Aug. (Beinecke Library, Osborn Collection, Blathwayt Papers, Box 19); May to Blathwayt, 19, 21 Aug. 1697 (NAI, May-Blathwayt Corres., 1697–8, MS 3070).

194. Lords Justices to Shrewsbury, 26 Aug., 7 Sept. in *Cal. SP (Dom.), 1697*, pp 331, 357; Winchester to Shrewsbury, 31 Aug., 9 Sept. in HMC, *Buccleuch and Queensbury*, ii, 545, 553; NA, PC2/77 f. 42; May to Blathwayt, 31 Aug. 1697 (NAI, May-Blathwayt Corres., 1697–8, MS 3070).

number of petitions by interested parties seeking the introduction of exempting provisos ensured that it could not simply be ushered through the familiar procedural hoops. However, it was less the deficiencies of the bill (and a number of 'not very considerable' clarifications were introduced at the Council Board) than the fact that it had been forwarded that bothered councillors.[195] Guided by the solicitor general, who brought it to their notice, it was maintained that it was 'an evading of Poining's Act' to present an amended version of a measure that had previously passed under the great seal of England. This was not a minor consideration but, because 'it was recommended from Ireland as a bill that would much conduce to the settlement of that kingdom', it was decided in this instance to allow the measure to proceed on condition that no future 'encroachments upon Poynings' Act by a side wind' were attempted. Ministers were encouraged to take this accommodating attitude by the assurance of Lord Chancellor Methuen that 'nothing of the same kind shall ever be offered at again', though they could take little comfort from the Irish lords justices' lengthy affirmation that they were responsible for nothing more than 'a technical infringement of Poyning's Law' when, if the Lords had had their way, 'a much more flagrant breach would have been the consequence'. James Vernon was certainly not appeased. He observed acidly on 9 October, in response to Methuen's claim that the transgression was less significant than what took place in the case of the measure to banish the regular clergy, that 'a lesser degree will hardly justify the persevering in an error'. Others felt equally strongly. As a result, the Privy Council authorised the lords justices of England on 26 October to write to Ireland to advise that 'care may be taken' to eradicate the 'irregular steps taken in preparing and transmitting certain bills out of Ireland'.[196]

This stern admonition could not be ignored, and both the Irish administration and Council made no effort to do so. Lord Galway, specifically, sought to reassure ministers that the steps taken in Ireland, though irregular, did not constitute an attempt to '*donner atteinte a Poini[n]gs Law*'.[197] None the less, the English Council had put down a clear marker that they would resist practices that circumvented the terms of Poynings' Law. This ought not obscure the fact that the involvement of both the English and Irish Councils in the initiation and certification of Irish legislation in 1697 assisted the development of a clearer understanding and

---

195. NA, PC2/77 ff 42, 56; Vernon to Williamson, 26 Oct. 1697 in *Cal. SP (Dom.), 1697*, p. 444.
196. Vernon to Shrewsbury, 7, 23, 25 Sept., 9 Oct. in James (ed.), *Vernon letters*, i, 345–6, 401, 406, 426; Vernon to Williamson, 24 Sept., Yard's Newsletter, 24 Sept., Minutes of proceedings of Lords Justices, 23, 24 Sept., 12 Oct., Methuen to Vernon, 27 Sept., 5, 6 Oct., in *Cal. SP (Dom.), 1697*, p. 394, 391–2, 425, 395, 397, 400–1, 416; Irish Lords Justices to English Lords Justices, 5 Oct. in [Malcomson (ed.),] *Irish official papers*, i, 18–19; NA, PC2/77 f. 55; Vernon to Blathwayt, 7 Sept. 1697 (Beinecke Library, Blathwayt Papers, Box 19).
197. Minutes of proceedings of Lords Justices, 9 Nov., Methuen to Vernon, 13, 17 Nov. 1697 in *Cal. SP (Dom.), 1697*, pp 465, 473, 475; Winchester to Shrewsbury, 13 Nov., Galway to Shrewsbury, 13 Nov. 1697 in HMC, *Buccleuch and Queensbury*, ii, 573; Vernon to Blathwayt, 12 Jan. 1698 (Beinecke Library, Osborn Collection, Blathwayt Papers).

definition of their respective roles and contribution to the process. More remained to be done clearly, since the unmistakeable implication of the outlawries and attainder bill was that Poynings' Law had still to reach a point when officials on both sides of the Irish Sea were in complete agreement on its application.

HEADS OF BILLS AT THE IRISH PARLIAMENT, 1697

While officials in Dublin and London were guided in the response they offered when problems arose with respect of Irish legislation in 1697 by a largely pragmatic determination to minimise the grounds for disagreement, the Irish executive was intent for equally pragmatic reasons to allow the Irish parliament the freedom to exercise a considerable degree of legislative initiative via the heads of bills process. The lords justices indicated as much in the speech opening the session by inviting the House of Commons to prepare heads of bills to raise money for the government of the kingdom and other purposes.[198] Interestingly, the term 'heads of bills', which was now employed routinely in Ireland, was not used in the address because ministers and officials in both kingdoms were eager that the Irish parliament did not expand on the right thereby granted. Thus, a reference in an early version of the speech 'recommending it to parliament to consider the heads of a bill for encouraging the linen manufacture' was deleted on the reasonable grounds that the bill was 'already lying before them'. More pertinently, an attempt by peers and MPs to establish a means 'for settling a method ... for the two Houses joining in the heads of bills to be presented to government' was resisted.[199]

This caution was understandable because both houses of the Irish legislature were eager to exercise the legislative initiative allowed them. This was manifest on the opening day of the session when the House of Commons established a committee to identify such measures as were prepared by them in 1695 that were transmitted to England. The ratification of a resolution four days later to the effect that a record should be made of the bills 'sent by this house to the chief governor' underscored their earnestness on this point.[200]

Of course, not all legislative initiatives that arose in parliament progressed as far as the Irish Privy Council. Some did not even receive a reading; in ten instances in which leave was given to prepare heads, no measure was presented.[201]

198. *Commons Jn. (Irl.)*, ii, 833–4; McGrath, *Making the constitution*, pp 123–4.
199. Minutes of the proceedings of the Lords Justices, 2, 16 July, Methuen to Vernon, 12 Aug. 1697 in *Cal. SP (Dom.), 1697*, pp 228–9, 252, 306–7. For instances of the use of the term 'heads of bill' to describe measures that arose in the Commons see May to Blathwayt, 19, 24 Aug., 14 Sept 1697 (NAI, May-Blathwayt Corres., 1697–8, MS 3070); Lords Justices to Vernon, 7 Jan. 1699 (NAI, Irish Correspondence, MS 2447 ff 41–2).   200. *Commons Jn. (Irl.)*, ii, 155, 157.
201. In five cases, nothing more was heard of the proposal after leave was given; in three instances leave was given to insert a particular clause, while in two further instances a scheduled reading was deferred (*Commons Jn. (Irl.)*, ii, 157, 158, 165, 168, 175, 176, 198, 206, 229).

In five further cases, heads did not advance beyond the first reading, while in three more they fell at committee.[202] As well as these, seven heads that made it through the Commons were either rejected at the Irish Council or held back.[203] The Irish Council was quite within its rights to do this and, when it saw fit, to amend heads prior to transmitting them to London, but there is little information with which to explore its treatment of heads of bills. This contrasts with its English counterpart where it can be shown that the Commons' measure 'for taking away the benefit of clergy' was significantly restructured. Amending legislation to the 1695 measure for suppressing tories was subject to one significant technical revision in respect of dating; while amendments were introduced also into proposals 'for avoiding of vexatious delays' in law cases; for the more easy recovery of small debts; for erecting lights in the city of Dublin; for the more easy obtaining partitions of lands, and 'for [the] redress of certain abuses in making pewter and brass'. By contrast, a proposal 'to prevent frauds by clandestine mortgages' and for raising £2,500 for the relief of the citizens of Bandon, which also arose with the Commons, passed unaltered.[204]

Since these bills were of modest or marginal import, the Irish executive was little agitated by their fate. The money bills were a quite different matter. The least problematic was that for granting an additional duty on tobacco and continuing the additional duty on beer and ale until 25 December 1702, which was approved by the English Council in October with one major and a plethora of smaller amendments appertaining to the management of the collection of the quit rent.[205] The omission of the word 'thousand' in the terminal date due to an oversight by the clerk of the crown, which was discovered when the bill was being engrossed, put it at risk, and it might not have made it to the statute book had the Irish administration not determined, rather than return the bill to London for correction, to introduce a correcting clause into another bill. This was not

202. *Commons Jn. (Irl.)*, ii, 175, 206, 207, 209, 221, 229, 232, 236.
203. These were heads of bills 'for registering deeds, conveyances and wills' (*Commons Jn. (Irl.)*, ii, 197); 'for the increase of the number of freeholders' and planting Protestants' (ibid., p. 209); 'for relief of creditors' (ibid., p. 183); 'for regulating the fees of the marshal of the four courts' (ibid., p. 208); 'for giving the subject equity against the King' (ibid., 210); for 'traversing inquisitions' (ibid.) and 'to prevent the illegal and undue charging and raising of money by grand juries' (ibid., p. 210).
204. An act for taking away the benefit of clergy (NA, PC2/77 ff 42, 50–51; *Commons Jn. (Irl.)*, ii, 221); An act to supply the defects … in an act for … suppressing tories (PC2/77 ff 46, 47–8; *Commons Jn. (Irl.)*, ii, 237); an act to prevent frauds by clandestine mortgages (PC2/77 ff 53, 57; *Commons Jn. (Irl.)*, ii, 237); an act for the more easy obtaining partitions of lands (PC2/77 ff 53, 57; *Commons Jn. (Irl.)*, ii, 237); an act for avoiding vexatious delays (PC2/77 ff 53, 58, 66–7; *Commons Jn. (Irl.)*, ii, 237); an act for redress of certain abuses in making pewter and brass (PC2/77 ff 53, 58, 66–7; *Commons Jn. (Irl.)*, ii, 237); an act for the more easy recovery of small debts (PC2/77 f. 62; *Commons Jn. (Irl.)*, ii, 237); an act fort erecting lights in the city of Dublin (PC2/77 ff 46, 54; *Commons Jn. (Irl.)*, ii, 237); and an act for raising £2,500 for the relief of the citizens of Bandon (PC2/77 ff 54, 56; *Commons Jn. (Irl.)*, ii, 237).
205. 9 William III, chap 4; NA, PC2/77 ff 46, 49–50; *Commons Jn. (Irl.)*, ii, 220.

welcomed at Whitehall but, since the problem was of the English Council's making, ministers did not stand in the way of the Irish administration on the point.[206] They entertained more serious reservations with the suggestion that a clause to the effect 'that the money should continue to go as it did during the continuance of the poll' should be added to the bill to grant a supply 'by raising money by way of a poll'. Perceived as an infraction on the royal prerogative, it was amended accordingly, but though MPs acceded they insisted on communicating their unease to the Crown. The lords justices tolerated this because of the importance of the point at issue, which otherwise encountered few problems on its way to become law.[207]

In the main, the lords justices were disposed to look benignly on the efforts of peers to advance heads of bills, though they too were carefully monitored.[208] The issue pursued by the Lords that most perturbed the Irish executive in 1697 was the attempt to advance a bill of rights, which Lord Chancellor Methuen labelled 'impertinent'.[209] Careful management ensured that a crisis was averted on this point, and the administration was in possession of enough legislation that had taken its rise in the Irish parliament during the 1697 sitting to transmit successive transmisses of fourteen, sixteen and three bills in late September, mid-October and early November.[210]

The receipt of these transmisses imposed a heavy administrative demand on the English Council. The fact that the bills were accompanied by short summaries or 'breviates' that were read before the full Council board assisted with their deliberations. These were aided further by dispatches from the lords justices of Ireland who, collectively and individually, offered commentaries on favoured bills.[211] The task of scrutinising thirty-three bills in the short time available was forbidding for all that, so it was understandable that in an attempt to spread the burden that the solicitor general was engaged to assist the attorney general.[212] As

206. Methuen to Vernon, 6 Nov., Lords Justices of Ireland to Lords Justices of England, 9 Nov. in *Cal. SP (Dom.), 1697*, p. 460; Shrewsbury to Lords Justices, 23 Nov. 1697 (NA, SP67/2 f. 92); McGrath, *Making the constitution*, p. 131.

207. 9 William III, chap 8; NA, PC2/77 ff 46, 47–8; *Commons Jn. (Irl.)*, ii, 237; Winchester to Shrewsbury, 31 Aug. in HMC, *Buccleuch and Queensbury*, ii, 545; Winchester to Vernon, 31 Aug. 1697 in *Cal. SP (Dom.), 1697*, p. 342.

208. For an indication that this was not a unanimous outlook see Winchester to [ ], 14 Sept. 1697 in *CSPD*, 1697, p. 369; for the ratification of bills see *Cal. SP (Dom.), 1697*, p. 398.

209. *Lords Jn. (Irl.)*, i, 628; Winchester to [ ], 14, 16 Sept., Methuen to Vernon, 16, 23 Sept. in *Cal. SP (Dom.), 1697*, pp 369, 380, 394.

210. Vernon to Blathwayt, 7 Sept. (Beinecke Library, Osborn Collection, Blathwayt Papers, Box 19); Lords Justices to Blathwayt, 14 Oct. 1697 (NAI, Lords Justices letterbook, 1697, MS 2454).

211. Lords Justices of Ireland to Lords Justices of England, 23 Sept., Galway to Vernon, 23 Sept. (2), Methuen to Vernon, 27 Sept., Minutes of the proceedings of the Lords Justices, 1, 15 Oct. 1697 in *Cal. SP (Dom.), 1697* pp 393, 401, 408, 427; Methuen to Somers, 27 Sept in [Malcomson (ed.),] *Irish official papers*, i, 18.

212. Minutes of the proceedings of the Lords Justices, 5, 7 Oct. 1697 in *Cal. SP (Dom.), 1697* pp 415, 417.

was now customary, the majority of bills, which required no more than a handful of technical or clarifying amendments, were processed with little delay. However, a number was deemed inappropriate to pass as currently presented. One of these was a bill 'for preventing abuses in making butter casks', which had arisen in the House of Commons. The problem in this instance centred on the so-called 'foreign clause', which sought to protect 'the interests of such Protestants as were either creditors to, or had purchased from those who were adjudged to be within the Articles of Limerick'. Perceived as nothing less than a surreptitious attempt to 'repeal ... some part of the late act for confirming the Articles' because it was not referred to in the accompanying 'breviate', officials were disinclined to return it. As it happened, they were provided with an unexpected way out of the difficulty when the discovery that there was a word missing from the additional duties bill necessitated the communication from Ireland of a remedial clause for inclusion in a bill still pending at the Council Board. Convinced that this was an ideal opportunity to resolve two problems at once, the Board decided on 22 November to replace the offending 'foreign' clause in the butter casks bill with the revenue bill clause.[213] It was an ingenious, if somewhat doubtful, undertaking that only failed to make it to the statute book because the Irish administration – persuaded that discretion was necessary – adjudged it wiser to hold the bill over for another session.[214]

Significantly, this was not the only occasion when problems traceable to faulty copying at Whitehall required remedial attention. A 'mistake in transcribing' the outlawries bill that meant a crucial reference to the year 1689 was rendered as 1697 could have resulted in this measure's rejection if the Irish administration had not authorised its silent correction.[215] This was a breach of Poynings' Law, but since nobody outside a select circle knew of the problem, it was successfully covered up. It did, however, reinforce the impression, already current in London, that the commitment in Ireland to adhere to the letter of Poynings' Law was far from complete. This impression was intensified in October as it emerged, firstly, that the tithe bill received on 30 September incorporated the controversial Henrician act relating to the payment of tithes that had been removed at the English Council board earlier in the year. Eager to make clear its disapproval of a practice that was only tolerated in the case of the outlawries bill because of the importance of the measure, the bill was laid aside.[216]

213. Minutes of the proceedings of the Lords Justices, 7, 8 Oct., Vernon to Williamson, 8 Oct. in *Cal. SP (Dom.), 1697*, pp 417, 418, 421; Vernon to Shrewsbury, 7 Oct. 1697 in James (ed.), *Vernon Letters*, i, 420–1; above, pp 95–6; Shrewsbury to Lords Justices, 23 Nov. 1697 (NA, SP67/2 f. 92); NA, PC2/77 f. 67.

214. Winchester to Shrewsbury, 2 Dec. 1697 in HMC, *Buccleuch and Queensbury*, ii, 585. The bill became law in 1698 (McGrath, *Making the constitution*, p. 131).

215. Vernon to Williamson, 19 Nov. 1697 in *Cal. SP (Dom.), 1697*, p. 478. The measure became law (Winchester to Shrewsbury, 20 Nov. 1697 in H.M.C., *Buccleuch and Queensbury*, ii, 578).

216. Minutes of the proceedings of the Lords Justices, 7 Oct. 1697 in *Cal. SP (Dom.), 1697* p. 418; NA, PC2/77 f. 46. Above, pp 92–3.

Comparable problems arose with the bill for 'the better security' of the King's 'person and government' that took its rise in the House of Commons. Anticipating a version of a similar act passed at Westminster in 1696, officials were taken aback when they received a bill that was 'clogged and altered' by the presence of a requirement that Catholics should take an oath of supremacy as well as allegiance. To compound matters, the Council board was bombarded with petitions from a veritable galaxy of eminent Catholics claiming that it was in contravention of the Articles of Limerick.[217] Determined to ensure that the bill mirrored the original English act, the law officers were instructed to delete the offending oath clause. They in turn advised a number of further alterations in respect of the administration of oaths and the imposition of the penalty of praemunire on defaulters to bring the measure into line with its English predecessor. Inevitably, such extensive emendation was not welcome in Ireland, where the bill was perceived as draconian and counter-productive. It was objected that the requirement to take an oath of supremacy was 'expressly contrary to the ninth of the Limerick Articles', which authorised only an oath of fidelity; that the 'penalty of praemunire' was 'too severe' and would 'provoke and exasperate' Catholics; and that the bill would lessen the value of land, discourage trade and industry and diminish the King's revenues. In addition, exception was taken to the exemption of Quakers on the grounds that it would encourage Catholics to convert to that religion and thereby to contribute to the propagation of 'blasphemy'. Such was the strength of opinion on the point that peers were only induced not to take the still more confrontational course of amending the bill there and then by the advice of the Lord Chancellor that this was in 'breach of Poynings' law'.[218] This did not inhibit the measure's rejection, which served in turn to remind English Privy Councillors that while they were at liberty to recast bills that took their rise in the Irish parliament, they could not assume that the Irish parliament would acquiesce in the changes they introduced. They were not unconscious of this, but they were unwilling to forward a measure they deemed objectionable. Thus when a bill to encourage linen production in Ireland (that took its rise in the House of Commons) was received at the English Council on 21 October, it was conveyed to the Council of Trade with instructions to consult with the attorney general on 'such alterations and additions … as they shall judge

217. The petitioners included the earl of Antrim, Viscount Fitzwilliam of Merrion, Colonel Nicholas Purcell, Colonel Henry Oxborogh, Colonel John Rice, John Galway, Nicholas Shea, Patrick Caddan, and 'several barristers' (NA, PC2/77 f. 51).

218. Yard to Williamson, 8, 12, 15 Oct., Vernon to Williamson, 15, 22 Oct. in *Cal. SP (Dom.), 1697*, pp. 419, 424, 429, 430, 440; Winchester to Shrewsbury, 23 Oct., 27 Nov., Methuen to Shrewsbury, 27 Nov. in HMC, *Buccleuch and Queensbury*, ii, 568, 583–4; NA, PC2/77 ff 46, 51, 54–5; Methuen to Somers, 24 Nov. 1697 in [Malcomson (ed.),] *Irish official papers*, i, 19; King to Southwell, 21 Dec. 1697 (TCD, King Papers, MS 750/1 f. 147); Reasons why some of the Lords could not assent to … an act for better security of his Majesty's person, [Dec. 1697] (BL, Ellis Papers, Add. MS 28941 ff 94–6); May to Blathwayt, 2 Dec. 1697 (NAI, May-Blathwayt Corres., 1697–8, MS 3070).

may make the same more effectuall to the purposes intended'. Several days were allocated to this task, but officials were unable to agree an appropriate set of modifications. As a result, the full Council adjudged that since 'the bill is so farr from answering the design expressed in the title' it was 'not ... thought fit to approve', and the bill was formally 'remitted'.[219]

The impact of the remission of this bill was mitigated by the suggestion that 'some good bill may be prepared for the effectuall setting up and carrying on of this manufacture', and by the decision, belatedly, to respond positively to a request from the Irish lords justices to animate a 'depending' bill from 1695 'for the relief of the subject against old dormant judgements', which had been passed over earlier in the year on the grounds that attempts to enact similar legislation at Westminster had failed. The bill was not acceptable to Irish MPs, however; forwarded from the Lords, it failed at the third reading stage in the Commons.[220] Moreover, it did not signal a more tolerant attitude to the deficiencies in Irish legislation. Quite the opposite; irritated by the errors detected in a series of bills received from Ireland – the 'foreign clause' in the butter casks bill particularly – the lords justices of England drew attention in October to the fact that 'that bills are many times incautiously drawn in Ireland'. Three weeks later, they instructed the lords justices of Ireland 'to take care to avoid sending over bills that have not been regularly proceeded on'.[221] Taken in tandem with the more specific concerns they articulated in respect of observing the terms of Poynings' Law, one could be forgiven for concluding that ministers and officials were suspicious as well as disapproving of Irish drafting practices in general, when it was specific infractions that were the issue. The number of Irish bills that were based closely on English bills, and the continuing readiness of the English Council to respond favourably to requests from Ireland that often minor measures should be returned helped keep problems of this ilk within reasonable bounds.[222] There was no identifiable reduction in the number of bills approved or increase in the time devoted to the scrutiny of measures as a result. A majority of the bills that were received were returned, and while this was not always accomplished sufficiently 'speedily' to avoid the necessity of unscheduled and extended adjournments of parliament,

219. NA, PC2/77 ff 53, 57, 65; *Commons Jn. (Irl.)*, ii, 177, 186, 196; O'Regan, *Archbishop William King*, pp 112, 114–15; [ ] to [ ], 12 Nov. 1697 in *Cal. SP (Dom.)*, *1697*, p. 470.
220. NA, PC2/77 ff 6, 52; *Commons Jn. (Irl.)*, ii, 321; Shrewsbury to Lords Justices, 3 Aug., Minutes of the proceedings of the Lords Justices, 8 Oct., Vernon to Williamson, 15 Oct. 1697 in *Cal. SP (Dom.)*, *1697*, pp 231, 420, 428–9; *Lords Jn. (Irl.)*, i, 654.
221. Minutes of the proceedings of the Lords Justices, 8, 28 Oct. 1697 in *Cal. SP (Dom.)*, *1697*, pp 421, 448.
222. Methuen to Vernon, 15 Oct. 1697 in *Cal. SP (Dom.)*, *1697*, p. 431. Minor measures so facilitated include a bill 'for setting up lights in Dublin' which was forwarded despite opposition in England (Vernon to Williamson, 22 Oct. in *Cal. SP (Dom.)*, *1697*, p. 440) and the bill for confirming the grants made to the earl of Romney (Lords Justices of Ireland to Lords Justices of England, 6 Nov. 1697 in *Cal. SP (Dom.)*, *1697*, pp 459–60).

such problems as were generated by delays were easily overcome.[223] Moreover, the fact that in a large proportion of cases amendments introduced at the English Council board tangibly improved prospective statutes also helped.[224]

Improved or not, amendments introduced at the English Council increased the likelihood of bills returned to Ireland in 1697 failing to secure the royal assent. This was the fate of a minority admittedly, and in most instances bills were rejected on substantive and pertinent grounds.[225] Among their number were six private bills transmitted in 1695. Two, appertaining to the confirmation of attainders, were not even presented. One of these was 'an act for confirming the attainders of Sir John Everard', which was heavily amended to secure guarantees of land possession given prominent Catholics. No less contentiously, bills to confirm grants to the earl of Romney (formerly Lord Sydney) and Lord Coningsby were also 'not offered to … parliament', because, in the case of the former, it did not include 'a saving … for the legal right of any person that may be thereby prejudiced'.[226] The four that were formally rejected were more varied in character, but given the sensitivies of Protestants to any measure that impinged, however slightly, on the interest of Protestant creditors and landowners, and the concern that family settlements were honoured, their rejection was not unanticipated.[227] The House of Lords, for its part, was particularly tender with respect to the Church of Ireland, and several church bills fell foul of the strong ecclesiastical presence in the upper house.[228] The Commons was less

223. Lords Justices of Ireland, 14 Oct., Vernon to Williamson, 2 Nov., Newsletter to Yard, 12 Nov. in *Cal. SP (Dom.), 1697*, pp 426, 454–5, 471; Winchester to Shrewsbury, 23 Oct. in HMC, *Buccleuch and Queensbury*, ii, 568; May to Blathwayt, 20 Oct., 24 Nov. (NAI, May-Blathwayt Corres., 1697–8, MS 3070); Lords Justices to Blathwayt, 26 Oct. 1697 (NAI, Lords Justices' letterbook, 1697, MS 2454). As well as the bills discussed above, seven other measures received at the English Council board were not reported in 1697 – bills 'to regulate the fees of sheriffs and executioners' (NA, PC2/77 f. 53); 'for the preservation of … game' (ibid.); 'for confirming estates and possessions' (ibid., f. 46); 'for the encouragement of Protestant strangers' (ibid. f. 53); 'to prevent Protestants from turning papists' (ibid., f. 53); 'to prevent charge and expence in elected members of parliament' (ibid., f. 46) and 'for the more speedy recovery of tithes and other ecclesiastical dues' (ibid., f. 46).

224. Vernon to Williamson, 29 Oct. in *Cal. SP (Dom.), 1697*, p 450; Methuen to Somers, 3 Nov. 1697 in Malcomson (ed.), *Irish official papers*, ii, 19.

225. Most notably in respect of the bill to protect the King's person (see above p. 98).

226. NA, PC2/77 ff 49–50, 65–6. May to Blathwayt, 6 Nov., 2 Dec. 1697 (NAI, May-Blathwayt Correspondence, 1697–8, MS 3070). The second attainder bill was entitled 'An act for confirming the outlawries and attainders of Richard Fagan and Wm Plunkett' (PC2/77 ff 61, 62).

227. See NA, PC2/77 ff 42, 47–8; *Commons Jn. (Irl.)*, ii, 229 (Browne bill); PC2/77 ff 6, 27; *Commons Jn. (Irl.)*, ii, 236; *Lords Jn. (Irl.)*, i, 663 (Burt bill); PC2/77 ff 42, 47–8; *Commons Jn. (Irl.)*, ii, 221 (Countess of Kilmarnock bill); PC2/77 ff 42, 54; *Commons Jn. (Irl.)*, ii, 221 (Shiel bill).

228. In addition to those such as the tithes and friars bills discussed above, measures such as the bills 'for building houses and making other improvements on Church lands' (*Lords Jn. (Irl.)*, i, 626; Foy to King, 10 Nov. 1797 (TCD, King Papers, MS 1995–2008 f. 553)); 'to enable ecclesiastical persons to make leases for three lives and one and twenty years' (PC2/77 ff 46, 50–1; *Lords Jn. (Irl.)*, i, 645); against simony (PC2/77 ff 46, 50–1; *Lords Jn. (Irl.)*, i, 647); 'for levying

predictable, but it did not behave fundamentally differently; thus, as well as rejecting the Privy Council bill 'for barring the remainders and reversions' on forfeited 'estates taile', and a bill for the relief of the subject against dormant judgements, it also scouted bills proposing to transfer the cathedral church of the diocese of Tuam to Galway, for 'building houses and making other improvements on Church lands' and against clandestine marriage.[229] Put beside the other measures that did not find favour, and Bishop William King's observation that 'we had rejected so many that we were ashamed to reject any more', it may appear that MPs and peers were just being difficult, when this was palpably not the case. Indeed, King's observation that 'severall [more] ought not to have passed' makes it clear that bills were only rejected when there were compelling reasons.[230]

King's contention that it was legitimate for parliament to reject a public bill that was 'clogged with ... additional clauses' introduced to satisfy 'private interests', or badly drafted because of 'the negligence or ignorance of clerks or the drawers' unskilfulness' was not shared at official level, where such problems were not so readily perceived.[231] King's particular *bête noir* was the manipulation of the process by private individuals. It was this that prompted him to oppose the bill for the better security of the King's person.[232] Moreover, this might not have been necessary, he implied, if the Irish parliament had the power to amend 'objectionable' provisions in what otherwise were good laws, but though King contended that his stance was entirely consistent with Magna Carta, the Privy Council had already made it clear that it would not seek the modifications to Poynings' Law necessary to meet his concerns.[233] Indeed, agreement on this point became less rather than more likely in 1698 as the perception grew among the Protestant interest in Ireland that 'their liberties and privileges [were being] invaded'. Referring to this very point, King observed emotionally that the key questions were 'whether the people of Ireland be slaves or freemen, [and] whether they be more the subjects of England than the people of England are the King's subject's'. In broad terms, King was inclined to the view that the people of Ireland were 'free', but regulations such as Poynings' Law, which stipulated that they

minister's money' (PC2/77 f. 46; *Lords Jn. (Irl.)*, i, 645) and 'for the reall union and division of parishes' (PC2/77 ff 46, 49–50; *Lords Jn. (Irl.)*, i, 644) were either lost or experienced a difficult time in the Lords. To these, one can add a bill 'for the better and more effectual levying and recovering certain duties to the church' that was returned but not presented (NA, PC2/77 ff 49–50). However, the Lords also rejected the bill to prevent butchers being graziers approved by the Commons (PC2/77 f 46, 49–50; *Commons Jn. (Irl.)*, ii, 224; *Lords Jn. (Irl.)*, i, 669).

229. King to Kildare, 25 Oct. 1697 (TCD, King Papers, MS 750/1 f. 114); NA, PC2/77 ff 25–6, 27, 28, 31, 46; *Commons Jn. (Irl.)*, ii, 176, 203, 231, 234, 217.
230. King to Southwell, 4 Dec., King to Clifford, 4 Dec. 1697 (TCD, King Papers, MS 750/1 ff 141, 138–40).
231. King to Kildare, 25 Oct. 1697 (TCD, King Papers, MS 750/1 f. 114).
232. King to Annesley, 10 Jan., King to Bishop of Sarum, 29 Jan. 1699 (TCD, King Papers, MS 750/1 ff 154–5, 165–8).
233. King to Southwell, 21 Dec. 1697 (TCD, King Papers, MS 750/1 f. 147).

could 'have no laws but what is approved by England', were perceived by him as a badge of enslavement.[234]

King did not allude in this context to the fact that the Irish legislature was allowed initiate legislation, and that it contributed substantially to the thirty acts of parliament (seventeen public and thirteen private) that made it to the statute book in 1697. He might also have observed that politics had emerged from the *impasse* caused by the 'sole right' issue, as Methuen's somewhat presumptuous claim that his stand in respect of the imposition of a duty on woollen exports meant that 'the sole right is much more removed from all controversy than by my Lord Capell's expedient' indicated.[235] Methuen, no less than King, was prone to exaggeration. The truth of the matter was that the 1697 session had determined little, other than to demonstrate further the viability of the heads of bill process as a means of allowing both Houses of the Irish legislature to participate actively in the making of law for Ireland. It had also demonstrated the strength of the commitment of officials in London to exercise their entitlement to curb as well as to control the legislative authority of the Irish parliament and brought about some further clarification in administrative procedure in the manner of the application of Poynings' Law. At the same time, the fencing that took place with respect of certain aspects of Poynings' Law indicated that practices as well as positions were not absolutely fixed. In the overall scheme of things, both the temper of parliament and its legislative output supported Methuen's positive assessment rather than King's resentful criticisms.[236] The parliamentary sitting held in 1697 was not so organised or tightly conducted as that of 1695. Yet, when problems were encountered, it was clear that the willingness to retain practices put in place in 1695 was stronger than the desire to tear them up and begin anew. At the same time, as the worried queries forthcoming from the English Council on occasion, and the procedural uncertainty that was still a feature of aspects of the way Poynings' Law was administered indicated, it could not be assumed that this would endure. The resentment articulated so vividly by William King certainly constituted a more challenging environment for the 1698–9 meeting of parliament than was the case in 1695 and 1697. This session would reveal if Capell's 'compromise' provided the basis for a viable long-term law-making arrangement to match the managerial system established in 1695.

THE 1698–9 SESSION

Impelled by the need for money to pay for the administration of the kingdom and to defray the expense of sustaining an augmented army establishment, preparations

---

234. King to Annesley, 19 May 1698 (TCD, King Papers, MS 750/1 ff 232–3); King to Canterbury, 1 Mar. 1698 (TCD, King Papers, MS 750/2 ff 50–1).
235. Methuen to Shrewsbury, 3 Feb. 1698 in HMC, *Buccleuch and Queensbury*, ii, 599–601.
236. Methuen to [Vernon], 24 Oct. 1697 in *Cal. SP (Dom.), 1697*, p. 443.

for a new session of parliament commenced in the early summer of 1698.[237] They took place against a backdrop of mounting political unease as English resentment at competition from Irish woollen goods propelled demand for the imposition of a prohibition on the importation of Irish woollens. The failure of a bill for this purpose, approved by the Westminster House of Commons in December 1697, to make it to the statute book offered some grounds for optimism that this could be avoided. But, the furore generated in England by the publication of William Molyneux's *ur-text, The Case of Ireland's being bound by acts of parliament in England, stated*, and the palpable anger in Ireland at the threat to the appellate jurisdiction of the Irish House of Lords arising out of the rival claims of the diocese of Derry and the London Society to the Foyle fishery ensured the atmosphere remained tense.[238]

It did not inhibit preparations for the session at the Irish Privy Council, however, and early in May 1698 the Council dispatched a transmiss with eleven bills to London; a second short transmiss of two bills was conveyed a short time later. This was in keeping with current practice, but whereas this was normally the occasion for the Irish Council to exercise its right to prepare original legislation, it chose on this occasion to communicate transmisses composed largely of heads of bills that had originated with the Irish House Commons in 1695 and 1697, and that had not then been forwarded. No explanation was offered by the Irish Council as to why it chose to pack the pre-session transmiss with heads of bills, though it was an implicit acknowledgement by the Council of its readiness to cede the initiative in inaugurating Irish law to the Commons.[239] Political calculation inevitably played an important part in the decision, but it was also of major constitutional import; ministers might, for this reason, have objected, but they took no identifiable exception. They may even have felt encouraged to animate a number of bills referred to the English Council in 1697 that had not been reported on at the time.[240]

The expectation that the Irish parliament would meet 'about the middle of September' set the context for the English Council's scrutiny of the thirteen bills

237. McGrath, *Making the constitution*, pp 134–5.
238. Ibid., pp 135–7; Vernon to Shrewsbury, 21 May, 2 June 1697 in James (ed.), *Vernon letters*, ii, 83–4, 93–4; P.H. Kelly, 'The Irish woollen export prohibition act of 1699; Kearney revisited', *Irish Economic and Social History*, 7 (1980), pp 20–44; Dickson, *Ireland: new foundations*, pp 46–9.
239. Of the eleven bills (NA, PC2/77 f. 89), six arose directly from heads forwarded in 1697; two from heads forwarded in 1695; most of the remainder were modified versions of bills considered but not approved in 1695 and 1697 (PC2/77 f. 8; *Commons Jn. (Irl.)*, ii, 145, 197, 208, 209, 210). The two additional bills were 'to prevent the undue raising of money by Grand Jurys', which was received on 12 May (PC2/77 f. 90) and 'for the preservation of the King's person and government' which is recorded on 7 July as having been received 'lately' (ibid., f. 106).
240. In contrast to 1697 when the clerk of the council was invited to establish how many bills were then 'depending', this does not appear to have been done in 1698, though a number of bills addressed at the Council Board were received in 1697. See below, p. 105.

received from Ireland.[241] Referred to the attorney and solicitor general 'jointly' for a report, their formal consideration, which commenced on 28 July, proved uncomplicated, as the fate of ten of the bills proved clear-cut.[242] Four were not reported and not heard of again;[243] while six were ordered to progress with little more than technical amendments appertaining to the date at which they would come into effect.[244] The amendments made to the bill for 'planting and preserving timber trees and wood' were more numerous and more significant,[245] but they were of modest import when compared with the experience of the bill for 'the recovery of the King's debts and for giving equity against the King'. Based on an act passed at Westminster in the 1540s (33 Henry VIII, chap 39), the Irish Privy Council chose to omit several clauses for the recovery of debt that were in the original, but the English Council was unwilling to approve such legislative cherry-picking unless the Crown was 'otherwise provided for by some express law in Ireland'. To this end, they invited the lords justices to provide them with 'an explanation', and when this was not forthcoming the original clauses were restored.[246]

The attitude of councillors to the redrafted version of the bill for 'the preservation of His Majesty's person and government' was equally firm. Consistent with the critical response afforded a similarly titled measure in 1697, attention focussed on whether the bill should be amended to 'exempt the Popish comprised within the Articles of Limerick' from taking the oath of supremacy. Anticipating this eventuality, the Irish Privy Council adopted the unusual expedient of conveying a clause, 'not as part of the bill but on a paper by itself to be added in case it should be thought fitt'. However, this did not have the endorsement of

241. Vernon to attorney general, 30 July 1698 in *Cal. SP (Dom.), 1698*, p. 363. On 9 September the prorogation of the Irish parliament was extended to 27 September (Vernon to Blathwayt, 9 Sept. 1798 (Beinecke Library, Blathwayt papers, Box 19)); Lords Justices to Blathwayt, 30 Aug. 1697 (NAI, Lords Justices letterbook, 1698, MS 2456).

242. Vernon to Delafaye, [1698] in *Cal. SP (Dom.), 1700–2*, p. 610; Yard to Blathwayt, 26 July, Vernon to Blathwayt, 29 July 1698 (Beinecke Library, Blathwayt Papers, Boxes 19, 20).

243. These were the bills 'to encrease the number of freeholders in this kingdom and planting the same with Protestants', 'for enabling the making leases of forfeited lands for three lives and planting the same with Protestants'; 'to enable lessees for years to serve on jurys' and 'for registering memorials of deeds' (NA, PC2/77 f. 89).

244. These were bills 'for the building and repairing of churches' (NA, PC2/77 ff 89, 106) 'for the more effectuall putting in execution ... an act for the erection of free schools' (PC2/77 ff 89, 107 111); 'for the relief and release of poor and distressed prisoners' (PC2/77 ff 109, 111–2); 'for regulating the fees of the marshalls of the four courts' (ibid.); and 'for traversing inquisitions' (PC2/77 ff 109, 111); Yard to Blathwayt, 2 Aug. 1697 (Beinecke Library, Osborn Collection, Blathwayt papers, Box 20).

245. NA, PC2/77 ff 89, 109, 111; Yard to Blathwayt, 5 Aug. 1697 (Beinecke Library, Osborn Collection, Blathwayt papers, Box 20).

246. NA, PC2/77 ff 89,109, 121–22; Vernon to Shrewsbury, 9 Aug. in James (ed.), *Vernon letters*, ii, 149; Yard to Blathwayt, 9 Aug., 30 Sept. 1698 (Beinecke Library, Osborn Collection, Blathwayt Papers, Box 20).

Lord Chancellor Methuen, who made his views known in person. Encouraged thereby to decline 'to make such a distinction between the Limerick men and the rest of the papists of Ireland' as the amendment proposed, the English Council took another step towards greater procedural probity by concluding that amendments 'ought to be transmitted ... in forme from the Council of Ireland', and that the bill should pass under the great seal with no more than a few clarifications.[247]

Having certified these nine measures, and four others received from Ireland in 1697 that were approved with few or no amendments, the English Council had good reason to anticipate that these bills would make it to the statute book without difficulty when parliament opened on 27 September, and that this would represent further progress towards applying Poynings' Law in a manner that was agreeable to all parties. However, the political atmosphere remained difficult, and it was this context that shaped the response in Ireland to a number of Privy Council bills prepared (ironically) as part of a well-intentioned attempt to meet concerns in both kingdoms in a fair and reasonable manner.[248] Persuaded that they could appease English hostility to Irish woollen imports and defuse Irish unease by pursuing the dual approach of 'encouraging the linen manufacture and discouraging the woollen manufacture in Ireland', the Commissioners for Trade and Lord Chancellor Methuen agreed in July that the 'heads of a bill or bills to this purpose' should be presented to the Irish parliament. Drafted at the Irish Council and received at Whitehall on 4 October, two bills were referred to the Commissioners for Trade 'to peruse ... and to make such amendments ... as they shall judge proper'. They were instructed specifically to calculate the 'impositions' that should 'be laid upon the woollen manufactures of Ireland exported' to set it on an equal footing with English woollen exports.[249] Heartened by the fact that, as James Vernon put it, 'the Council of Ireland have done their part', officials were hopeful that the proposed duty of two to four pence on woollens exported from Ireland would deflect 'clamour' in England.[250] They were less confident about

247. NA, PC2/77 ff 100, 105; Yard to Blathwayt, 29 July 1698 (Beinecke Library, Osborn Collection, Blathwayt Papers, Box 20).
248. The bill 'to encourage the building of houses and making other improvements on church lands', which was essentially the same measure that had been rejected in the Lords in 1697, was returned in 1698, as it had been in 1697, unaltered. Changes were authorised to bills 'for confirming estates and possessions held and enjoyed under the acts of settlement and explanation', for regulating 'the fees of sheriffs on executions', whose return was specifically requested from Ireland, and for preserving game, but they were only significant in the latter case. In this instance, a clause of some twelve lines was deleted: NA, PC2/77 ff 37–8, 46, 53, 105, 106, 109, 110, 111–12, 115–16; Newsletter, 5 Aug. in *Cal. SP (Dom.), 1698*, p. 372; Yard to Blathwayt, 6 Sept. 1698 (Beinecke Library, Blathwayt Papers, Box 20).
249. Yard to Blathwayt, 29 July, 5 Aug., 30 Sept., 4 Oct. 1698 (Beinecke Library, Blathwayt Papers, Box 20); Newsletter, 4 Oct. 1698 in *Cal. SP (Dom.), 1698*, p. 400; Lords Justices to Blathwayt, 30 Aug. 1698 (NAI, Lords Justices letterbook, 1698, M 2456); NA, PC2/77 f. 126; Horowitz, *Parliament, policy and politics*, pp 235, 241–2.
250. Vernon to Shrewsbury, 4 Oct. 1698 in James (ed.), *Vernon letters*, ii, 189–90.

Irish reaction, as the failure to mention the woollen bill in the opening speech indicated, and the session was not long under way when they were embroiled in difficulties arising out of the perception there that the proposed woollen bill was a supply measure.[251] As a result, the administration was put on the defensive when the Commons deemed the proposal to tax woollen exports inappropriate because it was a money bill, and set about preparing their own heads. Though the Lords Justices of Ireland, Galway and Winchester, were at pains in their account of events to emphasise that '*le mot de solo right n'a pas este prononce dans la maison*', it was on MPs minds. Moreover, there was no avoiding the fact that either the Privy Council bill or the Commons' heads must fall. The preference of the lords justices was that it should be the former because, as they pointed out, if the Privy Council rejected the heads that took their rise in the Irish parliament, MPs would reject the Privy Council's woollen and linen bills. More seriously, they hinted that the Commons apprehended that if they allowed the Privy Council woollen bill to progress it would be interpreted as a climbdown on the 'sole right', and this was to be avoided at all costs since the Commons had already signalled that they would not take kindly to this by embarking reluctantly on the preparation of heads of bills to provide a supply.[252]

This news was greeted with understandable unease by officials in England who were disinclined to concede further ground on the issue of 'sole right'. However, they were no less anxious to ensure the provision of an appropriate supply and the enactment of suitable linen and woollen bills. Persuaded for this reason that the politic thing to do was to approve the Privy Council woollen bill as it stood, it was agreed at Council on 13 October to send it to pass under the great seal *before* the report requested from the Council of Trade was received.[253] The linen bill was afforded a more thorough scrutiny. Robert Yard, the secretary to the lords justices, observed that it was subject to 'some little amendments', which may have been his true impression given the exceptional length of the bill, but a consideration of the twenty-three amendments introduced – a number of which involved the rewriting and introduction of new clauses – does not bear this out.[254] Moreover, the hopes

251. McGrath, *Making the constitution*, pp 139–41; Lords Justices to Blathwayt, 6 Oct. 1698 (NAI, Lords Justices letterbook, 1698, MS 2456).
252. Winchester and Galway to Shrewsbury (2), 10 Oct., Winchester to Shrewsbury, 27 Oct., Galway to Shrewsbury, 28 Oct. in HMC, *Buccleuch and Queensbury*, ii, 615–16, 617–18; Vernon to Shrewsbury, 13 Oct. 1692 in James (ed.), *Vernon letters*, pp 194–6; O'Regan, *Archbishop William King*, pp 113–15; McGrath, *Making the constitution*, p. 142.
253. Privy Council to Lords Justices of Ireland, 13, 18 Oct. in *Cal. SP (Dom.), 1698*, pp 616, 617; Vernon to Shrewsbury, 13 Oct. in James (ed.), *Vernon letters*, ii, 194–6; Yard to Blathwayt, 14, 18 Oct., Vernon to Blathwayt, 18 Oct. (Beinecke Library, Blathwayt Papers, Box 20); NA, PC2/77 ff 125, 127–9. The report of the Council of Trade, which was read at the Council Board on 18 October, concluded that a 40 per cent duty on 'the woollen manufacture exported out of Ireland ... would bring it to a par with the trade of England': Vernon to Blathwayt, 18 Oct. (Beinecke Library, Blathwayt Papers, Box 20).
254. Yard to Blathwayt, 14 Oct. 1698 (Beinecke Library, Blathwayt Papers, Box 20); NA, PC2/77 ff 125, 127–9.

entertained in England that the essentially sympathetic consideration accorded both bills would facilitate their early enactment proved unfounded as the presentation to the Commons of the heads of a woollen bill obliged the lords justices of Ireland to proceed gingerly on the issue. They held back their own bill hoping they would be permitted by ministers to drop the measure rather than provoke a disagreement, which they could not win, and ventured forward tentatively with the bill for encouraging the manufacture of flax and hemp. Significantly, it was repeatedly deferred after receiving its first reading on 4 November because it was 'look'd upon as a money bill', and was aversely noticed by those 'country gentlemen who think it is so … insisting upon the sole right'.[255]

Irish sensitivities on the subject of woollen exports were predictable, given their economic dependence on that commodity; their concerns were certainly heightened by the fact that English officials were reluctant to take them on board. James Vernon, for example, was unconvinced by the efforts of the Irish executive to assure him that the matter at issue with respect to the woollen bill was 'not on account of the sole right'. On a more positive note, he advised that practical politics demanded that 'if the Irish considered their interest in this matter, they would pass the woollen bill as it went from hence, for they will never have so good a bargain of it again'.[256] Few in Ireland concurred, but English sensitivities on this point were made still more explicit when William of Orange let it be known in respect of the 'pretence of the House of Commons of [the] Kingdom [of Ireland] to the sole right of beginning money bills amongst themselves' that he saw 'no reason to alter precedency [as defined in 1695] for a new plan'. He instructed the lords justices of England to inform the lords justices of Ireland 'that in case the sole right of beginning money bills be insisted on by the Commons there, their Lords[hip]s do in that case forbear at least to give the Royall Assent to any bills without his maj[es]ties express orders'.[257]

It seemed that a showdown was inevitable if, as some anticipated, the Irish parliament chose to make a stand on the matter of 'sole right', but news early in November that 'the House of Commons have agreed with the Committee for laying an additional duty on the woollen manufacture exported', but omitted the words that it should 'be towards supply' averted this prospect.[258] It also demonstrated once more that when faced with the stark choice of crisis or compromise, which in this case meant accepting a Privy Council bill or adhering rigidly to their position that such legislation should take its rise in the form of heads of bills only, compromise proved most appealing. This was made still

255. McGrath, *Making the constitution*, pp 143–4; *Commons Jn. (Irl.)*, ii, 262, 265, 266, 267, 270, 273, 274, 276, 277, 279, 280, 282; Yard to Blathwayt, 8, 18 Nov., 2 Dec. 1698 (Beinecke Library, Blathwayt Papers, Box 20).
256. Vernon to Shrewsbury, 25 Oct. in James (ed.), *Vernon letters*, ii, 206–8; see also Galway to Shrewsbury, 28 Oct. 1698 in HMC, *Buccleuch and Queensbury*, ii, 617–18.
257. Blathwayt to Lords Justices of England, 21/31 Oct., enclosed with Blathwayt to Lords Justices of Ireland, 21/31 Oct. 1698 (Beinecke Library, Blathwayt Papers, Box 20).
258. Yard to Blathwayt, 4 Nov. 1698 (Beinecke Library, Blathwayt Papers, Box 20).

clearer when MPs voted a generous supply of £139,000 without reference to the 'sole right'. Their mood remained crusty, none the less, as the support forth-coming for a motion calling for the disbanding of five Huguenot regiments underlined.[259] Furthermore, a bill for 'the better preservation of his Majesty's royal person and government' encountered problems as MPs objected to the proposition that 'all persons' should take the prescribed oath. Not to be outdone, peers too were 'very warm', and they chose 'to assert their jurisdiction in judicial matters' in the row over property rights between the Bishop of Derry and the London Companies.[260] James Vernon greeted the reports of these events with a mixture of anxiety and alarm: 'They have done so many extravagant things one upon the neck of another, that I cannot think them in a temper to bring anything to maturity if they were disposed to it', he observed dolefully.[261] Vernon was prompted to make this observation in response to reports that the bill for the preservation of the King's person was in trouble, but while it accurately mani-fested his unease at what he perceived as the inappropriate assertiveness of the Irish parliament (as evident, for example, in the suggestion that a *habeas corpus* and a bill of rights would be advanced), the reality was that the Irish parliament was merely exercising the right, conceded by Capell, to initiate legislation, albeit in a more active fashion than it had done either in 1695 or 1697.

In keeping with the pattern already identified for 1695 and 1697, leave was granted to MPs to introduce a significantly larger number of heads of bills than was presented for formal discussion. Among the eleven heads for which permission to introduce a bill was secured but where no bill ensued were measures to regulate fisheries, tolls, customs, fairs and markets, the practice of physic, the use of woollens and to make the river Shannon navigable.[262] There is no detectible trend in the type of bills, public or private (of which there were two)[263] that did not progress to a reading stage; this is true also of the seven public heads that did not negotiate the Commons.[264] For those that did, the Irish Privy Council could prove a difficult obstacle as six heads of (public) bills referred from the Irish House of Commons during the regular session were not transmitted to the

259. McGrath, *Making the constitution*, pp 142–6; Yard to Blathwayt, 28 Oct., 4, 15 Nov., Vernon to Blathwayt, 4 Nov. 1698 (Beinecke Library, Blathwayt Papers, Box 20); Lords Justices to Blathwayt, 25, 29 Oct., 17, 26 Nov. 1698 (NAI, Lords Justices letterbook, 1698, MS 2456).

260. Vernon to Blathwayt, 18 Oct., 1 Nov., Yard to Blathwayt, 25 Oct., 1, 4, 15, 22 Nov., 2 Dec., Lords Justices of Ireland to Lords Justices of England, 19 Nov. (Beinecke Library, Blathwayt Papers, Box 20); Lords Justices to Blathwayt, 15, 22 Oct. 1698 (NAI, Lords Justices letterbook, 1698, MS 2456); Yard to Williamson, 1 Nov., Ellis to Williamson, 1 Nov., in *Cal. SP (Dom.)*, *1698*, pp 410–11; Vernon to Shrewsbury, 25 Oct. 1698 in James (ed.), *Vernon letters*, ii, 206–8.

261. Vernon to Blathwayt, 1 Nov. 1698 (Beinecke Library, Blathwayt Papers, Box 20).

262. *Commons Jn. (Irl.)*, ii, 246, 250, 256, 257, 260, 268, 273, 278, 279, 291.

263. Heads of bills to enable John Baker, a minor, to raise money on his estate, and to enable the trustees for securing the debts of John Browne sell his estate (*Commons Jn. (Irl.)*, ii, 284, 290)

264. *Commons Jn. (Irl.)*, ii, 280 (blasphemy bill); 282 (malt bill); 282 (estates of minors bill); 282 (small tithes bill); 286 (reduction of interest bill); 291 (paper office bill); 306 (Protestant inheritance bill).

English Council. In the absence of a record of the Council's deliberations, it is difficult to identify a possible common cause, since the bills – for a ballast office for Dublin, the relief of 'the Galway prisoners', the regulation of the beef industry, the enlargement of Dame's Gate, the preservation of the liberty of the subject and provision for the poor – were diverse in theme. However, it is apparent from lobbying by absentee landowners against the attempt to provide Ireland with a poor law and the known dislike in England for any measure appertaining to the liberty of the subject that a combination of vested interest and knowledge of the pitfalls ahead at Whitehall were important considerations.[265]

Though English officials made no secret of their wish to 'bee rid of the Irish parliament' before their own assembled on 29 November, it was crucial to the reputation and standing of the Irish parliament that its meetings were conducted according to its own needs and requirements, and it was thus symbolically as well as administratively significant that the preparation of bills took considerably longer than anticipated. As a result, it was not until 12 December that the first of a number of transmisses with fourteen public and eight private bills was received at Whitehall.[266] A further pointer to future practice was provided by the fact that the main supply bill, which inaugurated a land tax aimed at raising £120,000, and a supporting bill authorising a high tariff on tobacco 'to compleat the supply … and to build and finish the barracks' were approved expeditiously and without amendment on 13 December.[267] Five other bills passed under the great seal on the same day,[268] and the ratification, again with no more than a handful of essentially minor amendments in three instances, of five public and three private bills over the following nine days later not just concluded the Privy Council's engagement with Irish legislation for the session, it manifested just how expeditiously and efficiently the English Council could deal with Irish bills when this was a priority.[269] Indeed, only two public bills transmitted at this time did not progress;

---

265. *Commons Jn. (Irl.)*, ii, 256, 282, 285, 290; Fitzgerald, 'Poverty and vagrancy', pp 233–5.

266. Vernon to Blathwayt, 28 Oct., 18 Nov., 2 Dec. (Beinecke Library, Blathwayt Papers); Vernon to attorney general, 12, 17 Dec., Ellis to Williamson, 13 Dec. in *Cal. SP (Dom.), 1698*, pp 426–7, 428; NA, PC2/77 ff 141–2; Lords Justices to Blathwayt, 5 Dec. 1698 (Lords Justices letterbook, 1698, MS 2456).

267. NA, PC2/77 ff 110, 142; Yard to Williamson, 16 Dec. in *Cal. SP (Dom.), 1698*, p. 427.

268. These were measures, 'for regulating the quartering and marching of soldiers'; 'against deceitful, disorderly and excessive gaming'; to encourage the building of houses and making other improvements on church lands'; 'for correcting … some words of an act entitled for encouraging … flax and hemp' and for 'explaining some doubts that may arise' in an act 'for confirming estates and possessions' (NA, PC2/77 f. 110).

269. The seven were measures 'for determining differences by arbitration'; 'to prevent papists being solicitors'; 'for reviving an act for reall union and division of parishes'; for 'the better management and disposall of the lands set apart for … the fort of Duncannon'; 'for regulating weights'; for restoring John Burke to his estate; to enable Sir William Parsons to charge his estate with £2,200 and to enable Hugh Morgan to raise £2100 on his estate (NA, PC2/77 ff 141–2, 143). The private bills that did not progress were those appertaining to Abel Ram, Edward Denny (against both of

the heads of a bill to encourage the importation of iron, which had experienced a difficult passage through the Commons because of opposition to the proposed duty of £4 to £5 per ton on iron exports, was referred to the Commissioners for Trade, but no report was forthcoming, while the bill to deprive 'papists' of jurisdiction in manor courts, which was targeted at Richard Martin of County Galway, was laid aside.[270]

Because the return from England of the sixteen bills (twelve public and four private) deemed suitable to receive the royal assent was delayed by contrary winds, the Irish lords justices endured an anxious few days at the beginning of January 1699 as they sought to calculate how long parliament need remain in session.[271] Acutely conscious that the thorny questions of the woollen and linen bills remained unresolved, the administration activated the heads of a linen bill, which had remained in limbo in committee since 30 November. Parallel with this they introduced an amending act 'to correct a mistake' in the linen manufacture bill. This caused more than a ripple of unease since the bill that it purported to amend had not yet received the royal assent, but it was modest compared with the reaction to the message from the lords justices pointing out 'that [since] our proceedings in the woollen manufacture bill was not so forward as to be likely to pass this session, as public necessity required ... their lordships thought they could not better express their great concern for us than sending us a bill in form, which was transmitted for that purpose from England'. Faced with the unpalatable implications of accepting the Privy Council woollen bill, battle was finally joined on the question of 'sole right'. The debate was 'long and warm', but the fact that when a division was called the administration enjoyed a healthy majority served to demonstrate not only that the Irish parliament accepted it had yielded on the principle of sole right in 1695 in return for the right to initiate legislation, financial legislation included, but also that the matter at issue was essentially one of detail.[272]

The ratification of an Act for laying an additional duty on woollen manufactures exported out of this kingdom rivalled the approval of two money bills, which placed the government of Ireland on solid financial foundations, as the Irish administration's most notable legislative achievement of the 1698 session. The money bills were enacted without drama and accorded the royal assent on 26 January.[273]

which petitions were presented), Edward Dean, the earl of Granard, and Lord Kingston (PC2/77 ff 141, 143).

270. NA, PC2/77 f. 141; *Commons Jn. (Irl.)*, ii, 260, 263, 264, 266, 267, 269, 270, 273, 274, 275, 277, 280, 285; King to Annesley, 2 Feb. 1699 (TCD, King Papers, MS 750/2/1 ff 64–5); Lords Justices to Vernon, 4 Mar. 1699 in *Cal. SP (Dom.), 1699–1700*, p. 83.

271. Galway to Vernon, 3, 9, 12 Jan. 1699 in *Cal. SP (Dom.), 1699–1700*, pp 2–3, 11, 17.

272. Palmer to [ ], 3 Jan. in *Cal. SP (Dom.), 1699–1700*, pp 3–4; McGrath, *Making the constitution*, pp 146–7; *Commons Jn. (Irl.)*, ii, 287; Lords Justices to Vernon, 14, 18 Jan. 1699 (NAI, Irish Correspondence, ii, MS 2447, ff 44, 45). I wish to thank Ivar McGrath for his assistance with this, and other, points in this chapter.

273. *Commons Jn. (Irl.)*, ii, 287, 291, 293, 294, 295, 296, 297, 298, 299, 301, 304, 307.

As well as these measures, 6 other public and 2 private bills returned in December also became law.[274] In all, 10 public and 2 private bills were approved by the Irish parliament in January 1699. Added to the 7 hills (6 public and 1 private) approved before that date, it brought the total for the session to 19. However, the fact that as many as 13 bills were lost during the same period (8 in the Commons and 5 in the Lords) indicates that the success ratio was not especially impressive. Moreover, when one takes on board Bishop King's conclusion that those 'rejected were of much greater moment to the kingdom than those that past', it is apparent that the arrangements for making law for Ireland within the restrictive parameters provided for by Poynings' law were far from fully developed.

King attributed the loss of so many bills in 1698–9 to the fact that 'they, either by the unskilfulness or malice of the drawers, were so clogged that they no ways answered their titles'. He also observed that because the concurrence of the Privy Councils of both England and Ireland was required to 'ease us' from any 'gall[ing]' law, it was incumbent on the Irish parliament to exercise particular discretion 'less we ty a knot we cannot unloose'.[275] It is clear from this that few if any of the thirteen bills were rejected without good reason, even if this was not always apparent. Thus, the bill for preserving the King's person was denied because it was 'of no real advantage to his majesty'; the bill for encouraging the manufacture of flax and hemp did not progress because it was 'too ambitious'; the act to prevent undue raising of money by grand juries was a rejected because 'it gave liberty to grand juries to raise money'; John Bourke's private bill could not be approved because it was a front to enable him to raise £9,000 on his estates for others; while the bill for reviving an act for the real union and division of parishes was simply 'of little use'. If it can be argued, based on this digest of reasons, that Irish peers and MPs were guided in their response to legislation by a healthy quotient of emotion and instinct, there were also important matters at stake in each case. For instance, opposition coalesced against the bill for the 'real union and division of parishes' because of the addition at the Privy Council of a clause 'that retrospected the act' and 'deprived severall good men of their livings'; six concrete objections were cited against the bill for regulating the quartering of soldiers, of which the entitlement to permit the free quartering of troops on the public for up to five years, no less than the proposal to build barracks, reflected genuine public concerns; while the earl of Inchiquin's private bill was 'thrown out' because it referred to lands 'not in his possession'.[276] In general terms, the grounds upon which the Lords rejected bills were more multi-factorial than was the case with the Commons. For instance, it was determined that rather than offer 'an express negative' to the bill for building and repairing churches, it should

274. 10 William III, chaps 6, 11, 12, 14, 15, 16 and 10 William III, chaps 2 and 3 (private); *Commons Jn. (Irl.)*, ii, 307.
275. King to Gilbert, 2 Jan., King to Annesley, 2 Feb. 1699 (TCD, King Papers, MS 750/2/1 ff 48, 64).
276. King to Annesley, 2 Feb. 1699 (TCD, King Papers, MS 750/2/1 ff 62–4); [ ] to [Somers], 26 Jan. 1699 in [Malcomson (ed.),] *Irish official papers*, i, 22.

simply be called for no more, though there was much that was wrong with it, including a problematic clause that was attributable to a 'mistake of the clerk'. Concern was also expressed in this instance and in the case of the bill 'for the erection of free schools' that it trespassed on the authority of the bishop, which was guaranteed to provoke objection in the Lords. However, the fact that there were also a number of major flaws in this bill, in the bills for the recovery of the King's debts, for regulating weights as well as for regulating the fees of sheriffs was more significant.[277] Bishop King was certainly persuaded that each of the thirteen bills failed for entirely legitimate reasons, and that this might have been the fate of a number of others. In this context, his observation that the business of the Irish parliament 'is not to make good laws, but to hinder ill ones [since this] is all that is left to us by Poinings Act' has a tempting aphoristic appeal, but it is belied by his acknowledgement that 'materiall' bills took their rise in the Irish parliament in the late 1690s. It bothered King that several (he instanced the bill of rights, the *habeas corpus* bill and a bill for a land registry) important bills 'were never returned', but had he taken stock and realised that no more than four of the nineteen acts approved during the 1698–9 session originated with the Irish Privy Council then he might have offered a more balanced and nuanced assessment.[278]

In reality, the 1698–9 session was a triumph neither for the government nor for parliament. Too many favoured legislative initiatives with both parties were lost. At the same time, the fact that nineteen bills made it to the statute book indicates just how far the Irish parliament had come as a functioning and working legislature since 1692. The money bills provide the most visible testament to this since, the preoccupation with the issue of sole right aside,[279] it demonstrated that the Irish MPs and peers were willing to accept that the price of possessing a parliament was an acceptance of the responsibilities that went along with it. In this respect, the heads of bills procedure constituted an appropriate compromise between the desire of Irish Protestants to make law for the kingdom of Ireland and the resolve of English ministers to possess a superintending authority. It was a compromise that had taken time to identify, and then to establish, but it seemed clearer in January 1699 than it had been in November 1695 or December 1697, that it both worked, and had much to offer all involved in the making of law for Ireland.

277. King to Annesley, 2 Feb. 1699 (TCD, King Papers, MS 750/2/1 ff 60–2).
278. Ibid. (f. 59).
279. Galway to Shrewsbury, 2 Feb. 1699 in HMC, *Buccleuch and Queensbury*, ii, 120.

Part Two

Monitoring the Constitution, 1703–82

CHAPTER THREE

Refining the process: the parliaments of Queen Anne, 1703–13

THE 1695 SESSION established that the Irish parliament would be afforded an active role in the making of law for the kingdom of Ireland by acknowledging its entitlement to initiate legislation in the form of heads of bills. Yet, because half the total number of legislative measures proposed in 1695 and closer to 60 per cent in 1697 took their rise in the Irish Privy Council, it remained a possibility that parliament and Council might share the privilege equally. The 1698–9 session demonstrated otherwise, as the precipitate collapse in the proportion of legislation arising with Council to less than one-third meant that the pendulum swung sharply and decisively in favour of parliament. It was this session that established that a majority of public bills, which accounted for 87 per cent of the legislation ratified by the Irish parliament between 1703 and 1800, would commence as heads of bills and that the Privy Council's role as the initiator of law would continue to decline.

The emergence of parliament, and particularly the House of Commons, as the main source of Irish law reflected the political reality that Irish Protestants were unwilling to accede to the subordinate and compliant role deemed appropriate in London for a dependent kingdom. This troubled ministers, as James Vernon, the secretary of state, testified when he observed in 1697 that 'if the Protestants in Ireland were not under some apprehension from the papists there, their thoughts would be then employed how they might get rid of their dependence on England'.[1] This was seriously to misjudge the motives of Irish Protestants; they harboured no wish to reconfigure the Anglo-Irish nexus in a manner inconsistent with the security of the connection. From their perspective, the problem was that English officials refused to allow Irish Protestants the full spectrum of constitutional rights to which they were entitled. Bishop King articulated the suspicion that fuelled this outlook with characteristic directness when he observed in 1697 that 'we and our affairs are so despised by those in the helm in England that they cannot afford us a reflection'.[2]

In reality, Irish affairs, and Irish bills specifically, were and continued to be attended to closely in England. The fact that the review of legislation received

1. Vernon to Shrewsbury, 12 Oct. 1697 in James (ed.), *Vernon letters*, i, 426.
2. Cited in O'Regan, *Archbishop William King*, p. 85.

from Ireland was, along with 'giving directions with respect to trade and the colonies, and hearing appeals from the plantations', chief among the responsibilities of the English Privy Council was indicative.[3] Moreover, the Council's structures continued to evolve to meet these needs. This was part of the ongoing refinement of the Council's administrative arrangements, of which the development of a more sophisticated committee system was a key component. The main innovation during the reign of William and Mary was the emergence of the committee of the whole council as the main forum of business. This may, as Turner has argued, have 'supersede[d] the limited committee' in so far as it was in this capacity that the Council dealt increasingly with a variety of issues. However, whereas this was not uncommon in the case of Irish bills during the 1690s, particularly when William was abroad, it was appealed to only in exceptional instances following the accession of Queen Anne in March 1702.[4] The more usual practice from this point was to refer Irish bills to the law officers for a report for presentation to Council. This arrangement continued until 1709 when a 'select committee' or 'committee of the board to consider Irish bills', subsequently designated 'the Lords of the Committee appointed to consider the bills transmitted from Ireland', was charged with the responsibility of overseeing the scrutiny of bills received from Ireland.[5]

This administrative innovation, allied to other procedural and practical refinements authorised during the reign of Queen Anne, ensured that Irish legislation was dealt with in a more systematic and uniform manner at the British Council from 1709. This was a logical corollary of the fact that meetings of the Irish parliament occurred with greater frequency and regularity from 1703. They did not yet observe the orderly pattern that was to ensure a parliamentary session every two years from the commencement of the Hanoverian era until the mid-1780s, but an important step was taken in this direction. Parallel with this, the Irish Privy Council's role in initiating legislation continued to decline. This occurred gradually, but the acceptance that it was unnecessary, consistent with the requirements of Poynings' Law, that due 'causes and considerations' were provided in respect of every parliamentary session, as distinct from every parliament, was significant. Bills continued to take their rise at the Irish Council, but they were soon dwarfed by the number of heads of bills arising with parliament. This did not preclude disputes or controversies, legislative as well as political, since, like its English (from 1707, its British) counterpart, the Irish Council used the powers it was provided with by Poynings' Law to veto and to amend heads of bills as it deemed appropriate.

3. Turner, *The Privy Council of England*, ii, 417.
4. One such instance was the bill to prevent the further growth of popery, which was referred on 5 January 1704; see below pp 123–4.
5. Turner, *The Privy Council of England*, ii, 202–3, 205–6, 363–4, 380–3, 386–92, 396–400; NA, PC2/82 ff 333, 347–8, 349, 370–1; PC2//83 ff 15, 16, 20–1 and passim; PC2/86 ff 45, 57, 63, 299, 321–2, 332; PC2/88 ff 358, 418; PC2/89 ff 123, 139.

Compared to the English/British Council, information on the operation of the Irish Council is sparse and tantalising, but there is good reason to suggest that it was no less scrupulous than its metropolitan equivalent in the manner in which it approached the task of scrutinising and putting bills in order that they could be certified under the great seal of Ireland and transmitted to London. In legislative terms, this helped ensure an increase of 54 per cent in the amount of law made in Ireland during the reign of Anne compared with that of William and Mary. The fact that one-third of the 385 legislative initiatives proposed between 1703 and 1713 made it to the statute book was also an improvement on the 1690s (Table 1; p. 159), and it suggests further that the heads of bills process was a reasonably efficient way of accommodating British and Irish differences and of making law for the kingdom of Ireland within the parameters of Poynings' Law.

PREPARING FOR PARLIAMENT, 1703–4

The four years and eight months that elapsed between the end of the 1698–9 session and the commencement of that of 1703–4 was the longest interval between meetings of parliament in Ireland between 1692 and 1800. This contributed to the loss of institutional memory that encouraged the English Council to seek in 1703–4 to assert powers in respect of the making of law for Ireland that might, had they not been resisted, have increased that Council's influence. However, parliament was enabled to capitalise on a weakened executive to assert the dominant role it had established for the first time in the late 1690s, and thereby not only to consolidate further the heads of bills process but also to inaugurate a pattern than was to ensure before the end of Queen Anne's reign that the heads of a bill was firmly established as the primary means of initiating legislation.

The failure to convene a parliament in Ireland prior to September 1703 was a result, in the first instance, of the generous supply voted by the Irish legislature during the 1698–9 session.[6] Political concerns prompted by dissatisfaction in Ireland at the prohibition imposed by Westminster in 1699 on the export of woollen goods, which exacerbated an already difficult economic environment, and by the resumption in 1700 of the lands forfeited by those complicit in the Jacobite wars also encouraged caution.[7] And there were difficulties in identifying a suitable person to head up the Irish administration, as Lord Shrewsbury, who was offered the lord lieutenancy in May 1700, was unable, for health reasons, to take up the position. Normal practice in this event was to appoint a 'new commission of justices', but this was precluded by the refusal of Lord Galway, who was prepared to take on the critical role of commander-in-chief, to serve 'at the head of the troops … under a commission'. Laurence Hyde, earl of Rochester, accepted the

6. McGrath, *Making the constitution*, p. 153.
7. Ibid., pp 153–4; J.G. Simms, *The Williamite confiscation in Ireland, 1690–1703* (London, 1956), pp 100–58; Dickson, *Ireland: New foundations*, pp 46–52; Hayton, *Ruling Ireland*, pp 71–83.

position of lord lieutenant in December, but though his instructions 'empowered' him 'to call a parliament' he was not authorised to do so.[8] More pertinently, by declining to reside in Ireland for the duration of his appointment, he set a precedent his successors chose to follow and that encouraged the practice whereby successive lords lieutenant confined their time in Ireland to the meeting of parliament. This did not have major implications in the short term because the pattern of parliamentary meetings remained irregular and because it was quite commonplace in the lord lieutenant's absence to entrust the government of the kingdom to commissions of lords justices that were predominantly English in personnel. However, as the Irish parliamentary managers, who were as crucial as heads of bills to the effective operation of Capell's 'compromise', assumed a more prominent presence on the commission of lords justices, the very structure of government served to reinforce the heads of bills arrangement.[9]

Discussions preparatory to a meeting of parliament, which were pursued fitfully from Rochester's appointment, accelerated as the date approached when, in the absence of new additional duties, the Irish exchequer would experience severe financial problems. As well as its financial advisability, the fact that issues of Irish concern were a subject of discussion at Westminster acted as an additional incentive with some.[10] They did not include the lords justices (Thomas Keightley, Thomas Erle and the earl of Mount-Alexander) to whom it fell to make the initial preparations until they were superseded by the appointment of James Butler, the second duke of Ormonde, as lord lieutenant in February 1703. These commenced, somewhat hesitantly, in the winter of 1702–3 when the lords justices responded to an enquiry conveyed by Lord Rochester with 'a rough list' of twelve items containing 'the substance or heads for such bills as may be properly prepared here before the meeting of parliament'.[11] Though this was not inconsistent with the procedures employed successfully in the 1690s, the transcription from the Irish 'Council books' of 'two letters [dating from 1695] ... relating to the orders from

8. Vernon to Shrewsbury, 13, 23, 28 May, 4, 8 June 1700 in James (ed.), *Vernon letters*, iii, 49, 58–9, 63, 69, 74; NA, PC2/78 f. 113; Instructions of Earl of Rochester, 28 June 1701 (NA, SP67/2 f. 216).

9. For a more considered account of Rochester's actions see 'The beginnings of the undertaker system' in Hayton, *Ruling Ireland*, pp 85–8.

10. McGrath, *Making the constitution*, pp 156–7. For Westminster and Irish issues, see St George Ashe to King, 17 Mar., 2, 25 Apr., King to Bishop Lloyd, 21 July 1702 (TCD, King Papers, MSS 1995–2008 ff 892, 901, 908, MS 1489/2 f. 59); Clyve Jones and Geoffrey Holmes (eds), *The London diaries of William Nicolson, bishop of Carlisle, 1702–18* (Oxford, 1985), pp 196–8.

11. Lords justices to lord lieutenant, 30 Jan. 1703 in *Cal. SP (Dom.), 1702–3*, pp 563. The list of bills printed out of place in *Cal. SP (Dom.), 1702–3*, pp 123–4 includes several previously prepared by the Commons (measures against clandestine marriages, for opening mines), and by the Lords (for relief against ancient bonds and judgements); it embraced measures that had previously been lost (against butchers being graziers), that targeted 'papists' (for preventing Protestants turning papists); that sought to advantages Protestants (to increase freeholders, and to enable Protestant lessees serve on juries), as well as measures appertaining to the importation of iron and staves, to protect salmon fry, to vest plus acres and undisposed lands and to provide for the payments of debts of minors.

England for calling of parliaments' for transmission to London is indicative of uncertainty as to how to proceed. The lords justices' continuing preference was that parliament should not be convened at this moment because of 'the poverty of the kingdom', but this was not a realistic option. Of greater import constitutionally and politically was the solicitor general's suggestion that, in order to avoid problems over the 'sole right' with respect of 'granting and … raising' money, the matter should be left 'wholly' to parliament and that they should proceed 'without any money bill being prepared or offered by the Crown'. This was not endorsed by the Irish Council, but the fact that it was made by such a high-ranking officeholder illustrates the depth of official unease, and why Lord Capell's administration was appealed to for guidance.[12]

Saliently, officials at Whitehall seemed less willing to be guided by the Capell precedent if this restricted their power to shape the legislative output of the Irish parliament. The instruction given the duke of Ormonde on 18 May 1703 that he should ensure that a money bill was included with those 'transmitted in form in order to be considered' at the English Council and in order that it should, if acceptable, be 'annexed to the commission which shall be sent … for calling and holding a parliament' captured their commitment to uphold the principle of dependence enunciated in Poynings' Law.[13] Consistent with this, the list of fourteen bills prepared by the Irish judges that the chief secretary, Edward Southwell, conveyed to Lord Nottingham on 8 June included 'an additional excise bill for one year'. The chief secretary was hopeful at this point that all would be 'ready to transmit in ten days'; in fact, it took eighteen to bring nine, of which the 'additional excise bill' was one, to a state of readiness to transmit to the English Council board.[14]

The Privy Council bills transmitted from Ireland were presented to the secretary of state, Lord Nottingham, on 1 July by William Wogan, the clerk to the chief secretary, who was charged with the task of ensuring the bills were properly represented and the intentions of the Irish Council made clear. In an attempt to expedite matters, in the hope that the deliberations of the Irish parliament could be 'ended before this in England meets', Nottingham promptly communicated the bills to Edward Northey, the attorney general, so he could 'consider of them before' they were formally presented to the Privy Council.[15] This was procedurally doubtful, and the irregularity of this action was compounded on 4 July when, having considered the bills 'in form', the Queen in Council adjudged that

12. Lords justices to Rochester, 30 Jan. 1703 in *Cal. SP (Dom.), 1702–3*, pp 563–4.

13. Nottingham to Ormonde, 18 May (NA, SP 67/3 f. 65); Note from Lord Lieutenant, 18 May 1703 in *Cal. SP (Dom.), 1702–3*, p. 722.

14. Southwell to Nottingham, 8, 12 June in *Cal. SP (Dom.), 1703–4*, pp 8–9, 13; Marsh to King, 24 June (TCD, King Papers, MSS 1995–2008 f. 1028); Ormonde and Council of Ireland to Nottingham, 26 June 1703 in *Cal. SP (Dom.), 1703–4*, pp 24–5.

15. Nottingham to Ormonde, 18 May, 19 June (NA, SP 67/3 ff 65, 66); Nottingham to Northey, 1 July (SP67/3 f. 67 calendared in *Cal. SP (Dom.), 1703–4*, p. 36); Wogan to Southwell, 3 July 1703 (BL, Southwell Papers, Add. MS 37673 ff 1–2).

eight should be referred to the attorney and solicitor generals for a report.[16] The bill omitted was that 'to prevent the further growth of popery', which was transmitted from Ireland in the knowledge that it might encounter problems. 'There are some clauses concerning [the treaties of] Limerick and Galway that ... you may think hard and inconvenient', the duke of Ormonde candidly avowed. Ormonde's comment suggests that he was less than enthusiastic about the bill. However, he 'could not conveniently hinder it' in deference to the strong support in Ireland for a measure that would, *inter alia*, penalise those who 'seduce or are seduced from the Protestant religion'; prevent Catholics disinheriting Protestant children; prohibit Catholics purchasing or inheriting estates currently in Protestant hands; and preclude papists from residing in Limerick and Galway. Northey felt more at liberty to suggest changes. His conclusion, on the basis of an initial assessment, that the bill required 'great amendments' may account for the failure of the Privy Council formally to refer it for a report on 4 July.[17] Curiously, it did not (as it ought) inhibit the Crown's law officers from reporting on the bill, for when William Wogan met with them on 6 July in the attorney general's chambers to 'draw up their report' on the Irish bills, Wogan noted their recommendation that the popery bill should not proceed in its present form because it contravened the Treaty of Limerick. The presentation of a petition by Viscount Fitzwilliam and Lord Bellew on behalf of the Catholics of Ireland against the bill had a bearing on their decision.[18]

The resolve of the law officers, revealed in their response to the bill, to ensure that only those measures that were appropriate and properly drawn should progress was also evident in their reaction to the remaining bills, only three of which – for continuing sanctions against tories and rapparees, for disposing of plus acres and for extending the existing prohibition on 'regulars and dignitaries from coming into this kingdom' to secular clergy – were deemed eligible to return immediately. Significantly, none was sent to progress without amendment. A high proportion of the authorised alterations appertained to 'literall mistakes and false spellings'; these vexed the attorney general who drew Wogan's attention to 'the interliniations and slovenly writing' that were a feature of 'all' Irish bills.[19] But there were serious matters of policy requiring attention in two instances. In the case of the 'plus acres' bill, reservations expressed at the proposition that the settling of fees was a matter for the Irish Privy Council, were left to the lord lieutenant to address, while the priests' bill was made 'temporary, less it should be

16. NA, PC2/79 f. 413.
17. Ormonde and Council Nottingham, 26 June, Ormonde to Nottingham (2), 27 June in *Cal. SP (Dom.)*, *1703–4*, pp 24–5, 25, 28; Wogan to Southwell, 3 July 1703 (BL, Southwell Papers, Add. MS 37673 ff 1–2).
18. Wogan to Southwell, 6 July (BL, Southwell Papers, Add. MS 37673 ff 3–4); NA, PC2/79 f. 414; J.G. Simms, 'The making of a penal law (2 Anne, c. 6), 1703–4' in Simms, *War and politics in Ireland*, pp 264–5.
19. Wogan to Southwell, 17 July 1703 (BL, Southwell Papers, Add. MS 37673, f. 11).

construed to infringe the Articles of Limerick by making it impossible in length of time for the papists to exercise their religion'. If this major alteration was indicative of the determination of the English Council in 1703 to shape important measures of policy, it was underlined by the acceptance of the law officers' recommendation that the bill to relieve 'subjects against dormant judgements, bonds and mortgages', James Stopford's private bill (which was deemed 'not very just'), and a measure recognising Queen Anne's title to the Crown, which was 'not thought necessary', ought not to proceed. In addition, both the proposal to protect woodlands by encouraging the importation of iron and staves and the supply bill were held over for 'further consideration'. This did not necessarily augur badly for either measure, but the fact that the Council made it known that their preference was that the tax should extend 'for three years at least' in order that 'an equal respect should be paid' to Queen Anne as was paid her predecessor was indicative of their determination to ensure that so that they should 'not be under the necessity of an annual parliament'.[20]

The certification of three bills was sufficient to permit the Queen to cause a commission to be issued to the duke of Ormonde empowering him to issue writs 'in the usuall manner for the calling a parliament', but it was a poor return from the nine bills originally transmitted. Acutely conscious, if they did not have more bills, that they must cede the initiative in making law to parliament, the Irish executive availed of William Wogan's presence in London to encourage the return of further bills.[21] Made aware that they had erred in not providing appropriate supporting documentation describing the purpose of each measure, and in not briefing William Wogan adequately 'to answer to any objections … made', the Irish administration scrutinised the 'objections which are made to the bills by Mr Attorney and Mr Solicitor' with a view to presenting a full justification of each contested measure.[22] The supply bill was their priority. They made their case stoutly.[23] Persuaded that the provision of an appropriate supply could be best advanced by leaving it to the Irish parliament to ensure the Queen would 'not be treated with less respect than her predecessors in the excise bill', councillors decided at the end of July to forward the bill with three inconsequential amendments.[24] This was encouraging from the perspective of the Irish administration;

20. Nottingham to Ormonde, 8 July 1703 (NA, SP67/3 ff 67–8 calendared in *Cal. SP (Dom.)*, *1703–4*, p 43); NA, PC2/79 f. 421; Godolphin to Southwell, 9 July 1703 (Beinecke Library, Southwell Papers, Box 1).

21. NA, PC2/79 f. 422; Wogan to Southwell, 10, 13, 17, 20 July 1703 (BL, Southwell Papers, Add. MS 37673 ff 7, 9, 11, 13).

22. Wogan to Southwell, 24 July 1703 (BL, Southwell Papers, Add. MS 37673 f. 15).

23. Edward Southwell maintained the bill 'was never intended to be only for a year', while the Duke of Ormonde observed that the bill was 'framed according to [the] precedent' set by Lords Sydney and Capell (McGrath, *Making the constitution*, pp 159–60; Ormonde to Nottingham, 15, 22 July, Southwell to Nottingham, 22 July, Memoranda on bills sent from Ireland, *c.* 22 July in *Cal. SP (Dom.)*, *1703–4*, pp. 46, 58–9, 55, 56; Wogan to Southwell, 29 July 1703: BL, Southwell Papers, Add. MS 37673 f. 17).

24. NA, PC2/79 f. 430; Nottingham to Ormonde, 31 July (NA, SP 67/3 f. 71 calendared in *Cal. SP*

so too was the certification of the iron and staves bill at the same time,[25] but the rejection of their argument that the bill to prevent the growth of popery should be returned on the grounds that 'the House [of Commons] here will certainly begin such a bill' demonstrated the limits of what they could achieve. Councillors were not unsympathetic at the same time to the object of the bill, and consistent with their willingness to intervene actively in Irish legislation, they chose finally on 30 July, nearly two months after it was received, to instruct the law officers 'to amend and frame the said act in such a manner' as 'may be a reasonable security to the Protestants and satisfactory to the people'.[26]

Directions such as these were unusual, but they are indicative of the procedural flexibility that still obtained when it came to processing Irish legislation. This was not without advantages, moreover, and an exploration of the experience of the bill to prevent the further growth of popery provides a revealing (if atypical) illustration of how the arrangements provided for under Poynings' Law could assist in the preparation of legislation that was acceptable to the Irish and English privy councils and, ultimately, to the Irish legislature, and how the additional procedural requirements necessary in this instance contributed to the evolution of a more fixed administrative process.

It was anticipated when the law officers were instructed to recast the bill to prevent the growth of popery that a revised bill would be ready in advance of the opening of the Irish parliament, which took place on 21 September. However, this did not prove possible. In its absence, the Irish Commons granted leave on 28 September to one of its members to prepare such a measure.[27] Spurred by this, and by enquiries from the Irish executive, which sought 'some intimation of what was likely to be approved', the committee of the Council overrode the objections of Attorney General Northey, and communicated a draft bill before it was considered by the Queen in Council. Inevitably, the draft diverged in several important respects from the bill received from Ireland, notably in not including a clause 'for disinheriting papists' because this was deemed 'too hard and ... not prudent while we are in allegiance with princes of that religion'. Similar considerations had prompted the excision, from an earlier draft, of clauses providing for the education of the orphaned 'children of papists in the Protestant religion, for giving the estates of such as at 18 do not become Protestant to the next Protestant of their kindred', and for the prohibition of Catholics from

(*Dom.*), *1703–4*, pp 69–70); Nottingham to Southwell, 31 July 1703 (SP 67/3 f. 71).

25. NA, PC2/79 ff 430–1; Ormonde to Nottingham, 22 July in *Cal. SP (Dom.)*, *1703–4*, p. 59; Memorandum of the Lord lieutenant and Council of Ireland, *c*. 22 July in *Cal. SP (Dom.)*, *1703–4*, pp 56–7; Nottingham to Southwell, 31 July 1703 (NA, SP 67/3 f. 71, calendared in *Cal. SP (Dom.)*, *1703–4*, p. 70).

26. Southwell to Nottingham, 22 July, Memorandum of the Lord Lieutenant and Council of Ireland, *c*. 22 July, Nottingham to Ormonde, 31 July in *Cal. SP (Dom.)*, *1703–4*, pp 55, 56, 69–70; NA, PC2/79 ff 430–31.

27. *Commons Jn. (Irl.)*, ii, 321; Southwell to Warre, 25 Sept., Northey to Warre, 5 Oct. 1703 in *Cal. SP (Dom.)*, *1703–4*, pp 133, 145.

inheriting property in Protestant ownership.[28] This notwithstanding, the draft received in Ireland incorporated a sufficient number of provisions 'against inducing Protestants to turn Catholic, sending children abroad for education, allowing Protestant property to be bought by Catholics and regulating the residence of Catholics in Limerick and Galway' to elicit a largely positive response. However, since it had not been reported at the English Council board and was not returned under the great seal of England, it could not be presented to the Irish parliament as a bill. Instead, the Irish administration made the draft available to the Commons. This was most unusual, but such was the eagerness of MPs to advance a comprehensive anti- popery bill measure they incorporated much of it verbatim into their own bill, and agreed 'some additions to the draft that was approved of in England' to prevent pilgrimages to St Patrick's Purgatory, to encourage the discovery of Catholic children educated abroad, to apply the law of gavelkind to the transfer of Catholic estates, and to prohibit Catholics inheriting from Protestants even in cases of inter-religious marriage. It could be argued that by doing this, the Irish parliament acceded to an expanded role for the English Council in the making of Irish law, but this was not their intention, and it was not the overt ambition of the lords of the English Council.[29]

Having agreed the heads of a bill 'to prevent the further growth of popery' that was a composite of the thinking of the Irish and English Councils and the Irish Commons on the subject, MPs affirmed their support for the measure by attending the Speaker when he presented it to the Lord Lieutenant. They were uneasy, as the Speaker made clear, lest its Catholic opponents would ensure the bill's emasculation or loss at either the Irish or English Councils, though the particular genesis of the bill meant that English Privy Council was unlikely to object unless the redrafted measure 'could be construed as a breach of the articles of Limerick or would be likely to be objected to by Catholic allies'.[30] This was established when, having negotiated the Irish Privy Council with no 'amendment of consequence', the bill was communicated to the attorney general on its arrival in London on 14 December, three days before it was formally referred to the law officers for a report.[31] The English Council was determined to proceed cautiously nonetheless, so in addition to referring a petition presented on behalf of the earl of Antrim and Viscount Fitzwilliam by two 'Popish agents' to the law officers, the

28. Nottingham to Southwell, 12, 14, 19 Oct. (NA, SP67/3 ff 78, 79; the first and third of these letters are calendared in *Cal. SP (Dom.)*, *1703–4*, pp 151, 162); Northey to [Nottingham], 16 Oct. 1703, Draft bill to prevent the further growth of popery in *Cal. SP (Dom.)*, *1703–4*, pp 160, 182–3; Simms, 'The making of a penal law', pp 265–7.

29. Simms, 'The making of a penal law', pp 265–7; *Commons Jn. (Irl.)*, ii, 340, 343, 350, 352, 373; Southwell to Nottingham. 23 Nov., 16 Dec. 1703 in *Cal. SP (Dom.)*, *1703–4*, pp 211, 236, see also pp 258–60.

30. Simms, 'The making of a penal law', pp 268–9.

31. Ibid., p. 269; Wogan to Southwell, 14 Dec. 1703 (BL, Southwell Papers, Add. MS 37673 ff 23, 25); Southwell to Nottingham, 28 Dec. 1703 in *Cal. SP (Dom.)*, *1703–4*, p. 248; NA, PC2/79 ff 473, 475.

Council acceded to the agents' request for 'copys of all acts as related to and [to] be heard on all acts as referred and related to them'. It was determined, furthermore, that the law officers' reports on the bill should be communicated not to the full Council but to 'a committee of the whole Council to consider, and to report their opinions [there]upon' to the Queen in Council.[32]

Discussion of the bill at the committee of the whole council took place over two days on 5 and 7 January, at the end of which the law officers were deputed to 'amend the bill upon the debate'. Because of the extent and complexity of the amendments at issue, it was mid-January before the revised bill was available. This delay encouraged speculation in Ireland that the bill might not be returned, which might have come to pass had the claim by the former lord justice of Ireland, Lord Coningsby, that proper procedure had not been followed because the draft bill communicated from the English Council had 'never been laid before ye House [of Commons]', received a sympathetic hearing. However, Coningsby's belated attempt to derail the bill was overcome, and once the measure was ready to present to the Council on 18 January, it was only a matter of time before it was ordered to progress and, following a few days further consideration, it was sent to pass under the great seal on 20 January.[33]

This was a setback for the 'popish agents' who had entertained high hopes, arising out of the time it took to scrutinise the bill, that they could 'defeat' the measure. In fact, as William Wogan's contacts made clear, this was never likely, though the bill was subject to extensive amendment.[34] This was not considered by Simms in his generally admirable reconstruction of the making of this law. He observed that 'the bill was approved by the English Council in a form that was considerably stronger than the draft [*sic*] sent over from Ireland', but this is an inadequate description of the multiplicity and magnitude of the amendments that were authorised. In keeping with the experience to date of Irish bills at the English Council, a large number were simple verbal or syntactical corrections, but five major amendments, which were among the most far reaching made to any bill in the course of the eighteenth century, were also approved. Extending in a number of instances to several thousand words, their purpose was to state more explicitly and, in some instances, to intensify the restrictions on Catholics retaining or acquiring property proposed in Ireland. Thus, the eldest son of Catholic parents who converted to the Church of Ireland could usurp his parents' title; Catholics were precluded from acting as guardians to 'any orphan' under twenty-one, who was required to be brought up as a Protestant and whose lands were to descend only to Protestants; while, in an allied clause, the prohibition in the bill

---

32. NA, PC2/79 ff 475, 477.

33. Wogan to Southwell, 4, 6, 13, 15, 20 Jan. (BL, Southwell Papers, Add. MS 37673 ff 31, 35, 41–2, 43–4, 47); Ormonde to Nottingham, 10 Jan., Nottingham to Ormonde, 18 Jan., Southwell to Nottingham, 18, 26 Jan., in *Cal. SP (Dom.)*, *1703–4*, pp 492, 500, 501, 509; PRO PC2/79 ff 490, 507, 2/80 f. 4; Simms, 'Making a penal law', pp 269–70.

34. Wogan to Southwell, 20 Jan. 1704 (BL, Southwell Papers, Add. MS 37673 f. 47).

received from Ireland on Catholics leasing and purchasing land from Protestants was extended to include inheritance. Still more critically, in a draconian late addition to diminish Catholic patrimonies, it was stated that property in Catholic ownership should pass between generations according to the law of gavelkind rather than primogeniture. Finally, and most infamously, the 'Test clauses', requiring officeholders to 'take the Eucharist according to the rite of the Church of Ireland', were introduced at the behest of English Tories.[35] Together, these amendments so extended an already lengthy bill, that it was calculated it would 'take up to five or six days in engrossing'.[36] This completed, the bill was returned to Ireland where, other than the Catholic interest, which persisted with its opposition, and some manifestations of disquiet from dissenters, the response was overwhelmingly positive. Some concern was expressed in the House of Commons about the implications for dissenters of the 'test' on the grounds that it promoted division within protestantism, but the calculation that Irish Whigs would conclude this was a price worth paying to secure so many anti-Catholic regulations proved well founded. When a vote was called there were not more than twenty negatives, and the act to prevent the further growth of popery received the royal assent on 4 March.[37]

Because the 1704 act to prevent the further growth of was a one-off, it established few administrative or legislative precedents that other bills were to follow. That said, the manner in which the Irish Privy Council, the Irish parliament (particularly the Commons) and the English Privy Council combined to devise the most comprehensive of all the Penal Laws illustrated that the suspicion, articulated by Archbishop King, that prevented many measures making it to the statute book in late 1690s had dissipated. The co-operative spirit manifest in this instance was more in keeping with the approach taken in 1695 when Capell had demonstrated that the aspirations of the Protestant interest in Ireland and the Crown could be accommodated. It might be cautioned that one ought not to draw such major conclusions from the history of one piece of legislation, especially when Irish Protestants had previously demonstrated that the threat posed to their religion, property and welfare took precedence over their expressed objections to Poynings' Law. However, this is precisely why the 1704 bill to prevent the further growth of is important. In this case, Irish Protestants were prepared not just to receive a bill that was the work of both Privy Councils and to embrace it within

---

35. The amendments are in NA, PC2/80 ff 8–21; Connolly, *Religion, law and power*, p. 273; David Hayton, 'Exclusion, conformity and parliamentary representation' in Kevin Herlihy (ed.), *The politics of Irish dissent* (Dublin, 1997), p. 54.

36. Wogan to Southwell, 29 Jan. 1704 (BL, Southwell Papers, Add. MS 37673 f. 53).

37. Fagan, *Catholics in a Protestant country*, pp 56–8; *An impartial relation of the several arguments of Sir Stephen Rice, Sir Theobald Butler and Councellor Malone at the bar of the House of Commons of Ireland, Feb. 22 and at the bar of the House of Lords, Feb. 28th 1703* ... (Dublin, 1704); Simms, 'Making a penal law', pp 274–5; *Commons Jn. (Irl.)*, ii, 394, 396, 400, 401, 402, 409, 411; Southwell to Nottingham, 4, 19 (2), 26 Feb. 1704 in *Cal. SP (Dom.)*, *1703–4*, pp 522–3, 537, 542–3.

the heads of a bill of their own devising, they agreed also to the revised measure returned from the English Council though this meant acceding to a version that, among other new and redrawn clauses, included a provision to penalise dissenters. Similarly, the acceptance by the English Council of a bill that had formally commenced in the Commons represented an important acknowledgement by the Crown of the right of the Irish parliament to prepare legislation. Most importantly of all, it revealed once more how a system of law-making for Ireland consistent with and perhaps even appropriate to the complex nature of the Anglo-Irish nexus and, in broad terms, with Poynings' Law could operate to mutual advantage and satisfaction.

PRIVY COUNCIL BILLS IN THE REIGN OF QUEEN ANNE

The proportion of bills to rise with the Privy Council during the twelve-year reign of Queen Anne fell appreciably from its 1690s level. Approximately 19 per cent of legislative initiatives arose at the Irish Council. However, since Privy Council bills were more likely than heads to be transmitted to London they accounted for 34 per cent of Irish bills received at the English/British Council. They featured most prominently in 1703–4 when the 20 Privy Council bills received comprised an impressive 39 per cent of the total. In 1709, by contrast, when only 7 were transmitted, they constituted a more modest 23 per cent (Table Four). Significantly, the Privy Council bills embraced private and public bills in near equal numbers (38 public, 35 private), though there was an identifiable decline in the proportion of public bills and a rise in the proportion of private bills as the reign progressed (Table Five; p. 163). The concerns of the Council's ecclesiastical and judicial members are also readily identifiable in the prominent presence among the public bills of measures appertaining to the union and division of parishes, blasphemy, profanity (1705) and infanticide (1707), the relief of creditors against fraudulent devises (1705), the advancement of justice (1707), small debts (1707), and writs of mandamus, warrants and recognisances (1711).[38] Private bills were less thematically diverse; their number per session fluctuated from a low of two to a high of eleven (Table 2; p. 160), but the sessional mean of 4–5 is indicative of the fact that by the reign of Anne the Irish Council conceived of private bills as a category of legislation that they could promote without provoking the Commons' resentment.

The largest transmiss of bills, comprising eight public and one private bill, was conveyed to London in 1703. This was in keeping with the explicit provision in Poynings' Law that due 'cause and consequences' were provided for issuing a

---

38. NA, PC2/80 ff 258–61; *Commons Jn. (Irl.)*, ii, 423, 430, 437, 462 (creditors' bill); PC2/81 ff 430–1, 436; *Commons Jn. (Irl.)*, ii, 540, 547, 554, 561, 562, 567, 568 (advancement of justice bill); PC2/81 ff 353, 366–8; PC1/6/60/3 (small debts bill); PC 2/83 ff 292, 313–5; *Lords Jn. (Irl.)*, ii, 397 (writs of mandamus bill); PC2/83 ff 291, 310–11, 313–5 (warrants and recognisances bill).

commission to convene a parliament in Ireland. Because parliament was not dissolved at the end of the 1703–4 session, it was not necessary for the Council to transmit bills in advance of the 1705 session, which commenced on 10 February. None the less, four Privy Council bills were conveyed to the English Council early in January and returned, after scrutiny, as proper 'to their being proposed to the parliament in Ireland'.[39] It is not apparent if the transmission of these bills at this moment was prompted by concern in Ireland to be seen to honour the practice in the 1690s whereby bills were sent in advance of each session, but if so, their return without an accompanying commission empowering the lord lieutenant to convene a parliament was a pointer to future practice. When preparations commenced in the spring of 1707 to convene a new session, the Irish Council chose not to cast bills *ab initio*, but to put existing parliamentary legislation in due order. 'We have used all diligence in finishing such bills as were recommended to our consideration by either house of parliament, or thought necessary against the next meeting', the Lords of the Irish Council informed their English counterparts on 12 April.[40] Five bills in all were transmitted to London in advance of the meeting of parliament, two of which can be identified positively with measures referred from the Irish parliament in 1705.[41] Another – for the better regulation of justices of the peace – may have had its origin in the 1705 bill 'for qualifying persons to be justices ... and sheriffs', but the only identifiable antecedent of the measure 'to prevent the destroying and murthering of bastard children' – the heads of a bill 'to oblige the parents of bastard children to maintain them' – did not emerge out of the House of Commons, and so never reached the Irish Council board.[42] More problematically, a bill comparable to the 1707 measure for 'better ordering of servants and day labourers' was 'refused' at the English Council board in 1705.[43] If this suggests that the lords of the Irish Council were less than frank when they described the five bills they communicated as the will of parliament (three of which became law), it is of lesser consequence than the fact that this was the last time in which bills were transmitted in advance of an ordinary session of the Irish parliament. There is no documented explanation for this, but it may have been prompted, Ivar McGrath has suggested, 'by a desire to avoid a repetition of the 1707's rejection of two of the government's three bills'. At any event, no bill

39. McGrath, *Making the constitution*, p. 178; Hedges to Ormonde, 16, 18, 23 Jan., 10, 27 Feb. 1705 (NA, SP67/3 ff 94–5, 96, 96–7, 101, 104). The bills were 'to prevent the illegal raising of money by grand jurys', 'for the more effectual suppressing of blasphemy', for the relief of creditors against fraudulent devices, and to repeal an act for the advancement of linen manufacture. For their experience at the English Council see PC2/80 ff 258–9, 260–1.

40. Irish Privy Council to Lord [ ], 12 Apr. 1707 (NA, PC/1/2/60/3).

41. These were bills 'for continuing ... an act for the more easie obtaining partitions of land in coparcenary, joint tenancy and tenancy in common' (*Commons Jn. (Irl.)*, ii, 464–5); for amending and continuing an act ... for the recovery of small debts (ibid., ii, 463, 464, 465, 466, 467).

42. *Commons Jn. (Irl.)*, ii, 432, 439, 442, 459, 460, 461; NA, PC2/81 f. 353, PC1/2/60/3.

43. *Commons Jn. (Irl.)*, ii, 425, 427, 438, 439, 495; NA, PC2/80 ff 314, 318–19, 361; PC2/81 f. 353; PC1/2/60/3.

was transmitted from the Irish Council *prior* to the commencement of the meeting of parliament in 1709, 1710 or 1711. Two bills were communicated in advance prior to the meeting of parliament on 25 November 1713, but since this was a new parliament they were *required* in order to obtain a commission so the lord lieutenant could cause writs to be issued for this purpose.[44]

The abandonment by the Irish Privy Council from 1709 of the practice of communicating bills prior to the commencement of a routine session of parliament was in keeping with the trend whereby the legislature, and particularly the Commons, consolidated its role as the primary initiator of law in Ireland. Since these initiatives took the form of heads of bills, no reservations were expressed in London. Moreover, the Irish Privy Council remained legislatively active, only now the percentage of bills taking their rise in that forum during as distinct from before the parliamentary session increased from 55 per cent in 1703–4 to the full complement in 1709 (Table Four; p. 162). Since this paralleled the absolute and proportionate decline in the number of public bills originating with the Irish Council (Table Two), it is apparent that the law-making role of the Irish Council continued to contract. This was masked somewhat by the number of private bills that took their formal rise in the Irish Council, but it was a logical outcome of the growing acceptance of the fact that parliament, and the House of Commons specifically, was deemed the more appropriate forum for the initiation of public bills. Furthermore, though there is no reason to suggest that such bills encountered more problems than was usual at either the English or Irish Council boards, the fact that over half (55 per cent) of the public bills emanating from the Irish Privy Council did not make it to the statute book is striking. Intriguingly, the pattern with respect of private bills is almost directly the reverse; based upon an overall success rate of 57 per cent, a minimum of two and more commonly four private bills were enacted during each of the six sessions of the 1703–11 parliament (Table Five).

In keeping with the implicit acknowledgement by the Irish Council that parliament, and the House of Commons specifically, was the primary source of Irish public bills, the Council refined its procedures to permit it to deal efficiently and expeditiously with heads of bills. This cannot be traced in any detail, but useful light is thrown on the process through the efforts of the Society of Friends (Quakers) to ensure that legislation emanating from the Irish parliament and Privy Council did not injure or diminish their interests.[45] Quakers were subject to the

---

44. McGrath, *Making the constitution*, pp 212, 234, 250, 267–8. The measure were 'for the better preventing mischiefs that may happen by fire' and 'for granting … an additional duty on beer, ales, strong waters, tobacco and other goods' (NA, PC2/84 ff 241–3).

45. The account that follows on Quaker lobbying is based on the Parliamentary Committee Minute book, 1699–1731 (Historical Library of the religious Society of Friends, MS YM N1), and I am grateful to John Bergin's pioneering work on this document, and to his generous sharing of his findings. See Bergin, 'The Quaker lobby and its influence on Irish legislation, 1692–1705', pp 9–36; and the abstract 'Principal measures concerning Quakers, 1692–1705' distributed to participants in the Early Modern Seminar, Trinity College, Dublin, 2004.

same legal disabilities as other dissenters, but their refusal to pay tithes and to swear oaths set them apart, and encouraged the dominant Church of Ireland interest to regard them with particular suspicion. This was not new of course; Quakers had contrived with some success during the Restoration era to resist attempts to confine their liberties and to curb their rights to freedom of expression, so it was entirely consistent that they should present a petition to Lord Sydney in advance of the 1692 parliament in respect both of their concerns on the matters of 'liberty of conscience' and oaths.[46] This petition was addressed to the Privy Council, but the abbreviated session proved a greater protection.

Three years later, the Quakers were presented with a more formidable challenge in the form of heads of bills 'for recovery of tithes', and they embarked then, and again in 1697 on an intense lobby of members of parliament to resist this and other measures. It is difficult to assay the effectiveness of their efforts, but it is surely significant that no specifically anti-Quaker legislation was approved. Be that as it may, the Quakers recognised that it was desirable to set their lobbying efforts on more solid grounds, for when parliament resumed in September 1703 they formed a committee that met while parliament was sitting and whose purpose was, as John Bergin describes it, 'the identification of bills prejudicial to Quakers, the preparation of arguments against such bills and the systematic personal lobbying of legislators'. To this end, the committee cultivated the Clerk to the Irish Council and individual councillors, and they were enabled with their assistance not only to acquire copies of relevant Privy Council bills and heads of bills, but also to present petitions. This was noteworthy, but in an action of still greater significance, it was agreed in December 1703, in response to a request, that the Quakers should be given a copy of a bill 'for the more easy recovery of tithes and other ecclesiastical dues' and permitted to present their arguments against it in person. This was not unimportant in ensuring this measure did not emerge from the Irish Council, and it set a precedent that others were to avail of. They were encouraged to do so, doubtlessly, by the fact that 'of eight proposed laws dealing with tithes and ministers' money, which gave rise to unease among Quakers between 1695 and 1705, not one was enacted'.[47] Their success rate with respect of legislation generally was less impressive, but the fact that of an estimated 23 measures 'concerning Quakers' proposed between 1692 and 1705, more were lost at the Irish Council (6) than at the Irish House of Commons (5), the Irish Lords (2), or the English Council (2) is compelling evidence of their effectiveness as lobbyists as well as of the preparedness of the Irish Privy Council to adapt its procedures. It is salient, at the same time that the Quakers met with more encouragement in Ireland than did Presbyterians and Catholics, which may explain why Ireland's Quaker community concentrated their lobbying on the Irish Council, while Catholics targeted their efforts on the English/British Council.[48]

46. Phil Kilroy, *Protestant dissent and controversy in Ireland, 1660–1714* (Cork, 1994), pp 241–3; Bergin, 'The Quaker lobby'.   47. Bergin, 'The Quaker lobby', pp 9–36.
48. Petition of Quakers, 9 Aug. 1711 (NAI, Notes by Isabel Grubb from petitions in Public Record

As the experience of the nine Privy Council bills transmitted to the English Council in the summer of 1703 has revealed (above, pp 119–25), each bill has its own history, yet they can be aggregated, though not always neatly, for analytical convenience. Excluding the 9 bills received in the summer of 1703, 64 bills were transmitted from the Irish to the English/British Council during the reign of Queen Anne. A minority, such as the tories and rapparees bill conveyed in July 1703, the bill 'for quieting ecclesiastical persons in their possessions', which was subject to a few modest amendments, and the bill for building parish churches, which was approved with one deletion to appease the bishop of Killaloe, had a trouble-free journey *en route* into law in 1704.[49] This was the experience also of the 1705 measures to repeal an act for the advancement of the linen manufacture, for the relief of creditors, and to prevent the illegal raising of money by grand juries; the proposals advanced in 1707 appertaining to the partitions of lands, and for the amendment of the law for the better advancement of justice, and the 1713 money bill imposing duties on alcohol and other imported goods.[50] By contrast, some measures were recommended for and subject to more material amendment. Thus, the 1707 measure to deter infanticide, which the Irish Council claimed was 'agreeable to the act in England', experienced the deletion of its final clause, while the 'useful' small debts bill presented during the same session was subject to a dozen or so alterations, some evidently significant, in order to eliminate ambiguities and lax expression.[51]

Every Privy Council bill did not reach the statute book, but the proportion of public bills of this type to fall at the hurdle of the English/British Council was smaller than was the case with respect of private bills. In 1703, for example, a proposal for erecting a ballast office at Dublin, which encountered resistance from a number of quarters in England, was set aside; while a measure to prevent abuses in collecting public money urged in 1710 was deemed 'not fitt for her Majesty's approbation'.[52] Significantly, a greater number of Privy Council bills failed to receive the royal assent because of opposition in Ireland to amendments

Office, 1915, p. 4); Reasons offered by Quakers against a bill for the more easy recovery of tithe, ca. 1710 (NAI, Calendar of miscellaneous letters and papers prior to 1760, f. 103); below, pp 149–50.

49. NA, PC2/79 ff 473–4, 484–7, 497–507; PC2/80 ff 4, 7, 8; *Lords Jn. (Irl.)*, ii, 59, 74; *Commons Jn. (Irl.)*, ii, 400, 401, 405, 406, 414.

50. 4 Anne, chap 3; NA, PC2/80 ff 258–9, 260–1; *Commons Jn. (Irl.)*, ii, 425, 483 (linen manufacture act); 4 Anne, chap 5; PC2/80 ff 258–9, 260–1; *Commons Jn. (Irl.)*, ii, 423, 483 (relief of creditors act); 4 Anne, chap 6; PC2/80 ff 258–9, 260–1; *Commons Jn. (Irl.)*, ii, 425, 483 (raising money by grand juries act); 6 Anne, chap 3; PC2/81 ff 353, 367–8; *Commons Jn. (Irl.)*, ii, 502, 560; *Lords Jn. (Irl.)*, ii, 166 (act for obtaining partitions of lands); 6 Anne, chap 10; PC2/81 ff 430–1, 436; *Commons Jn. (Irl.)*, ii, 540, 568 (act for the advancement of justice); 11 Anne, chap 1; PC2/84 ff 241–3; *Commons Jn. (Irl.)*, ii, 757, 758, 774 (additional duties act).

51. 6 Anne, chap 4; NA, PC1/2/60/3; 2/81 ff 353, 368; *Lords Jn. (Irl.)*, ii, 170; *Commons Jn. (Irl.)*, ii, 509, 560 (infanticide act); 6 Anne, chap 5; PC1/2/60/3; PC1/2/60; PC2/81 ff 353, 366–7; *Commons Jn. (Irl.)*, ii, 492, 560 (small debts act).

52. NA, PC2/79 ff 473–4; PC2/80 f. 55; Southwell to Nottingham, 1 Jan. 1704 in *Cal. SP (Dom.)*, *1703–04*, pp 481–2 (ballast bill); PC2/83 ff 14, 16, 36 (abuses in collecting bill).

introduced by the English/British Council. This can be cited with respect of the 1705 bill for 'the real union and division of parishes', which was strongly resisted in clerical circles; the 1707 bills for 'better ordering' servants and labourers and for regulating justices of the peace; the 1709 measures to combat counterfeiting and to dissolve a union and build parish churches in the diocese of Armagh, each of which was subject to extensive amendment and, in the case of the latter, transformed from a private into a public bill; and the 1711 and 1713 fire bills.[53] However, opposition to amendments agreed by the English/British Council was not the only reason Privy Council bills failed. In the case of the 1705 measures for 'suppressing blasphemy and prophaneness' and for taxing imported muslins and hops; the 1707 measures for the relief of debtors and for settling tithes in the archdiocese of Tuam; the 1709 grain and measures bill; the 1710 Dublin pavements bill, and the 1711 hides, union of parishes, writs of mandamus, and warrants and recognisance bills, which were returned unamended or with no more than a small number of 'verbal' amendments, resistance from interested parties in Ireland was sufficient to precipitate their demise.[54] This pattern can also be identified in respect of private Privy Council bills, whose treatment at the English/British Council board and, if returned, in Ireland was not without its distinctive features.

Of the private Privy Council bills presented during the 1703–4 session, the most singular was the Stopford bill vesting 'certain lands and hereditaments' in trustees so they could be sold for the payment of debts. There was nothing unusual about this, other than that the initial attempt by James Stopford, who was MP for Wexford, to obtain legal authority to do so was laid aside in July 1703. Unwilling for pressing family reasons to await a new session to try again, Stopford availed of his excellent political connections to push a revised measure through the Irish Council and personally to present 'full answers to the objections' that were raised. This was unusual, but it worked to Stopford's advantage, for though

53. NA, PC2/80 ff 318–19, 352; King to Bishop Vigors, 9 June, King to Lord Chancellor Cox, 12, 26 June 1705 (TCD, King Papers, MS 750/3/1 ff 178, 181–2, 190–1) (union of parishes bill); PC1/2/60/3; PC2/81 f. 353; *Commons Jn. (Irl.)*, 495 (servants and labourers bill); PC1/2/60/3; PC2/81 ff 353, 367–8; *Commons Jn. (Irl.)*, ii, 496 (justices of the peace bill); 8 Anne, chap 6; PC2/82 ff 347, 355–6, 360–2; *Lord Jn. (Irl.)*, ii, 293; *Commons Jn. (Irl.)*, ii, 625, 635 (counterfeiting act); Anne, chap 13; PC2/82 ff 348, 357–8, 385–6; *Lord Jn. (Irl.)*, ii, 300; *Commons Jn. (Irl.)*, ii, 631, 635 (Armagh parishes act); PC2/83 ff 292, 313–15 (fire bill, 1711); PC2/84 ff 241–3; *Commons Jn. (Irl.)*, ii, 743, 768 (fire bill, 1713).

54. NA, PC2/80 ff 258–9, 260–1 (blasphemy and profanity bill); PC2/80 312, 325 (duty on muslins and hops bill); PC2/81 ff 438–9, 446; *Commons Jn. (Irl.)*, 545, 549 (relief of debtors bill); PC2/81 ff 438–9, 450–1; King to Southwell, 23 Sept. 1707 (TCD, King Papers, MS 750/3/2 ff 153–5) (Tuam tithes bill); PC2/82 ff 347, 356, 360–2; *Lord Jn. (Irl.)*, ii, 293; *Commons Jn. (Irl.)*, ii, 625, 630 (grain and measures bill); PC2/83 ff 14–15, 29; *Commons Jn. (Irl.)*, ii, 671, 677 (Dublin pavement bill); PC2/83 ff 292, 312, 313–15; *Commons Jn. (Irl.)*, ii, 720, 723 (hides bill); PC2/83 ff 292, 311, 313–15; King to Annesley, 22 Oct. 1711 (TCD, King Papers, MS 2531 f. 358) (union of parishes bill); *Lords Jn. (Irl.)*, ii, 397; PC2/83 ff 292, 313–15 (writs of mandamus bill); PC2/83 ff 291, 310–11, 313–15 (warrants and recognisances bill).

his bill was extensively amended at the English Council board its passage into law was not interrupted.[55] By contrast, measures for the relief of Margaret Wall and John Power of Moylargy, County Waterford, which greatly occupied William Wogan in January 1704, did not emerge from the Council. Wall's bill encountered 'great opposition' because her father had obtained a divorce in a French ecclesiastical court that could only be reversed by the pope, while Power's was not allowed to progress because of the strong resistance to any action that was seen to favour a known Jacobite.[56] This outcome was always a probability when a private bill was contested because of the genuine commitment to provide fairly for all parties in family settlements. This may account for the rejection of the Harrison divorce bill in 1705; it certainly explains the loss of the Sir John King debts bill of 1710, while the Hammerton debt bill, which was amended, was lost on its return to Ireland in the same year. It was also a factor in respect of the bill for applying the surplus profits of the Erasmus Smith charity, which fell at a very late stage when it was established in a petition presented on behalf of Christ's Hospital, London, that the money at issue had been granted by Smith to the Hospital in 1680.[57] However, compared with public measures, it is not possible in a large number of instances to identify why a private Privy Council bill was rejected, though there was usually a substantive reason.[58] This was demonstrated on 10 July 1710 when the decision of the British Council that four private bills were 'not fitt for her majesty's approbation', caused (it was alleged) by the determined opposition of the earl of Anglesey, prompted a decision to refer the bills for further consideration. Significantly, in no instance was the decision reversed.[59] A less dramatic fate was to be subject to material amendment, which was the outcome in 1703–4 in the case of the measure to prevent the disinheriting of Garret Coghlan; in 1705 in the case of the Shelburne bill; and in 1707 in the case of the Ormonde bill.[60] The amendments authorised in these instances could be extensive, but they were on a small scale when compared with the extent of the

---

55. Above p. 121; NA, PC2/79 ff 413, 470, 477–8; Ormonde to Nottingham, 2 Oct. 1703 in *Cal. SP (Dom.), 1703–4*, p. 142; *Commons Jn. (Irl.)*, ii, 393, 394, 395, 397, 406, 414.

56. For the Wall and Power bills see NA, PC2/79 f. 484; Wogan to Southwell, 1, 4, 6, 15, 18, 29 Jan. 1704 (BL, Southwell Papers, Add. MS 37673 ff 29, 32, 35–6, 43–4, 53); Povey to Southwell, 29 Jan. 1704 (Beinecke Library, Osborn Collection, Southwell Papers, Box 2).

57. NA, PC2/80 ff 329, 361 (Harrison bill) (Dr John Bergin suggests that the main reason for the loss of the Harrison bill was that a divorce had not been secured in the ecclesiastical courts.); NA, PC2/82 ff 366, 383–4, 388–9 (Smith bill); PC2/83 ff 17, 18 36 (King bill); PC2/83 ff 17, 18, 26, 28, 42–3, 44; *Commons Jn. (Irl.)*, ii, 680, 681 (Hammerton bill).

58. For examples, the Gormanston private bill, which was received on 8 Sept 1707, received no further mention (NA, PC2/81 f. 442). In the case of the Jones bill in 1709, the advice of the Irish bills committee was 'not to pass the bill' (PC2/82 ff 397).

59. The bills appertained to the Maurice Fitzgerald, Theophilus Jones, Francis Smith and Richard Bolton (NA, PC2/83 ff 17, 36, 50, 75, 77); Annesley to King, 28 Nov., King to Annesley, 16 Dec. 1710 (TCD, King Papers, MSS 1995–2008 f. 1392, MS 2531 f. 239).

60. 2 Anne chap 7 (private); NA, PC2/79 ff 484–7; PC2/80 ff 30–1; *Commons Jun. (Irl.)*, ii, 396, 414 (Coghlan bill); 4 Anne, chap 1 (private); PC2/80 ff 318–19, 355–6; *Commons Jn. (Irl.)*, ii,

alterations approved in 1710 to remedy deficiencies in the bill providing for the payment of the debts of the duke of Ormonde; these extended over twenty-five expansive folios and necessitated the rewriting of the vast majority of the bill.[61]

A substantial proportion of private Privy Council bills negotiated the scrutiny of the English Council with few or no amendments.[62] And a majority encountered no problems on their way to receive the royal assent in Ireland, though this was not invariable. For example, the 1703–4 bill for the relief of Walter Butler, which sought to reverse his outlawry, was rejected on its return because, Edward Southwell noted, MPs 'had no mind to encourage anyone bred up in arms in foreign service'.[63] Privy council private bills that were subject to material amendment to clarify ambiguities in meaning and purpose were likewise generally well received. Indeed, other than church bills into which the introduction of 'a clause of residence' was described by Archbishop William King as the equivalent of inviting the bills to be rejected,[64] amendments made to private bills to safeguard a legitimate interest or to public bills to redress syntactical or legal defects were rarely contested.

THE MANAGEMENT OF HEADS OF BILLS, 1703–13

The lord lieutenant's pronouncement at the commencement of the 1703–4 session that, as well as debating the bills that had taken their rise in the Privy Council, he expected MPs and peers to propose 'such other laws as may yet be wanting for the establishment of the Protestant religion and the welfare of the

467, 483 (Shelburne bill); 6 Anne, chap 2 (private); *Lord Jn. (Irl.)*, ii, 212; PC2/81 ff 432, 439–42; *Commons Jn. (Irl.)*, ii, 554, 568 (Ormonde bill).

61. *Lords Jn. (Irl.)*, ii, 349; NA, PC2/83 ff 50–76; *Commons Jn. (Irl.)*, ii, 679, 680, 685.

62. Among their number are 2 Anne, chap 1 (private); *Lord Jn. (Irl.)*, ii, 57; NA, PC2/79 ff 484–7, 497–507; *Commons Jn. (Irl.)*, ii, 396, 414 (Ormonde bill); 2 Anne, chap 2 (private); *Lord Jn. (Irl.)*, ii, 68; PC2/79 ff 473–4, 497–507; *Commons Jn. (Irl.)*, ii, 403, 414 (Rosse bill); 4 Anne, chap 2 (private); *Lords Jn. (Irl.)*, ii, 121; PC2/80 ff 312, 353–5; *Commons Jn. (Irl.)*, ii, 472, 483 (Aylmer bill); 4 Anne, chap 7 (private); PC2/80 ff 312–14, 318–19, 339; *Commons Jn. (Irl.)*, ii, 463, 483 (Dawson bill); 6 Anne, chap 3 (private); PC2/81 ff 442, 449, 451; *Commons Jn. (Irl.)*, ii, 543, 568 (Doneraile bill); 6 Anne, chap 4 (private); *Lords Jn. (Irl.)*, ii, 231; PC2/81 ff 438–9, 450–1; *Commons Jn. (Irl.)*, ii, 564, 568 (St Andrew's parish bill); 8 Anne, chap 1 (private); PC2/82 ff 348, 362–4; *Commons Jn. (Irl.)*, ii, 620, 635 (Ranelagh bill); 8 Anne, chap 3 (private); PC2/82 ff 349, 363–4; *Commons Jn. (Irl.)*, ii, 620, 635 (Blundell bill); 10 Anne, chap 1 (private); PC2/83 ff 17, 41, 43; *Commons Jn. (Irl.)*, ii, 679, 685 (Grandison bill); 10 Anne, chap 5 (private); PC2/83 ff 17, 41, 43; *Commons Jn. (Irl.)*, ii, 683, 685 (Stoughton bill); 11 Anne, chap 4 (private); PC2/83 ff 393, 318, 327–8; *Commons Jn. (Irl.)*, ii, 711, 735 (Donnellan bill).

63. For the Burke bill see *Lords Jn. (Irl.)*, ii, 67; Thomas Doyle, 'Jacobitism, Catholicism and the Irish Protestant elite 1700–10', pp 11–12; NA, PC2/79 ff 484–7, 497–507; *Commons Jn. (Irl.)*, ii, 402, 412. Other bills that may be placed in this category include the Conway bill (PC2/80 f. 70).

64. King to Bishop Vigors, 9 June, King to Lord Chancellor Cox, 12, 26 June 1704 (TCD, King Papers, MS 750/3/1 ff 178, 181–2, 190–1).

kingdom' indicated that it was anticipated that parliament would play an active part in initiating legislation.[65] Eager to do so, and thereby to build on the achievements of the late 1690s, MPs and peers responded with a wave of legislative initiatives.[66] Over 70 per cent (272 out of 385) of the measures initiated during the reign of Queen Anne arose with the Commons. A striking 45 per cent of these did not proceed to the Irish Council, though the fact that in almost half of these instances permission to introduce the heads of a bill did not result in their presentation indicates that the attrition rate in the Commons was not as severe as the figures suggest. By contrast, the Lords was responsible for a modest 10 per cent of the total number of legislative proposals initiated during Anne's reign, which put it firmly behind the Commons and the Privy Council, and sustains the observation of the chief secretary, Joseph Addison, that the Irish Lords did 'little business'.[67] Because proportionately fewer (25 per cent) heads of bills that took their rise in the Lords were lost in that chamber, peers were responsible for 20 per cent of the 179 heads of bills forwarded to the Irish Privy Council between 1703 and 1713 (Table Four). Comprising 145 public and 34 private measures (Tables Two and Three), the task of scrutinising these to determine which should be transmitted to the English/British Council board had to be completed expeditiously in order that those deemed eligible would be available to be presented to the Irish parliament on its resumption after the mid-session recess that lasted on average between four and six weeks.

Though the operation of the Irish Council during Anne's reign remains particularly opaque, it is possible to gain some insight into its operation from incidental observations in the correspondence of a number of its members. It is clear from these that the minority of active councillors took the responsibility very seriously. For instance, when the bill to prevent the further growth of was being considered in 1703, Archbishop Narcissus Marsh invited his ecclesiastical colleagues, William King of Dublin and Richard Tennison of Meath, to his 'house … to consider a little more about a clause etc'.[68] This was uncharacteristic,

---

65. Cited in James, *Lords of the ascendancy*, p. 73.
66. One can gain a sense of their variety from a listing of the nineteen proposals for which leave to introduce a bill was sought in 1703 but no bill ensued. They were heads of a bill to oblige certain person to take the oath of abjuration (*Commons Jn. (Irl.)*, ii, 327); to prevent papists inheriting (ibid., 321); to give toleration to Protestant dissenters (ibid., 401); for vacating and laying aside the charter granted to the corporation of butchers (ibid., 344); for better collecting … the arrears of the poll tax (ibid., 359); for the encouragement of trade (ibid., 349); to encourage the making of earthen ware (ibid., 327); for regulating the privilege of parliament (ibid., 330); to employ and maintain the poor (ibid., 326); for regulating the practice of physic and chirurgery (ibid., 322); for making the river Shannon navigable (ibid., 322); for the real union and division of parishes (ibid., 360); to make the river Nore navigable (ibid., 351); to make a canal from Lough Neagh to Newry (ibid., 324); to make the river Barrow navigable (ibid., 324); to make the river Boyne navigable (ibid., 325); for regulating servants (ibid., 325); to take off the duty on rape seed (ibid., 330, 354); to encourage the linen manufacture (ibid., 322, 328, 354, 356, 360).
67. Quoted in Hayton, 'Ireland and the English ministers', p. 99.
68. See Marsh to King, 10 July 1703, King to Synge, 16 Jan. 1705 (TCD, King Papers, MSS 1995–2008, f. 1032, MS 750/3/1 ff 65–6).

particularly for Marsh whose dislike of 'world business', of which the preparing of bills was one of the most demanding of tasks, was well known. Despite this, bishops, who comprised six of the forty-two-member Council sworn in 1702, were among the most reliable and assiduous attendees at meetings of that body, which were held in the council chambers in the Custom House until they were consumed by fire in April 1711.[69] Their commitment was exceeded only by that of the judiciary, who were represented on the Council at this time by the chief justices of the major courts. They assumed the lion's share of the work of drafting bills, and of scrutinising and recommending amendments to the heads of bills transmitted from parliament. The 'generality of privy councillors', by contrast, offered little to the process, and they were frequently conspicuous by their absence when the Council was at its busiest 'readying' bills.[70] This was a chore that few councillors relished as it meant devoting long hours to ensuring that bills to be forwarded were put in proper order quickly so they could be certified for transmission to England. The number of heads received each session during Queen Anne's reign ranged from a low of 18 in 1711 to a high of 40 in 1703, though it was more usually in the low 30s. This was the case in 1705, and in 1707 when Archbishop King observed irritably that it was unreasonable to expect the Council to consider 32 bills in the space of eighteen days and not make mistakes.[71] King was one of the handful of councillors who took the task of preparing bills very seriously, for though he regarded it as 'drudgery', and lamented the time, effort and energy it demanded, he acknowledged that it was 'the most material part of their work'.[72] He was impatient for this reason with MPs who alleged that their bills were 'being ruined by amendments introduced at Privy Council'. Pointing to a number of bills that were 'lost … for want of two or three amendments proposed at the Board', he robustly defended the actions of the Council. He alleged, indeed, that in a number of instances the 'most that is good' about a bill 'was introduced in the Council', and unhesitatingly defended councillors actions in respiting bills that 'deserved' to be lost, and in amending bills that were presented in deficient form.[73]

69. McCarthy, *Marsh's Library*, pp 6–7; Royal warrant listing those to be sworn to Irish Privy Council, 27 June 1702 in *Cal. SP (Dom.)*, *1702–3*, pp 143–4; Marsh to King, 24 June (TCD, King Papers, MSS 1995–2008 f. 1028); King to Synge, 16 Jan. 1705 (ibid., MS 750/3/1 ff 65–6); King to Commissioners [of Customs], 8 July 1715 (ibid., MS 2533 f. 6); Order in Council, 18 Apr. 1711, Report, 21 Apr. 1711 (NAI, Calendar of miscellaneous letters and papers prior to 1760, f. 72); Affidavits and examinations relative to fire, 20 Apr. 1711 (NAI, Calendar of presentments, affidavits etc., f. 77).
70. Southwell to Nottingham, 12 June 1703 in *Cal. SP (Dom.)*, *1703–4*, p. 13; King to Synge, 2 Sept., 1707, King to Brodrick, 11 Sept. 1708 (TCD, King Papers, MS 750/3/2 ff 150, 244).
71. King to Synge, 2 Sept. 1707 (TCD, King Papers, MS 750/3/2 f. 150); Irish Council to Lord [ ], 12 Apr. 1707 (NA, PC1/2/60/3).
72. King to Southwell, 29 July, King to Synge, 2 Sept. 1707 (TCD, King Papers, MS 750/3/2 ff 142, 150).
73. King to Annesley, 16 Aug. (2), King to Synge, 2 Sept., King to Southwell, 8 Nov. 1707 (TCD, King Papers, MS 750/3/2 ff 143, 145, 150, 160–1).

As this implies, the number of heads of bills lost at the Irish Council during the reign of Queen Anne was significant, particularly during the first three sessions of the reign, when nearly two-thirds (24) of the total of 38 were lost.[74] It is not possible to offer a statistical perspective on the number of bills that was subject to amendment, but since the Council committees that examined individuals bills in detail chose to meet 'every morning' and the Council 'every afternoon' to 'hurry on the bills', it is likely that amendments were routine.[75] At the same time, the speed with which bills were processed offered little protection against mistakes. Influenced by this, some ecclesiastical and lay councillors chose deliberately not to attend when bills were being scrutinised to escape being implicated in the criticism by MPs to which the Council and councillors were routinely subjected for this reason.[76] Since 26 (24 public and 2 private) of the 38 heads of bills that were held back or 'thrown out' by the Irish Council originated with the Commons, this response is understandable. The overall loss of 21 per cent of all heads was not deemed excessive, however, and can be set in perspective by the fact that two-thirds of the 214 bills transmitted under the great seal of Ireland to the English/British Council between 1703 and 1713 commenced as heads of bills in the Irish parliament (Table Four).[77]

Heads of Irish bills were conveyed to England in one or two major transmisses each session during the reign of Queen Anne.[78] These transmisses could comprise as many as 30 bills, but 15 or less was usual. Because it was critical that the bills were communicated safely, dealt with expeditiously and, if the opportunity allowed or demanded, represented skilfully, the task was entrusted by the Irish administration to reliable officials rather than to ordinary messengers. William Wogan (encountered above) is the best known, though there were others. In reality, because they were seldom sufficiently informed to address the sort of

---

74. In 1703–4, a total of nine heads of bills (two from the Lords and seven from the Commons) was lost. These were heads for supplying defects in the act directing how the collectors shall receive crown, quit or composition rents (*Lords Jn. (Irl.)*, ii, 47, 48); for the more easy collection of tithes (ibid., 29, 34); to repeal ... the act ... which relates to the High Commission Court (*Commons Jn. (Irl.)*, ii, 346, 381); for building abridge over the river Shannon (ibid., 378, 390); to regulate the election of members to serve in parliament (ibid., 346, 363); to prevent the destroying of fry (ibid., 338, 444); to make the estates of minors liable to the payment of debts (ibid., 343, 373); for explaining the statute ... concerning the valuation of houses in corporations for the maintenance of ministers (ibid., 372, 379); declaring the qualifications of persons to be put into the commissions of the peace (ibid., 344, 368).

75. Southwell to Nottingham, 13, 27 Nov., 5, 8 Dec. 1703 in *Cal. SP (Dom.)*, *1703–4*, pp 196–7, 216–18, 221, 228–9.

76. Marsh to King, 24 June 1703 (TCD, King Papers, MS 1995–2008 f. 1028); King to Bishop St George Ashe, 13 Sept. 1707 (ibid., MS 750/3/2 f. 151).

77. Nottingham to Northey, 1 July 1703 in *Cal. SP (Dom.)*, *1703–4*, p. 36.

78. In 1703, two transmisses communicated in December contained twelve and twenty–two bills. Sundry others were communicated individually or in smaller groups (Nottingham to Northey, 14 Dec., Southwell to Nottingham, 8, 15, 18 Dec., Ormonde to Northey, 16 Dec. 1703 in *Cal. SP (Dom.)*, *1703–4*, pp 234, 235, 238, 236).

detailed queries posed by the Crown's law officers, they were, Wogan admitted, of limited use in this respect. None the less, they performed a useful role as a source of general information and as the eyes and ears of the Irish executive in London, since progress reports on the fate of Irish bills from English officials were rarely forthcoming.[79]

The English officeholder, other than the attorney general, with whom Wogan and other messengers had most communication, was the secretary of state for the southern department who was the primary point of contact between the English Council and Irish executive. He was also the person to whom bills from Ireland were conveyed. The expectation was that he would oversee their formal reception at the English/British Council and liase as necessary with the Irish adminis-tration, but, as already noted, Lord Nottingham (secretary of state, 1702–4) and his successor, Sir Charles Hedges (1704–6), authorised their direct communi-cation to the attorney general. Despite its procedural irregularity, this arrangement effectively received royal sanction when, in January 1705, Queen Anne authorised that four bills should be sent directly to the law officers 'to save time'.[80] In the normal course of events, such bills and the accompanying explanatory letters from the Irish Council and any petitions that were offered were presented formally at the English/British Council.[81] Significantly, the committee of the council, which emerged as the main forum of business at the Privy Council at the beginning of the eighteenth century did not engage routinely with Irish bills. A minority of critical measures only were referred to the committee, which responded as appropriate. Thus, the bill to prevent the further growth of popery that was agitated in 1703–4 was subject to a series of extensive amendments and additions at that forum.[82] In obvious contrast, the 'committee of the whole council', attended by the attorney and solicitor general, at which the measure 'for registering the popish clergy' was considered a few weeks later proved less eventful. On this occasion, it was determined, following a discussion attended by only four lords, to amend the bill 'in light of their debate'; three of the four amendments that were approved were of the nature of textual clarifications; but the fourth, which authorised the removal of twenty-three lines of text, involved the deletion of controversial clauses appertaining to the Catholic solicitors and the requirement that registering priests should take the oath of allegiance.[83]

Perhaps this experience shaped the response subsequently, for when bills 'to explain and amend' both the registration act and the act to prevent the further growth of popery were received in 1705 and 1707, they were conveyed directly to

79. Above, pp 121, 124; Wogan's letters to Edward Southwell survive in BL, Southwell Papers, Add. MS 37673–4.
80. Hedges to Ormonde, 16 Jan. 1705 (NA, SP67/3 f. 94).
81. See, for example, NA, PC2/80 f. 312; PC2/81 ff 430–1; Hedges to Ormonde, 24, 31 Apr. 1705 (NA, SP67/3 ff 108–9, 115).
82. Above pp 123–4.
83. NA, PC2/79 ff 484–7, 511; PC2/80 ff 31–2; Fagan, *Catholics in a Protestant country*, p. 58.

the law officers. In the first instance, there were no complications and the measure was forwarded with a few textual amendments.[84] However, the 1707 measure to amend the 'act to prevent the further growth of popery' was subject to a large number of petitions, arising out of which the full Council declined to approve the report presented by the law officers and referred the bill back to them 'to consider' This paved the way for the introduction of three and a half folios of amendments appertaining to the rights of inheritance of the Protestant eldest son of Catholic parents and to the superior rights of Protestants over Catholics, following which the bill was forwarded to take its chances in Ireland.[85]

    This was an unwieldy arrangement that may have served to increase the appeal of embracing the scrutinising of Irish bills within the evolving committee system. The first indication of this was provided on 9 June 1709 when, rather than the usual law officers, it was determined at the Privy Council to refer an unprecedented supply bill recently received from Ireland to 'a committee of the board to consider an Irish bill'. Comprising thirteen members – the lord chancellor, the archbishop of Canterbury, the lord treasurer, lord president, lord privy seal, lord steward, lord high admiral, the dukes of Somerset, Marlborough and Queensbury, the earl of Sunderland, Earl Wharton and the secretary of state, Henry Boyle – not all of whom were present to consider the bill, the committee promptly referred the bill to the attorney and solicitor general 'to consider'. They reported back the next day with a series of 'amendments and alterations' that were taken on board. A number of 'other amendments', which arose during the course of the discussion' were also 'agreed', and the bill was forwarded to a meeting of the full Council, in the presence of the Queen, which sent it to be engrossed so it could be returned to Ireland.[86] Encouraged by the facility with which this was done, it was decided on receipt of a large transmiss of bills from Ireland a month later that they should all be referred to a 'committee ... to consider Irish bills'. Indicatively, this committee showed some changes in personnel from its predecessor.[87] But this was of less importance than the fact that having identified and considered 'the petitions they believe[d] deserving to be heard', the committee prepared a report on the bills for 'her majesty at the board'. Since this was previously the responsibility of the Crown's law officers, it meant in effect that the role of the attorney and solicitor generals in the process of scrutinising Irish bills was being downgraded, though their legal knowledge and willingness to engage in the time-consuming task of scrutinising legislation meant they could not be done without. Arising out of this, it was agreed by the committee that it should be 'attended from time to time' by the attorney and solicitor generals.[88]

84. NA, PC2/80 ff 312, 315, 335.
85. NA, PC2/81 ff 438–9, 443, 445, 448, 451–2, 453, 456.
86. NA, PC2/82 ff 333, 335–6; McGrath, *Making the constitution*, pp 218–20.
87. It was largely the same committee save that the duke of Marlborough and earl of Wharton were replaced by Lord Chief Justices Holt and Trevor and Lord Coningsby (NA, PC2/82 ff 347–8).
88. NA, PC2/82 ff 347–8.

With this new mode of proceeding established, the Lords of the committee to consider Irish bills systematically scrutinised the legislation received from Ireland in 1709. It was clearly not councillors' favoured activity as attendance seldom exceeded five,[89] but this was enough to allow the committee to consider each measure and to prepare a report for the full Council.[90] Moreover, the experiment was adjudged a success since, following the receipt in 1710 of bills from Ireland, it was determined once more to refer the bills to a 'select committee' for a report. Significantly, the committee was larger on this occasion than it was a year earlier, but the addition of four members, raising its complement to eighteen, had only a temporary impact on attendance. Eight or nine lords were present at the initial meetings, but this soon reverted to the more usual five. A report to the effect that the 'attorney general found it inconvenient when the present bills came to be considered' that he did not possess 'the printed acts of parliament' passed in Ireland the previous session suggests that he may have played an active part in preparing the reports communicated by the Irish bills committee to the full council, but if this is so his presence is not attested by the minutes. At any event, there is no outward indication to suggest that it made a difference. The bills received were examined closely and those that the committee deemed appropriate to proceed with or without amendment were accepted by the Council board and forwarded to pass under the great seal in the usual way.[91]

Though the employment of an Irish bills committee to examine Irish bills worked efficiently in 1709 and 1710, the marginalisation of the Crown's law officers under this arrangement remained something of a problem. It was not the subject of written comment, but the fact that it was decided in September 1710 to refer bills received from the 'select committee' on Irish bills to the attorney general, and in a number of instances to both law officers for a report was clearly significant. This decision was taken ostensibly because it ensured the bills at issue met 'with the quickest dispatch', but it is more likely that the Irish bills committee recognised that it was more efficient to commission a report than to prepare it. It certainly proved so in 1711, when all the bills that were received were so referred. In the overwhelming majority of cases, the report presented was approved. However, the fact that in a number of instances the attorney general was requested to consider a measure 'further' or additional amendments were introduced suggests not only that the involvement of the law officers was closely monitored, but also that some doubts remained as to the merits of this means of proceeding.[92] These must be kept in perspective. Something similar had occurred in 1707 with respect of the amending measure to prevent the further growth of

89. NA, PC2/82 ff 370–1; Minutes of Clerk of Council 1670–1776 (PC4/1 ff 317–34).
90. NA, PC2/82 passim.
91. NA, PC2/83 ff 15, 16, 20–1, 24, 25, 26, 27 and passim; Dartmouth to Wharton, 13, 15, 20, 25, 27 July 1710 (NA, SP67/4 ff 3, 4, 5, 6).
92. NA, PC2/83 ff 291–2, 308–9, 310, 313–15, 318, 323–5 and passim; Dartmouth to Ormonde, 8 Sept. 1711 (NA, SP67/4 f. 41).

popery. On that occasion, when the report of the law officers was not 'approved' by the full Council, the bill was 'referred back' to them so they could 'consider it in the light of the debate on the bill they heard at Council', the 'particular cases referred to them which have been this day read at the board, and how far Protestants may be affected by the said bill'. They were also instructed to 'attend the Lord Chancellor and Lord Chief Justice' prior to reporting back to the Council.[93] However, this measure excepted, the law officers were empowered to deal with other bills in the usual way.

Acknowledgement that the involvement of both law officers was crucial to the efficient scrutiny of Irish bills was provided in 1713 when, following the receipt of bills from Ireland, it was determined by the Irish bills committee that they should be referred directly to the attorney and solicitor general. Since reports had been received from both in 1710 and 1711 this was more of a refinement than an innovation, but it was significant nonetheless because it established what became normative with respect of Irish bills. Essentially from this point onwards, bills transmitted from Ireland were received and read at the Privy Council before being referred to the Irish bills committee, which referred them for a report to the Crown's law officers.[94] Since this combined the reliance upon the law officers that had worked well during the early years of Queen Anne's reign with the sub-committee system subsequently employed it is hardly surprising that it was to endure. Furthermore, confidence was generated in the arrangement by the fact that the full Privy Council was disposed to accept the recommendations of the Irish bills committee. Indeed, there is only one instance during Queen Anne's reign when this was not the case; in the summer of 1711 the Irish Commons provided for the imposition of what amounted to a prohibitive duty on imported molasses. This was resisted by the Crown's law officers, who condemned the proposal as 'a restraining and binding of England'. They were supported in this conclusion by the Commissioners of the Customs, but fearful that such an important bill might be lost if it was returned to Ireland in a significantly amended form, and subject to intense lobbying from Ireland, the Council was induced to 'disapprove of the alteration made by the Committee of Council' and conveyed the bill for transmission with three minor syntactical alterations only.[95]

As this case illustrates, the new administrative procedures applied from 1709 imposed demands as well as conferring advantages. To work to optimal effect, co-ordination was required across the Irish Sea to ensure the processing of legislation dovetailed with the evolving pattern of the Irish parliamentary session, which comprised two distinct parts. Essentially, the first was taken up with debating the Privy Council bills and the heads of bills initiated by peers and MPs. This was

93. NA, PC2/81 f. 448.
94. NA, PC2/84 ff 241; Bolingbroke to lords justices, 3 Oct. 1713 (NA, SP67/4 f. 87).
95. NA, PC2/83 f. 291, 318, 323–5; F.G. James, 'The Irish lobby in the early eighteenth century', *EHR*, 81 (1966), p. 551; Dartmouth to Ormonde, 2 Oct. 1711 (NA, SP67/4 f. 43); McGrath, *Making the constitution*, pp 258–9.

followed by an adjournment when, as shown above, it was the responsibility of the Irish Council to transmit 'a sufficient load of bills' to the British Council in anticipation that enough would be returned in time to provide the Irish parliament with legislative business for the second part of the session.[96] However, because the number of bills that negotiated the Irish Council during a session was unpredictable, because all attempts to co-ordinate the meetings of the Irish and English/British parliaments and to time the receipt of bills from Ireland to coincide with a lull in the working cycle of the English/British Privy Council proved impossible, and because the consideration and processing of Irish bills frequently fell behind schedule, matters seldom ran entirely to plan. In 1703, for example, attempts to ensure that the meeting of the Irish parliament 'ended before this in England meets' were frustrated by problems encountered in Ireland in the preparation of the Privy Council bills. Subsequently, the resumption of the session was delayed by the extended length of time required to bring a series of measures including the bill to prevent the further growth of popery to an agreeable state at the English Council. Originally set for 20 January 1704, it was apparent to the secretary of state, Lord Nottingham, before the end of December that this date could not be met and he advised the Irish chief secretary, Edward Southwell, 'to continue the parliament by short adjournments', which is what was done, until 1 February.[97]

This was not invariably the practice, but it was not unusual for ministers and officials in London to advise the lord lieutenant to prolong the duration of the mid-session adjournment for a week, ten days or a fortnight because Irish bills were not ready to be returned.[98] To be sure, ministers did not do this on a whim. The promises they made in response to Irish urgings that bills would be 'dispatched with all possible speed' were sincerely made, but they were not always kept though the arrival in Dublin of a messenger with bills was sufficiently newsworthy to be reported in the press.[99] However, a majority of Irish bills deemed suitable to become law in Ireland were returned as rapidly as practicable, and with considerably greater expedition than was norm in the seventeenth century. This was particularly true of the vital financial legislation, which could be turned round in as little as a week, as in the case of the 1707 measure for 'granting to her majesty an additional duty on beer, ale, strong waters and other commodities'.[100]

---

96. King to Southwell, 2 Sept. 1707 (TCD, King Papers, MS 750/3/2 f 147); David Hayton, 'Ireland and the English ministers' (Unpublished D. Phil, Oxford University, 1975), p. 95.

97. Nottingham to Ormonde, 19 June, Nottingham to Southwell, 28 Dec. 1703 (NA, SP67/3 ff 66, 82); Southwell to Nottingham, 10, 26, 30 Jan. 1704 in *Cal. SP (Dom.)*, *1703–4*, pp 491, 509, 516; Ellis to Southwell, 12 Feb. 1704 (Beinecke Library, Osborn Collection, Southwell Papers, Box 1).

98. Sunderland to Pembroke, 16 Sept. 1707, Sunderland to Wharton, 21 July 1709 (NA, SP67/3 ff 157, 202).

99. Hedges to Ormonde, 15 Mar., 21 Apr. 1705, Dartmouth to Wharton, 4, 8, 11 July 1710 (NA, SP67/3 ff 105, 115, SP67/4 ff 2, 3); *Flying Post*, 9 Oct.; *Dublin Gazette*, 11 Oct. 1707.

100. 6 Anne I, chap 1; NA, PC2/81 ff 430–31, 436; *Commons Jn. (Irl.)*, ii, 523, 527, 530, 540, 543, 548, 550, 558, 560.

Two years later, when there was insufficient time to prepare a proper supply bill to extend duties 'on several foreign wares' before they were due to expire, approval was forthcoming for an emergency short money bill more quickly still. Anxious to ensure that there was no 'interval of time' between the expiry of the old act and the ratification of the full quota of taxes already 'upon the anvil', the Commons approved heads to this effect in four days. Six days later the measure was with the Irish bills committee, which examined, amended and sent it to be engrossed in one day. Returned soon after to Ireland, it received the royal assent within three days of its presentation to the Irish parliament.[101] In all, the process from seeking leave to receiving the royal assent took twenty-five days, which was one day less than it took to implement a similar measure in 1710.[102] While it might be suggested on these grounds that this practice could have been followed more generally, this would have been unrealistic. Both bills were regarded as priority items and the urgency with which they were handled at all stages reflected this fact. In broad terms, the management of Irish legislation improved over time independent of the emergence of the Irish bills committee, but it complemented it, and contributed to the greater effectiveness of the process.

Another helpful development was the improvement in the information forthcoming from the Irish Council on the content and purpose of each measure they forwarded. Advised of the problems caused in the summer of 1703 when their failure to provide explanatory missives to nine bills was the subject of critical comment, the Irish Council was more forthcoming thereafter and full use was made of their efforts. On 1 September 1707, for example, the heads of a supply bill and the accompanying 'covering letter ... from the lord lieutenant and Council' were both referred to the Crown's law officers.[103] As a result, the attorney and solicitor generals were equipped with critical details on the measures before them, which greatly assisted with their deliberations. On the downside, it meant they were heavily dependent on the information the Irish Privy Council chose to provide and, as seen above in respect of the Privy Council bills transmitted prior to the 1705 session, they were not averse to eliding awkward details.[104] It was not made an issue of on this occasion but, in 1710, following his appointment for a second term as attorney general, the vigilant Edward Northey enquired as to why 'none of the printed acts of parliament passed in Ireland the last year have been sent over'. His suspicions were aroused by a proposal for 'the encouragement of tillage', some of whose clauses bore close comparison with a

---

101. 8 Anne, chap 1; Addison to Sunderland, 3 June 1709 (BL, Blenheim Papers, Add. MS 61636 f. 40); NA, PC2/82 ff 335–6; *Commons Jn. (Irl.)*, ii, 594, 595, 596, 597, 609, 610, 611, 614, 615; McGrath, *Making the constitution*, pp 218–20.

102. 9 Anne, chap 1; NA, PC2/83 f. 7; *Commons Jn. (Irl.)*, ii, 648, 649, 656, 657, 659, 660, 661, 663, 665; Hayton, 'Ireland and the English ministers', p. 93; McGrath, *Making the constitution*, pp 236–7.

103. NA, PC2/81 ff 430–31; see also PC2/80 f. 334 for further reference to a 'letter' from the lord lieutenant.

104. Above, p. 127.

similar bill that had been 'remitted' in 1709, as well as by an amending bill to an act for planting and preserving timber trees and woods that had, he believed, been sent over 'last session'. The Irish bills committee believed his concerns were justified, though their unease derived from the failure to document 'several matters of fact' in a private bill on behalf of Henry and Sarah Stoughton, which meant they were unable to 'judge whether it is or is not' appropriate 'that this bill should passe'. Eager to deter such practices and to bring a greater degree of regularity to the process, the Irish bills committee formally recommended on 24 July 1710 'that after every session, a roll containing all the publick acts past that session ... signed by the proper officer may be transmitted [from Ireland] to this board', which the Queen in Council approved.[105]

Though the request was tactfully worded, the fact that it was issued in and communicated from London is significant since, as well as emphasising where the centre of power in Anglo-Irish relations rested, it drew attention in Ireland to the scrutiny to which Irish bills were subject by the attorney general. It would have been highly embarrassing, of course, if the chief law officer had conducted himself other than with strict probity given the critical tenor of his comments on much Irish legislation, but this can be said also of the solicitor general, and the other officers of state that participated in the process. Statistically, only a small number of Irish bills were referred to officials other than the law officers, but the practice of so doing with those bills where particular expertise was required was a further procedural refinement that became normative during the reign of Queen Anne. It was appealed to firstly in 1703 with respect of the heads of a bill 'for the encouragement of the hempen and flaxen manufacture' which was sent 'for a report' to the Lords Commissioners of Trade and Plantations 'to consider of that part thereof which relates to the exportation of that manufacture'.[106] Four years later, when the law officers were unable to answer the Council's queries as to whether a proposal to introduce premiums contained in a Commons' bill 'for the further encouragement and improvement of the hempen and flax manufacture' might prove 'detrimental to the trade of England', the matter was referred to the Commissioners of Customs. Significantly, their report was delivered to the law officers, and no substantive amendment was made as a result though it was directed that the premiums should be paid out of 'the present allowance ... for encouraging ... linen'.[107] Unlike the 1703 measure which did not become law, that of 1707 made it to the statute book, but the fact that both bills were referred for an expert report attests to the commitment at the English/British Council board to protect English commercial interests. This was manifest again in 1709 when a

---

105. Dartmouth to Wharton, 13, 15, 20, 27 (2) July 1710 (NA, SP67/4 ff 3, 4, 5, 6); NA, PC2/83 ff 28–9. Significantly, it did not deter the Irish Council from conveying similar bills in future; indeed, in 1711 a further tillage bill was relayed, while the fire bill that failed in 1711 was conveyed as a Privy Council bill in 1713.
106. NA, PC2/79 ff 473–4; *Commons Jn. (Irl.)*, ii, 361, 370, 395, 399, 404, 409.
107. NA, PC2/81 ff 449, 460, 464; 9 Anne, chap 6.

proposal to encourage the 'exportation of corn', which was referred to the lord high treasurer and passed on to the Commissioners of Customs 'for a report', did not emerge out of the Council.[108] Similarly, when the Commissioners of Trade and Plantations were requested in July 1710 to 'examine and report on' a measure to 'enforce such acts as have been made for the improvement of the linen manufacture', they invited the Governors of the Hamburgh Company to convey their sentiments. The Hamburgh Company was untroubled, whereupon the bill was returned to Ireland with a few modest amendments to become law.[109] The outcome was different a year later when a measure for 'the encouragement of tillage', 'postponed' on foot of a report from the attorney general, was promptly referred for an expert assessment to the Commissioners of Trade and Plantations. Their task officially was to assess the impact of the measure on 'the dominions', but it was the testimony of English corn merchants to the effect that, inclusive of the proposal to grant premiums, 'the bill would be very prejudicial to the corn trade of this kingdom' that proved compelling. The measure was forwarded to Ireland from the British Council board with thirty amendments that provided for an exception for Great Britain, an exclusion for meal, flour, biscuit and starch and an additional clause reserving the power to the Irish Privy Council 'to prohibit transportation when they pleased'. This was more than Irish MPs were willing to accept; the amended bill excited 'the greatest heat and clamour' in Ireland and it was lost in the House of Commons.[110]

A similar outcome ensued with respect of the measure to prevent the 'running of tobacco', which was referred to the lord high treasurer for his opinion in 1711. This did not trespass upon English commercial interests, but the insertion of a number of material revisions into the text of the bill was enough to ensure it was not allowed a second reading on its return to Ireland.[111] Six years earlier, the lord high treasurer approved the clause in the royal mines bill providing Lord Abercorn with compensation to the tune of £4,000 on condition that the sum was 'made good by a further supply'; while, in another such case in 1707, the lord high admiral was consulted in respect of a proposal for cleansing the port and erecting a ballast office in Dublin.[112] Because both of these measures became law, one cannot make a sustainable connection between the referral of an Irish bill to officials other than the law officers and the likelihood of its not making the statute

---

108. NA, PC2/82 ff 365, 371; James, 'The Irish lobby', p. 552.
109. NA, PC2/83 ff 14–15, 21, 38, 40; *Journal of the Commissioners for trade and plantations, 1709–15* (London, 1925), pp 171–2; *Commons Jn. (Irl.)*, ii, 660, 676, 678, 680, 684, 685.
110. NA, PC2/83 ff 291, 308, 317, 319, 324–5; *Journal of the Commissioners for trade and plantations, 1709–15*, pp 300–2; David Hayton (ed.), 'An Irish parliamentary diary in the reign of Queen Anne', *Analecta Hibernica*, 30 (1982), pp 110–16; King to Annesley, 22 Oct. 1711 (TCD, King Papers, MS 2532 f. 358); *Commons Jn. (Irl.)*, ii, 697, 699, 721, 722, 723.
111. NA, PC2/83 ff 14–15, 21, 37–8, 40; *Commons Jn. (Irl.)*, ii, 656, 661, 665, 676.
112. NA, PC2/80 ff 312, 334, 335, 344; King to Abercorn, 13 May 1705 (TCD, King Papers, MS 750/3/1 ff 166–7); *Commons Jn. (Irl.)*, ii, 428, 440, 463, 464, 467, 470, 475, 483 (mines bill); 6 Anne, chap 20; PC2/81 ff 430–1, 445, 460–1, 468 (Dublin port bill).

book. Rather, the key determinant as to whether commercial or financial guidance was sought was the purpose and content of the bill at issue.

A total of 40, or nearly 19 per cent of the public and private bills received at the English/British Council board were not deemed suitable to progress during the reign of Anne. Significantly, of the total received, the percentage of public bills lost (15 per cent) was little more than half that of private bills (27 per cent). This may have something to do with the fact that only three of the 22 public bills not to proceed arose with the Irish Council, and is consistent with the fact that it gave more time and attention to public bills. Perhaps, councillors were content to forward private bills, most of which were drawn elsewhere on behalf of the private interests that requested them, without the same attentive enquiry. Be that as it may, no bill was refused permission to progress at either the Irish or English/British Councils without reason, though the precise grounds are not always readily identifiable. Indeed, at the beginning of the reign (particularly with respect of objectionable private bills) it is often the case that the only official indication that a bill was deemed unsuitable at the English/British Council is the absence of any reference in the official minutes beyond the fact that it had been admitted.[113] The record became fuller as the reign progressed, though the language employed to indicate that a bill was not appropriate to proceed varied. It was signalled by the employment of the term 'rejected' in 1703–4 and 1707; 'refused' in 1705; 'layd (or 'laid') aside' in 1709 and 1710; and by recourse to the phrases the 'advice ... is not to pass the bill' or the bill was 'not fitt for her majesty's approbation' in 1709, 1710 and 1711.[114]

Focussing specifically on those measures that took their rise as heads in the Irish parliament, it is apparent that those lost at the English/British Council during the reign of Queen Anne fall into a number of distinct categories. In the first place, there were bills that appertained to constitutional rights such as that of *habeas corpus*, which ministers adjudged should not be extended to Ireland on five occasions.[115] Secondly, there were economic or commercial proposals that were deemed undesirable because they were contrary to British interests.[116] Thirdly,

---

113. For examples, the Wall bill and the Power bill, 1703–4 (NA, PC2/79 ff 484–7); the bill 'to prevent fees being taken in certain cases', 1705 (PC2/80 ff 312, 330–31); Gormanston bill, 1707 (PC2/81 f. 442); corn exportation bill, 1709 (PC2/82 ff 365, 371).

114. NA, PC2/80 ff 49, 55, 361; PC2/81 f. 453; PC2/82 ff 350, 397; PC2/83 ff 36.

115. The 1703, 1705,1707, 1709, 1710 proposals 'for better securing the liberty of the subject' (NA, PC2/79 ff 484–7; PC2/80 ff 55, 361; PC2/81 ff 438–9, 453; PC2/82 ff 347, 350, PC2/83 ff 14–5, 36).

116. For example, the 1709 proposal 'for the encouragement of the exportation of corn' (PC2/82 f 365, 371); and the 1710 measure 'for the encouragement of tillage' (PC2/83 ff 36, 75, 80).

117. The 1705 bills for regulating elections of members, for the better ordering of servants, and for the public registering of memorials (NA, PC2/80 ff 318–9, 361); the 1710 measures appertaining to the paying of quit, crown and other rents, and preventing abuses in collecting public money (PC2/83 ff 14, 16, 36); and the 1711 bill for the better securing what is given for pious and charitable uses (PC2/83 f. 291; SP67/4 f. 42).

there were administrative bills that were objectionable or that were presented in deficient form.[117] Fourthly, there were bills appertaining to legal issues that did not mirror English practice.[118] Fifthly, there were bills to which cogent opposition was expressed by particular interests;[119] and, sixthly and most numerously, there were private bills that were lost because of defective drafting or because the bill failed to make due and appropriate allowance for a variety of interested parties, usually family members.[120]

Though this listing indicates that the English/British Council was not reluctant to veto measures across the legislative range, councillors preferred where possible to bring Irish legislation into due form by amendment, and they had ready resort to this power. In all, nearly two-thirds (64 per cent) of Irish bills received were amended. The number and extent of these revisions varied greatly. Some 69 per cent of public and 54 per cent of private bills were modified in the course of Queen Anne's reign, but the sessional percentage ranged from a low of 47 per cent in 1710 to a high of 86 per cent in 1711. Perhaps the most vivid index of the scale of intervention is provided by the fact that the percentage of bills that proceeded unaltered through the English Council was smaller than the percentage that was respited. Only 17 per cent of bills negotiated the Council without some amendment. The sessional percentage, which in 1711 was a mere 9 per cent, never achieved one-third; it came closest at 32 per cent in 1707 (Table Three; p. 161). Moreover, there is no identifiable pattern to the bills that negotiated the English Council unaltered. In 1703–04, they included measures for building parish churches, for reducing interest to 8 per cent, and for erecting a workhouse in Dublin.[121] In 1705, the main supply bill enjoyed the same experience.[122] Indeed, it was sometimes the case that measures it was anticipated would require substantial amendment were subject to few changes. A case in point is provided by the proposal for 'registering the popish clergy', which was referred in 1704 to a committee of the whole council so the law officers could 'amend the bill upon the debate'. In the event, two meetings produced four amendments, only one of which (appertaining to popish solicitors) was material.[123] What is apparent is that the disposition to amend Irish bills, strongly manifest during the early sessions of the 1703–11 parliament, weakened in 1705 and 1707 when a majority were subject to a reduced number of frequently minor amendments.[124] A similar claim can be

---

118. Such as the 1705 bill to 'make process of law or equity being served ...' (NA, PC2/80 f 312); the 1707 and 1709 measures for qualifying persons to be justices of the peace (PC2/81 f. 453; PC2/82 ff 347, 350); the 1710 measure appertaining to the renewing of leases (PC2/83 ff 14–5, 36).

119. Such as the 1710 proposal against 'the engrossing and monopolizing of coals imported into the city of Dublin' (NA, PC2/83 ff 14–5, 19, 36).

120. As well as the private bills cited in note 113 this may be true of the Harrison divorce bill, and is true of the Philip's bill, 1705 (NA, PC2/80 ff 329, 361); and the Rawdon and White bills, 1710 (PC2/83 ff 17, 36, 50, 51, 75, 77).   121. NA, PC2/80 ff 4, 6.

122. NA, PC2/80 ff 312, 353–5; *Commons Jn. (Irl.)*, 450, 460, 466, 468, 471, 472, 473, 478, 483.

123. NA, PC2/79 ff 484–7, 511, PC2/80 ff 31, 32; Fagan, *Catholics in a Protestant country*, p. 58.

124. In this category of measures that made it to law that experienced a small number of

made for 1709, but what is more striking about the latter half of Queen Anne's reign coinciding with the establishment of the Irish bills committee, is that the combined percentage of bills that were lost and amended, which had dipped during the middle years of Queen Anne's reign, reverted to the higher levels it had achieved earlier in the reign (Tables Two and Four).

Furthermore, it is apparent where major amendments were deemed appropriate that the English/British Council was in principle committed to approve their incorporation even when, as in the case of supply bills, it risked causing problems in Ireland. This was the case throughout the reign, and an examination of those bills that made it to the statute book illustrates that the Irish parliament in turn was not ill-disposed in principle to accept amendments, though here again supply bills were a source of particular difficulty. Examples of bills subject to amendment that were approved are readily identifiable. In 1703, proposals to 'make it high treason ... to impeach the succession of the crown', to 'prevent butchers being graziers and to redress severall abuses in buying and selling cattle', and for the recovery of small debts required a solid list of corrections, clarifications and improvements.[125] In 1705 and 1707 the addition of clauses directing that measures to 'prevent ingrossing of coals in the city of Dublin', to prevent horse-stealing, and to empower justices of the peace to determine disputes about servants wages should remain in force for five years proved acceptable even when, as in the latter two instances, these were among a host of alterations that in the case of the horse-stealing bill meant, as well as the title, the scope and content of the bill was substantially altered.[126] Two years later, in 1709, the Irish legislature took an equivalently indulgent attitude to the addition of lengthy clauses to measures to limit the privileges of parliament and to discourage abduction because they were consistent with the thrust of the heads as they were originally formed and because they redressed weaknesses in the Irish draft.[127] This was the case also with respect of the amendments made to the bills appertaining to the

---

amendments are 4 Anne, chap 7; NA, PC2/80 ff 312, 337 (rape seed duty bill); 4 Anne, chap 9; PC2/80 ff 318–19, 350 (planting and preserving timber trees bill); 4 Anne, chap 10; PC2/80 f. 351(fees bill); 4 Anne, chap 13; PC2/80 ff 312, 349–50 (debt prisoners relief bill); 4 Anne, chap 14; PC2/80 ff 318–19, 353 (regulating weights bill); 6 Anne, chap 1; PC2/81 ff 430–1, 436 (additional duties on ale and beer bill); 6 Anne, chap 2; PC2/81 ff 430–1, 437 (registering deeds bill); 6 Anne, chap 6; PC2/81 ff 430–1, 456 (papist solicitors bill); 6 Anne, chap 7; PC2/81 ff 430–1, 437 (sheriffs fees bill); 6 Anne, chap 10; PC2/81 ff 430–1, 436 (amendment of law bill); 6 Anne, chap 14; PC2/81 ff 430–1, 446 (marching soldiers bill); 6 Anne, chap 15; PC2/81 ff 438–9, 454 (secret outlawries amendment bill); 6 Anne, chap 17; PC2/81 ff 438–9, 455 (suppressing lotteries bill).

125. NA, PC2/79 ff 473–4, 479; PC2/80 ff 4, 7.

126. 4 Anne, chap 8; NA, PC2/80 ff 313, 343; *Commons Jn. (Irl.)*, ii, 466, 469, 470, 471, 479, 483 (coal bill); 4 Anne, chap. 11; PC2/80 ff 318–19, 350–1; *Commons Jn. (Irl.)*, ii, 427, 445, 466, 467, 470, 473, 474, 478, 483 (horse stealing bill); 6 Anne, chap 13; PC2/81 ff 430–1, 455–6; *Commons Jn. (Irl.)*, ii, 499, 501, 502, 510, 512, 549, 55, 558, 561, 567, 568 (servants' bill).

127. 6 Anne, chap 8; NA, PC2/81 ff 438–9, 446–7; *Commons Jn. (Irl.)*, ii, 493, 497, 499, 501, 512, 545, 548, 553, 554, 558, 559, 560 (privilege of parliament bill); 6 Anne, chap 16; PC2/81 ff

registration of deeds, bills of exchange, hempen and flax, and the union of parishes, though once again the number, size and import of the amendments made was extensive and, in respect of the last of the bills cited, altered the intent of the original proposal considerably.[128] A similar pattern can be identified with respect to the 1710 and 1711 sessions when, as well as bills experiencing commonplace 'verbal' clarifications, approval was forthcoming for bills that required the addition and deletion of full clauses that meant in cases, such as the 1710 houghers bill, that the focus of the measure was fundamentally altered. In this instance, the original bill was targeted at a number of baronies in County Galway, whereas the measure that made it to the statute book was national in its focus.[129]

Proportionately, a higher percentage of public bills (69 per cent) than private bills (54 per cent) were subject to amendment at the English/British Council board during Anne's reign (Tables Two and Three). Otherwise the pattern of amendment to private bills compares closely with that of public bills; in other words, some measures were subject to extensive amendment in order to eliminate technical and other weaknesses, while others experienced no more than a handful of syntactical clarifications.[130] In a majority of cases, the amendments were introduced because the law officers or other officials identified changes that would enhance the bill as presented or because they sought to bring the measure into line with existing British legislation. The latter function was perceived as one of the

430–31, 447; *Commons Jn. (Irl.)*, ii, 493, 498, 500, 506, 515, 417, 544, 546, 548, 551, 567, 568 (abduction bill).

128. 8 Anne, chap 10; NA, PC2/82 ff 347, 355, 360–62; *Commons Jn. (Irl.)*, ii, 577, 582, 586, 620, 621, 622, 633, 635 (registering of deeds amendment bill); 8 Anne, chap 11; PC2/82 ff 348, 358–9, 360–2; *Commons Jn. (Irl.)*, 598, 604, 620, 621, 622, 632, 635 (bills of exchange bill); 8 Anne, chap 12; PC2/82 ff 345, 372–5, 388; *Commons Jn. (Irl.)*, ii, 591, 603, 614, 615, 616, 626, 627, 628, 630, 631, 633, 635 (hemp and flax bill); 8 Anne, chap 13; PC2/82 ff 348, 357–8, 360–2; *Commons Jn. (Irl.)*, ii, 627, 629, 631, 632, 633, 635; *Lords Jn. (Irl.)*, ii, 300 (dissolving parish union bill).

129. 9 Anne, chap 6; NA, PC2/83 ff 14–15, 29–30; *Lords Jn. (Irl.)*, ii, 331, 338, 343; *Commons Jn. (Irl.)*, ii, 673, 675, 676, 685 (taking away benefit of clergy bill); 9 Anne, chap 7; PC2/83 ff 14–6, 30–31; *Commons Jn. (Irl.)*, ii, 650, 653, 663, 664, 671, 672, 673, 676, 685 (butchers and graziers bill); 9 Anne, chap 8; PC2/83 ff 14–16, 30–31; *Commons Jn. (Irl.)*, ii, 645, 659, 665, 668, 669, 671, 673, 674, 679, 685 (payment of rents bill); 9 Anne, chap 9; PC2/83 ff 14–6, 30; *Commons Jn. (Irl.)*, ii, 650, 651, 656, 666, 667, 670, 671, 673, 674, 680, 685 (highways and roads bill); 9 Anne, chap 11; PC2/83 ff 14–6, 31; *Commons Jn. (Irl.)*, ii, 647, 652, 662, 671, 672, 674, 675, 680, 685 (maiming of cattle bill); 11 Anne, chap 2; PC2/83 ff 291, 310, 313–15; *Commons Jn. (Irl.)*, ii, 699, 703, 704, 705, 707, 720, 721, 723, 724, 727, 735 (preventing frauds bill); 11 Anne, chap 3; PC2/83 ff 292, 311, 313–15; *Commons Jn. (Irl.)*, ii, 700, 710, 717, 718, 721, 722, 728, 732, 735 (guardians bill); 11 Anne, chap 4; PC2/83 ff 292, 318, 319, 323–5; *Commons Jn. (Irl.)*, ii, 705, 710, 714, 721, 722, 725, 727, 728, 730, 735 (coals bill).

130. 8 Anne, chap 2 (private); PC2/82 ff 366, 384–5, 388; *Commons Jn. (Irl.)*, ii, 589, 596, 600, 601, 602, 624, 625, 626, 627, 633, 635 (Bellew bill); 8 Anne, chap 5 (private); PC2/82 ff 366, 381–3, 388; *Commons Jn. (Irl.)*, ii, 606, 607, 609, 616, 624, 625, 632, 635 (Plunkett bill); 10 Anne, chap 1 (private); PC2/83 ff 17, 41, 43; *Commons Jn. (Irl.)*, ii, 679, 681, 682, 685 (Grandison bill).

key merits of Poynings' Law, but ministers were also amenable to the introduction of amendments at the behest of individuals and interest groups where there were solid grounds. The most effective way to bring such matters to the attention of the Council was by means of a petition, for though the proportion of bills that were the subject of a petition was modest, the success rate was encouragingly high. In all, 17, or 8 per cent, of the bills received at the English/British Council were subject to petition. Coincidentally, the number of public and private bills that were the subject of petitions was virtually the same, but because they were fewer in number the proportion of private bills (12 per cent) was almost double that of public bills (6.1 per cent: Tables Two and Three).

More than half the petitions were submitted in respect of anti-Catholic measures promoted by the Irish legislature. Though Catholics did not hesitate to lobby against these bills in Ireland and, in the specific instance of the 1709 amending act 'to prevent the further growth of popery', to petition the Irish House of Lords, the number of petitions presented at the English Council board in 1703, 1705 and 1707 is indicative of their appreciation that this route offered more prospect of success.[131] They were encouraged to do this by the fact that the considerable diplomatic pressure they were able to marshal was also directed towards London.[132] As it happened, the changed domestic as well as international environment meant that the Crown and ministers were not as responsive to pressure from this quarter in the early eighteenth century as they had been in the 1690s, but Catholics sustained this strategy never the less. They commenced in 1703 when Viscount Fitzwilliam, Lord Richard Bellew and the earl of Antrim presented a number of petitions against the proposals 'to prevent popish priests from coming into this kingdom' and 'to prevent the further growth of popery', and requesting permission to be heard. As was the norm in these circumstances the petition was referred to the law officers who tended to look benignly on such requests, but their impact was modest because of the sensitivities of Protestant opinion in Britain as well as in Ireland. It may be that the introduction of a clause in the former limiting its duration to fourteen years or to 'the end of the next session of parliament' was in response to Catholic lobbying, but this cannot be demonstrated, and it is apparent that their intervention had no impact in the case of the latter.[133] Two years later in 1705, when the Irish Commons sought approval for an amendment to the act of the previous session for registering the popish clergy, a petition was presented by George Mathew and Denis Malony on behalf

131. For opposition to the 1709 measure see *Lords Jn. (Irl.)*, ii, 296; *The case of the Roman Catholicks of Ireland, in relation to a bill intituled (an act for securing the Protestant interest of this kingdom by further amending the several acts of parliament made against papists, and to prevent the growth of popery ...* (Dublin, 1709).

132. See Fagan, *Divided loyalties*, pp 32–4; Fagan, *Catholics in a Protestant country*, p. 49; C. Giblin (ed.), 'Catalogue of Nunziatura di Fiandra', *Collectanea Hibernica*, 4 (1961), pp 90–106, 107, 110–11; ibid., 5 (1962), p. 8; ibid., 13 (1970), pp 76–7, 80, 83–4, 86–7; ibid., 15 (1972), pp 10–14.

133. NA, PC2/79 ff 414, 421, 475.

of Catholics 'comprised within the Articles of Limerick' complaining that the measure was in breach of the Treaty; as a result, a clause was introduced limiting the duration of the act to three years.[134] This was a victory of sorts for the Catholic lobbyists, and it may be that they were heartened thereby to intensify their efforts in 1707. On this occasion, a total of six petitions (from Sir Robert Roebuck and John Blake; George Mathew of Thurles; Lord Mountgarret and the earl of Fingall; the earl of Antrim; Lord Bellew and the countess of Newburgh; and Thomas Daly) were presented against a further proposal to remedy deficiencies in the 1704 growth of popery act, and one (from Oliver Weston, Francis Glascock and Peter Dayly) against an amendment to the act 'to prevent papists being solicitors'. The primary sources of concern with respect of the former appertained to the clauses requiring Catholic converts 'to take the sacramental test' in order to inhibit insincere outward conformity and registered Catholic clergy to take the oath of abjuration. Anxious that these objections should be addressed, the Queen instructed the law officers to 'consider the particular cases referred to them … and how far Protestants may be affected by the … bill'. As a result, the bill was extensively amended. With these additions, and a smaller number of technical corrections to the solicitors' bill, both were forwarded to return to Ireland.[135]

As well as Catholics, a variety of corporate and individual interests appealed to the right to petition to blunt or to resist objectionable measures. Significantly, they registered greater impact than Catholic interests at this point. Thus, the protest of the Hollow Blades Company in 1705 that a bill for 'making process in law or equity' would impose 'great hardship' on the agents and attorney of the Company was grounds enough to have the measure 'laid aside'.[136] In 1707, a petition from the Lord Mayor and city of Dublin appertaining to the construction of a ballast office prompted a major amendment to a measure relating to Dublin Harbour to meet their concerns, while in 1710 the contention of 'several masters and shipowners' that, as well as other difficulties, the proposed coals bill would hasten the ruin of 'the whole coal trade' in the city was sufficient to ensure that it was 'laid aside.[137] However, success was not invariable. In 1703 when the East India Company and the merchants, linen drapers and others trading with Ireland protested against 'a very high duty, amounting in effect to a prohibition' in one of the main supply bills, their objections were overruled. In this instance, Irish

---

134. NA, PC2/80 ff 312, 315, 335; 4 Anne, chap 2.
135. NA, PC/81 ff 430–1, 33; 6 Anne, chap, 6; NA, PC2/81 ff 438–9, 443, 445, 448, 451–2, 453, 456; Fagan, *Catholics in a Protestant country*, p. 58; Fagan, *Divided loyalties*, p. 28; King to Southwell, 2 Sept. 1707 (TCD, King papers, MS 750/3/2 ff 147–8).
136. NA, PC2/80 ff 315, 343.
137. 6 Anne, chap 20; NA, PC2/81 ff 430–31, 445, 460–61, 468 (Dublin harbour bill); PC2/83 ff 14–5, 19, 36 (coals bill). It is noteworthy that a representative of the Lowthers of Whitehaven protested against the measure to the Commissioners of Trade and Plantations (*Journal of the Commissioners for Trade and Plantations, 1709–15*, p. 168); James, 'The Irish lobby', pp 552–3.

revenue and political needs took priority, though a petition from the countess of Dorchester seeking an exemption from the pension tax provided for in the same bill was taken on board.[138]

Petitions presented by, or on behalf of, individuals featured more commonly with respect of private than public bills. Moreover, because they conveyed in a majority of instances the genuine concerns of family members, they were frequently favourably received. This was the case, for example, with the bill to 'prevent the disinheriting of Redmond Morres', which was virtually completely rewritten on foot of a petition by Sir John Morres.[139] In 1707, the Council intervened to protect the portion of Mary Nugent, the wife of Francis Bermingham, with respect of the estate of Anne, viscountess dowager of Clanmalier, but it was less responsive to the petitions of a number of other interests in this case and in the case of the Hackett family.[140] This was the pattern for the remainder of the reign; where a persuasive case was made, as instanced by the petition of John, Lord Baron Kingston and his son against an act for vesting the estate of Sir John King; or the petition of Charles Humphreys with respect of the Hammerton bill, appropriate action followed. In the case of the former, the bill was respited, whilst in the latter instance the bill was returned to Ireland in an amended form though it did not become law.[141] However, when a petition failed to convince, as occurred in 1711, when the honourable Henry Power requested that a private bill in favour of Anne, countess of Tyrone, should not pass because it was 'very prejudicial' to his interests, the Privy Council recommended that the bill should be returned to Ireland to become law if it was consented to by Power's father, Lord Power.[142]

While the submission of a written petition generally ensured that objections to a bill were fully considered by the Crown's law officers, oral testimony could be offered to supplement a petition. This was done on a number of occasions. In addition, there were a small number of instances in which oral testimony was received in which a written petition was not forthcoming. This was the case, for example, with John Podmore, the clerk of the crown and peace for the province of Leinster, who objected in person to a measure advanced from the House of Commons in 1705 'to prevent fees being taken in certain cases'.[143] It is not apparent that his concerns were met, though John Coghlan manifestly enjoyed better fortune some weeks later when he secured the insertion of a clause

---

138. NA, PC2/79 ff 473–4, 475, 480, 497–507; Wogan to Southwell, 1, 4 Jan. 1704 (BL, Southwell Papers, Add. MS 37673 ff 29, 31–2; James, 'The Irish lobby ', p. 551; McGrath, *Making the constitution*, pp 176–8.

139. 2 Anne, chap 6 (private); NA, PC2/79 ff 469–70; PC2/80 ff 31–2.

140. 6 Anne, chap 1 (private); NA, PC2/81 ff 432, 433, 462, 463 (Clanmalier bill); 6 Anne, chap 7 (private); PC2/81 ff 432–3, 461 (Hackett bill).

141. NA, PC2/83 ff 17, 18, 36 (King bill); PC2/83 ff 17, 18, 42–3, 44; *Commons Jn. (Irl.)*, ii, 680, 681 (Hammerton bill).

142. 11 Anne, chap 1 (private); NA, PC2/83 ff 293, 296, 318, 326–8.

143. 4 Anne, chap 10; NA, PC2/80 ff 312, 330–1; 351; *Commons Jn. (Irl.)*, ii, 466, 467, 470, 475, 483.

providing for his children by his second wife in the Coghlan bill; Sir John Morres' audience with respect of the Morres bill was also not without impact.[144] Perhaps the best-documented illustration of this less formalised lobbying in action, also dating from 1705, is provided by 'the hempen and flaxen manufacture' bill, which was strongly resisted by the bishops of the Church of Ireland because it proposed that half the tithes on flax and hemp should be surrendered for eleven years. Spearheaded by the archbishop of Dublin, William King's, tireless lobbying of councillors climaxed, not in a petition as one contemporary maintained but, in an invitation to state his case before the Council. It too was not without effect; the decision initially was to continue the measure 'in force for three years', but difficulties remained and the bill was sent back to be rewritten. The resulting measure was more to King's liking though the procedures employed in this instance, which involved input from Ireland, verged on the irregular.[145]

There was, in addition to this, still more informal lobbying of individual politicians and councillors that had no identifiable impact on the way in which the English/British Privy Council dealt with Irish bills. Some of this, as instanced by the involvement of the Hamburgh Company by the Commissioners of Trade and Plantations in 1710 were conducted within normal procedures. More of it was not, but it does not appear to have had direct influence on the deliberations of the Privy Council. What is indisputable is that a majority of the bills (174 out of 214) received from Ireland successfully negotiated this body. This represented a success rate of 81 per cent, and interestingly, the percentage of public bill that succeeded (85 per cent) was greater than the respective percentage for private bills (73 per cent; see Tables Two, Three and Four).

BILLS AT THE IRISH PARLIAMENT, 1703–13

Because every measure that negotiated the English/British Council had to be approved unaltered by the Irish parliament in order to receive the royal assent and become law, the Irish parliament possessed the right of veto over all bills. The Irish parliament, and particularly the Commons, threatened frequently to use this power in an active fashion by opposing amended supply bills in order to assert their sole right to initiate money bills. However, these instances apart, other than occasional rhetorical flourishes to the effect that it was a matter of principle with

---

144. 4 Anne, chap 5 (private); NA, PC2/80 ff 312, 328–9; 355; Commons Jn. (Irl.), ii, 466, 468, 470, 472, 478, 483 (Coghlan bill); 4 Anne, chap 8 (private); PC2/80 ff 318–19, 329 357; Commons Jn. (Irl.), ii, 467, 470, 472, 475, 479, 483 (Morres bill).

145. 4 Anne, chap 4; NA, PC2/80 ff 312, 335–6, 368–9; O'Regan, Archbishop William King, p. 150; King to Vigors, 20 Apr., King to Hickman, 24 Apr., King to Synge, 28 Apr., King to Abercorn, 28 Apr., King to York, 1 May, King to St George Ashe, 28 Apr. (TCD, King papers, MS 750/3/1/ff 157, 149, 152–4, 155–6, 159, 151); Green to Henry King, 28 Apr. (ibid., MS 1995–2008, f. 1078); Hedges to Ormonde, 31 May 1705 (NA, SP67/3 ff 114–5); Vigors to King, 16 June 1705 (Holloden Papers, Bagenalstown, Co. Carlow, NLI Special List 416).

both houses of the Irish parliament that they disapproved of bills that took their rise in the Irish Privy Council and of heads of bills that were returned to them with amendments, the Lords and Commons of Ireland did not single out either. This can be demonstrated statistically by the fact that though 79 per cent of bills were forwarded amended from the English Council, 74 per cent made it to the statute book.

This notwithstanding, when parliament met for the first time during Queen Anne's reign, the Irish administration was appropriately nervous lest the five Privy Council bills submitted by the administration should encounter stern opposition. In fact, all made it expeditiously through the Commons. The plus acres, and the tories and rapparees bills were held up for some time in the Lords, but each was approved eventually.[146] In view of the ongoing controversy over the Commons' claim to possess the 'sole right' to initiate money bills, the administration was particularly pleased that the excise bill was ushered into law with comparatively little fuss. A handful of MPs sought to revive 'the old dispute of the sole right' on its initial presentation on 1 October, but agreed to waive 'that matter in respect to her majesty and the present governor', and the bill's progress was not delayed.[147] Indeed, to the administration's pleasure, MPs embarked promptly on the process of proposing their own supply bills to provide the additional money necessary for the government of the country.[148]

This did not mean that the question of the 'sole right' or what Archbishop King tellingly termed 'the great abuse of Poynings' Law' was no longer a matter of concern. Indeed, King maintained in 1707 that the intervention of the Irish Council 'to put our bills in form to be sent into England [was] quite contrary to the meaning of the act, which speaks nothing of the Privy Council but the Council of the realm which is altogether different'.[149] It was an issue on which strong opinions continued to be avowed, for when in 1709 the English Council amended a provision in the money bill that proposed to locate 'arms, ammunition and other warlike stores for the militia of this kingdom' in 'arsenals in the several provinces of this kingdom' by centralising storage 'in or near the city of Dublin',

---

146. For the supply act see p. 121. The others were an act for the encouragement of iron and staves (2 Anne, chap 2) which received the royal assent on 16 October (*Commons Jn. (Irl.)*, ii, 338); an act to prevent popish priests from coming into this kingdom (2 Anne, chap 3) which received the royal assent on 16 October (*Commons Jn. (Irl.)*, ii, 339); an act for quieting possessions and disposing of the undisposed and plus acres (2 Anne, chap 8) which received the royal assent on 4 March 1704 (*Commons Jn. (Irl.)*, ii, 414); and an act for continuing two acts against tories, robbers and rapparees (2 Anne, chap 13) which received the royal assent on 4 March (*Commons Jn. (Irl.)*, ii, 414).

147. [Southwell] to [Nottingham], 2, 16 Oct., Ormonde to Nottingham, 9 Oct. 1703 in *Cal. SP (Dom.)*, *1703–4*, pp 141, 160, 150; *Commons Jn. (Irl.)*, 325, 327, 330, 334, 338, 339.

148. [Southwell] to [Nottingham], 16 Oct., 23, 27 Nov., Nottingham to Ormonde, 25 Oct. in *Cal. SP (Dom.)*, *1703–4*, pp 160, 211, 216–18, 176; Nottingham to Ormonde, 26 Oct., Nottingham to Southwell, 26 Oct., 1703 (NA, SP67/3 f. 80). This skeletal account of a complex political as well as administrative process can be followed in McGrath, *Making the constitution*, pp 158–76.

149. King to Weymouth, 28 Mar. 1707 (TCD, King Papers, MS 750/2 f. 108).

former 'sole right' men were to the fore in challenging the alteration as an attack on the 'poor remains of our constitution'. The positions taken at this time were greatly complicated by intra and inter-party rivalry, but the larger question of constitutional principle was articulated by Stephen Ludlow, MP for Dunleer, who argued that the Commons should throw out such bills since this 'was the only method the house could make use of to show their resentment of such usage'. Others favoured comparing all money bills transmitted and returned since 1688; still others suggested 1661. The calculation of those who agitated this point at the time seems to have been that it was only by exposing the alterations to successive money bills and by 'exert[ing] the power of a negative … so often as the Queen and Council should exert their power of altering a bill especially if it related to money' that the Commons would be enabled 'to hinder Poynings' Law from doing all the mischief that it might do'. However, a majority of MPs were disinclined towards confrontation. They accepted the 'precedents' cited by 'those for the government' that 'an alteration in money bills was no new thing', and despite the ringing complaints of 'several zealous patriots' that 'the constitution was run through' the bill was approved.[150]

This was a relief to the secretary of state, the Earl of Sunderland, who was disposed to the view that because the Irish parliament 'do every day something or other to evade Poynings' Law, which has been the great security to keep that kingdom dependent upon the crown of England', MPs aspired both to 'effect an independency from England and to putt their parliament upon the same foot with your parliament of Great Britain'.[151] This was incorrect, and had ministers analysed the reception accorded the generality of bills returned to Ireland from the English Council, rather than take alarm at individual manifestations of dissatisfaction, they might have established more secure grounds for concern in the number of bills returned from England that did not make it to the Irish statute book. In all, 129 (87 public and 42 private) bills were granted the royal assent of the 174 (125 public and 49 private) bills that were returned to Ireland. This meant that 45 (26 per cent) of the total did not become law. Significantly, the percentage of public bills (30 per cent) that failed was more than double the percentage of private bills (14 per cent). Not surprisingly, given that the pattern of law-making identified above, 31 (69 per cent) fell at the Commons; 6 (13 per cent) failed to negotiate the Lords, and 8 (18 per cent) were not reintroduced (Tables Two and Four).

Perhaps the most unexpected feature of the bills that failed at this stage is that one cannot make a strong link with the number and importance of the

---

150. 8 Anne, chap 2; NA, PC2/82 ff 347, 353, 360–1; Sunderland to Wharton, 18 July (SP67/3 ff 205–6); Addison to Sunderland, 2, 6, 10, 12 Aug. 1709 (BL, Blenheim Papers, Add. MS 61636 ff 48, 50, 52–3, 54–5); Robins to Howard, 13 Aug. 1709 (NLI, Wicklow Papers, PC226–7); Connolly, *Religion, law and power*, p. 83; McGrath, *Making the constitution*, pp 222–9.

151. Boyle to Wharton, 9 Aug., Sunderland to Wharton, 12 June (NA, SP67/3 ff 208–9, 200–1); Godolphin to Marlborough, [16 Aug.1709] in G.L. Synder (ed.), *The Marlborough-Godolphin Correspondence* (3 vols, Oxford, 1975), iii, 134–6.

modifications introduced at the Irish or English Council boards. Indeed, in a surprising number of instances, bills that ran into difficulty sported few amendments. A case in point is the private bill for the relief of Walter Butler, which was rejected in 1704 because it was inconsistent with the 'severe law against popery' that had recently been approved and not because it was amended. In other instances, the reason a bill failed bore no connection to the amendments introduced at the English Council; for example, the heavily amended bill for the sale of John Browne's estate was lost in 1704 on a technicality – it ran out of time.[152] Overall, seven bills that negotiated the English Council unamended, and more than double the number that experienced modest verbal amendments failed to receive the royal assent in Ireland on their return. This is a high figure and, tempting as it may be, one cannot assume that these bills encountered problems because of amendments introduced at the Irish Council board. This was the case in some instances; the 1703–4 measure to prevent the illegal raising of money by grand juries was rejected by MPs because the Irish Council modified the penalty for judges that confirmed an 'illegal presentment'; and the blasphemy and profanity bill of the same session was lost because the Irish Council imposed a penalty of £1000 which was deemed 'too high'.

It is the case, however, that a significant number of bills failed because of resistance to amendments introduced at Whitehall; this appertained in the cases of the frauds and bankrupts bill of 1709, and the Hammerton private bill and the tobacco running bill of 1710.[153] More famously, the attempt in 1707 to amend the 1703–4 act to prevent the further growth of popery was rejected on its return because an amendment introduced at the English Council to allow a Catholic sell land to Protestants nullified a 'useful clause in the previous act' aimed at securing the rights of inheritance of Protestant heirs.[154] In other instances, bills were rejected by the Commons because they conferred powers that were deemed 'arbitrary and dangerous' (the 1703–4 bill for regulating sheriffs fees fits this category); because they were 'too severe' (for example, the oath taking bill of the same session);[155] or because they contained provisions extending the jurisdiction of the ecclesiastical courts (the blasphemy and profanity measures of 1703–4 and 1709) or the Privy Council (the 1711 tillage bill).[156] A number of bills also failed because of opposition to clauses introduced to satisfy pressure groups such as the

152. Southwell to Nottingham, 4 Mar. 1704 in *Cal. SP (Dom.)*, *1703–4*, pp 557–8; NA, PC2/79 ff 484–7, 497–507, PC2/80 ff 33–5; *Commons Jn. (Irl.)*, 412, 413.
153. NA, PC2/82 ff 365, 376–80, 388; *Commons Jn. (Irl.)*, ii, 627, 629, 631, 632 (bankrupts bill); PC2/83 ff 17, 18, 26, 28, 42–3, 44; *Commons Jn. (Irl.)*, ii, 680, 681 (Hammerton bill); PC2/83 ff 14–15, 21, 37–8, 40; *Commons Jn. (Irl.)*, ii, 676 (tobacco bill).
154. Hayton, 'Ireland and the English ministers', p. 132; Connolly, *Religion, law and power*, pp 276–7.
155. Southwell to Nottingham, 4 Mar. 1704 in *Cal. SP (Dom.)*, *1703–04*, pp 557–8; Wogan to Southwell, 20 Jan. 1704 (BL, Southwell Papers, Add. MS 37673 f. 61); *Commons Jn. (Irl.)*, ii, 404, 405, 406, 408, 409, 411 (for 1703–4 bills).
156. *Commons Jn. (Irl.)*, ii, 623, 624, 625, 631; Addison to Sunderland, 25 Aug. 1709 (BL, Blenheim Papers, Add. MS 61630 f. 64) (1709 blasphemy and profanity bill); NA, PC2/83 ff 324–5; D.W.

exemption provided for Dublin in the measure 'for the better regulation of all markets' and the restriction on the rights of exportation in the flax and hemp bill, both from 1703–4.[157] In addition, bills relating to the Church of Ireland, the duties and perquisites appertaining to offices, and debt and bankruptcy were especially vulnerable; and four of the eight bills returned but not presented to the Irish parliament fit this profile; two sought to introduce residency requirements for clergy and two appertained to the ever-contentious matter of fines and fees.[158]

The rejection by the Irish parliament of between 3 and 11 bills every session during the reign of Queen Anne contributed to ensure that the sessional legislative outcome never exceeded 30 statutes and was generally less than 20. While this was a modest return from the 385 legislative initiatives that took their rise during the reign and the 214 received at the English/British Council, the fact remains that 129 enactments were made in the course of the reign. This is the most salient testament to the capacity of Poynings' Law and the complex legislative procedures it spawned to accommodate the increased determination of Protestants in Ireland to make law for the kingdom consistent with the continuing commitment of English ministers 'to keep that kingdom dependent upon the crown of England'.[159]

CONCLUSION

An average of 18.4 bills were passed into law per session during Queen Anne's reign. Since this is less than the 21 registered during the reigns of William and Mary and William III, it could be argued that the process of law-making for Ireland was both less effective and less efficient between 1703 and 1713, but this is not a conclusion that can easily be sustained (Table One). Indeed, if one exempts the 'bungled' 1713 session, the sessional average of the two reigns is virtually indistinguishable.[160] Moreover, the total corpus of law made during the reign of Queen Anne was more than 50 per cent larger than was made during the previous reign, and it embraced a wider range of issues. Significantly, this included the ratification of further disabilities against Catholics and the development of the process whereby the Irish parliament provided the funds necessary to pay for the government of Ireland. The enactment of legislation in respect of both matters was frequently only achieved in the teeth of strong resistance in Ireland. But the fact that they reached the statute book meant that by

Hayton (ed.), 'An Irish diary in reign of Queen Anne', *Analecta Hibernica*, 30 (1982), pp 110–17; King to Annesley, 22 Oct. 1711 (TCD, King Papers, MS 2531 f. 358) (1711 tillage bill).

157. Southwell to Nottingham, 4 Mar. 1704 in *Cal. SP (Dom.)*, *1703–4*, pp 557–8.

158. PC2/80 ff 318–9, 352; King to Vigors, 9 June, King to Lord Chancellor Cox, 12 June 1705 (TCD, King Papers, MS 750/3/1 ff 178, 181–2) (union of parishes bill); PC2/81 ff 438–9, 450–1 (Tuam bill); PC2/83 ff 291, 310–11, 313–15 (1711 fees bill).

159. Sunderland to Wharton, 12 June 1709 (NA, SP, 67/3 ff 200–1).

160. Simms, 'The Irish parliament of 1713' in Simms, *War and politics in Ireland*, p. 286.

the end of Queen Anne's reign Irish Protestants not only possessed a recognised right to make law for Ireland, but also had initiated a body of anti-Catholic regulations to meet their concerns on that point and they had asserted their claim to raise the main supply bills that provided the finance to pay for the administration of the kingdom.[161] In return, parliament agreed not just to provide the money, but even to approve supplementary short money bills when they were required to protect against a revenue shortfall. Moreover, it was accepted in practice, if not always in argument, that the Irish Privy Council could initiate legislation and that the Irish and English/British Privy Councils could respite and amend legislation rising with it.

Of course, tensions and resentments remained, and these were capable of spilling over and generating crises and difficulties virtually without warning particularly in respect of amended supply bills and Privy Council bills, which were precisely the points on which Irish MPs sought to assert their legislative authority. Because the outcome in a majority of instances during Queen Anne's reign was nothing more than the loss of an item or a few items of legislation, a majority of these 'crises' were short lived and without major legacy. None the less, their loss was not without consequence – individual as well as national. Thus the repeated refusal of the English/British Council to allow the extension of the right of *habeas corpus*, to export agricultural commodities on the same terms as Englishmen – to cite but two instances – struck at the constitutional rights of Irish subjects and at the commercial rights of the kingdom as a whole. This rankled, and while resentments were kept within tolerable bounds during Anne's reign, they did not go away. Indeed, significantly, the last meeting of parliament – the brief and difficult short session held over four weeks between 25 November and 24 December 1713 – concluded with a row as to whether Poynings' Law legally entitled the Irish Privy Council to alter heads of bills. The context was provided by the requirement (uncontested on all sides) that the Irish Council was obliged to transmit a number of bills to its British equivalent 'in order to the calling of a new parliament'. Pursuant to this, the Irish Council prepared two bills, one of which was the obligatory money bill, and transmitted them in September 1713. Approved with 'some small amendments', and returned 'annexed to the commission [issued] under the great seal of Great Britain for calling and holding a new parliament', the proposal 'for the better preventing … fire' was rejected by the Irish parliament.[162] Significantly, the short money bill was ratified, but not before it was caught up in a further round of party conflict as a result of which MPs headed by the prominent Tory Mathew Forde, the MP for Downpatrick, requested leave to introduce the heads of a bill 'for the better regulating the

161. For studies of this see Maureen Wall, *The penal laws, 1691–1760* (Dundalk, 1976); McGrath, *Making the constitution*, chapters 5–7.

162. King to Annesley, 14 Nov. 1713 (TCD, King Papers, MS 750/4 f. 134); Bolingbroke to Lords Justices, 14 Sept. (2), 3 Oct. (NA, SP67/4 ff 85, 87); NA, PC2/84 ff 241; *Commons Jn. (Irl.)*, ii, 743, 753, 765, 768.

manner of preparing and transmitting heads of bills'. His object was to embarrass the Whigs, and to this end Tories argued that the power claimed by the Irish Council to alter bills 'sent to them from either House of Parliament before the Council transmits them for England' was 'highly prejudicial to the country, because Her Majesty on some occasions could not know the sense of her people through the alterations their bills, after they had passed the Lords and the Commons, might meet with at the board'. Forde's object was for Irish heads of bills to be transmitted intact to England, and for the Irish Council's amendments to be sent separately. There was some support in principle for the idea of altering Poynings' Law since it acted 'against the interest of the Kingdom and [as] a great cramp on the constitution', but the realisation that there was no prospect of any alteration being achieved caused Forde to drop the motion.[163] This outcome, dissatisfying as it was in many respects, symbolised the reality of the impact Poynings' Law had on the making of law in Ireland; it was, as many MPs acknowledged, an encumbrance that greatly complicated the process, but it was unlikely to be amended since so long as 'it was an advantage, the crown would hardly part with it'.[164] Indeed, the royal instruction conveyed via the British Privy Council by Queen Anne on 31 July 1710 that the Irish parliament should prepare a bill to encourage clerical residence indicated how more difficult the situation could have been.[165] In this context, the refinements made to the application of Poynings' law between 1703 and 1713 not alone improved its operation they affirmed rather than diluted the role of the Irish legislature in law making and, thereby, demonstrated that there was no good reason why it should not continue.

163. NA, PC2/84 ff 241–3; *Commons Jn. (Irl.)*, ii, 757, 758, 761, 762, 767, 768, 769, 772, 774; D.W.
       Hayton (ed.), 'An Irish parliamentary diary in the reign of Queen Anne' in *Analecta Hibernica*,
       30 (1982), pp 128–9; McGrath, *Making the constitution*, pp 269–70, 274–5.
164. Hayton (ed.), 'An Irish parliamentary diary', p. 128.
165. NA, PC2/83 f. 44.

TABLE ONE
LEGISLATIVE OUTPUT OF THE IRISH PARLIAMENT, 1660–1800

Monarch	Public bills	Private bills	Total	Number of sessions	Average per session
Charles II, 1661–6	46	8	54	5	10.8
William and Mary, 1692–4; William III, 1695–9	62	22	84	4	21
Anne, 1703–13	87	42	129	7	18.4
George I, 1715–26	95	36	131	6	21.8
George II, 1727–59	325	58	383	17	22.53
George III, 1761–1782	415	73	488	13	37.53
George III, 1783–1800	976	81	1057	18	58.7

Source: Irish Statutes.

TABLE TWO

THE LEGISLATION OF THE IRISH PARLIAMENT, 1703–13: PUBLIC BILLS

| | Ireland — Origins of (heads of) bills | | | Ireland — Lost heads of bills | | | | England — Irish Privy Council bills and heads of bills at the Privy Council | | | | | | Ireland — Bills at the Irish parliament | | | |
Session	Privy Council bills	House of Commons heads	House of Lords heads	House of Commons Leave only	House of Commons Rejected	House of Lords	Privy Council	Received	Respited/postponed	Amendments	No amendments	Petitions against	Approved	Not presented	Rejected Commons	Rejected House of Lords	Received royal assent
1703*	11	55	10	19	12	2	9	34	5	24	5	3	29	1	8	1	19
1705	7	39	2	5	10	2	8	23	5	15	3	2	18	3	1		14
1707	8	31	3	5	2	1	5	29	2	20	7	3	27	1	5	1	20
1709	3	37	10	4	16	2	6	22	3	15	4		19		5	1	13
1710	2	25	5	5	5		2	20	6	10	4	1	14		2		12
1711	5	18	4	3	3	1	3	17	1	15	1		16	2	3	3	8
1713	2	15	2	10	4		3	2		2			2		1		1
Total	**38**	**220**	**36**	**51**	**52**	**8**	**36**	**147**	**22**	**101**	**24**	**9**	**125**	**7**	**25**	**6**	**87**

Sources: NA, Privy Council Registers, PC2/78–84; Privy Council papers, PC1; Commons Journals (Irl.); Lords Journals (Irl.).
* The Privy Council bill to prevent the growth of popery, though not formally presented, is included as it was considered at the British Council and returned restructured.

TABLE THREE

THE LEGISLATION OF THE IRISH PARLIAMENT, 1703–13: PRIVATE BILLS

	Ireland							England						Ireland			
	Origins of (heads of) bills			Lost heads of bills				Irish Privy Council bills and heads of bills at the Privy Council						Bills at the Irish parliament			
				House of Commons		House of Lords	Privy Council								Rejected		
Session	Privy Council bills	House of Commons heads	House of Lords heads	Leave only	Rejected			Received	Respited/postponed	Amendments	No amendments	Petitions against	Approved	Not presented	Commons	House of Lords	Received royal assent
1703	9	22	1	7	8			17	5	11	1	1	12	1	2		9
1705	4	11		2				13	2	8	3	1	11		3		8
1707	5	6					2	9	1	3	5	2	8				8
1709	4	7	1	1	1	1		9	3	4	2	1	6				6
1710	11	4	1		1	1		14	7	6	1	2	7				6
1711	2	2	1					5		4	1	1	5		1		5
1713																	
Total	**35**	**52**	**4**	**10**	**10**	**2**	**2**	**67**	**18**	**36**	**13**	**8**	**49**	**1**	**6**		**42**

Sources: NA, Privy Council Registers, PC2/1; Privy Council papers, PC1; Commons Journals (Irl.); Lords Journals (Irl.).

TABLE FOUR

THE LEGISLATION OF THE IRISH PARLIAMENT, 1703–13: PUBLIC AND PRIVATE BILLS

	Ireland							England						Ireland			
	Origins of (heads of) bills			Lost heads of bills				Irish Privy Council bills and heads of bills at the Privy Council						Bills at the Irish parliament			
				House of Commons		House of Lords	Privy Council								Rejected		
Session	Privy Council bills	House of Commons heads	House of Lords heads	Leave only	Rejected			Received	Respited/postponed	Amendments	No amendments	Petitions against	Approved	Not presented	Commons	House of Lords	Received royal assent
1703	20	77	11	26	20	2	9	51	10	35	6	4	41	2	10	1	28
1705	11	50	1	7	10	1	8	36	7	23	6	3	29	3	4		22
1707	13	37	3	5	2	1	7	38	3	23	12	5	35	1	5	1	28
1709	7	44	11	5	17	3	6	31	6	19	6	1	25		5	1	19
1710	13	29	6	5	6	1	2	34	13	16	5	3	21	2	3		18
1711	7	20	5	3	3	1	3	22	1	19	2	1	21		3	3	13
1713	2	15	2	10	4		3	2		2			2		1		1
Total	**73**	**272**	**40**	**61**	**62**	**10**	**38**	**214**	**40**	**137**	**37**	**17**	**174**	**8**	**31**	**6**	**129**

Sources: NA, Privy Council Registers, PC2/1; Privy Council papers, PC1; *Commons Journals (Irl.)*; *Lords Journals (Irl.)*.

TABLE FIVE

THE EXPERIENCE OF PRIVY COUNCIL BILLS, BY SESSION, 1703–13

Session	1703–04		1705		1707		1709		1710		1711		1713		Total
Type of bill	Public	Private	Public	Private	Public	Private	Public	Private	Public	Private	Public	Private	Public	Private	
Number proposed	11	9	7	4	8	5	3	4	2	11	5	2	2	–	73
Number enacted	7	4	3	3	4	4	2	2	–	5	0	2	1	–	37
Number lost	4	5	4	1	4	1	1	2	2	6	5	–	1	–	36
Sessional total: proposed/enacted/lost	20/11/9		11/6/5		13/8/5		7/4/3		13/5/8		7/2/5		2/1/1		73/37/36

CHAPTER FOUR

An efficient arrangement: the operation of Poynings' Law under the early Hanoverians, 1715–60

THE ADMINISTRATIVE REFINEMENTS to the operation of Poynings' Law introduced during the reign of Queen Anne (1703–14) were honed by practice during the reigns of the first two Hanoverians. Spanning 23 sessions (6 during the reign of George I, 1714–27 and 17 during the reign of his son George II, 1727–60) held over a period of 45 years, Poynings' Law was applied with greater consistency during this period than during any phase in its history to date. This is not to imply that these sessions were predictable. For one thing, the number of acts admitted to the statute book oscillated sharply from a low of three during the contentious 1753 session to a high of 31 during the more business-like 1715–16 and 1735–36 sessions (Table Eight; p. 244). The average was 22.35, which was four more per session than was ratified during Queen Anne's reign (Table 1). As a result, the volume of Irish-made law increased greatly during the early Hanoverian period, though the application of Poynings' Law was not without incident, constitutional as well as administrative, and, inevitably, it had its share of critics. They are more readily identifiable, for obvious reasons, in Ireland than in England, but in an environment where the Westminster legislature was prepared in 1720 to assert its entitlement to make law for Ireland but disinclined thereafter to exercise that authority in a manner that significantly impeded or impinged upon the law-making function of the Irish legislature, the procedures provided for under Poynings' Law represented an effective accommodation of the respective ideals of Irish and English political opinion.[1] Moreover, those involved in the making of Irish law on both sides of the Irish Sea were largely content withthis arrangement because, the occasional assertions to the contrary notwithstanding, they were prepared to live with inconsistency in principle as well as with complexity in practice if this was the price of sustaining a secure Anglo-Irish connection and maintaining the ascendancy of the Protestant interest in Ireland.

1. A.G. Donaldson, 'The application in Ireland of English and British legislation made before 1800' (QUB, PhD, 1952), pp 222–56; J.C. Beckett [and A.G. Donaldson], 'The Irish parliament in the eighteenth century', *Belfast Natural History Society Proceedings*, 2nd series, 4 (1950–4), pp 29–37; Julian Hoppitt, *Failed legislation, 1660–1800: extracted from the Commons and Lords journals* (London, 1997).

This also accounts for their ambivalent response to attempts to legislate for Ireland at Westminster. There was, for example, no objection in Ireland in 1714 to the initiative of the British House of Lords in April to offer a reward for the apprehension 'alive or dead' of the Pretender if he should 'land or attempt to land in any part either of Great Britain or Ireland', and in June to deem it 'traitorous' to enlist men in Ireland 'to serve' in the Jacobite cause.[2] However, the response to the introduction, also in 1714, of a clause into a bill that sought to strike at the root of religious schism by diminishing the rights of dissenters in Ireland was quite different. Disinclined in principle to 'approve of your imposing that [the schism bill] or anything on the people of Ireland by a law to which they are no[t] partys', Archbishop King protested that any attempt

> to bind our liberty, property or conscience by laws where we have no representatives and where the dependence of Ireland is not concerned I take to be against the constitution or fundamental maxims of our nations … .[3]

This was not a view unique to King, but while some Irish Protestants were disposed reflexively to conclude that legislation appertaining to Ireland or to Irish interests introduced at Westminster must prove deleterious, others lobbied for, or for the amendment of such legislation. For example, when an amendment to the British act for naturalising foreign Protestants was considered at Westminster in 1723 and 1724, a number of memorials and petitions were forthcoming from Ireland requesting that this should not be done in a manner that advantaged the 'numerous issue of papists bred in principles destructive of our constitution in church and state'. Moreover, when this was not done to their satisfaction, the same interests promoted the adoption by the Irish parliament of the heads of a bill exempting 'the children or issue of any person who was born in Ireland, and was guilty of and concerned in the late rebellion in that kingdom'.[4] Interventions of this kind were uncommon, but the fact that they occurred is indicative of the ability of Irish Protestants to use the powers provided by Poynings' Law to advance their own legislative agenda, while ministers and councillors in Britain relied on the law to ensure that the legislative aspirations of Irish Protestants mirrored their image of a dependent Ireland.

2. Protestant Succession and Pretender, 5 Apr., Enlistment of soldiers act, 24 June 1714 in HMC, *House of Lords MSS*, n.s., x, 274–5, 371–2.

3. King to Annesley, 3 July 1714 (TCD, King Papers, MS 750/4 f. 176). For the schism bill see Clyve Jones and Geoffrey Holmes (eds), *The London diaries of William Nicolson, bishop of Carlisle, 1702–18* (Oxford, 1985), pp 605–6, 612; HMC, *House of Lords MSS*, n.s., x, 341, 345–7.

4. Lords Justices to Carteret, 4 Feb., Carteret to Law Officers and enclosed heads, 26 Mar. 1723 (NA, SP63/380); Carteret to Grafton, 26 Mar. 1723, 7 Mar. 1724 (NA, SP67/7 ff 143–4, 162); Grafton to Carteret, 28 Feb. 1724 (NA, SP63/383); Carteret to [ ], 8 Dec. 1724 (NA, SP67/8 ff 30–1).

THE IRISH PRIVY COUNCIL IN THE EARLY HANOVERIAN PERIOD

The death on 1 August 1714 of Queen Anne transformed the political landscape in Britain and Ireland, as the inauguration of the Hanoverian succession effectively negated the *raison d'être* of the party system that had flourished during Anne's reign.[5] George I was less attentive than his predecessor to administrative and political detail, but his subscription to an oath to 'preserve the settlement of the true Protestant religion' augured well for a continuation of the pattern of law-making that responded to the security agenda of the Protestant interest in Ireland.[6] This was a priority with the supporters of the new regime as the Tories, who had exercised a powerful, and contentious, sway in the corridors of power during the latter years of Anne, reluctantly passed the political baton to the Whigs. This was vividly and, as far as the making of law and future governance of the kingdom was concerned, tellingly demonstrated when the Tory-dominated Privy Council of Ireland refused to acquiesce in the appointment of a Whig lord mayor for Dublin though this was the wish of the English ministry.[7] Advised that 'Ireland will not be quieted until his majesty is pleased to alter the Council', the government determined on its dissolution and, following the issue of the order by George I on 30 September, a new Council was constituted in 'which all the persons who have acted irregularly in the great affair of the city of Dublin are left out'. Comprising 56 members, which was three more than there were at the time of Anne death, 25 were first-time appointees. Inevitably, they included, in the words of Archbishop King, some 'of the greatest note and fortune in the kingdom', but the initial optimism with which he greeted their appointment soon gave way to disquiet.[8] King's disquiet was fuelled by his perception that because most were 'strangers to the business' at the board and no more than '14 or 15 are in Ireland', the Council was ill-equipped to perform its essential duties. His fears seemed well-founded when the attendance at the early meetings, which took place in the Council chamber in a new complex of buildings at Dublin Castle designed by the surveyor general, Thomas Burgh, was 'very thin'. King was so perturbed he alerted the chief secretary, Joseph Addison, to the advisability of nominating 'some that are likely to be constant attendants', but this was not acted upon.[9] It

5. Linda Colley, *In defiance of oligarchy: the Tory party, 1714–60* (Cambridge, 1982); Hayton, *Ruling Ireland*, pp 85–95 and passim.
6. NA, PC2/85 f. 85.
7. For background see D.W. Hayton, 'The crisis in Ireland and the disintegration of Queen Anne's last ministry, 1712–14', *IHS*, 22 (1981), pp 193–215; McNally, *Parties, patriots and politics'*, pp 69–70; idem, 'The Hanoverian accession and the Tory party in Ireland', *Parliamentary History*, 14 (1995), pp 263–83.
8. McNally, *Parties, patriots and undertakers*, p. 70; Stanley to King, 17 Sept., Sunderland to King, 1 Oct. 1714 (TCD, King Papers, MS 1995–2008 ff 1520, 1526); George I to Irish Council, 30 Sept. 1714 (NA, SP67/6 ff 1–2); Privy Council of Ireland, 1714 (BL, Blenheim Papers, Add. MS 61630 f. 101).
9. NAI, Military entry book, 1711–13, MS 2553, ff 80, 82, 93; Petition of minister of St.

did not prove necessary; attendance oscillated between twelve and twenty during the parliamentary session, which was ample to permit the Council to fulfil its responsibilities in respect of the initiation and certification of Irish bills.[10]

The fact that the Council increased steadily in size during the reign of George I and the first half of that of George II served also to diminish the need for additional appointments. The precise configuration of the pattern of appointing to the Council remains to be delineated but its membership, which numbered 66 in 1725, fell to 60 in the late 1720s before the addition of 17 members between 1729 and 1733 briefly raised its ranks to an unprecedented 74. It subsequently contracted, as deceased councillors were not replaced.[11] Indeed, Lord Chesterfield's observation in 1746 that 'the Council door has not been opened … [for] seven or eight years' when he oversaw the addition of eight new members is indicative of a trend that caused the Council, which had already contracted to 65 by 1739, to fall further to 59 by 1761.[12] Though a body of this size was, Primate Boulter argued reasonably in 1729, still too large for efficiency or easy management, the main problem with the Council was less its size than the 'great many unnecessary members who … never attend', with the result that it was not possible always 'to make up a quorum'. In order to address this problem as well as to advance his own anglicising vision, Boulter urged in the late 1720s that 'the English interest' should be reinforced. He was enabled to make some progress by ensuring that the Englishmen he ushered onto the upper reaches of the judicial and ecclesiastical benches were also elevated to the Privy Council, though the composition of the body remained overwhelmingly Irish because it suited successive lords lieutenant to promote Irishmen to appease the demand of the Protestant interest for preferment.[13]

As this suggests, the Irish Council during the Hanoverian era was composed of a combination of the holders of the major offices of state, four or more members of the ecclesiastical bench of the Church of Ireland, a substantial number of peers of the realm, and a smattering of eminent commoners who achieved membership by virtue of their stature as borough-owners or influence in the House of

Werburgh's, June 1715 (NAI, Irish Correspondence, 1697–1798, ii, MS 2447 f. 171); King to Addison, 9, 14 Oct., 9 Nov. 1714 (TCD, King Papers, MS 750/4 ff 220, 221, 225).

10. McNally, *Parties, patriots and undertakers*, p. 50. The attendance at other times varied greatly, based on the evidence of the number of signatures appended to proclamations.

11. Ibid., p. 50; List of Irish Privy Council, 9 Jan. 1725 (NA, SP67/8 ff 35–6); Boulter to Newcastle, 10 Mar. 1729 in *Letters written by Hugh Boulter, lord primate of all Ireland* (2 vols, Dublin, 1770), p. 286; List of the Lords and others of the Irish Privy Council, 23 Aug. 1733 (NA, SP63/396).

12. F.E. Ball, 'Some notes on the judges of Ireland in the year 1739', *Journal of the Royal Society of Antiquaries of Ireland*, 34 (1904), p. 27; Chesterfield to Newcastle, 11 Mar. 1746 (NA, SP, 63/409); A list of the Irish Privy Council, [June 1761] (PRONI, Wilmot Papers, T3019/4121).

13. Burns, *Irish parliamentary politics*, i, 261; McNally, *Parties, patriots and undertakers*, p. 52; King to Southwell, 3 Oct. 1727 (TCD, King Papers, MS 750/9 f. 30); Boulter to Newcastle, 26 Aug. 1727, 16 Jan. 1728, 10 Mar. 1729 in *Boulter letters*, i, 157–8, 167–8, 285–6; Chesterfield to Newcastle, 11 Mar. 1746 (NA, SP63/409).

Commons. It was, Primate Boulter repeatedly emphasised, not a combination best calculated to protect, and even less to advance the interests of England in Ireland. Moreover, many peers as well as commoners were appointed in the full realisation that they were unlikely to prove effective councillors.[14] The expectation was that the men of business, and particularly the judiciary, would carry their less informed colleagues, which accounts for Boulter's preoccupation with ensuring that Englishmen were well represented among the main judicial officeholders in the land.[15] It was a concern endorsed by Edward Willes, who was chief baron of the Court of Exchequer for nine years between 1757 and 1766; he observed that it was 'of more consequence to be cautious of making a privy counc[ello]r than a peer and, as the law [officers] have generally some considerable influence [there]…, it is very material to make proper persons the L[or]d Chanc[ello]r and the three chief judges'.[16] Few in Ireland with experience of the Council would have disagreed that it was desirable to elevate 'proper persons' to that body, but whereas all were in agreement that ability was a *desideratum*, they were far from unanimous on what was the optimal political outlook.

As was the case during the reign of Queen Anne, information on the way in which the Irish Council acquitted itself of the task of preparing bills and processing heads of bills during the early Hanoverian era is fragmentary. It was, as Archbishop King repeatedly observed, demanding work but, this notwithstanding, there is no evidence to suggest that councillors ever reached an agreed definition of their role, though some individuals had no doubts as to their purpose. Chief Baron Willes, for example, maintained that it was 'their duty to watch that thru' party heat or power in either house [of the Irish parliament], nothing may pass that may be in general detrimental to Ireland or ag[ains]t the legal prerogative of the crown, or the interest of England when it clashes w[i]th the interest of Ireland'.[17] Thus, Willes unhesitantly approved the rejection in 1757 of the heads of a bill to alter the constitution of the city of Dublin on the grounds 'that it w[oul]d be improper and dangerous to advise his Majesty to propose a bill to p[arliament] for changing the constitution of corporations', and was disapproving in 1759 of a measure for placing judges commissions on the same basis as applied in England because to accede would be to agree 'to lessen the power of the Crown and increase the power of the Commons'.[18] Archbishop King did not disagree with Willes in respect of the merits of his first two criteria, but his priority was to protect the interests of the Church of Ireland. To this end, in 1719 King led an ecclesiastical group that included Edward Synge, the archbishop of Tuam, and

14. Chesterfield to Newcastle, 11 Mar. 1746 (NA, SP63/409).
15. Boulter to Carteret, 26 Aug. 1727 in *Boulter letters*, i, 156; Patrick McNally, 'Patronage and politics in Ireland, 1714 to 1727' (PhD, Queen's University Belfast, 1993), pp 165, 177–8.
16. Willes, Legal and political reminiscences on Ireland, 1757–8 (WRO, Willes Papers, MS 2, p. 67).
17. Ibid.
18. Ibid., p. 44; Willes, Memorandum on debates etc. in Irish Houses of Parliament, [1759–60] (WRO, Willes Papers, pp 42–3).

John Stearne, the bishop of Clogher, in resisting 'a parcell' of bills 'very mischievous ... to the church'.[19]

Though this might suggest that vested political interests exerted decisive influence on the fate of heads of bills, measures submitted to the Irish Council for certification were subject to due process. This was in keeping with the commitment of the Council to conduct its business in a regular manner, symbolised by the decision in the wake of the fire in 1711 to acquire copies of the rules and precedents of the British Council. Like its British counterpart, the Irish Council constituted itself into a committee for the purpose of scrutinising bills, and the evidence suggests that public bills were forwarded to sub-committees for examination. This may have obviated the necessity of public bills being referred, as was the practice at the British Council, to the Crown's law officers. In the normal course of events, the law officers could be applied to, but since they were not invariably members of the Council, their participation was secondary to that of the chief justices and the lord chancellor, and on occasion bills were readied for transmission to London without legal assistance.[20]

This was not acceptable to councillors. Indeed, Archbishop King's observation in 1722 that it was common practice to include one or more of the senior lawyers on Council committees bears out his contention that 'a great many things can't be done without the presence of the chief justices or [lord] chancellor'. The expectation, certainly, was that legal expertise would be available to all Council committees; otherwise the work of the Council as a whole could grind to a halt.[21] This does not seem to have happened during the early Hanoverian period, but the lack of ready legal assistance did cause delays – of as much as ten days in 1723–4, King admitted ruefully – in the preparation of bills for transmission.[22] This was uncommon during the 1720s both because the chief justices generally made themselves available, and because there was a core group of councillors which, on the evidence of a handful of signed privy council letters, rarely amounted to more than twenty and was more usually in the low teens, contributed to the task of preparing legislation.[23] The commitment demanded was considerable, as Archbishop King indicated when he confided in November 1723 that he had devoted eight to nine hours a day over a period of three weeks to the task. This

---

19. King to Annesley, 10 Nov., King to Southwell, 12 Nov. 1719 (TCD, King Papers, MS 750/5 ff 200, 210–11); see also King to Tennison, 17 Dec. 1723 (MS 2537 f. 37).

20. 1719, 1722 and 1723 can be instanced: see King to Southwell, 18 Aug. (TCD, King Papers, MS 750/5 f. 195); Bolton to [Craggs], 20 Aug., Webster to Delafaye, 20 Aug. 1719 (NA, SP63/377); King to Hopkins, 15 May 1722 (MS 750/7 f. 112); King to Annesley, 5 Dec. 1723 (MS 2537 ff 33–5).

21. King to Hopkins, 15 May 1722 (TCD, King Papers, MS 750/7 f. 112); James Kelly (ed.), *The letters of Lord Chief Baron Edward Willes 1757–62* (Aberstywyth, 1990), p. 22.

22. King to Annesley, 5 Dec. 1723, King to Southwell, 28 Jan. 1724 (TCD, King Papers, MS 2537 ff 33–5, 66–7); see also Bolton to [Craggs], 20 Aug. 1719 (NA, SP63/377).

23. For examples, see Irish Privy Council report on bills, 31 Oct. 1723 (NA, SP63/381); Irish Privy Council letters, 24 Jan., 6 Feb. 1730 (BL, Hardwicke Papers, Add. MS 35872 ff 26, 35–6).

was exceptionally onerous, but the need to ensure their prompt dispatch meant that the work of preparing bills was generally performed under conditions of great pressure.[24]

King continued to find such circumstances trying, though the frequency with which it was reported from Dublin during the traditional mid-session recess that the Council was fully occupied 'closely examining, amending and altering heads of bills' indicates that he did not do so unassisted.[25] The task he and his colleagues undertook was made more demanding certainly by the sheer number of bills to be considered. This varied from session to session, but the thirty-five to forty-five bills presented for scrutiny during the 1715–16, 1719–20, 1723–4 and 1729–30 sessions was exceptionally burdensome.[26] A more familiar problem, but one that was no less time-consuming, was caused by the defective drafting of public bills communicated from parliament and the private bills presented by individual interests. Officials were prepared at the outset of the reign of George I to look indulgently upon the fact that the public bills 'needed more consideration than usual', on the grounds that they were 'generally drawn up by young members'. Attitudes hardened over time, and the ongoing submission of bills that were 'crude enuff [*sic*] so that they want greatly to be amended', 'penned in a language unparliamentary', 'crewdly [*sic*] and unskilfully drawn', replete with 'inaccuracy' or 'ill-prepared' was regarded increasingly as tiresome and unwelcome.[27]

It certainly highlighted the necessity of having legal expertise at hand, because while precedent served as a reliable guide with respect of a majority of public bills, private legislation could generate exceptional problems. King conceded as much in 1719 when he observed of a particular transmiss bearing private bills that it was 'with great difficulty that they are modelled to the consent of the parties'. Four years later, councillors determined formally to pass 'no private bills without the presence and assistance of a judge or two and of the attorney and solicitor general' because of the need to examine 'deeds of settlement' and to scrutinise 'the consents of all who were judged necessary ... or [had] a saving allowed for them'.[28] This could not always be guaranteed, but because a significant number of private bills attracted petitions, affidavits, bills in chancery and other legal

24. King to Annesley, 25 Nov., 5 Dec., King to Maule, 28 Nov., King to Southwell, 2 Dec. 1723 (TCD, King Papers, MS 2537 ff 24–5, 27, 30, 33–5).
25. Nicolson to Wake, 21 Dec. 1725 (Gilbert Library, Wake Papers, MS 27 f. 388; BL, Add. MS 6116 f. 294); Harrington to Newcastle, 4 Feb. 1748 (NA, SP63/410); Dorset to Newcastle, 12 Dec. 1737 (Northumberland Record Office, Potter Papers, MS 650/C/24).
26. Galway to Stanhope, 22 Mar. 1716 (NA, SP63/374); King to Southwell, 18 Aug., 10 Nov. 1719 (TCD, King Papers, MS 750/5 ff 195, 203); King to Cork, 17 Dec. 1723 (ibid., MS 2537 ff 39–40); Coghill to Southwell, 22 Jan. 1730 (BL, Southwell Papers, Add. MS 21112 f. 107).
27. Galway to Stanhope, 22 Mar. 1716 (NA, SP63/374); King to Southwell, 18 Aug. 1719, 28 Jan., 1724 (TCD, King Papers, MS 750/5 f. 195, MS 2537 ff 66–7); Nicolson to Wake, 28 Oct. 1721 (Gilbert Library, Wake Papers, MS 27 ff 304–5); Coghill to Southwell, 22 Jan. 1730 (BL, Southwell Papers, Add. MS 21112 f. 107).
28. King to Southwell, 18 Aug. 1719, 26 Dec. 1723 (TCD, King Papers, MS 750/5 f. 195, MS 2537 f. 43).

instruments from interested parties, the practice of referring these to one or more, usually to two, judges for a report was extended. The fact that this arrangement was persisted in is an indication of its value, and it proved helpful to councillors to determine the merits of individual bills.[29] In a further attempt to ensure that private bills were properly drawn, both the Irish Council and the House of Lords, where an increasing proportion of private bills took their rise from the early 1720s, insisted that a petition was presented requesting leave to introduce a private bill and, from 1739, required that a notice was posted at the Four Courts or Tholsel in Dublin two months in advance to alert interested parties.[30] These administrative refinements, notwithstanding, there were occasions, such as the 1723–24 session, when the unavailability of legal guidance meant bills were transmitted to England full of 'imperfections'. King did not hesitate to attribute responsibility in this instance to the Crown's law officers, who were so fearful of antagonising MPs by altering a Commons' measure that 'it was with difficulty that we coul'd obtain either of them', and to the failure of the judiciary 'to attend' meetings of Council committees. Obliged in their absence to assume responsibility for supervising the clerks whose function it was to prepare a fair copy of each bill, King conceded that the checking normally performed with the assistance of a senior clerk by a small number of lords of Council did not take place, thereby permitting bills to leave Ireland with more mistakes than was usual.[31]

Given the potential legal, political and constitutional issues that could arise with any piece of legislation, the involvement of jurists and the employment of a committee arrangement to allow for the close scrutiny of every bill was well advised. There is no specific information on the composition and operation of these committees, but Archbishop King's references to meetings of 'the committees of Council' as well as to 'committees and Councils' suggests that draft bills and heads were allocated among a number of sub-committees, which reported to the committee of Council.[32] Debate at this forum could be 'very strong' on occasion, as Edward Weston observed in January 1748 in respect of the resistance offered by the lord chancellor and chief judges to the so-called Newtown Act, since it was the committee that determined which amendments were introduced and recommended whether bills should progress.[33] It was in

29. NAI, Calendar of miscellaneous letters and papers prior to 1760 ff 110, 153, 168, 182, 212, 218, 267, 269, 270, 282, 299, 305; Calendar of miscellaneous letters and papers, 1760–89, f. 1; Index of departmental letters and papers, 1760–89, ff 51–3, 55, 56, 57, 58, 59, 60, 64, 65, 69, 70, 73, 74, 78, 79, 85.

30. Annesley to King, 21 Jan. 1724 (TCD, King Papers, MS 1995–2005, f. 2059); NAI, Calendar of miscellaneous letters and papers prior to 1760, ff 109, 111; *Faulkner's Dublin Journal*, 28 July 1741.

31. King to Southwell, 28 Jan. 1724 (TCD, King Papers, MS 2737 ff 66–7).

32. King to Hopkins, 15 May 1722, King to Annesley, 25 Nov., 5 Dec., King to Maule, 28 Nov., King to Southwell, 2 Dec. (TCD, King Papers, MS 750/7 f. 112, MS 2537 ff 24–5, 27, 30, 33–5).

33. Burns, *Irish parliamentary politics*, ii, 92–3; Weston to Wilmot, 18 Jan. 1748 (PRONI, Wilmot Papers, T3019/960); Ryder to Ryder, 19 Jan. 1748 in Malcomson (ed.), *Irish official papers*, ii, 27–8; Carteret to [ ], 29 Jan. 1726 (NA, SP67/8 f. 116).

committee, for instance, in February 1716 that Archbishop King and his then allies – the bishop of Dromore, John Stearne, and the bishop of Clogher, St George Ashe, and Lords Castlecomer and Abercorn – 'strenuously opposed' the suggestion that dissenters be admitted 'to bear commissions for ten years in the army' in a measure appertaining to the security of the king's person, and in 1719 that Archbishop Edward Synge of Tuam and Bishop Stearne of Clogher were able to secure the amendment and rejection of a number of 'very mischievous' bills.[34] It was here, in 1723, that the heads of a bill for 'continuing several temporary statutes' received from the Commons with an objectionable 'indemnifying ... clause in favour of certain Protestant dissenters', securing them from prosecution for 'fornication' in the Church of Ireland ecclesiastical courts, was rewritten. Understandably apprehensive lest the presence of the dissenter marriage clause should prompt the rejection of the measure in the Irish Lords on its return from London, those aspects of the bill that were adjudged 'an absolute necessity' were preserved in the 'temporary laws bill', while the 'clause about Presbyterian marriage' constituted the basis of a new bill 'for the further amendment of the law' that was forwarded, much against the wishes of the bishops, and received at the British Council board on 24 December 1723.[35] It was in the committee of the Council also, as Edward Willes records, that a controversial corn premium bill in 1757 was permitted to advance.[36]

Willes does not provide much in the way of a description of the discussion that took place on the corn bill. His account of the debate to determine whether Lord Clanbrassil's registration of the Catholic clergy bill would be received is more revealing since it indicates not only that some (controversial) bills were afforded extensive discussion, but also that, on occasions, it was debated whether a bill should even be referred to a sub-committee. It is apparent from this that all points of view were afforded a hearing even when, as in this instance, the Council was 'very much divided as to the general propriety of the bill' being proposed. It is particularly striking in this case that the decisive factor in tipping the balance against the measure arose out of the discussion, and that the outcome, when it was decided, was close; the bill was defeated on a division by fourteen votes to twelve with the lord lieutenant in the minority.[37] In so far as one can tell, it was only necessary in a minority of contentious instances to appeal to a division to determine the fate of a measure. As a mode of proceeding it had the virtue of decisiveness, but in those cases in which a bill was 'warmly debated', it could also leave a legacy of ill feeling. This is exemplified by Archbishop King's angry observation, in response to the lord lieutenant's employment in 1719 of his

34. Lords Justices to Stanhope, 24 Feb. 1716 (NA, SP63/374); King to Annesley, 10 Nov. 1719 (TCD, King Papers, MS 750/5 f. 200).
35. NA, PC2/88 f. 412; Grafton to Carteret, 15 Nov., Grafton to [ ], 14 Dec. 1723 (NA, SP63/382); King to Gibson, 10 Jan. (TCD, King Papers, MS 2537 f. 50); Nicolson to Wake, 4 Feb. 1724 (Gilbert Library, Wake Papers, MS 27 ff 337–8).
36. Willes, Legal and political reminiscences, p. 16.

'casting vote' to resist King's attempt to introduce a clause into the dissenter relief bill that would have allowed non-conformists to be prosecuted in ecclesiastical courts for not conforming to the Church of Ireland, that he was wrong to do so since he did not have 'the majority of the Councill'.[38] King's reasoning seems particularly flawed in this instance, but it may be that he was influenced by the fact that this was the second occasion that he was on the losing side by 'one vote'; in February 1716, the Council had rejected by the same margin his argument that it was 'impolitic and of no advantage' to admit dissenters to the army for a limited time, though he and other 'members of [the] Church of Ireland' made clear their 'disgust' with what they characterised as an attempt to 'to repeal the test ... for ever'.[39] Such incidents were rare but not unique, since, nearly half a century later in the spring of 1760, Chief Baron Edward Willes joined the other law lords in protesting at the outcome of a close decision on a private bill appertaining to the transfer of lands. The lands at issue, which had been granted to the first earl of Ranelagh (d.1712) for the support of charity schools in Athlone and Roscommon and which were administered by trustees, were in the process of being transferred to the Incorporated Society for Promoting English Protestant Schools in Ireland. The main source of difficulty centred on the fact that Edward Synge, the bishop of Elphin, who was receiver of the charity's rents, had, contrary to the wishes of the trustees, secured the introduction of a clause into the bill exonerating him from repaying £1200 that, he maintained, had been lost as a result of the failure of Lennox's Bank. When this came to the notice of the Irish Council, the lord chancellor, John Bowes, and two chief judges were 'all of the opinion that the claim ou[gh]t not to stand w[i]thout the consent of the trustees', but they were outvoted 7 to 3, and the clause was allowed to remain. Unwilling to accede to majority opinion, the three 'law lords' persisted in opposition and, for the first time in memory, no law lord signed the privy council letter that accompanied the bill to London.[40]

Such disagreements, notwithstanding, councillors were not discouraged from resolving matters by a show of hands, and a number of votes of four to three in a council committee of seven are recorded from the 1750s. Yet, it is surely significant that the preferred means of sidelining unwelcome or controversial legislative measures was to propose that their consideration should be postponed to a distant day, 'or in plain English thrown out'.[41] On occasions, councillors were

37. Ibid., pp 33–40; Connolly, *Religion, law and power*, p. 293.
38. King to Tennison, 1 Aug., King to Southwell, 12 Nov. 1719 (TCD, King Papers, MS 750/5 ff 189, 210–11); King to Charlemont, 7 Nov. 1720, printed in *Analecta Hibernica*, 2 (1931), pp 65–6.
39. Lords Justices to Stanhope, 16 Mar. (NA, SP63/374); King to Wake, 24, 26 Mar. 1716 (TCD, King Papers, MS 2533 ff 160–71, 172).
40. Willes, Memorandum on debates, 1758–9 (WRO, Willes Papers, pp 72–3). The trustees carried the struggle against the bill, unsuccessfully, to the British Council (NA, PC2/107 ff 339–40, 352–4, 363–5), but the measure reached the statute book (*Commons Jn. (Irl.)*, vi, 207, 212, 214, 225, 227, 228, 233).
41. Willes, Memorandum on debates, 1759–60, pp 27, 46–7, 72–5.

assisted to decide on a bill by hearing evidence from interested parties. Since this was regular practice at the British Council board, it may be that the Irish Council followed the lead of its metropolitan equivalent in this respect, as well as in respect of the practice of accepting petitions, and that both were resorted to more frequently than the occasional reference suggests. One body that certainly saw merit in this arrangement was Dublin Corporation. It intensified the practice it had pursued since the 1690s of opposing measures prejudicial to metropolitan interests by appealing directly to the Privy Council 'to be heard'. This did not always prove advantageous. The receipt of oral testimony in 1757 did not assist the Corporation bill at issue, but this result did not dissuade the Corporation from continuing to mount an active lobby on a wide range of issues and, when it was deemed appropriate, from seeking 'to be heard' at the Council board.[42] The submission of a petition and the hearing of counsel in 1723 against a clause vesting the power of weighmaster of Cork in the two MPs for the city constituency was also without effect. But the hearing of counsel in December 1739 in respect of the measure to amend the 1695 act for disarming papists was welcomed by the lord lieutenant, the duke of Devonshire, as an appropriate means to 'free it from objections', while the submission in 1760 of a petition to safeguard family settlements entered into by bankers that were unable to meet their debts may also have proved useful.[43]

Though the tentativeness of this reconstruction of the procedures of the Irish Council illustrates that much about the operation of that body in respect of the making of law remains opaque, it can be suggested that the Council became more effective and efficient at processing bills and heads of bills over time.[44] The most salient indicator is provided by the fact that the consideration afforded bills at the Irish Council and the process of readying them for transmission to London proceeded in an increasingly regular manner. As a result, fewer bills were respited at the Irish Council in absolute and proportionate terms between 1731 and 1760 than was the case between 1715 and 1730 (Table 8). And, in a further manifestation of greater administrative regularity, letters (generally brief) outlining the content of bills for the information of the Crown's law officers and the members of the British Council were increasingly forthcoming. When these were ready, the way was clear for the bills to be gathered into three or more sizeable transmisses for communication to the British Council.[45]

42. Sir John Gilbert (ed.), *Calendar of ancient records of Dublin* (19 vols, Dublin, 1889–1945), vi, 128–9, 207–8; ix, 19; x, 192–4, 203–8, 360, 409–12; xi, 383–6; xii, 173–4, 539–45.

43. Grafton to [ ], 14 Dec. 1723 (NA, SP63/382); Willes, Legal and political reminiscences, p. 44; Memorandum on debates, 1759–60, p. 61; Devonshire to Newcastle, 27 Dec. 1739 (SP63/402).

44. King to Southwell, 26 Dec. 1723 (TCD, King Papers, MS 2537 f. 43); McNally, *Parties, patriots and undertakers*, p. 51.

45. For examples see BL, Hardwicke Papers, Add. MS 36136 ff 206–7, Add. MS 36138 ff 129–30; Dorset to Newcastle, 17 Jan. 1734 (PRO SP63/397); Irish Council to Holdernesse, 29 Dec. 1753, 7, 12 Jan. 1754 (SP63/413); and for correspondence indicating the regularity of the process Clutterbuck to [ ], 3 Feb. 1730, Cary to Delafaye, 5 Jan. 1734, Harrington to Newcastle, 4 Feb. 1758 (NA, SP63/392, 63/397, 63/410); Devonshire to Fox, 17 Jan., 3 Feb., 9, 30 Mar., 1 Apr.

Once bills had negotiated the Irish Council, the priority of the Irish executive was to ensure their expeditious communication to London in order that they could be returned in timely fashion. In the case of public bills this was an official responsibility, while the conveyance of private bills, which generally took place separately, was the responsibility of 'the persons concerned in them' who usually entrusted it to agents.[46] The safe and expeditious communication of bills could not be assumed, however, not least because the messengers charged with conveying official documents between Dublin and London regularly encountered delays due to bad weather and other complications.[47] This prompted the lord justice, the earl of Galway, to suggest in October 1716 that, as well as the normal communication of the main transmiss along the Liverpool/ Holyhead–Dublin route, 'duplicates' of matters of 'business or intelligence' should be conveyed via the more northerly port of Portpatrick to Donaghadee. Galway was prompted to make this suggestion by the wish to obviate the delays caused by westerly winds that prevented regular sailings from Holyhead, but while the logic of his proposition ensured it was immediately acceded to in respect of urgent dispatches, practical considerations seem to have ensured that it was not implemented with respect of Irish bills at this point.[48] Inevitably, delays were experienced. In 1719, for example, Carmichael the messenger was obliged to hire a vessel at Carnarvon to enable him to return with six bills. In 1723, the lord lieutenant contemplated hiring a ship to convey the 'last parcel of our heads of bills' because of the unavailability of 'common pacquet boats'.[49] Three years later, in 1726, the loss on the Irish Sea of the ship carrying bills necessitated the preparation of duplicates; in 1728, the transmission of bills from Ireland was delayed by strong 'contrary winds'; while, in 1731, the money bills were held up at Holyhead for '3 or 4 days ... by contrary winds'.[50] Though there was little that could be done in such circumstances other than wait and, if need be, to extend the adjournment of

1756 (SP63/414 ff 19–22, 29–31, 97–9, 126–8, 130–2); Bedford to Pitt, 10 Jan., 9, 22 Mar. 1758, 6, 22, 27 Mar., 3 Apr. 1760 (SP63/415, 63/418).

46. Devonshire to Fox, 17 Jan. 1756 (NA, SP63/414 ff 19–22); Potter to Wilmot, 1 Apr. 1746 (PRONI, Wilmot Papers, T3019/734).

47. Delays could be prolonged: in January 1737, the lord chancellor was 'detained' for 'near a month' at Parkgate 'by contrary winds' (Mathew to Fitzwilliam, 27 Jan. 1737: NAI, Pembroke Estate Papers, 97/46/1/2/2/2/4); in 1748, post was held up for an exceptional '6 weeks' (ibid., 27 Jan. 1748, 97/46/1/2/5/57); in June 1762, contrary winds ensured it took the Quaker Joseph Oxley six days to make the journey from Liverpool to Dublin – three days to get to Holyhead from Liverpool and three further days to reach Dublin (Joseph [Oxley]'s offering to his children (Historical Society of Pennsylvania, AM 1095 ff 196–7)).

48. Galway to Methuen, 30 Oct. (NA, SP63/374); Methuen to Galway, 20 Nov. 1716 (NA, SP67/7 f. 17).

49. Addison to Sunderland, 2 Aug. (BL, Blenheim Papers, Add. MS 61636 f. 49); Webster to Delafaye, 6, 15 Oct., Bolton to Craggs, 10 Oct. 1719 (NA, SP63/378); Nicolson to Wake, 14 Dec. 1723 (Gilbert Library, Wake Papers, MS 27 f. 331).

50. Carteret to Southwell, 9 Jan. (BL, Southwell Papers, Add. MS 38016 ff 3–4); Carteret to [ ], 13 Jan. 1726, Carteret to Newcastle, 30 Jan. 1728 (NA, SP67/8 f. 113, 67/10 f. 22); Cary to Delafaye, 8 Dec. 1731 (NA, SP63/394).

parliament, which was not unusual, officials did at least contrive to ensure that bills being returned to Ireland encountered minimum delay by using the express 'flying pacquet' or by instructing the postmaster at Liverpool personally to oversee their immediate and efficient dispatch. Moreover, from the early 1730s it became the norm also to communicate a duplicate set via Portpatrick.[51] This did not prevent delays caused by bad weather, and by the need to repair the packet boat, but it helped to ensure that before long it was more commonplace for the resumption of the session in Ireland to be postponed for 'want of business' because of the tardy processing of Irish bills at the British Council rather than because of delays in their physical transmission between Dublin and London.[52]

THE OPERATION OF THE BRITISH PRIVY COUNCIL, 1715–60

To be fair, officials in Britain during the early Hanoverian era generally needed little encouragement to deal efficiently with Irish bills because they did not wish to complicate proceedings at the Irish parliament.[53] This was, for obvious reasons, a matter of even greater concern for Irish officials, and they did not hesitate to bring pressure to bear on ministers and officials in London if a delay was likely. They did so with respect of individual bills, such as the corn bill proposed in 1716, that MPs in Ireland had 'set their affections very much upon'; money bills that had to receive the royal assent within a limited window of time;[54] and even, on occasion, whole transmisses.[55] The priority of the Irish administration was that bills were returned quickly, and with this in mind transmisses were accompanied routinely by requests that bills were assured of an 'early return' or were afforded 'all possible dispatch', 'all convenient dispatch', 'all convenient expedition', or some equivalent phrase.[56] Significantly, such entreaties were received

51. Clerk of Council to Postmaster General, 27 Mar. 1745, 5 Dec. 1749, 2 Mar. 1750, 3 Dec. 1755, 27 Nov. 1757, 7 Dec. 1759 (NA, PC2/98 f. 445, 2/101 ff 376, 479, 2/104 f. 537, 2/105 f. 636, 2/107 f. 211); Dorset to Newcastle, 14 Feb. 1733 (NA, SP63/396); Potter to [ ], 12 Jan. 1739 (Northumberland Record Office, Potter Papers, 650/C/24).

52. Waite to Wilmot, 24 Feb., 5 Apr. 1750 (PRONI, Wilmot Papers, T3019/1494, 1533); Delafaye to [ ], 4 May 1716, Webster to Delafaye, 22 Sept., 15 Oct. 1719 (NA, SP63/374, 63/378); Carteret to Newcastle, 19 Mar. 1728, 10 Feb., 25 Mar. 1730 (NA, SP67/10 ff 38, 98, 99); Bedford to Granville, 8 Mar. 1758 in Malcomson (ed.), *Irish official papers*, ii, 186.

53. Carteret to Bolton, 20 Dec. 1721 (NA, SP67/7 f. 100); Grafton to Devonshire, 15 Dec. 1737, Walpole to Devonshire, Jan. 1738, Wilmot to Devonshire, 21 Jan. 1742, Hartington to Devonshire, 23 Jan. 1742 (PRONI, Chatsworth Papers, T3158/41, 45, 198, 200); Bedford to Harrington, 16 Feb., 10 Mar. 1748 (NA, SP67/11 ff 158, 178).

54. In 1731, the 'early transmission of money bills' was deemed worthy of congratulatory notice: Newcastle to Dorset, 23 Nov. 1731 (NA, SP67/9 f. 143).

55. Galway to Stanhope, 28 Dec. 1715, Delafaye to [ ], 30 Jan., Galway to Stanhope, 4 Apr. , Galway and Grafton to Stanhope, 30 Jan., 22 May 1716 (NA, SP63/373, 63/374); Bolton to [Craggs], 14 Aug. 1719 (SP63/377); Cary to Delafaye, 2, 29 Jan. 1732 (NA, SP63/395).

56. Galway to Stanhope, 4 Apr. 1716, Bolton to [Craggs], 14 Aug., Bolton to Lords Justices, 15 Aug.

sympathetically. And it became a familiar feature of the dispatches acknowledging the receipt of Irish bills for the secretary of state for the southern department to promise that they would be afforded 'all possible dispatch', or that he would see to it personally that they were referred to the attorney and solicitor generals so that they could 'make their report upon them with all possible speed'.[57]

Consistent with this, the secretary of state rarely delayed communicating bills and the accompanying explanatory letters to the Council Office in order that they could be 'laid [promptly] before the King in Council' for referral to the Crown's law officers.[58] This was largely a matter of form, as an order to this effect was issued by the Privy Council on 9 September 1715. Comprising a simple instruction that 'the severall bills ... together with the letter from the Privy Council be referred to the attorney and solicitor generals to examine the same and to report to a committee of council', it was clearly anticipated that the role of the law officers should be subordinate to the Irish bills committee. The most patent testimony that this was the intention is provided by the fact that, though the law officers were invited from 1716 to attend the committee when Irish bills were being considered, the committee alone was authorised to determine what 'alterations and amendments' they 'conceive proper'.[59] This remained the case during the reign of George I, but from the early 1730s the orders in council directing the law officers to 'examine all the bills ... transmitted from Ireland during the ... session of parliament' provided that they should 'report from time to time their opinion with what alterations and amendments are proper to be made' to the Irish bills' committee.[60] It is not apparent what prompted this change to the wording of the order as it served only to give formal recognition to the role already played by the law officers rather than to inaugurate an administrative departure. This is not to deny it significance. It gave the law officers a direct and powerful input into the amendment of Irish law at the British Council board that was to endure until 1782.

1719 (NA, SP63/374, 63/377); Boulter to Newcastle, 10 Feb. 1726 in *Boulter letters*, i, 51; Carteret to Newcastle, 21 Feb., 7 Mar. 1728 (NA, SP67/10 ff 31, 37); Dorset to Newcastle, 20 Nov. 1733, Devonshire to Newcastle, 22 Nov. 1737, 19 Nov. 1739 (NA, SP63/396, 400, 402).

57. Stanhope to Lords Justices, 3. 10 Apr. 1716 (NA, SP67/6 ff 137, 141); Addison to Bolton, 17 Oct. 1717, Carteret to Bolton, 11 Nov. 1721, Newcastle to Carteret, 3 Feb., 7 Mar. 1728, Holderness to Dorset, 9 Jan. 1752, Fox to Hartington, 29 Nov. 1755, Pitt to Bedford, 23 Mar. 1758 (NA, SP67/7 ff 19, 94, 67/9 ff 38, 93, 67/12 ff 9, 48, 86); Newcastle to Dorset, 24 Feb. 1732 (NA, SP63/375); Lord President to Hartington, 29 Nov. 1755 (NA, PC1/31/A78); Devonshire to Wilmot, 30 Mar. 1756 (PRONI, Wilmot Papers, T3019/2789).

58. Stanhope to Lords Justices, 3, 10 Apr. 1716 (NA, SP67/6 ff 137, 141); Addison to Bolton, 17 Oct., 2 Nov. 1717, Carteret to Bolton, 11 Nov., 7 Dec. 1721, Bedford to Hartington, 10 Mar. 1750, Holdernesse to Dorset, 23 Nov. 1750, 9 Jan. 1752, Fox to Hartington, 22 Nov. 1755, Pitt to Bedford, 10 Apr. 1760 (NA, SP67/7 ff 19, 22–3, 94, 99, SP67/11 f. 178, SP67/12 ff 7, 9, 47, 101).

59. NA, PC2/85 f. 279.

60. NA, PC2/91 f. 474; PC2/92 f. 273; PC2/954 f. 420; PC2/97 ff 19–20, PC2/100 f. 444; PC2/102 ff 340–1.

It was the law officers' responsibility also to assess the merits of the petitions that were presented in respect of some 7 per cent of the measures received at the Council board during the reigns of George I and George II. While this was comparatively straightforward in those cases in which one petitioner was involved, multiple petitions were presented in several instances in respect of measures against Catholics and for protecting the creditors of banks.[61] Moreover, some petitioners sought to reinforce their case by making an oral presentation or, in what may have been an innovation, by having an oral presentation made on their behalf by counsel at which supplemental information and additional explanations were offered. Every petition was not successful, but the readiness with which the Crown's law officers, first, and the Irish bills committee, second, responded to a well-made case meant that legislation was routinely altered to allay concerns. In addition, petitioners could seek to challenge the report of the law officers or, on those rare occasions when a petition was presented too late to be considered by them, seek to have their concerns taken into account at the Irish bills committee. In 1748, for example, Viscount Taaffe and others, who entertained serious reservations with respect of a measure 'to restrain foreign education' were not just provided with the text of the bill, they were allowed 'time to consider the report' of the attorney and solicitor general. Two years later, in an instance in which 'popish agents' were allowed the same privilege, the petitioner's conclusion that the revised bill was 'still very improper' ensured the measure was returned for further scrutiny by the Irish bills committee.[62]

The bills received by the British Council were conveyed to the attorney and solicitor general in the main in lots of the same size as they were transmitted out of Ireland.[63] Other than a small number of mainly commercial bills upon which it was deemed appropriate to seek specialised guidance from bodies such as the Commissioners of Customs, each was the subject of an original report written by the law officers. This normally took a standard form; it recommended whether the bill should proceed or not, and in those cases in which this was contingent on amendments being made, listed the recommended changes in sequence by the skin, line and place in which they were required.[64] Invariably presented above their names as the joint work of the attorney and solicitor generals, the only instances in which this practice was not observed in the early Hanoverian era occurred when one of the law officer's was unable to participate due to illness; then the report was presented under one name.[65]

---

61. See below, pp 214–15.
62. Minutes of proceedings on foreign education, 15 Feb., law officers' report, 12 Mar. 1748 (NA, PC1/6/9 ff 1–6); PC2/100 ff 544, 573, 579; law officers' report on … regulating agents, receivers and attorneys, 13 Mar., Petition, Irish bills committee minute, 16 Mar. 1750 (PC1/6/18, 19 ff 1–3); PC2/101 ff 458, 469–70, 498.
63. For examples of these orders in council see BL, Hardwicke Papers, Add. MS 35872 ff 15–17, MS 36138 f. 221.
64. For examples see law officers' reports, 13 Mar. 1750 (NA, PC1/6/8, 18).
65. As in December 1721 when the illness of the solicitor general ensured that the attorney general,

As the authors of the report that was the focus of the Irish bills committee and of the full Council's engagement with each item of Irish legislation, successive attorney and solicitors general were well placed to shape the content as well as the direction of Irish law. The evidence suggests that they did not seek to use their position in an obvious manner to advantage either kingdom, when public matters were at issue, or individuals, when they scrutinised private bills. While this obviously reflects well on the integrity of successive incumbents, the fact that five of the nine men who held the senior office of attorney general served as solicitor general prior to their promotion assisted to create a situation in which the British officials who subjected Irish bills to closest scrutiny brought an exceptional measure of experience to the task. This was made possible by the fact that three of the nine men who were attorney general during the reign of the first two Hanoverians held the position for ten years or more. The longest serving was Dudley Ryder, who was attorney general for seventeen years between 1737 and 1754. Previously, Philip Yorke held the position for all but a few months between 1724 and 1734, while Edward Northey's two terms (1701–07, 1710–18) meant he served in the office for a total of fifteen years. At the other end of the scale, no fewer than six attorneys general held the office for very short terms, but the potentially disruptive impact of this was mitigated by the fact that four had previously served as solicitor general. The attorney general with the briefest service was Robert Henley (seven months in 1756–7); otherwise nobody held the position for less than two years. The fact that three of the nine holders of that office during the reigns of George I and George II subsequently became lord chancellors and four became chief justices suggests that the law officers were an exceptionally well-informed body of men.[66]

While the wealth of legal knowledge and experience they brought to bear was important, the fact that the law officers had to present written reports to the Irish bills committee ensured that the process was conducted in a thorough and administratively efficient fashion. Stipulated by an order in council just prior to the opening of each session of the Irish parliament, the importance attached to the management of Irish legislation at the Council board was highlighted by the Irish bills committee's emergence during the reign of George I as one of the Council's main committees. This was not entirely straightforward. Authorised at the outset of the reign to 'report to his majesty at this board what alterations and amendments they conceive proper' to be made to Irish bills, the ability of the

Robert Raymond, compiled the report (Attorney General's report on four Irish bills, 5 Dec. 1721 (NA, PC1/3/98)).

66. Melikan, 'Mr Attorney general and the politicians', pp 68–9. Then other incumbents and the time they spent in office were: Nicholas Lechmere, 2 years, 1718–20, previously solicitor general 1714–15; Robert Raymond, 3–4 years, 1729–34, previously solicitor general 1710–14; John Willes, three years, 1734–7; William Murray, 2.5 years, 1754–56, previously solicitor general 1742–54; and Charles Pratt, 4.5 years, 1757–62. Robert Henley was solicitor general between 1751 and 1754.

committee to operate efficiently was diminished by the failure of a majority of its nominated members to attend with any regularity. Constituted in 1715 with eleven members plus the law officers who possessed attendance rights only, the committee was augmented to fourteen in 1717. This was too large, and it was determined in August 1719, coinciding with the establishment of a quorum at three, to limit the committee to ten. This was not an apposite number; 'twice' in 1719, the Council 'could not sit for want of the attendance ... to make a quorum' with the inevitable result, the under-secretary, Charles Delafaye, observed, that 'our Irish bills which should have all possible dispatch given them [are] retard[ed]'. As a result, it was decided to take the rather drastic action of adding 'all the Lords of the Council in town' to the committee.[67] This was not an ideal expedient, but a comparable practice was resorted to during the mid-1720s when, following the establishment of an Irish bills committee of thirteen, membership was augmented on two occasions by the nomination of sixteen (1723) and fourteen (1725) additional members. This raised the membership of the committee to the high twenties by the later years of George I's reign.[68] The accession of George II brought the practice of doubling the size of the Irish bills committees by the nomination of additional members to an end. Committees of sixteen (1729), seventeen (1727 and 1733) and eighteen (1728, 1731 and 1735), with a quorum of three, were standard between then and the early 1740s when twenty or more was set as the new norm for the remainder of the reign of George II.[69]

In keeping with its fluctuating size, membership of the Irish bills committee was not an *ex officio* entitlement. The incumbent lord chancellor, archbishop of Canterbury, lord treasurer, lord president, lord privy seal, lord steward, lord chamberlain, master of the rolls, the chancellor of the exchequer and two chief justices were normally nominated, but though they were generally present at Council meetings conducted in the presence of the King, their attendance was distinctly less faithful when Irish bills were being considered in committee. Things might not been so if more Irishmen were members but, other than the earl of Abercorn who sat on the committee during the early 1740s, the only recorded instance of an Irish peer being added to the Irish bills committee occurred in 1758 when the earl of Hillsborough was nominated.[70] Otherwise, membership of the committee remained top-heavy throughout the period 1715–60 with the holders of major government and church office in Britain, who chose carefully the meetings that they deemed it necessary to attend. As a result, it was rare for

---

67. NA, PC2/85 ff 279, 331, 354; PC2/86 f. 45; PC2/86 ff 299, 332. More generally see Turner, *The Privy Council of England*, ii, 37, 150, 193–7, 202–3, 205–6, 363–4, 376, 380–3, 386–92, 394, 396–400, 408–9, 411, 416–17, 427.
68. NA, PC2/88 ff 358, 418; PC2/89 ff 123, 139; PC1/4/16.
69. NA, PC2/90 ff 53,224; PC2/91 ff 87, 475; PC2/92 f. 257; PC2/93 ff 243; PC2/98 f. 57; PC2/99 f. 244; PC2/101 ff 366–7; PC2/103 f. 504; PC2/104 f. 526; PC2/105 ff 614–15; PC2/107 f. 187.
70. NA, PC2/98 f. 57; PC2/106 f. 70; Lists and Index Society, *Ministerial meetings in the reign of George I*, vol. 224 (London, 1987), pp 32, 35, 37, 83, 84.

attendance at meetings of the Irish bills committee to exceed six. Eight and nine are recorded at four of the fourteen meetings held during 1733–4 and 1735–6, but no more than three and four were present on a total of six occasions.[71] It could be, as the chief secretary, Lord Duncannon, observed ruefully in December 1743, 'a most difficult matter to get people to attend at the council', and most English councillors were seldom sufficiently animated by everyday Irish legislation to do so readily.[72] This ensured, the best intentions of those with responsibility for administering the Anglo-Irish nexus in Great Britain notwithstanding, that delays were not unusual. Some – for example, those attributable to the indisposition of the lord chancellor and the unavailability of the judiciary in 1719 – were unavoidable; others such as were caused by the reluctance of 'gentlemen' to leave their country seats to attend to public business were not. Delays attributable to personality clashes, such as occurred in 1742 when the lord president was 'pique[d]' by the failure of the duke of Devonshire to 'write to him'; administrative foul-ups (though exceptionally rare) attributable to the 'imperfect' record keeping of the clerks of the council, and unexpected problems, such as were caused in 1760 by the unnecessary comparison of new and old bills, were certainly avoidable.[73]

Saliently, the management of money bills proceeded without complication. This can be attributed largely to the fact that, because they were essential to the smooth administration of the kingdom of Ireland and, by extension, to the maintenance of a harmonious Anglo-Irish nexus, they were given priority. Always included in the first transmiss communicated from Dublin each session, they were invariably the first bills to negotiate the British Council. Such expeditious treatment was encouraged by frequent urgings from Dublin Castle, and the positive spirit in which these urgings were received.[74] It is significant also that money bills on average required fewer 'amendments and alterations' than almost any other category of legislation. Indeed, by the end of the reign of George II such amendments as were made appertained to minor matters of meaning, and were, in the words of the president of the Council, Lord Granville, 'such as are usually made for preserving the right of amending those bills'.[75]

71. NA, PC2/86 ff 57, 321–2; Lord Chancellor's attendance at Irish bills committee, 1729–31 (NA, PC1/13/69); Lords present at the several committees for Irish bills, 1733–4, 1735–6 (PC1/13/69/1).

72. Duncannon to Devonshire, 29 Dec. 1743 (PRONI, Chatsworth Papers, T3158/272); *Ministerial meetings … of George I*, p. 19.

73. Stanhope to Lords Justices, 6 June 1716 (NA, SP67/6 f. 151); Bolton to [Craggs], 20 Aug., Webster to Delafaye, 24 Aug., 19 Sept. 1719 (NA, SP63/377); Carteret to Bolton, 29 Nov., 30 Dec. 1721, Townshend to Carteret, 27 Nov. 1729 (NA, SP67/7 ff 97, 102, 67/9 f. 111); Willes to [ ], 12 Mar. 1736 (NA, SP63/399); Wilmot to Devonshire, 26 Jan. 1742 (PRONI, Chatsworth Papers, T3158/202); Granville to Bedford, 25 Mar. 1760 (NA, PC1/31/A78); Bedford to Granville, 1 Apr. 1760 in Malcomson (ed.), *Irish official papers*, ii, 236.

74. Burns, *Irish parliamentary politics*, i, 211; Carteret to Newcastle, 18 Nov. 1729, Newcastle to Devonshire, 3 Dec. 1737 (NA, SP67/10 f. 90, 67/11 f. 60); Dorset to Newcastle, 6 Nov. 1735, Devonshire to Newcastle, 22 Nov. 1737, 19 Nov. 1739 (NA, SP63/398, 63/400, 63/402).

75. Granville to Bedford, 7 Dec. 1759 (NA, PC1/31/A78).

The prompt progress of money bills through the British Council was assisted by the Privy Council letters that now accompanied all bills.[76] While it may appear from their ostensibly formulaic character that they were deserving of little notice, this is belied by the importance attached to them by the Crown's law officers. This was made clear in 1728 when, having acknowledged that 'the nature and design of the bills in general is very well explained in the letters transmitted by ... the Privy Council of Ireland', the Lords of the British Council yet observed that they did not provide sufficient 'information ... especially with regard to particular customs and constitutions in Ireland, which may be varied or affected by the bills transmitted'. Arising out of this, it was agreed by the King in Council 'that for all the future due care may be taken to transmit with the bills all such necessary lights and informations as may serve more fully to explain such parts and clauses thereof as are most liable to any doubt or objection'.[77] Nine years earlier, when a comparable difficulty arose in respect of private bills because of 'the absence of any reference in the letters transmitted ... from the Irish Council ... that the facts alleged in those bills were proved to the satisfaction of the Council or that the proper parties were consenting thereto', the Irish Council assured its British counterpart that such consents as were required were routinely obtained. The then lord lieutenant, the duke of Bolton, harboured certain reservations about the procedures followed at the Irish Council but, as in 1728, the eagerness of both sides to resolve the matter ensured there was no dispute, and the bills at issue made it to the statute book.[78] This outcome could not be assumed; the failure in 1732 'to furnish ... proper proofs' in respect of a private bill appertaining to the sale of an estate caused the law officers to decline to make a report.[79]

The disposition of the British Council to observe Poynings' Law, but to do so in a manner that did not give cause for offence in Ireland, is illustrated further by the tendency, increasingly common as the reign of George II progressed, to define the alterations made to Irish bills as 'inconsiderable', 'small and literal', 'verbal', 'immaterial' and 'such as make no alteration in the intent and meaning'.[80] As this suggests, and as the tone and content of the general correspondence bears out, the government officers whose responsibility it was to oversee the management of legislation performed this task with quiet efficiency. Credit for this rests with no individual, though the duke of Newcastle, in his capacity as secretary of state for

76. For three examples see NA, PC1/7/89. The printed votes of the House of Commons were also communicated 'for the information of the Lords of the Council, who are to consider the bills of parliament' (Liddell to Leicester, 6 Jan. 1746 (NAI, Irish Correspondence, i, MS 2446)).
77. Newcastle to Carteret, 15 Apr. 1728 (NA, SP67/9 f. 96).
78. NA, PC2/86 ff 260–3, 332, 344; Webster to Delafaye, 15, 17 Oct., Bolton to Lords Justices, 17 Oct. 1719 (NA, SP63/378); Carteret to Newcastle, 30 Apr. 1728 (NA, SP67/10 f. 42).
79. Newcastle to Dorset, 24 Feb. 1732 (NA, SP63/375).
80. Carteret to Bolton, 16 Dec. 1721, Newcastle to Dorset, 24 Jan. 1732, Harrington to Dorset, 30 Nov. 1733, Newcastle to Dorset, 26 Nov. 1735, 30 Jan. 1736 (NA, SP67/7 f. 100, 67/9 ff 144, 178, 282, SP67/11 f. 24); Irish bills passed at Council, 27 Jan. 1732 (NA, SP63/395); Granville to Devonshire, 29 Nov. 1755, 5 Feb. 1756 (NA, PC1/31/A78).

the southern department from 1724 to 1746, set the standard. Newcastle guided each transmiss expeditiously through the Privy Council, facilitated open communication, and coaxed and encouraged with such effect that, during the reign of George II, successive lords lieutenant commenced their preparations to return home prior to the return of the final bills from the British Council.[81] Furthermore, good will was promoted by the willingness of ministers to shower praise on the Irish executive for the effective management of sessions when things went well.[82]

Once the Irish bills committee had considered the report of the law officers and any other information it deemed pertinent, and reached a decision as to whether an Irish bill should be respited or recommended as suitable to become law with or without amendments, it was forwarded to a meeting of the full Council, which invariably took place in the presence of the King. This was largely routine, as the Council, happy in most instances during this era to accept the guidance of the Irish bills committee, concentrated on the vital procedural steps of ordering that bills deemed suitable to become law should be conveyed to the clerk of the Council for duplication and engrossment so they could be passed under the great seal. Responsibility for overseeing the first of these tasks was entrusted to the attorney general, and the second to the lord chancellor. The latter was also responsible for overseeing the preparation of commissions empowering the lord lieutenant of Ireland to give the royal assent to such bills as were returned that 'shall be agreed' by the Irish parliament.[83]

The procedure adopted in this respect mirrored that employed during the years of the later Stuarts, and it was followed with the same attention to detail that was a characteristic of the British Council's engagement with Irish bills. However, because some bills, and, on occasions, a significant number, were 'respited' every session, suspicions were voiced in Ireland that this could be avoided if the public bills were better represented. Significantly, it was on one such occasion – the 1723–4 session when four public bills were respited – that this sentiment was expressed most openly. Archbishop King, for example, observed that

> our private bills have an easier and quieter passage than our public ... because the private bills are commonly accompanied with a particular agent, who is acquainted with the circumstances of the case and prepared to

81. Burns, *Irish parliamentary politics*, ii, 40–1; Bishop of Down to Ryder, 20 Feb. 1746 in Malcomson (ed.), *Irish official papers*, ii, 20; Chesterfield to Newcastle, 1 Apr. 1746 (NA, SP63/409); Devonshire to Wilmot, 16 Jan., 3 Apr. 1756 (PRONI, Wilmot Papers, T3019/2747, 2796).

82. Newcastle to Devonshire, 20 Oct. 1737 (NA, SP67/11 f. 58); Granville to Devonshire, 14 Apr. 1756 (NA, PC1/31/88A).

83. See, for examples, NA, PC2/94 ff 322–3; 2/100 ff 461–4, 531–5; BL, Hardwicke Papers, Add. MS 35872 ff 118, 130, 249 and Add. MS 35873 ff 19, 21, 22, 23, 33, 35, 37, 39, 45, 259; Add. MS 35874 ff 19, 20, 21, 43, 44, 46, 47, 48, 49, 50, 52, 117, 119 and following.

answer the objections, and prosecute them with ready money from place to place and sollicite them in every office, whereas the publick go with a messenger that knoweth nothing of the matter, leaves them in the office and lets them shift for themselves.[84]

King speculated that the reason for this was the wish of successive lords lieutenant to retain the £100 or £200 that could be used to advantage in hiring agents for their 'own servants', but while this may well have been a factor it was not the only consideration. The then lord lieutenant, the duke of Grafton, resisted the suggestion that he should employ qualified agents on the grounds that 'he, by his situation, was the only agent we ought to look for, and that … he would look on it as an affront if such a thing were attempted'.[85] Others took a different opinion. As described above, Chief Secretary Southwell made good use of William Wogan during the duke of Ormonde's viceroyalty, while Joseph Addison found equal use for the services of Edward Young, his under secretary, later the same decade.[86] Moreover, following the accession of George I to the throne, Lords Justices Grafton and Galway authorised Alexander Stevenson to assist Fisher who was already employed in 'soliciting the dispatch of … bills through the several offices in England'.[87] Perhaps because they lacked Wogan's drive, neither Stevenson nor Fisher made a particular impression, with the result that it was soon being observed that 'the public business of Ireland suffers … for want of some proper agent to present it and that some of the publick bills are likely for that cause to miscarry'.[88] The situation was to continue to give cause for concern. In 1724, Edmund Gibson, the bishop of London, responded to Archbishop King when the latter observed angrily, following the forwarding of a measure 'for accepting the solemn affirmation' of Quakers in lieu of an oath, that since 'two Quakers have more interest with the government and parliament than 22 bishops and ten lords … the proper remedy would be the appointment of some person …to attend the bills here'; Gibson advised that the person given this important responsibility should 'be upright and impartial'.[89] A person to fit this bill was identified soon after when Baron Carteret, later Earl Granville, recruited Edward Southwell to represent Irish bills on his behalf in London.[90] This improved

84. King to Southwell, 11 Jan. 1724 (TCD, King Papers, MS 2537 ff 53–4); see also King to Cork, 10 Jan., King to London, 10 Jan., King to Southwell, 8 Feb. 1724 (ibid., ff 49, 52, 74–5).
85. King to Wake, 28 Jan., 15 Feb. 1724 (TCD, King Papers, MS 2537 ff 63, 79–80).
86. Above pp 119–21; James, 'The Irish lobby', p. 550; McGrath, *Making the constitution*, p. 220.
87. Grafton and Galway to Stanhope, 24 Dec. 1715 (NA, SP63/373).
88. Saville to King, 29 Oct. 1717 (TCD, King Papers, MS 1995–2008 f. 1832).
89. On this episode see Grafton to Carteret, 9, 15 Nov. 1723 (NA, SP63/382); King to Southwell, 2 Dec. 1723, King to Gibson, 10 Jan., 1 Feb., King to Wake, 15 Feb., Robinson to King, 18 Feb. (TCD, King Papers, MS 2537 ff 28, 50, 69, 79, MSS 1995–2008 f. 2066); Nicolson to Wake, [ca. 17 Dec. 1723], 14, 27 Jan. 1724 (Gilbert Library, Wake Papers, MS 27 ff 333, 335); *A collection of protests of the Lords of Ireland from 1634 to 1770*, pp 75–80.
90. Carteret to Southwell, 1 Mar. 1726, Coghill to Southwell, 3 Jan. 1730 (BL, Southwell Papers,

matters, and the merits of this arrangement were sufficiently obvious that it was set on solid foundations in 1740 by the appointment of Robert Wilmot as resident secretary to the lord lieutenant. Over the following thirty-two years, spanning twelve viceroyalties, Wilmot dealt with a wide range of business appertaining to the Anglo-Irish relationship, of which the expedition of legislation through the British Council was one of the most important.[91]

If the skill with which Southwell and Wilmot represented Irish legislation at the British Privy Council vindicated their use, the effectiveness of those agents employed on their behalf during the reign of Queen Anne ensured that Irish Catholics continued to employ lawyers to represent their interests during the reigns of the first two Georges. They were particularly active during the 1730s when they contrived with some success to resist efforts to extend and to tighten the penal laws.[92] As a result, Catholics were one of the main employers of agents throughout this period, and though Irish Protestants were more than a little irritated that their legislative intentions were frustrated as a result, they were torn between endeavouring, as they contrived in 1750 and 1756, to curb their activities by law, and appointing agents of their own to represent bills in which they had an especial interest.[93] Bishop Synge favoured the latter course in 1753; as a member of the Linen board, he recommended the employment of an agent to represent the bill to prevent a repetition of the 'mutilat[ion]' experienced by a linen bill in 1751. Thirteen years later what Lord Chancellor Bowes termed 'a wild scheme' to send a Commons' representative to explain Irish bills was well received in Ireland because it was believed that many popular bills failed to negotiate the British Privy Council for lack of information.[94] This idea was not pursued, though MPs revisited this idea on occasions when they adjudged that their presence would hasten the return of a bill.[95]

Add. MS 38016 f. 7, Add. MS 21122 ff 103–6); Carteret to Southwell, 12 Jan. 1728 (NLS, Watson Collection, MS 578 f. 180). For an example of Southwell's activities see Southwell to Yorke, 6 Feb. 1729 (BL, Hardwicke Papers, Add. MS 36136 ff 216–17).

91. Johnston, *Great Britain and Ireland*, pp 78–80; Magennis, *The Irish political system*, p. 43; PRONI Wilmot Papers, T3019 passim; Wilmot to Devonshire, 21 Jan. 1742, 28 Nov. 1755 (PRONI, Chatsworth Papers, T3158/198, 1001).

92. Fagan, *Catholics in a Protestant country*, pp 63–6; below, pp 235–6.

93. W.P. Burke, *Irish priests in penal times* (Waterford, 1913), p. 308. A bill for regulating agents, recoverers and attornies that rose in the Irish Commons in 1750 and was promoted at a high level in Ireland was approved with amendments by the British Council, but lost in the Commons on its return (*Commons Jn. (Irl.)*, v, 66, 68, 69, 70; PC2/101 ff 458, 469–70, 498, 503–4; law officers' report, 13 Mar. 1750 (PC1/6/18); Petition and Irish bills committee minute, 16 Mar. 1750 (PC1/19 ff 1–3); Weston to Wilmot, 17 Feb., 6 Mar. 1750: PRONI, Wilmot Papers, T3019/1504). For insights into Catholic concerns and efforts to resist this see Mathew to Fitzwilliam, 1, 14 Feb., 7 Apr. 1750, 13, 20 April, 4, 6 May 1756 (NAI, Pembroke Estate Papers, 97/46/1/2/5/53, 75, 76, 77, 79, 80, 81).

94. Magennis, *The Irish political system*, pp 77, 186; Johnston-Liik, *History of Irish parliament*, i, 305–6.

95. Kelly, *Henry Flood*, p. 125.

There were interests, of course, that had recourse to more direct and rewarding form of lobbying. Members of the Church of Ireland ecclesiastical bench (Archbishops Boulter and King and Bishop Nicolson notably) appealed on a regular basis to leading ecclesiastics of the Church of England (particularly to the archbishop of Canterbury, William Wake, and the bishop of London, Edmund Gibson, who were members of the British Council) to use their best efforts to press for the amendment or respiting of legislation they judged contrary to the interests of protestantism. They also, on occasions, encouraged the 'chief judges' of Ireland to intervene with the British lord chancellor, attorney and solicitor general to expedite bills they favoured, and to appeal to others whom they thought might be well disposed. Irish law officers also intervened on occasions, though the best examples, by Chief Baron John Bowes in the late 1740s, appertained to private as well as public bills.[96] Moreover, the response to such lobbying was not always as expected as the negative response of Sir John Stanley and Lord Palmerston to Archbishop King's request in 1726 to secure the insertion of a clause in a glebes bill illustrates. Unwilling to intervene because they were 'too ignorant of the rights of the severall interests', they advised King 'to prepare the heads of a bill against the next meeting of parliament with the consent of all parties'.[97] Such rebuffs did not deter lobbying, but they helped to confine it to those with appropriate contacts. One such figure was Nathaniel Clements, the deputy vice treasurer of Ireland, who called on the services of William Blair, the clerk of the British Council, in 1760 to assist in ensuring that the bill for the relief of the creditors of his failed bank was afforded proper consideration.[98] Few were as well placed as Clements; as a result, the bulk of the requests for 'assistance at council' conveyed from Ireland were from churchmen, and appertained to measures touching on church leases, parish unions, tithes, the maintenance of curates, and the rights of Quakers and dissenters. Secular matters were not ignored, but the majority of their correspondence appertained to church issues.[99]

In some instances, the principal advocates of a bill felt obligated to lobby on its behalf because they had invested heavily in its enactment. In respect of public bills, this investment took the form of effort and endeavour rather than money since most of the expense associated with the enactment of public bills was

---

96. Bowes to Ryder, 11 Feb. 1746, 18 Jan., 23 Feb. 1748 in Malcomson (ed.), *Irish official papers*, ii, 19, 27, 29.
97. King to Stanley, 21 Jan. and reply, 1 Feb. 1726 (TCD, King Papers, MS 750/8 ff 78–9, MSS 1995–2008 f. 2141); Bishop of Down to Ryder, 19 Jan. 1748 in Malcomson (ed.), *Irish official papers*, ii, 27.
98. Blair to Clements, 28 Feb., 15, 20 Mar. 1760 (TCD, Clements letterbooks, MS 1742/63, 65, 66). I wish to thank Dr A.P.W. Malcomson for these references.
99. As note 89; Boulter to London, 11 Jan., 17, 24 Feb., 13 Apr., Boulter to Wake, 13, 24 Feb. 1728 in *Boulter letters*, i, 165, 172–5, 175–9, 178–9, 168–71, 188–9; Howard to King, 27 Apr. 1716 (TCD, King Papers, MS 1995–2008 f. 1775); Nicolson to Wake, 2 Nov., [17 Dec.] 1723 (Gilbert Library, Wake Papers, MS 27 ff 329, 333); King to Wake, 17 Dec., King to Annesley, 1 Nov. 1723 (King Papers, MS 2537 ff 37, 19–20).

embraced within general administration. The process was not cost-free, none the less, and considerable expense was incurred in the form of fees and other charges due a variety of officials along the line. Information on this subject is fragmentary, but in the early eighteenth century the clerk of the Irish council received £5, rising to £6 2s., for each bill for which he was responsible for 'putting in form'. The costs incurred on these grounds alone were not inconsiderable as the evidence of payments of £120, £202 8s. and £140 11s. 4d. made in 1706, 1717 and 1719 suggests. In addition, the 'extraordinary clerks employed in copying and preparing copys' of bills had to be paid (£20 in 1705), though this cost was modest compared with the £199 4s. paid to the Irish attorney and solicitor generals 'for transmitting bills for England' and the bounty of £100 provided at the same time to messenger/agents such as William Wogan, John Medicott and Edward Young 'for carrying acts of parliament to England'.[100] Agents could also earn once-off payments in respect of particular bills. William Wogan, for example, was paid £30 by Archbishop King to monitor 'church bills' in 1708, while Thomas Allan, who worked on behalf of Lord Townshend in 1772 submitted a claim for £150 for attending the law officers and Council in respect of two money bills.[101]

Legal counsel too required payment, which proved a problem in the case of public bills that were subject to petition since, Lord Duncannon observed in 1748, no procedure existed for paying them.[102] Inevitably, the sums earned by agents and counsel were small compared with those paid the law officers of Great Britain, who between them received £21 for every bill they examined in the early eighteenth century, and who were the recipients of payments of £200 per session by the 1770s. In addition, payments had to be made to the secretary of state's office, the Council office and the clerk to the crown. In all, approximately one thousand pounds was 'transmitted to several persons in Great Britain for their fees and trouble' each session during the reign of George I.[103] By the early 1750s this figure had risen to £1200 since this was the amount Robert Wilmot received from the Irish parliament for disbursement at the end of each session until the

100. Fees due the clerk of the Council in Ireland, 1705, Warrants on the concordatums in 1705, State of the Concordatum 1705–06 (Gilbert Library, Privy Council Papers, 1640–1707, MS 205/59, 64, 68); 'Documents of Kilkenny Corporation', *Journal of the Royal Historical and Archaeological Association of Ireland*, 4th series, i (1870), p. 277; Payments on letters from George I, 1715–17 (NA, SP63/375); Payments made on King's letters, 1719–21 (NA, SP63/380).

101. King to Southwell, 9 Oct. 1708 (TCD, King Papers, MS 2531 f. 2); Allan to Townshend, 24 Oct. 1772 (Beinecke Library, Osborn Collection, Townshend Papers, Box 5).

102. Duncannon to [Wilmot], 5 Feb. 1748 (PRONI, Wilmot Papers, T3019/972).

103. An account of fees received at the Council office in Dec. 1703 by Edward Southwell (Folger Library, Southwell Papers, Privy Council office papers, 1678–1705 f. 35); 'Documents of Kilkenny Corporation', *Journal of the Royal Historical and Archaeological Association of Ireland*, 4th series, i (1870), p. 277; Payments on letters from George I, 1715–17 (NA, SP63/375); Payments made on King's letters, 1719–21 (NA, SP63/380); Meredyth to Wilmot and enclosure, 10 Mar. 1764 (PRONI, Wilmot Papers, T3109/4814–5); Wilmot to Townshend, 24 Apr. 1772 (Beinecke Library, Osborn Collection, Townshend Papers, Box 7); Johnston-Liik, *History of Irish parliament*, i, 219.

early 1770s. Of this sum, £200 each went to Wilmot and to the clerk of the English Council and £800 to their offices 'for dealing with Irish parliamentary business'.[104] This was only half the total cost as the payments to 'officers' in Ireland as well as England sanctioned by royal letter in 1746 amounted to £2297. Since a considerable part of this sum remained with the lord lieutenant as part of the perquisites of office, it is tempting to conclude, as many contemporaries alleged, that the fees on public bills were extravagant, when this was really not the case.

Significant though such charges were, the cost of bringing a public bill into law was modest when compared with the charges incurred by private acts. The arrangement in the eighteenth century was quite different to that which operated in the early seventeenth century when the Commons stipulated in 1614 that instead of a parliamentary charge £5 should be given 'to the poor'. This proved unsatisfactory and, from 1695 the payment of parliamentary fees followed a complex schedule approved by the House of Lords. Amounting to nearly £30 for a bill of average length, it authorised payments of £5 to the speaker and the gentleman usher of the black rod, £1 to the yeoman usher, £2 to the doorkeepers, £1 10s. to the serjeant at arms and a charge per skin to be paid to a variety of clerks involved in the process of certification and engrossment.[105] Saliently, these charges constituted only a minor part of the total costs incurred by those seeking a private act of parliament, as the itemised list of expenses paid in 1706–7 by the trustees of Sir Thomas Hackett's estate illustrates. They incurred charges of £410 5s. 3d. in respect of their efforts to secure legislative approval for a bill to allow them sell Hackett's estate, but the costs associated with bringing the act into execution raised the total to £947 15s. 6d. This was a substantial sum, and more was to follow for, as happened occasionally in such cases, a second act was required, which incurred further costs amounting to £1735 18s. 5d.[106] Expenses of this magnitude were exceptional because the trustees of the Hackett estate were more dependent on 'agents' than was normal, but since the alternative – a private act at Westminster, which was the option sought by some[107] – was still more expensive, private legislation was clearly not to be embarked upon without considerable resources.[108]

Given the financial implications it is hardly surprising that, on occasions, what manifestly were private bills were designated 'public' to 'avoid paying fees'.[109]

---

104. Waite to Wilmot, 21 May 1752, 4 July 1770 (PRONI, Wilmot Papers, T3019/1899, 6106); Magennis, *The Irish political system*, p. 43; Chesterfield to Lords of Treasury, 19 Apr. 1746 (NAI, Irish Correspondence, i, MS 2446).

105. *Commons Jn. (Irl.)*, i, 17; *Lords Journal (Irl.)*, i, 569–70.

106. The charges in passing and soliciting Sir Thomas Hackett's bill, 28 Feb. 1706 (Gilbert Library, Hackett Trustee Papers, MS 223 f. 81); Mark Tierney, *Murroe and Boher* (Dublin, 1966), pp 198, 206–7; 4 Anne, chap 3 (private); 6 Anne, chap 7 (private).

107. See, for example, Carteret to Newcastle, 26 Jan. 1728 (NA, SP67/10 ff 19–21).

108. King to Lord Kingston, 31 Oct. 1722 (TCD, King Papers, MS 750/7 f. 23).

109. A good example is the measure 'for funding and regulating the hospital founded by Richard

This practice was sharply criticised by the Crown's law officers in the 1770s, but the fees charged in Ireland on private bills were a matter of such disquiet that in the Lords in 1780 Lord Mountmorres proposed 'a conference of both houses [of parliament] to ascertain' the fees 'on the passing of private bills'. This was rejected as inappropriate, and it was determined instead to establish a committee 'to take the matter into consideration'. Little came of it, and the matter was back on the agenda six years later when it was claimed by agents that the fees to be paid on private bills in Ireland were higher than in Britain.[110] Not surprisingly, the officers of the House of Commons were vigilant to assert their entitlement to fees on all private bills when, as happened on a number of occasions, attempts were made by corporate interests to designate private bills as public.[111] Most such proposals were rebuffed, but the issue remained live not least because various attempts were made, usually by MPs, to designate any private bill that could be interpreted as having a public dimension a public bill. The most noteworthy category of bills to which this occurred were turnpike roads bills, which were designated as public bills in 1729 and in 1760 and, as such, entitled 'to pass ... without fees'.[112] This did not secure turnpike bills against all fees because the address seeking royal approval for this action was not proceeded with, but it ensured that charges, which in two instances in the early 1760s amounted to a respectable £180 and £135, were kept within bounds.[113] Despite this, road bills continued to be lumped in the public mind, if not in the statute book, with private bills. The implication – that the latter were somehow less weighty than public bills – also proved enduring,[114] though peers as well as MPs sought to ensure that the processing of private bills was as stringent as it was in the case of public bills. To this end, the House of Commons ordered in 1703 that heads of private bills should only be offered for consideration subsequent to the presentation of a petition. Practical difficulties associated with securing the return of private bills in time to receive the royal assent was also a matter of concern, and prompted a suggestion from Dublin Castle that the lord lieutenant should have the 'discretion in giving the royal assent' to private bills. Not surprisingly, this was not acceded to, and since it would have diminished the right of the Irish parliament to veto amended bills it was never a likely prospect. Indeed, there was a stronger current

Stephens' (3 Geo II, chap 33); see Southwell's remarks, [Feb. 1731] (BL, Hardwicke Papers, Add. MS 36136 ff 214–15).

110. *Lord Jn. (Irl.)*, v, 159, 671; Heron to Porten, 26 Feb., Buckinghamshire to Hillsborough, 28 Feb. 1780 (NA, SP63/468 ff 316, 328–9); *Freeman's Jn.*, 11 Feb. 1786.

111. *Lords Jn (Irl.)*, iii, 765–6.

112. *Lords Jn (Irl.)*, iv, 183; *Commons Jn. (Irl.)*, v, 377; vi, 209, 212; x, 167; David Broderick, *The first toll roads: Ireland's turnpike roads, 1729–1858* (Cork, 2002), pp 50–1.

113. Fees for turnpike bills, [Mar. 1764] (PRONI, Wilmot Papers, T3019/4815, 4816).

114. Spencer to Price, 5 July 1747 (NLW, Puleston Papers, MS 3580 f. 65); Conolly to [Delafaye], 20 Aug., Webster to [Delafaye], 27 Sept. 1719 (NA, SP63/377, 378); King to Annesley, 2 Mar. 1727 (TCD, King Papers, MS 750/8 f. 183).

of opinion within the Irish legislature that aspired to extend rather than to accede to the diminution of the authority of the Irish parliament in the making of law.[115]

THE POLITICS OF POYNINGS' LAW, 1715–60

Though the atmosphere in which Irish and British executives applied Poynings' Law during the reigns of George I and George II was predominantly harmonious, there was an enduring *undercurrent* of opposition to the law in Ireland throughout this period. It was certainly manifest at the outset of George I's reign when the requirement that appropriate cause must be shown to allow the King to issue a commission authorising the holding of a parliament in Ireland in 1715 proved unexpectedly troublesome as the privy councils in both jurisdictions contrived to complicate what should have been a straightforward business. One of the main reasons for this, inevitably, was the Irish administration's eagerness not to provide MPs with any reason to reanimate the matter of the 'sole right'.[116]

Preparations for the first parliament of the Hanoverian era commenced in the late spring of 1715 when, following the receipt from London of authorisation to convene a new parliament, the Irish Privy Council gathered to commence 'the necessary preparations ... to transmit proper bills to open the session'. Little progress was made initially because of the absence of the law officers and judiciary on circuit, but there was broad agreement on the principles by which the Council should operate. Firstly, in order to preserve the royal prerogative in respect of financial legislation, it was agreed that a money bill should be 'the first' bill to be prepared while, secondly, in an acknowledgment that the right of initiating law should rest with parliament, it was determined not to transmit 'many bills'. Justified on the grounds that, in the words of Archbishop King, it was 'more convenient to let [MPs] prepare heads and present them to the Lord Lieutenant, who brings these heads to the Privy Council to be formed into bills there', the still more revealing observation that this was 'the usual method' occluded the more obvious conclusion that the Irish Council did not aspire to assert its primacy over parliament in the making of law, it anticipated a further contraction in the role it had played during Queen Anne's reign.[117] King had little to say on this point as delays and other problems ensured the task of preparing bills at the Council board took longer than expected, but three were ready for transmission by the beginning of September.[118]

115. *Commons Jn. (Irl.)*, ii, 305; Carteret to [ ], 22 Feb. 1726 (NA, SP67/8 f. 123); *Lords Jn. (Irl.)*, iii, 458; Webster to Delafaye, 15 Oct. 1719 (NA, SP63/378).
116. Burns, *Irish parliamentary politics*, i, 53–7.
117. King to Tennison, 1 Mar. 1715 (TCD, King Papers, MS 2533 f. 150); King to Sunderland, 28 Mar., 1715 (MS 750/4 ff 246–7).
118. King to Addison, 3 May, 7 July, King to Delafaye, 4 June (TCD, King Papers, MS 750/4 ff 254, 54A, 258); King to Fitzwilliam, 6 July 1715 (MS 2533 f. 4); NA, PC2/85 f. 279.

Having received and referred the three bills to the law officers for scrutiny, the British Council's disposition to facilitate the Irish administration was demonstrated by the expeditious way in which the money bill and a bill for recognising George I's title to the throne were approved. Neither was forwarded without comment; in the case of the money bill the date on which the designated duties were to come into being was advanced by three weeks, while the recognition bill, which was returned unaltered, was sent back (though it was deemed unnecessary) simply because it was essential that 'there should be one bill for the House of Lords in Ireland to open the session withall'.[119] However, the third measure, which sought 'to prevent his majesty's subjects listing themselves in foreign services', was 'laid aside as unnecessary' because Ireland was included in a British act of a similar purport passed in 1714.[120] This was a legitimate reason for setting aside the bill, but the fact that it was one of only three Privy Council bills presented the Irish administration with an unexpected difficulty. The problem did not relate to the issuing of a commission to permit a meeting of parliament, which was forthcoming, but to the fact that since only two bills were returned, one of which (the recognition bill) had to be sent to the Lords, the Irish executive was being invited to commence the session by presenting a money bill to the Commons, which was procedurally invalid. 'The money bill', Archbishop King explained, 'cannot be sent to the Commons because they can't begin a session with it; before they receive such a bill it is necessary that they enquire whether any supply be needful and vote it, for to grant it before they vote were very preposterous'. King's expressed preference was that the enlisting bill was returned, heavily amended if necessary, simply to negotiate the opening of the session, but this did not find favour with his colleagues or with English officials.[121] Ministers adjudged instead that the Irish administration should prepare a 'new transmiss of two bills ..., the one for opening the session in the House of Commons, the subject matter of which ... may not be liable to any objection, the other for annulling the Palatinate of Tipperary', but before this instruction reached Dublin, the Irish Council prepared a new transmiss of three bills. Since, in their estimation, 'a bill for anulling the Tipperary Palatinate' should 'most properly take its rise in the Commons', they explicitly ruled this out, and opted instead for bills to deter arson, to facilitate conveyancing, and the original money bill so the date of its commencement could be moved forward to 1 December.[122] With parliament scheduled to open on 12 November, time was pressing, and in order to meet this deadline, the arson and conveyancing bills were examined directly and sent to pass under the great seal at the British Council without

119. NA, PC2/85 ff 279, 282–4.
120. NA, PC2/85 f. 282l; see King to Molineux, 8 Oct. 1715 (TCD, King Papers, MS 2533 ff 105–6).
121. King to Delafaye, 24 Sept. (TCD, King Papers, MS 750/4 f. 277); also King to Stearne, 6 Oct., King to Stanhope, 7 Oct. 1715 (MS 2533 ff 98–9, 99–102).
122. Stanhope to Lords Justices, 3 Oct. 1715 (NA, SP67/6 f. 76); King to Stanhope, 7 Oct., Lords Justices to Stanhope, 15 Oct., Galway to Stanhope, 21 Oct. 1715 (NA, SP63/373); O'Regan, *Archbishop King*, p. 222.

reference to the law officers or the Irish bills committee. This was now unusual, but it was quite legal. So too was the decision to decline to amend the money bill on the grounds, Secretary of State Stanhope explained, that 'it is much better that there should be a retrospect ... than that a money bill sent from here to Ireland should be returned *again* with any change in it, tho' only of the date'.[123] As a result, the Irish administration had four Privy Council bills with which to conduct the opening of parliament.[124]

Because of the problems they encountered in preparing for the session, the Irish administration was gratified that the recognition and money bills negotiated both houses of the Irish legislature 'with greater expedition than usual'. The recognition bill met with no resistance, but opinion was palpably less unanimous in respect of the money bill. Conscious that it would not be politic to resist its implementation, a 'Tory lawyer', Henry Singleton, 'moved a question that for the future the House [of Commons] should not receive any bill of the like kind that first did not take its rise in their House'. Singleton was supported by a number of 'young members, who otherwise are not ill affected', but despite the introduction of 'several other questions relating to the same,' the administration was relieved when MPs voted by 177 to 57 to proceed to the order of the day rather than support the objectors.[125] Prompted by these events to proceed gingerly in respect of the 'sole right' of the Irish legislature to raise money, the Irish executive not alone did not oppose publicly the introduction into the main money bill of a provision for a 20 per cent absentee tax in return for a larger than usual two year's money supply, it alerted the secretary of state 'of the danger there might be in making any alterations in this bill on your side, lest the same should give a handle to dispute ... here and consequently risk the loss of the whole subsidy'. Determined that this should not come to pass, the British Council approved the bill with a handful of minor amendments that had no bearing on the proposed tax, which pre-empted those of 'the Cork squadron' led by St John Brodrick who had calculated that the clause providing for the tax would be deleted at the Privy Council and that this deletion would 'give them a pretence for throwing ... out' the whole bill.[126]

Having failed in this instance to assert the 'sole' authority of the House of Commons to initiate money bills, MPs affirmed their adherence to the substantive point by resolving in May 1716 that 'no money bill be read in this house' prior to the reception of the report of the Committee of Accounts.[127] However, they were

123. NA, PC2/85 ff 293–4; Stanhope to King, 23 Oct., Stanhope to Lords Justices, 24 Oct. 1715 (NA, SP67/6 ff 81, 82).

124. Stanhope to Lords Justices, 10 Nov. 1715 (NA, SP67/6 f. 110).

125. Lords Justices to Stanhope, 23 Nov. 1715 (NA, SP63/373); Walton, *'The King's business'* , p. xiv.

126. Lords Justices to Stanhope, 24 Dec., Delafaye to Pringle, 24 Dec. 1715, Delafaye to [ ] (NA, SP63/373, 63/374); Burns, *Irish parliamentary politics*, i, 57–9, 61; McNally, 'Patronage and politics', pp 195–6; NA, PC2/85 ff 331, 332, 333–5; *Commons Jn. (Irl.)*, iii, 53, 54, 55, 59, 66, 68, 72, 73; 2 Geo I, chap 3.

127. *Commons Jn. (Irl.)*, iii, 91.

not to be provided with many opportunities to build on this in the years immediately following, as the British and Irish executives contrived to ensure that the heads of bill process met the legislative requirements of Ireland. Constitutional matters did not simply fade into the background, meantime, but the long-simmering dispute as to whether the final court of appeal in Irish law cases lay in the Irish or British House of Lords shifted the focus from Poynings' Law and the question of the 'sole right'. This state of affairs was not to endure, for once it became clear that ministers were determined not only to uphold the claim of the British Lords that it was the court of final appeal but also to affirm the entitlement of the Westminster legislature to make law for Ireland resentment soon found vigorous voice.[128] The main focus of comment was the appellate jurisdiction, but statements such as that made by the House of Lords in October 1719 that the kingdom of Ireland was a 'distinct dominion, and no part of the kingdom of England, [and that as a result] none can determine concerning the affairs thereof, unless authorized thereto by the known laws and customs of this kingdom' reverberated through the kingdom.[129] Archbishop King was characteristically forthright. He 'stood to his old doctrine of independency; and strenuously avow'd that no acts made by a parliament of Great Britain signified more than by-laws of a court of Py-Powder [in Ireland], unless confirmed by our own two Houses'.[130] English-born bishops, like William Nicolson of Derry, were appalled by such observations, which they interpreted literally. A more discriminating review of the spectrum of responses of Irish Protestants to the history of English/British law-making for Ireland would have indicated that attitudes were palpably more varied and nuanced.[131] What is patent is that the decision to give statutory authority in 1720 to the claim that the British parliament could legislate for Ireland stimulated constitutional discussion, and that this was not without implication for the way that Poynings' Law was perceived and applied.

The earliest indication of the impact of the enactment of the Declaratory Act on constitutional perceptions and attitudes in Ireland was provided during the banking crisis of 1720–1. With suspicion of English motives at fever pitch, elements of Irish opinion counselled against acceding to the proposal to found a Bank of Ireland on the grounds that since a 'dependent Kingdom' like Ireland was neither empowered to 'make laws nor [to] repeal them', it was in their interest

128. See Isolde Victory, 'The making of the Declaratory Act of 1720' in Gerard O'Brien (ed.), *Parliament, politics and people* (Dublin, 1989), pp 9–29; D.W. Hayton, 'The Stanhope–Sunderland ministry and the repudiation of Irish parliamentary independence', *EHR*, 113 (1999), pp 610–36; Burns, *Irish parliamentary politics*, i, 9–12, 93–105. It is significant also that William Molyneux's *The case of Ireland ... stated* (1698) was reprinted in Dublin in 1720.

129. *A collection of the protests of the Lords of Ireland*, pp 49–51.

130. Nicolson to Wake, 6 Oct. 1719 (Gilbert Library, Wake Papers, MS 27 ff 241–2).

131. See, inter alia, D.W. Hayton, 'The "country" interest and the party system 1680–*c*.1720' in Clyve Jones (ed.), *Party and management in parliament, 1660–1784* (Leicester, 1984), pp 60–3; Carteret to Pelham, 22 Feb. 1725 (NA, SP67/8 ff 43–4); above, pp 115, 157–8.

'to be very cautious' and not to 'pin any thing down upon ourselves, the consequence whereof are at least doubtful'.[132] Guided by such considerations, discontented members of the House of Commons targeted the actions of the Privy Council, and particularly the 'alterations ... made in the heads of bills'. To this end, they claimed that 'some bills (as they are returned) have not one line in them of the original draught'. This was quite misleading, but it accurately reflected the rising dislike in Ireland of the fact that both the Irish and British Councils felt at liberty to make whatever amendments they pleased to parliamentary legislation.[133] MPs singled out in particular the Irish Council's practice of introducing clauses vesting in or reserving powers to the Council. In its defence, Archbishop King and others justified the amendments made on the grounds that they were 'necessary' to remedy errors, verbal as well as legal, in the heads of bills received from the Commons, but MPs' unwillingness to accept this explanation was clearly demonstrated on January 1722 when they threw out three bills for this reason. A worried Bishop Nicolson apprehended that this was a prelude to a direct assault on 'the shackles of Poynings', but this was not the case.[134] Attention remained focussed on the Irish Council, to the discomfort of the dozen or so councillors who were also MPs. It cannot be shown that this had any implications for the manner in which heads of bills were processed at the Irish Council board, but it did discourage some councillors from participating in the scrutiny of Commons' legislation, and heightened the sensitivity of the Council at large to the fact that their amendments could precipitate the rejection of bills.[135] Specifically, it may have contributed to the loss in 1724 of the Privy Council bill for the further amendment of the law, which was strongly resisted by bishops because it proposed to void prosecutions 'already commenced in the ecclesiastical courts' against dissenters 'for fornication or clandestine marriages' conducted by their own clergy.[136] In view of this, it is hardly surprising that the most swingeing criticisms of Poynings' Law at this time were articulated by Archbishop King, who was provoked by such episodes and the crisis over Wood's halfpence to observe that Ireland's constitutional integrity had been compromised by British actions and that 'we should never be right till Poynings' etc. law were abrogated'.[137]

132. Rowley, *An answer to a book*, pp 4–5, cited in Gerald McCoy, 'Local political culture in the Hanoverian empire: the case of Ireland, 1714–1760' (DPhil, Oxford, 1994), p. 92.

133. Nicolson to Wake, 6 Jan. 1722 (Gilbert Library, Wake Papers, MS 27 ff 262–3).

134. Ibid.; above, p. 170; King to Southwell, 9 Jan. 1722 (TCD, King Papers, MS 750/7 ff 67–8); McNally, *Parties and patriots*, p. 51.

135. King to Southwell, 9 Jan. 1722, 26 Dec. 1723, King to Gibson, 10 Jan. 1724 (TCD, King Papers, MS 750/7 f. 65, MS 2537 ff 43, 50).

136. NA, PC2/88 ff 412, 419–20, 461–3; law officers' report, 1 Jan. 1724 (PC1/3/120 ff 1–2); Grafton to Carteret, 15 Nov. 1723 (SP63/382); King to Southwell, 8 Feb. 1724 (TCD, King Papers, MS 2737 f. 74).

137. O'Regan, *Archbishop William King*, p. 306.

King's sensitivities on the subject of Ireland's constitutional rights meant he was an awkward presence when, following the accession of George II to the throne in June 1727, it fell to the Irish Privy Council once more to provide due 'cause' why a writ should be issued for calling a new parliament. Having concluded that it was in Ireland's interest to convey 'some indifferent bills, which would give us no great concern whether they past [*sic*] or not' if the House of Commons chose, as he apprehended, to reject them on the grounds that 'they had their rise in the Council', King declined to sign the Privy Council letter that accompanied the five bills to London.[138] This was unusual, but since there were eight other signatories, little notice was taken. The key matter, as far as the Irish administration and British Council were concerned, was the inclusion in the transmission, 'in conformity to the usage which has been observed', of a money bill. None of the other measures were included in fulfilment of any requirement; the presence of a corn and tillage regulating bill was a well-meaning response to prevailing famine conditions, while the proposals to extend the time available to those who wished to 'qualify themselves' according to the 1704 anti- popery law, to encourage the construction of bridges, and to require 'some years conversion in papists before they practise the law' were well calculated to appeal to Irish Protestants.[139] The members of the British Council were not quite so convinced of their utility for, following the usual scrutiny, the recommendation of the Irish bills committee that the lawyers, and corn bills should be respited and that the other three should pass with amendments was endorsed. The amendments authorised were largely of the nature of clarifications and refinements, but the deletion of a clause appertaining to the imposition of 'a further additional duty upon brandy and spirits above proof' in the money bill, and the introduction of a £5 limit on certain repairs into the bridge bill indicate that a number of substantial amendments were also sanctioned.[140] Significantly, no reservations were expressed in Ireland at this, and there was no more than muted protest from Ireland at the loss of two bills.[141]

The largely trouble-free negotiation by three Privy Council bills of the British Council in 1727 ensured not alone that a writ for a new parliament was issued in a timely fashion, but that the sole right was less of an issue in 1727–8 than it had been in 1715–16.[142] This is not to suggest that the realisation that the Westminster

---

138. King to Southwell, 29 Aug. 1727 (TCD, King Papers, MS 750/9 f. 9); Privy Council letter, 19 July 1727 (NA, PC1/4/55 ff 3–4).

139. Boulter to Carteret, 20 July 1727 in *Boulter letters*, i, 151–2; Privy Council letter, 19 July 1727 (NA, PC1/4/55 ff 3–4).

140. Order in Council, 29 July, Abstract of proceedings in the Privy Council, 29 July–12 Aug. (NA, PC1/4/55, 56); NA, PC2/90 ff 52, 66–7, 68 79–80; Southwell to King, 29 July, 15 Aug. (TCD, King Papers, MS 1995–2008 ff 2166, 2168); Carteret to Lords Justices, 25 Aug. 1727 (NAI, Irish Correspondence, i, MS 2446).

141. Boulter to Carteret, 24 Aug., 23 Sept. 1727 in *Boulter letters*, i, 153, 162.

142. On writs see King to Southwell, 5 Aug. 1727 (TCD, King Papers, MS 750/9 f.2); NA, PC2/90 f. 68).

legislature had no intention of using the powers provided by the Declaratory Act aggressively to make law for Ireland had prompted a change in attitude in respect of Poynings' law. Irish opinion remained tender on this point, so when the political atmosphere disimproved in the difficult economic environment of the late 1720s and in the aftermath of the death on 30 October 1729 of William Conolly, it was inevitable that it should become a focus of attention during what one insider labelled 'the most troublesome session I ever knew'.[143] The root cause of the Irish administration's problems was the requirement that they raise extra funds to meet the 'great deficiencies which must be made up' in the revenue. Obliged, as a result, to accede to the implementation of two money bills – a 'greater' money bill encompassing the usual taxes and a 'lesser' bill with new taxes – there was considerable unease in Ireland lest a proposal to levy a 20 per cent tax on all Irish salaries and pensions held by absentees, which was provided for in the second bill, should fall at the British Council.[144] This was not the case. The 'greater' money bill negotiated the Council 'without any amendment', whilst the 'lesser' bill, though it was the subject of a petition from the manufacturers of wrought silk at London and Canterbury objecting to the proposed tax on imported British silks, experienced twenty-two amendments.[145] Described in London as 'just and reasonable', the lord lieutenant, Lord Carteret's instinctive inclination to accept that they had been made 'for very good reasons' weakened as it became clear that this was not the perception in Ireland. Saliently, attention focussed not on 'the alteration with relation to the silk' but the many smaller amendments, which were more resistant to easy explanation. Still confident that MPs would approve the bill rather than lose the taxes contained therein, the lord lieutenant and his advisers lobbied tirelessly to counter the bill's critics who deemed it emblematical of the abuses permitted by Poynings' Law. Common sense ultimately prevailed, and both measures went on to receive the royal assent, but the intense emotions generated were a warning to the British Privy Council against introducing amendments that were not essential.[146]

Three months later, the Irish executive was taught an even sharper lesson when MPs rejected a bill 'for the more effectually preventing riots and unlawful con-

143. Burns, *Irish parliamentary politics*, i, 239–53; McNally, *Parties, patriots and undertakers*, p. 137; Tickell to Delafaye, 4 Jan. 1730 (NA, SP63/392); Gallagher to St George, 13 Dec. 1729 (NA, St George Papers, C110, Box 46 f. 741); Boulter to Newcastle, 30 Oct. 1729 in *Boulter letters*, i, 266.

144. Burns, *Irish parliamentary politics*, i, 254–5; Lloyd to O'Brien, Sept. 1729 in Fagan (ed.), *Stuart papers*, i, 153; Coghill to Southwell, 8, 13 Nov. 1729 (BL, Southwell Papers, Add. MS 21122 ff 91–2, 95); Boulter to Newcastle, 13 Nov. 1729 in *Boulter letters*, i, 168.

145. NA, PC2/91 ff 86–7, 89, 90–1, 92–3, 93–5; Townshend to Carteret, 4 Dec. 1729 (NA, SP63/391).

146. Carteret to Southwell, 9, 26 Dec. (BL, Southwell Papers, Add. MS 38016 ff 11, 17); Carteret to Newcastle, 14, 22 Dec. 1729, 3 Jan. 1730 (NA, SP67/10 ff 93, 94, 97); Carteret to Townshend, 14 Dec., Clutterbuck to Delafaye, 14 Dec., Carteret to Newcastle, 22, 25 Dec. (NA, SP63/391); Coghill to Southwell, 20, 25 Dec. (BL, Southwell Papers, Add. MS 21122 ff 97–100, 102); Boulter to Newcastle, 16, 20 Dec. 1729 in *Boulter letters*, i, 272–3, 274.

federacys' that had arisen at the Irish Council. Primate Boulter, who articulated the shared conviction of councillors that the bill was 'absolutely necessary for the preservation of the public peace', was astounded. It was, he observed (inaccurately), 'the first time' that a bill that had negotiated the Irish and British Councils and the Irish House of Lords 'has been in plain defiance of our constitution, thrown out *for rising in the Privy Council*'. He was as familiar as other participants in the business of making law for Ireland with the predisposition of MPs to 'abuse the Privy Council' for interfering with bills that had their rise in the Commons, but their action on this occasion was manifestly more serious.[147] In common with most of his colleagues, Boulter reluctantly acceded to the logic of Archbishop King's analysis that there were compelling political reasons to leave the initiation of most legislation to the Commons, but this did not and, from his perspective, ought not to preclude the Privy Council exercising its constitutional right to do likewise.

What Boulter's anger failed to acknowledge was that the trend registered during the reigns of William and Mary and Anne, whereby the volume of legislation to take its rise at the Privy Council board declined as a proportion of the total, intensified during the early Hanoverian era. This was hardly apparent during the 1715–16 session when, as well as the five that were prepared in order to provide cause for calling a parliament, an additional six bills (three private and three public) were communicated from the Irish Council in the course of the session. Significantly, two of the three public bills – measures appertaining to the conduct of suits at law and St Werburgh's church – were rejected by the Irish parliament on their return, while all three private bills made it to the statute book.[148] As if chastened by this experience, the number of bills arising with the Irish Council declined in the sessions immediately following, till a situation was arrived at in the 1721–2 session (for the first time since the initiation of Poynings' law) that no bill was initiated by the Irish Council. This was a sensible response to the heightened sensitivity of Irish opinion in the wake of the ratification of the Declaratory Act for, as the mood ameliorated thereafter, five Privy Council bills were forwarded in 1723–4. Unusually, all were private bills. This was a product,

147. NA, PC2/91 f. 154; Irish Privy Council letter, 27 Jan. 1730 (BL, Hardwicke Papers, MS 36138 ff 210–11); *Lords Jn. (Irl.)*, iii, 124, 126; *Commons Jn. (Irl.)*, iii, 639; Boulter to Newcastle, 19 Mar. 1730 in *Boulter letters*, i, 287; McNally, *Parties, patriots and undertakers*, p. 52; Connolly, *Religion, law and power*, p. 95.

148. The public bills were 'for the further avoiding frivolous and vexatious suits in law' (NA, PC2/85 ff 293–4; *Commons Jn.(Irl.)*, iii, 43, 51); 'for rebuilding and enlarging the parish church of St Werburghs' (PC2/85 ff 361, 367, 374, 377; *Commons Jn. (Irl.)*, iii, 78, 88), both of which did not become law, and An act for the real union and division of parishes (PC2/85 ff 360, 363, 405, 409–10), which became law (2 Geo I, chap 14). The three private bills, which became law, were 2 Geo I, chap 5 (private); PC2/85 ff 355, 367, 374–5, 377; *Lords Jn. (Irl.)*, ii, 526; *Commons Jn. (Irl.)*, iii, 104, 106, 112 (Hammerton bill); 2 Geo I, chap 6 (private); PC2/85 ff 355, 367, 375, 377; *Commons Jn. (Irl.)*, iii, 96, 99, 101, 106, 112 (Friend bill); and 2 Geo I, chap 7; PC2/85 ff 401–2, 402–3; *Lords Jn. (Irl.)*, ii, 532; *Commons Jn. (Irl.)*, iii, 107, 108, 109, 112 (Harris bill).

in the first instance, of the fact that there was a backlog in this area arising out of the failure to approve any private bills in 1721–2 and, in the second, of the greater resort by interests seeking private legislation to the Privy Council.[149] On this occasion, four of the five bills were approved.[150] There was to be no repeat of this in the sessions that followed as parliamentary opposition to the Privy Council's legislative activities through the 1720s ensured that, other than the 1727–8 session, when the number of Privy Council bills was inflated by the requirements of a new parliament, the number of bills that took their rise at the Irish Council board did not exceed two in any session.[151] Inevitably, the rejection of the riot bill in 1730 ensured this trend was intensified rather than reversed as, following the ratification of one (a bill to prevent the throwing of fireworks) and the rejection by the Commons of another Privy Council bill in 1731–2, no further public bills originated with the Council until 1743–4.[152] In that session, a measure was advanced to allow the King's Inns sell and lease property; this negotiated both the British Council and the Irish Lords, but was rejected by the Commons.[153] A similar fate awaited the tillage bill of 1745–6, prompted in part at least by 'a flaming speech against bills taking rise in Council' by the influential master of the rolls, Thomas Carter, while, in 1750, the British Council responded to intense lobbying from Ireland by respiting a Council bill permitting Church of Ireland ecclesiastics to exchange and to divide lands.[154] Indeed, the only public bill arising

149. As, for example, in the case of the Erasmus Smith bill in 1723 (Irish Privy Council to Lords Justices, 31 Oct. 1723 (NA, SP63/381)).

150. Those approved were bills 'for the further application of the rents and profits of the lands and tenements … given by Erasmus Smith' (NA, PC2/88 ff 352, 369–71, 372–3; *Commons Jn. (Irl.)*, iii, 373, 374, 375, 376, 377, 389; 10 Geo I, chap 1 private); to enable Lord Blayney sell part of his estate (PC2/88 ff 392, 428–9, 442–6, PC1/3/120 ff 12–13; *Lords Jn. (Irl.)*, ii, 793; *Commons Jn. (Irl.)*, iii, 384, 385, 386, 387, 389); for the sale of part of the estate of James Stevenson (PC2/88 ff 392, 431–33, 442–6, PC1/3/122 ff 10–11, 16–17; *Lords Jn. (Irl.)*, ii, 794; *Commons Jn. (Irl.)*, iii, 384, 385, 387, 389); and for Lady Blessington's jointure (PC2/88 ff 375, 424–5, 442–6, PC1/3/122 ff 4–6; *Lords Jn. (Irl.)*, ii, 796; *Commons Jn. (Irl.)*, iii, 386, 387, 388, 389). The private bill that did not secure approval was 'for the sale of the estate of Edward Kelly of Fidane' (PC2/88 ff 416, 440, 446–7).

151. Above, p. 195; the Privy Council initiated in 1727–28 a bill 'for preventing embezzling' by servants and the destruction of engines (1 Geo II, chap 24). As well as the riot bill discussed above, the Council initiated in 1729–30 a bill 'for the better discovery of judgements in the courts' (3 Geo II, chap 7).

152. 5 Geo. II, chap 12 (fireworks act). The bill lost in 1731–2 appertained to the union and division of parishes (NA, PC2/91 ff 527–9, 568, 572–4; *Lords Jn. (Irl.)*, iii, 185, 191; *Commons Jn. (Irl.)*, iv, 53, 54).

153. NA, PC2/98 ff 110–11, 122–4, 133–5; *Lords Jn. (Irl.)*, iii, 570, 573; *Commons Jn. (Irl.)*, iv, 437, 438.

154. Fletcher to Wilmot, 23 Apr. 1746 in Walton (ed.), *The King's business*, p. 4; Bishop of Down to Ryder, 10 Apr. 1746 in Malcomson (ed.), *Irish official papers*, ii, 21; NA, PC2/99 ff 408, 426–7, 435–7, PC2/101 ff 481, 489, 497–8; PC1/6/18 f.5; *Lords Jn .(Irl.)*, iii, 639, 645; *Commons Jn. (Irl.)*, iv, 503, 504, 505. The 1750 church lands bill was deemed 'bad and dangerous' (Weston to Waite, 24 Feb. 1750 (PRONI, Wilmot Papers, T3019/1494); Bishop of Down to Ryder, 10 Mar. 1750 in Malcomson (ed.), *Irish official papers*, ii, 33).

with the Irish Council to make it to the statute book between 1732 and 1760 was a measure appertaining to financial presentments at the court of King's Bench, which was approved in 1756 (Table Six; p. 242).[155] The situation was somewhat more encouraging with respect of private bills; three of the six that took their rise as the Irish Council board during the reign of George II received the royal assent. Significantly, the three that were not unsuccessful were respited at the British Council board rather than rejected by the Irish House of Commons.[156]

Forty-one bills in all were initiated at the Irish Council board during the reigns of the first two Georges. This represented 4.4 per cent of the bills to arise during this period, but this figure masks the striking decline – from 8 per cent during the reign of George I to 2.6 per cent during the reign of George II – in the proportion of measures that originated at that forum over this period (Table Eight; p. 244). Omitting for the purpose of this argument, the ten Privy Council bills that were initiated to provide due cause for the calling of parliaments in 1715 and 1727, the decline of the Privy Council as a law-making body is even more stark. Whereas 75 per cent (eight private and four public) of Privy Council bills made it to law during George I's reign, only 47 per cent (three private and four public) did so during the longer reign of George II. The abandonment by the Privy Council of its power to initiate ordinary legislation was prolonged and somewhat fitful, but it was apparent by 1730 that it would do so no more than occasionally.

The eclipse of the Privy Council as a law-making body resulted in a significant transfer of power from the executive to the legislature. It was only a short step from this to the conclusion that the interventions of the British Council were also unjustified, but whereas this argument could be sustained by a particular reading of Poynings' Law, it was not widely embraced. Significantly, it was inconsistent with the viewpoint, widely accepted in Ireland at this time, that '*England* is the Principal Kingdom, and *Ireland* an accessory to it'.[157] The pamphleteer John Browne, for example, suggested in 1731 that 'it could be no way below the dignity of our parliament to send a select committee to wait on their sovereign for his assent to such bills as they judge necessary for the honour of his majesty and the welfare of their fellow subjects'.[158] Yet, when it emerged in the autumn of 1731 that Robert Walpole's British ministry was actively contemplating 'tacking' a clause to a bill communicated from Ireland in order to repeal the 1704 sacramental

155. 29 Geo II, chap 14; NA, PC2/105 ff 113, 141, 146–8; *Commons Jn. (Irl.)*, v, 396, 401, 406, 408.
156. 7 Geo. II, chap 2 (private); NA, PC2 /92 ff 348, 438–40, 442–3; PC1/5/22 ff 3–4; *Commons Jn. (Irl.)*, iv, 147, 148, 152 (Graham act); NA, PC2 /93 ff 326, 388–90, 398–9; *Commons Jn. (Irl.)*, iv, 216, 218, 219, 220, 223 (Nuttall act); NA, PC2/94 ff 398, 451, 461–2; *Lords Jn. (Irl.)*, iii, 419, 42; *Commons Jn. (Irl.)*, iv, 281, 282, 283, 285 (Coote act); these became law. NA, PC2/92 ff 347–8; PC1/5/22, 23 (Maynard bill); PC2/93 ff 326, 402 (Bolton bill); PC2/95 ff 516, 639, 659 (Stafford estate bill) were respited.
157. The words quoted are by Archbishop Synge, cited in McNally, *Parties, patriots and undertakers*, p. 183.
158. John Browne, *Reflections upon the present unhappy circumstances of Ireland in a letter to … the lord archbishop of Cashel* (Dublin, 1731), pp 13–15.

test required of Presbyterians, it was confidently forecast in Ireland that any such measure would 'certainly be flung out in the House of Commons or dropt in the House of Lords without a division'.[159] Significantly, peers chose this moment to reanimate a proposition previously advanced in 1695, 1703 and 1716 that heads of bills 'prepared' in the Lords should be communicated to the Commons 'for their consideration and concurrence before they are laid before the government'. Such an arrangement, which was promoted on the grounds that it would 'very much facilitate the passing of bills', was given added impetus when MPs undertook to do likewise in December 1733, intensifying unease in official circles that this was 'a material innovation' that was 'not to be admitted' on the grounds that it must make it more difficult in future to amend or to veto bills emanating from the Irish legislature. This obliged the duke of Dorset to make clear his disapproval, but though this was important in ensuring the negation of the resolution by 102 votes to 27 in the Commons in January 1734, MPs were guided in this action – not by opposition to the principle but by resentment at the fact that the Lords had snubbed a bill to limit tithes that took its rise with them.[160]

The inability of the two houses of the Irish parliament to agree to present legislation jointly to the Irish Council and the unwillingness of the Irish executive to acquiesce in this practice reflected the prevailing disinclination to favour constitutional innovation. This outlook would certainly have been reinforced was it generally known that among other major constitutional changes, Irish Jacobites favoured the repeal of Poynings' Law.[161] There was no strong voice calling for such a radical *démarche* in Protestant Ireland during the 1730s or during most of the 1740s. However, as the prevailing consensus sustained by the undertaker system degenerated, however temporarily, into quasi-factionalism during the late 1740s and early 1750s, criticism of Poynings' Law appreciated. Inevitably, the outspoken municipal radical Charles Lucas was one of its sharpest critics, but since he was looked upon with especial disfavour in parliamentary circles he was in no position to make an issue out of this.[162] The expanding fissures within the

159. McCoy, 'Local political cultures in the Hanoverian Empire', pp 171–2; Clayton to Clayton, [Jan. 1732] (Beinecke Library Osborn Collection, Sundon letterbook 2 ff 109–10 printed in Thompson ed., *The memoirs of Lady Sundon*, ii, 18–21; Barrymore to Price, 12 Jan. 1732, Kingsbury to Price, 24 Nov. 1733 (NLW, Puleston Papers, MS 3582 f. 1, MS 3584 f. 19); Burns, *Irish parliamentary politics*, ii, 20–2; Magennis, *The Irish political system*, p. 26.

160. MacNally, *Parties, patriots and undertakers*, p. 42; James, *Lords of the ascendancy,* p. 132; Magennis, *The Irish political system*, pp 26–7; *Lords Jn. (Irl.)*, ii, 10, iii, 244, 245, 249, 256, 271; *Commons Jn. (Irl.)*, iii, 100, 105; iv, 93, 119; Galway to Stanhope, 15 June 1716 (NA, SP63/374); Burns, *Irish parliamentary politics*, i, 66–7; *A collection of protests of the Lords of Ireland*, pp 94–5, 96–7; Wainwright to Dodington, 2 Jan., Cary to Dodington, 10 Jan. 1734 in HMC, *Reports on private collections, vi: Eyre Matcham MSS*, pp 57–8; Cary to Delafaye, 10 Jan. Wainwright to [ ], 16 Jan., Dodington to Newcastle, 17 Jan., Newcastle to Dorset, 5 Feb. 1734 (NA, SP63/397).

161. Burns, *Irish parliamentary politics*, ii, 38; Fagan (ed.), *Stuart papers*, i, 264–5.

162. Hill, *From patriots to unionists*, p. 89; Walpole to Devonshire, 21 Feb. 1738 (NA, SP63/401).

undertaker system could not be so easily papered over, however, particularly when Henry Boyle, who had dominated domestic politics for a generation, perceived that he could advantageously animate the question of the 'sole right' in the early 1750s to demonstrate his indispensability to the Irish administration. It is salient that Boyle did not choose to appeal to his 'country parts' as a matter of principle, but in order to make a political point, as the sole right issue was now fought not on the right of the Irish parliament to raise revenue but on its claim to possess the sole entitlement to dispose of the surplus currently in the Irish exchequer, which was contested by ministers who insisted that the royal consent was necessary.

This emerged as a legislative issue for the first time in 1749, but it assumed serious proportions in 1751 when the heads of a bill that arose in the Commons 'for the payment of the principal sum of £120,000 in discharge of ... the national debt' was transmitted to the British Council without the anticipated 'reference to the King's prior consent'; mention was made instead to the King's 'gracious recommendation'. Happy that the measure should become law, but only if the royal prerogative was upheld, the bill was sent to be engrossed and returned contingent on the addition of a clause signifying that the King gave his 'consent' to the allocation of the proposed sum. The Irish executive was uneasy with this amendment, but though they apprehended problems in the Irish parliament, the combination of Primate Stone's effective lobbying and Henry Boyle's unwillingness to fight a battle he could not win ensured the amended measure advanced to become law.[163] However, two years later when relations between Boyle and the Irish executive had broken down, he was disinclined to be so forbearing. He was guided and advised by Anthony Malone, who had let it be known 'that no consideration whatsoever should prevail upon him to agree to that preamble [acceding to the previous consent] being inserted in the bill for paying off the national debt which returned from England last session' because it would be a betrayal of 'the libertys of the people ... not [to] oppose it'. The Irish administration countered by alleging that this amounted to an attack on the royal prerogative, but unable to insist on the inclusion of an appropriate 'previous consent' clause, they allowed the measure, which proposed to allocate £77,500 to the discharge of the national debt, make its way through the Irish parliament and Council.[164] Ministers and officials in London were less than pleased, and impelled by the King, who was determined to uphold the royal prerogative against dilution and by the conviction that royal displeasure should be made clear, it was determined at the British Council not only to amend the bill to reflect this fact but

163. 25 Geo II, chap 2; NA, PC2/102 ff 363–4, 378–9, 383–5; Johnston-Liik, *History of the Irish parliament*, i, 114–15; Magennis, *The Irish political system*, pp 66–8; Sackville to Wilmot, 28 Nov., Wilmot to Weston, 11 Dec. 1751 (PRONI, Wilmot Papers, T3019/1822, 1831); Burns, *Irish parliamentary politics*, ii, 128–30.

164. *Commons Jn. (Irl.)*, v, 190; Sackville to Pelham, 15 Nov. 1753 (Nottingham University Library, Newcastle of Clumber Papers, NeC 1581/1, copy in PRONI, Wilmot Papers, T3019/2204); Sackville to Wilmot, 16 Nov. 1753 (T3019/2205); Burns, *Irish parliamentary politics*, ii, 161–3.

also to upbraid the Irish administration. So, when on 27 November the Irish bills committee recommended the insertion in the money bill of a more explicit statement of the royal consent than had been appealed to in 1751 it was also agreed on the following day that the full Council should address a letter to its Irish counterpart 'signifying to them that the addition of the clause is absolutely necessary for the support of ['s] prerogative and dignity, and for preserving the regularity of the proceedings in his parliament in Ireland'. Signed by eighteen councillors, this represented an unambiguous affirmation by both and his ministers of their determination not to accede to any modification of the operation of Poynings' Law.[165]

Faced with the option of backing down, and surrendering his power and influence in the Irish parliament, Boyle felt he had no alternative but to oppose the modified money bill. His decision set him on a collision course with the Irish administration that climaxed on 17 December 1753 when he and his allies successfully ensured the bill's rejection by 122 votes to 117. Some on the government side apprehended that this was the first step *en route* 'to flinging off the English government'. But though the rejection of the King's consent was deemed 'unjustifiable', and elicited an expression of his majesty's 'highest displeasure', most of the forecasts of a major Anglo–Irish constitutional crisis proved unfounded as the government contrived successfully to defuse what was essentially a political row before it escalated into a constitutional dispute.[166] Despite this, the public's exposure to Poynings' Law, symbolised by the publication of the letter of the British Council of 28 November in a pamphlet on the dispute, helped to animate the voice of political patriotism, and it encouraged the articulation of the view that Ireland was being denied its right to make law unencumbered, by 'oppression'.[167] Critical to this, was the emergence of a patriot 'party' headed by Edmund Sexten Pery, William Brownlow and Robert French, who were to the fore in raising the matter of Poynings' Law. They focussed in particular on the role of the Irish Privy Council. Persuaded (like an increasing number of Irish commentators) that the Irish Council was acting in error in

165. Burns, *Irish parliamentary politics*, ii, 164–5; NA, PC2/103 ff 514, 515–6, 518–19, 525; British to Irish Council, 28 Nov. 1753 and reply (BL, Hardwicke Papers, Add. MS 35870 ff 235–7); Adderley to Charlemont, ca. 18 Dec. 1753 in HMC, *Charlemont*, ii, 190–91; Magennis, *The Irish political system*, pp 76–9 passim.

166. Burns, *Irish parliamentary politics*, ii, 169–70; Sackville to Wilmot, 15, 18 Dec., Waite to Wilmot, 18 Dec. (PRONI, Wilmot Papers, T3019/2224, 2226, 2227); Tuam to Ryder, 18 Dec. 1753 in Malcomson (ed.), *Irish official papers*, ii, 3607; Dorset to Holdernesse, 14 Jan. 1754 (NA, SP63/413).

167. *The cabinet, containing a collection of curious papers relative to the present political contests in Ireland* (London, 1754), pp 49–50; *An account of the revenue and national debt of Ireland, with … a speech to the parliament of Henry, Lord Viscount Sydney, lord lieutenant, in the year 1692, as also an order of council, and several resolutions of the House of Commons, extracted from the journals …*(London, 1754); Magennis, *The Irish political system*, pp 15, 86; Bob Harris, *Politics and the nation: Britain in the mid-eighteenth century* (Oxford, 2002), p. 203.

exercising 'that negative power they used of refusing to send bills over to England', they chose to challenge the operation of Poynings' Law on this, its most vulnerable point, in the 1757–8 session.

Robert French initiated the attack in November 1757 when he sought information on the number of heads of bills passed by the Commons during the previous two sessions in order to establish how many measures had failed to negotiate the Irish Council, and he pressed successfully for the establishment of a Commons' committee to investigate the fate of all bills. Pursuant to this, French and Pery sought to introduce regulatory legislation; they invited MPs early in December to permit them to bring 'in heads of a bill to explain and amend Poynings' Law' to ensure that all 'heads of bills pass'd by this house' were presented to the Crown. However, when Pery moved formally for leave to introduce such a bill, it was denied, 102 votes to 76, on the grounds 'that Poynings' Law is considered by the English as the palladium of the dependence of Ireland upon England, and that for many prudential reasons it was not proper to raise a jealousy of that import in England'.[168] This was a tame outcome to the sequence of debates focussing on the Irish Council's entitlement to initiate bills and to veto and amend heads of bills referred to it, but the readiness of MPs in April 1758 to pronounce 'that private and clandestine applications to procure alterations in heads of public bills … are unconstitutional and of dangerous consequence to the public', which was an unmistakeable reference to the Irish Council, is indicative of the fact that attitudes were changing. So too was the decision of John Monck Mason to publish an extended commentary on the failure to admit of Pery's and French's bill in which he not just defended the legitimacy of their attempt 'to root out those abuses which have sprung up under the influence' of Poynings' Law, he offered a detailed analysis of the history and purpose of the law to demonstrate that the Irish Privy Council's claim to possess the right to initiate bills and to amend heads received from the legislature was 'an unwarranted usurpation' of power.[169] This remained the key patriot argument against Poynings' Law in the eighteenth century, and it was well established as a prominent trope in public discourse by the end of George II's reign.[170]

168. A gentleman of Ireland [John Monck Mason], *Remarks on Poynings' Law and the manner of passing bills in the parliament of Ireland* (Dublin, 1758), pp 34–40; Willes, Legal and political reminiscences, 1757–8 (WRO, Willes Papers 2, pp 16–27); *Commons Jn. (Irl.)*, vi, 45, 47, 49; Harris, *Politics and the nation*, p. 229.
169. [Monck Mason], *Remarks on Poynings' Law*, passim, but especially pp 5, 25.
170. Burns, *Irish parliamentary politics*, ii, 216; Walton, *The King's* business, p. lxxxi; *Commons Jn. (Irl.)*, vi, 106; A list of heads of bills, *Universal Advertizer*, 20 May 1760.

THE IRISH PARLIAMENT, THE IRISH PRIVY COUNCIL AND THE
MAKING OF LAW, 1715–60

The virtual eclipse of the Irish Privy Council as a law-making body during the
early Hanoverian era meant inevitably that parliament became the primary source
of Irish legislation. In all, 96 per cent (888 out of 929) of legislative measures
inaugurated between 1715 and 1760 took their rise as heads of bills. Most of these
arose in the Commons, which was the assembly of origin of 85 per cent. This was
an increase of 15 per cent on the position during the reign of Queen Anne, but
it is salient that this figure did not grow further thereafter because the Lords
became more legislatively active. From a level of 11 per cent during Anne's reign
(Tables Four), the proportion of heads of bills arising with peers climbed to 13
per cent during the reign of George I and to 15 per cent during the reign of
George II. The corollary of this was that the percentage of heads to arise in the
Commons fell modestly from 87 per cent during the reign of George I to 85 per
cent during the reign of his successor (Table Eight). This pattern was replicated
by the average number of heads of bills initiated each session; this rose in the
House of Lords from 5.16 to 5.88 and fell in the Commons from 35 to 32.17,
though the sessional average (22.53) was marginally greater during the reign of
George I than it was during the shorter reign of his predecessor (21.8) (Table
One; p. 159). This can be accounted for by the fact that the average number of
laws made throughout the period oscillated appreciably. Indeed, as was the case
during the reign of Queen Anne (Table Four; p. 112), the reign of George I
commenced with a flurry of legislative activity that was not sustained. George II's
reign followed a similar pattern, but the decline that is observable during the
middle years of the reign was not enduring, and the final decade witnessed a
recovery to the levels registered in the late 1720s (Table Eight; p. 244).

Inevitably, a significant proportion of heads of bills did not progress. As the
place of origin of the overwhelming majority, this was inevitably more of a feature
of the operation of the House of Commons than it was of the Lords where a
modest 6 per cent of the heads of bills initiated between 1715 and 1726 and 9 per
cent initiated between 1727 and 1760 failed to advance (Table Eight). In 15 per
cent of instances in which leave was given by the Commons to introduce a bill
during the reign of George I, no bill ever transpired; during the reign of George
II, this occurred in only 8 per cent of instances.[171] Remarkably, during the ten
sessions that were held between 1737 and 1756, there are only fourteen instances
of leave to introduce a bill being granted in which no bill was forthcoming. In
might be concluded that this was a consequence of the fact that this was a
quiescent period in the history of the Irish parliament, but this is not the reason;
rather it is indicative of a pattern of law-making that was more efficient than

---

171. The figures were comprised as follows: 26 or 13.5 per cent of public heads and 5 or 10 per cent
    of private heads were lost during the reign of George I, as against 7 per cent (42) public heads
    and 1.33 per cent (1) private during the reign of George II (Tables Six and Seven).

previously. Thus, the percentage of public and private heads of bills presented in the Commons that failed to proceed fell from 16 per cent (33 out of 210) during the reign of George I to 14 per cent (79 from 547) during the reign of George II (Table Eight). Consistent with this, the percentage of failing public heads arising in the Commons fell from 19 per cent to 15 per cent during the same period.[172] In all, the percentage of heads of bills (public and private) initiated in the Irish parliament during the reign of George I that failed to progress to the Irish Council (27 per cent) was noticeably larger than that which failed (20 per cent) during the reign of George II (Table Eight).

A total of 175 heads of bills, 132 of which were public and 43 private, were forwarded from the Irish parliament to the Irish Privy Council during the reign of George I; and 515, comprising 445 public and 70 private heads of bills progressed during the reign of George II. Of these totals, 21 heads (13 public: 10 per cent; and eight private: 19 per cent) did not negotiate the Irish Council during the reign of George I. This represented 12 per cent of the total, which was nearly 2 per cent greater than the percentage that were lost during the reign of his successor. A similar pattern is identifiable in respect of the experience of bills at the Irish Council during the reign of George II. The 11 per cent (47 from 445) of heads of public bills that were respited or postponed at that stage between 1727 and 1760 was marginally larger than it was between 1715 and 1727, though the percentage of private bills to fall declined significantly to 9 per cent (Tables Six, Seven and Eight). In specific terms, the actual number of bills to fall at this hurdle each session ranged from zero in 1717–18 to 9 in 1759–60, and averaged 3.3 and 3.1 per session during the reigns of George I and George II respectively.

It is not possible to tell in the majority of the 74 instances in which heads of bills failed to negotiate the Irish Council board why this happened. It certainly had little to do with the house of parliament from which they originated as, proportionate to the number received, the percentage of Lords heads (12 per cent) that failed at this hurdle was not dramatically different from the percentage of Commons heads (10 per cent). Moreover, the bills span the full range of issues that occupied the Irish parliament during the early Hanoverian era. Fourteen were private bills, eleven of which rose with the Commons and three with the Lords, though an unknown number of private bills, such as the Robinson estate bill promoted in 1721 and in 1724, presented directly to the Privy Council also failed at this stage.[173] The fact that in this, and other, instances, private bills with powerful supporters did not progress reinforces the conclusion that there were compelling reasons why particular heads languished.[174] This appears to have been

172. These percentages and figures are calculated from the information tabulated on Tables Six, Seven and Eight. Saliently, the overall percentage of private bills that fell was up from 2 per cent (one from 49) during the reign of George I to 5 per cent (four from seventy-five) during the reign of George II.

173. Carteret to Bolton, 30 Dec. 1721 (NA, SP67/7 ff 102–3); King to Southwell, 11 Jan. 1724 (TCD, King Papers, MS 2537, ff 55–6).

174. The heads were the Carter estate bill (1719–20) (*Commons Jn. (Irl.)*, iii, 194, 195, 199); a bill for

the case also with respect of public bills. In 1716, for example, an attempt by the Lords to block the Commons' efforts to permit Dissenters to bear arms by 'excepting them from the sacramental test for ever in the militia and for ten years in the army' by preparing a bill of exactly 'the same title and much the same purpose but without the above mentioned clause' failed when the Lords' bill was laid aside at the Council board; debate focussed thereafter on the Commons' bill, which was modified in the teeth of intense ecclesiastical resistance to permit dissenters to bear arms for the duration of the present crisis only, and this helped to ensure the measure was rejected by the Commons on its return.[175] Despite this outcome, the Lords had recourse to the same tactic again in 1719; on this occasion their heads of a bill for the relief of dissenters was respited on the grounds that its purpose was 'to give more strength' to the opponents of a comparable Commons' measure in the Lords. It did not succeed, though opposition in the Lords was particularly vigorous.[176]

The refusal of councillors to nod through church and anti-popery bills was a source of anxiety to Englishmen on the Irish ecclesiastical bench, who shared Bishop Nicolson's unease that many Irish Protestants were, as he put it, 'afraid of provoking our Roman neighbours'.[177] In point of fact, equally problematic, deficient or controversial bills appertaining to the ascertaining or levying of fees by officeholders (1715–16, 1725–6), for preventing clandestine marriage (1721–2, 1725–6), for regulating the making of pewter and brass (1719–20, 1723–4), for preventing bribery and corruption at elections (1729–30, 1731–2), for 'continuing several temporary statutes (1731–2, 1735–6, 1737–8), and for 'securing the liberty of the subject' by extending the right of *habeas corpus* (1743–4, 1749–50, 1751–2, 1755–6), were routinely rejected.[178] Few of these measures enjoyed a difficult

the relief of Patrick Ryan (1721–22) (*Commons Jn. (Irl.)*, iii, 271, 274, 279, 280); Mervyn estate bill (1721–2) (*Commons Jn. (Irl.)*, iii, 278, 281, 283); Countess of Antrim jointure bill (1721–2) (*Commons Jn. (Irl.)*, iii, 283, 285, 287); Eccles bill (1721–2) (*Commons Jn. (Irl.)*, iii, 279, 282, 285, 287); Mary Dowdall relief bill (1723–4) (*Commons Jn. (Irl.)*, iii, 349, 350, 352, 354); Hamilton of Killileagh estate bill (1725–6) (*Commons Jn. (Irl.)*, iii, 428, 429, 431); Waller trustees bill (1725–6) (*Lords Jn. (Irl.)*, ii, 819, 863); Theophilus Jones trustees bill (1727–8) (*Commons Jn. (Irl.)*, ii, 523, 542); Heaton lands bill (1737–8) (*Lords Jn. (Irl.)*, iii, 383, 385); Earl of Barrymore trustees bill (1737–8) (*Lords Jn. (Irl.)*, iii, 374); Andrew Savage trustees bill (1745–6) (*Commons Jn. (Irl.)*, iv, 479, 483, 487); Edmond Sexten Pery lease bill (1753) (*Commons Jn. (Irl.)*, v, 184, 186, 188, 190, 192); and the creditors of John Fitzgerald bill (1759–60) (*Commons Jn. (Irl.)*, iv, 163, 169, 170, 171).

175. *Lords Jn. (Irl.)*, ii, 504, 506; Grafton to Stanhope, 15 Feb., Lords Justices to Stanhope, 24 Feb. (NA, SP63/374); King to Wake, 15 June 1716 (TCD, King Papers, MS 2533 ff 248–9). King was delighted that the bill was lost in the Commons despite his forecasts that it would fail in the Lords where opposition was even more entrenched.

176. Webster to Delafaye, 1 Oct. 1719 (NA, SP63/378); *Lords Jn. (Irl.)*, ii, 630, 641. The Commons' bill became law (6 Geo I, chap 5) despite the intense opposition of peers (James, *Lords of the ascendancy*, pp 63–4).

177. Quoted in McNally, *Patronage and politics in Ireland*, p. 162; for Nicolson see F.G. James, *North Country bishop: a biography of William Nicolson* (New Haven, 1956), pp 256–7.

178. *Lords Jn. (Irl.)*, ii, 540, 542, 829, 832 (officers' fees bill); *Lords Jn. (Irl.)*, ii, 703, 706, 831, 839

passage *en route* to the Council board, but heads of bills that did frequently encountered difficulties with councillors. This is true, for instance, of a measure pursued in 1733–34 for regulating trials in high treason cases; of the heads of a bill for the relief of insolvent debtors that enjoyed a tortuous passage through the Commons in 1745–6; of the controversial attempt in 1753 to compel Arthur Jones Nevill to make good the defects of several barracks, and of the 1756 proposal to provide for the discharge of fees when accused were acquitted.[179]

Some indirect insights are offered into the process by the experience of heads of a bill for *habeas corpus* that were lost in 1743–4 and 1755–6. In the former instance, the bill fortuitously 'slipped through the committee of Council', and might have made it through the full Council had the lord lieutenant, the duke of Devonshire, not precipitated its rejection when he made it clear that he believed it was 'contrary to my duty to sign a letter to recommend it' because the measure would have 'interfered with those acts of Henry 8th and Edward 6th by which persons guilty of treason in Ireland may be tried for it in England'.[180] The measure was afforded a warmer reception in 1755, but it failed to progress once more because, in the judgement of the highest officers of state, it was inappropriate.[181] In 1747–8, the heads of a bill for naturalising Jews, thereby giving them full rights to own property, came to grief in an equivalent fashion because, it was believed, it was improper to advantage an 'enemy to all Christians'.[182]

As these examples bear witness, many heads of bills were lost at the Irish Privy Council because those charged with determining whether they should proceed felt there were material constitutional or religious reasons, rather than minor matters of detail or drafting deficiencies, why they should not become law. This is vividly attested by the record Chief Baron Edward Willes made of debate at the Council board in the late 1750s on a number of bills. The most animated was on the heads received from the Lords 'for a general register of priests'. Promoted by the earl of Clanbrassill, its object was to put in place a more efficient system of clerical registration that, consistent with the repeal of the discredited provision inaugurated in 1704 prohibiting the replacement of registered Catholic clergy, offered legal recognition to Catholic clergy contingent on their subscription to an oath that one Protestant moderate deemed acceptable to all 'but those that are

(clandestine marriage bill); *Commons Jn. (Irl.)*, iii, 587, 588, 593, 600, 601, 605, 606, iv, 28, 31, 32, 36 (bribery and corruption bills); *Lords Jn. (Irl.)*, iii, 165, 167, 319, 330, 396, 397 (temporary statutes bill); *Commons Jn. (Irl.)*, iv, 420, 421, 427, 429, v, 24, 25, 26, 108, 113, 115, 119; v, 248, 284, 309, 310 (*habeas corpus* bills).

179. *Commons Jn. (Irl.)*, iv, 77, 79, 82, 83, 85, 88, 89, 90, 91, 92 (treason bill); ibid., iv, 459, 465, 466, 468, 473, 474, 476, 478, 487, 489 (insolvent debtors bill); ibid., v, 197, 201, 204, 208, 209, 210 (Neville bill); ibid., v, 249, 284, 321, 313, 323, 328, 329, 330, 358, 359 (fees bill).

180. Devonshire to Newcastle, 25 Dec. 1743 (NA, SP63/405).

181. Tuam to Ryder, 15 Dec. 1755 in Malcomson (ed.), *Irish official papers*, ii, 58; Conway to Wilmot, 16 Dec. 1755 (PRONI, Wilmot Papers, T3019/2728).

182. Down to Ryder, 16 Dec. 1747, 19, 20 Jan., Stone to Sackville, 18 Jan. 1748 in Malcomson (ed.), *Irish official papers*, ii, 26, 27, 28, 36.

absolutely devoted not only to the Church but [also] to the court of Rome'. Having overcome vigorous opposition in the Lords, the heads encountered still further resistance at the Council board from Willes, among others. 'Convinced in my conscience the bill was a very dangerous one', the chief baron 'took a large share in opposing the bill'. He justified his stand on the grounds, firstly, that the measure was nothing less than 'an establishm[en]t of popery by a law, for this was not only to licence a present priest in each parish, ... it p[ro]vided for their succession'. Secondly, he adjudged that the 'toleration of popery' that would result was 'contrary to the set[t]led maxims and politicks of Great Britain and Ireland from the time of the Reformation', and opined that it would be 'very extraordinary ... to reverse those politicks at once without any visible reason for doing so and establish[ing popery] by a law'. And thirdly, he observed that the proposal was contrary to 'the 1st and 27 Eliz[abeth] ag[ains]t priests coming into England or any other dominion belonging to the Crown of England', and that its implementation 'might occasion such a clashing of laws as might be of very bad consequence' since it would 'give mankind a very strange notion of the incon-sistency of the laws of the Crown of Great Britain that in England 'tis death for a priest to exercise the functions of his religion and in Ireland he is not only licensed to do it, but the governm[en]t gives him a safe passport to come into it in order to exercise it'. These were weighty considerations, and they helped ensure that the discussion at the Council board, which was 'very much divided as to the general propriety of the bill', 'took up many days'. Willes shouldered the burden of responsibility for making the 'legal' case against the measure, the Primate the religious case, and it was Willes' ability to elicit an admission from Clanbrassill that he had in mind to introduce a further measure 'to allow four popish bishops, one in each province' that proved decisive. Unwilling to accept that a whole category of Penal Laws would be rendered null and void, the Council determined on a division, 14–12, to reject the measure though it was favoured by the lord lieutenant, the duke of Bedford.[183]

The disinclination to endorse major legislative innovation, vividly attested to by the response of councillors to Clanbrassill's clerical registration bill, was further manifest in the response to the heads, communicated from the House of Commons, 'for better regulating the elections of the lord mayor, aldermen, sheriffs and officers of the city of Dublin'. This bill proposed to divide the city into wards in order to make the elections to the Corporation 'more popular', but Willes and his Council colleagues so disliked the fact that the bill sought to 'change the constitution of the City of Dublin' they declined to allow it to proceed on the grounds that 'it would be improper and dangerous to advise his

---

183. Leland to Clanbrassill, 31 Oct. 1757 (Roden Papers, PRONI, Mic147/9); Willes, Legal and political reminiscences, 1757–8 (WRO, Willes Papers 2, pp 37–42); Fagan, *Divided loyalties*, pp 110–11; Rigby to Wilmot, 19 Jan. 1758 in Walton (ed.), *The King's business*, p. 184; Barry to Orrery, 24 Jan. 1758 in Countess of Cork and Orrery (ed.), *The Orrery papers* (2 vols, London, 1903), ii, 130–1; Burns, *Irish parliamentary politics*, ii, 248–9; *Lords Jn. (Irl.)*, iv, 87, 93, 96, 98.

Majesty to propose a bill to p[arliament] for changing the constitution of corporations'.[184] A proposal, emanating from the Commons in 1759–60, to alter the terms upon which judges held their commissions, from *ad bene placitum regis to quam diu se bene gesserint*, encountered a similar response. Persuaded that if the measure became law, not only would the judicial bench 'be in continual fear of the Commons and consequently under their influence whereas now ... they are under the power of the Crown', but also that the independence of the Privy Council would be compromised, which must have 'the effect of weak[en]ing Poynings' Law and consequently the independency [*sic*] of this kingdom on England', Willes succeeded in having the bill sidelined.[185]

Equivalent considerations were brought to bear during the same session with respect to the heads of a bill that proposed to allow 'all persons indicted of treason or felony ... council [*sic*] as in civil cases'. Promoted by Edmond Sexten Pery in response to the refusal of a judge on the Munster Circuit to allow a defendant's counsel speak on his behalf, Willes's contention was that if 'all judges here would give the same indulgence as in England' there would be no need for such a regulation, and having been assured that this was, and would continue to be the case, it was determined the bill should be 'thrown out'.[186] A proposal from the Commons to raise the qualifications of justices of the peace that was likewise adjudged 'unnecessary' met with the same fate. And so too did a bill to abolish fees on turnpike bills; the latter was subject of a petition from the deputy clerk of the Council on behalf of those who stood to experience a considerable loss of income if the bill received the royal assent, and the bill was rejected both because of difficulties that would be encountered in its implementation as well as because it was deemed improper to 'take away a private right without making compensation'.[187] Equally practical considerations prompted Dublin Corporation to petition against a bill that proposed to vest the administration of Dublin Harbour in a corporation established for that purpose, but the factor that ensured its rejection was the realisation that it was inconsistent with the 'prerogative of the Crown [to make] a corporation by act of parliament'.[188]

Edward Willes observed on one occasion of the operation of the Irish Privy Council that heads of bills were 'frequently thrown out ... [that] attack the royal prerogative of the Crown or the interests of the King of Great Britain'.[189] This was an accurate statement in so far as it went, but as the examples considered

184. Willes, Legal and political reminiscences, 1757–8 (WRO, Willes Papers 2, p. 44); *Faulkner's Dublin Journal*, 25 Mar. 1758; *Commons Jn. (Irl.)*, vi, 65, 73, 83, 84, 87, 88, 89, 91, 93.
185. *Commons Jn. (Irl.)*, vi, 160, 170, 174, 183, 186, 188; Willes, Memorandum on debates, 1759–60, pp 42–6.
186. *Commons Jn. (Irl.)*, vi, 125, 138, 147, 150; Willes, Memorandum on debates, 1759–60, pp 23–7.
187. *Commons Jn. (Irl.)*, vi, 199, 205, 206, 213, 214, 215; Willes, Memorandum on debates, 1759–60, pp 62–3, 72–6.
188. *Commons Jn. (Irl.)*, vi, 189, 199, 203, 205; Willes, Memorandum on debates, 1759–60, pp 69–71.
189. Willes, Memorandum on debates, 1759–60, p. 44.

above testify, these were not the only grounds. The Irish Council took an essentially conservative approach to the legislation it scrutinised, and it reacted instinctively against innovation where the case was less than compelling. As a result, some potentially valuable law was lost at the Irish Council board, but since this could be justified in the context of upholding the royal prerogative, maintaining constitutional equilibrium and a harmonious Anglo-Irish connection, protecting private and corporate interests, and best practice few councillors would have disagreed with Edward Willes that theirs was a valuable and important role.

Though 8 per cent of the heads of bills received at the Irish Council were respited and an unknown number were amended, 67 per cent of the bills and heads of bill prepared (175 from a total of 262) were forwarded to the British Council during the reign of George I and 72 per cent (482 from 667) during the longer reign of his successor. Numbering 657 legislative items *in toto* – 113 (17 per cent) of which were private measures, and 544 (or 83 per cent) public – this represented 71 per cent of the total of Privy Council bills and parliamentary heads of bills initiated between 1715 and 1760 (Table Eight; p. 245).[190]

IRISH BILLS AT THE BRITISH PRIVY COUNCIL, 1715–60

The legislative aspirations of the Irish ruling elite during the early Georgian era, as expressed in the bills and heads of bills received at the British Council board in numbers ranging from a high of 40 in the 1715–16 and 1735–6 sessions to lows of 17 in 1741–2 and 16 in the truncated 1753 session, were significantly reshaped by their experience at this forum. This is tellingly indicated by the fact that 78, or 12 per cent of those received, were not returned, which was comparable to the proportion (11 per cent) of heads that stumbled at the Irish Council board. Significantly, and consistent with the pattern already identified at the Irish Council, the proportion that failed during the reign of George I (14 per cent) was higher than it was during the reign of his successor (11 per cent). The fact that the latter figure includes twelve measures that were stranded at the British Council when the 1753 session came to a premature halt reinforces this trend.[191]

190. Analysed as public and private legislation, this comprises 132 public heads and bills and 43 private heads initiated during the reign of George I, which represented 65 per cent of public (203) and 74 per cent of private bills and heads of bills. For the reign of George II, the figures are 412 (or 70 per cent of the total of 586 public measures) and 70 (or 86 per cent of the 81 private measures). In all, 657 (or 71 per cent) of the total of 929 heads and heads of bills made it to the British Council (Tables Six and Seven).

191. The heads, most of which would have been returned and all of which rose with the Commons, were: for continuing several revenue laws; for continuing several temporary statutes; for licensing hawkers and pedlars; for amending an act for the preserving of game; for allowing further time to officeholders to qualify; for amending the tillage encouragement act; for the relief of insolvent debtors; for amending an act for buying and selling corn; for regulating free schools; for amending the Clonmel–Doneraile bill; the Mallow–Killarney bill (*Commons Jn.*

However, since the distribution over time of those bills that did not progress does not conform to a consistent pattern (though there were a number of sessions in which no public bill – 1737–8, 1747–8, 1751–2, 1755–6 – or no private bill – 1715–16, 1717–18, 1719–20, 1725–6, 1737–8, 1741–42, 1743–4, 1749–50, 1751–2, 1755–6, 1757–8, 1759–60 – was respited or postponed (Tables Six and Seven; pp 243 and 244), it is apparent that each bill was assessed on its merits.

This is not to claim that there was no pattern to the examination of bills at the British Council, though the task of identifying it is somewhat obscured by the fact that, in a minority of cases, either the law officers made no report or the report was not noted.[192] What is more striking with respect of a significant proportion of the bills respited, postponed or not reported, is that they failed to proceed because they were deemed 'inconsistent with the interest of England'.[193] The protection afforded English economic interests is exemplified by the rejection of successive tillage bills. This practice, already established during Anne's reign, was continued on the receipt on 2 January 1716 of heads of a bill for 'the encouragement of tillage and the buying and selling of corn'. Transmitted to London with the request that it should be returned because MPs deemed it 'highly beneficial', it was referred to the Commissioners of Customs who singled out the proposed increase of bounties on grain exported from Ireland and the manner in which they would be administered. However, their most material concern appertained to the fact that, because 'prices of corn in Ireland appear to be much lower than in this kingdom, … any encouragement given for exporting corn from Ireland will be a discouragement to the exportation of corn out of Great Britain'. Since a comparable bill had negotiated the British Council in 1711, only to be rejected in Ireland on its return, officials in Dublin protested that because the

---

(*Irl.*), v, 190, 193, 194, 196, 197, 199, 200, 201, 202, 203, 204, 205, 206, 207, 208, 209, 210, 211, 212, 213; NA, PC2/104, ff 2, 3, 17–18, 29–30).

192. For example, measures upon which no report was made include that 'for further explaining and amending … acts … for erecting lamps in the city of Dublin, 1735–6 (NA, PC2/93 f. 325; *Commons Jn. (Irl.)*, iv, 188, 191, 193, 196, 199, 200) and for making a turnpike road from Assolas, County Clare (1759–60) (NA, PC2/107 f. 340; *Commons Jn. (Irl.)*, vi, 176, 209, 214). Bills 'respited' upon which no further information is available other than this fact include that for 'securing the freedom of parliament by further qualifying the members to sit in the House of Commons' (1719) (NA, PC2/86 ff 305, 309; *Commons Jn. (Irl.)*, iii, 188, 195, 198, 199); 'the better regulation of partnerships' (1735–6) (NA, PC2/93 ff 286, 295, 309; *Commons Jn. (Irl.)*, iv, 182, 185, 189); to prevent defrauding of creditors (1735–6) (NA, PC2/93 ff 289, 338, 352; *Commons Jn. (Irl.)*, iv, 189, 192, 194, 196); to prevent inconveniencies by privilege of parliament (1739–40) (NA, PC2/95 ff 520, 637–8, 659; *Commons Jn. (Irl.)*, iv, 298, 299, 300, 305, 306, 308, 310, 311, 313, 314); for the encouragement of tillage (NA, PC2/99 ff 326, 388, 416; *Commons Jn. (Irl.)*, iv, 465, 466); to oblige Arthur Jones Neville to deliver contracts etc. 1757–8 (NA, PC2/106 ff 65, 103; *Commons Jn. (Irl.)*, vi, 84, 85, 92); to prevent mischiefs by retailers of spirituous liquors (1757–8) (NA, PC2/106 ff 62, 74; *Commons Jn. (Irl.)*, vi, 74, 76, 77); and for the relief of debtors (1759–60) (NA, PC2/107 ff 286, 359–60, 365; *Commons Jn. (Irl.)*, vi, 181, 194, 195, 196).

193. Wake to King, 14 Nov. 1717 (TCD, King Papers, MS 1995–2008 f. 1835).

Commissioners of Customs were wrongly informed about Irish grain prices, their report should not be accepted. They lobbied strongly in the early months of 1716 to have the decision reversed, but despite their best efforts to identify 'some method of making this affair more palatable to England', the differences over the price of grain in Ireland could not be resolved and the Council finally determined in April, on the advice of the Irish bills committee, that the measure should be 'postponed'.[194] The inevitable disappointment experienced in Ireland at this outcome was eased by a determination to succeed at the next opportunity and a similar bill was presented in 1717. Once again, the measure was referred to the Commissioners of Customs, who reiterated their previous observation that the cheaper price of grain in Ireland and the proposed bounties would allow Irish exporters 'undersell ... British subjects at foreign markets', and the bill was once more 'respited to a further opportunity'.[195] This was provided two years later, but despite the duke of Bolton's efforts to impress on officials the 'great stress' attached to the measure in Ireland, the outcome was no different then or in 1721, except that on these occasions the Irish bills committee did not feel obliged to appeal to the Commissioners of Customs to assist them in their deliberations.[196] This was the outcome once more in 1727 when a Privy Council tillage bill was respited, and in 1745 when a further bill of this nature was not allowed to progress.[197]

Though tillage constitutes the fullest illustration, a similar result was registered in other instances in which Irish economic aspirations threatened English vested interests. Thus in 1732, a petition presented on behalf of the London company of gold and silver wiredrawers claiming they would be injured by a proposal to tax gold and silver lace hastened the end of this bill, while in 1734 and in 1736 Irish attempts to encourage the 'employment of the poor by prohibiting the use and

---

194. *Commons Jn. (Irl.)*, iii, 14, 22, 25, 36, 37, 39, 42, 43; NA, PC2/85 ff 331, 332, 364; Minute of Irish bills committee, 7 Jan., Extract of letters from Lords Justices to Stanhope, 28 Dec. 1715–28 Mar. 1716, Report of Commissioners of Customs, 11 Jan. 1716 (PC1/3/41/1,3, 4, 5, 6); Galway to Stanhope, 28 Dec. 1715, Lords Justices to Stanhope, 22 Jan. Delafaye to [ ], 30 Jan., Galway and Grafton to Stanhope, 15, 24 Feb., 2 Mar., 22 May 1716 (NA, SP63/373, 63/374); Stanhope to Lords Justices, 14 Jan., 5 Feb. and enclosure, 9, 25 Feb. 1716 (NA, SP67/6 ff 119, 125, 127–9, 130, 133); Burns, *Irish parliamentary politics*, i, 57, 63–4; Webster to Delafaye, 15 Aug. 1719 (SP63/377).

195. *Commons Jn. (Irl.)*, iii, 123, 125, 127, 130, 133; NA, PC2/86 ff 44–5, 63; Tickell to Webster, 19 Oct., Addison to Bolton, 19 Nov. 1717 (NA, SP67/7 ff 19–20, 26–8); Hutchinson to King, 26 Oct., 1 Nov., Wake to King, 14 Nov. 1717 (TCD, King Papers, MS 1995–2008 ff 1830, 1837, 1835). Significantly, Archbishop King maintained that the Commissioners were right in respect of grain prices (King to Whitshed, 30 Nov., King to Canterbury, 21 Dec. 1717 (ibid., MS 2535 ff 31, 37).

196. *Commons Jn. (Irl.)*, iii, 188, 189, 190, 252, 253, 256, 259, 264, 269; NA, PC2/86 ff 299, PC2/87 ff 353, 380, 391; Webster to [Delafaye], 11 July, 15, 30 Aug., 10 Sept., Bolton to [ ], 31 July, Bolton to [Craggs], 14 Aug. 1719 (NA, SP63/377).

197. NA, PC2/90 ff 52, 68, PC2/99 ff 326, 388, 416; Irish Privy Council letter, 19 July 1727 (PC1/4/55 f. 3).

wear of ... wrought silks' and other luxury fabrics were subject to petitions from the East India Company and the linen drapers of London; as a result, the bills were rejected because it was adjudged that they would 'be prejudicial to the trade of Great Britain'.[198]

English political concerns also featured prominently among the reasons why Irish bills foundered at the British Council. This was true particularly when the royal prerogative or the conduct of foreign policy were at issue. This was highlighted during the reign of George I when an attempt on four occasions to reduce the amount of quit rent, crown rent and composition rent paid to the Crown by Irish landowners was denied as 'not proper to pass' despite claims that it is 'very much desired by the gentlemen of this kingdom'.[199] Some forty years later, an attempt to limit the duration of parliament was 'respited' on similar grounds; disparaged by the then lord lieutenant, the duke of Bedford, as 'a most flagrant' illustration of the 'eagerness' he detected in Ireland to 'intrench ... on the prerogative', the bill was decisively rejected.[200] In a related instance, when the Irish parliament sought in 1750 to empower the lord lieutenant and Council to make such regulations 'as they shall think proper' to combat the spread of disease in cattle, the law officers' report that the measure was unnecessary because a British statute already provided for such an eventuality ensured it was 'respited'.[201]

The disinclination to approve proposals emanating from the Irish parliament that sought either to tighten the existing disabilities against Catholics or to inaugurate new ones was equally revealing of the power of the British Council to shape the legislation of the Irish parliament for political reasons. The turning point in this respect was reached in 1723 when the heads of a bill 'for explaining and amending the acts to prevent the further growth of and for strengthening the Protestant interest' was received. Prompted by the exasperation of Irish Protestants that 'milder methods have been so frequently despis'd and elud'd' as well as by the 'the vast swarm of popish priests who infest and impoverish this kingdom and are continually negotiating against the Government', it was commonly held, in the words of the duke of Grafton, that this severe measure was 'a necessary support of the Protestant interest in this kingdom'. As a result of the 'fiery ordeal (as hot as Purgatory itself)' it endured at the Irish Privy Council, a number of draconian provisions were ameliorated, but since it was still envisaged

198. NA, PC2/91 ff 527–9, 541–2, 571, 574, PC2/92 ff 347, 393, 415, PC2/93 ff 286–7, 295, 309; law officers' report on silk bill, 27 Mar. 1734 (PC1/5/21 f. 3); Irish bills, 27 Jan. 1732 (NA, SP63/395).
199. NA, PC2/85 ff 360, 363, 383, PC2/86 ff 44–5, 49, 305, 309, PC2/87 ff 353, 380, 391; King to Wake, 21 Dec. 1717 (TCD, King Papers, MS 2535 ff 37); King to Hutchinson, 26 Oct. 1717 (King Papers, MS 1995–2008 f. 1830); Bolton to [Craggs], 14 Aug., Webster to Delafaye, 15 Aug., 10, 17, 22, 29 Sept. 1719 (NA, SP63/377, 378)
200. NA, PC2/106 ff 7, 23, 24–5; Bedford to Pitt, 4 Jan. (NA, SP63/415); Grenville to Bedford, 3 Feb.1758 (PRONI, Bedford Papers, T2915/4/10).
201. NA, PC2/101 ff 480, 488–9, 497–8; law officers' report, 13 Mar. 1750 (PC1/6/8 f. 4); *Commons Jn. (Irl.)*, v, 72.

that all registered priests would be oblige to subscribe to the oath of abjuration, Archbishop King legitimately described the measure as 'barbarous'. Irish Catholics certainly agreed, for not alone did Lord Caher, Lord Esmond and George Butler petition the British Council to countermand the measure, others lobbied sympathetic 'foreign ministers' in London and their superiors across the continent, and it paid dividends when the law officers declined to make a report on the bill and it was let lapse.[202]

Given the close co-operation that was a feature of the relationship of the Irish parliament and the British Privy Council in the introduction of the Penal Laws, this was a highly significant action. More importantly, it set a precedent that was followed in 1726 when no reports were forthcoming on two anti-Catholic measures – bills to explain and amend the laws 'to prevent papists purchasing lands' and for obliging 'converts to breed their children Protestants'.[203] Thereafter, the political climate at the British Council grew still colder towards Irish efforts to tighten the bonds of repression against Catholics. An attempt in 1727 to extend the time that had to elapse before converts from Catholicism were allowed practice law was 'respited'.[204] In 1733–4, measures to tighten the existing laws against regulars, bishops and converts, to enforce the registration procedures and to void 'all marriages celebrated by popish priests or fryars' were let fall unreported.[205] A number of further attempts were made in 1734 and 1744 to advance measures to annul marriages conducted by Catholic clergy, but these too were respited.[206]

Though the failure of these anti-Catholic regulations is indicative, first and foremost, of the diplomatic priorities of Great Britain rather than of any sustained rethink of the merits of penalising Catholics, the fact that prominent Catholics presented petitions in a number of these cases is illustrative of the effectiveness of this form of lobbying.[207] This conclusion is undergirded by the

---

202. *Commons Jn. (Irl.)*, iii, 347, 357, 361, 362, 363, 364, 366; NA, PC2/88 ff 415–16, 433; Patrick Fagan, *An Irish bishop in penal times: the chequered career of Sylvester Lloyd* (Dublin, 1993), pp 47–52; Connolly, *Religion, law and power*, pp 282–4; O'Regan, *Archbishop King*, pp 328–9; King to Southwell, 2, 26 Dec. 1723, 11 Jan, 1724 (TCD, King Papers, MS 2537 ff 29, 43, 55); Grafton to Carteret, 15 Nov. 1723 (NA, SP63/382); Nicolson to Wake, 18 Nov., 14 Dec. 1723 (Gilbert Library, Wake Papers, MS 27 ff 330–31, 332); Townshend to Walpole and enclosure, 25 Dec.-5 Jan. 1723–4 (BL, Townshend Papers, Add. MS 37634 ff 201–04); John Brady (ed.), *Catholics in the eighteenth-century press* (Maynooth, 1966), pp 40–1; [ ] to Crawford, 22 Dec. 1723 (NA, SP78/179/347); Fagan, *Stuart Papers*, i, 41 note 2; Fagan, *Divided loyalties*, pp 52–4; C. Giblin (ed.), 'Nunziatura di Fiandra', *Collectanea Hibernica*, 5 (1962), pp 110–13.

203. NA, PC2/89 ff 141, 142, 152; Abstract of an act, Feb. 1725 (BL, Southwell Papers, Add. MS 34777 f. 86); Connolly, *Religion, law and power*, p. 290.

204. NA, PC2/90 ff 52, 68; Irish to English Council, 19 July (PC1/4/55 f. 3); Southwell to King, 15 Aug. 1727 (TCD, King Papers, MS 1995–2008 f. 2168).

205. NA, PC2/91 ff 527–30, 542, 571, 595–6; Connolly, *Religion, law and power*, p. 291.

206. NA, PC2/92 ff 327, 334, 337, PC2/98 ff 110, 114, 139; law officers' report, 20 Feb. 1734 (PC1/5/16 f.2); Devonshire to Newcastle, 25 Dec. 1743 (NA, SP63/405). See also below, pp 238–9 for Catholic opposition to bills in 1748 and 1750.

207. Catholics presented a number of petitions against the 1723–24 measure for explaining and

frequency with which the case made by petitioners contributed to the decision to respite or to postpone a measure. This was the outcome, for example, with respect of the 1723–24 measure 'for preventing abuses ... by millers, bakers and farmers', which was opposed by the bakers of Dublin as well as by a number of private interests.[208] Two years later, the presentation by George Mason, a Dublin silk weaver, of a petition in which he maintained that a proposal to 'encourage the making of silk crapes' would materially injure his livelihood prompted the rejection of this measure.[209]

The clearest illustration of the efficacy of petitioning is provided by the fact that four of the six private bills that failed to negotiate the British Council during George I's reign and seven of the eighteen lost between 1715 and 1760 were subject to petitions presented by interested parties requesting that they should not be disadvantaged by the ratification of the bill at issue. Petitions were not always sufficient in and of themselves to prevent a bill proceeding, as instanced by the four petitions presented over two different sessions against a measure 'for the relief of the creditors of James Leathley', and others in which it was alleged that they asserted claims against the estate of the controversial deputy vice-treasurer, Sir William Robinson, 'contrary to law'; however, in the latter instance, they cast sufficient doubt for the Council to adjudge that the bill was 'not fitt for ... royall approbation'.[210] A similar judgement was reached in respect of a private bill 'to enable John Bingham ... to pay his debts', which was the subject of a petition from Richard Fitzwilliam. In this instance, the absence 'both of certainty and proof' was sufficient to warrant the decision that the bill was 'not fit to be approved'.[211] The Privy Council was well capable of arriving at such judgements without prompting,[212] but they were more likely to do so when it was made plain that the material interests of spouses, children, siblings or other interested parties would be aversely affected, or where there was some doubt about the legality or *bona fides* of the facts on which a bill was based.[213] In such cases, the eagerness of

amending the acts to prevent the growth of (NA, PC2/88 ff 415–6); the 1725–6 measure to oblige converts to raise their children as Protestants (PC2/81 f. 141), while counsel was heard on their behalf in 1732 against the measures for banishing regulars and others and for registering Popish clergy (PC2/91 f. 571). See Colin Haydon, *Anti-Catholicism in eighteenth-century England: a political and social study* (Manchester, 1993), chapter 4.

208. NA, PC2/88 ff 412, 465; law officers' report, 6 Jan. 1724, Privy Council minute, 24 Dec. 1723, Petition, PC1/3/121 ff 1–5, 6, 7, 9).

209. NA, PC2/89 ff 140, 173, 189; Order in Council, 25 Jan. 1725, Mason's petition, 1725/6 (BL, Hardwicke Papers, Add. MS 35872 f. 1)

210. NA, PC2/87 ff 423, 438, 444–5, 471; PC2/88 ff 391, 440, 446–7; Irish Council letter, 22 Nov. 1723 (NA, SP63/382).

211. NA, PC2/88 ff 375, 392, 411.

212. NA, PC2/88 ff 416, 440, 446–7 (Kelly bill); PC2/88 ff 392, 440, 446–7 (Mervyn bill); PC2/91 ff 582, 595–6 (Moore bill); PC2/92 ff 347–8, 440; law officers' report, 2 Apr. 1734 (PC1/5/22–3) (Maynard bill); PC2/95 ff 516, 639, 659 (Strafford bill); PC2/99 ff 423, 427, 437 (Fitzherbert bill).

213. See, for examples: NA, PC2/88 ff 375, 394; King to Southwell, 21 Dec. 1723, 11 Jan. 1724

councillors and the law officers to do nothing that could be construed in any way 'to barr the right of any person' without due and adequate compensation or that might be deemed to 'break into the general rules of property' was usually reason enough to precipitate the rejection of a measure.[214]

An equal concern to prevent any infringement of existing statute law accounted for the rejection in 1721 and, again, in 1723 of an amending bill 'for the maintenance and execution of pious uses'. The problem in this instance was that the measure conveyed from Ireland required the relaxation of the statutes of mortmain to accommodate charitable giving, which was not acceptable, and there was nothing bishops of the Church of Ireland could say in its favour to induce a change of mind.[215] Similarly, the rejection in January 1724 of a measure to amend an act preserving the inheritance and property rights of Church of Ireland ecclesiastics was justified on the grounds that it contravened legislation dating from the mid-1630s and would 'advantage ... present possessors of ecclesiastical dignities ... in prejudice to their successors'.[216] Comparable considerations, only in this instance not to allow landlords 'to break in upon the property' without permission of lessees or tenants, precipitated the rejection of a measure to amend an act for 'the further encouragement of finding and working mines', while the belief that privately agreed contracts could achieve as much as the 'corporations' mooted in measures advanced in 1735 and in 1739–40 for the better regulation of partnerships proved decisive in ensuring the rejection of both these bills.[217] It is apparent from these examples that bills were only rejected when there were legal, political and strategic reasons to do so. The fact that private bills were respited on equally solid grounds reinforces this conclusion, and it gains further weight from the high proportion of bills that were returned in an amended form.[218]

*　*　*

(TCD, King Papers, MS 2537 ff 41–2, 55) (Henry King bill); PC2/90 ff 258, 288–9, 292; Petition of William Knox, 4 Apr. 1728 (PC1/4/70) (Fleming bill); PC2/93 ff 326, 338, 369–70 (Campbell bill); PC2/100 ff 545, 571–3; law officers' report, 12 Mar. 1748 (PC1/6/8 f. 4) (Ashe bill); PC2/100 ff 545, 600–12; law officers' report, 12 Mar. 1748 (PC1/6/8 ff 4–5) (Cusack bill).

214. NA, PC2/90 ff 258, 289–90, 292; law officers' report, 3 Apr., Irish bills committee report, 3 Apr. 1728 (PC1/4/71 ff 21–2, 7–8) (Fleming bill – 1727–8); PC2/91 ff 173, 205, 213; Petition, 21 Feb. 1729, Order in Council, 21 Feb., Irish Privy Council letter, 24 Jan. 1729: BL, Hardwicke Papers, Add. MS 35872 ff 28, 29, 31, 31) (Fleming bill – 1729–30); PC2/93 ff 326, 402 (Bolton bill).

215. NA, PC2/87 ff 392–3, 417, 432, 438; PC2/88 ff 352, 362, 364; Irish Council letter, 31 Oct., law officers' report, 15 Nov. 1723 (PC1/3/116 ff 4, 3); Gibson to King, 23 Nov., Annesley to King, 25 Nov. 1723 (TCD, King Papers, MS 1995–2008 ff 2054, 2055); King to Southwell, 2 Dec., King to Gibson, 2 Dec., King to Annesley, 5 Dec., King to Wake, King to Southwell, 26 Dec.1723 (King Papers, MS 2537 ff 29, 31–2, 34–5, 36, 46).

216. NA, PC2/88 ff 412, 422, 465; law officers' report, 1 Jan. 1724 (PC1/3/120 ff 4–7). Archbishop King believed this measure 'pernicious' (TCD, King Papers, MS 2537 f. 24).

217. PC2/91 ff 154, 165; PC2/93 ff 286, 295, 309; PC2/95 ff 501, 518, 539–41; Legge to Devonshire, 24 Jan. 1740 (PRONI, Chatsworth Papers, T3158/132).

218. For example, see the law officers' reports on the Ashe and Cusack bills, 12 Mar. 1748 (NA, PC1/6/8 ff 4–5).

Almost 75 per cent of the bills received at the British Council board between 1715 and 1760 were returned to Ireland with amendments. This dwarfed both the proportion of bills that was respited (12 per cent) and the 14 per cent that negotiated the Council unaltered. Moreover, it was ten per cent greater than was the case during the reign of Queen Anne, though, as in Anne's reign, there was considerable variation between sessions.[219] There was also an identifiable variation between public and private bills; the proportion of private measures subject to amendment during the reign of George II (63 per cent) was significantly less than the proportion of public measures (77 per cent). This was the reversal of the situation during the shorter reign of George I though the percentage of private bills amended (77 per cent) exceeded the proportion of public bills (73 per cent) by only four per cent. Despite this, the percentage of bills amended at the British Council board during the reigns of George I and George II was very similar; 74 per cent of public and private bills received between 1715 and 1726 and 75 per cent of those received between 1727 and 1760 were amended (Table Eight; p. 244). But what is more striking still is that during the reign of George II, the proportion of measures that were amended fell from 87 per cent during the nine sessions spanning the years 1727 to 1744 to 61 per cent during the eight sessions held between 1745 and 1760. The proportion of bills that proceeded without amendment oscillated still more sharply. At 13 per cent during George I's reign, it plummeted to 3 per cent between 1727 and 1744 only to rise to 27 per cent between 1745 and 1760 (Table Eight).

Despite the variation in the percentage of measures ordered for amendment, the process itself was virtually unchanging. In almost all cases, the required amendments were identified by the crown's law officers. In a small number of instances, usually appertaining to matters of trade, commerce and finance, guidance was obtained elsewhere. The bodies appealed to were the Commissioners of Customs, the Commissioners of Trade and Plantations, the Commissioners of the Admiralty and the Commissioners of the Treasury. For example, the Commissioners of the Treasury were invited in March 1728 to communicate their views on a measure to prevent 'frauds and abuses ... in customs and excise' and for setting duties on a range of goods. In 1717, the Commissioners of the Admiralty were requested to identify 'any objections' they might have to a measure 'for the preserving all such ships and goods' forced ashore on the Irish coast.[220] The bodies appealed to with greatest frequency were the Commissioners of Customs and the Commissioners for Trade and Plantations. It was the latter, for example, that was charged in September 1719 with reporting on an Irish measure 'for the more effectual preventing the running of goods', but the legislation that demanded their closest attention appertained to the wish of the

219. Above, p. 146.
220. 4 Geo I, chap 4; NA PC2/86 ff 44–5, 48, 50, 51–2 (ships and goods bill); 1 Geo II, chap 6; PC2/90 ff 257, 258, 280–2 (frauds and abuses in customs bill); 6 Geo I, chap 8; PC2/86 ff 312, 326, 327–31 (the running of goods bill).

Irish parliament to extend the 'encouragements' in place to foster 'the hempen and flaxen manufacture'. Thus, in 1716, a bill to this end was referred to the Commissioners for Trade and Plantations, while similar measures received in 1719 and 1723 were referred to the Commissioners of Customs. Five years later, in March 1728, it was the turn once more of the Commissioners of Trade and Plantations though, significantly, on this occasion they were invited to consider the bill 'for the further improvement of the hempen and flaxen manufactures' in tandem with 'a minute' from the Commissioners of Customs.[221]

If it appears from this, that the British Council was less than certain to whom they should best appeal for expert commercial advice in respect of Irish bills this would be misleading. Moreover, they felt a diminishing need to seek such guidance during the reign of George II. This was due in no small part to the fact that as Council members became more familiar with, and accepting of Irish efforts to promote the linen industry, such bills as were received for 'improving the hempen and flaxen manufacture' were dealt with in the ordinary way without the need to consult more widely.[222] Indeed, on the few occasions that consultation with others did take place during the 1730s and afterwards it was as likely as not to be done within the Council framework, as happened in 1734 when the law officers left it to the Irish bills committee to consult with the Commissioners of Customs to establish if it was wise to approve a clause in a measure appertaining to the sale of meal and grain that set a 'quarter' at forty stone (rather than the usual twenty-eight) since it must be 'prejudicial to His Majesty's revenue'.[223] However, when commercial guidance was required, as in 1738 with respect of an Irish measure to promote fisheries, the Irish bills committee did not hesitate to invite the Commissioners of Customs 'to consider whether there be anything contained therein which may be prejudicial to His Majesties revenues or the trade and commerce of this kingdom', or to authorise amendments to appease worried merchant fishermen and others in Cornwall and Devon.[224]

As this indicates, the efficient and largely trouble-free authorisation of amendments to so many bills was facilitated by the implicit conviction of all parties to the process of bill scrutiny, and it is highly significant that the reports prepared by the law officers for the Irish bills committee and the recommendations made by the Irish bills committee between 1715 and 1760 were

221. 2 Geo I, chap 13; NA, PC2/85 ff 360, 363–4, 382–3, 389–90; *Journal of the Commissioners for trade and plantations, 1714/15–18* (London, 1924), pp 133–4 (1716); 6 Geo I, chap 7; PC2/86, ff 312, 316, 325, 327–31 (1719); 10 Geo I, chap 2; PC2/88 ff 373–4, 395–400, 409, 418, 418–19, 451–6 (1723); 1 Geo II, chap 11; PC2/90 ff 257, 275, 282, 290–1 (1728).

222. 7 Geo II, chap 10; NA, PC2/92 ff 347, 392–3; law officers' report, 27 Mar. 1734 (PC1/5/21 f. 3) (flax bill).

223. 7 Geo II, chap 15; law officers' report of 'Act for buying and selling all sorts of corn and meal by weight', 20 Feb. 1734 (NA, PC1/5/16 ff 4–7).

224. 11 Geo. II, chap 14; NA, PC2/94 ff 398, 400–2, 448, 458–60; Walpole to Devonshire, 16 Feb., Wilmington to Devonshire, 6 Mar. 1748 (PRONI, Chatsworth Papers, T3158/46, 49).

queried in only a small proportion of instances.[225] Moreover, the preferred option on such occasions was to refer the measure at issue back to the law officers for a new or additional report. This is what occurred in 1725–6, for example, in respect of two measures; the bill to extend the allocation of the coal duty authorised in 1719 to help with the construction of Christ Church in Cork city to assist three other churches was returned to the law officers with the direction that the duty should be confined to 'the finishing of Christ Church' and should extend for seven rather than the proposed 21 years; while the bill 'for the more effectual transporting of felons and vagabonds' was returned with the instruction that the law officers should 'reconsider [the measure] and make such alterations' as the bills committee directed. The instructions offered were not always so explicit; in 1721, a measure to amend a tenant fraud act was sent to the law officers 'to reorder some clauses'; in 1748, a controversial attempt to reinforce the ban on 'foreign education' was returned with the request that 'further amendments' should be made; while, in 1734, a measure for the further encouragement of trade by admitting ships to invoice their loadings was simply 'sent back'.[226]

Sometimes, matters were not so straightforward. In 1734, measures 'for the amendment of the law in relation to popish solicitors' and for securing the payment of bankers' notes were subject to two reports, both of which were taken on board by the Irish bills committee.[227] It is not clear in these cases if the Irish bills committee formally requested the second report having identified deficiencies in the first, but this is likely. This certainly is what happened in other instances; it occurred, for example, in 1740 with respect of a measure 'to explain, amend and make more effectuall' the 1695 act for 'disarming papists'; in 1742, when a measure for the better regulation of partnerships was referred with explicit instructions to limit the size and capitalisation of partnerships; and in January 1758, when measures appertaining to the supply of coal to Dublin and to the prevention of combinations inflating the price of coal in the city were 'referred back' to the law officers with an instruction 'to inform themselves of all other bills of the same nature ... and to report their further opinions on the two bills'.[228] The full

225. In this context, it is noteworthy that the minute long employed by the clerks of the Council to note the deliberations of the Irish bills committee read 'Their Lordships are pleased to take into consideration the aforesaid act, and report their opinion thereupon, according to the several amendments made by the Attorney and Solicitor general' (Minutes of clerks of Council 1670–1776, *sub* 13 Jan. 1724, 27 Mar. 1729, 1, 4 Mar. 1738, 29 Apr., 13 Dec. 1771, 28 Apr. 1772: NA, PC4/1 ff 429, 533, 808–9, 811, 1156–8, 1171, 1187).

226. 12 Geo I, chap 2 (private); NA, PC2/89 ff 140–41, 153, 162–3 (Christ Church, Cork bill); PC2/89 ff 130, 153, 155–7, 164–5; Privy Council letter, 9 Nov. 1725 (PC1/4/17 f. 17) (transportation bill); 8 Geo I, chap 2; PC2/87 ff 353, 375, 379–80, 385–7 (tenants fraud bill); law officers' report on bill for encouragement of trade, 27 Mar. 1734 (PC1/5/21 f. 2); Minutes of Irish bills committee on foreign education bill, Mar. 1748 (PC1/6/9 ff 3–6).

227. 7 Geo. II, chap 5; two reports of law officers, 20 Feb., 5 Mar. 1734 (NA, PC1/5/18 ff 1–8; PC2/92 ff 296, 355–8, 362–4, 415, 435–8, 441–2; law officers' report on payment of bankers' notes, 7, 27 Mar. 1734 (PC1/5/19 ff 4–6, PC1/5/21 ff 4–5).

228. 13 Geo II, chap 6; NA, PC2/95 ff 520, 641, 643–6, 656–7 (disarming papists bill); 15 Geo II,

Council likewise had recourse to this strategy on occasions; it did so in 1736 when it requested that measures 'for the more effectuall preventing clandestine marriages' and for repairing the Kilcullen–Kilkenny road should be sent back to the law officers 'to consider further thereof'; and in 1738, the law officers were invited 'to revise' their report on a proposal to repeal part of an act relating to the inheritance and property rights of Church of Ireland ecclesiastics.[229]

It was, of course, procedurally more appropriate for the Council to refer bills back for 'reconsideration' to the Irish bills committee, and for the committee to make the decision to involve the law officers. This was the decision taken in 1719 with respect of the euphemistically titled proposal 'for securing the Protestant interest', which contained the notorious provision that would have allowed for the castration of 'unqualified Popish priests', and the controversial Dissenter relief bill of the same session. As a result, the 'castration' provision was deleted from the first measure and a clause introduced exempting Quakers in the second, following which both bills were deemed proper to receive the royal assent should they be approved by the Irish parliament. The same procedure was pursued in 1719 in respect of the private bill to enable John Bingham 'to settle a competent jointure' on his wife; in 1734, in the case of a proposal for securing the 'payment of bankers' notes'; and, in 1745, when there were problems with an amending bill in respect of the rights of purchasers.[230] Alternatively, such revisions as were required could be made without formally involving the law officers, which occurred on a handful of occasions only. In January 1726, the Irish bills committee approved four amendments over and above those suggested by the law officers to a controversial measure against forestallers, regraters and ingrossers; in March 1728, following the receipt of oral testimony from Hans Hamilton, the bills committee introduced a lengthy clause into a measure for the relief of debtors exempting Hamilton from arrest for debts incurred by his father; while, in 1745, the committee recast a whole clause prepared by the law officers to a proposal to amend the law in respect of common recoveries.[231] This approach had

chap 7; PC2/97 ff 41, 59–60, 62–2, 64–6 (partnerships bill); 31 Geo II, chaps 14 and 15; PC2/106 ff 7, 23, 74, 102, 111–12; Granville to Bedford, 3 Feb. 1758 (PC1/31/A78) (coal and combinations bills).

229. 9 Geo II, chaps 11, 24; NA, PC2/93 ff 325, 332–3, 352, 384–6, 290, 303–04, 309, 337–8, 350 (clandestine marriage bill; Kilcullen road bill); 11 Geo II, chap 15; PC2/94 ff 355, 381–2, 389–91, 431–2, 446 (ecclesiastics' property rights bill).

230. 6 Geo I, chap 5; NA, PC2/86 ff 299, 301–3, 304–5, 315, 326–7, 327–31 (dissenters relief bill); PC2/86 ff 312, 322–3, 332, 334, 344, 346; *The Postman*, 15 Sept. 1719 (securing the Protestant interest bill); 6 Geo I, chap 3 (private); PC2/86 ff 313, 317, 327, 338, 340–3 (Bingham bill); PC2/92 ff 327, 360, 364, 415, 435–8, 441–2 (purchasers rights bill); law officers' report on payment of bankers' bill (PC1/5/21 ff 4–5); Cary to Dodington, 4 Feb., 28 Mar. 1734 in HMC, *Report on various collections, vi: Eyre Matcham*, pp 58–9, 60; PC2/99 ff 371, 405–7, 416, 425–6 (bankers notes bill).

231. NA, PC2/89 ff 140–1, 149–51, 162–3 (forestallers bill); 1 Geo II, chap 25 (Hamilton bill); PC2/90 ff 257, 290, 296–7, 298–9; Irish bills committee report, 8 Apr. 1728 (PC1/4/72 ff 3–4); PC2/99 ff 371, 405–7, 416, 425–6 (common recoveries bill).

the advantage, as far as the Irish bills committee was concerned, of ensuring that such amendments as were made were couched in precisely those terms that the committee favoured, but the time required to do so explains why this was not commonly resorted to. In 1745, it took the committee two meetings to agree on the extensive amendments introduced into a measure aimed primarily at 'preventing … subjects from entering into foreign service'. The multiple petitions presented in 1748 against measures for 'quieting corporations' (the Newtown Act) necessitated the devotion of two days to the consideration of this bill, while an unsustainable six days was allocated to the consideration of the bill to restrain foreign education in the same session.[232]

If it was prepared to allocate the time required to do so, the Irish bills committee was perfectly entitled to put its stamp upon every legislative initiative emanating from Ireland. This was graphically illustrated in 1730 when, instead of acceding to the law officers' recommendation that a measure to allow tenants for life alienate up to twenty acres 'as a perpetual glebe' was not fit to receive the royal assent, they forwarded the bill without amendment and it was law within four months.[233] It was provided in 1734 with a rare opportunity to determine the shape of a bill 'to prevent frauds and abuses' in the export of bay yarn when the law officers' report on the bill offered the committee the options either of forwarding the measure with 19 or with 79 amendments based upon their response to a provision in the measure that would, if approved, 'greatly affect the woollen trade of Great Britain'. Significantly, this did not set a precedent that the law officers sought to exploit. As the small number of instances in which the Irish bills committee chose to accept some and reject others from the lengthy lists of amendments presented to them by the law officers illustrates,[234] the committee did not deem it necessary to assess individually the merits of the manifold amendments that were routinely presented to it. This is true also of the full Council's response to the report it received from the Irish bills committee, though there were exceptions. Potentially, the most controversial was the decision in January 1716 to amend the main supply bill of the 1715–16 session; forwarded from the Irish bills committee in January 1716 with the recommendation that it should pass with one amendment, it was sent for engrossment with a dozen

---

232. 19 Geo II, chap 7; NA, PC2/99 ff 325, 388, 402–04, 411–13 (foreign service bill); 21 Geo II, chap 10; PC2/100 ff 522, 560, 563–6; Petitions of Alexander Stewart and others, 26 Feb., Petition of Irish Society, 29 Feb. 1748 (PC1/6/7 ff 1–2) (Newtown bill); PC2/100 ff 544, 573, 574, 579, 580–81; law officers' report on foreign education, 12 Mar. 1748 (PC1/6/8 f. 2); Petition, minutes etc. on foreign education bill (PC1/6/9 ff 3–6); Petition of Viscount Taaffe, [Feb. 1748] (PC1/2/48/1) (foreign education bill).

233. 3 Geo II, chap 12; NA, PC2/91 ff 134, 145, 149–50; law officers' report, 24 Jan. 1730 (NA, PC1/4/105 f. 68); *Commons Jn. (Irl.)*, iii, 636, 637, 651.

234. 7 Geo, chap 9; NA, PC2/92 ff 327–8, 359–60, 362–4; law officers' report, 7 Mar. 1734 (PC1/5/19 ff 2–3) (bay yarn fraud bill); 7 Geo, chap 13; PC2/92 ff 327–8, 359, 362–4; law officers' report, 7 Mar. 1734 (PC1/5/19 ff 1–2) (tillage bill).

syntactical clarifications by the full Council.[235] On rare occasions, rather than accept the recommendation of the Irish bills committee and approve a bill with amendments, the Council chose, as in January 1724 with respect to the measure to prevent abuses by millers and bakers, to authorise its rejection.[236]

The fact that the proportion of bills (75 per cent) amended at the British Council greatly exceeded the percentage that was respited (12 per cent) constitutes the most compelling evidence that the preferred response of the British Council to problems identified in the legislation received from Ireland was to bring it into line by amendment. Consistent with this, the nature and extent of the amendments that were sanctioned spanned the range of possibilities from virtual total rewriting to minor corrections aimed at eradicating syntactical and legal imprecision. This can be illustrated by reference to the experience of the supply bills. Because the voting of funds was vital to the efficient administration of the kingdom of Ireland and because of sensitivities over the question of the 'sole right', the ratification of the key financial bills received from Ireland was critical to the successful outcome of the session. Arising out of this, and the repeated affirmation by the Irish administration of the desirability that such bills should be returned expeditiously and with as few amendments as possible, English ministers and officials were disinclined to offend Irish sensitivities on this point.[237] Thus, the practice established early in the reign of George I that money bills would be subject only to minor 'literal' amendments proved enduring. For example, following agreement that a money bill should be included among the bills transmitted from Ireland as reason to call a new session in 1715, the two money bills communicated in 1717 were returned in short order with only seven amendments which provided for the rectification of minor syntactical lapses.[238] The outcome was similar in 1721, in 1723 and in 1725, for though the number of amendments ratified in the latter years was between forty and fifty, most of these related to the replacement of 'your majesty' by 'his majesty'. On only one occasion −1719 − was the main money bill returned unaltered.[239]

Matters continued thus during the reign of George II. Indeed, since the amendments made were similar in character from year to year, it is tempting to conclude that both parties were engaged in a complex legislative ritual epitomised by further instances, as in 1727–8, when the phrase 'your majesty' was changed to

235. NA, PC2/85 ff 331, 332, 333–5.
236. NA, PC2/88 ff 412, 465; law officers' report, 6 Jan. 1724 (PC1/3/121 ff 1–5).
237. Above, pp 176–7; Newcastle to Dorset, 29 Nov. 1731 (NA, SP67/9 f. 143); Walpole to Newcastle, 21 Feb. 1738, Devonshire to Newcastle, 24 Nov. 1741, 25 Dec. 1743 (NA, SP63/401, 404, 405); Bedford to Granville and reply, 26 Nov., 7 Dec. 1759 (PC1/31/A78).
238. 4 Geo I, chaps 1 and 2; NA, PC2/86 ff 44–5, 48, 49, 50–2. For example, these included the replacement of 'excellect' with 'excellent', 'from' with 'for', etc.
239. 6 Geo I, chap 4; NA, PC2/86 ff 305, 308, 310; 8 Geo I, chap 1; PC2/87 ff 353, 376–7, 385–6; 8 Geo I, chap 1; PC2/88 ff 352, 359–60, 362–4; 12 Geo I, chap 1; PC2/89 ff 123, 124–5, 128–9; law officers' report, 20 Nov. 1725 (PC1/4/17 ff 1–2).

'his majesty'.[240] Since this was consistent with the transformation of the heads of a bill into a bill, it sustains the observation of the secretary of state, Viscount Townshend, in 1729 that 'no alterations [are] made but what appeared ... to be just and reasonable'.[241] A majority of the amendments introduced into successive money bills during the long reign of George II were minor, in the sense that they did not constitute a material alteration either of meaning or of import. They were, as British officeholders were prone to describe them, 'only literal', but while it was correctly assumed as a result that they would 'create no difficulties in the passing of these bills', it would be a misjudgement to describe them as trivial or insignificant.[242] Each was introduced to remedy an identifiable deficiency. Moreover, the British Council did not refrain from approving larger and more substantive amendments if they were deemed necessary.[243] This was more likely in those years when the money bill received from Ireland differed in some material way from its predecessors. Thus in 1741–2, the measure granting the Crown 'a further additional duty on wines' and other commodities was re-titled to reflect more accurately its purpose. Significant amendments were authorised in 1733 to the measure 'for granting ... a further additional duty on wine' and other commodities. But, invariably, once the teething problems associated with innovative provisions, particularly in the financial domain, were negotiated, and key money bills could be transmitted with the observation that they were 'the same as that passed last session', they were rarely the subject of more than a handful of minor amendments.[244] In the main, these were of the nature of grammatical, syntactical and expressive corrections, such as were imposed in 1747–8 and 1749–50 when 'their' was amended to 'the', 'green' to 'raw', 'herein' to 'therein' and 'thereunto' to 'hereunto' in successive money bills. Amendments of this ilk were also commonplace during the mid- and late 1750s when one, two or three literal amendments to money bills were the norm.[245] Ironically, in contrast to the 1710s when money bills occasionally negotiated the British Council

240. 1 Geo II, chap 4; NA, PC2/90 ff 223, 234–5, 238–9.
241. Townshend to Carteret, 4 Dec. 1729 (NA, SP63/391).
242. Newcastle to Dorset, 29 Nov. 1731 (NA, SP67/9 f. 143); Memorandum on Irish bills, 12 Feb. 1739/40 (BL, Spencer Compton Papers, Add. MS 45733 f. 68); Granville to Bedford, 7 Dec. 1759 (PC1/31/A78).
243. For example, the money bills of 1731 (5 Geo II, chaps 1 and 2; NA, PC2/91 ff 475, 485, 487–9); of 1749–50 (23 Geo II, chaps 1, 2 and 3; PC2/101 ff 370–1, 372–4, 480, 484–5, 489–92); of 1755–6 (29 Geo II, chaps 1, 2, 3; PC2/104 ff 537, 539–41, PC2/105 ff 8, 25, 26–8) and 1759–60 (33 Geo II, chaps 1, 2 and 3; PC2/107 ff 205–6, 207, 208–10).
244. 15 Geo II, chap 2; NA, PC2/97 ff 20, 21–2, 23–5; 7 Geo II, chaps 2; PC2/92 ff 257–8, 259–60, 260–1; Irish Privy Council letter, 20 Nov. 1733 (SP63/396).
245. 9 Geo II, chaps 1, 2; PC2/93 ff 258, 259–60, 260–1; 15 Geo II, chaps 1, 2; PC2/97 ff 20, 21–2, 23–5; 17 Geo II, chaps 1, 2; PC2/98 ff 58–60, 64–7; 19 Geo II, chaps 1, 2; PC2/99 ff 246, 247, 249–50, 257, 258, 264–5; 23 Geo II, chaps 1, 2; PC2/101 ff 370–1, 372–4, 480, 484–5, 489–92; 29 Geo II, chaps 1; PC2/104 ff 537, 539–41; 31 Geo II, chaps 1; PC2/105 ff 631, 632, 634–5; 33 Geo II, chaps 1, 2; PC2/107 ff 205–6, 207, 201–10.

without amendment, they were now consistently returned with at least one amendment in order, as the President of the Council, Lord Granville, explained in 1759, to 'preserve the right of amending these bills'.[246]

Ministers and officials were encouraged to make such pronouncements because of the perception, reinforced by the Money Bill dispute, that Irish Protestants sought at every opportunity to assert their legislative independence from Great Britain. This was not the case of course, as the history of Poynings' Law and the fact that the constitutional dimension to the Money Bill dispute was prompted by the British Privy Council's assertion of the royal prerogative in respect of the allocation of the money surplus then in the Irish exchequer both attest.[247] It is notable also that the amendment by which this assertion was made was a short phrase, which provides a cautionary warning against underestimating the import of the multiplicity of minor textual corrections and clarifications approved each session. The fact that some measures were subject not to one but to dozens of what the secretary of state routinely described as 'verbal' or literal amendments emphasises just how problematic it is to minimise their significance since even the smallest alteration could in the right circumstances generate a constitutional crisis.[248] There was little risk of this in practice other than at moments of particular political sensitivity. For this reason, the merit of persisting with the concept of the 'minor amendment' to define these routine syntactical and verbal changes made to so many Irish bills is best attested by the sort of changes made in the 1730s and 1740s to such legislative perennials as the bills for the renewal of temporary statutes, the encouragement of hemp and flax manufacture, for allowing officeholders more time to qualify pursuant to the act to prevent the further growth of popery, for recognising the right of Quakers not to make oaths, and for the encouragement of tillage.[249] It is also reasonable similarly to categorise a majority of the amendments made routinely to the bills presented session after session during George II's reign appertaining to the construction or repair of turnpike roads, the relief of insolvent debtors, the protection of game, and the regulation of juries, sheriffs and petty constables though they were sometimes more material. The point can be illustrated by reference to ten road bills considered at the British Council in the winter of 1735–6 all of which were recommended to pass with an average of between thirty and forty amendments, a majority of which related to the inclusion of a clause exempting parks, gardens,

---

246. Granville to Bedford, 7 Dec. 1759 (NA, PC1/31/A78).

247. For the money bill dispute, see above, pp 201–2.

248. For example the heads of a bill that arose with the Irish Commons in the late autumn of 1721 for 'quieting and securing possessions' experienced some 63 minor corrections (8 Geo I, chap 4; NA, PC2/87 ff 419–20, 425–6, 433–5; *Commons Jn. (Irl.)*, iii, 253, 260, 268, 271, 279, 280, 281), the heads obliging proprietors to make fences some 40 (8 Geo I, chap 5; NA, PC2/87 ff 392, 395–7, 407–9; *Commons Jn. (Irl.)*, iii, 261, 262, 269, 277, 278).

249. Exceptions to this include the popery qualification bill of 1735, which was rejected on its return (PC2/93 ff 286, 292–3, 304–6; *Commons Jn. (Irl.)*, iv, 205, 207, 212); and the flax and hemp amending bill of 1752 (PC2/102 ff 553, 2/103 ff 3, 18–22; *Commons Jn. (Irl.)*, v, 153).

orchards, planted yards, tree-lined walks or avenues, paddocks, and deer parks from being built upon. This was not an unimportant reservation, but in common with the amendments sanctioned in the course of the 1733–4 session requiring the insertion of a reference to 'geldings' in another sequence of road bills, they can plausibly be defined as corrections rather than changes.[250] The number of amendments sanctioned in such cases could reach fifty, though they usually ranged between eleven and twenty, and many were subject to far fewer. Saliently, the decline in the average number of 'literal' amendments that were approved was paralleled by the increased number of bills that were returned unaltered; in other words the proportion of bills subject to less than ten 'minor' amendments appreciated during the 1740s and, by the 1750s, many were subject to five or less (Table Eight).[251]

Though eclipsed numerically by those requiring minor alterations, there were few sessions when some Irish measures were not subject to major amendment. The experiences of bills so categorised span the range of possibilities from extensive rewriting to the addition or deletion of full clauses. Examples of the former are not abundant, but the 1723 measure for the encouragement of mining, which was subject to circa one hundred amendments, in some cases involving the rewriting of full clauses, and the clandestine marriage legislation pursued in 1750, which was virtually completely rewritten, fit this category. The 1733 equity court bill, which was strongly lobbied for on the grounds that it was necessary 'for preserving the English and Protestant interest' in Ireland to curb the 'influence of popish lawyers', is another. In this instance, the Crown's law officers sanctioned not only a change of title but also rewrote the bill to focus firmly on the 'relief of mortgagees' and ensured, in the process, that the legal procedures provided for were clear and unambiguous. The 1733 corn weight measure bill was amended likewise; as well as a change to the title and a host of essentially minor technical clarifications arising from the alteration of the date in which the measure would take effect, whole sections were rewritten.[252] Compared with the extensive revisions required in these instances, the effort required to bring measures to proper form where the problem could be pinpointed to one clause or section, was palpably less onerous. In a significant proportion of such cases, the favoured solution was either to delete or to add a full clause or section. The number of measures from whom clauses were deleted comfortably exceeds those to which clauses were added. A comparatively uncomplicated example is provided by the

---

250. 9 Geo II, chaps 14, 15, 17, 18, 19, 21, 22, 23, 24, 26; NA, PC2/93 ff 287, 290, 293–4 296–7, 298–300, 302–3, 304–9, 337–8, 350, 365–6, 372–3, 386–8, 397–8; 7 Geo II, chaps 16, 17, 18, 19, 20, 21, 22, 23, 24, 25; PC2/92 ff 348–50, 368–9 370–1, 372–3, 375–9, 395–7, 413–14.

251. As well as Table Eight, this observation is based upon an examination of the experiences of Irish bills in the 1740s and 1750s.

252. 10 Geo I, chap 5; NA, PC2/87 ff 374, 400–4, 407–9 (mining bill); 23 Geo II, chap 10; PC2/101 ff 459, 473–4, 475–8 (clandestine marriage bill); 7 Geo II, chap 14; PC2/92 ff 327, 398–401; law officers' report, 27 Mar. (PC1/5/21 ff 5–7); Dorset to Newcastle, 17 Jan. 1734 (SP63/397) (equity court bill); 7 Geo II, chap 15; PC2/92 ff 327m 350–4, 362–4; law officers' report, 20 Feb. 1734 (PC1/5/16 ff 4–7) (corn weight measure bill).

attempt in 1716 to make the existing law against 'the maiming of cattle … more effectual'. In this instance, as well as introducing amendments excising loose and careless references to 'barbarous' acts and defining precisely the nature of the offence that was the measure's target, the British Council authorised the deletion of a full clause at the end of the bill.[253] The response to a measure to amend an act to prevent frauds by tenants and to introduce quarantine regulations in 1721 was comparable; in both instances, the offending clauses were replaced with clauses deemed more appropriate.[254]

The law in respect of the provision of glebes for Church of Ireland clergy was more complex, for when a bill amending the 1704 act 'for the exchange of glebes' was addressed in November 1721, it was determined, amid a host of minor amendments, to delete those sections ('put in' at the Irish Council) that empowered the archbishop of Dublin 'to grant to resident cures forty acres of glebe land … out of his demesne and mensal lands' on the grounds that this could not be done 'without lessening his archbishoprick'. All reference to the augmentation of the deanery of Cloyne was also removed. Archbishop King did not mask his 'dissatisfaction' at this outcome, since it obliged him 'to settle tithes of his own purchasing (instead of transferring others from his own see) on the poor vicarages in his diocese', but though the bill's passage was delayed, it did become law.[255] King's displeasure was understandable given his personal interest in the measure but, as in the instance of the bill to raise £13,500 'for finishing and regulating' Dr Steevens' Hospital, the offending sections were adjudged incompatible with existing regulations.[256] Most public bills did not engage so closely with the financial concerns of individuals, and were seldom subject to major alterations of this kind as a result. This was the case, for example, with the 1736 measure 'for the further encouragement of … flaxen and hempen manufactures', which had a nine-line clause appertaining to sanctions deleted; it was true also of the recasting of a measure for promoting the planting of trees, which had to be completely restructured arising out of a decision to excise all reference to the 'enclosing and preserving of woods', and of an amendment to a bill to encourage building on church lands, which experienced the loss of eighteen lines.[257] Moreover, it was not unusual for this to happen to several bills in one session. In a repeat of what happened in 1735–6, whole clauses were deleted from measures in 1742 to renew a number of expiring statutes, to facilitate the payment of rents

---

253. 2 Geo I, chap 22; NA, PC2/85 ff 360, 363, 391, 395, 399–400.
254. 8 Geo I, chaps 2, 3; NA, PC2/87 ff 353, 375, 379–80, 385–7, 419–20, 430–2, 433–5 (tenants fraud bill; quarantine bill).
255. 8 Geo I, chap 11; NA, PC2/87 ff 353, 377–9, 385–6; *Commons Jn. (Irl.)*, iii, 293, 294, 297, 299, 301, 306; Alterations in the bill for the exchange of glebes, 29 Nov. 1721 (NA, SP67/7 ff 98–9); Nicolson to Wake, 13 Jan. 1721 (Gilbert Library, Wake Papers, MS 27 ff 276–7).
256. 3 Geo II, chap 23; NA, PC2/91 ff 156, 203–5, 209–11; Privy Council letter, 25 Jan. 1729 (BL, Hardwicke Papers, Add. MS 35872 ff 18–19).
257. 9 Geo II, chaps 4, 7, 13; NA, PC2/93 ff 286–7, 324, 325, 333–5, 348–50, 362–3, 371–2.

and to encourage mining, and in 1744 a number of clauses were objected to in a transportation bill and a major deletion approved to a measure to combat forgery.[258] Significantly, this did not prevent these bills being accepted in Ireland.

The number of Irish bills to which major additions were made at the British Council board during the early Hanoverian era was modest. One might have anticipated considerable activity in respect of commercial bills given the number respited but, other than an exception for English muslins incorporated into the flax and hempen act of 1745, there were no additions of note.[259] The most controversial addition was to the 1719 proposal 'for exempting … Protestant dissenters … from certain penalties'. This bill was hotly contested, and the heads only negotiated the Irish Council after a 'long and warm debate' on the casting vote of the lord lieutenant. As a firm opponent of the measure, Archbishop King remained hopeful that the measure might yet be remodelled to his satisfaction at the British Council. The report of the law officers, which was received at the Irish bills committee on 19 August, went some way to meet his concerns and those of the rest of the bishops of the Church of Ireland who were opposed to any concessions inconsistent 'with our constitution in church and state', by recommending a lengthy list of clarifications. However, when the bill was referred back to the Irish bills committee by the full Council 'to revise', a new section was added to the bill providing for Quakers and 'in favour of persons under prosecution who had not qualified themselves'. The perception among some in Ireland was that the clause could be interpreted as offering 'greater … exemption from all penal statutes' to those 'who had qualifyed themselves before such prosecutions', but others contended that 'it repeals the whole Act of Uniformity'. This was not the case, but the protest offered in the Lords that the measure, which became law in its amended form, was a threat to 'the security of the Church of Ireland, as at present by law established', was indicative of the strength of feeling it generated.[260] No such resentments were directed at the addition in 1728 of a new clause (one of 68 amendments) making the new Dublin workhouse corporation liable for all suits, actions, claims and demands incurred by its predecessor; by the addition in 1732 of a clause to a measure to enable 'ideots and lunaticks' to enter into legal agreements with respect of property; and by a similar addition with respect of juries in case of 'actions at law' arising out of the 'improvement of barren and waste lands and bogs', or by the addition made in 1742 to a butchers' bill.[261]

258. 15 Geo II, chaps 6, 8, 10; NA, PC2/97 ff 41, 48, 50–2, 57, 58, 64–6 (expiring estate bill; rents bill, mining bill); 17 Geo II, chaps 4, 11; PC2/98 ff 110, 113–14, 129–32 (transportation bill; forgery bill).

259. 19 Geo II, chap 6; NA, PC2/99 ff 371, 405, 411–13.

260. 6 Geo I, chap 5; NA, PC2/86 ff 299, 301–3, 304–5, 315; O'Regan, *Archbishop King*, p 253; Burns, *Irish parliamentary politics*, i, 82–9; Nicolson to Wake, 9 July 1719 (Gilbert Library, Wake Papers, MS 27 ff 224–5); King to Canterbury, 1 Aug., 10 Nov., 1 Dec. 1719 (TCD, King Papers, MS 750/5 ff 189, 206–7, 216–20); Webster to Delafaye, 6, 15, 22 Oct., Bolton to Craggs, 12 Oct. 1719 (NA, SP63/378); *A collection of protests of the Lords of Ireland*, pp 70–2;

261. 1 Geo II, chap 27; NA, PC2/90 ff 257, 273–5, 276–8 (Dublin workhouse bill); 5 Geo II, chaps

There was little or no objection in Ireland to the addition or deletion of clauses at the British Council board when it was apparent that the changes made enhanced a bill. Moreover, the definition of 'enhancement' applied in this context was elastic since, as well as infringements of the royal prerogative, which was guarded against in the most material amendment introduced into the 1728 measure for keeping parliament in being for six months after the demise of a sovereign, it embraced changes like that made the merchant seamen act of 1732 which stipulated that recovered monies should go to the Bluecoat School rather than the 'poor of the parish'.[262] It might be suggested that since the latter measure was 'taken chiefly from an English [act] for the same purpose', there should have been little need for this or any of the nine other amendments it received.[263] However, such considerations did not weigh heavily with members of the British Privy Council. They sanctioned whatever amendments they believed were justified. And because a high proportion appertained to the law and to its administration, where the case in favour of an amendment was often compelling, this gave credibility to the process as a whole.

This point can be illustrated by examples from throughout the early Hanoverian period. In May 1716, for example, the British Council determined that the proposal that 'insolvent debtors' should be transported was too draconian, and it provided instead for twelve months' 'hard labour' in the House of Correction.[264] Five years later, a measure for the better transporting of felons was extensively amended, as a result of which the title was rewritten and a reference to bonds being null and void was deleted.[265] The commitment, visible in this instance, to ensure that, in so far as possible, the rights, procedures and entitlements provided under Irish law dovetailed with those operating in England provided the rationale for a large number of amendments. It was further manifested by the amendment authorised in 1716 to limit to two years the time during which 'actions, suits, bill and indictments' could be brought on the matter of forfeitures.[266] It was evident again in 1726 when the oath of office provided for in a measure for better regulating the office of sheriff was altered to conform to that taken in England, and a sequence of sanctions against errant sheriffs, including public whipping, were adjudged 'unreasonable' and summarily deleted.[267] And, it

8, 9; PC2/91 ff 527–30, 535, 542–4, 567–8, 572–4 (idiots bill; juries bill); 15 Geo II, chap 9; PC2/97 ff 41, 49, 50–2 (butchers bill).

262. 1 Geo II, chap 7; NA, PC2/90 ff 257, 266–7, 276–8; 5 Geo II, chap 13; PC2/91 ff 582, 590–1.
263. Cary to Delafaye, 29 Jan. 1732 (NA, SP63/395).
264. 2 Geo I, chap 23; NA, PC2/85 ff 361, 363, 382–3, 389–90.
265. 8 Geo I, chap 9; NA, PC2/87 ff 392–3, 416–17, 418–19.
266. 2 Geo I, chap 20; NA, PC2/85 ff 353–4, 366, 368–72. Comparable amendments were introduced in 1719 to a bill to prevent 'the ingrossing and regrating of coals', which stipulated, *inter alia*, that appeals against prices had to be submitted within ten days and actions and suits within a year (6 Geo I, chap. 2; PC2/86 ff 305, 308–9, 311).
267. 12 Geo I, chap 5; PC2/89 ff 141, 144–7, 162–3, 170, 187. A similar concern was demonstrated in 1730 to ensure that the law in respect of sheriffs and sub-sheriffs was properly couched (3 Geo II, chap 9; PC2/91 ff 134, 144–5, 149–51).

was manifest in 1730 when the law officers were so ill at ease with an amending act preventing under-sheriffs and sheriffs' clerks from acting as sub-sheriffs for more than a year, on the grounds that, 'contrary to the general rule of law', it involved self-incrimination, they requested that the law should extend for no more than four years.[268] However, it was most vividly highlighted by the measure proposed in 1726 to curb 'forestallers, regraters and ingrossers' and to regulate the price and assize of bread, which was drastically restructured by the excision of all reference to forestalling on the grounds that it was 'unnecessary and improper'; the measure proposed in 1728 for the further encouragement of mining, which was conceived to be 'unreasonable' because it 'empower[ed] landlords to enter upon the estates of their lessees contrary to their contracts without … consent'; and the measure proposed in 1734 appertaining to the payment of bankers' notes, which the law officers adjudged 'very unreasonable and extreamly unjust' because it proposed to subject 'all the real and leasehold estates of bankers to the payment of their notes'.[269]

A series of comparable interventions were prompted by the wish to confine the eagerness of Irish Protestants to penalise Catholics and converts from Catholicism. This accounts for the removal in March 1728 from the Catholic disfranchising act of a clause that would have disbarred Protestant men married to Catholics women who had not converted within twelve months of marriage.[270] Likewise, the fitful efforts of the Irish parliament to implement a body of law to combat the thorny problem of clandestine marriage were frustrated by the disinclination of the British Council to approve new sanctions targeted at Catholic clergy.[271] And when, in 1755–6, the Irish parliament sought to discourage Catholics serving in the French military by making it treasonable, the British Council responded by recategorising it as a felony.[272]

The British Council was even more determined to protect fiscal and propertied interests in public bills. This can be illustrated, in the first instance, by citing the amendments introduced in 1728 to the law on the construction of roads providing that any 'overplus' should be returned, and to the insertion of an indemnification from legal challenge for those who gave land 'seized in fee simple' for religious purposes.[273] Two years later, clarifications were sanctioned to protect leaseholders

268. 3 Geo II, chap 9; NA, PC2/91 ff 134, 144–5, 149–51; law officers' report, 24 Jan. 1730 (PC1/4/105 ff 63–6).

269. NA, PC2/89 ff 140–1, 149–51, 162–3 (forestallers etc. bill); PC2/90 ff 240, 253–4, 255–6; law officers' report, 18 Mar. 1728 (PC1/4/67 ff 6–7) (mining bill); PC2/92 ff 327, 360, 364, 415, 435–6, 441–2; law officers' report … on bankers' notes (PC1/5/19 ff 4–6) (bankers bill).

270. 1 Geo II, chap 9; NA, PC2/90 ff 257, 267–8, 276–8; in 1746, the British Council introduced an amendment to an Irish election measure requiring that voters would have registered 6 months before an election (19 Geo II, chap 11; PC2/99 ff 372, 404–5, 411–13).

271. 9 Geo II, chap 9; NA, PC2/93 ff 325, 332–3, 352, 385–6, 396–7; 19 Geo II, chap. 13; PC2/99 ff 326, 349, 353–5; 23 Geo II, chap 10; PC2/101, ff 459, 473–4, 475–8.

272. 29 Geo II, chap 5; NA, PC2/105 ff 7, 24, 26–8.

273. 1 Geo II, chaps 13, 15; NA, PC2/90 ff 240, 250–2, 255–6, 257, 265–6, 276–8; law officers' report on clerical residence, 18 Mar. 1728 (PC1/4/67 ff 1–3).

'adjoining the new Parliament house', but as had already been demonstrated in 1717 in the case of the Tuam bill, which was amended to ensure the interests of the Crown and others were not injured by the power granted to the archbishop to 'sett leases of part of his demesne lands', existing legitimate property interests were assured of protection.[274] This was emphasised repeatedly over the following decades when extensive amendments were authorised in a number of high-profile bills to protect creditors in the case of bank failures to protect the interests of family members, and named creditors who might otherwise have been collateral victims.[275]

The readiness to intervene to protect the interests of individuals in public bills emphasises just how difficult it could be on occasion to draw a clear distinction between a public and a private bill. Indeed, in the case of the measure 'for finishing and regulating' Steevens' Hospital, a private bill was 'made ... publick' to 'avoid paying fees'.[276] This also provides an explanation for the fact that there was only a moderate difference of 6 per cent in the percentage of public bills (76 per cent) and private bills (70 per cent) that were sent for amendment. Significantly, the percentage of private bills to negotiate the hurdle of the British Council unaltered (14 per cent) increased, in line with the pattern for public bills, from the mid-1740s, and is symbolised by the fact that during the 1751–52 sessions the three private bills received were forwarded without amendment, as well as by the fact that the average number of amendments made to private bills was below average during the 1750s.[277] At the same time, as was the case with public measures, the range and extent of the amendments agreed in the case of private bills varied according to what the Crown's law officers perceived was required. This meant that a minority of private bills was subject to extensive amendment, that some required only minor corrections but that most required a varied combination of both. In the former category, and accounting for a majority of the substantive amendments made to private bills, were additions introduced to protect the interests of family members. These varied considerably in content, scope and character from simple insertions such as were added to the Ford bill in 1716 to protect the jointure of Mary Ford, and to the Blessington bill in December 1723 to secure the jointure of Martha, Lady Blessington; to significant

274. 4 Geo I, chap 14; NA, PC2/86 ff 44–5, 49, 51; 3 Geo II, chap 8; NA, PC2/91 ff 154, 182–3, 206–8.

275. 9 Geo II, Chap, 27; NA, PC2/93 ff 325, 367–8, 374–5; 29 Geo II, chaps 21, 23; PC2/105 ff 152, 161–2, 163–5; 31 Geo II, chap 12; PC2/106 ff 62–4, 73, 80–2.

276. Dr Steevens' bill, [Feb. 1730] (BL, Hardwicke Papers, Add. MS 36136 ff 14–15).

277. The 1751–2 measures were the Kilmore bill (NA, PC2/102 ff 528–9, 532, 542–3; *Commons Jn.(Irl.)*, v, 117, 120, 147, 148, 156); Fitzherbert bill (PC2/102 ff 529, 532, 543–4; *Commons Jn.(Irl.)*, v, 115, 117, 121, 146, 147, 148, 154); and the Frend bill (PC2/102 ff 533, 544–5; *Commons Jn.(Irl.)*, v, 149, 150, 151, 156; *Lords Jn. (Irl.)*, iii, 793, 804, 819, 823). In 1757–8, of the six private bills approved, three secured approval without amendment and two with one amendments and one with three literal amendments (PC2/106 ff 48, 64, 70, 72–3, 80–2, 102–3, 104, 112–15).

deletions and additions, such as were made to the Smith debt bill of 1717, the Coolbanagher lands bill of 1719, the Percy and Blayney bills of 1723 and the Butler and Morres bills of 1726 to protect the interests of family members.[278] Examples of private bills requiring mainly minor literal corrections are the Ely trustees' bill of 1716, which, in keeping with the fact that all the concerned parties were 'agreed' on its terms, primarily involved correctives to misspellings, the Smith bill of 1717, the Morgan debt bills of 1719, the Longfield lease, the O'Hara estate, the Bell estate and the Cooke bills of 1723, the Parsons' bill of 1728 and many more.[279]

Private bills were generally assured of a trouble-free passage through the Privy Council when 'the several persons concerned … have given their consents to it'.[280] *Per contra*, when consent was not forthcoming, it fell to the Council to ensure that a fair balance was struck, and they were disinclined, as they made clear in the report recommending the rejection of the O'Hara estate bill in 1728, 'to exclude anybody who may have a claim'.[281] For the same reason, the law officers promoted the introduction in 1726 into the Pyke estate bill of an amendment that provided that all creditors would be paid 'according to the nature of their respective securities in proportion to the sum or sums of money raised' by the sale of the property, and, in 1736, authorised a comparable amendment in respect of the interests of the creditors of the bankers, Joseph Nuttall and William McGuire.[282] In 1734, a measure for the relief of the creditors of Samuel Morris was allowed proceed contingent on the admission of an extensive amendment to protect the rights of Arthur, earl of Anglesey.[283] Care was taken also to protect against misfortune, particularly with respect of women and minors, as evidenced

278. 2 Geo I, chap 3 (private); NA, PC2/85 ff 355, 367, 373, 377 (Ford bill); 4 Geo I (private), PC2/86 ff 55–6, 60–1, 65 (Smith bill); 6 Geo I, chap 7 (private); PC2/86 ff 313, 316–17, 336–7 (Coolbanagher lands bill); 10 Geo I, chaps 3, 5 (private); PC2/88 ff 375, 392, 422–3, 428–9, 442–6; law officers' report on Blayney private bill, 3 Jan. 1724 (PC1/3/120 ff 12–13) (Percy and Blayney bills); 10 Geo I, chap 11; PC2/88 ff 375, 424–5, 442–6; law officers' report on Blessington bill, 3 Jan. 1724 (PC1/3/122 ff 4–6) (Blessington bill); 12 Geo I, chaps 5, 8; PC2/89 ff 142, 143, 176, 183, 190–1 (Butler and Morres bills).

279. 2 Geo I, chap 1 (private); NA, PC2/85 ff 345, 367, 372–3; Countess of Drogheda to King, 25 Mar. 1715 (TCD, King Papers, MS 1995–2008 f. 1604); King to Sunderland, 2 Apr. 1715 (King Papers, MS 750/4 f 248); 6 Geo I, chap 8; PC2/86 ff 313, 317, 336, 340–3 (Morgan bill); 10 Geo II, chaps 4, 7, 8, 9; PC2/88 ff 374, 375, 391, 405–6, 409–10, 416, 426–8, 429–31, 437–9, 424–6; law officers' reports on Cooke estate bill, on O'Hara bill, 3 Jan. 1724 (PC1/3/122 ff 7–15) (Longfield, O'Hara, Bell, Cooke bills); 12 Geo I, chap 1 (private); PC2/89 ff 130, 151–2, 163–4; PC2/90 ff 258, 287–8, 292; Irish bills committee report, 3 Apr. 1728 (PC1/4/71 ff 5–6, 19–20) (Parsons' bill).

280. Irish Privy Council letter on Molesworth bill, 9 Nov. 1725 (NA, PC1/4/17 f. 6).

281. NA, PC2/90 ff 289–90; Irish bills committee report, 3 Apr. 1728 (PC1/4/71 ff 7–8, 21–2).

282. NA, PC2/89 ff 175–6; PC2/93 ff 326, 388–90, 398–9 (Nuttall and McGuire). For other illustration of the care taken of creditors see PC2/93 ff 391–2 (Fleming bill).

283. 7 Geo II, chap 1 (private); NA, PC2/922 ff 348, 401–4, 414–15; law officers' report, 2 Apr. 1734 (PC1/5/22).

by the amendments (sometimes extensive) to the measures for the provision of the younger children of John Odell, Charles Coote of Cootehill, County Cavan, Caesar Colclough of Mocorry, County Wexford and Stephen Rice of Mount Rice, County Kildare.[284] At the opposite end of the human cycle, the interpretation of last wills and testaments was also accorded close attention particularly when it concerned a bequest to establish a charitable endowment. In 1728, it was necessary to rewrite completely the Bishop Foy charitable foundation bill to ensure that the wishes of the bishop, as expressed in his will, were honoured, while the measure to inaugurate the charity endowed by Hugh Rainey of Magherafelt ten years later also required extensive amendment.[285]

As well as identifiable deficiencies in measures, amendments were authorised in respect of a number of private bills in response to petitions emanating from a variety of interested parties. More than three quarters of all the petitions presented to the British Council during the early Hanoverian era concerned public bills, but the proportion (10 per cent) of private bills that was the subject of a petition exceeded that of public bills (6.25 per cent) by a noticeable margin. That apart, there was no difference in the manner in which petitions were assessed. All petitions, and the oral evidence that was sometimes heard, were taken seriously, though by no means all had the impact their presenters anticipated. The petition presented in 1719 against the measure 'for the relief of the creditors of Sir Maurice Eustace' is a case in point. Having previously negotiated the British Council in April 1716 only to fall in the Irish Commons, it was something of a surprise when Charles Baldwyne presented a petition seeking the introduction of an amendment to protect his interests; he was refused and the bill was forwarded unaltered to become law.[286] A more predictable outcome ensued in the winter of 1723–4 when the presentation of petitions contributed to the decision to respite three private bills,[287] and in the spring of 1728 and 1730 when the evidence contained in a number of petitions helped to persuade the Irish bills committee on two successive occasions that it was not appropriate 'to break into' the existing estate settlement to enable Michael Fleming, the brother of Lord Slane, to pay his father's debts.[288] However, when a more acceptable version of the measure was

284. 3 Geo II, chap 3 (private); NA, PC2/91 ff 173, 200–1, 210–12; Irish Privy Council letter, 6 Feb. 1730 (BL, Hardwicke Papers, Add. MS 35872 ff 35–6); PC2/94 ff 398, 451, 461–2 (Odell bill); 13 Geo I, chap 2 (private); PC2/95 ff 505, 580–2 (Rice bill); 19 Geo II, chap 4; PC2/99 ff 338, 387–8, 415–16 (Colclough bill).
285. NA, PC2/90 ff 258, 284–7, 292; Irish bills committee report, 3 Apr. 1728 (PC1/4/71 ff 9–14) (Foy bill); PC2/94 ff 428, 451–2, 463–4 (Rainey charity bill).
286. NA, PC2/85 ff 361, 367, 376–7; 6 Geo I, chap 1 (private); PC2/86 ff 314, 334, 340–3.
287. NA, PC2/88 ff 375, 391, 392, 394, 406–7, 411, 440, 446–7; Irish Privy Council letter, 22 Nov. 1723 (SP63/382); Southwell to King, 23 Jan. 1724 (TCD, King Papers, MS 1995–2008 f. 2060).
288. NA, PC2/90 ff 258, 288–9, 292, PC2/91 ff 173, 205, 213; Petition of William Knox, 4 Apr. 1728 (PC1/4/70); Petition and other papers re Fleming bill, 21 Feb. 1730 (BL, Hardwicke Papers, Add. MS 35872 ff 28, 29, 31, 32).

presented in 1736, the objections of Lord Fleming were not deemed compelling, and the bill was forwarded, albeit with significant amendments.[289]

By this date, too, the high point of the presentation of petitions in the case of private bills had passed. They continued to be presented in a smaller proportion of instances (Table Seven; p. 243) and, where they offered a substantiated case, to cause bills to be both amended and lost.[290] The pattern of petitioning was comparable with respect of public legislation (Table Six; p. 242) since, of the 34 public measures against which petitions were presented between 1715 and 1760, 23 date from the period 1715 to 1732, and 10 from the years 1747 to 1758. Significantly, the fall-off in the presentation of petitions coincides with the decline in the number of measures that were respited and the increased number returned to Ireland without alteration. But the point can be better illustrated by reference to the fact that, though 7 per cent of Irish bills considered at the British Council board during the early Hanoverian era were the subject of petitions, there was a sharp decline in the percentage subject to petitions during the reign of George II (Table Eight).

Petitions were submitted to the British Council by interested parties in the expectation that they would convince the law officers and the generality of privy councillors either to respite or amend as appropriate the legislation against which they were presented. Given their well-chronicled impact during the reign of Queen Anne, it was logical that the number of petitions presented should increase following the Hanoverian succession, and 14 per cent of bills were subject to petitions during the reign of George I. Interested parties were certainly encouraged to pursue this avenue by the positive response to a number of private objections to public proposals during the 1715–6 session. Perhaps the most successful applicant was the dowager Duchess of Ormonde who had good reason to object to the proposal to dissolve the Tipperary palatinate and to vest the estates of James, duke of Ormonde in the Crown. Lobbying on behalf of herself and other family members, she contended the measure 'deprived' them 'of their rights and just debts', and her intervention was vindicated by the addition of an amendment of several thousand words that went some way to meet her concerns.[291] The Quakers also had good reason to be pleased with the response to their petition in 1719 against a clause in the bill 'for the further amendment of the law' since, contrary to the expressed opposition of the 'spiritual Lords who thought the ecclesiastical jurisdiction reduced by it', they secured an amendment that allowed them to make a 'solemn affirmation (in lieu of an oath)'.[292] And,

289. NA, PC2/93 ff 360, 391–2, 401–2; *Common Jn. (Irl.)*, iv, 175, 182, 189, 216, 217, 220, 222, 223.
290. NA, PC2/93 ff 326, 338, 369–70, 376 (Campbell bill, 1736); PC2/94 ff 402–3, 415, 452, 452–6, 463–4; Minutes of the Clerk of the Council, 1670–1776 (PC4/1 f. 810); *Commons Jn. (Irl.)*, iv, 254, 264, 266, 267, 268, 269, 279, 283, 285, 286 (Reddy bill); 21 Geo II, chap 8 (private); PC2/100, ff 512–13, 514–15, 555–60; *Commons Jn. (Irl.)*, iv, 563, 565, 566, 567 (Walsh bill).
291. 2 Geo I, chap 8; NA, PC2/85 ff 353–4, 355–6, 362, 391–2, 396–8, 399–400.
292. 6 Geo I, chap 6; NA, PC2/86 ff 317–18, 323–4, 327–31; Bolton to Craggs, 24 Oct. 1719 (NA, SP63/378); Nicolson to Wake, 31 Oct. 1719 (Gilbert Library, Wake Papers, MS 27 ff 244–5).

though the amendments that resulted were by no means so far-reaching, the petitions presented in 1716 by the earl of Burlington on his own and on behalf of other aristocrats against a plan to prevent the destruction of salmon fry on the grounds that 'property to a very great value would be taken from them', and in 1717 by Lord Dunkellin, John Asgill (the owner of Rosse Castle) and others objecting to the proposal to vest 'several lands, tenements and hereditaments' upon which barracks were located in the Crown also proved worthwhile.[293] This set a pattern that was to endure for the remainder of the reign of George I and the reign of George II, when the percentage of bills that were the subject of petition fell to 4.5 per cent. The measure subject to the largest number of petitions during George II's reign was the bill for the 'relief of the creditors' of Burton's bank, which was the subject of eight petitions in the spring of 1734. Amenable to protect those with loans to bankers, the law officers recommended an extended series of 'unusually explicit' amendments and alterations numbering 158 in all and extending over thirteen tightly written folio pages that included most of the petitioners by name.[294] Indeed, when the matter came before the Council again in 1758, and was once more the subject of a petition, this time by the administrator of the estate of one of the original petitioners, an amendment was introduced to ensure that no creditors would be obliged to accept a composition for their debts without their written 'consent'.[295]

As well as individuals, petitions were also forthcoming from corporate interests whose object was not redress but, as one contemporary put it, 'to defeat' objectionable legislation. In 1723, for example, extensive amendments were introduced into a measure for 'amending the several laws ... in force for encouraging the hempen and flaxen manufacture' in response to objections, articulated in petitions, raised by dealers in Irish linens and yarns in Lancashire and Cheshire.[296] Seven years later, in response to the concerns expressed by merchants from Exeter, London and Bristol and the inhabitants of Tiverton, Dorset, at the duties laid in Ireland on wool exports which, they claimed, led directly to an increase in the smuggling of wool to France, and aided the French secure a 20 per cent competitive advantage over English producers, the British

---

Interestingly, when the matter of accepting the 'solemn affirmation' of Quakers was addressed in law in 1723, it negotiated the British Council as well as the Irish parliament without much difficulty despite the strong reservations of the Church of Ireland hierarchy (10 George I, chap 8; PC2/88 ff 374, 400, 407–9; Grafton to Carteret, 9, 15 Nov. 1723 (SP63/382); King to Southwell, 2 Dec. 1723, King to London, 10 Jan., 1 Feb.1724 (TCD, King Papers, MS 2537 ff 28, 50, 69); *A collection of protests of the Lords*, pp 75–80).

293. 2 Geo I, chap 21; NA, PC2/85 ff 360–1, 363, 382–3, 388, 390 (salmon fry bill); 4 Geo I, chap 7; PC2/86 ff 55, 56, 58, 63–5 (barracks bill).

294. 7 Geo II, chap 26; NA, PC2/92 ff 348, 360–1, 373, 457–71 (Burton's bank bill).

295. 31 Geo II, chap 12; NA, PC2/106 ff 63–4, 73, 80–2.

296. 10 Geo I, chap 2; NA, PC2/88 ff 395–400, 409, 451–6; Minutes of the clerks of the Council 1670–1776, 3 Jan. (PC4/1 f. 421); Irish bills committee report, 13 Jan. (PC1/3/124 ff 1–5); King to Canterbury, 28 Jan. 1724 (TCD, King Papers, MS 2737 f. 63) (hempen and flax bill).

Council sanctioned the insertion in an Irish measure for the encouragement of tillage of a clause removing all duties on wool, bays and woollen yarns exported to Ireland.[297] Another interest to lobby successfully were the coal owners, merchants and masters trading in coal between Britain and Ireland, who petitioned in 1724 and in 1726 against an attempt to make the 1719 act for the more effectual preventing the engrossing and regrating of coals perpetual, and in 1728 against a measure to prevent price combinations on the grounds that they were 'very prejudicial' to the 'trade and navigation of Great Britain'.[298]

The amendment of bills to accommodate British commercial interests was a source of resentment in Ireland, but this did not deter Irish interests from following their example. In 1723, the mayor, sheriff and commonalty joined with the merchants and traders of Cork city to oppose the suggestion that two MPs would be made weighmasters for life. Since this regulation had been introduced at the Irish Council board, the Irish bills committee was reluctant to authorise its alteration but the measure was amended agreeably to empower the corporation to nominate their successors.[299] The Irish interest that employed the right to petition to best advantage to defeat or to remodel measures were Catholics. They were assisted by the greater reluctance of English officials from the mid-1720s to approve penal restrictions to petition successfully in 1728 for the deletion of a sequence of clauses that were more onerous than the prevailing regulations in Britain and that would, had they been sanctioned, have precluded recent converts from Catholicism practising as barristers.[300] Six years later, the presentation of three petitions from groups of leading Catholics, including Lord Mountgarret and Lord Caher, and some interested Protestants, ensured that Protestants married to Catholics would not be penalised and that such sanctions as were invoked against those who infringed 'the law in relation to Popish solicitors' did not include the death penalty.[301] This was a welcome concession given the antipathy Irish Protestants continued to bear Catholics in the professions, and the value of petitioning was further illustrated in 1740 when the Irish parliament

297. 3 Geo II, chap 3; NA, PC2/921 ff 155, 183–6, 206–09. Ironically, Irish concerns in respect of the bill at the British Council centred on the provision to encourage the draining and improving of low grounds and unprofitable bogs in the midland counties (see Coghill to Southwell, 3 Jan., Carteret to Southwell, 28 Jan., 9, 26 Feb. 1730 (BL, Southwell Papers, Add. MS 21122 ff 103–06, MS 38016 ff 21, 23, 25–6); Irish Privy Council letter, 3 Jan. , Southwell to Attorney General and enclosure, 6 Feb. 1730 (BL, Hardwicke Papers, Add. MS 36136 ff 116, 216, 217).

298. 6 Geo I, chap 2; 10 Geo I, chap 4; NA, PC2/88 ff 412, 456–8, 461–3; law officers' report, 8 Jan., affidavit of James Lowther, 3 Jan., affidavit of Philip Peck, 7 Jan., Irish bills committee report, 13 Jan. 1724 (PC1/3/123 ff 1–9); PC2/89 ff 140–1, 177–8, 187–9; 1 Geo II, chap 21; PC2/90 ff 256, 282–4, 290–1; Petition of coal merchants of Britain, Apr., Petition of Philip Knightley, 4 Apr. 1728 (PC1/4/68 ff 1–3).

299. 10 Geo I, chap 9; PC2/88 ff 412, 413–14, 458–61, 461–3; Irish bills committee report, 13 Jan. 1724 (PC1/3/124 ff 6–9).

300. 1 Geo II, chap 20; NA, PC2/90 ff 256, 293–6, 298–9.

301. 7 Geo II, chap 5; NA, PC2/92 ff 296, 355–8, 262–4; law officers' reports, 20 Feb. 1734 (PC1/5/18 ff 1–8).

sought to tighten up the regulation in respect of Catholics bearing arms; on this occasion the British Council responded to the petition of Lord Mountgarret by including an exemption for any nobleman and those covered by the treaties of Limerick and Galway.[302]

Interestingly, exceptions sought in 1717 by members of the now defunct Tory party were treated less favourably. Thus in the case of the measure to 'strengthen ... the Protestant interest' in the town of Galway, petitions from a number of erstwhile Tory interests headed by John Staunton claiming that they and other 'loyal subjects' would be 'deprived of their libertys and freeholds' unless an appropriate exemption was 'inserted in their behalf' were not acceded to though the bill was amended in a number of different ways. The outcome was the same with respect of a similar measure for Kilkenny. In this instance, a petition presented by a number of Tory aldermen threatened with political margin-alisation if the bill transmitted from Ireland became law was set aside on the grounds it had arrived too late to be considered as, due to the exceptional efforts of an agent on behalf of Kilkenny Whigs, the measure made its way through the British Council in forty-eight hours and had completed its passage before the measure's opponents presented their petition.[303] As this emphasises, petitions did not always produce the hoped for result. In 1719, for example, the petitions of Thomas Domvile, who opposed the measure 'for cleansing and repairing the water courses' leading from the river Dodder to the city of Dublin, and Joseph Fitzsimon, a prisoner in the Dublin Marshalsea, who protested at his exclusion from a bill for the relief of insolvent debtors, had no effect.[304] In 1748, when Edward Walsh petitioned against a proposal to amend the law in relation to fines and common recoveries, the changes made to the measure were less directly relevant than those made to a private bill with a similar title. And similarly, though the controversial 'Newtown bill', which made it legal for corporations to elect non-resident burgesses and other officers, was the subject of a number of petitions from a variety of individual and corporate interests, all of which asserted that they 'would be greatly and prejudicially affected thereby', the amendments that were introduced did not meet their concerns.[305] Petitions from English

---

302. 13 Geo II, chap 6; NA, PC2/95 ff 520, 641, 643–6, 656–7; List of business for the Irish bills committee, 29 Feb. 1740 (Beinecke Library, Great Britain Files).

303. 4 Geo I, chap 15; NA, PC2/86 ff 54, 57, 63–5; Hutchinson to King, 29 Oct., 1 Nov., Whitshed to King, 2 Nov. 1717 (TCD, King Papers, MS 1995–2008 ff 1831, 1837, 1833) (Galway bill); 4 Geo I, chap 16; Addison to Bolton, 26 Nov. 1717 (NA, SP67/7 f 28); Wake to King, 26 Nov. 1717 (King Papers, MS 1995–2008 f. 1838); Wharton to Addison, 26 Nov. 1717, Hackett to Warren, 26 Nov. 1717 (NA, Prim Collection, nos 43, 41) (Kilkenny).

304. 6 Geo I, chaps 16, 17; NA, PC2/86 ff 312, 316, 317–18, 323, 327–31.

305. 21 Geo II, chaps 10, 11; NA, PC2/100 ff 507–08, 514, 522, 556–60, 563–6; Petition of Irish Society, 29 Feb., Petition of Alexander Stewart etc., 26 Feb. 1748 (PC1/6/7 ff 1–3); Duncannon to Wilmot, 24 Dec. 1747 (PRONI, Wilmot Papers, T3019/952). For other examples see 29 Geo II, chap 22; PC2/105 ff 152, 160, 163–5 (Willcocks and Dawson bill); 31 Geo II, chap 14 (Dublin coals bill); in this instance a petition from the Lord Mayor and Corporation was presented, but the bill was forwarded unaltered (PC2/106 ff 7, 23, 74, 102).

commercial interests likewise fell on deaf ears, as the failed protest in 1729 of the London and Canterbury manufacturers of wrought silks against the imposition of an additional duty on British silks imported to Ireland, and in 1751 of merchants trading with Ireland against an Irish corn bill indicates.[306]

BILLS AT THE IRISH PARLIAMENT, 1715–60

Eighty-eight per cent or 579 of the 657 heads and privy council bills received at the British Council board during the reigns of George I and George II were returned to Ireland. Since the vast majority of these had originated with the Irish parliament, the expectation was that they would make it to law, but the unacceptability of amendments introduced in the Irish and British Councils combined with the suspicion with which MPs, particularly, regarded legislation rising in the Lords ensured that 64 public and one private bills, or 11 per cent of the total returned, did not receive the royal assent (Tables Six and Seven). Disaggregated, five did not become law because they were not presented to the Irish parliament, eleven because they were unacceptable to the Lords, and 49 because they were unacceptable to the Commons. The pattern of losses oscillated from zero to six per session, but it does not observe any identifiable temporal pattern; twenty bills were lost during the reign of George I, and 44 during the reign of George II (Table Eight).

Though the surviving record offers little by way of clues, it is hardly a coincidence that the five bills that were not presented to the Irish parliament for approval were either contentious measures or had been extensively amended. The former criterion applies in the case of the 1716 bill to allow Quakers subscribe to an 'affirmation' rather than an oath and to amend the 1703 act to prevent the further growth of popery, and the latter to the 1728 mines bill and the controversial trade and bankers' bills of 1733–4.[307] Similar concerns were registered in respect of other measures, but more were lost because MPs were disposed to look with disfavour on bills that did not arise with them. The rejection of bills that arose with the Irish Privy Council was a clear affirmation of the determination of MPs to assert their authority to initiate legislation,[308] and it was given added weight by the fact that some twenty per cent (13) of the bills that foundered in the Commons took their rise as heads in the Lords.

In some cases, the Commons' action can plausibly be accounted for by reference to legitimate objections to the bills' content. This is the case, for

---

306. 3 Geo II, chap 2; NA, PC2/91 ff 86–7, 92–3, 93–5 (money bill); 25 Geo II, chap 15; PC2/102 ff 526, 528, 530–1 (corn bill).
307. NA, PC2/85 ff 360, 363, 391, 395, 399–400 (Quaker and amending bill); PC2/90 ff 240, 253–4, 255–6 (mining bill); PC2/92 ff 347, 397–8; PC1/5/21 f. 2 (trade bill); PC2/92 ff 327, 360, 364, 415, 435–38, 441–2; law officers' report ..., 7 Mar. 1734 (PC1/5/19 ff 4–6) (bankers bill).
308. Above, pp 197–8.

instance, with bills for the preservation of game lost in 1721 and 1736 which experienced numerous, albeit largely verbal, amendments at the British Council; the 1723 bill to prevent malicious maiming and wounding, and the only private measure to fall – the bill for the relief of the creditors of Maurice Eustace; this was rejected in the House of Commons in June 1716, having been amended extensively at the British Council.[309] However, a striking number of bills that arose as heads in the Lords and that were subject either to little or no amendment also failed to make it to the statute book because the Commons disagreed fundamentally with the approach taken by peers or believed legislation of this kind was unwarranted. This explains the loss of the measure for 'the more easy recovery of small tithes' in 1719 which was rejected, Archbishop King observed caustically, because MPs wanted to do nothing 'that would be an ease to the Church' and, perhaps, the bill for the better maintenance of curates, which empowered bishops to erect chapels of ease for the convenience of 'inhabitants ... six or more miles from their places of publick worship'.[310] More strikingly, it accounts for the loss during the 1750s of six bills, all of which negotiated the British Council without amendment, because MPs were intent on affirming the primacy of the House of Commons in initiating legislation.[311] The significance of this is underlined by the fact that during the Hanoverian era not only were few bills that took their rise in the Lords lost in the Lords on their return, but also that few bills that arose in the Commons were lost in the Lords. There were only two in the former category – a comparatively innocuous records bill that failed in 1728, and the controversial foreign education bill of 1748. As described above, the latter was substantially amended at the British Council on foot of concern that it infringed 'immunities' conceded by the Treaty of Limerick, and that it left no

309. NA, PC2/87 ff 419–20, 429, 433–5; *Lords Jn. (Irl.)*, ii, 708, 714, 730; *Commons Jn. (Irl.)*, iii, 303, 304, 305 (game bill, 1721); PC2/93 ff 286, 291–2, 304–06; *Lords Jn. (Irl.)*, iii, 307, 316, 334, 337; *Commons Jn. (Irl.)*, iv, 210, 215 (game bill, 1736); PC2/88 ff 352, 360, 362–4; *Lords Jn. (Irl.)*, ii, 752, 753, 769; *Commons Jn. (Irl.)*, iii, 227; Privy Council letter, 31 Oct., law officers' report, 15 Nov. 1723 (PC1/3/116 ff 2, 4–5) (maiming bill); PC2/85 ff 361, 367, 376–7; *Commons Jn. (Irl.)*, iii, 104 (Eustace bill). Significantly a comparable bill finally received the royal assent in 1719 (6 Geo I, chap 1 (private)).

310. NA, PC2/86 ff 317–18, 325, 327–31; *Lords Jn. (Irl.)*, ii, 611, 634. 652; *Commons Jn. (Irl.)*, iii, 227, 228, 230, 232, 234; King to Southwell, 12 Nov. 1719 (TCD, King Papers, MS 750/5 f. 211) (small tithes bill); PC2/88 ff 352, 361–2, 362–4; *Lords Jn. (Irl.)*, ii, 754, 767; *Commons Jn. (Irl.)*, iii, 370, 371, 372; Privy Council letter, 31 Oct., law officers' report, 15 Nov. 1723 (PC1/3/116 ff 2, 5) (curates bill).

311. NA, PC2/101 ff 459, 473, 475–8; *Lords Jn. (Irl.)*, iii, 733, 740, 753, 758; *Commons Jn. (Irl.)*, iii, 75, 76 (bastards bill); PC2/105 ff 31, 115, 120–2; *Lords Jn. (Irl.)*, iv, 44, 45, 60, 65; *Commons Jn. (Irl.)*, v, 398, 399, 405, 406 (parishes bill); PC2/105 ff 31, 115, 120–22; *Lords Jn. (Irl.)*, iv, 42, 45, 60, 65; *Commons Jn. (Irl.)*, v, 398, 399, 401, 402 (cure of souls bill); PC2/105 ff 8, 48, 142, 146–8; *Lords Jn. (Irl.)*, iv, 39, 40, 60, 65; *Commons Jn. (Irl.)*, v, 398, 402, 403 (stewards bill); PC2/106 ff 7, 22, 23–4; *Lords Jn. (Irl.)*, iv, 91, 95, 116, 119; *Commons Jn. (Irl.)*, v, 91, 92, 94, 95 (fire bill); PC2/107 ff 337, 350, 360–2; *Lords Jn. (Irl.)*, iv, 110, 173, 190, 191; *Commons Jn. (Irl.)*, vi, 227, 229, 230 (statutes bill).

incentive for guardians, and intense Catholic opposition, but it was still expected to become law. However, such was the determination of Catholics to overturn the bill that they took their opposition into the House of Lords and they achieved a notable triumph when the bill was dropped in committee.[312] Saliently, only two of the eight Commons bills not to progress through the Lords were formally rejected in that house. The first – an attempt to prevent minors marrying without parental permission – foundered on the eminently practical grounds that the decision of the British Council to bring forward the date when the bill should come into effect did not provide sufficient time to alert the public that it was a felony offence.[313] The second, and more infamous measure of 1719, 'for securing the Protestant interest', which was returned to Ireland without the offending 'castration' clause, but which had 'many beneficial clauses', ran into the sands in the Lords because 'the clause to prevent leases being granted in reversion to Papists and for revoking those already made since the popery Act ... [of] 1703' was incompatible with reversionary leases.[314] Perhaps, influenced by this experience, a number of controversial bills that negotiated the Commons and were 'sent to the Lords' were never presented to the upper house. It was an anti-climactic *denouement* for measures as varied as the 1719 marriage bill, the 1730 Newgate prison bill and the 1746 Jewish naturalisation bill, though it did mean that they were never formally rejected.[315] Moreover, this outcome was probably slightly preferable than the experience of the 1752 measure permitting the sale of King's Inns properties; uniquely, it negotiated both the Lords and the Commons but it never became law because it did not receive the royal assent.[316]

The increasing dominance of the House of Commons in the making of law for the kingdom of Ireland that is a feature of the early Hanoverian era is highlighted by the fact that not only were MPs responsible for rejecting a majority of the bills that failed at this final stage, but also that a high proportion of those that rose with

312. NA, PC2/90 ff 257, 264–5, 276–8; *Lords Jn. (Irl.)*, iii, 38, 40, 62, 64 (records bill); above, p. 221; *Lords Jn.(Irl.)*, iii, 701, 703, 707; Some observations upon a bill ... entitled ... to restrain foreign education, [Feb.–Mar. 1748] (Nottingham University Library, Newcastle of Clumber Papers, MS NeC 1598); Fagan, *Catholics in a protestant country*, p. 71; Mathew to Fitzwilliam, 11 Feb. 1748 (NAI, Pembroke estate Papers, 97/46/1/2/5/53).

313. NA, PC2/86 ff 55, 58–9, 63–5; King to Canterbury, 21 Dec. 1717 (TCD, King Papers, MS 2535 ff 36; *Commons Jn. (Irl.)*, iii, 125, 142, 150, 161, 163, 166, 167; *Lords Jn. (Irl.)*, ii.

314. Above, p. 220; NA, PC2/86 f. 334; Bolton, *Irish parliamentary politics*, i, 92; Burke, *Irish priests in penal times*, p. 200; Fagan, *Catholics in a Protestant country*, pp 59–60; Webster to Delafaye, 22 Sept., 29 Oct., Bolton to Craggs, 31 Oct., 3 Nov. 1719 (NA, SP63/378).

315. NA, PC2/86 ff 317–8, 324, 327–31; *Commons Jn. (Irl.)*, iii, 225, 228, 229, 230, 231, 235 (marriage bill); PC2/91 ff 153, 163–4, 168–70; *Commons Jn. (Irl.)*, iii, 637, 639, 640, 641 (Newgate bill); PC2/99 ff 326, 349, 353–5; *Commons Jn. (Irl.)*, iii, 495, 497, 498 (Jews bill); PC2/102 ff 553–4, 2/103 ff 2, 18–22; *Commons Jn. (Irl.)*, v, 151, 152 (corn bill, 1752); PC2/105 ff 145, 155–6; *Commons Jn. (Irl.)*, v, 396, 397, 400 (murder bill, 1756); PC2/106 ff 62, 71–2, 78–80; *Commons Jn. (Irl.)*, vi, 98, 99 (presentment bill, 1758).

316. NA, PC2/102 ff 529, 2/103 ff 5, 26–7; *Commons Jn. (Irl.)*, v, 110, 111, 112, 113, 150, 151, 152, 155.

them did not proceed because of objectionable amendments made at the Irish and British Councils. Identifying examples of the former is not without hazard, but they include the diluting of the clause in relation to dissenters and the test in the controversial 1716 measure for further securing the King's 'person and government', and the addition of a clause to the 1723 flax bill reserving to the Irish Council the 'power of inspecting (and approving) the bye-laws' of the Linen board. Moreover, as the observation in respect of the latter and the case of a 'hawkers and pedlars bill' indicates, the fact that the Commons rejected both bills with 'indignation' offers further evidence of the passion the interventions of the Irish Council could arouse.[317] This is only slightly less true of the amendments made at the British Council, for it is noteworthy just how heavily amended were many of the bills that fell by the wayside in the Commons. The 1726 forestallers bill, which was utterly recast by the elision of that part of the text relating to forestalling and restricted to regulating the price and assize of corn is an example. This revised bill, which was described as 'of pernicious consequence', prompted so many 'complaints' that even Primate Boulter was induced to question the judgement of the English attorney general.[318] Others, such as the 1726 workhouse bill prompted only slightly less irritation.[319] The pattern as the reign of George II progressed was simply for amended bills that were disliked by MPs to be lost in the Commons without especial fuss, and the fact that some were heavily amended is an indicative guide as to why this happened.[320]

CONCLUSION

Five hundred and fourteen public and private bills received the royal assent and became law in Ireland between 1715 and 1760 from the 929 bills and heads of bills to take their rise at the Irish Privy Council and Irish parliament. This represented a success rate of 55 per cent (Table Eight). Interestingly, the experience of public and private bills diverged quite significantly, from just over half (53 per cent) in

---

317. Above pp 206, 234; *Commons Jn. (Irl.)*, iii, 95, 98, 99, 100; Nicolson to Wake, 13 Jan. 1721 (Gilbert Library, Wake Papers, MS 27 f. 275); NA PC2/87 ff 392, 399; *Commons Jn. (Irl.)*, iii, 295, 298 (hawkers and pedlars bill, 1721); PC2/87 ff 392, 400–01; *Commons Jn. (Irl.)*, iii, 295, 298 (hemp and flax bill, 1721).

318. NA, PC2/89 ff 140–1, 149–51; Nicolson to Wake, 10 Mar. 1726 (BL, Wake Papers, Add. MS 6116 f. 299); Boulter to Newcastle, 22 Mar. 1726 in *Boulter letters*, i, 54–5.

319. PC2/89 ff 140–1, 178–81, 187–9; Nicolson to Wake, 10 Mar. 1726 (BL, Wake Papers, Add. MS 6116 f. 299); *Commons Jn. (Irl.)*, iii, 446, 448, 450 (workhouse bill).

320. NA, PC2/97 ff 41, 60–61, 64–6; *Commons Jn. (Irl.)*, iv, 391, 392 (tillage bill, 1742); PC2/97 ff 42, 57, 64–6; *Commons Jn. (Irl.)*, iv, 391, 392 (livestock stealing bill, 1742); PC2/99 ff 371, 405–07, 416, 425–6; *Commons Jn. (Irl.)*, iv, 500, 501, 503 (common recoveries bill, 1746); PC2/101 ff 458, 469–70, 498, 503–04; Petition, Minutes of Irish bills committee, 16 Mar. 1750, law officers' report, 13 Mar. 1750 (PC1/6/19 ff1–3, PC1/6/18); *Commons Jn. (Irl.)*, v, 80 (agents bill, 1750).

the case of public bills to more than two-thirds (68 per cent) in the case of private bills, but the fact that the proportion of all bills to make it to law appreciated from 50 per cent to 58 per cent, between the reigns of George I and George II is testament to the constancy in the manner with which Poynings' Law was applied and in the pattern of law-making during this period (Tables Six and Seven). This conclusion is strengthened by the constancy in the number of laws made per session over the period (Table 1). However, this situation was about to change as the effective working arrangement that had lasted for near half a century came under increased pressure from the 1760s as the willingness of politicians and public to live within the restrictive parameters defined by Poynings' Law diminished. The most visible manifestation of the fact that the effective arrangement in place during the early Hanoverian era was no longer tenable is provided by the acceleration in the volume of law proposed and enacted per session, but the most significant indication was the intensifying demand to amend Poynings' Law itself.

TABLE SIX

THE LEGISLATION OF THE IRISH PARLIAMENT, 1715–60: PUBLIC BILLS

| | Ireland — Origins of (heads of) bills | | | Ireland — Lost heads of bills | | | | | England — Irish Privy Council bills and heads of bills at the Privy Council | | | | | | Ireland — Bills at the Irish parliament | | | |
| | | | | House of Commons | | Lords bill | House of Lords | Privy Council | | | | | | | | Rejected | | |
Session	Privy Council bills	House of Commons heads	House of Lords heads	Leave only	Rejected				Received	Respited/postponed not reported	Amended	Not amended	Petitions presented	approved	Not presented	Commons	Lords	Royal assent
1715–16	8	31	3	4	3			3	32	3	22	7	2	29	2	3		24
1717–18	1	28	3	4	8		1		19	2	14	3	3	17			1	16
1719–20	2	31	5	5	5			4	24	3	13	8	5	21		1	2	18
1721–2		29	4	4	5			1	23	3	20	–	–	20		4		16
1723–4	1	25	6	7	4			2	19	4	15	–	5	15		4		11
1725–6		24	3	2	7			3	15	3	12	–	4	12		2		10
1727–8	6	22	10	2	2			3	31	2	29	–	2	29	1		1	27
1729–30	2	32	3	5	1		1	3	27	2	23	2	1	25		1	1	23
1731–2	2	33	8	7	3			2	31	4	26	1	1	27		5		22
1733–4		33	4	6	4	1		2	31	2	29	–	–	29	2	1		26
1735–6		45	7	1	9			2	34	4	30	–	–	30		3		27
1737–8		22	7	1	2		2	5	19		17	2		19				19
1739–40		21	4	1	3			1	20	2	18		1	18		2		16
1741–2		17	4	2	3		1	1	14	1	13			13		2		11
1743–4	1	23	2	3	3		1	2	17	2	15			15		2		13
1745–6	1	30	3	1	7			1	25	1	21	3		24		3	1	21
17474 8		18	5	1	6		1	1	14		13	1	3	14				13
1749–50	1	23	6	1	2		1	1	25	3	17	5	1	22		3		19
1751–2		31	5	1	5			3	27		20	7	1	27		2	2	23
1753		20		1	3			1	15	11	3	1		4		1		3
1755–6	1	32	10	1	5		2	6	29		31	8	2	29		4	1	24
1757–8		44	6	5	12			5	28	4	15	9	3	24		2	2	20
1759–60		40	2	4	5			8	25	4	7	14		21		3		18
Total	26	654	110	68	107	1	10	60	544	60	413	71	34	484	5	48	11	420

Sources: NA, Privy Council Registers, PC2/1; Privy Council papers, PC1; *Commons Journals (Irl.)*; *Lords Journals (Irl.)*.

TABLE SEVEN

THE LEGISLATION OF THE IRISH PARLIAMENT, 1715–60: PRIVATE BILLS

	Ireland — Origins of (heads of) bills			Ireland — Lost heads of bills					England — Irish Privy Council bills and heads of bills at the Privy Council						Ireland — Bills at the Irish parliament			
				House of Commons			House of Lords	Privy Council								Rejected		
Session	Privy Council bills	House of Commons heads	House of Lords heads	Leave only	Rejected	Lords bill	House of Lords	Privy Council	Received	Respited/postponed not reported	Amended	Not amended	Petitions presented	approved	Not presented	House of Commons	House of Lords	Royal assent
1715–16	3	5	1	1					8		8			8		1		7
1717–18	1	1							2		2			2				2
1719–20		7	3					1	9		5	4	1	9				9
1721–2		7		2				4	1	1			1					
1723–4	5	13	2	1	1	1	1	1	16	5	11		3	11				11
1725–6		9	1	1				2	7		7			7				7
1727–8		5	1					1	5	2	3		1	3				3
1729–30		5	1						6	1	5		1	5				5
1731–2		4							4	1	3			3				3
1733–4	2	2			1				3	1		2		2				2
1735–6	2	4	2						6	2	4		2	4				4
1737–8	1	2	2					2	3		3		1	3				3
1739–40	1	4	2		2				5	1	4			4				4
1741–2		3			1				3		3			3				3
1743–4		1							2		2			2				2
1745–6		4	2					1	5	1	4			4				4
1747–8		8	3	1					10	2	6	2	1	8				8
1749–50		2							2		2			2				2
1751–2		2	1						3			3		3				3
1753		2						1	1	1								
1755–6		2							2		2			2				2
1757–8	6	6							6		3	3		6				6
1759–60		5						1	4		2	2		4				4
Total	15	103	21	6	5	1	1	14	113	18	79	16	11	95		1		94

Sources: NA, Privy Council Registers, PC2/1; Privy Council papers, PC1; *Commons Journals (Irl.)*; *Lords Journals (Irl.)*.

TABLE EIGHT

THE LEGISLATION OF THE IRISH PARLIAMENT, 1715–60: PUBLIC AND PRIVATE BILLS

	Ireland								England						Ireland			
	Origins of (heads of) bills			Lost heads of bills					Irish Privy Council bills and heads of bills at the Privy Council						Bills at the Irish parliament			
				House of Commons												Rejected		
Session	Privy Council bills	House of Commons heads	House of Lords heads	Leave only	Rejected	Lords bill	House of Lords	Privy Council	Received	Respited/ postponed not reported	Amended	Not amended	Petitions presented	approved	Not presented	House of Commons	House of Lords	Royal assent
1715–16	11	36	4	5	3			3	40	3	30	7	2	37	2	4		31
1717–18	2	29	3	4	8		1		21	2	16	3	3	19		1	1	18
1719–20	2	38	8	5	5			5	33	3	18	12	6	30		4	2	27
1721–2		36	4	6	5			5	24	4	20		1	20		4		16
1723–4	6	38	8	8	5		1	3	35	9	26		8	26		4		22
1725–6		33	4	3	7		1	5	22	3	19		4	19		2		17
1727–8	6	27	11	2	2			4	36	4	32		3	32	1		1	30
1729–30	2	37	4	5	1		1	3	33	3	28	2	2	30		1	1	28
1731–2	2	37	8	7	3			2	35	5	29	1	1	30		5		25
1733–4	2	35	4		5	1		2	34	3	29	2		31	2	1		28
1735–6	2	49	7	6	9			2	40	6	34		1	34		3		31
1737–8	1	24	9	1	2		2	7	22		20	2	1	22				22
1739–40	1	25	6	1	5			1	25	3	22		1	22		2		20
1741–2		20	5	2	4		1	1	17	1	16			16		2		14
1743–4	1	24	3	3	3		1	2	19	2	17			17		2		15
1745–6	1	34	5	1	7			2	30	2	25	3		28		3		25
1747–8		26	8	2	6		1	1	24	2	19	3	4	22			1	21
1749–50	1	25	6	1	2		1	1	27	3	17	7	1	24		3		21
1751–2		33	6	1	5			3	30		20	10	1	30		2	2	26
1753		22		1	3		2	2	16	12	3	1		4		1		3
1755–6	1	34	10	1	5			6	31		23	8	2	31		4	1	26
1757–8		50	6	5	12			5	34	4	18	12	3	30		2	2	26
1759–60		45	2	4	5			9	29	4	9	16		25		3		22
Total	41	757	131	74	112	1	11	74	657	78	490	89	44	579	5	49	11	514

Sources: NA, Privy Council Registers, PC2/1; Privy Council papers, PC1; *Commons Journals (Irl.)*; *Lords Journals (Irl.)*.

1. Thomas Wentworth, 1st Earl Stafford (1593–1641), lord deputy and lord lieutenant of Ireland, 1633–41 (detail from engraving by George Virtue after Anthony Vandyke), who demonstrated in the 1633 parliament how Poynings' Law could be used effectively to control the Irish parliament (author's collection).

2. Roger Boyle, first earl of Orrery (1621–79), lord justice of Ireland (1661–2) (portrait, artist unknown, reproduced in Kathleen M. Lynch, *Roger Boyle, first earl of Orrery* (Knoxville, 1965)). Orrery was a leading figure in the government of Ireland and Restoration parliament.

3. James Butler, 1st duke of Ormonde (1610–88), lord lieutenant of Ireland, 1662–9 (mezzotint by Robert Dunkarton after David Loggan). It was during Ormonde's viceroyalty that the heads of bill process was first employed by the Irish House of Commons (National Portrait Gallery).

4. Henry Capell, 2nd Baron Capell of Tukesbury (1638–96), lord justice, 1793–5, and lord deputy of Ireland, 1695–6 (miniature, water colour on vellum, by John Hoskins). Capell was central to the 'compromise' that in 1695 paved the way for the House of Commons to initiate a majority of legislation in the form of heads of bills. (National Portrait Gallery).

5. William King, archbishop of Dublin, 1703–29 (portrait, oils, by Ralph Holland, Trinity College, reproduced in Charles King, *A great archbishop of Dublin: William King* (London, 1908) from which the present illustration is drawn). King was an active member of the Irish Privy Council and intermittently a lord justice of Ireland, 1714–23.

6. Philip Yorke (1691–1756), 1st Earl Hardwicke, successively solicitor general (1720–4), attorney general (1724–33) and lord chancellor (1737–56) (mezzotint by John Faber jr, after portrait by Michael Dahl). As a law officer, he reviewed many Irish bills on behalf of the Irish bills committee of the British Privy Council.

7. Edward Thurlow, Baron Thurlow (1731–1806), lord chancellor of Great Britain, 1778–92 (mezzotint by Samuel William Reynolds after Sir Joshua Reynolds). In his capacity as attorney general, Thurlow applied Poynings' Law strictly during the 1770s (National Portrait Gallery).

8. Henry Flood *(left)* (1734–1790), MP and leading patriot (lithograph by J.W. Allens after engraving by C. Clayton). Flood was an assertive advocate of legislative independence, whereby in 1782 the powers available to the executive under Poynings' Law were profoundly curtailed (author's collection).

9. *(above)* Henry Grattan (1746–1820), MP and leading patriot (detail by J. Godby from a drawing by A. Pope). By reason of the leading part he played in securing the amendment of Poynings' Law in 1782, the Irish parliament achieved legislative independence. Grattan was immortalised in the nineteenth century when the phase of Irish parliamentary history, 1782–1800, culminating in the Act of Union, became known as 'Grattan's parliament' (author's collection).

CHAPTER FIVE

The erosion of legislative dependence: Poynings' Law, 1761–82

THE CRITICISMS ARTICULATED in Ireland in the 1750s of Poynings' Law were expressed with still more intensity during the early decades of the reign of George III. During the 1770s in particular, a loose but increasingly powerful coalition of interests inside and outside parliament demanded that the Irish legislature was put on the same constitutional footing as its Westminster equivalent. The reforms required to bring this about were resisted by ministers, who, to employ the fashionable metaphor of the day, not alone perceived the kingdom of Ireland as a dependent daughter, when the Anglo-Irish conceived of them as equal sisters, they prized the fact that Poynings' Law and the Declaratory Act accorded it statutory definition.[1] Much as they aspired to do so, ministers were not in a position to maintain the constitutional *status quo*, and they were obliged in 1782 to accede to the fundamental dilution of the legislative dependence of the Irish parliament. This was more clear-cut in respect of the Declaratory Act than Poynings' Law, but the latter is a more accurate barometer of change in the atmosphere in which the legislative dependence of Ireland operated in the two decades before 1782. What happened was that in response to intensifying opposition in Ireland, changes in practice and emphasis ensured a less interventionist attitude to Irish legislation. This followed a fitful rather than a progressive pattern because the demand for constitutional reform developed along similar lines, and because key officials in the early 1770s resisted the tendency to apply Poynings' Law less strictly. Both the Irish and British Privy Councils continued, as this suggests, applying Poynings' Law in accordance with well-established practice, but they did so in a manner that took cognisance of the political mood in Ireland. Thus, the Irish Council was content to cede the right to initiate legislation still further to parliament, while the British Council responded to Irish criticism of its role by respiting fewer bills and approving fewer amendments. They were encouraged to do so by the increased amount of law being made, which increased the burden of administration associated with scrutinising Irish bills, yet they authorised few changes in bureaucratic practice. This notwithstanding, the application of Poynings' Law in a less interventionist manner anticipated the significant constitutional changes agreed in 1782.

1. See Thomas Bartlett, '"A people rather made for copies than originals": the Anglo-Irish, 1760–1800', *International History Review*, 12 (1990), pp 11–25.

THE IRISH PRIVY COUNCIL AND THE ADMINISTRATION OF POYNINGS' LAW, 1761–82

The accession of George III to the throne in succession to George II, who died on 29 October 1760, prompted a major change in the personnel dealing with Irish legislation. This was a product in the first instance of the general election that followed the dissolution of the Irish parliament that sat for the duration of George II's reign. This was crucial in so far as it accelerated the process whereby a new, more outspoken, generation entered politics, and a more vigorous patriot voice came to be heard.[2] Parallel with this, the personnel at the head of both the British and Irish executives also changed. Since the replacement of lords lieutenant was a regular event, this had little obvious impact. However, the combined effects of the mounting realisation in Britain that secure and stable government in Ireland grounded upon the twin pillars of non-residential English lords lieutenant and powerful Irish undertakers was no longer assured, and the need to improve the structures of imperial government to cope with the requirements of an expanded empire in the aftermath of the Seven Years War (1756–63) encouraged new thinking. The canvassed options included a legislative union, a lord deputy and residential lords lieutenants. The latter was preferred, but though the Grenville ministry determined in February 1765 that future lords lieutenant should reside in Ireland for the duration of their appointment, the instinctive caution of the British government in respect of Ireland ensured the decision was not implemented. None the less, this decision, which was prompted by the death of Henry Boyle and Primate Stone, whose celebrated power struggle in the 1750s had exposed the limitations of existing political arrangements, symbolised (however simplistically it has been portrayed at times) the end of a stable undertaker system. This was hardly apparent during the mid-1760s as a succession of short-term lords lieutenant were as dependent as their predecessors on undertakers, but the outward signs of stability masked a less certain environment characterised by a more assertive parliament, an increasingly vocal politicised public, less assured undertakers and wary ministers.[3] The uncertainty this encouraged was exacerbated by the instability at the heart of British politics that, during the 1760s, produced a succession of short-lived ministries and, during the 1770s, by the gathering crisis that culminated in war in 1775 with the American colonies.[4] The impact of this on British policy towards Ireland was

---

2. See R.B. McDowell, *Ireland in the age of imperialism and revolution 1761–1800* (Oxford, 1979), pp 212–14; James Kelly, *Henry Flood: patriots and politics in eighteenth-century Ireland* (Dublin, 1998), chapter 3.

3. James Kelly, 'The origins of the Act of Union', pp 246–8; idem, *Prelude to Union: Anglo-Irish politics in the 1780s* (Cork, 1992), pp 19–20; M.J. Powell, 'The reform of the undertaker system: Anglo-Irish politics 1750–67', *IHS*, 31 (1998–9), pp 19–36; Eoin Magennis, *The golden age of the undertakers*, p. 110 ff.

4. On this see John Brewer, *Political ideology at the accession of George II* (Cambridge, 1976); Stephen Conway, *The British Isles during the American War of Independence* (Oxford, 2002), passim.

never straightforward, but one little-appreciated result was a degree of flexibility in the application of Poynings' Law.

One of the main consequences of the inability of the authorities in Britain and Ireland to apply Poynings' Law during the 1760s and 1770s in the restrictive manner to which they had long appealed was the virtually total eclipse of the Irish Privy Council by parliament. This was a logical outcome of a process that can be traced back to the 1690s, as the lords justices acknowledged in November 1760 when they observed that 'since the sitting of parliaments have been more regular, the framing of bills originally in the [Privy] Council has become less and less frequent, and has been for many years past almost totally disused'.[5] The Irish Council might have specified that the number of bills for which they bore responsibility had fallen from eight in the 1730s to one in the 1750s, and that it was consistent with this trend that the Council did not seek in the 1760s or 1770s to initiate any bill other than those that it was obliged to propose 'as the causes for calling a parliament'. To this end, the Irish Council initiated a total of nine bills (4 in 1760–61, 2 in 1769 and 3 in 1776 (Table Eleven; p. 312) between 1760 and 1782. This represented 1.01 per cent of the total number of bills and heads of bills prepared between 1761 and 1782, and their preparation did not pass without incident as the sensitivity of Irish opinion on the matter of the 'sole right' further diminished the Privy Council as a source of law by curbing its authority to initiate money bills.[6]

It is ironic that the Irish Council played an important part in the process whereby this came about, though this was less a function of the lack of commitment of a minority of its members and of the Irish executive to uphold its traditional role than their incapacity to resist the assertion by the Irish parliament of its 'sole right' to legislate for Ireland and, in particular, to initiate all financial legislation. The fact that as a result of the Octennial Act of 1768, new parliaments were called every eight years was also important. It ensured that the controversial matter of the Privy Council's claim to make financial law could not be conveniently sidelined, as it was for most of the thirty-three year reign of George II, and it is not a coincidence, therefore, that the Council effectively ceded this right in 1776, in the run-up to the opening of the second Irish parliament arising from the Octennial Act.

Preparations for the first parliament of George III's reign commenced in November 1760 when the lords justices – Lord Shannon, Primate Stone and John Ponsonby – suggested that the Irish Council should meet to determine the bills to be transmitted to the British Council as 'the causes for calling a parliament' in order that 'the proper steps [could be taken] towards preparing them'. Conscious

5. Lords Justices to [Bedford], 23 Nov. 1760 (NAI, Irish Correspondence, 1697–1798, i, MS 2446), printed in *The representation of the L[ord]s J[ustice]s of Ireland, touching the transmission of a Privy Council money bill previous to the calling of a new parliament in two letters addressed to the duke of Bedford* (Dublin, 1770), pp 3–4.
6. See McGrath, 'Central aspects of the eighteenth-century constitutional framework', p. 33.

of the potential difficulties, they asked the lord lieutenant, the duke of Bedford, 'whether on the present occasion it was necessary or expedient' to include a money bill.[7] Since the lords justices had neither sought nor received direction from London on this crucial point, their action was problematical, as became clear when it emerged that opinion at the Council board was sharply divided. The inclination of those such as Lord Chancellor Bowes and Chief Baron Willes, who believed their first duty as councillors was to protect the royal prerogative, was that precedent should be followed and a money bill transmitted because 'the giving up an asserted right in the crown' would persuade those at the helm of Irish politics that 'this country cannot be governed but by those of their own choosing'. A majority felt otherwise. Influenced by the ebullient chancellor of the exchequer, Anthony Malone, who maintained that any infringement of the rights of the Irish parliament to appropriate a supply would 'raise such a flame in the House of Commons as he w[oul]d not answer for the consequence', the weight of opinion adjudged, in the words of the lords justices, that they should transmit 'such bills only as can be liable to no exception'. They justified this mode of proceeding by reference to the fact that the Irish Council no longer sought to initiate bills during the session, as well as by the fact that, by a strict reading of Poynings' Law, it was appropriate that the Irish Council should transmit ordinary bills when it must excite 'fears and jealousies of the most dangerous kind' by presenting a money bill.[8] Pursuant to this, the Irish Council prepared two bills – a measure to allow persons in office more time to qualify pursuant to the 1704 popery law and a measure for the more effectual assigning of judgements – for transmission so they could 'be laid before his majesty' in Council as providing 'the causes and considerations for calling a parliament in Ireland'.[9]

The British Privy Council was distinctly unimpressed. When the two bills were presented at the Council board for formal consideration on 3 December, the report of the Irish bills committee was accompanied by Lord Sydney's rejection of the claim of 'sole right' by the Irish Commons in 1692 and the judges' opinion of the same year affirming the right of the Irish council to raise money bills and to transmit them to London. The thrust of the Irish bills committee report – that the bills received from Ireland were 'insufficient to answer' the purpose for which they were transmitted because they did not include a money bill – was accepted by the large attendance of thirty-two councillors that gathered to consider the matter. Everybody present did not concur with the duke of Devonshire that it was critical that the Council insisted upon the transmission of a money bill because

7. As note 5.
8. Burns, *Irish parliamentary politics*, ii, 301–2; Bowes to Secker, 23 Dec. 1760 (Lambeth Palace Library, Secker Papers, vol. 2) (I wish to thank Dr Marie-Louise Legg for this reference); Willes to [ ], 15 Dec. 1760 (WRO, Willes Papers, 3); Lords justice to Bedford, 23 Nov. 1760 (NAI, Irish Correspondence, 1697–1798, i, MS 2446).
9. Lords justice to Bedford, 26 Nov. (PRONI, Bedford Papers T2915/10/5); Privy Council to Bedford, 26 Nov. in *Cal. HO papers*, 1760–5, p. 6; Lords Justices to Holdernesse, 26 Nov. 1760 (NA, SP63/418); Burns, *Irish parliamentary politics*, ii, 302–3.

the Irish action 'was one step towards throwing off their dependency on England'. But the readiness of those who were present to sign the letter to the Irish Council in which it was made explicit that the bills transmitted 'do not contain causes and considerations sufficient for the calling a new parliament, nor are agreeable to former precedents' was indicative of their wish to uphold the practice of dependence inherent in the way Poynings' Law was traditionally interpreted and applied.[10]

The stand taken by the British Council presented the Irish Council with a serious problem. Some councillors latched initially onto the phrase 'agreeable to former precedents', and concluded hopefully that it would suffice if they transmitted a major bill that was not a money bill. A minority, headed by the marquess of Kildare,[11] the Lord Chancellor and chief judges, who were more receptive to instruction on such matters, reached the opposite conclusion and adjudged that they had no alternative but to transmit a supply bill. However, they could not convince a majority of their colleagues to uphold what Chief Justice Willes termed 'his majesty's undoubted prerogative in this kingdom of proposing a Mon[e]y Bill to his parliament' and, amidst rumours that the lords justice were contemplating resignation and the Dublin crowd planning disorder, it was decided to postpone further consideration until mid-January.[12]

Since parliament was not scheduled to meet until October 1761, this was a prudent decision. The difficulty was that all the signs from England pointed to the conclusion that ministers were disinclined to accommodate Irish concerns on the point. Indeed, it was even suggested there that this was a manufactured crisis 'contrived and ... raised entirely by the Lords Justices', and that the 'delay' in making a decision on the point was a tactic 'to mollify and manage here, and perhaps yield, to get the power of doing more mischief'.[13] Another, stronger strand of opinion, represented by the earl of Bessborough – John Ponsonby's elder brother and former chief secretary of Ireland, who had made his career in England – held that the lords justices had behaved 'very foolishly' in not transmitting a money bill because, he observed dramatically, if the British Council acceded 'to this offered alteration', it must result inevitably in 'an attempt to repeal Sir Edward Poyning's laws [*sic*]' and the 'ruin' of Ireland'.[14] Richard Rigby,

10. NA, PC2/108 ff 79–80, 81–2, 82–5, 93; British to Irish Council, 3 Dec. 1760 (NAI, Irish Correspondence, 1697–1798, i, MS 2446); P. Brown and K.W. Schweizer (eds), 'The Devonshire diary', *Camden*, 4th series, 27 (1982), pp 61–2.
11. Kildare's role in this affair can be followed most closely from his letters to Henry Fox of 18, 20, 22 December 1760 (BL, Holland House Papers, Add. MS 51426 ff 159–65). These letters are printed from copies in the Bedford papers in Malcomson (ed.), *Irish official papers*, ii, 250–2.
12. Willes to [ ], 15 Dec. 1760 (WRO, Willes papers 3); Lords Justices to [Bedford], 27 Dec. 1760 (NAI, Irish Correspondence, 1697–1798, i, MS 2446); Bowes to Dodington, 25 Dec. 1760 in H.M.C., *Reports on various collections*, vi, 75–6; Ponsonby to Bessborough, 10 Dec. 1760 (PRONI, Chatsworth papers, T3158/1630); Ryder to Ryder, 16 Dec. 1760 in Malcomson (ed.), *Irish official papers*, ii, 63; Burns, *Irish parliamentary politics*, ii, 303–5.
13. Fox to Bedford, 30 Dec. 1760 in Lord John Russell, *The correspondence of John, fourth duke of Bedford* (3 vols, London, 1842–6), ii, 428.
14. Bessborough to Devonshire, 18 Dec. (PRONI, Chatsworth Papers, T3158/1631); Rigby to Bedford, 20 Dec. 1760 (PRONI, Bedford Papers, T2915/10/69).

the current chief secretary, was still more critical. He observed of the long dispatch communicated by the lords justices to the duke of Bedford on 27 December, in which they maintained that their purpose was to pre-empt 'trouble and animosities' that it was 'extraordinary', 'absurd' and 'disingenuous'. Bedford did not disagree.[15] Only William Pitt manifested any sympathy for the position of the lords justices, and while this ensured that the cabinet advised Bedford on 7 January 'to write an exhortatory letter' to the lords justices requesting them 'to reconsider' their stance, no compromise was offered. Indeed, in despatches on 8 and 17 January, Bedford affirmed that it remained the 'unanimous opinion' of ministers that the Irish Council 'should not have deviated from the ancient usage of certifying a money bill as one of the causes and considerations for calling a new parliament', and that they should now prepare a money bill to serve as a 'proper cause'.[16] Though this seemed to leave the Irish Council with little room to manoeuvre, their refusal, by 15 votes to 9, to acquiesce in Lord Kildare's suggestion that they should transmit 'the usual ... full money bill' when they gathered on 23 January indicated that they had no intention simply of backing down. Yet they were eager, like their British counterparts, for a solution, and a majority was drawn to Lord Carrick's compromise proposition that they should forward a supply bill to continue additional duties for three months such as was agreed in the 1758–9 session. Strong reservations were expressed by supporters of the royal prerogative that this suggestion 'encroached on the claimed rights of the Crown' and did not meet the criteria 'anciently' employed, but the fact that it was a money bill proved compelling, and it was agreed at a meeting of the Privy Council on 24 January to forward it along with 'a bill continuing the calling of juries by ballot'. This was not to the liking of Lord Chancellor Bowes, Chief Justice Yorke, Chief Baron Willes, Lord Kildare and a number of others who, having failed to secure support for the 'usual' bill, declined to be associated with 'sending these two bills'. At the other extreme, Lord Antrim and Hercules Langford Rowley demurred on the grounds that 'they would never certify any kind of money bill'.[17]

Given the difficulties experienced in securing agreement for what Archbishop John Ryder of Tuam tellingly labelled 'the compromise three month supply bill', the British Council board agreed reluctantly to accept it. Many, like the president of the council, Lord Granville, were less than content to do so, but they consoled themselves by concluding that because the Irish Council had 'submitted', the supply bill was sufficient to satisfy the requirements of Poynings' Law. It was

15. Rigby to Bedford, 1 Jan. 1761 in *Bedford Corres.*, iii, 1–2; Lords Justices to Bedford, 27 Dec. 1760 (NAI, Irish Correspondence, 1697–1798, i, MS 2446); Bedford to Lords Justices, 3 Jan. 1761 in Malcomson (ed.), *Irish official papers*, ii, 255.
16. Rigby to Wilmot, 7 Jan. 1761 (PRONI, Wilmot Papers, T3019/3963); Bedford to Lords Justices, 8, 17 Jan. 1761 (NAI, Irish correspondence, 1697–1798, i, MS 2446).
17. Lords Justices to Bedford, 24 Jan., Ryder to Wilmot, 31 Jan. 1761 (PRONI, Wilmot Papers T3019/3972, 3979); Bowes to Dodington, 2 Feb. 1761 in HMC, *Reports on various collections*, vi, 77–9; Yorke to Rigby, 24 Jan., Bowes to Bedford, 25 Jan. 1761 in Malcomson (ed.), *Irish official papers*, ii, 257–60; Burns, *Irish parliamentary politics*, ii, 309–10.

approved with two minor amendments in late February and returned to Ireland.[18] Of the remaining Privy Council bills, that for regulating juries was respited on the advice of the Crown's law officers, while those 'for the more effectual assigning of judgements' and to allow officeholders more time to qualify pursuant to the act to prevent the further growth of popery were deemed 'proper to be passed'.[19] As a result, the attorney general was authorised to prepare a commission for issuing an order for calling a new parliament in Ireland.[20]

With three of the four bills transmitted from Ireland formally approved, preparations could commence for the meeting of parliament. It helped that the predominant reaction in Ireland was one of relief that the money bill was 'accepted', as this helped to diffuse the ill feeling generated in diverse quarters.[21] However, the implications of the episode were far from clear. According to Robert Burns, 'the lords justices and a majority of the Irish Privy Council had successfully defied the lord lieutenant, the English [*sic*] cabinet, and the English [*sic*] privy council' and 'an unprecedented degree of political and constitutional independence from an English [*sic*] government had been asserted by the Dublin administration'.[22] Ivar McGrath's assessment is more measured; noting that the transmission of a supply bill was 'crucial for the upholding of Poynings' Law and the Crown's prerogative', he observed that the fact that the Irish Council's request to transmit only 'such bills only as can be liable to no exception' was declined allowed British councillors to claim that they had prevailed. This notwithstanding, there is no denying that the acceptance of a lesser money bill was something of a climbdown.[23] For, as McGrath has pointed out:

> the 1761 bill did not re-impose the much-expanded schedule of duties voted biennially in the main Supply Act for the purposes of providing income towards the government's revenue at large. Instead, the bill re-imposed the more specialised and, in terms of amount and scope, restricted appropriated duties voted in the secondary Supply Act for accommodation of the national debt. As such, the 1761 compromise represented a further diminution in the importance of Poynings' Law and the crown's prerogative.[24]

18. Rigby to Bedford, 2 Feb. 1761 in Malcomson (ed.), *Irish official papers*, ii, 260; NA, PC2/108 ff 191–2, 208–09, 213–15; Waite to Wilmot, 6, 10 Feb. 1761 (PRONI, Wilmot Papers, T3019/3983, 3986).
19. NA, PC2/108 ff 191–2, 209–10.
20. NA, PC2/108 f. 215; Lords Justices to Bedford, 7 Apr. 1761 (NAI, Irish Correspondence, 1697–1798, i, MS 2446).
21. Burns, *Irish parliamentary politics*, ii, 310–12; Waite to Wilmot, 6, 10, 13, 22 Feb. 1761 (PRONI, Wilmot Papers, T3019/3983, 3986, 3988, 3998); Henley to Willes, 17 Feb. 1761 (WRO, Willes Papers, 8).
22. Burns, *Irish parliamentary politics*, ii, 311.
23. McGrath, 'Central aspects of the eighteenth-century constitutional framework', p. 21; Lords Justices to [Bedford], 23 Nov. 1760 (NAI, MS 2446); Kelly, 'Monitoring the constitution', p. 98; Rigby to Bedford, [ante 2 Feb. 1761] in Malcomson (ed.), *Irish official papers*, ii, 260.
24. McGrath, 'Central aspects of the eighteenth-century constitutional framework', p. 22.

The implications of this for the process of making law for Ireland would only became clear in time, but there were signs in the run up to the opening of the session in October 1761 that it might prove of immediate advantage to the Irish parliament.

The newly-installed lord lieutenant, the earl of Halifax, certainly seemed disposed to accept that it would be so, for when he was made aware of 'the constant and strenuous opposition which has been made by the House of Commons here to the passing any bill concerning money which had not taken its rise, and received whatever was essential of its form among themselves', he sought permission to allow the Privy Council money bill 'to perish quietly' lest it should become an object of 'public notoriety'.[25] Ministers were understandably unhappy. Reminded 'how much the King has already departed from what has been constantly complied with, and what His Majesty might reasonably have expected', it was made clear that since any further concession on this issue must 'diminish' the rights of 'the Crown and Privy Council of Great Britain', it was 'not a proper conjuncture to add further concessions to those His Majesty has already been graciously pleased to make or to suffer this bill to be dropped'.[26] This was not what Halifax wanted to hear, but the instruction proved less troublesome than he apprehended because the administration had the support of 'the late Lords Justices' in the House of Commons. The outspoken MP for Dublin city, Charles Lucas, 'oppos'd [the money bill] vehemently and argued that upon the title of it, it ought to be rejected'; but, though his arguments appealed to many on the opposition benches, they made little impression in the division lobbies.[27] Equally encouragingly, MPs agreed to provide the money necessary to pay for the administration of the kingdom for the normal duration of two years by approving appropriate heads of supply bills, while the British Council assisted by returning both promptly with 'two or three literal amendments solely for preserving the right of amending such bills'.[28]

To outward appearances, the trouble-free ratification by parliament of the Privy Council and Commons' money bills suggested that the acceptance of a compromise money bill as 'proper cause' for calling an Irish parliament was politically astute in that it neutralised hotheads like Lucas, who were intent on challenging the entitlement of the Privy Council to initiate legislation. The ease with which the main items of financial legislation made it through parliament in 1763–4, 1765–6 and 1767–8 seemed to confirm this impression,[29] while the advice

25. Halifax to Pitt, 11 Oct. 1761 (NA, SP63/419).
26. Egremont to Halifax, 20 Oct. 1761 (NA, SP63/419).
27. Halifax to Egremont, 30 Oct., 20 Nov. 1761 (NA, SP63/418, 419); Cavendish to Wilmot, 14, 17 Nov., Waite to Wilmot, 14, 19 Nov. 1761 (PRONI, Wilmot Papers, T3019/4220, 4223, 4222, 4226); 1 Geo II, chap 2; *Commons Jn. (Irl.)*, vii, 64, 67, 68, 69, 70, 73.
28. Granville to Halifax, 5 Dec. 1761 (NA, PC1/31/78A); PC2/108 ff 191–2, 208–9, 213–15; I Geo III, chap 2; I Geo III, chap 5; PC2/109 ff 23, 41, 60–1; law officers' report, 11 Feb. 1762 (PC1/7/11).
29. Winchelsea to Hertford, 10 Dec. 1765 (NA, PC1/31/A78); 3 Geo III, chaps 1 and 2; PC2/110

given the incoming attorney general, Fletcher Norton, by the clerk of the British Council, William Sharpe, in 1763 'that no material alterations are ever made in the ... money bills, ...[other] than some small literal amendments in order to preserve the right to the crown to amend such bills' suggested that Poynings' law could continue to be applied unchanged so long as the British Council did so sensitively.[30] Officials on both sides of the Irish Sea were eager to sustain this impression, and while those in Ireland could point to the fact that the Privy Council's legislative inactivity during the 1760s and 1770s demonstrated the truth of the Lords Justices' assessment in 1760 that the right to frame bills 'has been for many years past almost totally disused', the difference now was that this was effectively a matter of policy. It was not stated openly, of course, and given the readiness of both the British and Irish executives and a majority of MPs to live with this inherently ambiguous situation and the practice of only calling a general election on the death of the monarch, it might have long remained thus had the ratification of the Octennial Act in 1768 not rendered this impossible.[31]

In contrast to 1760–1 when the drama associated with the certification of a Privy Council money bill took place behind the scenes, controversy was very public in 1768–9. Conscious of the potential pitfalls, the secretary of state for the southern department, the earl of Shelburne, alerted the lord lieutenant, Lord Townshend, well in advance that the inclusion of a money bill among the bills communicated from Ireland as reason for calling a parliament was 'a point, which must not be given up'.[32] Townshend expressed no unease, and he was enabled with the warm support of the Privy Council to ensure that a money bill granting for three months the duties appropriated for payment of the national debt and a measure for allowing officeholders further time to qualify pursuant to the popery laws were 'unanimously' endorsed for transmission to London by the beginning of June 1768. Their experience at the British Council proved uneventful; the bills were received, reported and approved as suitable to become law in Ireland by 13 June with two minor amendments, and writs were issued soon after for calling a parliament, which finally assembled in October 1769.[33] However, in contrast to 1761 when the opponents of Poynings' Law in the House of Commons offered

ff 162, 163–4, 165–7; *Commons Jn. (Irl.)*, vii, 245, 247, 258, 259, 261, 262, 263; 5 Geo III, chaps 1 and 2; PC2/111 ff 433, 436–7, 437–9; Conway to Hertford, 9 Dec. 1765 (NA, SP67/13 f. 37); *Commons Jn. (Irl.)*, viii, 58, 59, 60, 67, 68, 69, 72, 73; 7 Geo III, chaps 1 and 2; PC2/112 ff 521–2, 523, 525–7; Shelburne to Townshend, 12 Dec. 1767 (SP67/13 f. 52); law officers' report on duties bill, 3 Dec 1767 (PC1/8/90 f. 1); *Commons Jn. (Irl.)*, viii, 207, 208, 213, 214, 215, 216.

30. Sharpe to Norton, 7 Dec. 1763 (NA, PC2/110 f. 162).

31. For the ratification of the Octennial act see Kelly, 'Monitoring the constitution', p. 102; Thomas Bartlett, 'The Townshend administration' in Bartlett and Hayton, *Penal era and golden age*, pp 88–112.

32. Shelburne to Wilmot, 9 Mar. 1768 (PRONI, Wilmot Papers, T3019/5710).

33. Townshend to Shelburne, 31 May, 4 June, Shelburne to Townshend, 14, 21, 24 June in *Cal. HO papers, 1766–9*, pp 344, 347, 350–1; Waite to Wilmot, 2 June (PRONI, Wilmot Papers, T3019/5710); NA, PC2/113 ff 198, 199, 202; Minutes of Clerks of Council, 13 June 1768 (PC4/3).

only token resistance, political disquiet with the style as well as the direction of
Lord Townshend's government was such that, as well as a more determined
patriot phalanx, major undertaker interests chose, as in 1753, to register their
dissatisfaction by joining with the patriots to resist the money bill as incompatible
with the Commons' 'sole right' to initiate all financial legislation. Led by Edmond
Sexten Pery and Lucius O'Brien, they inflicted an embarrassing defeat on the
administration on 21 November when, having first rejected a motion that the
money bill should be sent for a second reading on the following day, they voted by
94 votes to 71 that the bill should be 'rejected because it did not take its rise in this
house'.[34]

Since this was the first time since 1692 that a money raising bill originating
with the Privy Council had been rejected, there was no evading the conclusion
that MPs were challenging the claim, long acknowledged under Poynings' Law, of
the Irish Privy Council to initiate supply legislation. Sydney had responded in
1692 by promptly proroguing the session in the vain belief that it would cause the
Commons to back down. Townshend was less impulsive. He was disinclined to
embark on any action that could precipitate a constitutional crisis in the absence
of instructions from London, and because he realised that any attempt to
prorogue parliament before the usual supply bills were agreed would cripple the
exchequer and must 'be the ruin of this country'.[35] Determined to avoid this
eventuality at all costs, Townshend deferred any public expression of disapproval
of the Commons' actions while MPs prepared the heads of two supply bills.
These proceeded uneventfully through the Irish and British Councils and
completed their parliamentary passage on 26 December when they received the
royal assent.[36] Having thereby secured the financial basis of English government
in Ireland, and bought himself time, Townshend prorogued the sitting.[37]

Townshend's speech justifying his decision and his accompanying protest drew
heavily on that uttered by Lord Sydney. In reality, as Ivar McGrath has argued, if
one assesses events in terms of where the authority to raise money rested, the lord
lieutenant's decision to order the prorogation *after* the supply had been voted
'represented a significant stand-down', since it acknowledged that this was a

---

34. Thomas Bartlett, 'The Irish House of Commons' rejection of the "Privy Council" money bill:
a reassessment', *Studia Hibernica*, 19 (1971), pp 70–6; Kelly, *Henry Flood*, p. 135; McGrath,
'Central aspects of the eighteenth-century constitutional framework', pp 24–5; *Commons Jn.
(Irl.)*, viii, 323.

35. McGrath, 'Central aspects of the eighteenth-century constitutional framework', pp 25–6;
Clements to Macartney, 8 Dec. 1769 (PRONI, Wilmot Papers, T3019/5998).

36. Waite to Wilmot, 12, 23 Dec. (PRONI, Wilmot Papers, T3019/5999, 6002); Garnett to
Hardwicke, 29 Nov., 18, 22, 23–25 Dec. 1769 (BL, Hardwicke Papers, Add. MS 35609 ff 106,
112, 120, 118); 9 Geo III, chap 1; NA, PC2/114 ff 164, 165, 166–7; Irish bills committee report.
12 Dec., Irish Privy Council letter, 6 Dec. 1769 (PC1/9/33 ff 1, 3–4); *Commons Jn. (Irl.)*, viii,
338, 339, 340, 345, 346, 353, 354.

37. Garnet to Hardwicke, 20 Dec. 1769 (BL, Hardwicke Papers, Add. MS 35609 f. 114); McGrath,
'Central aspects of the eighteenth-century constitutional framework', p. 26.

Commons' function, which Sydney had refused to do.[38] The fact that (unlike 1761) the Privy Council money bill did not make it to the statute book in 1769 underlines this point. And yet, the Irish Privy Council's legal entitlement to initiate bills remained unimpaired; the admission of the Council bill allowing officeholders further time to qualify to the statute book indicated that MPs were unwilling *a priori* to deny the Council the right to initiate law.[39]

The inescapable implication of events in 1769 was that the Irish Council would find it difficult on any future occasion to assert its right to frame money bills, and its failure to present even a token number of bills during the five sessions that constituted the 1769–76 parliament suggested that the Council and the Irish executive both believed that this was now a redundant power. The hostility of Irish public opinion certainly encouraged this, and it was thus hardly surprising that when it fell to Earl Harcourt in 1776 to oversee the preparations for a new parliament that he concluded it was not in the interest of the Irish administration and, probably not in the interest of the Irish Privy Council, that 'the causes and considerations' communicated from Ireland 'for calling a parliament' included a money bill. Harcourt cited the lords justices' 'long letter' of 23 November 1760 in support of his contention, but his case was primarily grounded upon his recognition that the 'considerable alteration in the disposition of the Commons', which he attributed, simplistically, to the Octennial Act, had made MPs 'more dependent upon their constituents and more afraid of offending the people, the body of whom are, to the last degree, jealous of this power'. He was acutely conscious also that the events of 1769 made the matter 'so peculiarly offensive' that any attempt to present a Council money bill was bound to stoke still tender political emotions, and that it was best for this reason not to excite 'great jealousies and animosities' by communicating a money bill from the Irish Council.[40]

Though Harcourt was instinctively inclined to look for a way around rather than to engage difficult issues head-on, his conclusion that the presentation of a Privy Council money bill to the Irish parliament would meet with strong resistance was well informed. It was, he explained to the secretary of state, Lord Weymouth, an issue that 'rests very much on the minds of the people', and it was 'considered by the most sober part of them, as injurious to the dignity and rights of the House of Commons'. Even Charles Agar, the bishop of Cloyne, who was not normally disposed to favour constitutional innovation, advised that it would be politically counter-productive to press the matter at this time:

> There is not I believe one sensible man in this kingdom who does not know
> that the Privy Council has the very same rights to originate a money bill that

---

38. McGrath, 'Central aspects of the eighteenth-century constitutional framework', pp 26–7.
39. On this see 9 Geo III, chap 2; NA, PC2/113 ff 198, 199, 201–2; *Commons Jn. (Irl.)*, viii, 288, 328; *Lords Jn. (Irl.)*, iv, 506).
40. Harcourt to Weymouth, 20 (2), 26 Mar. 1776 (NA, SP, 63/452 ff 296, 298–300, 332).

it has to originate any other bill. Nor is there a sensible man in the kingdom, I believe, who ever wishes to see a Privy Council money bill passed into a law. Such bills have invariably been rejected, and with very bad humour. They have always produced discontent, ferment and ill will. ... [W]here is the good policy in persevering in a custom productive only of bad consequences? Are the rights of the Crown best ascertained by presenting such bills and having them constantly rejected, or by claiming the right and prudently withholding the exercise of it? If the object were to raise money, that money could be obtained in this way (which it cannot), and that it could not be obtained by a more eligible mode, I should at once applaud and approve a Privy Council money bill. But what is the case at present? Why this. The parliament has granted most cheerfully full and ample supplies for two years.

Agar further justified the impolicy of presenting a Privy Council money bill to the Irish parliament on the grounds that the latter was no longer an infant institution, and that it would be absurd for ministers to insist on the communication from the Irish Council of a money bill at this moment 'when no money was wanted' because current duties and taxes did not expire until December 1777.[41] The problem was that few in London were willing to accept the validity of these arguments. Agar's uncle, Welbore Ellis, observed simply that it was incumbent upon the Irish Council to transmit a money bill 'because it is the constitution'; he also opined that there was no justification for parliament being 'out of humour' on the matter because it was empowered 'by that constitution [in] the exercise of its full, clear, independent option of acceptance or negative', which 'no ministry ... no lord lieutenant ... have ever disputed'.[42]

Few interpreted constitutional issues with the relentless logic Welbore Ellis was able to bring to bear,[43] but ministers concurred that they could not in law be expected to accede to Harcourt's request. Advised by Lord Weymouth, the secretary of state, that the King wished to adhere to 'constant usage', the lord lieutenant was informed that a 'new parliament cannot [be] summoned unless a money bill be transmitted as a cause for its calling'.[44] With no alternative but to comply, the Irish Council did as instructed and, having established a committee to perform the task, certified three bills, one of which was a money bill, and forwarded them for consideration at the British Council board. Though the speed with which the bills were processed was exceptional, the fact that the Irish Council complied without demur seemed to suggest that a majority of its members were content to uphold the royal prerogative in respect of money bills

41. Agar to [Ellis], 5 Apr. 1776 (PRONI, Normanton Papers, T3719/C/10/1); McGrath, 'Central aspects of the eighteenth-century constitutional framework', p. 28.
42. Ellis to Agar, 13 Apr. 1776 (PRONI, Normanton Papers, T3719/C/10/2).
43. Malcomson, *Charles Agar*, passim.
44. Weymouth to Harcourt, 26 Mar. 1776 (NA, SP63/452 ff 324–9).

regardless of the political consequences.[45] Harcourt was less easy. His priority was to ensure that the short session he planned to inaugurate the new parliament proceeded smoothly to allow for his early departure from his Irish posting, so when he was made aware that the procedures of the House of Commons demanded that a money bill was considered by the committee of accounts which, based on the precedent of 1769, took more than a month, or that MPs voluntarily agreed to 'depart from standing orders to allow reading of the money bill on the understanding government will not press it further', he did not delay bringing the matter to the notice of his superiors.[46] This posed ministers with a dilemma. So far everything had gone according to plan from their perspective, as the three bills transmitted from the Irish Council each negotiated the British Council without difficulty.[47] Faced now with the choice either of insisting that the sitting Irish parliament should last as long as required to consider these bills in order to comply fully with Poynings' Law or accepting that they had taken the matter as far as was currently feasible, Weymouth reluctantly acceded to the latter view. Though it remained his conviction that it was 'desirable that the money bill should be read', it was, he conceded, 'not very important what may become of it, provided it appears in the journals of the House [of Commons] that it has had an existence as the cause and consideration of calling the parliament'.[48] This is what happened, though it is not clear if Weymouth anticipated that the bill would be formally rejected. Taken together with the fact that only one of the three bills to take their rise at the Irish Council – the innocuous qualification measure – made it to law, it was now apparent that that the power of the Irish Council to initiate legislation had been reduced to no more than a symbolic shadow of its former reality.[49] The main beneficiary of this was the Irish Commons which finally – eighty-four years after it had famously made this assertion – effectively possessed the 'sole right' to initiate financial legislation. What they did not enjoy, and what parliament could never possess so long as Poynings' Law remained unamended, was the sole right to initiate law. They had to share this with the Irish Privy Council though the fact that only four Privy Council bills (2 in 1761, 1 in 1769, and 1 in 1776) made it to the statute book between 1761 and 1782 constitutes the most telling illustration of just how negligible a power it had become.

* * *

45. Harcourt to Weymouth, 3, 6, 21 Apr. 1776 (NA, SP63/453 ff 67, 93–5, 159).
46. Harcourt to Weymouth, 17 Apr. 1776 (NA, SP63/453 ff 149–53).
47. Minutes of the Clerks of Council, 1764–95 (NA, PC4/2, 18 Apr. 1776); PC2/119 ff 511, 512, 518–9, 519–21; Weymouth to Harcourt, 21 Apr. 1776 (SP67/15 f. 119).
48. Weymouth to Harcourt, 1 May 1776 (NA, SP63/453 ff 222–3).
49. 16 Geo III, chap 1; *Commons Jn. (Irl.)*, ix, 296, 299. The third bill, for continuing an act to prevent frauds committed by bankrupts, was only accorded a first reading (*Commons Jn. (Irl.)*, ix, 296).

Despite this further attenuation of its legislative function, the Irish Privy Council continued to play a key role in the process of making law for Ireland. It is stretching the point to maintain, with the Lords Justices of Ireland, that 'the constitution was still in every material point preserved by the power exercised by the Council in amending inaccuracies, supplying defects, or supplying the whole of what seemed to be improper', but this illusion was shared by others. The English lord chancellor, Lord Camden, observed in 1765 that 'the Council ... is ... of equal importance of either branch of the legislature', while the influential under secretary, William Knox, maintained in 1767 that 'the Privy Council comprise the second branch of the legislature' in Ireland because of the weakness of the Lords.[50] What is undeniable is that the Irish Council continued to play an important part in the process of making law because its role in certifying heads of bills received from the legislature remained unchanged.

The Council constituted in June 1761 comprised sixty-four members and it engaged with the task of scrutinising and certifying Irish legislation in exactly the same way as its predecessor.[51] In keeping with established practice, only a minority of councillors participated, and attendance only achieved respectable levels when contentious measures were at issue: 24 were in attendance at the crucial discussions in January 1761 on transmitting a money bill; an exceptional 33 were present to vote 17–16 in favour of forwarding the heads of a bill for limiting the duration of parliament in February 1762; 27 were reported present in July 1780 to approve a controversial tenants' bill, and 19 appended their signature to the Privy Council letter forwarding a sugar bill in 1782.[52] The number in attendance when more routine legislation was at issue were more modest; 8 to 16 was average, but significantly they included most of the holders of high office though this could mean, as the lord chancellor, Lord Lifford, observed in 1768, devoting five to six hours a day to the task of examining heads of bills.[53]

Because of the greater assertiveness of MPs, councillors were disposed to proceed cautiously.[54] The number of heads of bills referred for their consideration in the 1760s differed little from the number presented during the later years

50. Camden to Grafton, 29 Sept. 1765 in William Anson (ed.), *Autobiography and correspondence of Augustus Henry, third duke of Grafton* (London, 1898), pp 162–3; Lords Justices to [Bedford], 23 Nov. 1760 (NAI, Irish Correspondence, 1697–1798, i, MS 2446); William Knox, *Extra official state papers* (London, 1789), appendix, pp 4–5.
51. Lords Justices to Halifax, 28 Apr. (NAI, Irish Correspondence, 1697–1798, i, MS 2446); Halifax to Pitt, 17 June 1761 (NA, SP63/419).
52. As note 17; Irish Privy Council letters, 17 Mar. 1762 (PC1/7/15), 24 Dec. 1765 (PC1/8/5); 26 Mar. 1766 (PC1/15/30); 1 June 1780 (PC1/12/17); 20 Nov. 1781 (PC1/12/96 ff 3–5); Waite to Wilmot, 8 Feb. 1762 (PRONI, Wilmot Papers, T3019/4285); Halifax to Egremont, 12, 19 Feb. 1762 (NA, SP63/421); *Hibernian Journal*, 3 July 1780.
53. Lifford to Grafton, 31 Mar. 1768 (Ipswich and East Suffolk Record Office, Grafton Papers: PRONI T2959/2/8).
54. For evidence of the Commons assertiveness see the consideration of the committee of comparison below, pp 303–4, and the resolutions of 24, 25 June 1778 (*Commons Jn. (Irl.)*, ix, 502, 504).

of George II, but the 1770s witnessed a dramatic acceleration, as the average number of legislative initiatives per session increased from 43 to 73 (Table Nine; p. 310). Compared with the Commons, which was responsible for over 90 per cent of heads of bills, and which was more active during the 1770s than at any moment in its history to date, the Lords was virtually somnolent. Indeed, the Lords possessed such a reputation for legislative inactivity that it was observed in 1771 that 'the church is more likely to furnish business in the House of Lords this session'.[55] It so happened that this trend was not to continue; the Lords shook off its legislative lethargy in the 1770s; four-fifths of bills and heads of bills that took their rise in the Lords between 1761 and 1782 post-date 1771 (Table Eleven; p. 312).

Whether they rose with the Commons or the Lords, the heads of public bills received at the Irish Council board were referred to a subcommittee of council, and private bills to one or (more usually) to two members of the judiciary for a report.[56] Reports were presented, generally in a written form, to the lords of the committee of the Irish Council, which recommended whether or not a bill should be forwarded and, if so, whether it should do so with or without amendments. The committee was also empowered to receive petitions, such as that presented in 1762 when the mayor of Limerick appealed against a bill 'for regulating the Corporation of Limerick', and to hear the statements of counsel, such as were offered on behalf of the Catholic Committee against a quarterage bill in 1772 and in support of an oath of allegiance in 1774.[57] The hearing of petitions and the admission of counsel could add considerably to the time required to process the heads of a bill, which was significant since delays at this point could, as in 1780, necessitate 'an additional adjournment of parliament'.[58] In practice most heads of bills were dealt with clinically, but heads of controversial measures for limiting the duration of parliament advanced in the 1760s, and for Catholic and Presbyterian relief in 1778 and 1780 were the subject of animated debate.[59] The destruction of the papers of the Irish Council precludes an assessment of the number of bills that were amended, but it is not unreasonable to assume, based on the Council's decision to respite a total of 13 per cent (85) of the 656 heads communicated from parliament between 1761 and 1782 that it was not uncommon (Table Eleven).

55. Bishop Garnett to Hardwicke, 12 Nov. 1771 (BL, Hardwicke Papers, Add. MS 35610 f. 75). A certain wistful longing was also expressed for more politically active primates.

56. The vesting of the task in the judiciary may reflect the fact that the attorney general, though 'a servant of the Privy Council', was not a member (Halifax to Northumberland, 22 Oct. 1763 (NA, SP67/13 f. 17)).

57. NAI, Index to departmental letters and official papers, 1760–89, ff 51, 52, 53, 565, 57–8, 63–4, 65, 69–70, 75, 79, 82; Heron to Porten, 29 June 1780 (NA, SP63/470 f. 5); Maureen McGeehin, 'The activities and personnel of the General Committee of the Catholics of Ireland, 1767–84' (MA, UCD, 1952), p. 10; Fagan, *Catholics in a Protestant country*, p. 161; R.D. Edwards (ed.), 'The minute book of the Catholic Committee', *Archivium Hibernicum*, 9 (1942), p. 26.

58. Heron to Porten, 29 June 1780 (NA, SP63/470 f. 5).

59. James Kelly, '1780 revisited: the politics of the repeal of the test act' in Kevin Herlihy (ed.), *The politics of Irish dissent* (Dublin, 1997), pp 74–92; Buckinghamshire to Hillsborough, 21 Dec. 1779 (NA, SP, 63/407 ff 295–6); below, pp 274–5.

Interestingly, though the number of heads of bills appertaining to public issues lost at the Irish Council (72) greatly exceeded those appertaining to private affairs (13), the proportion of private bills that was not certified (14 per cent) was larger than the proportion of public bills (13 per cent) (Tables Nine and Ten). More significantly, both the number and proportion of heads of bills respited during the 1776–82 parliament (18 or 6 per cent of the total) was lower than during the parliaments of 1761–68 (30 or 12 per cent) and 1769–76 (37 or 12 per cent). It is tempting to attribute this to the appreciating calls for the reform of Poynings' Law, but the oscillating pattern of respiting within parliaments cautions against this. This is not to say that no conclusions are possible. It is noteworthy that those sessions during which the fewest bills were respited (2 or less) were the most difficult - 1761–2, 1769, 1771, 1781–2 (Table Eleven). One can also attribute the refusal to certify as many as fifteen bills during the 1771–2 session in large part to the intervention of Lord Townshend.[60] He was particularly concerned to ensure that no measure for the payment of unfunded premiums and bounties advanced, and the Council usually accepted the guidance of the executive on such matters.

Moreover, during most of the period, but particularly during the 1761–68 parliament, the Irish Council showed no obvious disinclination to respite popular heads of bills. In 1763–4, for example, the thirteen measures that were not forwarded included heads of bills for limiting the duration of parliament, for altering the terms of judges' commissions, to extend the right of *habeas corpus* to Ireland, a private bill to help relieve the creditors of Dillon's Bank, and several law and order measures advanced to combat agrarian violence.[61] In 1765–6, more private than public bills were delayed, and only one could be described as popular.[62] The situation was comparable during the 1770s. A number of controversial popular measures – a sequence of quarterage bills (1772, 1774, 1775, 1778) and a *habeas corpus* bill (1776) – were not certified,[63] but a majority of the bills that failed at the Irish Council appertained to more quotidian concerns, such as the administration of justice (transportation, the qualification of justices of the peace, the fees of sheriffs), church affairs (including the question of the tithe on flax), the promotion of the movement of grain, the development of fisheries, road bills, and so on.[64]

60. Townshend to Rochford, 10 Apr. 1772 in *Cal. HO papers, 1770–2* p. 478.
61. See *Commons Jn. (Irl.)*, vii, passim; Magennis, *Irish political system*, p. 163.
62. Waite to Wilmot, 5 Jan., 16, 17 Mar. 1762 (PRONI, Wilmot Papers, T3019/4253, 4316, 4318); the bill referred to was the Heads of a bill for the better securing the freedom of parliament by ascertaining the qualification of knights, citizens and burgesses of parliament, which was proposed by Charles Lucas.
63. *Commons Jn. (Irl.)*, viii, 469, 471, 495, 501, 518, 521, 523, 529, 530 (quarterage bill, 1772); ibid., ix, 79, 82, 88, 91, 92, 96, 104, 105 (quarterage bill, 1774); ix, 415, 424, 432, 458, 461 (quarterage bill, 1778); ibid., ix, 267 (*habeas corpus* bill).
64. *Commons Jn. (Irl.)*, viii, 480, 490, 505, 507, 508 (transportation bill, 1772); ibid., viii, 410, 469, 481, 486, 510, 513 (church leases bill, 1771); ibid., ix, 85, 104, 106, 109 (church leases bill, 1774); ibid., ix, 28, 59, 67, 83, 123, 126, x, 212, 261 (tithe bills, 1774, 1780); ibid., viii, 405, 426, 456,

In accordance as they negotiated the Privy Council, certified bills were assembled into transmisses for conveyance to London. During the 1760s, a maximum of five transmisses was required during any session, though the uneven preparation of bills meant that the number of bills conveyed ranged from two, three or four, which was not unusual for the first or second transmiss carrying the money bills, to ten in the third and, occasionally, to twenty or more in subsequent transmisses.[65] During the 1770s, as the number of bills eligible for transmission appreciated, an additional sixth transmiss was added, simply to maintain some equilibrium between the number of bills being certified in Ireland and the number being received at any time at the British Council.[66] In keeping with established practice, each bill was communicated with a descriptive letter from the Irish Council. These typically described in which house a measure arose, its relationship with existing legislation, its main provisions and its purpose. As a result, they ranged considerably in length. In instances in which a measure was being re-enacted, the letter simply stated this fact, and it could normally be accommodated in the compass of half a page. This was true also of the letters accompanying road bills, which typically stated that the measure at issue was 'of the same nature with several bills passed for the like purposes with some alterations and amendments', while in the case of private bills it was explained that 'the several facts and recitals therein contained have been fully approved' and that 'all partys concerned … have consented thereto' after an equally formulaic fashion.[67] However, where more information was required adequately to define the nature, purpose and intent of a bill, the letters expanded accordingly, and missives of two, three, four and even six pages were not uncommon. Such letters also frequently incorporated a statement as to whether the measure was recommended or not.[68]

Parallel with the transmission of a bill and its Privy Council letter, legislation of importance to the Irish administration frequently elicited additional communications, of a variety of imports and purposes. Some, especially those appertaining to money bills, took the form of requests from the lord lieutenant

458, 459, 462, 466, 470, 471 grain bill, 1771); ibid., viii, 457, 462, 507, 516, 520 (fisheries bill, 1772), ix, 182, 206, 220, 222 (fisheries bill, 1775), x, 142, 145, 148 (fisheries bill, 1780).

65. Northumberland to Bedford, 31 Mar. 1764 (NA, PC1/7/76/1); Hertford to Conway, 30 Mar. 1766 (SP63/424); Shelburne to Townshend, 23 Apr. 1768 (SP67/13 f. 74); Townshend to Shelburne, 5 Apr. 1768 in *Cal. HO papers, 1766–9*, p. 332; Townshend to Rochford, 27 Mar. 1771 in *Cal. HO papers, 1770–2*, pp 231; Harcourt to Rochford, 9 Dec. 1773 in *Cal. HO papers, 1773–5*, p. 111; Harcourt to Weymouth, 20 Feb. 1776, Buckinghamshire to Weymouth, 30 Nov. 1777, 6, 16, 21 Apr. 1778, Buckinghamshire to Hillsborough, 15 June, 3 July 1780 (SP63/452 f. 134, SP63/458 ff 212–5, SP63/459 ff 272–4, 318–19, 336–42, SP63/469 ff 344–5, SP63/470 f. 44); Eden to Porten, 21, 30 Nov., Carlisle to Hillsborough, 28 Nov., 29 Dec. 1781 (SP63/477 ff 95, 144, 123–4, SP63/480 ff 3–4).

66. Townshend to Rochford, 10 Apr. 1772 in *Cal. HO papers, 1770–2*, p. 477

67. Privy Council letters, NA, PC1/7/15; PC1/7/75/3, 5, 7; PC1/7/80/3, 5, 7; PC1/8/18 ff 17–20; PC1/8/19 ff 41, 47; PC1/8/2/3; PC1/9/15 f. 3; PC1/9/13 ff 7–10, 15; PC1/9/14 f. 7; PC1/123/100 f. 7.

68. For example, see NA, PC1/7/77; PC1/7/15; PC1/7/80/3, 5, 7; PC1/82, PC1/83.

and chief secretary that bills were returned with all possible speed to facilitate the easeful management of the Irish parliament.[69] Others, from officials, took the form of lobbying requests addressed to Robert Wilmot, or later to William Knox, to encourage them to use their influence to facilitate the return of a bill or bills in an orderly fashion or, more usually, unamended to guarantee their passage into law.[70] The most interesting were those from the head of the Irish executive to the secretary of state from the southern department because they effectively superseded the Privy Council letter.

Successive lords lieutenants and chief secretaries had long prepared dispatches for transmission in tandem with the communication of bills to London. The character and content of these communications varied according to the personality of the author and the matter at issue, but in general terms they fell into two categories – pro-forma letters alerting officials to the arrival of an Irish transmiss, and political letters to ministerial and administrative colleagues that explained why a particular measure or measures should be approved, amended or respited. This practice persisted into the reign of George III, when it became commonplace for lords lieutenant to sign a covering note to the secretary of state for the southern department that accompanied the transmiss with the bills and privy council letters. In the main these were routine and perfunctory in the early 1760s,[71] though some, such as those composed by the duke of Northumberland and the earl of Hertford in the mid-1760s, went further and explained why particular bills should be returned.[72] The transformation of the lord lieutenancy from a non-resident to a resident officeholder in the late 1760s prompted an intensification of this practice, with the result that longer, more personalised dispatches became commonplace. Significantly, having first demonstrated his unwillingness to intercede in support of favoured items of legislation in 1768, it was Lord Townshend's practice during the early 1770s to communicate detailed commentaries on those bills that he believed should not be returned. For instance, he recommended in 1771 that a proposal 'to prevent the distilling of spirits from wheat' and a number of other bills should not be returned on the grounds that they must prove 'injurious to the revenue'. He also suggested amendments, as in

69. Waite to Wilmot, 1 Dec. 1765, Macartney to Wilmot, 27 Apr. 1772 (PRONI, Wilmot Papers, T3019/5137, 6292); Harcourt to Rochford, 1 Dec. 1773 in *Cal. HO papers, 1773–5*, p. 110; Harcourt to Gower, 28 Feb. 1776 (NAI, Index to departmental letters and official papers, 1760–89, i, 46); Harcourt to Weymouth, 14 Mar. 1776, Buckinghamshire to Hillsborough, 1 Aug. 1780, Carlisle to Hillsborough, 28 Nov. 1781 (NA, SP63/452 ff 233–4, SP63/470 f. 172, SP63/477 f. 121).

70. Waite to Wilmot, 31 Mar. 1764, 8 Apr. 1766, Meredyth to Wilmot, 6 Apr. 1764 (PRONI, Wilmot Papers, T3019/4825, 5209 4826); Heron to Knox, 15 July 1778 (NLI, Heron Papers, MS 4135).

71. See, for example, Northumberland to Bedford, 29 Nov. 1763 (NAI, Irish Correspondence, 1697–1798, i, MS 2446).

72. Halifax to Granville, 5 Jan. 1762 (NA, PC1/31/A78); Northumberland to Halifax, 31 Mar. 1764 (SP63/423); Hertford to Winchilsea, 30 Nov., 4, 24 Dec. 1765 (NAI, Irish Correspondence, 1697–1798, i, MS 2446).

the case of the 1771–72 proposal for granting duties for the purpose of promoting inland navigation, which he recommended was restricted to two years.[73] As these examples suggest, Townshend's interventions were prompted by his commitment to place the government of Ireland on solid financial as well as political foundations, so when he deemed it of assistance, he appended documentation from the commissioners of the revenue, extracts from legislation, and practical guidance as to what bills 'merit the first consideration, from which can be judged what bills may be postponed with the least inconvenience, should there not be time for completing the whole'.[74] Such advice was of considerable value to the British Council board, but it was also politically risky. Moreover, it was time consuming to prepare, and it is significant that the earl of Harcourt, who possessed little of his predecessor's restless energy, expressed his intention in 1773 'to make my dispatches as little voluminous as possible'. This notwith-standing, Harcourt was as eager as Townshend to indicate those bills he wanted on the statute book and he too conveyed his views in letters to the secretary of state.[75] It paid dividends in both instances, as the response to Irish bills at the British Council board was invariably guided by the opinions of successive lords lieutenants.

Given its effectiveness, it is not surprising that the Earl of Buckinghamshire, and his chief secretary Richard Heron, continued this practice. Like Harcourt, Buckinghamshire was less than eager at the outset, being content to provide little more than *pro forma* covering notes with each transmiss in which he observed that the enclosed bills were 'fully explained in the letters which accompany them … from the Privy Council'.[76] However, when the political temperature increased in the late 1770s, he too prepared letters in which he outlined the history and intent of particular bills he wished to progress. In the 1777–8 session, for example, these appertained to the establishment of a militia, the encouragement of fisheries, the development of 'wide and convenient' streets in Dublin city, and the advancement of trade through the equalisation of duties,[77] while, in the more difficult session

---

73. Townshend to Shelburne, 5 Apr. 1768 (NA, PC1/9/19 ff 9–11); Townshend to Shelburne, 26 Mar. 1768 in *Cal. HO papers, 1766–9*, pp 319–20; Townshend to Rochford, 27 Mar., 5 Dec 1771 in *Cal. HO papers, 1770–2*, pp 231–4, 333–4.

74. Townshend to Rochford, 31 Mar., 10 Apr. 1772, 5 Dec 1771, Rochford to Townshend, 2 May 1771 in *Cal. HO papers, 1770–2*, pp 470–2, 477–8, 249–51.

75. Harcourt to Rochford, 9 Dec.1773, 28 Apr., 25 May 1774 in *Cal. HO papers, 1773–5*, pp 111–12, 209, 216–7; Harcourt to Weymouth, 20, 28 Feb. 1776 (NA, SP63/452 ff 132–5, Gilbert Library, Harcourt Papers, MS 93 ff 355–6).

76. Buckinghamshire to Weymouth, 30 Nov. 1777, 6 Apr. 1778, Buckinghamshire to Hillsborough, 22 Jan., 10 Apr., 3 July 1780 (NA, SP63/458 ff 212–5, SP63/459 ff 272–4, SP63/468 f. 96, SP63/469 f. 31, SP63/470 f. 44).

77. Buckinghamshire to Weymouth, 21 Apr., 1, 17 May (NA, SP63/459 ff 336–42, 460 ff 27–31, 121–2, 305–8); Buckinghamshire to Weymouth, 2 July, Heron to Knox, 15 Apr., 4, 15 July (NLI, Heron Papers, MS 4135); Buckinghamshire to North, 22, 29 Apr., 1 May in *Life of Grattan*, i, 305–7, 320–1, 323; Buckinghamshire to Gower, 16 Apr. 1778 (NA, Granville Papers, 30/29/3/9).

of 1779–80, he was still more forceful in pressing the main supply bill, free trade legislation, the repeal of the sacramental test act, the army bill and the tillage bill.[78] Inevitably, given the political pressure he came under, Buckinghamshire's successor, the earl of Carlisle, was also forthcoming with his opinions on how Irish bills should be managed.[79] It proved less than wholly effective in this instance because the strength of patriot opposition to the practice of respiting and amending heads at the Irish Council inhibited councillors, which perforce limited the freedom of action of the lord lieutenant. The fact that only one of the 90 heads received at the Irish Privy Council during the landmark 1781–82 session did not progress is indicative of the fact that having effectively ceded its entitlement to initiate law, the Privy Council's power to reject heads of bills received from the legislature was fast becoming redundant.

THE OPERATION OF THE BRITISH PRIVY COUNCIL, 1761–82

Five hundred and eighty bills – 87 per cent of which were public and 13 per cent private – were transmitted from the Irish to the British Council between 1761 and 1782. This represented 65 per cent of the number of legislative initiatives proposed in the Irish parliament, for as well as the 85 heads of bills that were respited at the Irish Council board a further 204 (25 per cent) did not emerge from the Commons, while exactly a quarter (19 from 76) of the heads proposed by the Lords did not progress (Table Eleven). Despite this high attrition rate, the average of 45 bills received at the British Council board each session was substantially higher than the early Hanoverian average of 28.56 (Table Eight).

The transmission of the 580 bills and heads of bills from Dublin to London, which was managed at Dublin end by the under-secretary at Dublin Castle, Thomas Waite, and at the London end by successive clerks to the council and the lord lieutenant's resident secretary in England, was entrusted to messengers who could be depended upon to perform the task efficiently and expeditiously.[80] There were delays, due primarily to adverse weather conditions. Potentially the most serious occurred in December 1763 when, as a result of a 'hurricane' on the Irish Sea, the packet carrying the messenger John Finlay with the all-important money bills was blown so severely of course that it was feared 'lost', and orders were given to prepare and to transmit 'duplicates'. As it happened, the duplicates were not required as Finlay, who was one of a roster of messengers, had disembarked

---

78. Buckinghamshire to Hillsborough, 2, 5, 6 Dec. 1779, 9 May, 21 June (2), 3 July, 16 Aug. 1780 (NA, SP63/467 ff 188–90, 189, 183–4, 208–9, SP63/469 ff 199–200, 375–6, 377, SP63/470 ff 48–9, 260–2); Buckinghamshire to Hillsborough, 28 May 1780 in *Life of Grattan*, ii, 93–5.

79. Carlisle to Hillsborough, 28 Nov., 29 Dec. (2) 1781, 21 Mar. 1782 (NA, SP63/477 ff 123–4, SP63/480 ff 1–3, 413).

80. Weston to Blaquiere, 29 Dec. 1775 (NAI, Index to departmental letters and papers, 1760–89, i, 349).

safely at Cardigan Bay and made the more time-consuming journey through Wales to London. Meanwhile, the difficulties associated with crossing the Irish Sea obliged the lord lieutenant to have recourse to the duplicates of the Irish bills made at the British Council, which were communicated to Dublin via Portpatrick and Donaghadee.[81] Duplicates were rarely required, but they continued to be prepared at the British Council board and to be returned synchronously with, if via a different route than, the originals.[82] This helped to ensure against delays caused by the tardy return of bills, reference to which featured routinely in the correspondence that passed across the Irish Sea when parliament was sitting, and to serve as a backup on those rare occasions when bills were damaged in transit. In one such instance, in 1768, the Irish bills committee recommended that a measure to amend a public roads bill should be respited because 'the original [had] been obliterated and made illegible by sea water'.[83]

English officials, particularly successive clerks of the council, of whom William Sharpe (1731–67) and Stephen Cotterell (1767–1810) have left a distinct archival imprint, assisted Irish bills to negotiate the British Council by advising the law officers of what was expected of them when politically sensitive bills were at issue, and by informing them when amendments were acceptable to petitioners.[84] The clerks also contrived to spur the law officers to examine bills expeditiously. This was matter of ongoing concern, and it prompted a steady flow of assurances from the British Council that Irish bills were being afforded 'all possible dispatch', and genuine expressions of gratitude in Ireland when bills were returned in a 'short' time.[85] Some secretaries of state and other officials were particularly attentive since as well as acknowledging that receipt of bills, indicating in advance which bills were being returned, and the nature of proposed amendments, they provided updates when delays occurred and, when it was helpful, conveyed copies or abstracts of minutes and reports on the deliberations of the Crown's law officers,

81. Waite to Wilmot, 5, 8, 10, 15 Dec., Finlay to Wilmot, 12 Dec. (PRONI, Wilmot papers, T3019/4732, 4744, 4748, 4749, 4753); Northumberland to Halifax, 8 Dec. (NA, SP63/422); Northumberland to Halifax, ca 10 Dec. 1763 (PRONI, Alnwick Papers, T2872/42).
82. Hillsborough to Buckinghamshire, 16 Dec 1779, 11 May 1780 (NA, SP63/467 f. 229, 469 f. 189).
83. Waite to Wilmot, 21 Apr. 1764, Macartney to Wilmot, 19 Apr. 1772 (PRONI, Wilmot Papers, T3019/4841, 6291); Heron to Porten, 26 Feb. 7 Aug. 1780 (NA, SP63/468 f. 316, SP63/470 f. 230). For the 1768 roads bill see NA, PC2/113 ff 125, 168, 175; Minutes of Irish bills committee, 10 May 1768 (PC1/9/19 f. 2); *Commons Jn. (Irl.)*, viii, 209, 239, 243, 244, 245, 256, 257.
84. Law officers' report on Lagan Navigation bill, 9 Mar. 1764 (NA, PC1/7/74/1); Sharpe to Norton, 7 Dec. 1763 (PC2/110 f. 162).
85. Conway to Hertford, 4 Mar. 1766, Rochford to Harcourt, 13 Dec. 1773, Weymouth to Harcourt, 19 Mar. 1776, Weymouth to Buckinghamshire, 3 Dec. 1777 (NA, SP67/13 f. 40, SP67/14 f. 114, SP67/15 f. 109, SP67/16 f. 5); Waite to Wilmot, 17 Dec. 1767 (PRONI, Wilmot Papers, T3019/5640); Sharpe to de Grey, 11 Dec. 1769 (NA, PC2/114 f. 164); Shelburne to Townshend, 8 Dec. 1767, 23 Apr. 1768 (NA, SP67/13 ff 50, 74); Townshend to Weymouth, 18 Dec 1769 in *Cal. HO papers, 1766–9*, p. 543; Weymouth to Buckinghamshire, 24 Feb., 18 July 1778, Hillsborough to Buckinghamshire, 31 Jan. 1780 (NA, SP63/459 f. 85, SP63/460 f. 338, SP63/468 f. 114); NAI, Index to departmental letters and official papers, 1760–89, i, f. 45 ff.

the Irish bills committee and, on occasion, the full Council.[86] Care was also taken
to impress on Irish officials that the changes made to particular bills did not make
any 'material alteration in the enacting part'. These and other amendments and
corrections were routinely described as 'literal', 'verbal', 'not material' or, more
rarely, as 'not worth notice'.[87]

Despite the eagerness, demonstrated in such communications, to ensure that
the making of law for the kingdom of Ireland proceeded with minimal difficulty,
complicating delays could not be avoided. Other than inclement weather, one of
the main causes of delay was the unavailability of the law officers or key privy
councillors. The reasons for this varied from their absence 'out of town' to the
need to fill a vacant office. Thus the interval between the promotion of Charles
Pratt, who served as attorney general from 1757 to 1762, to the judiciary and the
appointment of Charles Yorke to succeed him was the occasion of a 'long delay'
in 1762, while the fall of Lord North's government threatened a similar problem
in 1782.[88] The demands of British politics could also create difficulties, as was
demonstrated in 1771 and 1777 when 'the business of parliament' and the
exigencies of 'public affairs' inhibited the law officers or the Irish bills committee
from engaging with Irish bills for a number of days.[89]

Such delays could complicate the Irish administration's plans for a session, but
they seldom created major problems because, other than the incidents cited above,
the law officers and the Irish bills committee proved attentive to Irish concerns.[90]
Indeed, the process of examining and certifying Irish legislation was so fully
integrated into the work of the Council that it was sufficient in 1761 to order 'that
the usual committee be appointed to examine the bills transmitted from Ireland'

86. Rochford to Townshend, 15 May (2) 1772 in *Cal. HO papers, 1770–2*, p. 498; Irish bills, 12 Apr.,
    18 April–11 May, Rochford to Harcourt, 14 May 1774, Weymouth to Harcourt, 16 Dec. 1775 in
    Cal. HO Papers, 1773–5, pp 202, 211, 213, 501; Rochford to Harcourt, 15, 20, 26 Apr., 14 May
    1774 (NA, SP67/14 ff 130, 131–2, 133–5); Minutes of proceedings of Irish bills committee, 26
    May 1778 (NLI, Heron Papers, MS 4135); Weymouth to Harcourt, 10 Dec 1775, 28 Feb., 26
    Mar. 1776 (SP67/15 ff 76–8, 102, 113); Weymouth to Buckinghamshire, 18 July 1778 (SP67/16
    f. 34); Weston to Heron, 24 July 1778 (NAI, Irish correspondence, ii, MS 2447 f. 275); Cotterell
    to Blaquiere, 28 Feb., 7, 9, 22 Mar. 1776, Bathurst to Carlisle, Dec. 1781, Reports on bills,
    1760–80 (NAI, Index to Departmental letters and official papers, 1760–89, ff 46, 48–9, 341–89);
    Hillsborough to Carlisle, 19 Jan., 15 Mar. 1782 (SP63/480 ff 78–80, 358).
87. Northumberland to [Halifax], 16 Feb. 1762 (NA, PC1/31/A78); Weymouth to Harcourt, 16, 29
    Dec 1775, 14 Feb. 1776 (NA, SP67/15 ff 76–8, 82, 97); Gower to Harcourt, 29 Dec. 1775
    (PC1/31/A78); Carlisle to Hillsborough, 7 Dec. 1781, 10 Mar. 1782 (SP63/477 f. 177,
    SP63/480 f. 348); Gower to Halifax, 6 Apr. 1762, Bathurst to Carlisle, 1, 17 Dec. 1781
    (PC1/31/A78); Buckinghamshire to Hillsborough, 15 May 1780 (SP63/469 f. 224).
88. Abdy to Devonshire, 15 Dec. 1761 (PRONI, Chatsworth Papers, T3158/1642); Northumberland
    to [Halifax], 16 Feb. 1762 (NA, PC1/31/A78); Bathurst to Carlisle, 30 Mar. 1782 (NAI, Index
    to departmental letters and official papers, 1760–89, f. 50).
89. Gower to Townshend, 2 May 1771, Gower to Harcourt, 22 Feb. 1774, Gower to Buckinghamshire,
    Dec. 1777 (NA, PC1/31/ A78).
90. Harcourt to Gower, 28 Feb. 1776 (NAI, Index to departmental letters and official papers,
    1760–89, f. 46); Bedford to Granville, 1 Apr. 1760 (PRONI, Bedford Papers, T2915/9/13).

and the reports of the law officers. In practice, the Irish bills committee was anything but 'usual', for while the quorum remained unchanged at three, the membership of the committee oscillated from a low of 15 in 1765 to a high of 37 in 1777. Charged with receiving the reports prepared by the law officers, the primary duty of the committee was to recommend to the King in Council 'what alterations and amendments they conceive proper' to enable an Irish bill to pass under the great seal of Great Britain.[91] The Committee, which rarely attracted an attendance of more than six or seven, was well disposed to accept the law officers' recommendations. These were submitted as a joint report in a majority of instances, but individual reports became more common in response to the rapid rise in the number of bills referred for consideration in the late 1770s. Significantly, the number of instances in which the law officers were not in agreement also rose.

A good example of the latter, dating from the spring of 1774, was the heads of a bill to secure the interests of defendants 'on trials by *nisi prius* or at bar'. Adjudged by the solicitor general, Alexander Wedderburn, to be 'a beneficial regulation' that did not require any amendment, the attorney general, Edward Thurlow, was scathing. Dismissing the measure presented as 'no more than [the] short incorrect notes of an idea which has been little considered and remains wholly undigested', he accepted that the issue the measure sought to address – 'the delay and expence of bills of exceptions, demurrers to evidence and special verdicts' – was an appropriate subject for legislative attention. However, he was unable to accede to the 'total subversion of the law' that was proposed and the bill was 'postponed' as a result.[92]

Disagreement as complete as this was unusual, since the law officers were enabled in a majority of cases not only to present joint reports on most bills but also to gather as many as five or six together and to present them on one document.[93] In the main, these reports avoided indulging what one might describe as opinions; they simply offered a recommendation accompanied by a list of amendments for the Irish bills committee to consider, and the Committee manifested its implicit trust in the law officers' expertise by routinely approving them without demur.[94] However, on occasions the law officers did not provide such clear-cut guidance, but left it to the bills committee to judge whether a bill should be amended or respited. In 1772, for instance, they presented an extensive report, replete with a sequence of material amendments to a bill 'to regulate the election' of MPs that

91. NA, PC2/108 ff 191, 588–9; PC2/111 f. 422; PC2/114 f. 131; PC2/115 f. 79; PC2/117 ff 336–7; PC2/121 f. 339; PC2/127 f. 33.

92. NA, PC2/117 ff 486; law officers' report, 11 May 1774, (PC1/10/19 ff 1–3).

93. Irish bills committee minutes, 6 Mar. 1776, 15 Jan., 28 Feb. 1782 (NA, PC1/15/81/3, PC1/12/100, 102); law officers' reports, 3 Apr. 1764, 26, 27 June, 11 July, July 1780 (PC1/7/77 ff 1–3; PC1/12/18 ff 5–7, 11, 13, 15, 17, 19, 21, 23, 27, PC1/12/21, 1/12/23).

94. For examples see NA, PC1/10/100 ff 1–34, PC1/10/102 ff 1–6; PC1/7/77/1–3; PC1/7/80/1; PC1/7/81/6; PC1/8/18 ff 5–10; PC1/9/113, ff 10–14; PC1/9/114 ff 3–10; PC1/8/19 ff 5–8.

would, if approved, have required the rewriting of an important section of the measure, but the Irish bills committee recommended the bill was respited, and this is what occurred.[95] This was unusual and, two years later, the law officers showed that they could also argue strongly in favour of a bill – in this case a bill for 'quieting the titles and possessions of his majesty's subjects' in Ireland – which they recommended on the grounds that, unlike the version presented in April 1772 that they had recommended should not advance, 'the preamble ... proves the sense of the Commons of Ireland that an act of this nature ought to flow from the grace of the Crown'. They were less pleased with a proviso 'saving all estates vested in the Crown in consequence of the Rebellion of 1688', because it did not fully cite the relevant clauses from comparable English bills, but they anticipated that the measure could be amended appropriately. However, the Irish bills committee was not persuaded and the bill was respited.[96] The Irish bills committee was equally decisive in 1776 in respect of a bill for continuing the 1748 barracks bill, for though the law officers found much to criticise in the manner in which the bill was drafted and presented, and rewrote a large section to reflect the fact that the building of new barracks was the responsibility of the barracks board, they anticipated it would be returned in an amended form. However, the Irish bills committee felt otherwise and recommended that the bill was respited, which is what occurred.[97]

The law officers and Irish bills committee were at liberty, of course, to seek expert advice though, following on the pattern established during the early Hanoverian period, they did so in a minority of instances only, and not always dextrously. For instance, when a measure for 'the better regulating the collection of the revenue' and 'preventing fraud' was received in 1762 it was found to include a new book of rates specifying the duties to be paid on goods entering Irish ports. This represented a departure from previous practice, which had relied on the discretion of revenue officers, yet the bill was not referred to the Commissioners of Customs as one might have anticipated. Instead, the book of rates was 'laid aside' and referred to the Lords of the Treasury, who were invited 'to direct the Commissioners of the Revenue in Ireland to prepare an account before the next session of parliament in Ireland of the duties hitherto payd and payable on the articles comprised in that book with the difference of the duties now proposed and ... their reasons for the expediency thereof'.[98] This did not appeal to the Treasury, which thought it 'more proper to refer the same to the

---

95. NA, PC2/116 ff 163, 243–4, 247; law officers' report, May 1772 (PC1/9/119 ff 8–12).
96. NA, PC2/116 ff 149, 232, 240 (1772 measure); PC2/117 ff 485, 2/118 ff 3, 12–13; law officers' report, 18 Apr. 1774 (PC1/10/14 f. 19) (1774 measure). This matter is further considered below p. 275; see also Carlisle to Hillsborough, 22 Dec. 1781 (NA, SP63/477 f. 203).
97. NA, PC2/119 ff 370–1, 444, 456–7; law officers' report, 12 Mar. 1776 (PC1/11/12 ff 15–22); Weymouth to Harcourt, 18 Mar. 1776 (SP63/452).
98. Law officers' report on an act ... for better regulating the collection of the revenue, 8 Apr. 1762 (PC1/7/16 ff 1–4); Irish bills committee, 8 Apr. 1762 (PC2/109 ff 192–3, 199).

Commissioners of the Customs', who concluded in February 1764 that because the book disadvantaged several English goods it must be 'a very great discouragement of the importation of British commodities into Ireland'. Having reached this determination, the book of rates was referred once more to the Treasury for a 'report'.[99] In 1764 also, the Irish bills committee unhesitatingly referred a measure for 'the further encouragement of tillage' to the Commissioners of Customs, thereby indicating that where matters of bounties were at issue they did not have any problem seeking expert advice, though there was to be little call for their services again before 1780 when, arising out of the concession to Ireland of free trade, the Privy Council 'thought fit to refer … all bills where the equalisation of duties is required … to the several boards … competent to ascertain those points'.[100]

As well as the Commissioners of Trade and Plantations, the Commissioners for Customs, the Treasury and so on, the law officers drew actively on the expertise of Sir Robert Wilmot who continued in the capacity as 'resident secretary' to the lord lieutenant in London until 1772. The beneficiary of a superb working relationship with the under-secretary at Dublin Castle, Thomas Waite, whose exceptional abilities were acknowledged by his elevation to the Irish Privy Council in 1771, it was to Wilmot that requests were submitted for copies of the Irish statutes and other documentation required to facilitate the scrutiny of Irish bills.[101] Wilmot also assisted in responding to the requests of law officers for information on points of concern, but it was as an intermediary between Dublin Castle and the British Privy Council that he was at his most useful. It was in this capacity that Wilmot responded to urgent appeals from Dublin Castle to 'send us back our bills as fast as possible', and kept the Irish administration informed on their progress.[102] This was not always easy as the crown's law officers were frequently 'so hurried with business' that Irish legislation had to compete for attention, but Wilmot's unrivalled understanding of the process and his skill as an intermediary meant that he was often influential.[103] Following Wilmot's death in 1772, his son Robert Wilmot, became the lord lieutenant's secretary in England until 1775 when he was succeeded by Robert Weston and John Jenkinson.

---

99. Whately (secretary to Treasury) to Clerk to Council, 14 Mar. 1764 (PC1/3058); law officers' report, 17 Apr. 1764 (PC1/15/23); Irish bills committee minute, 18 Apr. 1764 (PC2/110 ff 380–1).
100. Council order, 18 Apr. 1764 (NA, PC2/110 ff 391–2); Bathurst to Buckinghamshire, Aug. 1780 (NA, PC1/31/A78). Five bills were so referred in 1780 – two to the Commissioners for Customs and three to the Commissioners for trade and plantations. See below pp 295–7.
101. Dickson, *Ireland: new foundations*, pp 146–7; Hardwicke to Wilmot, 5 Jan., Waite to Wilmot, 8 Jan., 6 Feb. 1761 (PRONI, Wilmot Papers, T3019/3961, 3964, 3983).
102. Waite to Wilmot, 10 Apr. 1762, 13 Apr. 1772, Wilmot to Campbell, 21 Apr., Temple to Wilmot, 8, 12 Sept. 1768, Macartney to Wilmot, 19 Apr. 1772 (PRONI, Wilmot Papers, T3019/4323, 6289, 5735, 5810, 5813, 6291); Wilmot to Lees, 20 Apr. 1771 (Raynham Hall, Townshend Papers).
103. Wilmot to Lees, 16 Apr. 1771 (Raynham Hall, Townshend Papers); Hertford to Wilmot, 3 May 1768 (PRONI, Wilmot Papers, T3019/5749). I wish to thank Dr Eoin Magennis for references from the Townshend Papers at Raynham Hall.

Significantly, none were so effective as Wilmot senior. Perhaps, it was this that prompted Lord Townshend to instruct Thomas Allan, whom he employed as 'his personal representative in London' between 1769 and 1772, to represent the rum and revenue bill with the law officers and Council in 1772.[104]

Prompted by this, as well as by the realisation that representatives and agents performed a useful role, a variety of such individuals were resorted to or employed by political and other interests to lobby on their behalf. The best connected was Henry Seymour Conway, the brother of the then lord lieutenant, the earl of Hertford, and sometime secretary of state, who supplied the duke of Grafton in 1766 with his 'brother's letters on the subject of ... Irish bills' in the expectation that Grafton would 'make such use of them as you might judge proper in relation to the passing of these bills thro[ugh] our Council'.[105] This was neither a desirable nor a replicable arrangement but, in July 1778, Richard Heron, the chief secretary, liaised actively with William Knox, the under secretary to the colonial department, with respect of a number of bills appertaining to Anglo-Irish trade and Catholic relief, and raised with him the merits of employing 'a solicitor ... to attend the progress' of one such bill.[106] In 1778 and 1780, established church interests, opposed in principle to the 'rash, precipitate and injudicious attempt to repeal at once all the laws that were made to secure the constitution' by limiting the rights of Catholics and Dissenters, lobbied like-minded members of the British Council such as Welbore Ellis and the archbishop of Canterbury. They were unsuccessful, and it is significant that, having failed to persuade his colleagues of the wisdom of replacing the sacramental test with a declaration, Ellis chose to absent himself rather than 'stand in the very awkward situation of debating it in the Council with all the members against me'.[107]

For those with less direct or no personal access to the corridors of power, petitioning remained an option, and a variety of municipal bodies, commercial interests, political pressure groups, and individuals presented petitions.[108] The law officers and Irish bills committee responded positively with sufficient regularity to encourage a significant, but diminishing, number of such appeals during these years (Table 11). To assist them in their efforts, bodies like the Catholic Committee were advised by sympathisers like Gorges Edmond Howard, to hire

---

104. Johnston, *Great Britain and Ireland*, pp 79–80, 82; Allan to Townshend, 24 Oct. 1772 (Beinecke Library, Osborn Collection, Townshend Papers, Box 5).
105. Conway to Grafton, 12 Apr. 1766 (Ipswich and East Suffolk Record Office, PRONI T2959/2/3).
106. Knox to Heron, 6, 16, 23 July (RIA, Knox-Heron letters, MS G.5.1); Heron to Knox, 4, 15 July 1778 (NLI, Heron Papers, MS 4135).
107. Agar to Ellis, 24 Jan, 1778, 1 Feb. 1780, Ellis to Agar, 1 Mar. 1780 (PRONI, Normanton Papers, T3719/C/12/ 10B, C/14/5, 9).
108. A good example is the 1774 bill 'to explain and amend several laws for the preservation of salmon fry', which was the subject of petitions from Thomas Conolly, the duke of Devonshire, the corporation of Limerick and the corporation of the plantation of Ulster (law officers' report, 10 May 1774 (PRONI, Shannon Papers, D2707/A2/2/14)).

an agent in London 'to transact business ... and to attend the attorney and solicitor general there'. To this end, Daniel Macnamara, a lawyer, was retained following his initial recruitment to promote a mortgage bill in 1768, while others employed individuals for more defined tasks on an *ad hoc* basis.[109] Thus Limerick Corporation secured the services of J. Palmer of Lincoln's Inn to represent them in 1774; Hugh Hammersley represented meal merchants opposed to the bakery trade bill in 1764 and, as previously noted, Chief Secretary Heron contemplated hiring a lawyer based at Lincoln's Inn to act on his behalf in 1778. Agents proved especially useful when the Irish bills committee allowed interested parties the opportunity to comment on amendments posited by the crown's law officers, as, for example, in 1780 when 'counsel on both sides' was called in and heard on the tenants' bill.[110]

While the engagement of agents, lawyers, and other lobbyists can be said to have assisted the Council in its work, they were of little use in dealing with some of the congenital problems encountered with respect of Irish measures. The most persistent, and irritating, was the perennial problem of lax drafting. Writing to Lord Townshend in May 1772, the then secretary of state, the earl of Rochford, lamented that 'the [Irish] bills in general are drawn with so little accuracy and precision, as to occasion great trouble and loss of time in examining and correcting them'.[111] This point was reiterated, even more forcefully, two years later. In a letter to Bishop Charles Agar, an exasperated Welbore Ellis observed:

> The transmisses of heads of your bills were sent over with a shameful negligence of the law officers of the crown of that kingdom, who I am persuaded never cast their eyes over them, for they are usually filled with faults which would disgrace even a diligent copying clerk. It would be an insult to the commonsense as well as dignity of the Council to pass such things under the great seal.

Ellis supported his case by reference to the 'verbal absurdities' that required correction in the stamp bill, but he was even more appalled by the wording of the clause of the tontine bill regulating the payment to be made to nominees; this, he maintained, was so badly drawn it must, if approved, 'have subverted the whole plan of the bill'. Given this experience, Ellis did not conceal his impatience with

---

109. G.E. Howard, *Miscellaneous works in prose and verse* (3 vols, Dublin, 1782), i, pp li–ii; McGeehin, 'Activities and personnel of the Catholic Committee', pp 6–7, 57; Garnett to Waite, 2 Apr. 1772 (PRONI, Wilmot Papers, T3019/6288); *Hibernian Journal*, 20 Mar. 1776.

110. Limerick petition, 1774 (NA, PC1/10/20 f. 22); Irish bills committee minute on Kilworth-Cork road bill, 26 Mar. 1764 (PC2/110 ff 330–1); Petition of Woodruff Drinkwater, [5 Apr. 1764] (PC1/7/88 f. 3); Minutes of Clerk of Council, 1704–95, 5 July 1780 (PC4/2); Heron to Knox, 4 July 1778 (NLI, Heron Papers, MS 4135).

111. Rochford to Townshend, 9 May 1772 (NA, SP67/14 f. 54). Some bills were lost for this reason: the north-west fishery bill was 'so full of mistakes and inaccuracies' it was 'considered impracticable to execute it' (*Cal. HO papers, 1770–2*, p. 177).

Irish criticism of the interpolations introduced into Irish bills by the British Council; they were, he protested, not introduced to alter meaning or sense but 'verbal alteration[s] occasioned by the negligence of the transcribers' and the 'slovenly manner in which your bills come over'.[112]

Somewhat surprisingly, Lord Harcourt agreed with Ellis that 'the inattention of the Irish in general to business and the carelessness with which the parliamentary official business is conducted is ... a constant occasion of unnecessary trouble to the ministry and to the Privy Council in England', but he did not see how it could 'well be avoided'. He certainly had few ideas on how things might be improved, and it remained a feature of Irish bills.[113] Its most obvious manifestation is provided in the plenitude of avoidable orthographical and syntactical errors introduced each session by the clerks charged with copying bills since they constitute the most vivid testament of the inadequacy of the checking procedures that were employed. This was, on occasion, a source of embarrassment, such as chief secretary Heron experienced in 1778 in respect of the duty-equalizing bill when it transpired that the version conveyed to William Knox contained an extraneous clause. Clearly irritated, Knox requested with admirable reserve that 'the clerk who made that copy ... will be more careful in future not to insert in his copies things that are not in the original'. However, the explanation he was provided by Heron did little to inspire confidence in the Castle bureaucracy:

> There has been a jumble in my office with respect of the copies, which were sent you of the export bills. They were, I perceive, made from draughts, which had been settled but before they had passed the House, the parts you objected to having been struck out, as you will see by the enclosed copies.[114]

Other than drawing the matter to the attention of Irish officials, British councillors were as short of ideas as Harcourt as to how Irish drafting practices might be improved. This notwithstanding, they did seek on a number of occasions to address recurring problems. Having objected to several bills in the 1770s on the grounds that they did not observe the convention of dealing separately with public and private issues, they directed in 1780 that 'matters of public and private concern' should not be included in the same bill.[115] They were eager also to ensure that proposals requiring public funding did not deplete the

---

112. Ellis to Agar, 1 Jan. 1774 (PRONI, Normanton Papers, T3719/C/8/1).
113. Harcourt to Jenkinson, 1 May 1774 (BL, Liverpool Papers, MS 38208 ff 64–6) printed in A.D. Madden and D.K. Fieldhouse (eds), *Imperial reconstruction, 1763–1840: select documents* ... (Oxford, 1985), pp 80–1.
114. Knox to Heron, 16 July (RIA, Knox-Heron letters, MS G.5.1); Heron to Knox, 16 July 1778 (NLI, Heron Papers, MS 4135).
115. NA, PC2/125 f. 196; Hillsborough to Buckinghamshire, 4 July and reply 9 July 1780 (NA, SP63/470 ff 17, 75).

hereditary revenue by insisting that funding was voted equal to the cost of proposed bounties. Lord Townshend was so concerned when this was not the case in the early 1770s that he personally intervened to recommend that a number of measures were amended or postponed at the British Council. Indeed, in 1771 the Council explicitly expressed 'His Majesty's disapprobation' in respect of the bill to provide a premium on the carriage of corn coastwise, and urged Townshend 'to use his utmost endeavours to discourage all attempts of the kind for the future'.[116] The practice did not end, however, for when the Irish parliament had not complied by 11 December 1775 with a resolution it entered into in March 1774 to fund corn bounties above £35,000, the Irish bills committee directed Lord Weymouth to write to Earl Harcourt 'expressing the surprise of the Privy Council that care was not taken to restore, in one of the money bills, to His Majesty's revenue, a sum equal to the excess of the corn bounties' and recommending 'that a clause be inserted in some future bill of this session for that purpose'. They also stressed that they could 'not be expected … [to] consent to the renewal of the act for the encouragement of tillage' otherwise. The Irish administration maintained in response that the 1774 resolution only enjoined the Irish parliament 'to make provision *from time to time*', but its failure to do so properly ensured that the matter resurfaced on several further occasions in the course of the decade. As a result, the tillage bill was respited in 1776, and its duration significantly shortened in 1778 when the Council drew attention once more to the reservation expressed in December 1775.[117]

IRISH LEGISLATION AT THE BRITISH COUNCIL, 1761–82

The exchanges between Dublin and London over successive tillage bills in the 1770s highlight the continuing reliance of the British Council on the powers vested in it by Poynings' Law to regulate the legislative output of the Irish parliament. This is demonstrated still more strikingly by the 43 heads of bills received from Ireland that were respited. Proportionately, this represented 7.4 per cent of the bills and heads of bills received at the British Council board, which was a significant reduction on the position during the early Hanoverian period when the figure was 12 per cent but, in an indication of increasing uncertainty on the Council as to how best to respond to the increased manifestations of assertiveness in Ireland, the percentage oscillated during the three parliaments that met during this period between 9 per cent in 1761–8, 12 per cent in 1768–76

116. Rochford to Townshend, 2 May 1771 in *Cal. HO papers, 1770–2*, pp 249, 251.
117. NA, PC2/119 f. 243; Minutes of the clerk of the Council 1764–95, 11 Dec. 1775 (PC4/2); Weymouth to Harcourt, 14 Dec. and reply 21 Dec. 1775 in *Cal. HO papers, 1773–5*, pp 500, 505; Weymouth to Harcourt, 14 Dec. 1775, 18 Mar. 1776 (NA, SP67/15 ff 74–6, 108); Weymouth to Buckinghamshire, 30 May 1778 (SP63/460 ff 150–2); PC2/122 ff 116–17, 122–3; Reports and proceeding at Council chamber, 26 May 1778 (NA, SP63/460 ff 154–6).

and 3 per cent in 1776–83 (Table Eleven). The increasing disinclination of the British Council to respite Irish bills to which this attests can be accounted for first and foremost by reference to the sensitivity of councillors to the mounting resentment at the practice evident in Ireland. It is especially noteworthy in this context that the 3 per cent of bills lost at the British Council board between 1776 and 1782 was the smallest in the history of the operation of the heads of bills arrangement. Moreover, the two bills that were lost at the British Council board during the 1781–2 session were private bills and they failed to progress, not because they were badly drawn (indeed, they negotiated the Irish bills committee without amendment), but because the Irish parliament adjourned before they could negotiate the Privy Council.[118]

Many reasons were offered for respiting Irish bills in the 1760s and 1770s, but the commitment of councillors to uphold the royal prerogative and to maintain Britain's primacy remained one of the most important. They contrived also to ensure that not only the law, but legal practice in Ireland conformed to that in England, and that individuals as well as interests were not disadvantaged by the emergence of a strong patriot voice. The effect of this in Ireland was to create an impression of the Privy Council as a reactionary body that was intent on restricting the entitlement of the kingdom of Ireland to enjoy the same rights as England. The nature of the changes proposed varied, but whether they appertained to the constitution, the political system or legal practice the disposition of the British Council to uphold the *status quo* remained strong though it was often obliged to accede to Irish pressure for reform. The demand to limit the duration of parliament is a case in point.

The limitation of the duration of parliament was one of the most warmly debated issues in Ireland from the late 1750s. The proposition that received most public support was that parliaments should last for seven years, and with this in mind the heads of a number of septennial bills were forwarded to the British Council during the 1760s. Having experienced a difficult passage through the Irish parliament and negotiated the Irish Council by one vote in February 1762, hopes were high that this septennial bill might make it to law. However, the Crown's law officers, Charles Yorke and Fletcher Norton, were uneasy. Their instinct was to reject the measure on the grounds that the bill represented 'a most essential alteration in the fundamental constitution of Ireland, it having hitherto remained in the power of the King, by virtue of his undoubted prerogative to continue any parliament called in that kingdom, even during his whole reign, as well as to dissolve it, at his pleasure'. However, they were equally conscious that, because the proposition before them was 'a political consideration of so high a nature', the final decision would be political, and it was on these grounds, in the absence of a formal recommendation from the Irish bills committee, that the bill

---

118. NA PC2/127 ff 427, 463–4; *Commons Jn. (Irl.)*, x, 332, 341 (Gore bill); PC2/127 ff 427, 463–4; *Commons Jn. (Irl.)*, x, 350, 355 (Nicolson bill).

was not ordered to be returned to Ireland.[119] Two years later, when a similar bill was received, the law officers were more decisive. Guided by their previous experience, they advised postponement on this occasion because 'this bill imports a restraint on his majesty's prerogative in Ireland and an essential alteration of the constitution of that kingdom, which may be attended with many great inconveniences'. Their advice was taken.[120] These concerns proved enduring, moreover, for when a further bill to limit the duration of parliaments was received in 1767–8, the law officers made a similar report, but the recognition that the measure was 'an object of great political consideration' which, if advanced, would 'be probably productive of some good and useful effects in the present state of Ireland' ensured their observations were accompanied by the recommendation that if the bill was to become law it should only do so in a modified form. The amendments they proposed were significant; they involved deleting the preamble, and changing both the duration of parliament and its date of commencement. Yet such was the relief that the principle of limited parliaments had been agreed that these patriots, who traditionally were among the sharpest critics of Poynings' Law, offered no objections, and the bill became law.[121]

As welcome as the compromise on the duration of parliament was in Ireland, the British Council board proved resistant otherwise to proposals that infringed the royal prerogative and that altered the constitutional *status quo*. In respect of the former, two attempts (in 1772 and 1774) to introduce a measure 'for quieting the titles and possessions' of subjects were respited because of the failure adequately to make clear that 'an act of this nature ought to flow from the grace of the crown'.[122] This concern was also cited in the negative report on a 'similar' measure pursued in 1780 'for the general quiet of the subject', on the grounds that it too did not proceed 'from the grace of the Crown'.[123] More significantly, it was identifiable in the reluctance, particularly manifest in respect of the 1762, 1768 and 1776 tillage bills, to approve unfunded bounties because their introduction would deplete the hereditary revenue, and in respect of the cost to the exchequer of the anti-distilling bills of 1771 and 1772 and the quit rent bill of

119. Law officers' report, 5 Mar. 1762 (NA, PC1/7/13/1–2; PC2/109 f. 93; Halifax to Egremont, 4, 8, 11, 23 Dec. 1761, 12, 19 Feb. 1762 (NA, SP63/419, 421); Waite to Wilmot, 26 Jan., 8 Feb., Bowes to Wilmot, 28 Jan. 1762 (PRONI, Wilmot Papers, T3019/4275, 4285, 4277); Cavendish to Wilmot, 5 Dec. 1761 (PRONI, Chatsworth Papers, T3158/1641).

120. NA, PC2/111 ff 543, 576, 589; law officers' report, 24 Mar. 1766 (PC1/8/18 f.3); Waite to Wilmot, 6 Feb. 1766 (PRONI, Wilmot Papers, T3019/5178).

121. NA, PC2/112 ff 25–6; Law officers' report on an act for limiting the duration of parliament, 10 Jan. 1768 (PC1/9/4 ff 7–8); Minutes of clerk of Council, 1 Feb. 1768 (PC4/3); Shelburne to Townshend, 2 Feb. 1768 (BL, Lansdowne Abstracts, Add. MS 24138); Kelly, *Henry Flood*, pp 124–6; *Biographical, literary and political anecdotes of several of the most eminent persons of the present age* (3 vols, London, 1797), i, 107–9; HMC, *Charlemont*, i, 26–7.

122. NA, PC2/117 ff 485, 2/118 ff 3, 12–13; law officers' report, 18 Apr. 1774 (PC1/10/14 f. 19) (1774); PC2/116 ff 149, 232, 240 (1772).

123. NA, PC2/125 ff 79, 288, 298; law officers' report, 27 July 1780 (PC1/12/27 f. 5).

1772.[124] The cost to the hereditary revenue of financing the creation of a militia was also singled out in the law officers' report as the main reason why it was inappropriate to proceed with this measure in 1776, though it is likely that the doubtful 'wisdom of raising so great a force ... at this time in Ireland' weighed equally heavily.[125] Equivalent concerns to uphold the royal prerogative contributed to the decision to respite the badly drawn north-west fishery bill the same year; it was the recommendation of the law officers that 'the parties, who ... applied for the bill' would be better served if they sought a charter from the crown.[126]

The commitment of the Privy Council to preserve the constitutional *status quo* in Ireland accounts for the decisions taken in 1766, 1768, 1774 and 1780 to reject bills proposing to introduce *habeas corpus*, which were denied on the grounds that conditions 'are not yet safe and expedient in Ireland, where the Roman Catholic religion is still so prevalent [and] tumultuous disorders and insurrections so frequent and dangerous'. Even the addition to the 1766 bill of a clause permitting the suspension of *habeas corpus* by proclamation should this prove warranted did not allay concerns, and councillors were encouraged to adhere to this position, in the early 1770s at least, by Earl Harcourt and members of the Irish judiciary who argued that *habeas corpus* was 'unnecessary'.[127] Attempts in 1766, 1776 and 1780 to alter the terms upon which the judiciary were appointed from royal pleasure to good behaviour foundered for the still more clear-cut reason that it was inconsistent with Poynings' law to seek to alter 'a fundamental part of the constitution [of Ireland] that all judicial offices and offices of accompt should be holden during ... pleasure ... without serious and urgent occasion'.[128] More modest efforts to

124. Above, pp 262–3; NA, PC2/109 ff 116, 190, 196 (tillage bill, 1762); PC2/113 ff 118, 151, 159; Minute of Irish bills committee, 10 May 1768 (PC1/9/19 f. 2); Townshend to Shelburne, 26 Mar. 1768 in *Cal. HO papers, 1766–9*, pp 319–20 (tillage bill, 1768); PC2/119 ff 344, 445; British to Irish Council, 11 Dec 1775 (PC1/10/9); law officers' report, 12 Mar. 1776 (PC1/11/12 ff 1–3); Weymouth to Harcourt, 18 Mar. 1776 (SP63/452 ff 247) (tillage act, 1776); Rochford to Townshend, 2 May 1771 in *Cal. HO papers, 1770–2*, pp 249–51; PC2/115 ff 136, 163, 171 (distilling bill, 1772); PC116 ff 150, 232, 240; law officers' report, 12 May 1772 (PC1/9/118 ff 5–7) (quit rents bill, 1772).

125. NA, PC2/119 ff 381, 467, 482; law officers' report, 13 Mar. 1776 (PC1/11/13); Irish bills committee minute, [Mar. 1776] (PC1/15/81/24).

126. NA, PC2/116 ff 150, 219, 227; law officers' report, 7 May (PC1/116 f. 17); Rochford to Townshend, 9 May 1772 (SP67/14 f. 54); above, p. 271 fn 111.

127. Above, p 260; NA, PC2/111 ff 570, 606, 613; PC2/113 ff 13, 131,143; PC2/117 ff 469, 492, 501; PC2/125 ff 88, 196); Irish Council letter, 29 Mar. 1766, law officers' report, 6 May 1766 (PC1/8/21 ff 7, 9); Yorke to Conway, 18 Mar. 1766 (BL, Hardwicke Papers, Add. MS 35892 ff 44–5); Northington to Hertford, [1766] (PC1/31/A78); law officers' report on an act for the better securing the liberty of the subject, 18 Apr. 1768 (PC1/9/11 ff 1–2); Harcourt to Rochford, 6 Mar. 1774 in *Harcourt Papers*, ix, 173–6. In 'Notes for a speech', 9 Mar. 1758, Philip Yorke observed that it was not appropriate to extend the *habeas corpus* act to Ireland because it was 'not safe for the King's Protestant subjects there' (P.C. Yorke, *The life and correspondence of Philip Yorke, earl of Hardwicke* (3 vols, Cambridge, 1913), iii, 11).

128. NA, PC2/111 ff 570, 606, 613; PC2/119 ff 344, 402, 412; PC2/125 ff 88, 196; Northington to

reform the political process met with a similarly negative response. Thus, attempts in 1764 and in 1768 to secure 'the freedom of parliament by ascertaining the qualifications of knights, citizens and burgesses in parliament', and in 1768, 1772 and 1774 to regulate the election of members to serve in parliament, were all denied.[129]

Attempts to alter legal or judicial practice or that would prove injurious to individual or interests were received no more favourably arising out of an equivalent resistance to alter legal practice. The law officers' observation of a well-meaning Irish proposal in 1761–2 'to regulate proceedings in courts of equity' that the advantage that would arise from preventing injunctions that were not accompanied by affidavits in order to prevent 'vexatious delays' would 'prejudice substantial justice in many more' cases, ensured this measure's postponement.[130] Comparable concerns attributable to the failure to fix 'properly the legal marks of bankruptcy' contributed to the loss of a measure to prevent frauds by bankrupts in 1766, and to the rejection of a measure appertaining to trials by *nisi prius* in 1774. This reflected poorly on those responsible for drafting this bill, but, as seen above, problems of this kind were ongoing. They were a feature of legislation that was, as the attorney general, Edward Thurlow, observed pointedly in 1774, 'little considered and … undigested', or that was founded on a misunderstanding of the thrust and purpose of the English statute upon which it was based. This latter was the case with respect of the 1774 measure for regulating the trials of peers, whereas an attempt in the same session to prevent litigation among the poor was rejected on the reasonable grounds that the problem it purported to solve could be redressed by civil bills.[131]

A number of private bills were also deemed deficient on legal grounds. In the case of the measure to enable Sydenham Singleton of the city of Dublin to raise

Hertford, [1766] (PC1/31/A78); law officers' report, 28 Feb. 1776 (PC1/11/9); Attorney General's report, 26 June 1780 (PC1/12/18 ff 9–10).

129. NA, PC2/110 ff 356, 385; *Commons Jn. (Irl.)*, vii, 284, 295, 327, 331 (qualification bill, 1764); PC2/113 ff 125, 168, 175; *Commons Jn. (Irl.)*, viii, 224, 242, 249, 251 (qualification bill, 1768); PC2/113 ff 125, 168, 175; Rough minute of Irish bills committee, 10 May 1768 (PC1/9/19 f. 2); *Commons Jn. (Irl.)*, viii, 243, 244, 247, 252, 255 (election regulating bill, 1768); PC2/116 ff 163, 243–4, 247; law officers' report, May 1772 (PC1/9/119 ff 8–12); *Commons Jn. (Irl.)*, viii, 410, 457, 472, 477, 487, 494, 500, 505, 524 (election regulating bill, 1772); PC2/117 ff 481, 519, 531; law officers' report, 15 Apr. 1774 (PC1/10/9 ff 13–14); Harcourt to Blaquiere, 28 Apr. 1774 (Gilbert Library, Harcourt Papers, MS 93 ff 126–7); *Commons Jn. (Irl.)*, ix, 25, 66, 82, 83, 84, 86, 92 (election regulating bill, 1773–4).

130. NA, PC2/109 ff 144, 193; Irish Council letter, 13 Mar., law officers' report, 8 Apr. 1762 (PC1/7/17/1–2); *Commons Jn. (Irl.)*, vii, 108, 112, 114, 116, 152.

131. NA, PC2/111 ff 570, 596, 606, 613; law officers' report, 10 Apr. 1766 (PC1/8/21 f. 1 (bankrupts bill, 1766); PC2/117 ff 486; law officers' report, 11 May 1774 (PC1/10/19 ff 1–3) (nisi prius bill, 1774); PC2/117 ff 481, 492, 501; law officers' report, 12 Apr. 1774 (PC1/10/7 f. 40) (peer trials bill, 1774); PC2/117 ff 482; law officers' report, 14 Apr. 1774 (PC1/10/9 f. 31) (poor litigation bill, 1774).

£10,000 on his estate, the law officers deemed the proposal 'unjust and improper' because Singleton, who was a tenant for life only, had made no provision to compensate his eldest son.[132] Their judgement with respect of a hotly contested measure to relieve the creditors of William Howard, a Dublin merchant, was even more severe because the bill proposed to give an 'unaccountable preference' to one creditor at the expense of the remainder. Alerted to this by a number of interested parties, the law officers advised that the measure ought not to be returned because it was 'contrary to the rule and order of law' and 'dangerous in the example'; the Privy Council concurred.[133]

Next to their opposition to proposals to make the Irish parliament more responsive to its electorate and to extend their constitutional rights, the most explicit illustration of the legal and political conservatism of the British Council is provided by their unease with initiatives by vested interests in Limerick in 1762 and in Dublin during the 1770s to alter the political and economic balance of power within these cities. What was at issue with respect of Limerick was an attempt, promoted by a body of 'independent free citizens', to increase the influence of freemen on the corporation by altering the 'mode of electing magistrates'. Determined to resist what they described as an attempt 'to subvert the charter of the city', which had been pursued unsuccessfully at the Irish Council board in March 1762, counsel and agents on behalf of the magistrates and common council of Limerick Corporation resumed the struggle in London in April. Because of the magnitude of the issues involved, the law officers produced an exceptionally detailed report urging the postponement of the bill, on the grounds that, as well as its being 'unusual for the legislative power to regulate corporations', it merited rejection because it tended 'totally to change the constitution, rights of election and powers of government in a corporate city without the actual consent, or at least acquiescence of all its members'. The law officers acknowledged that 'the abuses complained of in the management of the revenues of the city of Limerick were very great', but their perception that the proposed solution was 'not adapted to the mischief' convinced them that the solution was not 'to restore the election of magistrates and all the powers of government to the freemen at large'.[134]

Twelve years later, the law officers were faced with an equally divisive local issue when the lord mayor, corporation, merchant traders and inhabitants of Dublin joined together to petition against a measure promoted by the Revenue Commissioners to purchase ground closer to the sea upon which to locate a new custom house. This was a powerful coalition, and its impact was augmented by their arguments that the relocation of the Custom House would 'diminish the

132. NA, PC2/116 ff 63, 244, 247–8; law officers' report, 17 Feb. 1772 (PC1/9/119 f. 13).
133. NA, PC2/116 ff 180–1, 232, 260–3, 265; law officers' report, 26 May 1772 (PC1/9/120 ff 1–4); Rochford to Townshend, 29 May 1772 in *Cal. HO Papers, 1770–2*, p. 504
134. John Ferrar, *The History of Limerick* (Dublin, 1787), p. 87; NA, PC2/109 ff 148, 193; PC1/3058.

value of their properties', would render the newly built Exchange 'totally useless', prove more hazardous to shippers, and, in the estimation of London merchants and insurers, increase insurance costs. These points made a powerful impression on the law officers, and they were influenced further by the argument that the cost would fall on the hereditary revenue to recommend that the bill should not proceed.[135] The Irish bills committee concurred. However, they were obliged to revisit the issue in the winter of 1775–6 when a new bill was received from Ireland. This measure was subjected to even more petitions and to more representations, as a result of which the committee met to consider the bill on an exceptional four occasions. Persuaded that the bill could be made acceptable if the Irish Revenue Commissioners were made answerable to the Treasury and undertook 'to treat and agree with the owners', they directed the law officers to make the required changes. This was done, but the revised measure failed to negotiate the Irish bills committee and it was ordered to be 'postponed'.[136] There is no readily identifiable explanation for this, though suggestions that private interests were able to bring influence to bear cannot be discounted.[137] However, one ought not to underestimate either the influence or persistence of metropolitan interests, as the lobbying in 1778 of Dublin Corporation and several bodies of freeholders ensured that a proposal to pave, light and clean the streets of Dublin was also lost.[138]

Though the controversy over the Custom House might have suggested otherwise, the law officers were disposed in the main to ensure that obstacles were not put in the way of economic activity. They were unable, therefore, in 1776 to approve a measure 'for the further promotion of trade by allowing interest on book debts' on the grounds that its ratification would discourage the repayment of the principal and thereby 'injure' rather than 'promote trade'. Four years later, they displayed an equivalent commitment to protect the 'security of the creditor' by rejecting a proposal 'to regulate partnerships' on the grounds that this attempt 'to exempt … anonymous partners from being liable to the debts, engagements or losses of their partnership beyond the shares of the capital stock and the produce', and to protect them from the implications of the bankruptcy laws was 'detrimental to credit in trade by diminishing the security of the creditor'.[139]

* * *

135. NA, PC2/117 ff 480, 492–3, 514; PC2/118 ff 27, 29–30; Petition of merchants of Dublin, 1774 (PC1/3058); law officers' report, 10 May 1774 (PC1/10/20 ff 12–15).
136. NA, PC2/119 ff 281, 282, 285, 299, 345, 356, 358–9, 472; Memorial of London merchants, 15 Jan. 1776 (PC1/11/1); law officers' report, 21 Mar. 1776 (PC1/15/81 ff 32–3).
137. Edward McParland, 'Strategy in the planning of Dublin 1750–1800' in L.M. Cullen and P. Butel (eds), *Cities and merchants* (Dublin, 1986), p. 103; Malcomson, *Archbishop Charles Agar*, pp 143–8.
138. NA, PC2/122 ff 73, 75, 104–5, 176, 187.
139. NA, PC2/119 ff 282, 320, 334; law officers' report, 6 Feb. 1776 (PC1/11/3 f. 5); PC2/125 ff 191, 240, 252; law officers' report, 11 July 1780 (PC1/12/21 f. 1); Buckinghamshire to Hillsborough, 16 Aug. 1780 (PC1/12/33 ff 2–3).

The increased disinclination of the British Privy Council to respite Irish bills illustrated by the decline in the proportion of bills that experienced this fate from 12 per cent during the early Hanoverian period to 8 per cent during the 1760s and 1770s was mirrored by a comparable decline, from 75 to 50 per cent, in the proportion of bills ordered for amendment. More strikingly, the proportion of measures that were forwarded unaltered rose steeply from 14 per cent to 43 per cent over the same time period (Tables Eight and Eleven). Interestingly, this downward trend was not consistent, as the proportion of bills amended and left unaltered during the 1761–8 parliament (50 and 40 per cent respectively) regressed (to 58 and 32 per cent) during the 1769–76 parliament before climbing to 41 and 56 per cent between 1776 and 1782 (Table Eleven).

The decline in the proportion of bills and heads that were returned to Ireland in an amended form during the first two decades of the reign of George III is a useful index of the impact on the British Council of the mounting opposition in Ireland to the application of Poynings' Law. Significantly, this cannot be linked to formal changes in administrative policy. Indeed, since once invariably troublesome measures appertaining to difficult issues, such as the encouragement of flax and hemp production and the collection of the quit rent, negotiated the British Council without amendment or with mere syntactical tweaking, even when they were the subject of petitions, it could be suggested, the frequent comments to the contrary notwithstanding, that it was due simply to improved drafting at the Irish end.[140] This had a bearing, undoubtedly, as bills that were routinely renewed invariably enjoyed smooth passages once there was clear agreement on their content. However, it does not account for the pattern identifiable during the 1763–4, 1767–8 and 1781–2 sessions when exceptional numbers of bills were returned unaltered (Table Eleven), or with respect of whole categories of legislation such as private bills (Table Ten) whose experience was similar. This is not to imply that the British authorities oscillated unpredictably between applying Poynings' Law in a forceful and in a relaxed manner. Rather, there were occasions and issues that encouraged a less assertive approach. An excellent instance is provided by the 1767 supply bill, which included a provision imposing a twenty per cent tax upon absentee placemen and pensioners. Since a similar tax, authorised in 1729, had only been repealed in 1753 there was no objection to the tax *per se*, only to the absence of a clause empowering the King to grant exemptions. With this in mind, the secretary of state, the Earl of Shelburne, instructed Robert Wilmot in December 1767 to check for precedents for '*substantially* alter'd' money bills but conscious of the likely difficulty the amendment of this measure could create in Ireland, the bill was returned subject to two 'literal' amendments only. It was a prudent move, because to have done otherwise would be to risk causing Lord Townshend, then at the outset of his

---

140. 3 Geo III, chap 22 (quit rent act); 3 Geo III, chap 12 (flax act); 3 Geo III, chap 34; 5 Geo III, chap 9 (hempen and flax act, 1763, 1765)

administration, serious embarrassment. There were some who interpreted actions such as these as evidence that the British government was 'afraid' of discommoding Irish opinion, but this was not so. Rather it was a case of ministers concluding that it made no sense to make a costly stand on this comparatively minor matter when there were more important issues pending.[141]

This is not to imply that the Council was disposed in the 1760s and 1770s to apply Poynings' Law in an *à la carte* fashion. If this was so, they would surely not have deemed it appropriate to approve the host of minor, syntactical amendments corrections to which a significant proportion of bills were subject. There are a myriad of examples, such as the replacement of 'then' for 'that' and 'delitory' for 'deletary' in the 1762 drugs and medicines bill; the introduction of 'persons' for 'person' in the 1764 Dublin Society bill; the excision of 'and' in line 17 of the 1765 rum duty bill; the addition of 'the' at a number of points to a variety of other bills during the same session; and the replacement of 'may' with 'shall' in the 1778 Dublin circular road bill.[142] Yet syntactical lapses (such as these and the plenitude of misspellings, wrong tenses, duplication of words, the misuse or omission of prepositions and definite articles)[143] that evaded Irish officials demanded correction since they derived in many instances from mistakes perpetuated by clerks in the course of copying and engrossing bills. In the normal course of events, the location and correction of such faults was accepted by all participants as an intrinsic benefit of the process and, other than the anticipated formulaic reference to 'literal' or 'verbal' amendments, they were rarely the subject of comment. This is not to say that they were perceived as of no significance. The entitlement of the British Privy Council to amend Irish bills derived its legal

---

141. NA, PC2/112 ff 521–3, 525–7; Waite to Wilmot, 3, 22 Dec., Shelburne to Wilmot, 9 Dec., Rigby to Wilmot, 14 Dec. 1767 (PRONI, Wilmot Papers, T3019/5631, 5650, 5633, 5638); Townshend to Shelburne, 3 Dec., Shelburne to Townshend, 19 Dec. 1767 (NA, SP63/425); law officers' report, 11 Dec. 1767 (PC1/8/90 f. 1).

142. 1 Geo III, chap 14; NA, PC2/109 ff 144, 151, 161–2; *Commons Jn. (Irl.)*, vii, 76, 110, 114, 143, 148, 154, 156, 158, 159, 166, 172 (drugs and medicines bill, 1762); 3 Geo III, chap 14; PC2/110 ff 328, 361, 363–5; *Commons Jn. (Irl.)*, vii, 270, 287, 292, 338, 341, 343, 344, 347 (Dublin Society bill, 1764); 5 Geo III, chap 5; PC2/111 ff 449, 465, 467; law officers' report, Irish bills committee minute, 10 Feb. 1765 (PC1/8/5/1, 3); *Commons Jn. (Irl.)*, viii, 71, 72, 100, 104, 107, 110 (rum duty bill, 1765); 5 Geo III, chap 7; PC2/111 ff 543, 547–8, 549–51; *Commons Jn. (Irl.)*, viii, 54, 76, 127, 128, 130, 135, 152 (fisheries bill, 1765); 5 Geo III, chap 15; PC2/111 ff 569, 601–2, 609–10; *Commons Jn. (Irl.)*, viii, 107, 113, 115, 118, 121, 137, 140, 144, 145, 148, 153 (temporary statutes bill, 1765); 17 and 18 Geo III, chap 10; PC2/122 ff 22, 64, 88–9; *Commons Jn. (Irl.)*, ix, 359, 410, 426, 474, 476, 477, 491 (Circular road bill, 1778).

143. For examples, see 11 and 12 Geo III, chap 7; NA, PC2/116 ff 149, 193–4; ('landed' for 'loaded' and 'ale for 'also'); 15 and 16 Geo III, chap 5; PC2/119 f. 230 ('preferred' is misspelled 'prefered', 'usage' as 'usuage' and 'of' as 'off'); 15 and 16 Geo III, chap 8; PC2/119 ff 279, 281, 286–7 ('subsidy' is misrendered 'subsidie'); 17 and 18 Geo III, chap 6; PC2/121 ff 505, 521, 526–7 ('separate' is misrendered 'seperate'); 17 and 18 Geo III, chap 19; PC2/122 ff 52, 118, 133–7 ('damming' is misspelled 'damning'); 19 and 20 Geo III, chap 44; PC2/125 ff 234, 258–9, 265–7 ('practible' is a misrendering of 'practicable'); 19 and 20 Geo III, chap 31; PC2/125 ff 233, 261, 265 ('sins' is a mistake for 'sums').

authority from Poynings' Law, which meant that each of the 'literal' amendments approved between 1761 and 1782 was potentially politically sensitive. The fact that nobody chose to make an issue of such changes during most of this period ought not to obscure this. Of course, this was not the impression that ministers wanted to foster; indeed, their insistence on making 'literal' amendments to the money bills offered the contrary impression. However, they effectively acknowledged this was not the case during the 1779–80 session when, rather than endorse a raft of familiar minor amendments, the Irish bills committee forwarded supply and other bills unaltered that in any other year and at any other point in the session would only have progressed with amendments.[144]

While this action confirms that a significant percentage of the syntactical and orthographic amendments forwarded from the British Council were not strictly necessary, the fact that the inclusion of such minor correctives did not provoke an adverse reaction in Ireland encouraged officials to persist with this practice. As a result, though the percentage of bills returned in an amended form fell during the late 1770s, a high proportion of those returned with amendments in 1777–8, 1779–80 and virtually all 25 returned with amendments in 1781–2 were subject to literal amendments only. These included bills that were referred back to the Irish bills committee in order that their date of commencement could be altered so that it did not antedate their enactment.[145] The alteration of 'your majesty' to 'his majesty' between three and forty-eight times in the supply bills forwarded between 1774 and 1778 can be placed in the same category of minor but necessary alterations.[146] But the fact that clerical errors (omissions, additions, misspellings), abbreviations, orthographic and syntactical mistakes also feature prominently is consistent with the observation that Irish opinion was well disposed to accept amendments made at the British as well as Irish Council boards that clearly improved a measure.[147]

144. 19 and 20 Geo III, chaps 1–3, 5; NA, PC2/124 ff 444, 449–50, 450–3; law officers' report, Irish bills committee minute, 13 Dec. 1779 (PC1/11/183 ff 1, 3, 5, 7,9). Law officers' reports advocating the corrections of the spelling of 'seperate', 'merchandizes', aforesd, sd, commissionrs etc. were allowed pass, when other recommendations to the same effect can be shown to have been embraced (17 and 18 Geo III, chap 16; 19 and 20 Geo III, chap 11).

145. 17 and 18 Geo III, chaps 21, 34, 38–40; NA, PC2/122 ff 25, 26, 53, 120, 121, 133–41, 172, 174–6, 183–6; 19 and 20 Geo III, chaps 14, 15, 18, 21, 22; PC2/125 ff 177–8, 193, 194–5, 203–06, 219, 220, 221–4; Solicitor general's report, 30 June 1780 (PC1/12/19 f. 3). Others acts to experience the alteration to the dates they were implemented include 19 and 20 Geo III, chaps 47 and 48; PC2/125 ff 192, 238–9, 249–51.

146. 13 and 14 Geo III, chaps 1 and 2; NA, PC2/117 ff 353–4, 355–8, 358–61; *Commons Jn. (Irl.),* ix, 59, 60, 69, 70, 71, 72; law officers' report on granting several duties, Dec. 1773 (PC1/9/147 ff 1–3); 15 and 16 Geo III, chaps 1 and 2; PC2/119 ff 230, 234, 237–8, 245–7; *Commons Jn. (Irl.),* ix, 222, 223, 224, 234, 243, 244, 246, 248, 249, 250; 17 and 18 Geo III, chaps 1, 2, 3 and 4; PC2/121 ff 387, 389–92, 392–4, 397–9; *Commons Jn. (Irl.),* ix, 377, 378, 379, 392, 394, 396, 397, 398.

147. See above, pp 152–3, 157, 302; for examples see note 125 above and 21 and 22 Geo III, chap 1; PC2/127 ff 59, 65–6; Memorandum upon Irish bills, 30 Nov 1781 (SP63/477 f. 138) ('plantacions'

This was also true of many of the larger and, by definition, more material amendments that were also approved in significant numbers. The identification of what constitutes a major amendment from the bald listings provided in the minutes of council is not unproblematical since even the smallest changes could exert a profound impact on the purpose of a particular clause and, by extension, of a measure. This is well illustrated by reference to the 1768 bill 'for limiting the duration of parliament' which, as well as an essentially cosmetic redrafting of the preliminaries, was changed in respect of two words only, but the effect of the alteration of 'seven' to 'eight' and '74' to '68' was profound, since this much sought-after bill was transformed from a 'septennial' to an 'octennial act', and the date of the general election from 1774 to 1768.[148] Comparable examples can be cited from among the long sequence of changes that were approved to many bills, but major amendments are generally readily identifiable since they reflected the well-established commitment at the British Council to ensure the law in Ireland mirrored that in force in Britain. This was achieved in different ways. In some instances, objectionable provisions were overcome by the simple excision of an offending clause. This was the solution adopted with respect of the 1762 measures to regulate the price of coal in Dublin by establishing 'public coal yards', which experienced the loss of sixteen crucial lines, and the related measure for continuing several temporary statutes, from which all reference to an act 'to prevent the excessive rise of coals ... in Dublin' was removed.[149] A bill to allow Catholics to take out mortgages on the security of land in Protestant ownership and to provide 'for the security of Protestant purchasers' was altered equally decisively; it was retitled and forwarded minus the clause appertaining to mortgages that made it attractive to Catholics.[150]

changed to 'plantations'); 21 and 22 Geo III, chap 2; PC2/127 ff 60–1, 65–6; SP63/477 f. 138 ('shou'd' corrected to 'should', 'devyce' to 'device', 'colum' to 'column'); 21 and 22 Geo III, chap 3; PC2/127 ff 61–2, 65–6; SP 63/477 f. 139 ('commr' to 'commissioner'); 21 and 22 Geo III, chap 5; PC2/127 ff 68, 76–7, 80–1 ('for' corrected to 'or'); 21 and 22 Geo III, chap 16; PC2/127 ff 237, 268, 280–4 ('exrs' corrected to 'executors', 'therein' to 'thereon' etc.); 21 and 22 Geo III, chap 17; PC2/127 ff 262, 271, 289–90 (repeat of 'such'); 21 and 22 Geo III, chap 20; PC2/127 ff 186, 190, 197–8 ('recognzance' corrected to 'recognizance', 'facia' to 'facias', 'specially' to 'speciality' etc.); 21 and 22 Geo III, chap 38; PC2/127 ff 238, 270, 281–5 ('comptent' corrected to 'competent'); 21 and 22 Geo III, chap 39; PC2/127 ff 265–6, 270–1, 288–9 ('exor' expanded to 'executor'); 21 and 22 Geo III, chap 43; PC2/127 ff 387, 409, 413–6 ('mustard' corrected to 'mustered'; 'messuages' to 'messages' etc.); 21 and 22 Geo III, chap 54; PC2/127 ff 388, 410, 413–6 (ransoming).

148. 7 Geo III, chap 3; NA, PC2/111 f. 522; 2/112 ff 25–6; law officers' report, 10 Jan. 1768 (PC1/9/4 ff 7–8); Minutes of clerk of council, 1 Feb. 1768 (PC4/3); Shelburne to Townshend, 2 Feb. 1768 (BL, Lansdowne Papers, Add. MS 24138); Seamus Cummins, 'Extra-parliamentary agitation in Dublin in the 1760s' in R.V Comerford et al. (eds), *Religion, conflict and coexistence in Ireland* (Dublin, 1990), pp 118–34; Noble to Shirley, 3 Dec. 1767 (PRONI, Shirley Papers, D3531/A/5 p. 20).

149. 1 Geo III, chap 10; NA, PC2/109 ff 115, 190, 195–6; Irish Privy Council letter, 9 Mar. 1762 (PC1/7/15) (Dublin coal, 1762); 1 Geo III, chap 17; PC2/109 ff 144, 189, 195–6 (temporary statutes, 1762).

150. 1 Geo III, chap 12; NA, PC2/109 ff 144, 188–9, 195–6; O'Brien (ed.), *Essays of Maureen Wall*,

As eager as officials at the British Council were to resist changes to the law that, by advantaging Catholics in Ireland, would encourage demands for change in Britain, they had more obvious reasons to be on the alert to safeguard British commercial interests. This is demonstrated by the response to successive heads of bills conveyed from Ireland that sought to replace the extant books of duty rates, which dated from 1661–2 and 1727, with a new book that incorporated valuations 'upon many articles of trade and manufacture of England' that were less favourable. Presented first in the 1762 measure 'for better regulating the collection of the revenue', the bill encountered formidable opponents in the East India Company, which objected to the clauses relating to tea, tobacco and spirits on the grounds that such goods would be able in the future to enter Ireland duty-free, and in the 'merchants and manufacturers of glass', who claimed that the new duties 'had doubled and, sometimes, trebled beyond the old rate'. Determined that duties that would injure the 'English revenue' and act as a disincentive to glass production should not be permitted, the law officers and, following them, the Irish bills committee recommended that the book of rates should be 'laid aside' pending the receipt of a report from the Irish revenue commissioners 'before the next session of the duties hitherto payd and payable on the articles in that book', and the excision of the clauses objected to by the East India Company.[151] This did not prevent the measure becoming law, but the matter of Irish duty levels was not resolved, and two years later the Irish Privy Council communicated another revenue bill incorporating the 'same book of rates'. Informed by the report of the British Commissioners of Customs that the new duties would serve as 'a very great discouragement of the importation of British commodities into Ireland', the bill was forwarded with amendments similar to those approved in 1762: all reference to the book of rates was excised and a clause making specified goods duty free was deleted.[152] Since, parallel with this, the Privy Council recommended once more that the book of rates should be examined by the Treasury Commissioners, the expectation was that the matter would soon be resolved, but this was not so and all reference to the proposed book of rates was deleted from the revenue bill once again in 1766.[153]

As well as prompting a stand-off in respect of the book of rates, the advice of the Commissioners of the Customs guided the law officers and the Irish bills committee when they moderated the bounties favoured in Ireland in the 1766 proposal for the further encouragement of trade and limited the duration of the

p. 89; Cathaldus Giblin (ed.), 'Nunziatura di Fiandra', *Collectanea Hibernica*, 10 (1967), pp 131–2.

151. Above, pp 268–9; 1 Geo III, chap 7; NA, PC2/109 ff 144, 192–3, 198, 199; law officers' report, 8 Apr. Deposition on behalf of glass manufacturers, 7 Apr 1762 (PC1/7/16/1–5).

152. 3 Geo III, chap 21; NA, PC2/110 ff 328, 380–1, 386–8; Whately to [ ], 14 Mar. 1764 (PC1/3058); Irish bills committee report ..., 17 Apr. 1764 (PC1/15/23).

153. Order in Council, 18 Apr. 1764 (PC2/110 ff 391–2); 5 Geo III, chap 16; PC2/111 ff 570, 601, 609–10; Winchilsea to Hertford, 14 May 1766 (PC1/31/A78).

scheme to six years.[154] Two years later, an innovative provision to permit the duty-free importation of wood and iron from the American plantations included in a measure for the further improvement of the revenue was also deleted.[155] Strikingly, neither this nor any of the previous interventions was the cause of protest in Ireland because they were within the parameters of what Irish public opinion was prepared to accept at that point. However, when in 1765, a clause was introduced into a measure to prevent the exportation of corn granting 'the King and Privy Council of Great Britain' a power 'reciprocal with that vested by the said bill in the Lord Lieutenant and Privy Council of Ireland' to prohibit corn exports, it provoked a strong reaction from Charles Lucas in the Commons, and from five peers who protested in the Lords that it struck at the constitutional rights of Ireland. In truth, it broke no new constitutional ground; the British Privy Council was simply affirming a right the Crown had long possessed.[156]

It so happened that this was one of the rare protests directed during the 1760s at a measure that had originated as the heads of a bill, because there were few cases in which the amendments introduced at the British Council touched so directly on points of constitutional sensitivity. More typical were the five folios of changes proposed to mitigate 'the rigorous and severe penalties' provided for in the heads of a bill 'for the more effectually amending the publick roads'. These were admitted to ensure justices of the peace did not 'intimidate and discredit ... subordinate officers of the peace in the execution of their duty'.[157] Similar motives prompted the amendment of the measure to prevent abuses by justices of the peace and the halving of the penalties provided for in the insolvent debtors bill in 1762; the legal exemption of bailiffs from prosecution proposed in the salmon poachers' bill in 1764; the extension of the time from three hours to five days allowed to provide a defendant with the copy of an indictment in cases of high treason; and the clause introduced to protect those falsely arrested and imprisoned for debt in 1768.[158]

As well as its ongoing commitment to ensure the proper administration of justice, the British Council was no less eager to ensure that proper administrative

---

154. NA, PC2/111 ff 601, 609–10, 630, 606, 608, 632–3; law officers' report, 6 May, Commissioners of Customs report ..., 21 May, Privy Council report, 27 May 1766 (PC1/15/30).

155. 7 Geo III, chap 27; NA, PC2/113 ff 125, 165, 171–2; Irish Council letter, 5 Apr. 1768, Townshend to Shelburne, 5 Apr. 1768 (PC1/9/19 ff 7, 9–11).

156. NA, PC2/111 ff 433, 440–1, 442–3; [Winchilsea] to Hertford, 13 Dec. 1765 (PC1/31/A78); Hill, *From patriots to unionists*, pp 101–7; *A collection of the protests of the Lords of Ireland*, pp 101–7.

157. 5 Geo III, chap 14; NA, PC2/111 ff 570, 602–05, 610–11; law officers' report, 6 May 1766 (PC1/8/21 ff 23–6); Winchilsea to Hertford, 14 May 1766 (PC1/31/A78).

158. 1 Geo III, chap 11; PC2/109 ff 115, 189, 195–6 (justices of peace, 1762); 1 Geo III, chap 16; PC2/109 ff 144, 212–14, 214–15 (insolvent debtors, 1762); 3 Geo III, chap 35; PC2/110 ff 356, 379, 386–8; law officers' report, 18 Apr. 1764 (salmon poachers, 1764); 5 Geo III, chap 21; PC2/111 ff 570, 602, 610–11; law officers' report, 6 May 1766 (PC1/8/21 f. 11); Winchilsea to Hertford, 14 May 1766 (PC1/31/A78) (high treason, 1766); 7 Geo III, chap. 25; PC2/113 ff 125, 150, 157–8 (debtors bill, 1768).

procedures were followed. To this end, it was specified that the reference to the 'collector of the county' in the corn preservation and public infirmary bills of 1768 should yield to that of 'vice-treasurer'.[159] The failure to honour the fact that justices of the peace were *ex officio* trustees necessitated the amendment of a sequence of road bills to resolve confusion on this point.[160] In addition to officeholders, a number of road bills were amended to protect the interests of the owners of private property, notably the earl of Hillsborough, who secured the exemption of four manors on his estate from the requirement to pay duty to fund the Lagan navigation.[161] A further manifestation of this concern was provided by the omission of Theobald Wolfe, on the request of Thomas Newland, from a measure for the relief of insolvent debtors. But the commitment to protect individual or family interests was, inevitably, called upon more frequently in respect of private bills; the inclusion of a clause in the Evans/Freke estate bill to ensure the heirs of John Evans were not left destitute and the attention accorded petitioners who feared they would be put at a disadvantage is indicative that this commitment remained strong.[162]

* * *

The orderly manner in which Poynings' Law was applied over several decades began to show signs of strain in the early 1770s. There were two reasons. In the first place, the impact of Lord Townshend's decision to reside for the duration of his viceroyalty and to build up a strong Castle interest rather than rely on the undertakers transformed domestic politics. In the short term, it prompted an intense power struggle as established and aspiring undertakers joined forces in an *ad hoc* arrangement with the vocal if still numerically modest patriot connection to resist what was widely caricatured as a despotic administration. Townshend eventually prevailed, but the longer-term consequence was that Irish politics became increasingly sharply aligned along a Castle-patriot axis, and that political engagement became more confrontational.[163] This was particularly noticeable following the outbreak in 1775 of the American War of Independence.

---

159. 5 Geo III, chap 18; NA, PC2/111 ff 570, 630, 633–5; law officers' report, 13 May 1766 (PC1/8/24 f. 3) (corn bill); 5 Geo III, chap 20; PC2/111 ff 570, 629–30, 633–5; Winchilsea to Hertford, 14 May 1766 (PC1/31/A78) (public infirmaries, 1766).

160. 3 Geo III, chaps 30–2, 36, 37; NA, PC2/110 ff 314, 328, 356, 357, 382 383, 388–9; law officers' report ..., April 1764 (PC1/7/81 ff 5, 6).

161. 3 Geo III, chap 6; NA, PC2/110 ff 170, 271, 279, 282–3; Hillsborough petition, Feb. 1764 (PC1/15/24); law officers' report, 7 Mar., Irish bill committee report, 9 Mar. 1764 (PC1/7/74/1–3); Irish Privy Council letter, 29 Mar. 1764 (PC1/7/86 f. 5).

162. 23 Geo III, chap 23; PC2/111 ff 570, 590, 602; President of the Council to Hertford, 14 May 1766 (PC1/31/A78); Petition of Loughlin Sullivan, 11 Apr. 1764 (PC1/7/84/5); law officers' report on bill for relief of creditors of William Bryan (PC1/7/84/1).

163. See, inter alia, Bartlett, 'The Townshend administration', pp 91–112; 'Viscount Townshend and the Irish revenue, 1767–73' in *RIA proc.* 79C (1979), pp 153–75; Kelly, *That damn'd thing*

Secondly, changes in personnel at the legal helm in Britain, which brought Edward Thurlow and Alexander Wedderburn to the offices of attorney and solicitor general, ensured that a more inquisitorial approach was taken to Irish bills. Thurlow was the more assertive. Appointed solicitor general in March 1770 and attorney general ten months later, he owed his rise to eminence to his membership of the Bedford faction, but it was, John Robinson noted, Thurlow's 'superior abilities' and 'sound … judgement' allied to his forensic skill as a lawyer (he possessed, Horace Walpole observed, a 'solid and deep understanding that penetrated the marrow of an argument') that distinguished him from a majority of his contemporaries. These were his positive attributes; on the negative side, Thurlow acquired a well-deserved reputation for irascibility. He was certainly 'impatient of what he regarded as inefficiency', with the result that, while he earned the grudging admiration and respect of those who recognised his talents, he was actively disliked. This did not bother Thurlow, who was unconcerned that many found him 'overbearing in his opinions', and it was hardly surprising, given his conviction that Britain's colonial possessions should accept their dependent position that he did not extend the sequence of law officers who were content to apply Poynings' Law efficiently rather than strictly.[164]

Thurlow possessed the strength of conviction to leave his mark on the way Irish bills were addressed at the British Council on his own, but this was made still more likely by the appointment of Alexander Wedderburn as solicitor general in January 1771. A Scot and a member of the Grenvillite faction, Wedderburn was also a talented lawyer, but whereas Thurlow was guided by knowledge and by conviction, Wedderburn's star was personal advancement. His object was high office, and while the solicitor generalship satisfied his aspirations for the moment, he was a restless presence in the position. To make matters still more uncertain, Thurlow and he disliked each other. This did not preclude co-operation in the scrutiny of Irish bills, but it introduced an additional degree of unpredictability at a time of augmented uncertainty.

Because of the disruption caused the pattern of parliamentary meetings caused by Townshend's prorogation of parliament in December 1769, Thurlow and Wedderburn's first opportunity to examine Irish bills as a team occurred during the abbreviated Irish session held in the spring of 1771. The absence of supply bills from the legislative menu they were invited to assess made the task easier, and most of the bills were forwarded with little fuss. The fact that it was deemed appropriate to add a clause to four bills stipulating that they should expire at the

---

called honour, part II; James Kelly, *Sir Edward Newenham MP, 1734–1814: the life and politics of a radical Protestant* (Dublin, 2004), chapters 3 and 4.

164. This character sketch of Thurlow draws on Robert Gore-Browne, *Chancellor Thurlow* (London, 1953); Namier and Brooke (eds), *History of parliament: the House of Commons 1754–90*, iii, 529–31; G.M. Ditchfield, 'Lord Thurlow' in R.W. Davis (ed.), *Lords of parliament: studies, 1714–1914* (Stanford, 1995), pp 64–78; I.R. Christie, *The end of North's ministry, 1780–82* (London, 1958), pp 8–9 and the sources cited therein.

'end of the next session of parliament' was noteworthy, but this was consistent with the Privy Council's decision in 1768 that a measure to encourage tillage and navigation by providing a bounty on the transport of corn by sea should remain in force only until 24 June 1770.[165] Moreover, it was a rational response to the tendency of the Irish parliament to assume financial commitments without voting a specific sum for their payment.[166] The law officers rejection of the petition presented on behalf of several trades against the measure to ban 'brick burning' in the vicinity of Dublin was equally justifiable, while the amendments they advanced in respect of a proposal for calling by-elections seemed also to suggest that Poynings' Law would continue to be applied by them in a familiar fashion.[167] The one, telling, pointer that this might not be so was provided by the response to the proposal 'to regulate the trial of controverted elections'. As an Irish version of a British act, no difficulties were anticipated, and the solicitor general's view that the bill was suitable to become law with the addition of a number of amendments 'to facilitate' its implementation, such as had been deemed necessary at Westminster, seemed appropriate. The Irish bills committee certainly thought so, but what should have been a straight forward decision was complicated by the assertion of the attorney general, who submitted a separate report, that the core proposal of the bill that 'a new judicature' of fifteen persons would assume responsibility for determining contested elections constituted 'a mighty change in the constitution of parliament and ... tranch[ed] deep upon the principle of it'. Though there were occasions previously (due usually to illness) when the report on a bill received by the Irish bills committee came from one rather than both law officers, the submission of separate and irreconcilable reports was unprecedented. Obliged, as a result, to decide between them, the Irish bills committee accepted

165. 11 Geo III, chap 1; NA, PC2/115 ff 137, 161, 167–9 (temporary statutes); 11 Geo III, chap 2; PC2/115 ff 137, 161, 171, 178–9, 180–1 (temporary statutes); 11 Geo III, chap 3; PC2/115 ff 136, 159–60, 167–9 (Dublin coal); 11 Geo III, chap 13; PC2/115 ff 137, 160, 167–9 (revenue fraud); PC2/113 f.150; Shelburne to Townshend, 7 May 1768 in *Cal. HO papers, 1766–9*, p. 332 (tillage).

166. See generally, Eoin Magennis, 'Coal, corn and canals: the dispersal of public moneys, 1695–1772' in Hayton (ed.), *The Irish parliament in the eighteenth century*, pp 71–86; 11 & 12 Geo III, chap 4; PC2/115 ff 482, 2/116 ff 84, 91–2; law officers' report, 12 Dec. 1771; Irish bills committee, 25 Feb. 1772 (PC1/9/107, 1, 3); Rochford to Townshend, 29 Feb. 1772 (SP67/14 f. 44): the duration of this act, which relates to the promotion of inland navigation was reduced from 21 to 7 years; 11 & 12 Geo III, chap 26; PC2/116 ff 161, 231, 239–40; law officers' report, 12 May 1772 (PC1/9/118 f. 3): the duration of this, the Lagan Navigation act, was reduced to nine years. It is noteworthy that a measure to encourage tillage by providing a bounty on the land carriage of corn to Cork was respited in 1768 because no provision was made to fund the bounty (PC2/113 ff 151, 159, PC1/9/19 f. 2).

167. 11 Geo III, chap 6; PC2/115 ff 137, 153–4, 158–9, 166–8; Petition of master builders ..., 18 Apr., law officers' report, Apr. 1771 (PC1/9/81 ff 3–6); Wilmot to Lees, 20 Apr. 1771 (Raynham Hall, Townshend Papers) (brick burning bill); 11 & 12 Geo III, chap 10; PC2/115 ff 136, 159, 167–9 (by-election bill).

the direction of the solicitor general and forwarded the bill for engrossment with the amendments and additions he advised.[168]

Since the attorney general was the senior of the two law officers, this was a significant rebuff. Moreover, Thurlow must have felt the slight, though it did not cause him to alter his attitude or his approach. Mention has already been made of the fact that the percentage of bills respited and amended increased during the 1769–76 parliament, but it is apparent also that the proportion of bills recommended for major amendment likewise appreciated. The nature of the amendments proposed in a majority of instances during the 1771–2 session did not differ materially from those proposed in the 1760s. They embraced clauses altering the duration of bills (inland navigation bills); technical and verbal enhancements (the supply bill); and the addition (Grand Canal bill), deletion (the bankrupts, mortgage and burial bills) and recasting (corn bounties and Cork bills) of clauses to ensure public bills were put in appropriate form.[169] Furthermore, Thurlow and Loughborough were so determined to uphold the distinction between private and public bills, they made a particular point of this matter. They touched on this in their reports on the Lagan navigation and Sackville Street bills late in April 1772, and registered their unease on 7 May in respect of the Cork Infirmary bill, of which it was noted the 'principal object of the bill' could have been better achieved by a charter of incorporation, and the Limerick navigation bill, which was, they adjudged, a 'purely private bill … declared to be a public act without any sort of reason'. However, it was the marriage of two 'distinct' bills, one public – a proposal obliging creditors to keep turnpike roads in repair – and one private – a scheme to enable Agmondisham Vesey to enclose part of an old road – in a purported turnpike bill that galvanised them to take a stand. Persuaded that the public part of the bill was 'manifestly unjust' because it placed the burden of checking that turnpike roads between assize towns were kept in good order on judges on circuit, which was 'below the dignity and character of their offices', they successfully urged the excision of the public part of the bill and effectively turned what remained into a 'private' bill.[170]

168. 11 Geo III, chap 12; NA, PC2/115 ff 136, 160, 167–9; Solicitor General's report, 24 Apr., Attorney General's report, 23 Apr. 1771 (PC1/9/80 ff 1–2, 4–5).

169. As note 149; 11 & 12 Geo III, chap 2; NA, PC2/115 ff 481, 487–8, 490–2 (supply); 11 & 12 Geo III, chap 31; PC 2/116 ff 159, 218, 227; law officers' report, [7 May 1772] (PC1/116 ff 11–2) (Grand Canal); 11 & 12 Geo III, chap 8; PC 2/116 ff 151, 183, 189–91; law officers' report, 28 Apr. 1772 (PC1/9/112 ff 5–7) (bankrupts); 11 & 12 Geo III, chap 10; PC 2/116 ff 160, 194, 198–201; law officers' report, 30 Apr. 1772 (PC1/9/113 f. 9) (mortgage); 11 & 12 Geo III, chap 22; PC 2/116 ff 150, 194–5, 198–201;law officers' report, 30 Apr. 1772 (PC1/9/113 f. 9) (burial); 11 & 12 Geo III, chap 9; PC 2/116 ff 159–60, 194, 198–201 (corn bounties); 11 & 12 Geo III, chap 18; PC 2/116 ff 151, 184–5, 192; law officers' report, 28 Apr. 1772 (PC1/9/112 ff 15–6) (Cork).

170. 11 & 12 Geo III, chap 23; NA, PC2/116 ff 160, 217–8, 225–7; law officers' report, 7 May 1772 (PC1/9/116 ff 7–8) (Cork Infirmary); 11 & 12 Geo III, chap 26; PC2/116 ff 161, 231, 239–40; law officers' report, 12 Apr. 1772 (PC1/9/118 f. 3) (Lagan Navigation); 11 & 12 Geo III, chap 13; PC2/116 ff 123, 184, 189–91; law officers' report, 28 Apr. 1772 (PC1/9/112 f. 11) (Sackville

Though the acceptance of the law officers' report on the Vesey/turnpike bill suggested that the Irish bills committee was content to be guided by the recommendation of the law officers, as was the case traditionally, their refusal in some instances to accept the report and, in others, to accept it in part only, was indicative of the unease of the Irish bills committee at the tone and content of some of the reports prepared by Wedderburn and Thurlow. This was not without precedent; it had previously happened in the 1720s, but it was more manifest at this point. In some instances, the points of difference were small. For example, the bills committee's disinclination to take on board the law officers' suggestion in the Oakboy bill that 'haggard' should be altered to read 'hay yard' was common sense, while the alteration of the bill's term was a common place amendment. The points at issue in respect of the bankrupts' and Lagan navigation bills were more significant, but the bills committee's selection was not exceptionable.[171] In other cases, the difference was more substantial. The law officers would, for instance, have deemed it appropriate that the Limerick navigation bill should be rejected because it appertained to private interests and was presented 'without a certain information about them', but this suggestion was ignored and the bill was returned.[172] They likewise felt that the measure appertaining to the requalification of judges and for the remitting of prisoners to be tried 'where the crimes were committed' was 'unnecessary and unfit to pass into law', but the Irish bills committee accepted their recommendation in respect of the former matter only.[173] The committee was more decisive in the case of both the Cork Infirmary and Sackville Street bills. In the case of the Cork Infirmary bill, as well as ignoring the law officers' contention that the bill should not proceed in its current form because it was private, councillors forwarded it with minor amendments when the officers urged that it should only 'proceed' if two clauses appertaining to the trustees and the purchase of property 'on mortmain' were excised.[174] Their judgement was still more categorical in respect of the Sackville Street bill, which the law officers claimed was 'merely private, exceedingly ill-drawn and unfit to pass into law in its present shape' and, because they did not possess the requisite

Street); 11 & 12 Geo III, chap 24; PC2/116 ff 160, 183, 189–91; law officers' report, 28 Apr. 1772 (PC1/9/112 f. 9) (Limerick Navigation); 11 & 12 Geo III, chap 35; PC2/116 ff 159, 219, 227; law officers' report, 7 May 1772 (PC1/116 ff 13) (Vesey bill).

171. 11 & 12 Geo III, chap 5; PC 2/116 ff 112–3, 113–4, 116–7; law officers' report, Mar. 1772 (PC1/9/109 ff 3–4); Suffolk to Townshend, 18 Mar. 1772 (SP67/14 f. 46); 11 & 12 Geo III, chap 26; PC2/116 ff 161, 231, 239–40; law officers' report, 12 Apr. 1772 (PC1/9/118 f. 3) (Lagan Navigation); (11 & 12 Geo III, chap 8; PC 2/116 ff 151, 183, 189–91; law officers' report, 28 Apr. 1772 (PC1/9/112 ff 5–7) (bankrupts).

172. 11 & 12 Geo III, chap 24; PC2/116 ff 160, 183, 189–91; law officers' report, 28 Apr. 1772 (PC1/9/112 f. 9) (Limerick Navigation).

173. 11 & 12 Geo III, chap 34; PC2/116 ff 123, 220–1, 224–5; law officers' report, Irish bills committee minute, 5 May 1772 (PC1/9/115 ff 1, 5–7).

174. 11 & 12 Geo III, chap 23; NA, PC2/116 ff 160, 217–18, 225–7; law officers' report, 7 May 1772 (PC1/9/116 ff 7–8) (Cork Infirmary).

information, 'impossible to be corrected by us'. The Irish bills committee concluded differently; it adjudged that the bill was acceptable and forwarded it without amendment.[175]

The operational and attitudinal tension between the law officers and the Irish bills committee exposed in the course of the 1771–2 session was further in evidence in 1773–4 as the commitment of both men, and of Thurlow in particular, to uphold the legislative authority of the British Council collided with greater frequency with the pragmatic determination of a majority of councillors to avoid problems with an increasingly assertive Irish parliament. This was demonstrated at the outset of the session when, following their receipt of the main supply bills, the Irish bills committee declined to accede to a suggestion from the law officers to include an amendment in the bill for funding the national debt which proposed that rather than apply the book of duty rates referred to in the bill, imports should be taxed 'according to the[ir] real value at the time of importation'.[176] The law officers felt justified in making this suggestion because the goods referred to in the bill were not 'mentioned' in the book of rates, but the Irish bills committee was unwilling to take the risk of modifying such an important measure 'lest', it was explained to earl Harcourt, 'it might appear in Ireland that the duty was originated here, and thereby have given occasion for opposing the whole bill'.[177] It proved a wise call, and the major supply bills made it into law without difficulty.

This was not the end of the money bills, however. In order to meet the requirements of the hard-pressed Irish exchequer for additional income, two new revenue raising measures – a tontine scheme and a stamp tax – were subsequently received. Both, but particularly the latter, were contentious, and the hope of the Irish administration was that they would encounter no problems at the British Council. This aspiration proved unjustified as, in common with previous new money bills, the law officers found much demanding their attention. Extending in one case over eight pages and in the other over four, their reports recommended the extensive rewriting and redrafting of a number of clauses, particularly in the tontine bill, and a host of syntactical corrections and verbal clarifications. Though they would have preferred if it had been otherwise, faced with such a clear delineation of the manifold 'absurdities and errors' in the bills, the bills committee had little option but to take a majority on board, and both bills were returned to Ireland in a much revised state.[178] Irish opinion was disinclined to perceive merit

175. 11 & 12 Geo III, chap 13; PC2/116 ff 123, 184, 189–91; law officers' report, Irish bills committee minute, 28 Apr. 1772 (PC1/9/112 ff 2, 11).
176. 13 & 14 Geo III, chap 38; NA, PC2/117 ff 18, 19–21.
177. 13 & 14 Geo III, chap 2; NA, PC2/117 ff 353–4, 355–6, 358–61; law officers' report, Dec 1773 (PC1/9/147 ff 1–3); Rochford to Harcourt, 17 Dec. 1773 in *Cal. HO papers, 1773–5*, p. 114.
178. NA, PC2/117 ff 354, 362–4, 368–9; law officers' report, 16 Dec. (PC1/10/2 ff 19–24); Irish bills committee minute, 16 Dec. 1773 (PC1/9/148 ff 1–5) (tontine bill); PC2/117 ff 354, 364–7, 368–9; law officers' report, 16 Dec. (PC1/10/2 ff 3–8); Irish bills committee minute, 16 Dec. 1773 (PC1/9/148 ff 3–5) (stamp bill).

in the amendments made, and MPs responded angrily to what they described as the 'very many material differences' they identified in both instances. Encouraged by Walter Hussey, the MP for Athy, an influential, and not exclusively patriot, interest concluded that 'it was necessary to give the most early and striking opposition to such an infringement of the privileges of the Commons'.[179] The response in England to the reports of 'uproar', 'confusion' and 'distress' in Ireland that accompanied the rejection of the bills was ambiguous. The former chief secretary William Gerard Hamilton opined, with characteristic bluntness, that the Irish claim that 'the Privy Council in England have no right to alter a money bill' was 'a pretty conceit'.[180] However, even those like Hamilton who were hostile to such manifestations of Irish assertiveness did not object strongly when, following the receipt of revised tontine and stamp bills from Ireland, the Privy Council deemed it appropriate they should be returned with a few minor alterations. Councillors were assisted to reach this decision by the fact that the newly drafted bills had 'adopted the greatest ... and the most important part ... of the amendments' that the law officers had 'thought proper to recommend'. What was more significant was that they overruled all but two 'very inconsiderable' but 'absolutely necessary' amendments from a longer list received from the law officers to the revised bills.[181]

Though both these measures enjoyed a comparatively trouble-free passage into law, the fact that the Irish parliament nominated a committee to compare the versions returned to them in January with the heads they conveyed in December indicated that the anxiety of councillors to ensure they did not discommode Irish sensibilities was justified.[182] Guided by this, the Irish bills committee continued to consider carefully the reports it received from the law officers. They rejected fewer reports in 1773–4 than they had in 1771–2, but this has to be seen in the context of the fact that the proportion of Irish bills that proceeded unaltered was greater. Moreover, the committee was disposed not to decline to agree to amendments unless they were absolutely necessary because, as Lord Rochford informed Earl Harcourt when returning the proposal to amend the 1756 tillage act, which was transmitted from Ireland without a provision for paying the proposed bounty, 'the King's servants' were sincerely disposed 'to do nothing seriously embarrassing to your administration'.[183] In this instance, the law officers

---

179. Below, p. 305; *Finn's Leinster Journal*, 29 Dec. 1773.
180. Waller to Macartney, 24, 25 [Dec. 1773] in Bartlett (ed.), *Macartney in Ireland*, p. 183; Hamilton to Pery, 12 Jan. [1774] (PRONI, Additional Pery Papers, T3052/33).
181. 13 & 14 Geo III, chap 5; NA, PC2/117 ff 403, 404, 409–10; law officers' report, 8 Jan. 1774 (PC1/10/2 ff 14–7); Irish bills committee report 10 Jan. 1774 in *Cal. HO papers, 1773–5*, p. 166; Rochford to Harcourt, 14 Jan., 22 Feb. 1774 in *Harcourt Papers*, ix, 156–7, SP67/14 f. 244; Leveson-Gower to Harcourt, 14 Jan. 1774 (PC1/31/A78) (tontine bill); 13 & 14 Geo III, chap 6; PC2/117 ff 403, 404, 409–10; law officers' report, 8 Jan. 1774 (PC1/10/2 ff 9–11; Hamilton to Pery, 12 Jan. [1774] (PRONI, Additional Pery Papers, T3052/33) (stamp bill).
182. *Commons Jn. (Irl.)*, ix, 76.
183. 13 & 14 Geo III, chap 11; NA, PC2/117 ff 476, 518, 526–8; law officers' report, 12 Apr. 1774

simply suggested that the text of the measure might be amended to ensure that the bounty did not depress the hereditary revenue. They took a firmer stand in other cases, but in a majority of instances in which it appeared to councillors that an amendment might injure the prospects of a measure, the Irish bills committee declined to take it on board. This was true, for example, of the revenue fraud bill and the Lagan Navigation bill. In the case of the former, the law officers' proposal that the final clause, which related to the collection of the revenue, should be set on the same perpetual grounds as the rest of the bill, was ignored, while, in respect of the latter, the financial and taxation issues that featured prominently among the longer list of amendments proposed for the Lagan navigation bill ensured they too were not accepted.[184]

The law officers do not seem to have resented the manner in which the Irish bills committee responded to their reports. It may be that they were conscious of the fact that their inability always to agree a joint report did not increase their moral authority. In the sole instance of this during the 1773–4 session, the Irish bills committee chose, in a repeat of its decision in 1772, to accept Wedderburn's recommendation that a controverted election bill was appropriate to become law though Thurlow adhered steadfastly to his opinion that 'it was too great an innovation' and should not be returned.[185] They were in agreement on the proposed oath of allegiance, which was, they observed in May 1774, 'founded in wisdom, humanity and justice', though they did tentatively suggest that it would be improved if the reference to the pope's 'dispensing power' was amended.[186] This was not taken up, but more significantly the tentativeness that was a feature of this report was the predominant attribute of several other late session reports. There is no ready explanation, other than that it was a logical outcome of a process that in 1774 seemed *more* about appeasing the Irish legislature, even when bills were described as 'inaccurate', 'useless' or 'mischievous', than it was about correcting errors or ensuring bills were entirely consistent with British law. [187]

This was a noteworthy turnabout on prevailing practice to this point.[188] Since it was a matter of practice rather than of rule, it was not anticipated that it would become a permanent arrangement, but the impact on Irish opinion of the

(PC1/10/9 ff 17–8); Rochford to Harcourt, 20 Apr. 1774 in *Cal. HO papers, 1773–5*, p. 203.

184. 13 & 14 Geo III, chap 8; PC2/117 ff 469, 488, 497–8; law officers' report, Irish bills committee report, 12 Apr. 1774 (PC1/10/7 ff 9–10, 3) (revenue fraud); 13 & 14 Geo III, chap 12; PC2/117 ff 476, 490, 499–500; law officers' report, 8 Apr., Irish bills committee, 12 Apr. 1774 (PC1/10/7 ff 25–32, 6).

185. 13 & 14 Geo III, chap 15; PC2/117 ff 481, 491, 498–9; Solicitor General's report ..., Attorney General's report ..., 11 Apr., Irish bills committee minute, 12 Apr. 1774 (PC1/10/7 ff 32, 34–5, 6).

186. 13'& 14 Geo III, chap 35; PC2/117 ff 481, PC2/118 ff 26, 27–9; law officers' report, 5 May, Irish bills committee report, 10 May 1774 (PC1/10/20 ff 9–11, 2).

187. 13 & 14 Geo III, chaps 45, 46, 47; PC2/117 ff 413, 480, 485, 2/118 ff 18, 19–22; law officers' reports, 6 May, Irish bills committee reports, 6 May 1774 (PC1/10/18 ff 16,14, 18, 2) (chalkers, badging the poor and Dublin baking trade bills).

188. Kelly, 'Monitoring the constitution', pp 105–6.

outbreak in 1775 of hostilities between the Crown and colonists in North America obliged councillors to tread still more carefully. This did not immediately deter the Council from approving amendments to Irish bills, as the high proportion (75 per cent) that was ordered for amendment in 1775–6 attests, but the number fell sharply thereafter (Table Eleven). Consistent with this, the proportion of those subject to major amendment also fell as the law officers and the Irish bills committee contrived to avoid any intervention that could be interpreted as confrontational, particularly with respect to the money bills.[189] This was highlighted in 1776 when in order to secure parliamentary sanction for the release of troops on the Irish army establishment for service in North America, the Irish attorney general Philip Tisdall inserted enabling clauses in a supplementary money bill. The British law officers were troubled by this, but they overcame their doubts as to 'whether the preamble ... carr[ied] the appearance of interfering with the King's undoubted prerogative of disposing the military force of the state', though they could not 'discover, in the matter of the bill, a reason for returning it'.[190] It is evident from this that the law officers adopted the practice in 1775–6 of noting contentious or doubtful points that would previously have prompted a recommendation that a bill should be respited or heavily amended.[191] This left it to the Irish bills committee to decide, and while the committee was not averse to doing so, they intervened on fewer occasions in 1775–6 to overturn, or to accept only in part, the report received from the law officers. They did not, for example, accede to the law officers' recommendation that a measure to explain 'several acts ... relating to the exchange of glebe lands' to 'enable tenants for life to exchange with schools and churches' under more favourable conditions was 'unnecessary'. Two years later, when the law officers deemed an amendment to the 'chalkers' act 'unfit to pass into law' because it did not distinguish between 'a very slight injury' and an 'atrocious one', the bills committee demurred once more and this measure went on to become law.[192] The Irish bills committee also exercised its right, as with the 1776 bill for regulating the trials of peers, to refer a bill back for specific amendments and to introduce amendments of their own, but it did so sparingly.[193]

The measure for regulating the trials of peers was referred back so it could be 'rendered conformable to the statute passed in England'. Though this point was

189. Above, pp 291–2.
190. 15 and 16 Geo III, chap 10; PC2/119 ff 370, 372–3, 374–6; R.E. Burns, 'Ireland and British military preparations for war in America in 1775', *Cithara*, ii (1963), p. 57; Harcourt to Weymouth, 19 Feb. 1776 (NA, SP63/452 f. 65); law officers' report, 26 Feb. 1776 (PC1/11/8 f. 11)
191. The best example is 15 and 16 Geo III, chap 15; NA, PC2/119 ff 370, 395–7, 408–9; law officers' report, 27 Feb. 1776 (PC1/11/8 ff 1–5).
192. 15 and 16 Geo III, chap 17; NA, PC2/119 ff 282, 372, 402, 410–12; law officers' report, 26 Feb. 1776 (PC1/11/78 ff 1–5) (glebes); 17 and 18 Geo III, chap 11; PC2/122 ff 25, 64, 82–4; law officers' report, 5 May 1778 (PC1/11/80 f. 3) (chalkers).
193. 15 and 16 Geo III, chap 29; NA, PC2/119 ff 254, 324, 395, 408–09; law officers' report, 6 Mar. 1776 (PC1/15/81/1) (peers); 15 and 16 Geo III, chap 23; PC2/119 ff 382, 429, 451–2; law officers' report, 12 Mar. 1776 (PC1/11/12 f. 7) (army pensioners).

seldom made quite so explicitly, this remained one of the primary purposes of the process of scrutiny to which Irish bills were subject. Yet because Irish MPs in the late 1770s were more vocal than ever in asserting their right to make law for the kingdom of Ireland untramelled by Poynings' Law, compliance with their instructions was not always forthcoming. It has already been shown that the British Council was unable to induce the Irish legislature to provide specific funding for the payment of bounties sanctioned in successive tillage bills. This concern was raised also with respect of the 1776 measures for promoting fisheries and for supplying the poor of Dublin with coal, but though the law officers averred in their report on the former that 'there never can be a reason for granting a bounty by act of parliament but when a fund is ... provided for paying it', funding was not voted.[194] Guided by these experiences, among other alterations, a limit was imposed in 1776 on the duration for which bounties would be available to subvent flaxseed imports, while two years later a similar restriction was introduced into the measure to provide bounties to promote 'the flaxen and hempen manufactures'.[195]

Perhaps influenced by their fitful success in regulating the granting and administration of bounties, as well as by the problems they encountered in protecting the hereditary revenue, the Privy Council directed that 'all the bills where the equalisation of duties is required' arising out of the concession in the winter of 1779–80 of 'free trade' should be subject to the 'minute attention ... of the several boards ... competent to ascertain these points'.[196] What this meant in practice was that two measures received from Ireland were scrutinised by the Commissioners of Customs and four by the Commissioners of Trade to establish if there was any provision in the bills that would 'operate materially to the prejudice of Great Britain' and, if so, to ensure that 'the particulars mentioned in [each] bill [was] put on the same footing as the trade of Great Britain'. With this in mind, a report was submitted in respect of each bill to the law officers who reported, as usual, to the Irish bills committee, which, in two instances, also sought further guidance from the lords of the treasury. As a result, none of the six measures was forwarded without amendment, but the observations in respect of the proposal 'for ... better regulating the corn trade' that 'no provision in this [bill] ought to give cause of uneasiness' and in respect of the 'tobacco' bill that it 'put the trade of Ireland on the same footing with that of this kingdom' were typical of what occurred in five of the six measures as they made their way into law. Thus amendments to provide adequately for trade beyond the Cape of Good

194. 15 and 16 Geo III, chap 19; NA, PC2/119 ff 254, 424–5, 450–2; law officers' report, 6 Feb. 1776 (PC1/11/3 f. 1) (fisheries); 15 and 16 Geo III, chap 32; PC2/119 ff 382, 426, 451–3; law officers' report, 12 Mar. 1776 (PC1/11/12 f. 9) (temporary statutes).
195. 15 and 16 Geo III, chap 4; NA, PC2/119 ff 227, 241–2, 245–7; law officers' report, 11 Dec. 1775 (PC1/10/100 ff 12–4) (flax seed); 15 and 16 Geo III, chap 7; PC2/121 ff 505, 520–21, 526–7 (flax and hemp).
196. Bathurst (President of the Council) to Buckinghamshire, Aug. 1780 (NA, PC1/31/A78).

Hope and to correct some errors in the schedule of duties were introduced into the bill 'for the advancement of trade'; the bounty on biscuit exports was excised and a number of clarifications were introduced into the export regulations in the corn trade bill; the size of the casks in which tobacco was imported was set down in the tobacco bill; the Faroe Islands were embraced within the linen export bill; while a reference to the provision of a bounty on the export of biscuit was removed, and new clauses added with respect of corn and grain to the tillage bill.[197]

The bill that encountered most difficulties appertained to the regulation of the sugar trade. Received from Ireland with the claim that the duties fixed on muscavado, white and refined sugar of a colonial origin were set at a rate 'similar to that paid on the same articles in Great Britain', and those from elsewhere set at a prohibitive level 'in order to preserve the manufacture of refining in Great Britain and Ireland', the bill and a petition from the sugar refiners of London were referred to the Commissioners of Trade and Plantations. It was the Commissioners task to establish 'what duty should be laid in Ireland on refined sugar from Britain so as to leave British and Irish refiners as near as possible in the same situation they have hitherto been', and since the London refiners alleged that the duty proposed in Ireland 'was in effect a prohibition', the Commissioners entered into a 'minute investigation' of the issues involved. This necessitated taking evidence from the London refiners, the Commissioners of the Customs and William Knox, the under secretary, over several days. The report they issued did not satisfy the Irish bills committee which called in the ubiquitous London refiners, and it was referred back for additional information 'on the value of molasses, scum and bastard sugars', as well as for a statement on the duty required 'to prevent the ordinary importation of foreign sugars to the prejudice of the British or West India trade'. This necessitated further consultation with the London sugar refiners, arising out of which the Irish bills committee concluded that the level of duties imposed on foreign sugar imported to Ireland, on refined sugar imported from Great Britain and on muscavado imported from the West Indies should be raised significantly. They would have preferred to raise them still

197. 19 and 20 Geo III, chap 11; PC2/125 ff 191, 285–6, 295–6; law officers' report, 27 July 1780 (PC1/12/27) (advancement of trade); 19 and 20 Geo III, chap 17; PC2/125 ff 191, 241, 263, 321–2, 295–6; Report of the board of Trade, 17 July, Irish bills committee minute, 3 Aug. 1780 (PC1/12/22, 29 ff 1, 14–5); *Journal of Commissioners of trade 1776–82*, pp 322–3, 324, 327 (corn trade); 19 and 20 Geo III, chap 23; PC2/125 ff 191, 229, 313–4, 320–1; Solicitor General's report, 6 July 1780 (PC1/12/20 ff 1–4); Irish bills committee minute, 3 Aug. (PC1/12/29 f. 1); Minutes of Clerk of Council, 1764–95, 6 July 1780 (PC4/2) (tobacco); 19 and 20 Geo III, chap 33; PC2/125 ff 191, 229, 314, 320–1; Solicitor general's report, 6 July, Minutes of Clerks of Council, 1764–95, 6 July 1780 (PC4/2); Irish bills committee minute, 6 July 1780 (PC1/12/20 ff 5–6); *Journal of Commissioners of trade 1776–82*, pp 324–5, 327 (linen and hempen manufacture); 19 and 20 Geo III, chap 24; PC2/125 ff 191, 241, 263, 316, 318–19, 321–2, 356–7; solicitor general's report ..., 11 July 1780 (PC1/12/20 f. 5); Report of the board of Trade ..., 17 July (PC1/12/22); Irish bills committee minute, 3 Aug. (PC1/12/29 f. 1); Minutes of Clerks of Council, 1764–95, 13, 18 July 1780 (PC4/2) (advancement of trade).

higher, but since their recommendation was enough to ensure the bill was decisively rejected in Ireland, the matter remained unresolved.[198]

Though the experience of these bills illustrates the continuing sensitivity of the British Council to be seen to protect British commercial interests, the tone of these reports was distinctly less assertive than those produced by Thurlow and Wedderburn in 1771–2 and 1773–4. None the less, the law officers did not deviate in their commitment to the high standards of legal analysis that was a feature of their reports, as revealed by their commentary on the bill for preventing revenue fraud:

> This bill repeals the duties now payable to His Majesty for bread and biscuit exported for which no reason is assigned either by the bill or the lord lieutenant's letter accompanying it. By the 33 Geo II, chap 10 sec 56, two-thirds of the duty of excise is drawn back upon exportation; by the 5 Geo chap 19, sec 10, 3d. a gallon more is drawn back upon which it is computed that no more excise will remain upon spirits exported than 1/3 d. per gallon. By the act of the present session 4d. a gallon is imposed as an additional duty on all spirits made in Ireland. The present bill recites that out of the last mentioned act, there hath been omitted *by mistake* a clause for allowing the *drawback* without stating what *drawback* in particular and proceeds to allow the drawback of *all the inland excise*. This stretch seems to be contrary to the policy of the former acts, which seem to have retained part of the inland duty upon exportation as a check upon a compensation for the frauds that would probably be committed by vending at home spirits pretended to be made for exportation. How far this object is material or how far it is compensated by the additional duty or how far even it was intended to draw back more than the additional duty is humbly submitted to your Lordships.[199]

Guided by forensic examinations of this ilk, the law officers identified and the Irish bills committee endorsed amendments, corrections and revisions to non-contentious bills during the 1770s that were as far-reaching as any made during the eighteenth century. The change of personnel, caused by Thurlow's promotion to the woolsack in 1778, which saw Wedderburn become attorney general and

---

198. NA, PC2/125 ff 177, 195, 230, 261–2, 311–13, 319, 320–1; Irish Privy Council letter, 1 June 1780 (PC1/12/17); Buckinghamshire to Hillsborough, 15 June (2) (SP63/469 ff 340, 344–5); law officers' report, 26 June (PC1/12/18 f. 13); *Journal of the Commissioners of trade and plantation, 1776–82* (London, 1938), pp 317–27; Minutes of Clerk of Council, 6, 13, 18 July 1780 (PC4/2); Irish bills committee minute, 18 July (PC2/1/12/24 ff 5–6), 3 Aug. 1780 (PC1/12/29 f.1); *Commons Jn. (Irl.)*, x, 186.

199. Law officers' report on *An act for the improvement of His Majesty's revenue and the more effectual preventing of frauds therein* ... (NA, PC1/11/8 ff 1–5). For a still longer example relating to the exchange of glebe lands see PC1/11/7.

James Wallace solicitor general, did not prompt any significant alteration in style, though there were a larger number of separate reports, which enabled Wallace to achieve a higher profile than was usual for solicitors general.[200] This did not disrupt the recent practice of the Irish bills committee cherry-picking from the list of recommended amendments presented by the law officers, as happened with respect of the attorney general's report on the army regulating bill in 1780. It also did not put an end to the practice of re-referring bills, such as those to prevent frauds by bankrupts and for the relief of tenants holding leases for lives, for particular amendment.[201] However, both were resorted to with less frequency by the early 1780s, as the law officers and the Irish bills committee found more ready agreement on the amendments they introduced into Irish bills. Thus, as well as the various changes already chronicled, in the course of the 1775–6, 1777–8 and 1779–80 sessions the British Council mitigated overly harsh penalties (plundering of ships bill);[202] secured extant property interests (roads and tenants bills);[203] prevented restrictive electoral legislation (potwalloping votes bill);[204] clarified defective drafting particularly in bills appertaining to the regulation of charitable institutions and charities (Foundling Hospital, Limerick House of Industry and Vaughan Charity bills),[205] and dealt judiciously with politically pregnant measures appertaining to Catholic relief, the establishment of a militia and the repeal of the requirement to subscribe to a sacramental test.[206]

They did this, moreover, while taking due notice of what Irish opinion was likely to accept. The most striking index of this is provided by the augmented number of bills that negotiated the British Council unaltered during the late 1770s (Table Eleven). Each session was unique, but the successful intervention of

200. See, for examples, NA, PC1/12/18, f. 1; PC1/12/19 f. 1.
201. 19 & 20 Geo III, chap 16; NA, PC2/125 ff 233, 315–6, 320–21; Attorney General's report, Irish bills committee minute, 3 Aug. 1780 (PC1/12/29 ff 19–23, 1) (regulating the army); 19 & 20 Geo III, chap 25; PC2/125 ff 247, 259–60, 284, 286–7, 265–7, 295–6; Solicitor general's report, 17 July, law officers' report, 26 July (PC1/12/23 ff 3, 9); Minutes of the Clerks of Council 1764–95, 26 July 1780 (PC4/2) (bankrupts fraud); 19 & 20 Geo III, chap 30; PC2/125 ff 234, 240–1, 278, 287–8, 295–6; Minutes of the Clerks of Council 1764–95, 22 July 1780 (PC4/2) (tenants bill).
202. 15 & 16 Geo III, chap 33; NA, PC2/119 ff 382, 429, 451–3; law officers' report, 12 Mar. 1776 (PC1/11/12 f. 11).
203. 15 & 16 Geo III, chap 13; NA, PC2/119 ff 283, 321–4, 333–4; law officers' report, [Feb. 1776] (PC1/11/2 ff 8–11) (roads bill); 19 & 20 Geo III, chap 30; PC2/125 ff 234, 240–1, 278, 287–8, 295–6; Minutes of the Clerks of Council 1764–95, 22 July 1780 (PC4/2) (tenants bill).
204. 15 & 16 Geo III, chap 16; NA, PC2/119 ff 283, 417–21, 423; law officers' report, 6 Mar. (PC1/11/11); Irish bills committee minute, 9 Mar. 1776 (PC1/15/81/6).
205. 15 & 16 Geo III, chaps 25, 35, 38; NA, PC2/119 ff 370, 381–2, 394, 427–9, 451–2, 463–5, 467–72, 478–80, 480–2; law officers' reports, 12, 22 Mar. 1776 (PC1/15/81/8–11, PC1/11/16 ff 7–10, 11–7).
206. 17 & 18 Geo III, chap 49; NA, PC2/122 ff 316–7, 354–5; Weymouth to Buckinghamshire, 24 July 1778 (NA, SP63/460 ff 354–6) (Catholic relief); 17 and 18 Geo III, chap 13; PC2/122 ff 51, 151–3, 167–9; Amendments to public bills, 10 June 1778 (SP63/460 ff 237–30) (militia); 19 & 20 Geo III, chap 6; PC2/124 ff 585–6, PC2/125 ff 1–2 (sacramental test).

the earl of Buckinghamshire in August 1780 in support of tillage and sugar bills offered a clear indication of the by now strong commitment to conciliate Irish concerns. Buckinghamshire was prompted to take this step by his receipt of minutes from the Irish bills committee which suggested that the tillage bill should be 'postponed' because 'no fund is provided by the bill for the payment of the bounties thereby granted', and the sugar bill set aside because the level at which the Irish bill set the duty on imported foreign sugar was 'not set high enough to answer as a prohibition and for the exclusive encouragement of the British sugar colonies'. Alarmed lest these concerns should derail two popular bills and prove right those critics of 'free trade' who argued it could only be secured by the concession to Ireland of legislative independence, Buckinghamshire pointed out to councillors that their unease in respect of the coastal bounties provided for in the tillage bill was unwarranted because it would be more than compensated for by a decline in 'inland bounties'. He conceded that in principle 'a specific fund should be provided for their discharge', but did not think this appropriate in this case. His position with respect of sugar was more conciliatory. He communicated a new bill, which took on board the 'several alterations' made at the Council, but his observation that 'the duty may easily be made agreeable to the opinions of the Lords of the Council … in a future session' made it clear that the tense political environment in Ireland was 'sufficient to induce a reconsideration' of both bills.[207]

The preparedness of the British Council to respond positively to Bucking-hamshire's last-minute intervention with respect of the tillage bill pointed forward to the 1781–82 session when, with the demand for legislative independence in Ireland in full cry, the British Council was at its most co-operative in the near three-hundred year history of Poynings' Law. The most striking measure of this is provided by the fact that an unprecedented 70 per cent of the Irish bills received at the British Council board were returned without amendment (Table Eleven). Moreover, it is clear that this was a result of intense activity behind the scenes as, even more so than Buckinghamshire, his successor, the earl of Carlisle, and his chief secretary William Eden, lobbied vigorously for the return of specific bills 'unaltered'. They were induced to do this in the first instance by the rejection on its return of a 'favourite' measure – the flax seed bill – because of the insertion of a reference to the Faroe Islands.[208] However, as the demand for legislative independence intensified, and as the threat of 'embarrass[ment] and disgrace' increased in parallel so too did the force of their rhetoric. Eden's characterisation of one amendment as 'a flimsy, absurd alteration of the most petulant and

---

207. For the tillage bill (19 & 20 Geo III, chap 34) see Solicitor General's report on tillage bill, 11 July (NA, PC1/12/20 f. 5); Irish bills committee minute, 3 Aug. (PC1/12/29 f. 1); Buckinghamshire to Hillsborough, 16 Aug., Porten to Clerk of Council, 20 Aug. 1780 (PC1/12/33 ff 1–4, the former letter can also be located at SP63/470 ff 260–2); for the sugar bill (19 & 20 Geo III, chap 35) see PC2/125 ff 355, 356–7; Buckinghamshire to Hillsborough (2), 16 Aug., Porten to Clerk of Council, 20 Aug. 1780 (PC1/12/32 ff 1–3, SP63/470 ff 263–5).
208. Eden to Hillsborough, 22 Dec. 1781 (BL, Auckland Papers, Add. MS 34418 f. 221).

offensive kind' and of its introduction as an act of 'criminal folly and hardened thoughtlessness', was his most categorical intervention, but it was only marginally more forceful than Carlisle's comment, and it served the useful purpose of putting ministers and councillors on the defensive and of ensuring that amendments that would otherwise have been approved were not proceeded with.[209] In the case of the tobacco trade bill, which was raised by both Carlisle and Eden, this ensured the unprecedented restoration of a clause respecting an £8 allowance 'for draught' for each hogshead on the grounds that the 'clause standing in the bill did not appear to the Lords of the Council of such importance as to weigh against any risque of the bill being thrown out in Ireland on account of the amendment'.[210] More importantly, it helped to ensure that sensitive bills were treated gingerly at the Council board, though this involved, as the secretary of state, Lord Hillsborough, informed Carlisle, 'dispensing with some forms and avoiding every possible cause of delay'.[211] In reality, the 'forms' to which Hillsborough alluded did not involve any significant deviation from established procedures. What was different was the responsiveness of the Council board to the increased number of requests received from Ireland that bills other than money bills were returned without 'alteration' so they did not fall on their return.[212] As a result, bills that would, at any other time, have been sidelined (respited or postponed) or returned with substantive amendments negotiated the British Council without difficulty. Among their number were measures to regulate the sugar trade, to promote the linen manufacture, to regulate the trials of controverted elections, to extend the right of *habeas corpus*, to combat revenue fraud, to facilitate the recovery of the King's debts, to regulate the corn trade, and many more.[213] Equally significantly, when the Council received a query from the duke of Portland in May as to why a 'popular bill [to regulate and encourage partnerships] ... earnestly expected by the mercantile part of the kingdom' had

---

209. Eden to Hillsborough, 21 Dec. 1781 (BL, Auckland Papers, Add. MS 34418 f. 224). Carlisle claimed that the amendment would 'break the credit and tranquillity of my government ... and [would] be followed by a long train of inconveniencies and hazardous consequences': Carlisle to Hillsborough, 18 Dec 1781 (NA, SP63/477 ff 193–4).

210. Clerk of Council to Attorney general, 14 Dec. (NA, PC2/127 f. 94); see also Carlisle to Hillsborough, 22 Dec 1781, Eden to Porten and enclosure, 20 Jan. 1782 (SP63/477 f. 203, 63/480 ff 91–4).

211. Hillsborough to Carlisle, 24 Dec. 1781 (NA, SP63/477 f. 195).

212. Eden to Porten, 3 Nov., Carlisle to Hillsborough, 29 Dec. 1781 (NA, SP63/477 f. 40, SP63/480 f. 8).

213. 21 & 22 Geo III, chap 6; NA, PC2/127 ff 67, 77, 80–2; law officers' report, 13 Dec. 1781 (PC1/12/96) (sugar trade); 21 & 22 Geo III, chap 8; PC2/127 ff 117, 134, 136–7 (linen manufacture); 21 & 22 Geo III, chap 10; PC2/127 ff 117, 134, 135–6 (controverted elections); 21 & 22 Geo III, chap 11; PC2/127 ff 118, 134, 135–6 (habeas corpus); 21 & 22 Geo III, chap 15; PC2/127 ff 222, 223–4, 228–9 (revenue fraud); 21 & 22 Geo III, chap 20; PC2/127 ff 186, 190, 197–8 (King's debts); 21 & 22 Geo III, chap 24; PC2/127 ff 237, 271, 281–5 (Catholic relief); 21 & 22 Geo III, chap 36; PC2/127 ff 238, 272, 282–5 (corn trade).

not yet been returned, the bill was immediately activated and returned.[214] And symbolically, when Barry Yelverton's bill 'to regulate the manner of passing bills and to prevent delays in summoning of parliament', which deprived both the Irish and British Privy Councils of the right they had long possessed under Poynings' Law to respite and to amend Irish bills was received on 28 June, it was promptly processed and returned without amendment.[215] Yelverton's act was not the last bill to be subjected to this procedure, but the expeditious manner with which it was certified was typical of the experience of a majority of bills in 1781–82.

Ironically, the non-interventionist approach favoured at this time did not suit those interests, such as Dublin Corporation, who had long employed the right to petition the British Council to resist objectionable legislation emanating from the Irish parliament. Reference has already been made to the skill with which they and others used this entitlement to delay the plans to move the Custom House downriver, and they contrived to use it again in 1782 to oppose legislation appertaining to the paving of the streets of the capital and for the 'improvement of the police'. They objected to the latter on the grounds that it constituted 'a most injurious attack upon their chartered rights' since it would, if enacted, empower 'strangers to act as magistrates within the … city', but, other than a few minor changes, both this and the paving bill were returned to Ireland virtually unaltered.[216] Other interests were more effective. On foot of a petition presented by the earl of Arran against the controversial 1780 tenantry bill on the grounds that it would 'involve every person … interested in … tenures [of leases for lives containing covenants for perpetual renewals] in tedious and troublesome disputes', the law officers' initial instinct was that the bill needed more consideration and should 'not [be] returned at present'. However, following the direction of the Irish bills committee that 'the objections which have been stated' by Arran should be reconsidered, the law officers introduced a page of amendments protecting the interest of landowners, and the bill was forwarded to become law.[217] Changes to protect the interests of individuals, as in the case of the 1776 elections bill which, if approved unaltered, would have raised the voting qualification in potwalloping boroughs to £20 and two years residency, and the 1780 bill vesting the estates of Sir Henry Cavendish in trustees so he could pay off his public debt also seemed to vindicate the value of petitioning.[218] However,

---

214. 21 & 22 Geo III, chap 46; PC2/127 ff 222, 332, 326, 333; Portland to Shelburne, [early May], Nepean to Clerk of Council, 6 May, Irish bills committee minute, 7 May 1782 (PC1/12/109).

215. 21 & 22 Geo III, chap 47; PC2/127 ff 423, 428, 430–3.

216. Above, pp 278–9; 21 & 22 Geo III, chap 60; PC2/127 ff 265, 278, 357–8, 364–6; Petition of Dublin Corporation, May 1782 (PC1/2/116 f. 3). The police bill was rejected by the Commons on its return.

217. 19 & 20 Geo III, chap 30; PC2/125 ff 234, 240–1, 278, 287–8, 295–6; Minutes of the Clerks of Council 1764–95, 13, 22 Jul. 1780 (PC4/2); law officers' report, 18, 27 Jul. (PC1/12/26 ff 5–8); *Freeman's Jn.*, 20 July 1780.

218. 19 & 20 Geo III, chap 51; NA, PC2/125 ff 325, 330, 336–7, 339–40; law officers' report, 17 Aug. 1780 (PC1/12/30 ff 5–6); Heron to Cavendish, 3 Aug. 1780 (SP63/470 f. 201) (Cavendish

the reality was that the percentage of bills subject to petition at the British Council declined from 7 per cent during the early Hanoverian era to 3.5 per cent between 1761 and 1782. There is no definitive explanation for this, as petitioners continued to be afforded a full hearing, but the greater willingness in the 1770s to deny the petitions of British mercantile interests, was undoubtedly a factor.[219] So too was the diminution in the need for Catholic interests to petition as the threat of penal legislation subsided. The upshot was that 537 or 93 per cent of the bills received at the British Council board were deemed suitable to return to Ireland to become law. This was an increase of less than five per cent on the percentage approved during the early Hanoverian period. But what this comparatively modest figure occludes is the many smaller and subtler changes that occurred in the manner in which Poynings' Law was applied. This was more in evidence during the late 1770s, and it ensured that the reality of Irish legislative dependence was significantly less confining during the 1781–2 session than it was twenty years earlier.

THE IRISH PARLIAMENT AND THE MAKING OF STATUTE LAW, 1761–82

Nearly 91 per cent of the bills returned to Ireland from the British Privy Council between 1761 and 1782 received the royal assent. In the main, this was without complication. Three days was the minimum time required for bills 'to pass through the Commons in due form', and the process could be even quicker in the Lords.[220] Delays were more likely to be incurred in the house of parliament in which bills had taken their rise, particularly when they returned in an amended form. Since the percentage of bills amended at the British Council was higher than the percentage of bills lost on their return (for the period 1761–82 they numbered 49: (9 per cent), which was down 2 per cent on the figure for the early Hanoverian period), it is apparent that, in keeping with custom and practice, MPs seldom objected to 'verbal' or 'literal' amendments when it was apparent that they improved a bill or, at the least, did not alter its thrust or purpose. As a result, most of the amendments made at the British and at the Irish Councils were incorporated into law. This was the case even for money bills, which were subject to closest scrutiny.

    bill); 15 & 16 Geo III, chap 16; PC2/119 ff 283, 312, 417–21, 423; law officers' report, 6 Mar., Petition of Sir James Cotter et al., 5 Feb. 1776 (PC1/11/11); Minute of Irish bills committee, 9 Mar. PC1/15/81/6); *Hibernian Journal*, 20 Mar. 1776 (elections).

219. 11 & 12 Geo III, chap 6; PC2/116 ff 150, 152–3, 161–2, 164–5; law officers' report, 15 Apr. 1772 (PC1/15/89); Rochford to Townshend, 23 Apr. in *Cal. HO papers, 1770–2*, p. 492; Gordon to [Townshend], 3 Apr. 1772 (Yale University, Sterling Library, English Misc MSS, 1766–72) (rum bill); 17 & 18 Geo III, chap 8; PC2/122 ff 25, 63–4, 82–4; Irish bills committee minute, 4 May (PC1/15/117); Petition of Norwich merchants, 15 Apr. 1778; Minutes of Clerks of Council 1764–95, 15 Apr. 1778 (PC4/2) (malsters).

220. Townshend to Shelburne, 21 May 1768 in *Cal. HO papers, 1766–9*, p. 341.

The main mechanism available to peers and MPs to establish if the heads of a bill that had taken its rise in the Irish parliament was returned to them in an amended form was the committee of comparison. This was not a new structure; an *ad hoc* committee of this nature had been established by the House of Lords in 1695, and many road and other bills were routinely compared from the early eighteenth century.[221] The Commons deemed it more appropriate to proceed otherwise. They ordered in 1734 that 'every member who brings in a bill do compare it with the heads sent from this house, and to report the alterations', but this did not prove successful; and it was only in the 1760s that an attempt was made to incorporate it into the routine workings of the House of Commons. In May 1764, it was resolved as a standing order 'that no bill shall pass the House until a committee of this House shall compare the transmiss with the original heads of a bill, and report if any and what alterations have been made therein to the House'.[222] Practical considerations dictated that this 'standing order' was not enforced, even with respect of money bills, though its existence encouraged its more frequent invocation in the routine of parliamentary business. The House of Lords, for example, determined in May 1766 to establish a committee to compare the bill 'to prevent … tumultuous risings' with the original transmiss.[223] What appears to have happened is that rather than an arrangement whereby a committee of comparison was automatically triggered by the admission of a bill, such bodies were only established on a motion of the House and that this was only resorted to in respect of money bills, and then not in all instances. Committees of comparison were requested in respect of other sensitive legislation, but, as in the case of money bills, they were usually appointed on a motion of the House *after* it had become apparent that the heads of a bill had been amended in a manner that was deemed objectionable.[224] This was the case, for example, with the 1765 bill to prohibit the exportation of corn, which enjoyed a difficult passage into law. Significantly, following the bill's approval, a motion affirming that 'the House was induced by the apprehension of a famine to pass the said bill, notwithstanding the addition annexed to it after the heads had been sent from the House, and that the same ought not hereafter be drawn into precedent' failed to receive the required support.[225]

Recourse to the committee of comparison, particularly with respect of money bills increased in the 1770s. This was a manifestation, in part at least, of the prevailing adversarial political atmosphere, but it was prompted in the main by the

221. James, *Lords of the ascendancy*, pp 75, 199 note 23; *Lords Jn. (Irl.)*, ii, 278.
222. *Commons Jn. (Irl.)*, iv, 133, vii, 357; viii, 67; David Lammey, 'A study of Anglo-Irish relations between 1772 and 1782, with particular reference to the 'free trade' movement' (PhD, QUB, 1984), p. 128.
223. *Lords Jn. (Irl.)*, iv, 378.
224. This conclusion is based on the index entry on the committee of comparison in the *Commons Journal*. This subject would repay more systematic analysis.
225. *Commons Jn. (Irl.)*, viii, 70, 74; Rigby to Wilmot, 29 Dec. 1765 (PRONI, Wilmot Papers, T3019/5149); Magennis, *The Irish political system*, pp 184–5.

heightened public disquiet with Poynings' Law that accompanied the emergence of a more assertive political patriotism.[226] In addition, there were incidents, such as occurred in 1771, when the implicit understanding that the British Council should introduce only 'literal' amendments to supply bills was breached. Ironically, this was by accident rather than by design. The main supply bill, which was received at the British Council board on 10 December 1771 was subject to the usual scrutiny, as a result of which it was amended at three points. Two of these were not 'inconsiderable', as the secretary of state, the earl of Rochford, disingenuously maintained, but the exemption of British herrings from the 'new duty laid upon herrings imported' and Hamburg linens 'passing thro' England' were hardly likely to stir the ire of a majority in the House of Commons. However, the bill also excluded a mention of 'cottons', which prompted an upsurge of disquiet. Suspicion that 'Ireland was meant to be sacrificed to Manchester in that branch of manufacture' caused the vocal patriot interest to cry foul, and resentful former undertakers joined with them in alleging 'that no less than the right of parliament, the constitution of this kingdom [was] at stake; [for] if we consented to the altering of a money bill, there was an end of parliament'. The chief secretary, George Macartney, was taken aback since he believed, with Lord Rochford, that the amendments made to the bill at the British Council were the 'usual inconsiderable alterations', so when he discovered, on comparing the original bill with the duplicate, that the reference to cotton had been omitted as a result of a 'clerical error' at the engrossing stage, he was not without hope that he might be able to appeal to MPs common sense and save the bill. However, the Commons were not to be mollified. Guided by Henry Flood, who argued forcefully that this was a matter of 'principle', and that any alteration, accidental or otherwise 'was an infringement of their rights', MPs refused to lay aside the defective bill and to recommence their consideration of the money bill with the duplicate. Persuaded that the whole affair was 'an experiment' orchestrated by 'despotic and tyrannical' ministers 'to try Irish passiveness', the Commons formally 'rejected' the bill on the suggestion that it should proceed to third reading stage.[227] Ministers and officials in Britain were understandably embarrassed that they had 'given an occasion of triumph to the opposition'. They were, as a consequence, particularly attentive to requests that the new supply bill was not altered 'in any national respect' and it was processed with 'extraordinary dispatch' on its way to become law.[228]

226. Below, pp 319–23.
227. NA, PC2/115 ff 481, 487, 490–1; law officers' report, 12 Dec. (PC1/9/97); Rochford to Townshend, 14 Dec. (SP67/14 f. 40); Garnett to Hardwicke, 21 Dec. (BL, Hardwicke Papers, Add. MS 35610 f. 101); *Hibernian Journal*, 23, 27 Dec. 1771; Townshend to Rochford, 21, 22 Dec. in *Cal. HO papers, 1770–2*, pp 351–3; Longford to Bective, 26 Dec. 1771 (NLI, Headfort Papers, F/5/91).
228. 11 & 12 Geo III, chap 1; NA, PC2/115 ff 481, 487, 490–1, 507, 507–8, 508–9; Rochford to Townshend, 28 Dec. 1771, Townshend to Rochford, 1 Jan. 1772 in *Cal. HO papers, 1770–2*, pp 355, 411; Thomas St George to Hardwicke, 1 Jan., 12 Feb. 1772 (BL, Hardwicke Papers, MS 35610 ff 113, 135); Waite to Wilmot, 30 Dec. 1771, Macartney to Wilmot, 1 Jan. 1772 (PRONI, Wilmot Papers, T3019/6259, 6171).

It was asserted privately that because the revised supply bill adopted 'the amendments made in England' to the initial bill, 'the House [of Commons] had in effect acquiesced in H[is] M[ajesty]'s prerogative', but this made no impression in Ireland. Moreover, the fact that the revised bill enjoyed a trouble-free journey onto the statute book, generated a measure of false confidence in both the British government and the Irish administration that no long-term damage had been done. This was not the case, for though it has been shown that the British Council's preparedness to confine the amendments it made to the main supply bills to 'verbal' and 'literal' matters during the 1770s assisted these bills become law, it did not prevent problems with supplemental supply bills such as the tontine and stamp measures introduced in 1773–4. Both these bills were rejected by the Irish parliament as a result, not of the number (though they were numerous in each instance) but of the import of a minority of the amendments introduced at the British Council. These, it was argued to a receptive audience of MPs, infringed 'the privileges of the Commons', and they responded in anticipated fashion by rejecting both bills, thereby obliging the Irish administration to prepare new versions in order that they could raise the required revenue consistent with the Commons' insistence 'that the English ministry [*sic*] should not dare to attempt any alteration of their bills'.[229] This ought to have established clearly the ground rules from the perspective of the Irish parliament, but two years later the problem arose again. In this instance, MPs used their power of veto to reject one of the main supply bills and the stamp bill for the session. Both bills were subject to many amendments, overwhelmingly of a minor character, but the reports of the committee of comparison in both instances indicated that a number of more significant amendments had also been made. The change that excited most attention was the omission of two clauses in the supply bill relative to the authorisation of 4000 troops on the Irish army establishment to serve abroad. This amendment gave rise, Harcourt confided, to more 'violent heats ... than have appeared ... since I came to Ireland', but resentment at the addition of a clause appertaining to the powers of officers of the stamp department' was also strong, and both bills were rejected.[230] The loss of five money bills in the Commons in three sessions amply attested to the determination of MPs in the early 1770s to assert their authority in respect of the raising of revenue, as well as to the disruption they could cause during any session in which their 'rights' were not acknowledged. The fact that no money bill was lost in similar circumstances in the subsequent six years indicated it was a lesson well learned.

229. Above, pp 291–2; NA, PC2/117 ff 354, 362–7, 368–9; law officers' report on stamp bill, on tontine bill, ... 16 Dec. 1773 (PC1/10/2 ff 3–8, 19–24); *Finn's Leinster Journal*, 29 Dec. 1773; *Commons Jn. (Irl.)*, ix, 74.

230. NA, PC2/119 ff 230, 235–6, 251–3; [John Almon], *Narrative of proceedings ... in the parliament of Ireland* (London, 1777), pp 118–23; Harcourt to Weymouth, 22 Dec. 1775 in *Cal. HO papers, 1773–5*, p. 506; Harcourt to Weymouth, 28 Jan. 1775 (SP, 63/451 ff 7–10); Harcourt to North (2), 21 Dec., Blaquiere to Germain, 30 Dec. 1775 (Gilbert Library, MS 93 ff 329, 332–6);

The House of Commons was not content to assert its authority solely in respect of money bills, however. As the place of origin of the overwhelming majority of heads of bills, it was eager to affirm its role as the source of all Irish legislation. They did so, among other devices, by rejecting more bills than the House of Lords. Nearly two-thirds of bills that failed on their return to Ireland came to grief in the Commons (Table Eleven), and many, like the money bills considered above, were rejected because of amendments introduced at the British Council. The evidential chain is not always complete, but a persuasive case can be made that this was so in respect of the 1762 and 1764 measures to regulate the baking trade, the 1762 measure to amend the law in relation to the flaxen and hempen manufacture; the 1764 Kilworth–Tipperary road bill, which was heavily amended in response to a petition; the Newcastle–Cork road bill; the 1774 measure for the improvement of the casual revenue; the 1774 salmon bill, which was amended in response to a battery of petitions from a variety of interests whose intervention secured the removal of the proposed ban on weekend fishing; and the sugar trade bill of 1780 in which the duty was altered.[231] The intervention of the Irish Council was hardly less welcome, but because of the lack of records it is particularly difficult to identify with certitude what bills were lost as a consequence of amendments made by that body. It can be established for a fact that the 1766 private bill for the relief of Hugh White and his creditors was 'rejected' by MPs because of the excision of a 'material paragraph' at the Irish Council because no such alteration was made at the British Council.[232] It is tempting to assume that this is true also of those bills that stumbled in the Irish parliament having negotiated the British Council either with no amendment or minimal alteration. If this is correct, it would explain the demise of bills for preventing frivolous and vexatious arrests and for improving the salaries of curates by better securing tithes in 1764; a bill to regulate building in Dublin city

Harcourt to North, 22, 24 Dec. 1775 in *Harcourt Papers*, x, 61–2, 66; *Commons Jn. (Irl.)*, ix, 244 (money bill); PC2/119 ff 234, 239–40, 245–7; Harcourt to Weymouth, 22 Dec. 1775 in *Cal. HO papers, 1773–5*, p. 506; *Commons Jn. (Irl.)*, ix, 244 (stamp bill).

231. NAI, PC2/109 ff 115, 190, 195–6; *Commons Jn. (Irl.)*, vii, 164, 165 (baking trade bill, 1762); PC2/109 ff 116, 150–1, 161–2; *Commons Jn. (Irl.)*, vii, 158, 159, 163 (flax and hemp, 1762); PC2/110 ff 264–5, 317–8, 330–1, 333–4; Petition of Cornelius O'Keeffe, 7 Mar. 1764 (PC1/3058); *Commons Jn. (Irl.)*, vii, 336, 337, 338, 339 (Kilworth-Tipperary bill, 1764); PC2/110 ff 356, 358, 381–2, 386–8; Petition of Woodruff Drinkwater, [5 Apr.], law officers' report, 14 Apr. 1764 (PC1/7/88 ff 3, 5); *Commons Jn. (Irl.)*, vii, 350 (baking trade, 1764); PC2/111 ff 568, 579, 586–7; *Commons Jn. (Irl.)*, viii, 137, 140, 144, 145 (Newcastle-Cork road, 1766); PC2/117 ff 481, 488–9, 497–8: law officers' report, 12 Apr. 1774 (PC1/10/7 ff 11–2); *Commons Jn. (Irl.)*, ix, 133, 134, 135, 136 (casual revenue); PC2/117 ff 482, 493, 520–21, PC2/118 24–5, 27–9; Petition of mayor of Limerick, 16 Apr. , law officers' report, 10 May 1774 (PC1/10/20 ff 7, 22); *Commons Jn. (Irl.)*, ix, 147, 151 (salmon, 1774); PC2/125 ff 177, 195, 230, 261–2, 311–13; law officers' report, 26 June 1780 (PC1/12/18 f. 3); Irish bills committee, 18 July 1780 (PC1/12/24 ff 5–6; *Commons Jn. (Irl.)*, x, 186 (sugar, 1780).

232. PC2/110 ff 357, 384, 391; *Commons Jn. (Irl.)*, vii, 351.

in 1766; a bankrupts' bill in 1778; flax bills in 1780 and 1782; a qualification bill in 1780; and Dublin police, freeholder registration, prisons and a road bill (Clonmel) in 1782, but other factors may also have played a part.[233] These were all lost in the Commons; the House of Lords was responsible also for the rejection of a significant number of bills that experienced little or no amendment at the British Council board. It may be that these were rejected because of amendments made at the Irish Council, though the strength of clerical opposition has also to be taken into account in a number of instances. This was certainly a factor in the demise in 1771 and 1774 of bills to allow Catholics lend money to Protestants on mortgage; it was probably the case with the 1774 measure to facilitate Church of Ireland clergy to reside in their benefices, which was subject to minor amendment only at the British Council board and, possibly the case with the 1782 measure to prevent the marriage of lunatics.[234] A less obvious argument can be made for the 1771 bill to prevent delays of justice, and the 1782 measure to continue several temporary statutes, which was the subject of a petition from Dublin Corporation, but if these bills were amended after an objectionable fashion at the Irish Council their failure to become law was facilitated by other factors.[235]

While is obvious why both houses of the Irish legislature resented the right of the Irish and British Privy Councils to interfere with their legislative deliberations, they were as intent as ever on resisting attempts to extend the authority of both Councils. This was a long-standing position and it explains the rejection by the Commons in 1768 of two quite different bills arising out of amendments (introduced at the British Council) extending to the British Council powers originally intended to apply only to its Irish equivalent.[236] Furthermore, both houses of the legislature continued to regard the legislative initiatives of the

233. NAI, PC2/110 ff 264, 278, 280–1; *Commons Jn. (Irl.)*, vii, 329, 331, 333, 338, 341, 353 (frivolous arrests, 1764); PC2/110 ff 356, 379, 386–8; *Commons Jn. (Irl.)*, vii, 350, 351, 354, 355 (curates salaries, 1764); PC2/111 ff 570, 573–4, 605, 612–13; *Commons Jn. (Irl.)*, viii, 137, 139, 1441, 143, 145 (Dublin building, 1766); PC2/122 ff 73, 153, 167–9; *Commons Jn. (Irl.)*, ix, 495, 497, 498 (bankrupts, 1778); PC2/124 ff 585–6, 2/125 ff 1–2; law officers' report, 22 Feb. 1780 (PC1/12/7); *Commons Jn. (Irl.)*, x, 86, 89, 90, 91, 97, 100, 165 (flax and hemp bill, bill, 1780); PC2/127 ff 69–70, 76, 80–1, 252, 271, 288–90, 265, 268, 278, 280–4, 357, 364–5, 388, 410, 413–16; *Commons Jn. (Irl.)*, x, 336, 337, 338, 339, 340, 341, 345, 347, 369, 371 (flax seed bill, freeholders bill, Dublin police bill, gaols bill, Clonmel roads bill, 1782).

234. NAI, PC2/115 ff 137, 160, 167–9; *Lords Jn. (Irl.)*, iv, 558, 564, 566 (mortgages, 1771); PC2/117 ff 448–9, 518, 526–8; *Lords Jn. (Irl.)*, iv, 759 (mortgages, 1774); PC2/117 ff 481, 515, 524–8; *Lords Jn. (Irl.)*, iv, 749 (clerical residence, 1774); PC2/127 ff 238, 271, 281–5; *Lords Jn. (Irl.)*, v, 238, 248, 298, 306 (lunatics, 1782).

235. NA, PC2/115 ff 137, 158–9, 167–9; *Lords Jn. (Irl.)*, iv, 557, 566 (delays of justice, 1771); PC2/127 ff 252–3, 269, 280–4; *Lords Jn. (Irl.)*, v, 288, 291, 298, 305 (temporary statutes, 1782).

236. This was an issue with respect of the 1768 bills to prevent the exportation and the distilling of corn (PC2/113 ff 118, 130–1, 133–5; Law officers, report, 18 Apr. 1768 (PC1/9/12 ff 1–2); *Commons Jn. (Irl.)*, viii, 259, 261, 263); and the alteration of judges commissions (PC2/113 ff 13, 150, 156–7; Whately to Grenville, 21 May 1768 in *Grenville Papers*, iv, 196–7; Waite to Wilmot, 12 May 1768 (PRONI, Wilmot Papers, T3019/5754); Townshend to Shelburne, 14 May 1768 in *Cal. HO papers, 1766–9*, p. 338; *Commons Jn. (Irl.)*, viii, 267, 270)

other with some suspicion, and to avail of the opportunity presented by the fact that each had to approve the other's bills to reject those they deemed objectionable. Significantly, the Lords were the more demanding in this respect. Four bills, each appertaining to issues that the episcopal bench jealously guarded, failed on these grounds. This embraced two bills (1762, 1764) to prevent the 'misapplication of money' donated for charitable purposes, a bill to enable Catholics to lend money to Protestants on mortgages of land (1772), and a measure that included the ascertaining of tithes on flax among its provisions.[237] In addition, seven further bills that took their rise in the Commons and that only needed the approval of the Lords to become law were not admitted for the consideration of peers in 1782. Since these embraced subjects as diverse as parliamentary reform, the education of Catholics, small debts, jury service and church leases, there is no obvious reason for this.[238]

In keeping with this pattern, only one bill returned from the British Council board was not presented to the Irish parliament for its consideration, and this would not have happened but for a 'mistake' at the Irish bills committee. The measure at issue appertained to the controversial subject of the tenure upon which judges held office. Forwarded by the law officers with the recommendation that it should be returned with an amendment providing for a role for the Irish Council in the dismissal of judges, the decision of the Irish bills committee to reject the law officers' report was not recorded in error and the bill was returned to Ireland in an altered form. The readiness with which Lord Shelburne owned up to the mistake helped to ensure it caused no ill feeling, and a new bill made it to the statute book before the end of the session.[239] Compared with the Lords, the Commons was more positive in its response to the smaller number of bills that arose in the Lords to which it had to respond. Only two – a measure dating from 1772 for the encouragement of timber and another dating from 1782 for the 'furtherance of justice' – were deemed inappropriate to become law and respited.[240]

237. NA, PC2/109 ff 116, 151, 161–2; *Lords Jn. (Irl.)*, iv, 245; *Commons Jn. (Irl.)*, vii, 154, 157, 158, 159 (charitable uses, 1762); PC2/110 ff 356, 379, 386–8; *Lords Jn. (Irl.)*, iv, 279, 305; *Commons Jn. (Irl.)*, vii, 350, 351, 355, 357 (charitable uses, 1764); PC2/116 ff 160, 204, 208–9; *Lords Jn. (Irl.)*, iv, 664; *Commons Jn. (Irl.)*, viii, 552, 553, 554, 556 (mortgages, 1772); PC2/116 ff 160, 196, 198–201; *Lords Jn. (Irl.)*, iv, 658; *Commons Jn. (Irl.)*, vii, 548, 459, 551, 552 (flax, 1772).
238. NA, PC2/127 ff 388, 410, 413–6; *Commons Jn. (Irl.)*, x, 370, 372, 373, 375 (elections); PC2/127 ff 265, 271, 281–5; *Commons Jn. (Irl.)*, x, 336, 339, 344, 345 (Catholic education); PC2/127 ff 265, 271, 281–5; *Commons Jn. (Irl.)*, x, 338, 341, 346 (juries); PC2/127 ff 252, 272–3, 282–5; *Commons Jn. (Irl.)*, x, 337, 340, 345, 347 (public roads); PC2/127 ff 388, 411, 416–18; *Commons Jn. (Irl.)*, x, 370, 374, 375 (mortgages); PC2/127 ff 422, 428, 430–33; *Commons Jn. (Irl.)*, x, 372, 375, 377, 378 (church leases).
239. 21 & 22 Geo III, chap 50; NA, PC2/127 ff 70, 269–70, 281–5, 387, 410–11, 416–18; *Commons Jn. (Irl.)*, x, 213, 220, 226, 355, 360, 361, 370, 371, 374, 376, 384, 385; Shelburne to Portland, 3 May 1782 (NA, HO122/1 ff 9–10).
240. NA, PC2/116 ff 123, 217, 224–5; law officers' report, 7 May 1772 (PC1/9/116 f. 5); *Lords Jn. (Irl.)*, iv, 590, 595, 657, 663; *Commons Jn. (Irl.)*, viii, 561, 563, 564, 565 (timber cultivation);

CONCLUSION

As a consequence of the fact that 48 bills acceptable to the British Council board failed to win the approval of the Irish legislature, a total of 488 acts made it to the Irish statute book between 1761 and 1782. An overwhelming 85 per cent of these were public bills and the remainder private, which was a rise of nearly four per cent on the proportion of public bills approved during the early Hanoverian era (Tables Six to Eleven).

Remarkably, the proportion of bills and heads of bills initiated in Ireland that made it to law remained virtually static at 55 per cent. Where the two periods diverged significantly was in respect of the volume of law that was made. An average of over fifteen laws more per session were enacted in the parliamentary sessions held between 1761 and 1782 than during the early Hanoverian era. This is the most convincing statistical pointer, not just of the increased busyness of the Irish legislature, but also of its increasing legislative ambitions. The fact that this occurred while Poynings' Law remained on the statute book indicates that the Law did not, of itself, curtail the legislative capacity of the Irish parliament. However, mounting resentment in Ireland at the legislative dependence it ordained combined with the preparedness of the Council in the late 1770s and early 1780s to apply the law in a manner that took greater cognisance of its critics indicated that for political as well as for legislative reasons its reform was now timely.

PC2/127 ff 252, 272, 282–5; *Lords Jn. (Irl.)*, v, 290, 291; *Commons Jn. (Irl.)*, x, 346, 347 (furtherance of justice).

TABLE NINE

THE LEGISLATION OF THE IRISH PARLIAMENT, 1761–82: PUBLIC BILLS

	Ireland			Ireland				England							Ireland		
	Origins of (heads of) bills			Lost heads of bills				Irish Privy Council bills and heads of bills at the Privy Council							Bills at the Irish parliament		
				House of Commons		House of Lords	Privy Council								Rejected		
Session	Privy Council bills	House of Commons heads	House of Lords heads	Leave only	Rejected			Received	Respited/ postponed	Amendments	No amendments	Petitions against	Approved	Not presented	Commons	House of Lords	Received royal assent
1761–2	4	31	1	3	4		2	27	5	18	4		22		2	1	19
1763–4		62	4	4	8		11	43	1	23	19	4	42		4	1	37
1765–6		52	2	2	13	2	3	34	4	25	5	3	30		2		28
1767–8		55	4	9	6		8	36	6	14	16		30		2		28
1769	2	13	1	10	1		1	4		3	1		4		1		3
1771		23	3	3	6		1	16	1	8	7	1	15			2	13
1771–2		71	11	5	16	2	15	44	4	25	15	2	40		3	2	35
1773–4		85	10	8	15	3	9	60	7	26	27	2	53		3	3	47
1775–6		70	4	6	12	2	8	46	6	34	6	2	40		2		38
1776	3							3		1	2		3				3
1777–8		73	8	6	12	4	8	51	1	28	22	2	50		1		49
1779–80		88	5	14	13	3	5	58	4	29	25	3	54		3		51
1781–2		90	12	8	10	3	1	80		24	56	1	80	1	6	9	64
Total	**9**	**713**	**65**	**78**	**116**	**19**	**72**	**502**	**39**	**258**	**205**	**18**	**463**	**1**	**29**	**18**	**415**

Sources: NA, Privy Council Registers, PC2/1; Privy Council papers, PC1; Commons Journals (Irl.); Lords Journals (Irl.).

TABLE TEN

THE LEGISLATION OF THE IRISH PARLIAMENT, 1761–82: PRIVATE BILLS

	Ireland							England						Ireland		
	Origins of (heads of) bills			Lost heads of bills				Irish Privy Council bills and heads of bills at the Privy Council						Bills at the Irish parliament		
	Privy Council bills	House of Commons heads	House of Lords heads	House of Commons		House of Lords	Privy Council	Received	Respited/ postponed	Amend-ments	No amend-ments	Petitions against	Approved	Rejected		Received royal assent
Session				Leave only	Rejected									House of Commons	House of Lords	
1761–2		9						9			9		9			9
1763–4		15		2			2	11		1	10	1	11	1		10
1765–6		13	3	1			4	9		5	4		9			9
1767–8		6						8		3	5	1	8			8
1769		1					1									
1771			1					1					1			1
1771–2		8	1					9	2	4	3		7			7
1773–4		7	1				1	7		6	1		7			7
1775–6		3	1		1		1	2		2			2			2
1776																
1777–8		12	3	2	1		4	8		1	7		8			8
1779–80		7			2			5		3	2		5			5
1781–2		9	1		1			9	2	1	6		7			7
Total		90	11	5	5		13	78	4	27	47	2	74	1		73

Sources: NA, Privy Council Registers, PC2/1; Privy Council papers, PC1; Commons Journals (Irl.); Lords Journals (Irl.).

THE LEGISLATION OF THE IRISH PARLIAMENT, 1761–82: PUBLIC AND PRIVATE BILLS

Session	Ireland — Origins of (heads of) bills: Privy Council bills	House of Commons heads	House of Lords heads	Lost heads of bills — House of Commons: Leave only	House of Commons: Rejected	House of Lords	Privy Council	England — Irish Privy Council bills and heads of bills at the Privy Council: Received	Respited/ postponed	Amendments	No amendments	Petitions against	Approved	Not presented	Ireland — Bills at the Irish parliament — Rejected: Commons	Rejected: House of Lords	Received royal assent
1761–2	4	40	1	3	4		2	36	5	18	13		31		2	1	28
1763–4		77	4	6	8		13	54	1	24	29	5	53		5	1	47
1765–6		65	2	2	13	2	7	43	4	30	9	3	39		2		37
1767–8		61	7	10	6		8	44	6	17	21	1	38		2		36
1769	2	14	1	10	1		2	4		3	1		4		1		3
1771		23	4	3	6		1	17	1	9	7	1	16				14
1771–2		79	12	5	16	2	15	53	6	29	18		47		3	2	42
1773–4		92	11	8	15	3	10	67	7	32	28	2	60		4	2	54
1775–6		73	5	6	13	2	9	48	6	36	6	2	42		2	2	40
1776	3							3		1	2		3				3
1777–8		85	11	8	13	4	12	59	1	29	29	2	58		1		57
1779–80		95	5	14	15	3	5	63	4	32	27	3	59		3		56
1781–2		99	13	8	11	3	1	89	2	25	62	1	87	1	6	9	71
Total	**9**	**803**	**76**	**83**	**121**	**19**	**85**	**580**	**43**	**285**	**252**	**20**	**537**	**1**	**31**	**17**	**488**

Sources: NA, Privy Council Registers, PC2/1; Privy Council papers, PC1; Commons Journals (Irl.); Lords Journals (Irl.).

Part Three

Legislative Independence, 1782–1800

CHAPTER SIX

The meaning and implications of legislative independence, 1782–1800

POYNINGS' LAW WAS AMENDED, not repealed, in 1782. As a result, the Irish legislature was liberated from the requirement to provide the Crown with the 'causes and considerations' necessary to obtain royal authorisation to assemble and, because it was no longer bound to secure prior approval for its legislative decisions, from the obligation to initiate legislation in the form of heads of bills. This important innovation, along with the repeal at Westminster (in 1782) of the Declaratory Act of 1720, and the ratification (in 1783) of the Renunciation Act, which formally recognised the right of the Irish parliament to make law, constituted the legal basis of the claim that the Irish parliament was 'legislatively independent' between 1782 and the Act of Union. However, because legislation arising with the Irish parliament still required the royal assent, which involved the attachment of the great seal of Great Britain, and this function remained with the British Privy Council, the bills of the Irish parliament continued to be conveyed to the British Council where they were examined, and reported on, in order to establish if it was proper they should pass and, on their return to Ireland, formally received the royal assent there in order than they should become law. This meant that the British Council was still entitled to veto Irish legislation and, though councillors sought in the main to employ other, less confrontational, strategies, the preparedness of the then lord lieutenant, the Marquis of Buckingham, to advise in 1788 that a bill he deemed 'absurd' should not be returned in order 'to keep up the practice of rejecting in the English [sic] Privy Council' indicates that it was not a redundant power.[1] Moreover, because the British Council maintained a large degree of procedural continuity in the way it engaged with Irish bills, ministers with responsibility for or interest in Irish affairs were still in a position after 1782 to monitor Irish legislation, and to use the avenues remaining to them to comment on content, to suggest amending legislation, which proved the preferred tactic in problematic cases and, on occasions, to decline to return objectionable bills. The role afforded the Irish Council after 1782 was narrower, but because it was the body responsible for certifying and conveying bills to Whitehall, which necessitated the attachment of the great seal of Ireland, it too continued to play a part in the process of making Irish law. At any event,

---

1. Buckingham to Grenville, 1788 (NA, HO100/23 f. 221; HMC, *Fortescue*, i, 315).

Poynings' Law continued to exert an influence (albeit much reduced) on the manner in which law was made in Ireland.

Though the relaxation in the intensity with which Poynings' law was applied, during the late 1770s particularly (chapter 5), indicates that the constitutional changes effected in 1782 can plausibly be presented as the culmination of a process rather than the outcome simply of political pressure, Poynings' Law would not have been modified but for the efforts of a coalition of patriot interests during the late 1770s and early 1780s. They did not promote a carefully conceived programme of constitutional reform, however, because of the inherent fissiparousness of the patriot interest meant they never developed an agreed plan, and because the reflexive eagerness of a majority of the Anglo-Irish political nation to do nothing that would endanger the Anglo-Irish nexus encouraged them to proceed in an *ad hoc* fashion. Yet, because these events are central to an understanding of the constitutional arrangements brought into being in 1782 and the subsequent history of Poynings' Law, it is appropriate that they are considered in the first instance.

REFORMING POYNINGS' LAW, 1760–82

Explicit criticism of Poynings' Law was muted until the 1750s because the representatives of the Protestant interest in Ireland were broadly content to operate within the parameters of the heads of bills process since it afforded them a major say in what law was made.[2] Moreover, overt opposition was inhibited by the fact that MPs contrived during this time both to curb the right of the Irish Privy Council to initiate law and to extend their own authority over the revenue-raising function. It was not until political consensus began to unravel in the 1750s, primarily as a consequence of the money bill dispute, that Poynings' Law became a political issue. This was hastened by the emergence of a stronger patriot interest in the House of Commons from the mid-1750s, while the growth of more assertive popular media, symbolised by the foundation in 1763 of the *Freeman's Journal*, and of a radical populist voice, whose most notable exponent was Charles Lucas, from 1761 to 1771 MP for Dublin, encouraged debate in the expanding public sphere.[3]

The primary focus of constitutional reform during the 1760s was provided by the demand to limit the duration of parliament. Support for a measure permitting general elections every seven or alternatively for ten years appreciated following the 1761 general election, but successive attempts in the early 1760s to give it the force of law foundered on the rocks of vested interests in the Irish and British

---

2. Above chapter 4, pp 152–3, 157.
3. See pp 152–3, 157; Robert Munter, *The Irish newspaper, 1660–1760* (Cambridge, 1966); Harris, *Politics and the nation*, p. 203; James Kelly, 'Political publishing, 1700–1800' in Raymond Gillespie and Andrew Hadfield (eds), *The Oxford history of the Irish book: the Irish book in English 1550–1800* (Oxford, 2005), pp 227–8.

Privy Councils.[4] Responding to the 'matchless arrogance' of the Irish Council in refusing to certify a septennial bill in the spring of 1764, the *Freeman's Journal* printed an extended analysis of Poynings' Law in which it was argued that the decision of the Irish Council to respite the bill was an abuse of power. The anonymous author of this commentary did not deny that the Council was acting legally in doing so, but he contended that it was a right that could only be justified in *extremis*, and that its application in this instance was an exercise in despotism.[5]

Charles Lucas took up and promoted this argument. Having denounced the insertion of a provision empowering the British Council to suspend the imposition of an embargo on grain exports in a bill for that purpose as the transfer of 'the dispensing power' from Ireland to Britain, he asserted simplistically in a public letter to the lord mayor, aldermen, sheriffs, commons, citizens and freeholders of Dublin in 1765 that Poynings' Law was responsible for creating a system whereby power was 'left to the arbitrary determination of one or two servants of the Crown, whose beings depend upon the breath of the Minister, and who approve, alter, or reject such heads of bills at his pleasure or their own'.[6] Lucas was strongly drawn to the argument, beloved of eighteenth-century advocates of reform, that the grievances of which they complained, in this case Poynings' Law, were inconsistent with the 'ancient constitution'. And in a 'second address' to the same metropolitan audience in 1766, he asserted that Poynings' Law was 'a breach of the original compact' empowering the legislature to make law; specifically, he alleged that by approving this measure, parliament had altered the constitution 'by alienating, transferring, diminishing, sharing [and] dividing the legislative power'.[7] Lucas and his allies were scornful of those who justified Poynings' Law, but for MPs like Alexander McAuley, who defended it as the outcome of a reforming impulse, or the controversialist William Henry, who welcomed the fact that it rendered the people of Ireland 'dependent upon the people of England', the position taken by Lucas was unwelcome because it threatened the stability of the Anglo-Irish connection.[8] This accusation was not made simply for rhetorical effect as the impact of the rejection of successive septennial bills and more general resentment at the interference by both the British and Irish Privy Councils with Commons' legislation prompted a renewed effort in the mid-1760s to make Poynings' Law a political issue. It commenced on 24 January 1766 with an attempt by Lucius O'Brien to convince MPs to agree a

4. Above, pp 260, 274–5; Kelly, 'Monitoring the constitution', pp 100–1.
5. *Freeman's Journal*, 17 Mar. 1764.
6. [Charles Lucas], *The address of Charles Lucas M.D. to the right honourable the lord-mayor, the aldermen, sheriffs, commons, citizens and freeholders of Dublin* (Dublin, 1765), p. 4; Vincent Morley, *Irish opinion and the American revolution, 1760–83* (Cambridge, 2002), pp 54–7.
7. Charles Lucas, *A second address to the right honourable the lord-mayor, the aldermen, sheriffs, commons, citizens and freeholders of Dublin* (Dublin, 1766), p. 10, cited in Gerald McCoy, 'Court ideology', p. 97.
8. Alexander McAuley, *Septennial parliaments vindicated* (Dublin, 1762), p. 5; William Henry, *An appeal to the people of Ireland* (Dublin, 1749), p. 10 cited in McCoy, 'Court ideology', pp 98–9.

resolution in favour of curbing the powers of the Irish Council. This was denied, but a month later, on 28 February, a request was made for leave to introduce the heads of a bill to 'explain' the 3 and 4 Philip and Mary, chap 4, passed in 1557, 'declaring how Poyning's [*sic*] Act shall be expounded and taken'.[9] This was 'negatived on division', 83 to 56, but Edmund Sexten Pery took everybody, including the procedurally ill-informed Speaker, John Ponsonby, by surprise when he moved a few days later that MPs should expunge a resolution agreed in 1614 by which the Commons acknowledged 'that the sole power and authority to transmit such bills as are to be prepared in parliament doth rest with the Lord Deputy and Council'. Since even the House of Lords was prepared at this point to assert that all bills that took their rise with them should be returned, it was probably less of a shock to officials than they suggested that Pery's motion was approved. It was troubling, none the less, and while Castle officials conspired with an embarrassed Ponsonby to neutralise the 'dangerous tendency' of Pery's motion by annulling 'the whole of the proceedings' on the spurious grounds that the clerk had made an 'error', the episode contributed to the growing strength of political feeling on the issue.[10]

This was underlined by the reception accorded these actions by an increasingly politicised public. The master, warden and brethren of the Guild of St Luke showed the way in the winter of 1765–6 when they lauded Lucas's effort 'to preserve the remnant of our constitution inviolate' by opposing the alterations made at the British Council to the heads of bill to prevent the exportation of grain. The Corporation of Weavers and other guilds in Dublin and elsewhere concurred, as support for the reform of Poynings' Law came to feature more prominently on the agenda of the parliamentary opposition and their supporters.[11] The limitation of the duration of parliament was commonly perceived as more realisable, and the key to the achievement of further reforms, but the amendment of Commons' bills by the Privy Council was regarded with increasing hostility. Henry Flood, the leading patriot of the day, made this apparent when he observed in the sixth of his Philadelphus letters, published in February 1768, that the Irish Privy Council was 'a sort of wen or excrescence that has grown out of the corruption of our constitution, and is nourished solely by its distemper'. He justified this disparaging depiction by reference to the old argument that the original purpose of Poynings' Law had been perverted since it was 'never meant to grant any additional privileges to the viceroy and council, or to abrogate from the senate any of its former rights', and that claims to the contrary were inconsistent with 'the letter or the spirit of the law':

9. *Commons Jn. (Irl.)*, viii, 105.

10. Seamus Cummins, 'Opposition and the Irish parliament', pp 211–2; A short sketch of the political history of Ireland (NLI, Joly Papers, MS 29 f. 41); *Lords Jn. (Irl.)*, iv, 378; Michael McDonagh, 'Journals of the Irish parliament', *Irish Ecclesiastical Record*, 10 (1917), pp 298–9; Magennis, *The Irish political system*, pp 187–8.

11. *Freeman's Journal*, 31 Dec. 1765, 4 Jan. 1766; Morley, *Irish opinion*, pp 54–5; *A letter to the right hon. J[ohn] P[onsonby] of the H[ouse] of C[ommons] of Ireland* (Dublin, 1767).

[U]pon a forced and unwarrantable construction of this very act, our Privy Council, these guardians of our constitution, have not only presumed to claim, but dared to exercise, powers which would, if submitted to, render our senates the meer [*sic*] pupils of these high mightinesses; to perform those exercises, and discuss those themes, only, that were marked out to them by their preceptors. For, because the reasons for summoning the senate are previously to be certified by them, they pretended to argue that a senate has no manner of right to propose or debate upon any one article which is not within their certificate. This is what they presume to claim. And also because they are to certify the cause for calling of a senate, they have assumed the sole right of certifying and transmitting the bills proposed by the senate ... Thus have this despotick council established themselves, *auctoritate sua*, into the rank of perpetual dictators ...[12]

Such negative perceptions of the actions of the Irish Council were reinforced by the apparent frequency with which 'popular' bills were lost at the British Council because, it was alleged, 'the unwarrantable interest of a single alien was preferred to the general advantage of the whole nation of Barataria [Ireland]'.[13]

Ministers could have denied this, of course, but whatever good will they earned in Ireland by acquiescing in the enactment in 1768 of the Octennial Act, it did nothing to ease concerns in respect of Poynings' Law. Flood, for example, was offended by the amendment of a measure altering the tenure upon which judges held office and a *habeas corpus* bill during the same session. However, his annoyance on this occasion was of minor import compared to the anger generated by Lord Townshend's prorogation of parliament in the wake of the House of Commons' rejection of the Privy Council money bill in December 1769.[14] Supporters of the administration aspired to deflect criticism by arguing that 'the subject should be understood ... not as involving any question of subordination or dependency', but a strong current of opinion in Ireland had arrived at the opposite conclusion, and focussed attention specifically on Poynings' Law, which was the subject of a brief but intense public debate in 1770.[15] Robert French was one of the first into print with a carefully modulated and well-received extended statement of the now familiar patriot argument that Poynings' Law, as currently applied, was contrary to what its framers intended, which was to limit the powers of the lord lieutenant and Council and not the legislature.[16] Charles Lucas

---

12. [Henry Flood], Letter VI from a native of Barataria in *Baratariana: a select collection of fugitive political pieces published during the administration of Lord Townshend in Ireland* (3rd ed., Dublin, 1777), pp 40–4; Kelly, *Henry Flood*, pp 122–5.
13. *Baratariana: a select collection*, p. 37.
14. Above, pp 253–5; Kelly, *Henry Flood*, pp 127–8; Bartlett, 'The Irish House of Commons rejection of the Privy Council money bill of 1769', pp 63–77.
15. Hely-Hutchinson to Hertford, 11 Jan. 1770 in HMC, *Donoughmore*, p. 265.
16. Robert French, *The constitution of Ireland and Poynings' Law explained* (Dublin, 1770).

concurred. Having expressed the view in his capacity as editor of John Lodge's historical work, *The usage of holding parliaments*, which (he argued) provided copious documentation to support this conclusion, he produced a trenchant, and characteristically convoluted critique of Poynings' Law in *The rights and privileges of parliament asserted*.[17] Taking as his basis the argument that 'each estate of the legislature has its prerogative', Lucas contended that it was crucial to the proper operation of the constitution that 'there can not ... exist a power that can legally control, interrupt or influence the debates or deliberations of either house [of parliament]'. His intervention was 'more a summary of established opposition positions than a development of anything new', but it was a useful 'compendium of argument' in support of the claim that the Protestant population of Ireland was 'by law entitled to the freedom, rights and privileges of Englishmen'.[18] Its impact was heightened, moreover, by the banality of the efforts of supporters of government to justify the role of the Privy Council on the grounds that 'this kingdom is deprived of the personal presence of the sovereign', and by reference to its historical record. The publication of a variety of other works advocating reform, including a reprint of William Molyneux's *Case of Ireland ... stated* with a topical introduction by Henry Flood, affirmed the criticisms of the Law's opponents.[19]

Though this surge in public interest in Poynings' Law was not accompanied by a focussed political campaign, because of the inability of the patriots to take the necessary organisational steps, the official expectation in advance of the short 1771 session was that the opposition would endeavour to use the first meeting of parliament since the prorogation to agitate the matter. In anticipation, Lord Townshend sought guidance as to how he should respond 'in case any intemperate motions should be carried against the right of the Crown as it stands by Poynings' Law'.[20] The anticipated motion was not long in coming, as the session was only in its third day when Henry Flood 'opened his grand question upon Poynings' law, and the right of the Commons in granting of money', but he was bested in the trial of political strength that ensued.[21] Unable to make any progress by this means, the patriots altered the point of their attack to bills that were

17. John Lodge, *The usage of holding parliaments* (Dublin, 1770); Charles Lucas, *The rights and privileges of parliament asserted* (Dublin, 1770).

18. Lucas, *The rights and privileges of parliament established*; Cummins, 'Opposition and the Irish parliament', pp 164–5.

19. *The policy of Poynings' Law fairly explained and considered* (Dublin, 1770, pp 8–11; [Richard Power], *A comparative state of the two rejected money bills in 1692 and 1769, with some observations on Poynings' Law, and the explanatory statute of Philip and Mary* (Dublin, 1770); William Molyneux, *Case of Ireland ... stated* (London, 1770), introduction; Kelly, *Henry Flood*, p. 143. See also the lengthy series of 20 public letters by 'Liberty' in the *Freeman's Journal*, 30 Jan.–22 Feb. 1770.

20. Townshend to Rochford, 27 Jan. 1771 in *Cal. HO papers, 1770–2*, p. 196.

21. Kelly, *Henry Flood*, p. 148; Townshend to Rochford, 28 Feb. 1771 in *Cal. HO papers, 1770–2*, p. 211.

subject to 'material', or what they deemed 'dangerous', alterations at the British Council board. Such attempts as they made during the 1771 spring session were rebuffed, but the unintended omission of 'cottons' in the great money bill of the 1771–2 session provided them with an unexpected opportunity in December 1771 to manifest the extent of their resentment at the interference with their legislative deliberations. Seized by the conviction that 'no[thing] less than the right of parliament and the constitution of this kingdom were at stake', MPs rejected the bill. As already described, a revised alternative made its way to law without much difficulty, but the episode had an enduring legacy as MPs were more willing thereafter to cite amendments made to bills at the Privy Council as reason enough to justify their rejection.[22] Their rhetoric suggested that they objected in principle to all amendments when, as Hercules Langrishe, the MP for Knocktopher made clear in March 1772, their focus was those 'material alteration[s] ... tending to the infringement of the constitution'.[23] This was a flexible definition that could be, and was, applied as opposition MPs deemed appropriate. For instance, when the measure to combat the Steelboys, which encountered a stormy passage on its way through the Commons, returned from the British Council with 'some amendments' in 1772, it was 'thought advisable to let it pass without a division on account of the necessity of the law'.[24] A number of MPs showed less flexibility in their opposition to a bill for better regulating the revenue and combating revenue fraud later in the same session, but though a committee of comparison was appointed, its report was not admitted and the bill progressed into law.[25]

If the appointment of a committee of comparison to identify the amendments made to money bills that had taken their rise as heads in the House of Commons constituted the most material outcome of the growing willingness of MPs to resist the 'material' alteration of their bills, it was clear from press comment and the request of Sir Edward Newenham, MP for Enniscorthy, on 6 May 1772 for lists of the bills that had passed the House of Commons and the bills that were transmitted to Great Britain' that this did no go far enough. Newenham's target was the Irish Privy Council. It was his conviction that the House of Commons could not 'any longer be justly stiled the representatives of the people of Ireland' if they acquiesced in a 'ridiculous and absurd' arrangement that allowed the Council 'to originate money bills' and to impede the progress of parliamentary legislation. In order to hasten the termination of the practice, he presented MPs on 18 May with a deceptively simple motion, which asserted 'that preventing the progress' of heads of bills that arose with the Commons 'tends to lessen the dignity and power of parliament'.[26] It was not endorsed, but the conviction that 'the theory of Poynings' Law, as it is held by the King's servants is a contradiction

22. *Hibernian Jn.*, 13 May, 23 Dec. 1771; above, p. 304.
23. *Hibernian Jn.*, 27 Mar. 1772.
24. St George to Hardwicke, 28 Mar. 1772 (BL, Hardwicke Papers, Add. MS 35610 f. 182).
25. *Hibernian Jn.*, 11 May 1772; *Commons Jn. (Irl.)*, viii, 546, 547, 548, 549, 550, 53, 554.
26. *Hibernian Jn.*, 27 Apr., 8, 18, 20 May 1772; *Commons Jn. (Irl.)*, viii, 556.

to the first principles of a free constitution [and] annihilates the original and incommunicable rights of parliament' took firmer hold.[27]

Indeed, it was articulated more strongly than ever during the 1773–4 session when, following Lord Harcourt's success in overcoming resistance to the enactment of the 'great money bill', MPs cited the number and scale of the amendments introduced into the tontine and stamp bills as reason to reject them. Councillors in Britain had no difficulty justifying the amendments cited as the logical consequence 'of the slovenly manner in which your bills come over'. It was alleged specifically that the stamp bill was 'full of verbal absurdities' and the tontine bill a litany of 'capital ... mistakes ... that ... subverted the whole plan of the bill', but these legitimate reservations cut little ice with the Irish Commons. In keeping with their recently adopted practice of referring money bills for a report from a committee of comparison, MPs felt they had no choice but to reject both measures when the extent of the amendments was revealed. Their feelings were memorably expressed by the fiery George Ogle, who proposed that the stamp bill 'should be thrown on the floor and the clerk ordered to kick it ignominiously out of the House'. Wiser counsels prevailed, with the result that not alone did MPs uphold the decorum of their chamber, but they manifested their determination to be seen to behave responsibly by agreeing in near record time to revised versions of both bills.[28] This may have encouraged some contemporaries to conclude that this was the end of the matter, but the unprecedented press speculation as to whether the bills would return with 'fresh alterations' was indicative of the disinclination any longer to acquiesce passively in the application of Poynings' Law.[29] This was sustained, if not fuelled, by ongoing controversy over the respiting of the heads of a bill to regulate the election of MPs, which Robert French pursued doggedly in the House of Commons in 1774.[30]

In the light of what had happened in the 1771–2 and 1773–4 sessions, one might have anticipated that the bill to grant the old and new additional duties would not encounter problems in 1775–6. But having detected the elision of two material clauses (appertaining to the deployment of 4000 troops abroad), the 'indignation' with which MPs were seized demanded that this bill and the stamp bill, which had also been amended, were rejected. New measures, which in the case of the money bill did not include the offending provision appertaining to the

---

27. *Hibernian Jn.*, 1 Dec. 1773.
28. Lammey, 'Free trade', p. 130; Ellis to Agar, 1 Jan. 1774 (Normanton Papers, PRONI, T3719/C/8/1); Rochford to Harcourt, 14 Jan. 1774 in *Harcourt Papers*, ix, 156–7; *Finn's Leinster Journal*, 24, 29 Dec. 1773, 26 Jan. 1774; *Hibernian Jn.*, 22, 24, 27, 29, 31 Dec. 1773, 28 Jan. 1774; Waller to Macartney, 27 Dec., Lill to Macartney, 31 Dec. in Bartlett (ed.), *Macartney in Ireland*, pp 184, 252; Harcourt to Rochford, 27, 30, 31 Dec. 1773 in *Cal. HO papers, 1773–5*, pp 120, 121–3; *Commons Jn. (Irl.)*, ix, 72, 74
29. *Hibernian Jn.*, 10, 19 Jan.; *Finn's Leinster Jn.*, 22 Jan. 1774.
30. PC2/117 ff 481, 519, 531; Harcourt to Blaquiere, 28 Apr. 1774 (Gilbert Library, Harcourt Papers, MS 93 ff 126–7); *Hibernian Jn.*, 20, 23 May, 15, 18 June; *Finn's Leinster Jn.*, 11, 15, 18 June 1774.

deployment of troops, were promptly readied, and the specific problem was overcome, but the source of the controversy – Poynings' Law – remained a matter of lively contention.[31] The most striking evidence for this is provided by the preparedness of the popular press to incorporate frequently technical discussions of the Law's evolution and operation into political discourse. The main thrust of the criticism emanating from that quarter was the familiar argument that the Irish Council was an 'unconstitutional board', and that its involvement disrupted 'the great equilibrium' between crown, lords and commons provided for by the constitution. It was asserted variously that there were five or six 'branches of the Irish constitution' – the King, lords, commons, British Privy Council, Irish Privy Council and the crown's law officers – when there ought to be three only, and that as a result 'the parliamentary mode of proceeding [employed in Ireland was not consistent with] that used in Great Britain'. Extended elaborations of the route an Irish bill must follow on its long journey into law made the difference explicit, and provided critics with evidence with which they affirmed not only that Ireland was being unjustly deprived of its rights, but also that the Irish Council was extending its powers. Misleading claims along these lines were sustained by reference to the experience of particular heads of bills that, one may plausibly assume, vested interests encouraged. For example, the heads of a bill for the relief of the creditors of William Howard, which was two months at the Irish Council board, was adduced in 1776 to illustrate how those seeking to evade responsibility could bring influence to bear to escape sanction for fraud.[32]

Expressions of public concern as to the fate of particular bills were also encouraged in the late 1770s by the actions of individual MPs who sought explanations for the delay in returning, or not returning as the case may be, favoured measures. George Ogle, for example, enquired of successive chief secretaries in 1776 and 1778 as to the fate of heads of bills to establish an Irish militia.[33] Greater resort was also made to the committee of comparison.[34] Previously invoked only to sustain the Commons' claim to possess the 'sole right' to initiate financial legislation, its usage was expanded in 1778 when critics of a controversial measure to relieve Catholics successfully overcame resistance to the establishment of a committee to compare the heads communicated from the Commons with the bill returned from the British Council board. Enabled, as a result, to establish formally that the clause to relieve dissenters had been removed, some MPs argued that the amended measure should be rejected on 'constitutional' grounds. The

31. [Almon], *Narrative of proceedings ...*, pp 118–23; *Finn's Leinster Journal*, 27 Dec. 1775, 6 Jan. 1776; Harcourt to Weymouth, 22 Dec. 1775 in *Cal. HO papers*, p. 506; Harcourt to North, 22, 24 Dec. 1775 in *Harcourt Papers*, x, 61–2, 66; Harcourt to Weymouth, 28 Dec. 1775, 8, 22, 27 Jan. 1776 (NA, SP63/451 ff 7–10, 71–4, 165–7); Kelly, *Henry Flood*, p. 227.
32. *Hibernian Jn.*, 1 Mar., 2, 9 Oct. 1776; Library of Congress, Cavendish parliamentary diary, vi, 257–60.
33. *Hibernian Jn.*, 3 Apr. 1776; Library of Congress, Cavendish parliamentary diary, x, 69–71.
34. *Hibernian Jn.*, 9 Oct. 1776; *Freeman's Jn.*, 20 Dec. 1777.

one-time leading patriot, William Osborne, was the most impressive; as a proponent of toleration, he protested that 'it was impossible to gratify the wishes or
indulge the best feelings of humanity without sacrificing to the object the rights
of parliament and the laws of the land'. Others protested after a more conven-
tional fashion that 'all ... who wish well to the constitutional legislature will be for
rejecting this bill', but once focus shifted from the 'constitution' to the matter of
relieving 'injustice', it was apparent that there was a majority for promoting the
bill and it was forwarded to become law.[35]

Instances such as this may have assisted in overcoming the strong resistance of
many MPs to the suggestion that Poynings' Law must be reviewed, but it
continued to have strong advocates. Sir William Osborne, notably, was content
to describe the Law in August 1778 as 'the bond of union between the two
kingdoms ... that every man who wishes the continuation of that union and
thoroughly understands the law will never desire ... to have repealed, or suffer ...
to be infringed'.[36] A current of powerful opinion continued to uphold this
position, but they were put firmly on the defensive by the concession of 'free
trade' in the winter of 1779–80, as thereafter the issue of the legislative rights of
the Irish parliament moved political centre stage and expressions of support for
constitutional reform proliferated.[37] The spring of 1780 was a crucial moment
because it was then that some of the patriots' loudest voices – Barry Yelverton and
Henry Grattan notably – openly signalled their commitment to pursue the repeal
of the Declaratory Act and the modification of Poynings' Law. Yelverton made
the running in respect of the latter, and he established his claim to pursue the
issue in parliament on 26 April 1780 when he argued in an 'eloquent and learned
speech' that in seeking support to amend Poynings' Law his object was to restore
the constitution to the situation that had prevailed between the thirteenth and late
fifteenth centuries when a proper constitutional equilibrium had existed between
Crown, lords and commons. In support of this position, Yelverton appealed to the
familiar patriot conceit that the Irish Privy Council had unwarrantably assumed
an active role in the law making process; he maintained equally dubiously that the
Council was intent on expanding rather than contracting its involvement when
constitutional principle demanded that the power of making law was vested in
parliament. Yelverton was supported by the main figures in the patriots' ranks,
who offered a variety of critical perspectives on the actions of the Irish and,
lesserly, on the British Council. He was opposed with still greater vigour by those
who were unconvinced by his argument that he did not aspire to constitutional
innovation, and by those, ill at ease at the raising of constitutional questions, who
protested that his motion showed ingratitude to Britain for free trade. Some of the

---

35. Cavendish's parliamentary diary, xiii, 21–5, 44, 159–60, 199, 286–93. The 1780 tenants bill was
     also sent for consideration by a committee of comparison (Callen, 'Cavendish's parliamentary
     diary, 1779–80', ii, 260).
36. Cavendish's parliamentary diary, xiii, 286–93.

exchanges during the debate were passionate, but the numbers were with the administration and Yelverton's motion was defeated by 130 votes to 105.[38]

Though they had lost, the fact that the opposition had performed so creditably in the division lobbies was an encouragement to them to persist with their campaign for the remainder of the long 1779–80 session. They certainly demonstrated resolve by taking an assertive line on a range of issues – the sugar duty and the mutiny bills notably – as well as by querying the fate of other amended, delayed and respited bills. In particular, Henry Grattan's objection to the insertion of a clause in the mutiny bill making the measure perpetual in contravention of Irish wishes highlighted the subordination of the Irish legislature to the British Council that an increasing number of MPs deemed intolerable. The Commons made its feelings plain by rejecting the amended sugar duties bill but were unsuccessful in their efforts to defeat the mutiny bill, and the session concluded, unsatisfactorily and inconclusively, on that note.[39]

This provided an opportunity for other, less elevated voices to make their opinion known in the press. Some, like the influential Owen Roe O'Nial echoed the patriots' position that they sought 'an explanation or amendment' and not the 'repeal' of Poynings' Law, in order to neutralise the worried prognostications of critics that any alteration of the constitution was dangerous. However, the now widespread impression that Poynings' Law was a force for ill – 'it fritters away the force of the national assemblies, divides their efforts, destroys their cooperation, and robs the united voice of the nation of that collected, constitutional, persuasive energy which it should always be supported in the bosom of its sovereign' – ensured that appeals along the lines expressed by O'Nial would not satisfy all, and it encouraged the publication of fuller commentaries on the law and its meaning for Ireland.[40] These took a stronger line against the measure than was the practice to date, and claims that the Law was 'flawed from its inception' seemed to sustain public expectations that appropriate concessions would be forthcoming during the 1781–2 session.[41]

Though constitutional reform remained a legislative priority with the Patriots in parliament and their supporters without, the likelihood of such reforms meeting their elevated expectations had diminished since parliament had adjourned in September 1780 as a consequence of changes to the personnel at the

37. [Frederick Jebb], *The letters of Guatimozin on the affairs of Ireland* (Dublin, 1779); Stephen Small, *Political thought in Ireland, 1776–1800* (Oxford, 2002), p. 78; *Dublin Evening Post*, 29 Feb. 1780.
38. Callen, 'Cavendish's parliamentary diary, ii, 154–67 passim.
39. Ibid., ii, 249–60, 263–78 passim; Small, *Political thought*, p. 94.
40. Owen Roe O'Nial's ninth letter, *Freeman's Jn.*, 22 Apr. 1780; [Charles Francis Sheridan], *A review of the three great national questions relative to a declaration of right, Poynings' law and the mutiny bill* (Dublin, 1781); Morley, *Irish opinion*, p. 267.
41. *Sketches of the history of Poynings' Law* (Dublin, 1780); [Hervey Redmond Morres], *Plain reasons for new-modelling Poynings' Law in such a manner as to assert the ancient rights of the two houses of parliament* (Dublin, 1780); York, *Neither kingdom nor nation*, p. 128. See also, Hervey Redmond Morres, *Considerations on the intended modifications of Poynings' Law* (London, 1780).

head of the Irish administration. The replacement late in 1780 of the earl of Buckinghamshire and his ineffectual chief secretary, Richard Heron, with the earl of Carlisle and William Eden restored confidence in the Irish executive. As a result, Dublin Castle was enabled not only to rally support among MPs and peers who were discomforted by the agitation of constitutional points but also to weaken the ranks of the patriots by drawing Denis Daly into office and by establishing a working relationship with Barry Yelverton. Matters went encouragingly well for the administration during the opening weeks of the 1781–2 session as it prevailed comfortably in all the divisions that mattered.[42] Officials were confident when constitutional issues were raised, that the Irish parliament would be guided by Yelverton's instinctive moderatism and that whatever changes, if any, proved necessary that they would be by agreement and with minimum fuss. Everything went according to plan until early December when news of the humiliation of the Crown's forces at Yorktown prompted Yelverton to postpone a motion for the 'consideration of Poynings' Law' to make way for a loyal address to the King. Yelverton's response was consistent with the traditional disposition of MPs to rally to the Crown during moments of crisis, but Henry Flood was quick to seize on the opportunity to affirm his claims to press the issue.

Having recently been liberated of the constraints of office, during which time he had been eclipsed as the leading patriot voice in the House of Commons, Flood was a disruptive presence on the opposition benches. A majority of his colleagues, many of whom admired his superior oratorical skills and analytical abilities, hoped he would join forces with Henry Grattan and Barry Yelverton to bring pressure to bear on the Irish administration to secure constitutional reform, but Flood was disinclined. Though many then and since have attributed his actions to ambition, Flood had good political reasons for acting as he did. Like others within the ranks of the patriot interest, he harboured doubts as to the purity of Yelverton's motives now that he was working with the administration. Still more significantly, Flood did not believe Yelverton's understanding of how Poynings' Law had come to be applied was correct, and this led him to conclude that Yelverton was intent on advancing a defective solution to the problem of Ireland's constitutional dependence. Had he known that Eden had assured Yelverton that the administration would remain neutral when he moved for leave to introduce legislation to amend Poynings' Law if he prompted a loyal address on 5 December, Flood's disquiet would have been still greater.[43] At any event, Flood was determined to press his own plan for the reform of Poynings' Law, though his estrangement from the Irish administration and the generality of patriots meant that, compared to Yelverton, he was not well positioned to do so successfully.

42. O'Brien, *Anglo-Irish politics in the age of Grattan and Pitt*, pp 47–54; McDowell, *Ireland in the age of imperialism and revolution*, pp 275–87.
43. Carlisle to Hillsborough, 5 Dec. 1781 (NA, SP63/477 ff 165–6); O'Brien, *Anglo-Irish politics*, pp 49–51.

Impelled by his belief in the correctness of his analysis of Poynings' Law and of the legislative remedies required to set matters right, Flood presented a delicately worded amendment for insertion in the address offered by Yelverton on 5 December that, a worried Carlisle observed, embraced 'a demand of recognition from Great Britain of the legislative independence of Ireland'. This was more than a majority of MPs deemed politic, and Yelverton's original proposition was carried comfortably.[44] Since this was always the likely outcome, Flood experienced no loss of face. At any event, his focus remained fixed on Poynings' Law and, determined that his ideas should be considered, he signalled his intention to 'make a motion relative to the law of Poynings in the Commons on 11 December'. Yelverton was sufficiently troubled by this turn of events, which threatened to undermine his own scheme, to assure MPs three days later that 'he had not deserted' the issue, but the more material outcome of this day's exchanges was that it demonstrated that Flood and Yelverton 'differ[ed] as to the mode' of proceedings they intended to adopt with respect of restoring the constitutional authority of the Irish legislature.[45]

Flood's interpretation of Poynings' Law was firmly grounded on the close study he had afforded the act and related legislation, the judgements arrived at by lawyers as to its meaning and implication, and the application of the Law over several centuries. He was sufficiently knowledgeable in the estimation of some of his friends that he might, had he wished, have presented the results of his researches to the public in a pamphlet.[46] However, he chose to reserve his sentiments for parliament and for the major speech (it took three and a half hours to deliver) he made to the House of Commons on 11 December 1781, in which he offered an elaborate statement of the case that the practice of the Irish Privy Council amending and respiting legislation arising with the Irish legislature was grounded on a misconception of the constitution as well as of Poynings' Law.

The constitution, Flood reminded his audience, possessed 'executive' and 'deliberative' arms each with 'its separate and distinct province':

> The *deliberative* authority of the state resting with the Houses of LORDS AND COMMONS, the *executive* with the KING. ... The constitution had invested the two Houses with the deliberate authority of propounding and framing laws, by which the people were to be governed, because they themselves were the people's representatives, and had given the King only a negative on the laws when proposed, because he was the executive officer, and had no occasion for any right of interference in the business of legislation; but just so much as was necessary to defend his own prerogative from the

44. *Parl. Reg. (Irl.)*, i, 119–29; Carlisle to Hillsborough, 5 Dec. 1781 (2) and addresses (NA, SP63/477 ff 156–9, 163–4); Kelly, *Henry Flood*, pp 295–6.
45. *Parl. Reg. (Irl.)*, i, 129, 149.
46. Malone to Charlemont, [ca. Dec. 1781] in HMC, *Charlemont*, ii, 401; [Henry Flood], Notes on Poynings' Law, n.d. (Birr Castle, Rosse Papers, C/4).

incroachments of other estates, which he was sufficiently enabled to do from a power of negativing any law which he thought might be injurious to that prerogative.

The problem, as Flood saw it, was that the right of 'participating in that constitution had been wrested from the people' by the 'corrupt and vicious construction and interpretation' of Poynings' Law and the explanatory act of 1557. As a result, instead of 'prevent[ing] the governors of Ireland from giving the royal assent to laws that might be injurious to the King', a 'false and vicious interpretation' that served to restrain the freedom of parliament now obtained. Flood adduced copious examples from British and Irish parliamentary history in support of his contention that 'the Privy Council here had no authority to alter any heads of bills before their transmission into Great Britain'; all that was required in order to fulfil 'the spirit' of Poynings' Law was that bills arising with the Irish parliament 'should be certified under the great seal'. It followed therefore, 'in order to restore the constitution to its native vigour', that it was incumbent upon the Irish parliament to approve a declaratory act affirming (as Flood put it at a later date[47]) 'the true intent and meaning of the Law'. However, if MPs agreed to follow Yelverton's alternative proposal which was to amend the Law, they were validating the 'corruption' and 'pusillanimity' that had allowed the Irish Privy Council to intervene in the law-making process.

Because both his diagnosis of the problem and his remedy for its solution were more palpably more assertive than those advanced by Yelverton, and therefore were more likely to encounter stiff official resistance, Flood was aware that most MPs would greet his recommendation sceptically. However, he was so convinced that his solution was the best way to quell the 'monster [the Privy Council]' that 'destroys the constitution' by 'stifl[ing] the voice of the people, and ... prevent[ing] the King from hearing' that he maintained any such attempt would be more beneficial than the formal approval of Yelverton's faulty scheme:

> he said that if the declaratory bill should pass the House of Commons, tho' it should not receive the Royal assent, yet the sense of the Commons being declared by the bill would operate in effect to his design of amending the practice in the constitution – whereas if a bill for altering the law should pass the House [of Commons], tho' it should not receive the Royal assent, it would nevertheless contain an acknowledgment that the law is agreeable to the present practice of the Privy Council, and would leave the evil acknowledged to exist in the law without succeeding in obtaining the remedy.[48]

47. On 28 February 1782 (*Parl. Reg. (Irl.)*, i, 305).
48. Carlisle to Hillsborough, 12 Dec. 1781 (NA, SP 63/477 ff 185–6).

Born out of their deep-seated reservations with what Lord Carlisle termed Flood's 'wild and extravagant ideas', MPs were not prepared either to embrace his analysis or his preferred mode of proceeding,[49] which was to invite the House of Commons to examine 'the precedents and records' in order to identify 'what the law ... and what the constitution of this country actually was'.[50] In common with the Provost, John Hely-Hutchinson, who took the lead in resisting Flood's proposition, many were impressed by his 'learned and eloquent oration' and sympathetic to his argument that 'the law of Poynings had not ... taken away the right of either House [of parliament] to originate laws'. However, they disagreed fundamentally with his contention that the Irish Privy Council had usurped the right of amending and respiting bills. Disinclined to be seen to reflect aversely on generations of councillors who were guided, Hely-Hutchinson argued, by 'their duty' to ensure that '[no]thing approach[ed] the throne, which was injurious or hurtful to the kingdom, or prejudicial to the royal prerogative', they rejected the core of Flood's argument. In view of this, it was inevitable that the administration should seek to pre-empt the anticipated attempt by Flood, 'upon the report of the committee', 'to form a declaration of rights'. It was a mode of proceeding, Hely-Hutchinson explained to a sympathetic House, 'that ... never should be used but in cases of the utmost necessity'. He placed the circumstances that had given rise to Magna Carta and the petition of rights in this category, but the Irish Privy Council was responsible for no 'abuse' demanding an equivalent response.[51]

Flood's inability to obtain the support of normally reliable patriots, one of whom observed revealingly that 'the indiscriminate violence of opposition is the parade, not the essence of patriotism', ensured his motion was rejected by a substantial margin. This was deeply disappointing to some on the opposition benches, of whom George Ogle, MP for County Wexford, was the most forthright. Anxious lest the disunity the debate had exposed in patriot ranks should undermine the prospects of constitutional reform, 'he lamented the unfortunate difference of opinion between the two great supporters [Yelverton and Flood] of the nation's rights against the law of Poynings'. However, his suggested way forward – a 'pathetic' entreaty to 'Flood to accommodate himself to the wishes of his friends and unite with Mr Yelverton in his mode of bringing forward heads of a bill – was naïve and impractical.[52] There could be no united patriot position on how Poynings' Law should be reformed after the debate of 11 December, though the impact of the disagreement on how to proceed was less debilitating than the 67 votes (in a division of 206) for Flood's proposal suggests.[53]

While the Irish administration was heartened by the rejection of Flood's intervention, the fact that there was a broad consensus within the House of

49. This phrase is taken from Carlisle to Hillsborough, 29 Dec. 1781 (NA, SP63/480 f. 14).
50. *Parl. Reg. (Irl.)*, i, 153–7.
51. Ibid., pp 157–9.
52. *Parl. Reg. (Irl.)*, i, 173.
53. Ibid., p. 174.

Commons and the political nation generally that some measure of constitutional reform was desirable encouraged them to look still more benignly at Barry Yelverton's scheme. As a result, when Yelverton finally sought leave on 18 December to present legislation that would 'take from the [Irish] Privy Council those rights which had unconstitutionally been wrested from parliament; to prohibit totally their power of altering bills, and instead of the words "we pray it may be enacted" to introduce these words "be it enacted"', he was afforded a palpably warmer reception than Flood a week earlier. The bill itself was a simple document.[54] There was no masking Yelverton's nervousness, however, for despite the assurance he had received from the chief secretary that his proposal 'commanded his particular attention', he was reluctant to enter into debate on the merits of his proposal with so formidable an adversary as Flood. Indeed, he was only prompted to make an extended statement in support of his proposition by Flood's provocative assertion that the proposed measure must prove 'not only insufficient, but detrimental and pernicious'. Yelverton maintained that it was the opinion of 'every lawyer' that 'by the act of the 3rd and 4th of Philip and Mary, the Privy Council have a *right* to *stop*, and if they please *to alter* our bills'. Flood disagreed. He accused Yelverton of misciting the 3rd and 4th of Philip and Mary and refuted his literal and restrictive interpretation of Poynings' Law, in a masterly reaffirmation of his contention that 'a declaratory law' that 'fix[ed] our constitution on a solid basis' was vastly preferable to Yelverton's scheme of 'a law to regulate the manner of certifying bills [whereby] we confessed our rights were taken away' when 'neither God nor man had given [MPs the] authority to destroy the people's rights'.[55]

Though Flood had the better of the argument, the weight of numbers arrayed against him meant that he was powerless to prevent Yelverton's motion advancing.[56] Significantly, his invitation (on 19 December) to the critics of a 'declaratory' act to 'point out the sentences' in Poynings' Law and its amendments 'that deprived parliament of the power to originate bills or that gave the [Privy C]ouncil of either kingdom power to alter bills after the meeting of parliament'

---

54. There is a copy of Yelverton's bill in NA, SP63/480 f. 16. It reads as follows: 'Whereas several doubts have arisen concerning the true construction and meaning of an act made in the tenth year of King Henry the seventh entitled An Act that no parliament be holden in this land until the acts be certified into England, and also of one other act made in the 3rd and 4th years of Philip and Mary entitled An Act declaring how Poynings' Act shall be expounded and taken. For the full and plain declaration of the true meaning and understanding of the said acts: We the [Lords], and Commons in parliament assembled pray it may be enacted and declared that the Lord Lieutenant or other Chief Governor or governors and Council of the realm of Ireland for the time being do and shall certify all such considerations, causes, tenors, provisions and ordinances as either House of parliament shall judge expedient to be established within the same realm of Ireland to His Majesty, his heirs and successors under the great seal of the same realm of Ireland without making any addition to, diminution from or alteration in the same, save putting the same into due form of law.'
55. *Parl. Reg. (Irl.)*, i, 184–6.
56. *Commons Jn. (Irl.)*, x, 276.

elicited abuse rather than engagement.[57] As if to acknowledge that it was pointless to proceed in this manner, Flood did not pursue his opposition for the moment, and attention shifted to the Irish administration, which had already concluded that some concessions to Irish opinion in respect of Poynings' Law were required if 'a permanent system of administration' was to be put in place. Convinced also that Yelverton's moderate proposition was infinitely preferable to Flood's 'wild' scheme, Lord Carlisle turned his attention to persuading his governmental colleagues.[58] To this end, he transmitted a copy of Yelverton's measure towards the end of December, and made clear his belief that it would, if ratified, neutralise Flood and 'become a fair occasion of quieting a question of much importance, which in its present state is a subject of continued agitation'. Since the bill had yet to be presented to the Irish parliament and, other than Flood, MPs had few fixed ideas as to what it should contain, Carlisle was optimistic that it could be amended in a manner that would satisfy interests on both sides of the Irish Sea. He went to far as to suggest to the secretary of state, Lord Hillsborough, that the heads 'might be amended and specifically worded so as to amount to a recognition of the whole present usage as practised under Poynings' law and merely to provide that the heads of all bills sent to the Lord Lieutenant and Council shall be transmitted to England'. This would not appease Flood, of course, but since he had already 'given notice of his intention' to oppose whatever bill was presented and nothing was to be gained by conciliating him, Carlisle concentrated his energies on eliciting the support of 'a great and respectable majority'. Persuaded by his discussions with 'men of the most moderate minds' that 'the power exercised by the Irish Privy Council in suppressing bills entirely and secreting from the sovereign the acts of either branch of the legislature' was the main point of Irish concern, he ventured to suggest that the issue could be resolved without any diminution in the royal prerogative 'by obliging the [Irish] Council to send the bills, accompanied with the recommendation of such amendments or rejections as they would otherwise adopt'. This was incompatible with the views articulated from most quarters in the Irish parliament. But Carlisle's perception that, other than 'money grants, ... there is, with few exceptions, a general disposition in both Houses [of the Irish parliament] to allow [alterations] with regard to all other bills', and to accept that 'there is and ought to be a power in the King and ... Privy Council to make such alterations and direct such rejections as may be deemed expedient', encouraged him to believe that a solution acceptable to all could be identified.[59]

Ministers were sceptical. Eager to do nothing to weaken the legal basis of the Anglo-Irish nexus, they ignored Carlisle's suggestion that Yelverton's draft bill

57. As note 53; Kelly, *Henry Flood*, p. 300.
58. Eden to Loughborough, 27 Dec. 1781, 12 Jan. 1782 in BL, Auckland Papers, Add. MS 34418 f. 221, *Auckland Corres.*, i, 326; Carlisle to Hillsborough, 29 Dec. 1781 (2) (NA, SP63/480 ff 3–7, 10–13).
59. Carlisle to Hillsborough, 29 Dec. 1781 (NA, SP63/480 ff 14–5).

could be recast in an acceptable form. Indeed, while they took especial care not to offend Irish sensitivities by embracing Ireland within a number of acts recently approved at Westminster, the advice forthcoming from London was that all attempts to modify Poynings' Law should be resisted. The administration was provided with time to rally its supporters by the Christmas recess, with the result that when Yelverton's bill received its first reading in the House of Commons on 13 February its prospects of making it to law had greatly receded. This was underlined fifteen days later when, on 'moving the committal of the bill', the attorney general maintained that it should be committed to a distant day.[60] The problem for the Irish administration was that their dominance in parliament was not matched by their ability to shape public opinion. The intervention of the Ulster Volunteers, who assembled a convention of delegates at Dungannon on 15 February, was particularly important in this respect since it energised a campaign for constitutional reform that had visibly running out of steam. Specifically, the ratification of resolutions, drafted by Flood and Grattan, pronouncing it 'unconstitutional, illegal and a grievance' for 'any body of men other than the King, Lords and Commons of Ireland to make laws to bind this kingdom' and 'that the powers exercised by the Privy Council of both kingdoms under, or under colour or pretence of the Law of Poyning are unconstitutional and a grievance' focussed the wavering attention of the public.[61] The political effects of this were not immediately apparent, as the temporising response to Yelverton's attempt on 28 February to progress his bill to committee, and the repeated rebuff of the efforts of Grattan and Flood during the previous week to advance their less specific agenda attest.[62] But before long 'the popular ferment increased', and as the 'friends of government' struggled to maintain control, Lord Carlisle was obliged to revert to his earlier position that 'public peace' could only be restored by appealing to 'the moderating' influence of the likes of Yelverton to dilute the 'jealousies and apprehensions' that threatened the very foundations of English government in Ireland.[63] As it happened, Carlisle was not to be given the opportunity to pursue this strategy as the fall of Lord North's government on 20 March brought the Whigs, led by Lord Rockingham, to power.

There was an expectation in Ireland following the change of government that, in the words of the military under-secretary, Charles Francis Sheridan, 'a declaration of the independency of our parliament upon yours will certainly pass our House of Commons immediately after the recess'. The question was how this was to be achieved, and what it would mean in practice. Lord Charlemont, the

---

60. Hillsborough to Carlisle, 24 Jan. 1782 (NAI, Index to departmental letters and papers, 1760–89, i, 256); *Commons Jn.(Irl.)*, x, 311; *Parl. Reg.(Irl.)*, i, 305–6.
61. Bristow to Ross, 17 Feb. 1782 (NA, SP63/480 ff 228–30); Grattan jr, *Life of Grattan*, ii, 204–6; Kelly, *Henry Flood*, pp 303–4.
62. Kelly, *Henry Flood*, pp 306–7; *Parl. Reg.(Irl.)*, i, 263–76; Carlisle to Hillsborough, 23 Feb. 1782 (2) (NA, SP63/480 ff 247–50).
63. Carlisle to Hillsborough, 19 Mar. 1782 (NA, SP63/480 ff 397–400).

éminence grise of the Irish patriots, was as eager as ever that they should present a united front, but he was unable to persuade Flood to join with Grattan and him in representing the Irish case to the new lord lieutenant, the duke of Portland. These discussions did not prove as fruitful as Charlemont, in particular, had anticipated, but once Grattan and he had made it apparent that the ministerial wish for a negotiated 'compact' – 'a new system and new arrangement of connection between the two kingdoms' – was incompatible with their determination that there should be no dilution of the 'incontrovertible rights' of Ireland all that remained to be worked out was the detail.[64] Little progress was made in advance of the resumption of the parliamentary session – adjourned to allow Carlisle vacate his Irish 'seat of thorns' so the duke of Portland could assume the reins of power – which took place on 16 April.[65]

In the absence of prior agreement between the leadership of the patriot interest – which at that moment meant Grattan and Charlemont – and the principals of the new administration, as to the constitutional reforms that were to be conceded to Ireland, the events of 16 April were to have a profound influence on the manner in which Poynings' Law was addressed. Had the administration had its way, MPs would have been content to approve a carefully modulated address in which the Crown agreed to 'take into their most serious consideration the discontents and jealousies which have arisen in this kingdom'. However, Grattan had other ideas, and consistent with a promise he made MPs prior to the adjournment to move for a declaration of rights, he proposed a lengthy amendment that, as well as asserting that 'there is no body of men competent to make laws to bind this nation, except the King, Lords and Commons of Ireland', affirmed that 'the practice of suppressing our bills in the Council of Ireland, or altering the same anywhere, to be another just cause of discontent and jealousy'.[66] Because it cited the British as well as the Irish Council, this was a more explicit statement of Irish dissatisfaction with Poynings' Law than Yelverton's draft legislation for certifying bills. It also negated the proposition advanced by Lord Carlisle late in December that the British Council might introduce amendments on behalf of its Irish equivalent, since it was now anticipated that the British Council would be stripped of this entitlement. The reluctant acquiescence of the British government, signalled by the lord lieutenant on 27 May, 'to acts to prevent the suppression of bills in the Privy Council of this kingdom, and the alteration of them anywhere' meant that heads of a new bill, or bills, to achieve this purpose was required.[67] This process was set in train on 31 May when the heads of Yelverton's 'certifying' bill were formally 'withdrawn', and leave was given to

---

64. Sheridan to Sheridan, 27 Mar. 1782 in *Life of Grattan*, ii, 214–15; Kelly, *Henry Flood*, pp 311–12; Kelly, *Prelude to Union*, pp 35–6; Sheffield City Library, Rockingham Papers, R1-2049.
65. Carlisle to Gower, 23 Mar. 1782 (NA, Grenville Papers, 30/29/1/5).
66. Grattan's amendment, 16 Apr. 1782 cited in Francis Dobbs, *A history of Irish affairs from 12 October 1779 to 15 September 1782* (Dublin, 1782), pp 70–3.
67. Kelly, *Prelude to Union*, pp 41–2; *Parl. Reg. (Irl.)*, i, 354.

prepare a new 'more perfect' measure to 'regulate the manner of passing bills and to prevent delays in summoning of parliaments'. Coincidentally, the task of presenting and arguing the merits of the bill fell to Barry Yelverton, recently appointed to the office of attorney general, and the bill (for, significantly, when presented it was called a bill rather than heads of a bill) was forthcoming within twenty-four hours.[68] Short, like its predecessor, the first clause of the new measure echoed the main (second) clause in Yelverton's 'certifying' bill in affirming that in the future 'the lord lieutenant, or other chief governor or governors and council of this kingdom ... shall certify all such bills and none other, as both houses of Parliament shall judge expedient to be enacted in this kingdom ... without addition, diminution, or alteration'. The second clause sought equally to confine the British Council; it stipulated that the Irish parliament would enact only those bills certified in Ireland that were 'returned ... under the great seal of Great Britain without addition, diminution or alteration'.[69]

Debate on what is commonly called Yelverton's bill began in earnest at the committee stage, which commenced on Thursday, 6 June. Since the bill mirrored Yelverton's idea of an amending act rather than Henry Flood's stated preference for a declaratory act, it was generally anticipated that he would not allow the occasion to pass without comment, and he did not disappoint. Convinced that the House of Commons was committing an egregious error in proceedings in this manner, Flood protested that Yelverton's redrafted bill was neither 'adequate to the idea held out and entertained by the nation' nor sufficient 'to do justice to the constitution'. Furthermore, he maintained haughtily, it was not to the kingdom's advantage to pursue expedient and deficient solutions that did not interdict the affirmation of the offending power in the future:

> They [MPs] ought either to declare against all usurpation, or by an effectual repeal to annihilate those pretensions in future. It was the opinion of the nine [judges] of Ireland [in 1692] that this act took away the power of originating bills, and gave it to the Privy Council. That should certainly be repealed, for he did not see by any effect in the present bill but the Privy Council might recal[l] this power under a corrupt ministry ... It was not to be supposed that the breed of the Straffords in political principles were yet extinct; and an arbitrary government might at some future period take advantage of the negligence of the present hour.[70]

Ireland, Flood insisted, was entitled to possess 'a similar constitution with England', but the proposed bill 'cut them off from that benefit' because it did not

---

68. *Commons Jn. (Irl.)*, x, 356; *Parl. Reg. (Irl.)*, i, 382–3. Yelverton was appointed to the office by Portland.

69. 21 and 22 Geo III, chap 47.

70. *Parl. Reg. (Irl.)*, i, 386–7. The reference to Strafford is to Thomas Wentworth, first earl of Strafford (1593–1641), lord lieutenant of Ireland. See above, pp 11–12.

contain a 'provision' to 'prevent the smothering of bills or explain the reasons of a silent negative'. In order to address this deficiency, he reiterated his recommendation that MPs should press instead for the 'express repeal of the law ... with a saving clause of such and such things as should be found necessary to retain'. Though this suggestion differed materially from the position Flood had taken in respect of Yelverton's 'certifying bill', the inherent logic of the proposition forced Yelverton into the telling admission that, while the current heads 'did not entirely restore what the constitution of England enjoyed, ... circumstanced as Ireland was now, it was the best calculated that could be devised'. Flood was not appeased. Having put his adversary firmly on the defensive, he intensified Yelverton's discomfort by pointing out that the history of Poynings' Law supported his contention that the only sure way permanently to extend the liberties of Ireland was by repealing, rather than by amending, the law since the original act

> had expressly provided that their bills should not be altered, and yet the English Privy Council had the effrontery to continue such alterations. No ambiguous words were sufficient to protect the rights of the weak against the strong, nor were the provisions of the present bill as explicit as the original law of Poynings. Lawyers might create doubts hereafter, and they should prefer certainty to doubt, by a repeal.[71]

Though Flood once more enjoyed, the perspicacious commissioner of the revenue, John Beresford, conceded, 'much the better of the argument', he still did not possess the political support necessary to translate his verbal triumphs into political victories.[72] Yelverton demonstrated that he was not disinclined to be accommodating by introducing a substantial amendment (comprising clauses three and four) to the effect that no bill would be 'certified into Great Britain as a cause or consideration for holding a parliament' in Ireland and that no parliament could be held in Ireland without a 'licence ... from his majesty' (clause four), but he was unwilling to meet Flood's primary objection. Flood refused to let the matter lie, and he contrived, during the ill-tempered debate on the third reading of the bill, to offer a substantial amendment ostensibly aimed at overcoming what he identified as a crucial weakness of the measure, but which, in fact, was nothing less than an attempt to remodel the bill to reflect his own view that a declaratory rather than an amending law was required:

> Whereas ... doubts have arisen on the construction of the law commonly called Poynings', and of the third and fourth of Philip and Mary, explanatory thereof: Be it enacted by the King's most excellent Majesty, by and with the advice and consent of the Lords Spiritual and Temporal, and Commons, in this present parliament assembled, and by the authority of the

71. *Parl. Reg. (Irl.)*, i, 388–9.

same, that the said law of Poynings, and the said third and fourth of Philip and Mary, be and stand repealed, save only as follows: that is to say, be it enacted that no parliament shall be holden in this kingdom until a licence for that purpose be had and obtained from his Majesty, his heirs and successors, under the great seal of Great Britain: And that all bills, considerations, causes, ordinances, tenors and provisions, of either or both Houses of parliament, shall be of right certified to his Majesty, his heirs and successors, unaltered, under the great seal of Ireland, by the Lord Lieutenant, or other chief governor or governors, and the council of this kingdom, for the time being; and that such bills, and no others, being returned unaltered, under the great seal of Great Britain, shall be capable of receiving the royal assent or dissent in parliament, according to his Majesty's commission, either for giving his assent or dissent to the same respectively.

Since it was unusual to amend a bill to this extent so late in its parliamentary odyssey, the House of Commons refused to take Flood's amendment on board. As a consequence, the bill that finally made its way from the Irish legislature to the British Council board conformed to what Barry Yelverton and other moderate patriots – Grattan, Hussey Burgh, Lord Charlemont – were prepared to accept.[73] What the bill, which negotiated the British Council without amendment,[74] authorised was that bills – as distinct from heads of bills – could take their rise in either house of the Irish parliament, and that they could be transmitted, complete and unaltered, from the Irish Privy Council to its British equivalent. The powers of the British Council were also much diminished, since the ratification of Yelverton's act meant that it was deprived of the authority to amend bills received from Ireland. It was still empowered to scrutinise Irish legislation, and it was not, as Flood had forewarned, explicitly deprived of the authority to postpone and to respite, but its primary function was to oversee the attachment of the great seal and the preparation of a commission empowering the lord lieutenant as the Kings's representative in Ireland to give each bill the royal assent so it could become law.

THE OPERATION OF LEGISLATIVE INDEPENDENCE

The 'act to regulate the manner of passing bills and to prevent delays in summoning of parliament', (21 and 22 George III, chap 47), fundamentally altered the manner in which law was made in Ireland. As established above, neither the British nor the Irish Privy Council was deprived completely of a role, but their

---

72. Beresford to Eden, 7 June (BL, Auckland Papers, Add. MS 34418 ff 470–71); see also Fitzpatrick to Dobbs, 1 June 1782 (NLI, Dobbs Papers, MS 2251 f. 95).
73. *Parl. Reg.* (Irl.), i, 387–97; Haliday to Charlemont, 7 June 1782 in HMC, *Charlemont*, i, 406–7.
74. NA, PC2/127 ff 423, 428, 430–3.

power to shape legislation was greatly diminished. In the case of the Irish Council, its function was reduced to that of certification which, post-1782, meant putting bills in order for the attachment of the great seal of Ireland so they could be transmitted to London. The fact that as well as attaching the great seal of Great Britain so they could receive the royal assent in Ireland, the British Council retained the authority to postpone and to respite Irish bills meant that it had not been disempowered to the same extent. Theoretically, it could have employed the requirement that bills could only become law in Ireland if they were returned to Ireland 'under the great seal of Great Britain' in an active fashion to justify vetoing problematic or objectionable legislation referred from Ireland.[75] The marquess of Buckingham said as much in 1788, and the attorney general, John FitzGibbon, made the same point when he informed MPs on 11 February 1789, in the course of the debate on the motion to address the prince of Wales to assume the regency of Ireland, that

> All bills, which pass the two houses here, which shall be certified into England, and which shall be returned under the Great Seal of England without any addition, diminution or alteration whatsoever, shall pass into law, and no other. By this you make the Great Seal of England essentially and indispensably necessary to the passing of laws in Ireland.[76]

The prime minister, William Pitt, was more tactful, but he made essentially the same point in the course of the debate on the merits of an Anglo-Irish union in 1799, when he observed that the great seal of Great Britain could only be 'put to an Irish bill' by the Lord Chancellor, who was guided in his actions by the cabinet.[77] This was a statement of legal and administrative fact; the political reality, as Pitt, who was prime minister for virtually all of the time that Ireland was legislatively independent, well knew was that the British Privy Council could not be seen to employ aggressively the power to reject Irish bills, because, William Knox observed tellingly, 'dreadful consequences follow trifling legislative disputes'. The aim of ministers, it was explained to Speaker Pery in September 1785, was 'to leave the government of Ireland to its parliament, exercising the King's negative only in extraordinary cases, and then with decision'.[78]

Guided by its wish to provide the Irish parliament with no reason to provoke a 'legislative dispute' that might weaken the Anglo-Irish connection, the British Privy Council was loath to employ the powers still available to it to interfere actively with the legislation transmitted from Ireland. The Council did 'veto' a

---

75. The phrase 'simple veto' to describe it was used by Denis Kennedy ('The Irish Whigs, administrative reform and responsible government, 1782–1800', *Éire-Ireland*, 8 (1973), p. 57).
76. *Parl. Reg. (Irl.)*, ix, 48.
77. Cited in R.B. McDowell, 'Parliamentary independence, 1782–9' in Moody and Vaughan (eds), *A new history of Ireland: iv*, 265.
78. Knox to Pery, 12 Sept. 1783 in HMC, *Emly*, ii, 175.

small number of measure (as shall be seen below), but the eagerness of ministers to do nothing that might reanimate the tension and ill feeling between the ruling elites in both kingdoms was symbolised by the failure to establish what administrative changes and technical refinements were required to give effect to Yelverton's Act prior to the commencement on 14 October 1783 of the 1783–4 session. Such caution was appropriate during the summer of 1783 when the question of the 'renunciation' by the Westminster legislature of its claim to make law for Ireland was a matter of dispute; the political instability that produced three governments in less than two years was also a factor, with the result that it was left to Lord Northington, who took charge of the Irish administration in the summer of 1783, to oversee the required administrative changes, and he made no attempt to do so until he had bills to transmit.[79] Thus, it was not until 3 December – the date of the first transmiss – that he conveyed the draft of a revised 'commission' empowering the lord lieutenant to give the 'royal assent to such acts as are to be hereafter passed into laws in this kingdom'.[80] It was in keeping with Northington's pragmatic style that he should proceed in this way, and it had the unintended effect of ensuring the preservation at both the British and Irish Councils of procedural arrangements for dealing with heads of bills that closely echoed those employed before 1782.

This was achieved by the simple expedient of making only those changes that were necessary to comply with the changed legal situation. What this meant in Ireland was that once bills negotiated the parliamentary chamber in which they took their rise, they were forwarded to the Privy Council for certification so they could be transmitted to London. Prior to Yelverton's act, the original rolls were transferred, but following its enactment, the originals were retained in the Lords Office and copies (prepared by the clerks of the Council) conveyed to the Council.[81] Since the Irish Council, which numbered 89 in 1784, no longer possessed the right to amend or to respite these bills, there was no particular reason for councillors, whose time was increasingly taken up with responding to petitions, preparing proclamations and issuing orders, continuing the practice of scrutinising bills. However, this is not what happened. On the basis of a small sample of incidental references, it appears that the Irish Council continued the practice of referring bills to committees of Council and that full and draft reports were submitted for formal consideration. Private bills were also scrutinised, but in these instances the

79. For the renunciation crisis see P.J. Jupp, 'Earl Temple's viceroyalty and the question of renunciation, 1782–3', *IHS*, 17 (1982), pp 299–317; Kelly, *Henry Flood*, pp 324–36.
80. Northington to North, 3 Dec. 1783 (2) (Beinecke Library, Osborn Collection, Northington Letterbook, ff 47–58).
81. *Dublin Evening Post*, 6 May 1786. The preservation of the 'original acts' permanently in the Lords Office was prompted by a report of a Lords' committee into the state of the rolls of parliament made in 1758. Prior to this, the 'original acts' with transcripts from 1715 were stored in a house in Latins Quarter, and only conveyed to the office of the clerk of parliament at the beginning of each session. Those antedating 1715 were kept permanently in the rolls office 'in disorder and confusion' (NA, SP63/415).

reports were prepared, as had long been the practice, by members of the judiciary.[82] Because no report has been located, it is not possible to comment on their content, but they were probably formulaic, and offered little by way either of general observation on the thrust of the measure or specific comment on deficient or problematic features. Whether this was the case or not, the copy bills received at the Irish Council were certified by the attachment of the great seal of Ireland, which was placed at the bottom left hand side, and by the preparation of a certificate from the lord lieutenant and Council. In addition, in a further manifestation of administrative continuity, a Privy Council letter describing the bill, the house in which it arose, its purpose, how it differed from preceding bills of this kind, why it was required and so on was readied in the usual manner. Since the lord lieutenant also prepared a covering note, which sometimes extended to a paragraph on each bill, the documentation accompanying each transmiss was quite extensive. This was emphatically the case at the outset of the 1783–4 session when the new procedural regime was brought into being. Subsequently, the covering notes prepared by lords lieutenants became perfunctory, and a majority of the Privy Council letters formulaic.[83]

The decision of the Irish Council to make as few changes as possible to established administrative practices was replicated by the British Council. Bills transmitted from Ireland were received at the Home Office, as the Southern Department became in 1782, from where they were transferred to the Privy Council. Once they were received at the Council they were conveyed, pursuant to the familiar order in Council made at the outset of every session, to the Crown's law officers 'to examine'. To assist them, the law officers also received the 'letters from the Lord Lieutenant and [Irish] Privy Council accompanying the said bills', and such petitions as might be presented to facilitate them to 'report from time to time their opinions thereupon'.[84] Other than on those rare occasions when one was unavailable,[85] the law officers continued to present joint reports, but because the Privy Council was no longer entitled to amend bills, the content of these documents changed significantly. Instead of the sometimes lengthy reports listing every amendment by skin and line, which were commonplace prior to 1782 and which, in specific instances, ran to many pages, the law officers' report simply stated that 'in our judgement this bill should receive His Majesty's assent and pass into a law'. Over time, a suitably tailored version of this formula was employed in reports devoted to large 'job lots' of bills.[86] 'Humbly submitted' to the

82. NAI, Index to departmental letters and official papers, 1760–89 ff 93, 97.

83. Northington to North, 3 (2), 4, 9, 11 Dec. 1783 (Beinecke Library, Northington letterbook, ff 47–55, 66–8, 68–9, 70–4); Northington to Stormont, 3, 4, 9, 11 Dec. 1783 (NA, PC1/16 no. 10, PC1/13/43 f. 11, PC1/31/78A); Privy Council letter, 25 Mar. 1788 (PC1/18/A17).

84. NA, PC2/128 f. 572, PC2/129 ff 14–15, 147, PC2/130 f. 37, PC2/146; Minutes of Clerks of Council, 1764–95, 28 Nov. 1783 (PC4/2).

85. See report on fourteen public and one private bill, 4 Apr. 1792 (NA, PC1/19/A24ii).

86. For examples, see NA, PC1/13/ 43, 44, PC1/16/12/1, PC1/18/A17, PC1/18/A21, A22, PC1/16/12 ff 1–127, PC1/18/A19, and as note 84.

'consideration' of the Lords of the Committee of Council' established 'to consider the Irish bills', the membership and operation of this committee also contracted as the task of dealing with Irish bills became less demanding. Constituted anew at the commencement of every session, its membership was halved with the appointment of a 17-member committee in 1783–4, and it was reduced still further in 1785 when 13 councillors were nominated. It remained at this level until 1795 when 16 members were appointed, and its number seems not to have fallen below 15 thereafter. In keeping with precedent, membership of the committee remained an *ex officio* courtesy offered to the archbishop of Canterbury, the lord privy seal, and lord steward, the lord chancellor and the president of the council, but the nomination of the home secretary, the prime minister and a succession of eminent cabinet figures – Lord Sydney, duke of Richmond, the earl of Westmorland, William Grenville, Lord Hawkesbury, Henry Dundas, the duke of Portland and Earl Camden – with particular knowledge of Ireland was more significant. Appropriately, the home secretary, who bore responsibility for Ireland, took charge of bringing Irish bills through the Committee.[87] It fell to him to remind colleagues to attend to ensure a quorum, which remained unchanged at three, and to chair meetings when nobody more senior was available. Since the Committee's work was largely routine and uneventful, it was necessary on occasion to 'beg [the] attendance' of specific cabinet members 'for half an hour' to enable business to proceed. Consistent with this, attendance at the Irish bills committee rarely exceeded four, and was generally no more than the minimum. These consisted usually of the home secretary, the president of the council, and one other, generally the foreign secretary, the chancellor of the exchequer or prime minister. This was usually sufficient to ensure that bills were 'returned as quickly as possible'.[88]

In keeping with the increasingly routine nature of the work conducted at the Irish bills committee, bills were forwarded for the consideration by the full Council in the presence of the King in substantially larger lots than was the case before 1782. Though this stage of the process at the British Council had become increasingly streamlined before 1782, it was still more so thereafter. This did not prevent George III from complaining in 1787 about the 'much hurry and want of regularity' in the management of Irish legislation,[89] but in truth while there was some hurry, there was little irregularity, since the Irish bills committee determined on 11 December 1783 the procedural adjustments that were required to comply

87. Draft note by Lord Sydney to Lords Carmarthen and Howe and William Pitt, 19 Apr. 1786 (NLI, Sydney papers, MS 52/P/13).

88. Johnston, *Great Britain and Ireland*, p. 101; NA, PC2/128 f. 572, PC2/130 f. 37, PC2/131 f. 24; PC2/132 ff 33–4; PC2/133 ff 30, 403; PC1/18/A19; PC2/134 ff 409–10; PC2/135 ff 185, 433–4; PC2/136 ff 443–4; PC2/137 f. 340; PC2/138 f. 70; PC2/139 ff 326–7; PC2/142; PC2/145 f. 154; PC2/151 f. 151; PC2/152 f. 293; PC2/154 f. 161; PC2/155 ff 311–17; PC2/136 ff 44–6, 478, 550; Minutes of Clerks of Council, 1764–95, 17 Mar. 1785 (PC4/20).

89. George III to Sydney, 6 May 1787 in Arthur Aspinall (ed.), *Later correspondence of George III, 1784–1812* (5 vols, London, 1962–70), i, 284.

with Yelverton's Act, and the wording of the various orders to enable bills to receive the royal assent in Ireland.

Though the procedures employed at the British Council after 1782 echoed those applied before that date, there were some modifications. The most notable arose from the decision to return the 'identical bills, which are certified to His Majesty by the Lord Lieutenant ... under the great seal of [Ireland]', when they were approved under the great seal of Great Britain. This meant that it was no longer necessary to engross Irish bills. This allowed for the more expeditious processing of Irish legislation, but it did cause a difficulty as to what 'should remain here as evidence of what bills came over'. It was proposed initially that 'the certificates from the Lord Lieutenant and Council of Ireland, which accompany each bill', should be retained, but this was not deemed appropriate. Instead, though some reservations were expressed as to its sufficiency, it was determined to make do with the warrant for passing the commission for the royal assent and the transcript of the bill conveyed from Ireland, which was requested when it was not provided; these were retained in the Council office.[90] In point of fact these were not the only records of what Irish bills 'came over'. The Council also retained a duplicate of the commission (the original draft of which was transmitted from Ireland by Lord Northington empowering the lord lieutenant to give the royal assent to a bill) prepared by the clerk of the council on the instruction of the attorney general (who in turn was acting on the instructions of the Council) annexed to each bill. Interestingly, in a further change of practice, the attorney general signed the commission rather than the bill, while the task of ensuring each bill 'passed under the great seal of Great Britain' was delegated to the lord chancellor. This seal was attached to the bill received from Ireland on the 'right side' (to complement the placement on the left side of the great seal of Ireland). Once this was done and the commission prepared, a formal order in Council was prepared and the bill or bills to which it pertained readied to be returned to Ireland.[91]

With the procedural and textual changes required to process Irish bills established before the end of 1783, the management of Irish legislation took a form that endured until the abolition of the Irish parliament in 1800. Some modifications were made to the wording of the commission granting the lord lieutenant authority to give the royal assent to bills in the intervening years, but they were matters of style rather than substance.[92] Indeed, because the task of attaching the great seal to Irish bills was essentially a matter of fulfilling

90. Portland to Camden, 26 May 1797 (NA, HO122/4 f. 137); King to Castlereagh, 20 June 1800 (NA, HO122/5 f. 169).
91. This and the preceding paragraph are based on the Minutes of the Clerks of Council, 11 Dec. 1783 (NA, PC4/3); Lord President to Northington, 12 Dec. 1783 (PC1/31/78A); PC2/128 ff 590–3; PC2/129 f. 89; Order in Council, 12 Dec. 1783 (C183/1); *Dublin Evening Post*, 6 May 1786.
92. NA, PC2/130 f. 277, PC2/135 f. 191; PC2/138 ff 56–7; PC2/147 ff 5–6.

procedural requirements, the case in favour of simplifying the frequently wordy content and form of orders and commissions was strong. It was part of the time-saving response that can be identified at all stages of the process from the formal minutes of proceedings at the Council board to the content of the orders in council that were prepared to accompany bills on their return to Ireland.[93] It was also logical because bills were dealt with increasingly at the British Council in groups of ten, fifteen or more, climaxing with 35 at the last formal meeting of the Irish bills committee on 26 July 1800, and because of the continuing pressures ministers, particularly the home secretary, were under to process bills with 'dispatch'. As a result, they were returned in equally large lots. Inevitably, there were delays due to the unavailability of key members, including the King, and the disinterest of ministers, but the process was so streamlined by the early 1790s that the majority of bills were turned round within ten days.[94]

This expeditious management of Irish bills was encouraged by the large amount of legislation that was forwarded from Ireland. In keeping with the pattern established between 1771 and 1782, an average of over ninety measures were initiated and more than sixty were transmitted to the British Council each session between 1783 and 1800 (Tables 12, 13 and 14: pp 355–7). One obvious reason for this was the removal from the Privy Councils of the power to respite and amend bills, but it was not the only factor. The reorganisation of finance and revenue law as a result of the disaggregation of the supply and appropriation bills was also significant, as was the opening up of new areas of legislative concern. As a result, the Irish parliament was more active making law during the 1780s and 1790s than at any moment in its history. This is all the more notable because the parliament met annually from 1785, and because the amount of law made in 1789, 1792 and 1794 was substantially below average (see Table 14). Significantly, the busiest three sessions in this period were also the busiest in the eighteenth century.

The bulk of the law proposed and made in the Irish parliament during the 1780s and 1790s rose in the House of Commons, which strengthened its already firm grip on this parliamentary function during the 1780s. In all, 92 per cent (or 1392) of the total of 1517 legislative initiatives for which leave was given between 1783 and 1800 commenced in the Commons (Table 14). Of the remainder, 124 or 8 per cent rose in the Lords. Saliently, 60 per cent of the Lords' bills were private

93. Orders in Council, 1783–90 (NA, C183/1 passim); PC2/130 ff 269, 281.
94. Minute of Irish bills committee, Mar. 1786 (NA, PC1/17/3); NA, HO 122/1–2 passim; Gower to Rutland, 6 May 1784, Camden to Rutland, 19 Mar. 1785, 3 Mar. 1787, Camden to Buckingham, 14 Mar. 1789 (PC1/31/78A); Buckingham to Grenville, 8 Apr. 1788 in HMC, *Fortescue*, i, 315; *Dublin Evening Post*, 2 May 1786; Draft note, 19 Apr. 1786 (NLI, Sydney Papers, MS 52/P/13); Sydney to Buckingham, 14 Mar. 1789 (HO122/2 ff 7–8); Dundas to Westmorland, 7 Aug. 1793, Portland to Fitzwilliam, 16 Mar., Portland to Camden, 28 May 1795 (HO122/3 ff 1, 123, 167); Portland to Camden, 16 Mar., 7 Apr. (2), 1796, 8, 28 June 1797, 18 Mar., 25 May 1798 (HO122/4 ff 44, 47, 142, 150, 205, 216); Portland to Cornwallis, 1, 18, 23 May 1799, 6 Apr. 1800, King to Marsden, 16 July 1800 (HO122/5 ff 79, 88, 92–3, 155, 171, 177–9, 181–3, 184–6).

(Table 13), in keeping with the fact that private legislation was seen as the Lords' responsibility primarily, and it is noteworthy in this context that the success rate of private bills (86 per cent) was better than that of public bills (74 per cent) in the upper house. F.J. James has drawn attention to the Lords' modest legislative impact by pointing out that only 12 public bills originating with peers made it to law between 1792 and 1797.[95]

One measure, entitled *An act for the King's most gracious, general and free pardon*, which was admitted to parliament via the Lords in August 1798, was presented as arising with the King, but this was a fiction. The bill arose with the Irish executive, and was conveyed to the British Council by the lord lieutenant. Considered at the Council board on 22 July, it caused councillors considerable 'embarrassment'. Having established that the only precedent for such a measure was (the lord chancellor, Lord Loughborough, reported to his Irish counterpart), 'the very peculiar case in 1660 when the act was grounded on the terms of the King's declaration from Breda offering free pardon under the Great Seal to all persons who should apply subject to such exception as the two houses of parliament should think fit', they were disturbed by the suggestion in the bill that 'all the exceptions' should be made by 'either houses of [the Irish] parliament'. Determined 'to suffer no interference' with the King's prerogative, such as this implied, the British Council would, was it empowered to do so, 'have framed the exceptions' themselves even if it did 'create some inconvenience on your side'. However, instead of this, they simply added a clause 'referring the exceptions to an act passed in the present session', which obliged the Irish parliament to legislate on this point, thereby securing the King's prerogative. This decided, the original measure 'was read at the [Council] board and signed by the King' on 22 July prior to its transmission to Ireland. The expectation was that it would become law in short order, but delays in its presentation prompted its recall and 'the preparation of another such act', which went through the same procedures prior to its transmission to Ireland, where it made it to the statute book in record time.[96]

A significant proportion of bills proposed in the Commons and the Lords did not become law. In all, 370 or 24 per cent of bills did not negotiate the Commons, which exceeded by a large margin the 5.5 per cent (74 bills) that failed in the Lords. The Lords was more active in practice than this figure suggest, since when one measures the proportion of bills to fail in the house in which they arose, the Lords' failure rate rises to 15 per cent. However, since a smaller proportion of Commons' bills fell in the Lords (5 per cent or 65 bills) than Lords' bills fell in the Commons (14 per cent or 17 bills), it is apparent that MPs were more legislatively assertive than peers. This observation is reinforced by the fact that the Commons' disapproval of interference by the Lords with its bills caused them to reject seven

95. James, *Lords of the ascendancy*, p. 40 note 40; *Lords Jn. (Irl.)*, vols 5–8.
96. 38 Geo III, chap 55; *Commons Jn. (Irl.)*, xvii, 373, 391; NA, PC2/151 ff 421, 424–8, 446–51; Loughborough to Clare, and enclosure, 23 July 1798 (NA, HO100/41 ff 312–8).

of their own bills that were modified in the upper house (Table 14). The Lords, for their part, sought in 1784 to assert their right to reject bills 'of aid or supply' that rose in the Commons that contained 'annexed clauses ... foreign to and different from the matter of said bill', but it did not sustain this assertion.[97] All told, 30 per cent (455) of the legislative initiatives that arose in the Irish parliament did not proceed to the Irish Council between 1783 and 1800. This was 5 per cent more than the proportion of bills that did not proceed between 1761 and 1782 (Table Eleven). However, when the proportion of bills respited at the Irish Privy Council is taken into account, the percentage of measures lost in Ireland between 1783 and 1800 was 5 per cent lower. The removal from the Irish Council of the power to reject bills can be shown therefore to have had an identifiable impact on the proportion of Irish bills that were forwarded to the British Council. Significantly, other than one bill – for defraying the expense of the militia for one year, which was 'sent to the lord lieutenant' on 25 March 1794 having passed all stages in the Irish parliament but was not forwarded to the British Council – no attempt was made to circumvent this.[98]

One thousand and sixty-one bills passed under the great seal of Ireland were received at the British Privy Council between 1783 and 1800. Though the number received each session ranged from a low of 26 in 1794 to a high of 110 in 1800, the sessional average for the period was over 60. This is comparable to the figures registered during the 1770s, but because the British Council was disinclined to use its power of 'veto', 99.6 per cent of the bills it received were sent to be returned. This was an unprecedented figure, and it is the most obvious register of the fact that 'legislative independence' had a tangible impact on the statute book. The British Council did express explicit reservations with respect of 3.2 per cent of the bills received from Ireland, but only four were deemed sufficiently objectionable to be laid aside.

The British Privy Council was understandably cautious in its response to Irish legislation in 1783–4.[99] This can be highlighted by the reaction to two bills of which John Foster's controversial proposal 'to secure the liberty of the press by preventing the abuses arising from the publication of traitorous, seditious, false and slanderous libels' is the best known. Prepared in response to an outburst of public anger in Dublin at the refusal of the Rutland administration to endorse calls for popular measures, the law officers (Richard Pepper Arden and Archibald McDonald) were sufficiently disquieted to express concern at what they perceived as the bill's draconian nature in their report to the Irish bills committee. Their unease was aroused in the first instance by the fact that the proofs required to demonstrate ownership of newspapers charged with libel were flawed and, in the second, by the apprehension that the powers granted to justices of the peace to

97. Charlotte Murphy, 'The Irish House of Lords, 1780–1800' (PhD thesis, University College Cork, 2003), pp 110–12.
98. *Commons Jn. (Irl.)*, xv, 326, 335, 337, 340, 341, 346, 347.
99. *Freeman's Journal*, 13 May 1784.

compel hawkers and other vendors 'to discover' the printers of any libellous publication would be abused. Precluded from recommending 'any alterations in the bill', the law officers confined themselves to listing their concerns and to inviting the Irish bills committee 'to determine whether the circumstances which induced the legislature of Ireland to pass this bill make it proper that it should receive his majesty's royal assent'.[100] As the first of its kind, the report was closely considered, but unwilling to risk antagonising Irish opinion by setting the bill aside, the lords of the committee took the safer option and determined it should be returned. They did not allow their unease to pass unrecorded, however. The secretary of state, Lord Sydney, explained to the duke of Rutland that the Council would have welcomed the opportunity to have amended the bill's offending clauses had that been possible.[101]

Parallel with this, the Irish bills committee singled out the omission of the 'exception for oyl' in a bill for facilitating trade and intercourse with the newly independent American states as a matter of concern. Apprehensive lest the bill as drafted would encourage the smuggling of American goods into Britain via Ireland, Rutland was advised 'to get a short [supplementary] bill prepared' to remedy the error, but the omission was dealt with instead by an order in Council.[102] This appeased ministers, who were less than content generally with the fact that Irish bills were, as Sydney put it censoriously, 'full of inaccuracys'.[103] Despite this, ministers and councillors remained disinclined to make an issue of the fallibility of Irish drafting practices other than when it was strictly necessary. Moreover, the solutions they identified were not transmitted to Dublin as instructions; rather they were presented as the answers to problems, which the Irish administration was expected to consider and, so far as it was possible, to act upon. Significantly, nobody in the Irish administration raised any objection with the fact that Irish bills were being subjected to such close scrutiny though it might have been argued that this was inconsistent with the spirit if not the letter of Yelverton's act, and more indicative of legislative 'dependence' than 'legislative independence'.

The close scrutiny that Irish legislation experienced during the 1783–84 session set the pattern for what was to follow. Understandably, more problems were identified during the 1780s when Irish legislators were still coming to terms with the implications of legislative independence than during the 1790s, but the disposition, demonstrated in 1783–4, to identify practical solutions to such

---

100. Law officers' report, 30 Apr. 1784 (NA, PC1/16/12 ff 105–06).
101. Minute of Irish bills committee, 30 Apr. 1784 (NA, PC1/12/18 ff 7–8); Sydney to Rutland, 1 May 1784 (NLI, Sydney Papers, MS 51/C/8).
102. Sydney to Rutland, 17 Apr. and reply 24 Apr. 1784 (NA, HO100/12 ff 330–2, 370–1); Sydney to Rutland, 1 May 1784 (NLI, Sydney Papers, MS 51/C/8).
103. Sydney to Rutland, 1 May (NLI, Sydney Papers, MS 51/C/8); Rutland to Sydney, 10 May 1784 (Suffolk Record Office, Pretyman Papers, HA119/T108/34); Sydney to Rutland, 6, 14 May 1784 in HMC, *Rutland*, iii, 93, 95–6.

problems as they arose proved enduring, though councillors made it clear that they were not disposed to permit bills to proceed that were either inconsistent with British interests or in breach of existing arrangements between the two kingdoms. This was made clear in 1785, when two bills were 'respited'. The first was a bill 'for granting bounties on gunpowder' exports, which met with resistance in the first instance because of 'a mistake in the ... calculation' of the level at which bounties should be set to keep them in line with those provided in England. However, it was the absence of a provision prohibiting the export of gunpowder to the West Indies and America that caused most difficulties. Determined to ensure that the level of duties and bounties in Britain and Ireland was kept uniform, the Irish bills committee expressed its 'fundamental objection to the bill' on the grounds that it was inconsistent with the proposed commercial union, which Pitt aspired to implement in 1785, and the free trade legislation of 1780.[104] It was also decided at the same time to reject a bill 'for preventing doubts concerning the parliament, Privy Council and officers civil and military on the demise of the crown, and for confirming letters patent'. No explanation was offered, but it may, as Gerard O'Brien has speculated, have had something to do with the 'failure' of Pitt's mooted commercial union.[105] No causal connection can be established but the fact that these were the first Irish bills to fall at this hurdle since 1782 suggests that the British Council may have been influenced in its actions by the expectation that the ratification of the commercial propositions would make it easier for them to shape Irish legislation. The fact that reservations were expressed in respect of three other bills transmitted in 1785 supports this conclusion.

The commitment, demonstrated in 1785, to ensure that the terms of the 1780 'free trade' legislation were observed strictly was a crucial consideration for British ministers and officials in their dealings with Irish bills during the 1780s and 1790s. This commitment was not absolute in so far as they were not unwilling to allow a bill to proceed that breached the principle of equality ratified in 1780 so long as the breach was temporary. This was made clear in the spring of 1785 when the members of the Irish bills committee observed that 'the enumeration of the duties payable ... upon the importation of ... refined sugar' in the bill 'for regulating the sugar trade' was deficient by 4s. 8d. Though eager to ensure that the duties levied in Ireland were 'equal to the duties imposed by the several English acts of parliament now in force', neither the Irish bills committee nor the full Council advocated that the bill was rejected because it was 'only an annual act'. They recommended instead the introduction of 'a short bill supplementing that under consideration ... to rectify the ... mistake' in the original.[106] This was

104. NA, PC2/130 ff 189, 252–4, 380; O'Brien, *Anglo-Irish politics*, p. 133.
105. NA, PC2/130 ff 270, 374, 380; O'Brien, *Anglo-Irish politics*, p. 133; Kelly, *Prelude to Union*, passim.
106. NA, PC2/130 ff 91, 93–4, 107–11; Minutes of the clerks of Council 1764–95, 17 Mar. 1785 (PC4/2); Sydney to Rutland, 19 Mar. 1785 (NA, HO100/16 ff 276–8).

the solution proposed also to remedy the omission of an 'exception with respect to the exportation of hay to Great Britain similar to the provision in the British act which authorises exportation to Ireland' in the hay bill, while the recommendation with respect of the revenue fraud bill was that the Irish parliament should 'pass a new bill to prevent this act from having a retrospect'. Significantly, the suggestion in this instance as well as in the instance of the hay bill that a 'new bill' should be prepared was presented as a request rather than as an instruction, which gave the Irish administration some room to manoeuvre. They pressed ahead with the hay and revenue bills, which received the royal assent shortly afterwards; in the case of the sugar duty bill, the Duke of Rutland's preparedness to recommend a short bill to remedy the error in the original measure ensured the matter was resolved satisfactorily.[107]

The co-operative attitude that characterised the exchanges between the lord lieutenant of Ireland, the duke of Rutland, and the home secretary, Lord Sydney, in respect of these bills was symbolised by Rutland's request in the aftermath of the sugar bill that 'at the conclusion of each session of the British parliament, authentic information may be sent to me of any addition or diminution or any other alteration whatsoever, which shall take place in the British duties'.[108] The British Council also had ideas as to how the problems of this nature might be averted. In 1785, they urged the early communication of bills to allow time for their 'due consideration' and, when this was not acted upon, they solicited the Irish book of rates for customs, excise and tariffs in 1786.[109] It was even suggested that in order to prevent 'future … difficulties' in respect of duties, which 'must bring on … alterations extremely prejudicial to both countries', the Irish administration should transmit 'in an early stage all such bills if not before they are brought in, an account of the articles upon which duties are to be imposed, or drawbacks or bounties granted, in order that information may be sent to Ireland of the exact amount of such duties, drawbacks or bounties laid or granted in Great Britain'.[110] Lord Sydney was prompted to propose this potentially significant encroachment on the legislative autonomy of the Irish parliament by the failure in 1786 bill of a bill for the advancement of trade to observe the terms of the 1780 'free trade' legislation, and the fact that difficulties were identified also with respect of the importation of tobacco.[111] Faced with 'the very disagreeable alternatives of either rejecting these bills as inconsistent with the agreement contained in the act of [the] year 1780 or of passing them … with a firm reliance

---

107. NA, PC2/130 ff 270, 281, 283, 283–5, 356, 359–61; Sydney to Rutland, 20 June, 18, 19 Aug. (NA, HO122/1 ff 44, 46, 48); Rutland to Sydney, 22 Mar. 1785 (NA, HO100/16 f. 285); *Commons Jn. (Irl.)*, xi, 406, 468, 481.
108. Rutland to Sydney, 22 Mar. 1785 (NA, HO100/16 f. 285).
109. Sydney to Rutland, 19 Mar. 1785, 14 Mar. 1786 (NA, HO100/16 ff 276–8, NLI, Sydney Papers, MS 51/C/57).
110. Sydney to Rutland, 14 Mar. 1786 (NLI, Sydney Papers, MS 51/C/57).
111. Sydney to Rutland, 16 Mar. 1786 (NA, HO122/1 ff 65–7); Camden to Rutland, 16 Mar (PC1/31/78A).

on the faith of equity of the parliament of Ireland that they will rectify these errors', ministers felt that they had no choice but to opt for the latter.[112] They clung to the belief that 'such difficultys' could be obviated by the early communication of information or of draft bills, but though an effort was made to pursue the former course, it did not prevent all problems.[113] In 1787, objections were expressed once more at the Irish bills committee to the 'bill for the advancement of trade' on the grounds that it too contravened the 1780 'free trade' legislation, by not providing for an equitable drawback on the re-export of wine to the British colonies or to North America. Because they were unwilling to respite such an important bill, it was returned to become law with the 'strongest' urging that such bills were transmitted earlier, and with a request that a supplementary bill rectifying the mistake was introduced if this could be accepted consistent with 'the practice of the parliament of Ireland'.[114]

Guided by such experiences, the clerk to the British Council invited the law officers to examine Irish bills closely on occasion to establish if they were consistent with the law in Britain. As a result, some specific changes were proposed but, as with all such recommendations, there was little identifiable follow-through.[115] Ironically, it was not duties, but concern at the identification of problems in May 1787 in revenue and manifest bills, which the chief secretary, Thomas Orde, was only prepared to address 'on the commencement of the next session', that prompted Lord Sydney to warn the duke of Rutland that the Privy Council would no longer return 'objectionable' bills:

> From our not being able to correct bills transmitted from Ireland, it becomes very necessary that their import should be more minutely attended to, and should any bills in future be sent over equally objectionable, the Council will feel it incumbent upon them to advise His Majesty to reject them, a measure which it is very much wished to avoid.[116]

The 'postponement' in 1788 of a bill 'for more effectually preventing deceits and frauds in the manufacture of cordage' can be interpreted as the first manifestation of this policy in action.[117] This bill was refused the right to proceed on the familiar grounds that if it was made law, 'the Irish trade to our colonies will be more beneficial ... than it can be exercised by His Majesty's British subjects'.

112. Sydney to Rutland, [16 Mar. 1786](draft) (NLI, Sydney Papers, MS 51/C/38).
113. Nepean to Orde, 2 Feb. 1787 (NA, HO122/1 f. 100).
114. NA, PC2/132 ff 91, 101–4, 104–6, 111; Minutes of clerks of council, 1765–95, 16 Mar. 1787 (PC4/2); Sydney to Rutland, 17 Mar. 1787 (NA, HO100/20 ff 215–20, 224–6); *Commons Jn. (Irl.)*, xii, 241.
115. These comments are based upon the experience of the bill to 'increase and encourage shipping and navigation' (NA, PC2/132 ff 152, 174–5, 177–9; Cotterell to Attorney general, 19 Apr. 1787 (ibid., f. 154); *Commons Jn. (Irl.)*, xii, 287.
116. Sydney to Rutland, 7 May 1787 (NA, HO100/21 ff 63–7).
117. NA, PC2/133 ff 88, 99; O'Brien, *Anglo-Irish politics*, p. 134; *Commons Jn. (Irl.)*, xii, 403.

If this policy was pursued consistently, other bills would also have fallen by the wayside, but when faced in March 1788 with the problem of what to do in respect of 'inaccuracies' identified in the annual bill 'for the advancement of trade', the spectre of the 'inconveniences [that] would be likely to arise from the detention of the bill' proved overriding, and this important measure was returned uncorrected once more.[118] Significantly, the five points identified as most in need of correction were communicated to Ireland, but the Irish administration was as powerless as the British Council to incorporate them into the bill. This elicited a further round of requests for information on bills conveyed from Ireland to assist the law officers, but it did not prevent further problems.[119]

The inclusion in 1789 of an exemption for France in a bill to regulate the importation of cordage put Irish law at odds with that of Great Britain, but the Privy Council chose once more to overlook the matter in deference to the other duties provided for by the bill, on condition that a supplementary measure was 'introduced during the present session'.[120] It is not clear that this request was complied with, but the Privy Council made it clear that its agreement could not be assumed by objecting during this session to two private bills on the grounds that they infringed the royal prerogative. This was clearly a matter upon which they believed there could be no scope for indulgence, since they also directed that the Lord Lieutenant and the Irish Council should be informed 'that care may be taken in future that no bills whereby the interest or prerogative of the Crown is affected be brought into and discussed in the parliament of [Ireland] without His Majesty's consent thereto having being first had and obtained in due form'.[121] Significantly, this problem did not arise again. However, in 1793, reservations were expressed about a private bill to confirm a compromise between George Cockburn and John Hussey on the grounds that it omitted 'the usual clause' saving 'the rights of the King and of all bodies politic and corporate not intended to be affected by the bill'.[122]

Problems were also identified on occasions in the supply bills, which featured prominently in the deliberations of the Irish bills committee and in the dispatches of the secretary of state. The issues raised in 1791 in respect of the main duty bill appertained to 'several inaccuracies and omissions' relating to trade with France arising out of the Anglo-French treaty of 1786, but what most displeased the Irish bills committee was the failure of the Irish administration to comply with the Council's recommendation of 16 March 1787 that bills relating to 'the equalization of duties or drawbacks ... should be sent over' with time 'for

118. Sydney to Buckingham, 13 Mar. 1788 (NA, HO122/1 f. 148).
119. Nepean to Fitzherbert, 13 Mar. 1788 (NA, HO122/1 f. 150).
120. NA, PC2/133 ff 422, 425–9; law officers' report, 17 Mar. 1789 (NA, PC1/18/A19); Sydney to Buckingham, 19 Mar. 1789 (NA, HO122/3 ff 9–10); *Commons Jn. (Irl.)*, xiii, 70.
121. NA, PC2/134 ff 14, 29–31, 36–9; *Commons Jn.(Irl.)*, xiii, 113, 114.
122. NA, PC2/138 ff 130–2, 142, 144–5; Dundas to Westmorland, 6 Apr. 1793 (NA, HO122/2 f. 159); *Commons Jn.(Irl.)*, xv, 189.

due consideration'.[123] Chastened by this reminder, steps were taken in Ireland to ensure it was not repeated, but three years later, the Irish administration was alerted to the inappropriateness of including a clause in a money bill that made reference to the Anglo-French treaty because Britain and France were now at war. This was a pardonable oversight, but it is indicative of the lack of precision in Irish drafting practices that the same problem was encountered in a similar bill in 1795, and in 1794 in a bill 'for preventing money or effects ... being applied to the use of the persons exercising the powers of government in France'; this transcript of a British act omitted a clause in the fourth section 'extremely essential' to the effectiveness of the measure.[124]

It is not clear how this problem was resolved, because there was no obvious means other than the supplemental bill to correct errors or omissions discovered at this late stage in a bill's journey to the statute book, and because the Irish parliament was unwilling to accede to supplementary laws. As a result, the Privy Council had little alternative but to set aside those bills to which it took particular exception. This was the fate in 1792 of a measure for the encouragement of naval recruitment by making it easier for sailors to remit wages, though the bill was a copy of a British measure and it was initiated at the suggestion of the home secretary, Henry Dundas.[125] An alternative strategy, employed by Dundas the same year, was to delay the progress of a bill until British concerns were satisfied. This happened in respect of a bill to 'encrease agriculture and commerce by establishing a reciprocal preference in the corn trade' between Britain and Ireland. Pressed for strongly by Dundas who engaged in extensive discussions with informed parties, including the Crown's law officers, to ensure that British interests were not disadvantaged, the bill presented to the Irish parliament on 1 February was grounded on an advanced draft received from Dundas. However, when the Irish bill omitted to acknowledge the distinctions in the weight of certain commodities, consideration of the bill at the British Council was 'postpone[d]' until Dundas was assured that 'a clause for correcting the defect ... in the table annexed to the ... corn bill' would be introduced into the revenue bill.[126] This was done, but the task of drafting a bill that applied uniformly in both kingdoms proved so labour-intensive and time-consuming as to be impractical on more than an occasional basis, and it was not replicated.

123. 31 Geo III, chap 1; NA, PC2/135 ff 504, 506, 508–09, 510–12, 514; Irish bills committee minute, 12 Mar. 1791 (NA, PC1/18/A22); Grenville to Westmorland, 15 Mar. 1791 (NA, HO122/2 f. 94).

124. 34 Geo III, chap 5; NA, PC2/139 ff 405, 410–2, 412–3; *Commons Jn. (Irl.)*, xv, 347; 35 Geo III, chap 4; NA, PC2/142 ff 236, 238–9; *Commons Jn.(Irl.)*, xvi, 99; 34 Geo III, chap 14; NA, PC2/139 ff 440, 462, 462–4; *Commons Jn. (Irl.)*, xv, 348.

125. NA, PC2/136 f. 551; Dundas to Westmorland, 25 June 1791 (NA, HO122/2 ff 105–06. An act along these lines was ratified in 1793, with some reservations (Dundas to Westmorland, 17 Mar. 1793 (NA, HO122/2 ff 156–7)).

126. 32 Geo III, chap 20; NA, PC2/136 ff 460, 467–8, 487–8, 489, 493–4; Privy Council minute, 12 Jan., Table of weights and report of James Rondeau, 7 Jan.; law officers' report, 14 Feb., 21

As is apparent from the experience of the bills just considered, the disinclination of the British Privy Council to be seen actively to encroach upon the 'independence' of the Irish legislature, ensured that the number of bills that were laid aside and about which reservations were expressed fell in the 1790s. Even fewer were subject to petition (Tables Twelve, Thirteen and Fourteen; pp 355 etc.). The 'first instance of a petition to be heard against any bill since 1782' dates from 1791, and it was prompted by the concern of the tanners of Dublin that the ratification of an amending bill 'to prevent frauds in the tanning of hides', which sought to increase the regulation of the tanning industry, would prejudice their livelihood. Referred to the law officers for a report, and heard before the Irish bills committee, officials were faced with the stark choice either of setting the bill aside or of approving it unaltered; their decision to take the latter option was made easy by the law officers' determination that no evidence was submitted in support of the claim presented in the petition.[127] The fact that William Jackson, who petitioned on behalf of Robert and Daphne Phaire, had no identifiable impact on the Phaire trustees' bill during the same session offered a further illustration of the futility of this course of action and no petitions were presented thereafter. It is ironic that this should be so, since the law officers found much about the Phaire bill to dislike, but though they brought their reservations to the notice of the lords of the Irish bills committee, the bill was forwarded to receive the royal assent in Ireland.[128] Significantly, the response was exactly the same in respect of the law officers' reports in respect of the Louth trustees' bill, with which they also expressed serious reservation, and Lord Mountjoy's reversionary lease bill, which, in the law officers' judgment, materially 'contradicted' the will of his grandfather, Luke Gardiner.[129] The law officers registered no protest in this instance, but given the low percentage of bills to which they raised objection that were set aside to this point, it was only to be expected. Moreover, it anticipated a practice that became normative from 1795 when the reservations of the law officers with Irish bills were conveyed to the lord lieutenant in Ireland so 'that you may give the necessary directions thereupon'.[130] It is not clear if appropriate action was taken other than on those occasions when it was convenient for the Irish administration

Mar. (NA, PC1/19/A24ii); Law officers' report and bill clause, 20 Jan. 1792 (NA, HO100/36 ff 87–91); Grenville to Westmorland, 7 Nov. 1791, Dundas to Westmorland, 19, 30 Jan., 14 Feb. (NA, HO122/2 ff 115, 123, 124, 133); Westmorland to Dundas, 2, 8, 22 Feb. 1792 (NA, HO100/36 ff 204, 230, 305–8).

127. 31 Geo III, chap 27; NA, PC2/136 ff 49, 56–8, 72, 73–4; law officers' report, 19 Apr., Irish bills committee, 21 Apr. (NA, PC1/18/A22); *Commons Jn. (Irl.)*, xiv, 440.

128. NA, PC2/136 ff 17, 73, 74–6; law officers' report, 18 Apr., Minute of Irish bills committee, 20 April 1791 (NA, PC1/18/A22); *Commons Jn. (Irl.)*, xiv, 440.

129. 31 Geo. III, chaps 1 and 2 (private); NA, PC2/136 ff 16–17, 72, 74–6; law officers' reports, 19 Apr. 1791 (NA, PC1/18/A22); *Commons Jn. (Irl.)*, xiv, 440.

130. NA, PC2/142 ff 237, 238–41; Portland to Fitzwilliam, 16 Mar. 1795 (NA, HO122/3 f. 123); Portland to Camden, 17, 21 Mar. 1797 (NA, HO122/4 ff 121); Wickham to Castlereagh, 6 Sept. 1798 (NA, HO122/5 f. 24).

to do so, and such was the anxiety in Great Britain to do nothing to discommode Irish opinion, which was aware even if it hesitated to make an issue of those bills that were set aside, that it was deemed preferable to persist with this ambiguity rather than press matters to a controversial resolution.[131]

One thousand and fifty-seven bills were returned to Ireland between 1783 and 1800 to receive the royal assent. This was conferred upon bills in large batches by the lord lieutenant, in a majority of instances close to or at the end of the session. Because lords lieutenant were resident officeholders, the idea that the task might be performed by deputy did not arise until the summer of 1799 when the expectation that Lord Cornwallis would be 'absent' during the summer rallying support for a legislative union prompted the suggestion that it might be appropriate to delegate the task to three 'commissioners'. The proposed panel included the lord chancellor, the archbishop of Armagh, Lord Shannon and three judges, but it did not prove necessary.[132] It also did nothing to diminish the eagerness of the Irish parliament to make law. More acts were added to the Irish statute book during the years 1783–1800 than at any time in the kingdom's history. It might be countered that the fact that the British Privy Council was in a position to veto Irish bills and suggest corrections and clarifications that the legislative independence of the Irish parliament was significantly qualified. The fact that the Irish executive regained control of parliament in 1783–4 and, except for the occasional crisis, maintained it, was also vitally important, but it cannot mask the legislative energy of the Irish parliament during the final decades of its existence.

Other than Pitt's scheme for a 'commercial union', there is little evidence to suggest that ministers or officials made much attempt to shape the legislative agenda of the Irish parliament during the early years of legislative independence. Quite the contrary; a majority of the controversial suggestions for the 'adoption' of English laws at this time came from the Irish legislature, and were made by politicians anxious to ensure, in the wake of legislative independence, that Ireland would identify such British laws 'advantageous to this country' as it was appropriate to adopt.[133] This proposition was not formally pursued, but within a few years bills that were accurately described as 'a transcript from the English ... act' reached the statute book on a regular basis.[134] Such borrowings were voluntary, but following the failure to bring about a 'commercial union' in 1785, ministers were less reticent about suggesting legislation that the Irish parliament should approve. This process commenced, appropriately, following the ratification

131. Hamden, in a public letter to Henry Grattan in *Dublin Evening Post*, 26 Apr. 1788, drew attention the loss of the cordage bill. In 1797, Grattan cited the loss of the 1785 gunpowder bill as a 'popular' grievance (Henry Grattan, *A letter on the nature and tendency of the Whig Club and of the Irish party* (Dublin, 1797), p. 19).
132. NA, PC2/152 f. 586. A similar suggestion was floated in 1749.
133. The quoted words were uttered by John FitzGibbon in the Irish Commons on 27 October 1783 (*Parl. Reg. (Irl.)*, ii, 29).
134. The reference, by Lord Kenmare, is to the 1787 riot act (Kenmare to Moylan, 23 Feb. 1787 in Evelyn Bolster (ed.), 'The Moylan correspondence', *Collectanea Hibernica*, 14 (1971), p. 93).

in 1786 of a 'new navigation bill' at Westminster, with the recommendation that Ireland would do likewise. Significantly, the bill that was enacted was drafted with the participation of key figures from both the British and Irish executives, and it paid off as the measure became law.[135] Others followed, notably in the early 1790s when a raft of major measures appertaining to the concession of Catholic relief (1792, 1793), limiting the civil list (1793) and establishing a reciprocal preference for corn (1792) were approved.[136] It was also not unusual, either, for the home secretary to request 'that a bill corresponding' to a specific measure bill approved recently at Westminster should be implemented in Ireland. The nature of the bills suggested varied, but a majority appertained to trade and taxation, and the request to the Irish administration to follow the British example and introduce a particular commercial regulation was generally justified by reference to the 'free trade' act of 1780 (10 George III, chap 10), which deemed it 'expedient' that Britain and Ireland should adhere to the same regulations.[137]

Trade and commerce remained areas in which ministers contrived successfully to ensure that Britain and Ireland possessed uniform regulations throughout the 1790s.[138] However, as the demands of war with France and the threat of internal disorder appreciated in the late 1790s, the interests of the two legislatures converged. Moreover, this was not always one-way. It is particularly noteworthy that as well as instructions from London authorising the introduction of particular bills, the Irish executive was invited periodically to transmit copies of bills it had originated to defeat 'the present treasonable and rebellious proceedings' because ministers had it 'in contemplation to pass a similar act' at Westminster.[139] As a result of this and the monitoring allowed under the extant terms of Poynings' Law, eighteen years of legislative independence did not generate the legislative chasm between the kingdoms of Britain and Ireland many apprehended in 1782. Indeed, the spirit of earnest co-operation and ideological solidarity that bound the executives in both kingdoms in opposition to revolution and in preserving the Anglo-Irish nexus allowed them to ensure that their legislative agendas were more

135. Sydney to Rutland, 16 Apr. 1786 (NA, HO100/18 ff 166–8); Sydney to Rutland, 13 Jan. 1787 (NA, HO122/1, f. 96); Kelly, *Prelude to union*, chapter 7.

136. Marianne Elliott, *Wolfe Tone* (London, 1989), pp 202–3; David Wilkinson, 'How did they pass the union? Secret service expenditure', *History*, 82 (1997), pp 223–51; Dundas to Westmorland, 22 June 1793 (NA, HO122/2 ff 169–70).

137. Grenville to Westmorland, 14 Feb. 1791, Dundas to Westmorland, 20 Mar. 1792 (NA, HO100/2 ff. 91, 134).

138. Grenville to Pelham, 21 Jan. 1797, Portland to Camden, 16 Feb., Wickham to Pelham, 24 Mar. 1798 (NA, HO122/4 ff 109, 198, 206); Portland to Cornwallis, 4 Mar. 1799 (HO122/5 f. 57).

139. Grenville to Pelham, 2 June 1797 (NA, HO122/4 f. 140); Portland to Cornwallis, 21 June 1798, 22 Mar. 1799, Wickham to Castlereagh, 2 July 1798 (HO122/5 ff 5, 8–9, 64). It is noteworthy in this context that nearly a quarter of the laws enacted in 1798 related to the 1798 Rebellion and its aftermath: Nial Osborough, 'Legal aspects of the 1798 rebellion, its suppression and the aftermath' in Thomas Bartlett et al. (eds), *1798: a bicentenary perspective* (Dublin, 2003), pp 437–68.

in harmony in the 1790s than they had been at any point in several decades. These were hardly sufficient grounds upon which to pursue or to base a legislative union, but they ensured that there were few real legislative obstacles in its way, which was not insignificant. The fact that the bill for a legislative union that was enacted in Ireland in 1800 mirrored the act passed at Westminster in 1799 was equally symbolically affirmative of the fact that by this date legislative independence was legislatively as well as politically redundant.

TABLE TWELVE

THE LEGISLATION OF THE IRISH PARLIAMENT, 1783–1800: PUBLIC BILLS

	Ireland — Origin of bills			Ireland — Lost bills (House of Commons)				Ireland — Lost bills (House of Lords)			England — Bills at the British Privy Council					Ireland — Irish parliament
Session	Royal bill	House of Commons	House of Lords	Leave only	Rejected	Lords' bills rejected	Commons' bills amended in Lords	Rejected	Commons' bills rejected	Bill not forwarded	Received	Laid aside	Reservations expressed	Petitions	Returned	Royal assent
1783–4		89	3	14	16				4		58		2		58	58
1785		110	6	9	24	3		3	10		67	2	3		65	65
1786		83	2	3	15	1		1	4		61		2		61	61
1787		85	5	5	16	4		1	4		60		4		60	60
1788		77	2	5	18	1		1	3		51	1	1		50	50
1789		63		2	17				2		42		1		42	42
1790		66	1	4	10	1			5		47				47	47
1790		1									1				1	1
1791		75	2	3	16	1	1		5		51		1	2	51	51
1792		55	4	1	11				5		42	1	1		41	41
1793		89	3	7	25		3		1		56				56	56
1794		43	1	2	12			1	2	1	26		2		26	26
1795		69	3	7	15	2					48		2		48	48
1796		72	2	2	11		1	1			59				59	59
1797		87	4	3	19	1	1	2	4		61		3		61	61
1798	1	101	4	8	11		1	1	2		83		2		83	83
1799		86	2	5	12	1			3		67				67	67
1800		117	6	6	12	1			4		100				100	100
Total	**1**	**1368**	**50**	**86**	**260**	**16**	**7**	**11**	**58**	**1**	**980**	**4**	**24**	**1**	**976**	**976**

Sources: NA, Privy Council Registers, PC2/1; Privy Council papers, PC1; *Commons Jn. (Irl.)*; *Lords Jn. (Irl.)*.

TABLE THIRTEEN

THE LEGISLATION OF THE IRISH PARLIAMENT, 1783–1800: PRIVATE BILLS

	Ireland		Ireland							England					Ireland
	Origin of bills		Lost bills						Bill not forwarded	Bills at the British Privy Council					Irish parliament
			House of Commons				House of Lords								
Session	House of Commons	House of Lords	Leave only	Rejected	Lords' bills rejected	Commons' bills amended in Lords	Rejected	Commons' bills rejected		Received	Laid aside	Reservations expressed	Petitions	Returned	Royal assent
1783–4	9	8						3		14				14	14
1785	5	7						2		10				10	10
1786	2	2								3				3	3
1787		8			1		2			6				6	6
1788		5								5				5	5
1789	1	3						1		3				3	3
1790		4								4		2		4	4
1790															
1791	1	4						1		4		3		4	4
1792		1								1			1	1	1
1793	1	8		1			1			8		1		8	8
1794															
1795	1	2								2				2	2
1796		5					2			3				3	3
1797	2	5					2			5				5	5
1798		2								2				2	2
1799		2					1			1				1	1
1800	2	8								10				10	10
Total	**24**	**74**		**1**	**1**		**8**	**7**		**81**		**6**	**1**	**81**	**81**

Sources: NA, Privy Council Registers, PC2/1; Privy Council papers, PC1; *Commons Jn.* (*Irl.*); *Lords Jn.* (*Irl.*).

TABLE FOURTEEN

THE LEGISLATION OF THE IRISH PARLIAMENT, 1783–1800: PUBLIC AND PRIVATE BILLS

	Ireland — Origin of bills			Ireland — Lost bills: House of Commons				Ireland — Lost bills: House of Lords		Ireland — Bill not forwarded	England — Bills at the British Privy Council					Ireland — Irish parliament
Session	Royal bill	House of Commons	House of Lords	Leave only	Rejected	Lords' bills rejected	Commons' bills amended in Lords	Rejected	Commons' bills rejected	Bill not forwarded	Received	Laid aside	Reservations expressed	Petitions	Approved	Royal assent
1783–4		98	11	14	16				7		72				72	72
1785		115	13	9	24	3		3	12		77	2	2		75	75
1786		85	4	3	15	2		1	4		64		3		64	64
1787		85	13	5	16	4		3	4		66		2		66	66
1788		77	7	5	18	1		1	3		56	1	4		55	55
1789		64	3	2	17				3		45		1		45	45
1790		66	5	4	10	1			5		51		3		51	51
1790		1									1				1	1
1791		76	6	3	17	1			6		55		3	2	55	55
1792		55	5	1	11				5		43	1	1		42	42
1793		90	11	7	25			3	1	1	64		2		64	64
1794		42	1	2	12			1	1	1	26		2		26	26
1795		71	5	7	16	2			1		50		2		50	50
1796		72	7	2	11		1				62				62	62
1797		89	9	3	19	1	1	3	4		66		3		66	66
1798	1	101	6	8	11		1	1	2		85		2		85	85
1799		86	4	5	12	1		1	3		68				68	68
1800		119	14	6	12	1			4		110				110	110
Total	1	1392	124	86	261	17	6	19	65	1	1061	4	30	2	1057	1057

Sources: NA, Privy Council Registers, PC2/1; Privy Council papers, PC1; Commons Jn. (Irl); Lords Jn. (Irl).

Conclusion

DURING THE PERIOD 1660–1800, Poynings' Law enabled the executive in Britain and Ireland to exert a determining influence on the deliberations of the Irish parliament by according the Privy Council's in both jurisdictions the authority to amend and to veto legislation emanating from that quarter. Yet, paradoxically, the Law also empowered the Irish parliament, as the shifting interpretation and application of the statute first permitted the Lords and the Commons of Ireland in parliament assembled to inaugurate a modest proportion of legislation in the form of heads of bills and, once this proved a workable arrangement, to expand the proportion of legislation that arose in this manner. Poynings' Law can, for this reason, be seen as emblematic of the political relationship – at once complex and ambiguous – in which Britain and Ireland were bound in the seventeenth and eighteenth centuries, for though Britain's dominant and Ireland's subordinate status can be said to be encapsulated by the Law, the respective positions of the two kingdoms was less rigidly defined than this binary description implies. As a result, some commentators have argued that resort to the term 'colonial' to describe the Anglo-Irish relationship is 'unhelpful and misleading' because 'the constitutional relationship between the colony [Ireland] and the metropolitan power [Britain]' was grounded on less than 'explicit dependence'.[1] This conclusion may not seem to accord sufficient significance to the fact that the executive at Dublin Castle was headed for most of the period 1660–1800 by an English/British appointee who was directly answerable to ministers and to the monarch as King or Queen of Great Britain rather than of Ireland, or to the implications of the ratification in 1720 of the Declaratory Act, which empowered the Westminster legislature to make law for Ireland. However, the political and administrative reality was palpably less clear cut, as the disinclination of successive lord lieutenants during the eighteenth century to reside in Ireland meant that responsibility for ordinary business, and the influence and authority this brought, passed to Irish lords justices, while Westminster was increasingly reluctant to legislate for Ireland other than when it could be seen to confer explicit advantage.[2] In the case of Poynings' Law, the incapacity to apply the measure during the late seventeenth and eighteenth centuries in the constricting manner pioneered by Thomas Wentworth in the 1630s is equally indicative of the limits of the capacity of the British authorities to rule Ireland in a wholly colonial fashion. But the fitful way in which the Irish parliament secured the right to initiate legislation in the shape of heads of bills in the 1660s and 1690s, and the

1. See, for example, McNally, *Parties, patriots and undertakers*, pp 29–30.
2. Significantly, it was announced publicly in Ireland in 1775 (*Hibernian Journal*, 28 June 1775) that three recent Westminster acts (for the promotion of fisheries, the encouragement of the

capacity of the British Council to respite and amend bills received from Ireland virtually at will in the early eighteenth century illustrates that Poynings' Law continued to bind the Irish parliament in a legislative nexus that, while effectively dependent, was inherently fluid. The fact that this changed over time, and in a manner that advantaged the Irish parliament, indicates that the nature of Irish dependence was not fixed. Yet, because the Irish parliament did not seek unconditional legislative independence when it contrived in 1782 to negate the more confining aspects of Poynings' Law, suggests that the definition of the political relationship in which the two kingdoms were bound as intrinsically colonial is not unjustified, though this is contingent on the employment of the term in a manner that is less strict than critics of its use would enjoin.

Because the interpretation and application of Poynings' Law changed significantly during the period 1600–1800, though the Law was only once subject to legislative amendment during that time, it can be appealed to as a barometer of the changing character of the Anglo-Irish relationship. The main reason the Law did not operate in a static fashion is to be found in the conviction of Irish Protestants, born out of their belief that, since they could not justifiably be deprived of access to the same rights as the Crown's English subjects, it was inappropriate that they were bound by restrictive constitutional arrangements. This would not have become an issue, of course, had the legislative union of the 1650s, whereby Ireland sent MPs to Westminster, satisfactorily accommodated the needs of both the English and Irish interests, but its failure to do so combined with disenchantment with government by executive in the wake of Wentworth's experiment in absolutism, meant that some form of parliamentary government was the only feasible option. This was made all the more likely by the fact that the outcome of the Civil War hastened the consolidation of the authority of parliament in England, and, as it was prepared to do with respect of its colonial dependencies in North America and the Caribbean, by the willingness of the King and his ministers to allow settlers committed to maintaining a relationship with England a direct say in the government and administration of such dependencies. This was not without its problematical aspects in the Irish case, since Ireland, unlike the American colonies, was a kingdom. But while Irish Protestants cited this in support of their claim to possess the same constitutional rights as Englishmen, they did so cautiously and, as evinced by their preparedness in the 1660s and 1690s to work within the parameters of Poynings' Law even when they pushed its interpretation to the limit, they did not seek directly to challenge the perception of Ireland's dependence shared across the English political nation. It was widely acknowledged in England that Ireland's status as a 'kingdom' entitled it to a parliament, but this did not inhibit their perception of Ireland as a 'colony', as a peer with major Irish interests observed pointedly in 1720.[3] By implication,

---

manufacture of 'rare' oils and the clothing and accoutring of the army) offered opportunities to Irish merchants.

3. Perceval to Dering, 5 Mar. 1720 (BL, Egmont Papers, Add. MS 47029 ff 22–5).

English politicians and officials were not prepared to allow that parliament the liberty to legislate free of restriction because they believed that the interests of those of English (or Scottish) ancestry settlers in Ireland, no less than those in America and the Caribbean, could not be assumed to dovetail with the primary interests of metropolitan Britain, and that, in the absence of a means to ensure statutory uniformity, differences and disagreements would emerge that must result over time in a loss of authority and control. It was this that made Poynings' Law so valuable to the Irish and English executives; it provided the Crown and its representatives with a ready-made set of constraints possessing the legitimacy of antiquity that required the Irish parliament to defer to the Irish and English/British Privy Councils.

Had the model of conciliar authority employed by Thomas Wentworth to make law for Ireland been adopted during the 1660s, the Irish legislature would have possessed little more than the negative power of vetoing legislative proposals that had taken their rise in the Irish Council. This remained the case in theory, but because it was unacceptable in practice to Irish Protestants, the King and his ministers went some way to meet Irish concerns. The *modus operandi* that epitomised this accommodation – the right to initiate legislation in the form of heads of bills – was achieved as a result, not of a formal agreement, but piecemeal over a number of decades as both parties evolved practical solutions to quotidian administrative and constitutional challenges within broad but flexible constitutional parameters. Yet, because this satisfied the aspiration of the Irish parliament to possess an active say in the making of law and the commitment of the British and Irish Privy Councils to exercise the powers it was provided by Poynings' Law, it constituted an appropriate compromise. As a result, the Anglo-Irish constitutional nexus possessed features, epitomised by the necessity to provide the 'causes and consequences' to secure authorisation to convene a parliament and the right possessed by the British Privy Council to respite and to amend prospective laws forwarded from Ireland, that were emphatically colonial in character. However, the ability of the Irish legislature to expand the concession to present heads of bills yielded in the 1660s into a near monopolistic claim with respect of the initiation of legislation a century later can be seen to contradict this conclusion, and may explain why Poynings' law has not been appealed to as frequently as it might be, as a litmus test of Ireland's colonial dependence in the seventeenth and eighteenth centuries.

The emergence of the heads of bills as a means to allow Irish Protestants to contribute directly to the making of law for Ireland enabled the Protestant elite to shape the law of the kingdom. Had this not happened, this role would have been performed by the Irish Privy Council, and by extension by the English Council, to which the Irish Council showed ready deference during the 1660s and 1690s. The deferential disposition manifest then did not endure because, in the first instance, it was recognised by the King and ministers that allowing the Irish legislature a more direct input in to the process was an effective way of retaining the goodwill of Irish Protestants and, in the second, because Irish Protestants were not prepared to acquiesce in the subordinate role the former experience demanded. They expressed their opinion on this matter respectfully in the 1660s, and assertively in the 1690s, with great effect. As a result, from the mid-1690s onwards not only did a majority of Irish law originate in parliament (with the House of Commons), but also reflected the concerns and preoccupations of Irish Protestants. The main casualty in this power struggle was the Irish Privy Council, since its ability to initiate legislation, other than that required to secure the authorisation of the Crown to allow parliament to assemble, was progressive curtailed and had all but become negligible by the early 1730s. It retained the powers to reject and to amend the heads of bills emanating from the legislature, but the refusal of the House of Commons to accept its entitlement to initiate legislation meant that it was soon to be neutralised as an active law making body.

This was a major boost to the status of the Irish legislature, but its incapacity to do likewise with respect to the English/British Privy Council was indicative of the determination in political circles in Britain to maintain its powers of colonial supervision. The procedures employed at the English Council when Irish legislation was received, applied with a lack of rigour and consistency in the late seventeenth century, were refined appreciably during the reign of Queen Anne, as a result of which the Council performed its supervisory role in respect of Irish bills with improved efficiency and effectiveness during the early Hanoverian period. One consequence of this was that some 12 per cent of Irish bills that were deemed inappropriate or deficient did not progress, while an imposing 75 per cent were returned with amendments, major and minor, in order to bring them into line with Irish legislation and to correct errors and mistakes.[4] The quantification of the extent of the intervention with respect of Irish legislation at the British Council, and of heads of bills at the Irish Council provides a more precise guide than has previously existed of the changing nature of legislative dependence during the eighteenth century. Saliently, the proportion of bills respited fell during George III's reign, but the capacity of the British Council to continue during the 1770s to continue to scrutinise Irish legislation as closely as it had done in the 1690s, even if it chose to do so with greater discretion, is indicative of the enduring colonial character of the Anglo-Irish nexus.

The intrinsically colonial nature of the Anglo-Irish relationship illustrated by the manner in which Poynings' law shaped both the process of law making in Ireland and the nature of the Anglo-Irish relationship is illuminated still further by a comparison of the system of legislative control that operated in Ireland with that applied to Britain's North American and Caribbean colonies.[5] The latter

---

4. See above, chapter 3.
5. As well as the sources identified in the footnotes, the next three paragraphs draw on E.B. Russell, *The review of American colonial legislation by the King in Council* (New York, 1915), and John Bergin, 'The laws of the American colonies' (unpublished paper, 2002). I wish to thank Dr Bergin for sharing his researches.

commenced during the Restoration era as the commitment to establish a uniform
pattern of colonial government encouraged the replacement of the extant diverse
pattern of plantation, proprietary and religious colonies with a more uniform
order of crown colonies characterised by a crown-appointed governor, an elected
house of assembly, and a council that combined the functions of an upper house
and a Privy Council. Because the houses of assembly could initiate law, though
they generally did so within recognised parameters, which meant that they did not
engage with matters of colonial trade and tended generally to respect the
instructions provided to royal governors on their appointment, ministers were
understandably eager to possess a more formal instrument than the extant power
of veto which was seen as cumbersome and inflexible. Poynings' Law, which had
proved its usefulness in Ireland in the 1660s, was a tempting model, and with the
extension of its application in mind the Commissioners for Trade and the
Plantations sought in the late 1670s and in the 1720s to apply a similar arrangement to Jamaica and Virginia, which, had it been agreed, would have empowered
them to initiate, and to amend as well as to veto bills. They were frustrated by the
refusal of the house of assembly in Jamaica to accept amendments introduced into
a bill in 1679, with the result that it remained the practice for the acts of the
colonial assembles to be transmitted to the Privy Council for examination to
establish if they were suitable to become law. Examined and reported on by the
solicitor general until 1700, they were subsequently referred to and scrutinised by
the Board of Trade, which reported to the Council. This process clearly bears
close comparison with what was applied in the case of Irish bills save that, in the
absence of the power to amend, the Privy Council was confined to deciding
whether a colonial act was suitable to come into force or not. Inevitably, despite
intense lobbying on behalf of individual colonial acts by agents acting at the
behest of colonial interests, some failed in controversial circumstances, but this
was of lesser consequence than the fact that the percentage of bills received from
the North American colonies that was 'disallowed' may have been smaller than the
percentage of Irish bills that was respited.[6] Direct comparisons are problematical
in the absence of a reliable sequence of American figures. However, estimations
that 5 per cent of the total number of bills presented from South Carolina were
challenged between 1719 and 1760, and that after 1760 an equivalent percentage
was disallowed for want of a 'suspending' clause have been offered, and other,
more limited, assessments, based on the experience of individual sessions, suggest
the percentage may have been higher in the late seventeenth century.[7]

Even if these figures are shown to be underestimates, the implication that more
bills from Ireland than from colonial America were lost at the British Council

6. J.R. Pole, *Political representation in England and the origins of the American Republic* (New York,
    1966), pp 29–31; James, 'The Irish lobby', p. 550; Richard Middleton, *Colonial America* (Oxford,
    1996), pp 148, 186, 330–1; R.J. Dircks (ed.), *The letters of Richard Cumberland* (New York, 1988),
    pp 45–51.
7. Middleton, *Colonial America*, pp 330–1; NA, PC2/77 f. 137.

implies that the parliament of Ireland was more legislatively dependent than the American houses of assembly. This is the assessment of John Philip Reid, who has made a suggestive, if not wholly accurate, comparison of their situations:

> Where American assemblies initiated legislation, in Ireland legislation was initiated either by the lord lieutenant and his council or the King and the British Privy Council. In the colonies, the colonial governor and then the King acting through his Privy Council exercised the veto. In Ireland the veto was not an executive but a parliamentary function.[8]

Significantly, this was the assessment also of some percipient members of the British Council. Welbore Ellis referred in 1774 to the 'very absurd but true [fact] that the legislatures of the colonies are more complete legislatures than the parliament of Ireland is' because the latter 'is but a council in the first instance of proposition of laws, which are to receive their efficacy in a great degree from the [British] Privy Council'.[9] Seen from this perspective, a case can be made that the Irish parliament compared unfavourably to the colonial assemblies, and that its disadvantageous situation was made still worse by the ability of some American assemblies in the eighteenth century to circumvent the veto of the Privy Council by voting money grants by resolution.[10]

If these were the only relevant factors, it could be argued that since it is commonly acknowledged that the American colonies were bound in a dependent colonial relationship with Britain, Ireland's political relationship with Britain in the seventeenth and eighteenth centuries must be described in the same terms. The problem is that the legislative, as distinct from the theoretical, reality is less clear-cut. Theoretically, the American assemblies were less tightly constrained because they possessed the authority to initiate legislation, rather than just heads of bills, and because the English/British Privy Council was not empowered to amend their acts. However, the advantage this gave has been exaggerated since the reality was that the American colonies initiated a smaller corpus and narrower range of legislation than the Irish parliament. Furthermore, the fact that the British Council did not possess the power to amend legislation received from the colonies meant that beneficial acts that would have been forwarded for approval in an amended form either fell by the wayside or were greatly delayed. The insistence on the inclusion in American acts of a 'suspending' clause also constituted an important qualification to the law-making function of the colonies since it meant that the Privy Council could determine when a colonial act came into force. However, even when these important practical restrictions are taken on board, the ability of the American house of assembly to establish 'a decisive leadership over both the colonial Council and the British governors' indicates that, in common

8. John Philip Reid, *Constitutional history of the American Revolution* (Madison, 1991), p. 205.
9. Ellis to Agar, 23 June 1774 (PRONI, Normanton Papers, T3719/C/8/4).
10. Pole, *Political representation*, p. 57.

with the Irish parliament, they too were able to mitigate the severity of their dependency. Because there is no absolute measure of this dependency in either the Irish or American instances, and no accepted scale against which it can be set, it may not be possible to assay precisely their relative positions. But what seems undeniable is that Ireland's political relationship with Britain was every bit as colonial as that of the American colonies.

It can be argued, of course, that because of their proximity, the interchange of personnel, and the greater assertiveness of the Irish legislature as the eighteenth century progressed that Britain and Ireland were not bound by a 'typical' colonial relationship, but this is to beg the question, since it is not apparent that there was or is such a thing. What is apparent is that, for all its inherent complexity and shifting import, Poynings' Law was sufficiently elastic to allow Irish Protestants exert an increasing say over the law that was made for Ireland consistent with their commitment to maintain a close and essentially dependent relationship with Britain. From this perspective, their readiness to compromise by acceding to bills that were subject to significant amendment at the British Council, and their acquiescence in the face of the denial of basic legal rights such as *habeas corpus* can be interpreted, not as evidence of the lack of principle or conviction that these were worthwhile, but as the price they were prepared to pay to uphold the close Anglo-Irish connection that was crucial to their long term security. Besides, the decision of the British Council in response to the growing assertiveness of Irish political opinion in the 1760s and, especially, in the late 1770s to increase the percentage of bills that were returned without amendment and to allow more controversial bills to progress diminished the need for Irish Protestants to follow the example of the American colonists and seek full independence, had they been inclined to take this route. Thus when, in 1782, the Americans were on the eve of establishing an independent state, Ireland's Protestants opted decisively for Barry Yelverton's moderate, if not very well thought through, scheme for legislative independence because this captured their wish to achieve a greater measure legislative latitude while maintaining the Anglo-Irish nexus. What they attained as a result was a flawed constitutional settlement that allowed the British Privy Council potentially major influence had they needed to exercise it. They chose not to, because London was enabled to use other strategies – its continued control of the Irish executive, the unreformed character of the electoral system, and, not least, the self-interested deference of Irish parliamentarians born out of the well-grounded perception of a majority of Irish Protestants that their security was dependent on the maintenance of the Anglo-Irish connection – to ensure that the constitutional changes implemented in 1782 represented the conclusion rather than the start of a process. This also explains why the constitution of 1782 culminated within two decades in an Anglo-Irish union rather than in full legislative independence. Forced by the late 1790s to choose between independence and a union, the membership of the Irish parliament voted to abolish a legislature that was then more active making law than it had been at any moment in its history because the right to make law was less valuable than the Anglo-Irish connection.[11]

Because it encapsulated, better than any other legal instrument, the co-operation and accommodation, suspicion and tension, attachment and mutual need that characterised the Anglo-Irish connection between 1660 and 1800, Poynings' Law was essential to the maintenance of a secure Anglo-Irish connection in which both participants acknowledged the respective entitlements and positions of the British and Irish elites within the existing parliamentary and conciliar structures. Without it, it is improbable that the Irish parliament could have been allowed to continue to sit for as long as it did, since there must sooner rather than later have arisen a constitutional crisis between the two kingdoms that would have required a decisive intervention comparable to that taken in the late 1710s that culminated in the Declaratory Act or to that taken in 1800 that resulted in the Act of Union to safeguard British authority in Ireland. With it, it was possible to permit the Irish parliament to function as the representative body of Irish Protestants because it meant that there was a complex and effective system of control that enabled the Crown and its ministers to ensure that the Irish parliament did not trespass into areas or engage with issues that must hasten the loosening of the Anglo-Irish connection. Moreover, as long as it functioned effectively, London felt little need to alter the legal basis of the connection. So when in 1703, 1707 and 1709, some Irish Protestants proposed a legislative union, London could afford to reject the suggestion because Poynings' Law was sufficient at that point to protect their interests while satisfying the aspirations of Irish Protestants to govern themselves. Its effective emasculation in 1782 thus brought the day closer when a union must prove compelling. This is what happened in 1800. It can thus be argued that the Irish parliament in the eighteenth century functioned as an efficient working assembly because of Poynings' Law rather than, as many argued then, and have continued to argue since, that it was unable to do so because of the constraints it imposed on the making of law in Ireland.

---

11. For a perspective on this see James Kelly, 'The act of union: its origins and background' in Dáire Keogh and Kevin Whelan (eds), *Acts of Union* (Dublin, 2001), pp 46–66.

Bibliography

PRIMARY SOURCES

I. MANUSCRIPTS

British Library, London
Auckland Papers, Add. MS 34418
Blenheim Papers, Add. MSS 61630, 61636
Egmont Papers, Add. MS 47029
Ellis Papers, Add. MS 28941
Hardwicke Papers, Add. MSS 35609–10, 36136, 36138, 35870, 35872–4, 35892
Historical and other tracts, Add. MS 27382
Holland House Papers, Add. MS 51426
Lansdowne Abstracts, Add. MS 24138
Privy Council Papers, Add. MS 30190
Liverpool Papers, Add. MS 38208
Opinion of Irish judges on sole right, 14 Feb. 1693, Add. MS 9715
Privy Council memoranda 1660–1708, Add. MS 35707
Spencer Compton Papers, Add. MS 45733
Southwell Papers, Add. MSS 21122, 34777, 37673–4, 38016
Townshend Papers, Add. MS 37634
Trumbull Papers, Add. MS 72566
Vernon Papers, Add. MS 40771
Wake Papers, Add. MS 6116

Harleian MS 6274

Folger Library, Washington
Southwell Papers

Gilbert Library, Dublin
Hackett Trustees Papers, MS 223
Harcourt Papers, MS 93
Privy Council Papers, 1640–1707, MS 205
Wake Papers, MS 27

Hampshire Record Office, Winchester
Normanton Papers (PRONI T3719)

Historical Society of Pennsylvania, Philadelphia
Joseph [Oxley]'s offering to his children, AM 1095

Lambeth Palace Library, London
Secker Papers

Library of Congress, Washington
Sir Henry Cavendish's parliamentary diary, 1776–89, volumes vi–xiii

National Archives of Ireland, Dublin
Calendar of miscellaneous letters and papers prior to 1760
Calendar of miscellaneous letters and papers, 1760–89
Calendar of presentments, affidavits and informations, 1703–80
Index of heads of bills, 1711–82, and transmisses, 1753–80
Index to departmental letters and official papers, 1760–89
Irish correspondence 1697–1798, MSS 2446–7
Isabel Grubb's notes from petitions in Public Record Office
Lords justices letterbooks, 1697, 1698, MSS 2454, 2456
May–Blathwayt correspondence, 1697–8, MS 3070
Military entry books, 1711–3, MS 2553
Pembroke estate Papers, MS 97/46
Prim Collection (PRI 38)

National Archives, Public Record Office, London
Chancery: parliament rolls, C65
Patent Rolls, C66
Chancery and Crown office: Irish Bills of the 1634–5 session, C86
Chancery and Crown office: Orders in Council, 1703–1800, C183/1–2
Granville Papers, 30/29
Home Office Papers (Ireland), HO100/16, 18, 20, 21, 36
Home Office Papers (Ireland), HO122/1–5
St George Papers, C110, Box 46
State Papers (France), SP78/179/347
State Papers (Ireland), SP63/373–480
State Papers (Ireland), SP66 Case B
State Papers (Ireland), SP67/1–16

Privy Council Papers
Minute and entry book of the Committee for Ireland, 1689–91, PC6/2
Minutes and papers of the clerks of the Council, 1670–1795, PC4/1–4
Privy Council Registers, PC2/53–155
Privy Council unbound papers, PC1/1–33, 1038.

National Library of Ireland, Dublin
Dobbs Papers, MS 2251
Headfort Papers, F/5/91
Heron Papers, MS 4135
Joly Papers, MS 29
Smythe of Barbavilla Papers, MS 41580
Sydney papers, MSS 51, 52
Wicklow Papers, PC226–7

National Library of Scotland, Edinburgh
Watson Collection, MS 578

National Library of Wales, Aberystwyth
Puleston papers, MSS 3580, 3582, 3584

Northumberland Record Office, Newcastle
Potter Papers, MS 650

Nottingham University Library, Nottingham
Newcastle of Clumber Papers, NeC 1581

Public Record Office of Northern Ireland, Belfast
Alnwick Papers, T2872
Bedford Papers, T2915
Chatsworth Papers, T3158
Grafton Papers, T2959
Additional Pery Papers, T3052
Roden Papers, Mic147/9
Shannon Papers, D2707
Shirley Papers, D3531
Wilmot Papers, T3019

Royal Irish Academy, Dublin
Knox-Heron letters, MS G.5.1

Sheffield City Library, Sheffield
Rockingham Papers, R1-2049

Suffolk Record Office, Ipswich
Pretyman Papers, HA119

Trinity College Library, Dublin
Clements letterbooks, MS 1742
King Papers, MSS 750/1–9, 1995–2008, 2531, 2533, 2535, 2537
Molyneux Papers, MS 890
Seventeenth-century political documents, MS 808

Yale University, New Haven
Beinecke Library: Osborn Collection
Blathwayt Papers, Boxes 19 and 20
Great Britain Files
Northington Letterbook
Southwell papers, Boxes 1 and 2
Sundon letterbook 2
Townshend Papers, Boxes 5 and 7

Sterling Library
English Misc MSS, 1766–72

Warwickshire Record Office,
Willes Papers (microfilm)

Private Collections
Holloden Papers (Bagenalstown, Co. Carlow, NLI Special List 416)
Rosse Papers (Birr Castle, Birr, County Offaly)
Tollemache Papers (Buckminster, Grantham, Lincs (HMC Report, no 1534))
Townshend Papers (Raynham Hall, Suffolk)

2. PRINTED PRIMARY MATERIAL: DOCUMENTS, MEMOIRS AND CORRESPONDENCE

Auckland: *The journal and correspondence of William, Lord Auckland*, ed. Bishop of Bath and Wells (4 vols, London, 1861–2).
Bedford: *The correspondence of John, fourth duke of Bedford*, ed. Lord John Russell (3 vols, London, 1842–6).

Boulter: *Letters written by Hugh Boulter, lord primate of all Ireland to several ministers of state in England, and some others ...*, ed. Ambrose Phillips (2 vols, Dublin, 1770).

Catholics: W.P. Burke, *Irish priests in the penal times* (Waterford, 1914).

Catholics: 'The minute book of the Catholic Committee, 1773–92, ed. R. Dudley Edwards, *Archivium Hibernicum*, 9 (1942), pp 1–172.

Catholics: *Catholics and Catholicism in the eighteenth-century press*, ed. John Brady (Maynooth, 1965).

Catholics: 'Catalogue of material of Irish interest in the collection *Nunziatura di Fiandra*' parts 2–9, (ed.) Cathaldus Giblin in *Collectanea Hibernica*, 3 (1960), pp 7–144; 4 (1961), pp 7–137; 5 (1962), pp 7–130; 9 (1966), pp 7–70; 10 (1967), pp 72–138; 11 (1968), pp 53–90; 12 (1969), pp 62–101; 13 (1970), pp 61–99.

Cumberland: *The letters of Richard Cumberland*, ed. R.J. Dircks (New York, 1988).

Devonshire: 'The Devonshire diary, 1759–62', ed. P. Brown and K.W. Schweizer, *Camden*, 4th series, 27 (1982).

Empire: *Imperial reconstruction, 1763–1840*, ed., A.F. Madden and D.K. Fieldhouse (Oxford, 1985).

Freke: 'Mrs Elizabeth Freke, her diary 1671–1714', ed. Mary Carbery, *Journal of the Cork Historical and Archaeological Society*, 2nd series, 16 (1910), pp 149–67; 17 (1911), pp 1–16, 45–58, 93–113, 142–54; 18 (1912), pp 39–47, 88–97, 151–9, 203–10; 19 (1913), pp 42–7, 84–90, 134–47.

Freke: *The remembrances of Elizabeth Freke, 1671–1714*, ed. R.A. Anselment, *Camden*, 5th series, 18 (Cambridge, 2001).

George III: *The later correspondence of George III*, ed. Arthur Aspinall (5 vols, London, 1962–70).

Grafton: *Autobiography and political correspondence of Augustus Henry, third duke of Grafton*, ed. Sir William Anson (London, 1898).

Grattan: *Memoirs of the life and times of the rt. hon. Henry Grattan* ed. Henry Grattan jr. (5 vols, London, 1839–46).

Grenville: *The Grenville papers*, ed. W.J. Smith (4 vols, London, 1852–3).

Harcourt: *Harcourt Papers*, ed. W.E. Harcourt (privately printed, 13 vols, 1876–1903).

Hardwicke: *The life and correspondence of Philip Yorke, earl of Hardwicke*, ed. P.C. Yorke (3 vols, Cambridge, 1913).

Irish official papers: *Eighteenth-century Irish official papers*, ed. A.P.W. Malcomson (2 vols, Belfast (1973–1990).

Irish parliament: 'An Irish parliamentary diary from the reign of Queen Anne', ed. D.W. Hayton, *Analecta Hibernica*, 30 (1982), pp 97–149.

Kilkenny: 'Documents of Kilkenny Corporation', *Journal of the Royal Historical and Archaeological Association of Ireland*, 4th series, 1 (1870), pp 268–77.

Macartney: *Macartney in Ireland, 1768–1772*, ed. Thomas Bartlett (Belfast, 1979).

Marlborough: *The Marlborough-Godolphin correspondence*, ed. G.L. Snyder (3 vols, Oxford, 1975).

Ministerial meetings: *Ministerial meetings in the reign of George I* (List and Index Society, vol. 224: London, 1987).

Moylan: 'The Moylan correspondence', ed. Evelyn Bolster, *Collectanea Hibernica*, 14 (1971), pp 82–142.

Nicolson: *The London diaries of William Nicolson, bishop of Carlisle, 1702–18*, ed. Clyve Jones and Geoffrey Holmes (Oxford, 1985).

Orrery: *A collection of the state letters of the rt hon. Roger Boyle, first earl of Orrery*, ed. Thomas Morrice (2 vols, Dublin, 1743).

Orrery: *The Orrery papers*, ed. Countess of Cork and Orrery (2 vols, London, 1903).

Rawlinson: 'Report on manuscripts in the Bodleian Library, Oxford: Rawlinson MS', *Analecta Hibernica*, 2 (1931), pp 1–291.

Stuart: *Ireland in the Stuart Papers, 1719–65*, ed. Patrick Fagan (2 vols, Dublin, 1995).

Sundon: *Memoirs of Viscountess Sundon*, ed. Mrs Katherine Thompson (2 vols, London, 1847).

Vernon: *Letters illustrative of the reign of William III from 1696 to 1708 addressed to the duke of Shrewsbury by James Vernon*, ed. G.P.R. James (3 vols, London, 1841).

Wilmot: *'The King's business': letters on the administration of Ireland, 1740–1761, from the papers of Sir Robert Wilmot*, ed. James Walton (New York, 1996).

Willes: *The letters of Lord Chief Baron Edward Willes, 1757–62*, ed. James Kelly (Aberstywyth, 1990).

3. RECORD PUBLICATIONS

Calendar of ancient records of Dublin, (ed.) Sir John and Lady Gilbert (19 vols, Dublin, 1889–1944).

Calendar of Home Office papers 1760–75 (4 vols, London, 1878–99).

Calendar of state papers, domestic series, 1603–1704 (84 vols, London, 1857–1972).

Calendar of state papers relating to Ireland, 1603–1703 (22 vols, London, 1860–1910).

Journal of the Commissioners for trade and plantations, 1709–15 (London, 1925).

Journal of the Commissioners for trade and plantations, 1714/15–18 (London, 1924).

Journal of the Commissioners for trade and plantations, 1776–82 (London, 1938).

4. PUBLICATIONS OF THE HISTORICAL MANUSCRIPTS COMMISSION

Buccleuch and Queensbury MSS, ii (London, 1903).

Charlemont MSS (12th Report, appendix 10, and 13th Report, appendix vii) (London, 1891–94).

Donoughmore MSS (12th Report, appendix ix) (London, 1891).

Downshire MSS, i (London, 1924).

Emly MSS (14th Report, appendix 9) (London, 1895).

Eyre Matcham MSS: Reports on various collections, vi (London, 1909).

Fortescue MSS, i (13th Report, appendix 3) (London, 1892).

House of Lords MSS, n.s, x, (London, 1914).

Rutland MSS, iii (London, 1894).

5. PARLIAMENTARY JOURNALS, PROCEEDINGS AND STATUTES

Journal of the House of Commons of the kingdom of Ireland, 1613–1800 (21 vols, Dublin, 1796–1802).

Journal of the House of Lords of the Kingdom of Ireland (8 vols, Dublin, 1782–1800).

[John Almon], *Narrative of proceedings ... in the parliament of Ireland* (London, 1777).

Callen, R.V., 'The structure of Anglo-Irish politics during the American Revolution: Cavendish's diary of the Irish parliament October 12 1779 to September 2 1780: edition of the partial text and a critical essay' (unpublished PhD thesis, University of Notre Dame, 1973).

The parliamentary register, or history of the proceedings and debates of the House of Commons of Ireland (17 vols, Dublin, 1782–1801).

The Statutes at large passed in the parliaments held in Ireland 1310–1800 (20 vols, Dublin, 1789–1800).

6. PAMPHLETS AND OTHER CONTEMPORARY PUBLICATIONS

An account of the revenue and national debt of Ireland, with ... a speech to the parliament of Henry, Lord Viscount Sydney, lord lieutenant, in the year 1692, as also an order of Council, and several resolutions of the House of Commons (London, 1754).

An account of the sessions of parliament in Ireland, 1692 (London, 1693).

An impartial relation of the several arguments of Sir Stephen Rice, Sir Theobald Butler and Councellor Malone at the bar of the House of Commons of Ireland, Feb. 22 and at the bar of the House of Lords, Feb. 28th 1703 ... (Dublin, 1704).

Baratariana: a select collection of fugitive political pieces published during the administration of Lord Townshend in Ireland (3rd ed., Dublin, 1777).

Biographical, literary and political anecdotes of several of the most eminent persons of the present age (3 vols, London, 1797).

[Browne, John], *Reflections upon the present unhappy circumstances of Ireland in a letter to ... the lord archbishop of Cashel* (Dublin, 1731)

The Cabinet, containing a collection of curious papers relative to the present political contests in Ireland (London, 1754).

The case of the Roman Catholicks of Ireland, in relation to a bill intituled an act for securing the Protestant interest of this kingdom by further amending the several acts of parliament made against papists, and to prevent the growth of popery ... [Dublin, 1709].

A collection of the protests of the Lords of Ireland from the first upon record to the end of the session in March 1770 (London, 1771).

Dobbs, Francis, *A history of Irish affairs from the 12th October 1779 to the 15th September 1782* (Dublin, 1782).

Ferrar, John, *The history of Limerick* (Dublin, 1787).

French, Robert, *The constitution of Ireland and Poynings' Law explained* (Dublin, 1770)

[Grattan, Henry], *A letter on the nature and tendency of the Whig Club and of the Irish party* (Dublin, 1791).

Harris, Walter, (ed.) *Hibernica* (Dublin, 1747–50).

Henry, William, *An appeal to the people of Ireland ...* (Dublin, 1749).

Howard, Gorges Edmond, *Miscellaneous works in verse and prose* (3 vols, Dublin, 1782).

[Jebb, Frederic], *The letters of Guatimozin on the affairs of Ireland* (Dublin, 1779).

[Knox, William], *Extra official state papers* (2 vols, London, 1789).

A letter to the right hon. J[ohn] P[onsonby], speaker of the H[ouse] of C[ommons] of Ireland (Dublin, 1767).

Lodge, John, *The usage of holding parliaments, and of preparing and passing bills of supply in Ireland* (Dublin, 1770).

[Lucas, Charles], *To the right honourable the lord-mayor, the aldermen, sheriffs, commons, citizens and freeholders of Dublin, the address of Charles Lucas* (Dublin, 1765).

[Lucas, Charles], *A second address to the lord-mayor, the aldermen, sheriffs, commons, citizens and freeholders of Dublin from Charles Lucas* (Dublin, 1766).

Lucas, Charles, *The rights and privileges of parliament asserted upon constitutional principles ...* (Dublin, 1770).

McAulay, Alexander, *Septennial parliaments vindicated* (Dublin, 1762).

Molyneux, William, *The case of Ireland being bound by acts of parliament in England ... stated* (London, 1770).

[Monck Mason, John] A gentleman of Ireland, *Remarks on Poynings' Law and the manner of passing bills in the parliament of Ireland* (Dublin, 1758).

[Morres, Hervey Redmond], *Plain reasons for new-modelling Poynings' Law in such a manner as to assert the ancient rights of the two houses of parliament* (Dublin, 1780).

[—], *Considerations on the intended modifications of Poynings' Law* (London, 1780).

The policy of Poynings' law fairly explained and considered, with seasonable advice to the people of Ireland (Dublin, 1770).

[Power, Richard], A barrister, *A comparative state of the two rejected money bills in 1692 and 1769, with some observations on Poynings' Law and the explanatory statute of Philip and Mary* (Dublin, 1770).

The representation of the L[ord]s J[ustice]s of Ireland, touching the transmission of a Privy Council money bill previous to the calling of a new parliament in two letters addressed to the duke of Bedford (Dublin, 1770).

[Sheridan, Charles Francis], *A review of the three great national questions relative to a declaration of rights, Poynings' Law and the mutiny bill* (Dublin, 1781).
Sketches of the history of Poynings' Law (Dublin, 1780).

7. NEWSPAPERS AND PERIODICALS

Dublin Gazette, 1707
Dublin Evening Post, 1780, 1786, 1788
Faulkner's Dublin Journal, 1741, 1758
Finn's Leinster Journal, 1773–6
Flying Post, 1707

Freeman's Journal, 1763–80, 1786
Hibernian Journal, 1771–6, 1780
The Postman, 1719
Universal Advertizer, 1760

SECONDARY SOURCES

I. PUBLISHED WORKS

Arnold, L.J., *The Restoration land settlement in County Dublin, 1660–1688: a history of the administration of the acts of settlement and explanation* (Dublin, 1993).
Ball, F.E., 'Some notes on the judges of Ireland in the year 1739', *Journal of the Royal Society of Antiquaries of Ireland*, 34 (1904), 1–19.
Barnard, T.C., 'Planters and policies in Cromwellian Ireland', *Past and Present*, 61 (1973), 31–69.
Bartlett, Thomas, 'Viscount Townshend and the Irish Revenue Board, 1767–73' in *RIA proc.*, 79C (1979), 153–75.
—, 'The Irish House of Commons' rejection of the "Privy Council" money bill of 1769: a reassessment', *Studia Hibernica*, 19 (1979), 63–77.
—, 'The Townshend viceroyalty' in Thomas Bartlett and D.W. Hayton (eds), *Penal era and golden age* (Belfast, 1979), pp 88–112.
—, 'Opposition in late eighteenth-century Ireland: the case of the Townshend viceroyalty' in *IHS*, 22 (1981), 313–30.
—, '"A people rather made for copies than originals": the Anglo-Irish, 1760–1800', *The International History Review*, 12 (1990), 11–25.
Beckett, J.C., 'Anglo-Irish constitutional relations in the later eighteenth century', *IHS*, 14 (1964), 20–38, reprinted in idem, *Confrontations* (London, 1972), pp 123–42.
Beckett, J.C., 'The Irish parliament in the eighteenth century', *Proceedings of the Belfast Natural History and Philosophical Society*, 2nd series, 4 (1951), 17–37.
Bergin, John, 'Poynings' Law in the eighteenth century' in *Pages: postgraduate research in progress* 1 (1994), 9–18.
—, 'The Quaker lobby and its influence on Irish legislation, 1692–1705', *Eighteenth-Century Ireland*, 19 (2004), 9–36.
Bottigheimer, K.S., *English money and Irish land* (Oxford, 1971).
Brewer, John, *Political ideology at the accession of George III* (Cambridge, 1976).
Broderick, David, *The first toll roads: Ireland's turnpike roads, 1729–1858* (Cork, 2002).
Burns, R.E., 'Ireland and British military preparations for war in America in 1775', *Cithara*, 2 (1963), 42–61.
—, *Irish parliamentary politics in the eighteenth century* (2 vols, Washington, 1989–90).
Christie, I.R., *The end of North's ministry, 1780–82* (London, 1958).
Clarke, Aidan, 'The History of Poynings' Law, 1615–41', *IHS*, 18 (1972–3), 207–22.
—, 'Colonial constitutional attitudes in Ireland 1640–60', *RIA proc.*, 90C (1990), 357–75.
—, *Prelude to restoration in Ireland* (Cambridge, 1999).
Colley, Linda, *In defiance of oligarchy: the Tory party 1714–60* (Cambridge, 1982).

Connolly, Sean, *Religion, law and power: the making of Protestant Ireland 1660–1760* (Oxford, 1992).

Conway, Stephen, *The British Isles and the American War of Independence* (Oxford, 2001).

Conway, Agnes, *Henry VII's relations with Scotland and Ireland 1485–1498* (Cambridge, 1932).

Cummins, Seamus, 'Extra-parliamentary agitation in Dublin in the 1760s' in R.V Comerford et al. (eds), *Religion, conflict and coexistence in Ireland* (Dublin, 1990), pp 118–34.

Curtis, Edmund, 'The acts of the Drogheda parliament, 1494–5, or "Poynings' Laws"' in Agnes Conway, *Henry VII's relations with Scotland and Ireland, 1485–1498* (Cambridge, 1932), pp 118–43.

Dickson, Dickson, *New foundations: Ireland, 1660–1800* (2nd ed., Dublin, 2000).

Ditchfield, G.M., 'Lord Thurlow' in R.W. Davis (ed.), *Lords of parliament: studies, 1714–1914* (Stanford, 1995), pp 64–78.

Donaldson, A.G., *Some comparative aspects of Irish law* (London, 1957).

—, 'Methods of applying English legislation in Ireland', *Bulletin of the Irish Committee of Historical Sciences*, no. 67 (1953), 4–5

Edwards, R. Dudley and T.W. Moody, 'The history of Poynings' Law: part 1, 1494–1615', *IHS*, 2 (1940–41), 415–24.

Elliott, Marianne, *Wolfe Tone: prophet of Irish independence* (New Haven, 1989).

Ellis, S.G, *Reform and revival: English government in Ireland, 1470–1534* (Woodbridge and New York, 1986).

Fagan, Patrick, *Catholics in a Protestant country: the papist constituency in eighteenth-century Dublin* (Dublin, 1998).

—, *Ireland in the age of the Tudors, 1447–1603: English expansion and the end of Gaelic rule* (London, 1998).

—, *An Irish bishop in penal times: the chequered career of Sylvester Lloyd OFM* (Dublin, 1993).

—, *Divided loyalties; the question of an oath for Irish Catholics in the eighteenth century* (Dublin, 1997).

Fenning, Hugh, *The Irish Dominican province, 1698–1797* (Dublin, 1990).

Gore-Browne, Robert, *Chancellor Thurlow* (London, 1953).

Greene, Jack P., *Peripheries and Center: constitutional development in the extended polities of the British empire and the United States, 1607–1788* (New York and London, 1990).

Harris, Bob, *Politics and the nation: Britain in the mid-eighteenth century* (Oxford, 2002).

Hayden, Mary, 'The origin and development of heads of bill in the Irish parliament', *Journal of the Royal Society of Antiquaries of Ireland*, 55 (1925), 112–25.

Haydon, Colin, *Anti-Catholicism in eighteenth-century England, c.1714–80: a political and social study* (Manchester, 1993).

Hayton, David, 'The beginnings of the "undertaker" system' in Thomas Bartlett and D.W. Hayton (eds), *Penal era and golden age* (Belfast, 1979), pp 32–54.

—, 'The crisis in Ireland and the disintegration of Queen Anne's last ministry, 1712–14', *IHS*, 22 (1981), 193–215.

—, 'The "country" interest and the party system c.1689–c.1720' in Clyve Jones (ed.), *Party and management in parliament 1660–1784* (Leicester, 1984), pp 37–86.

—, 'Exclusion, conformity and parliamentary representation' in Kevin Herlihy (ed.), *The politics of Irish dissent* (Dublin, 1997), pp 52–73.

—, 'The Stanhope-Sunderland ministry and the repudiation of Irish independence', *EHR*, 103 (1998), 610–36.

—, (ed.), *The Irish parliament in the eighteenth century: the long apprenticeship* (*Parliamentary History*, 20 no. 1 (2001)) (Edinburgh, 2001).

—, 'Ideas of union in Anglo-Irish political discourse, 1692–1720' in D.G. Boyce, Robert Eccleshall and V. Geoghegan (eds), *Political discourse in seventeenth- and eighteenth-century Ireland* (Basingstoke, 2001), pp 142–69.

—, *Ruling Ireland, 1685–1742: politics, politicians and parties* (Woodbridge, 2004).

—, 'Patriots and legislators: Irishmen and their parliaments, *c.*1689–*c.*1740' in Julian Hoppit (ed.), *Parliaments, nations and identities in Britain and Ireland, 1660–1850* (Manchester, 2003), pp 103–23.

Hill, Jacqueline, *From patriots to unionists: Dublin civic politics and Irish Protestant patriotism 1660–1840* (Oxford, 1997).

—, 'Convergence and conflict in eighteenth-century Ireland', *Historical Journal*, 44 (2001), 1039–63.

Hoppit, Julian, *Failed legislation, 1660–1800: extracted from the Commons and Lords journal* (London, 1997).

Horwitz, Henry, *Parliament, policy and politics in the reign of William III* (Manchester, 1977).

James, F.G., *Ireland and the empire, 1688–1770* (Cambridge, MA, 1973).

—, *North County Bishop: a biography of William Nicolson* (New Haven, 1956).

—, 'The Irish lobby in the early eighteenth century', *EHR*, 81 (1966), 543–57.

—, 'Illustrious or notorious? The historical interpretation of Ireland's pre-Union parliament', *Parliamentary Yearbook*, 6 (1987), 312–25.

—, *Lords of the ascendancy: the Irish House of Lords and its members 1600–1800* (Dublin, 1995).

Johnston, E.M., *Great Britain and Ireland 1760–1800: a study in political administration* (Edinburgh, 1963).

—, *Ireland in the eighteenth century* (Dublin, 1974).

Jupp, P.J., 'Earl Temple's viceroyalty and the question of renunciation', *IHS*, 17 (1971), 499–520.

Kelly, James, 'The origins of the Act of Union: an examination of Unionist opinion in Britain and Ireland 1650–1800', *IHS*, 25 (1987), 236–63.

—, *Prelude to Union: Anglo-Irish politics in the 1780s* (Cork, 1992).

—, 'Parliamentary reform in Irish politics, 1760–90' in David Dickson et al. (eds), *The United Irishmen* (Dublin, 1993), pp 74–87.

—, 'The glorious and immortal memory: commemoration and Protestant identity in Ireland, 1660–1800', *RIA proc.*, 94C (1994), pp 25–52.

—, *'That damn'd thing called honour': duelling in Ireland 1570–1860* (Cork, 1995).

—, *Henry Flood: patriots and politics in eighteenth-century Ireland* (Dublin, 1998).

—, '1780 revisited: the politics of the repeal of the test act' in Kevin Herlihy (ed.), *The politics of Irish dissent* (Dublin, 1997), pp 74–92.

—, 'The Act of Union: its origins and background' in Daire Keogh and Kevin Whelan (eds), *Acts of Union* (Dublin, 2001), pp 46–66.

—, 'Monitoring the constitution: the operation of Poynings' Law in the 1760s' in D.W. Hayton (ed.), *The Irish parliament in the eighteenth century: the long apprenticeship (Parliamentary History)*, 20 no. 1 (2001) (Edinburgh, 2001), pp 87–106.

—, 'Public and political opinion in Ireland and the idea of an Anglo-Irish union, 1650–1800' in D.G. Boyce et al. (eds), *Political discourse in seventeenth and eighteenth-century Ireland* (Basingstoke, 2001), pp 110–41.

—, *Sir Edward Newenham MP, 1734–1814: the life and politics of a radical Protestant* (Dublin, 2004).

—, 'The making of law in eighteenth-century Ireland: the significance and import of Poynings' Law' in Norma Dawson (ed.), *Reflections on law and history* (Dublin, 2006), pp 259–77.

—, 'Political publishing, 1700–1800', in Raymond Gillespie and Andrew Hadfield (eds), *The Oxford History of the Irish book, vol. 3: the Irish book in English, 1550–1800* (Oxford, 2006), pp 215–33.

Kelly, P.H., 'The Irish woollen export prohibition act of 1699: Kearney revisited', *Irish Economic and Social History*, 7 (1980), 22–44.

Kennedy, Denis, 'The Irish Whigs, administrative reform and responsible government, 1782–1800', *Eire-Ireland*, 8 (1973), 55–69.

Little, Patrick, 'The first unionists?: Irish Protestant attitudes to union with England, 1653–9', *IHS*, 32 (2000), 44–58.

McCarthy, Muriel, *All graduates and gentlemen: Marsh's Library* (Dublin, 1980).

McDonagh, Michael, 'The journals of the Irish parliament', *Irish Ecclesiastical Record*, 10 (1917), 289–301.

McDowell, R.B., *Ireland in the age of imperialism and revolution, 1761–1800* (Oxford, 1979).

McDowell, R.B., 'Colonial nationalism and the winning of parliamenary independence 1760–82' in T.W. Moody and W.E. Vaughan (eds), *A new history of Ireland: iv* (Oxford, 1986), pp 196–235.

Magennis, Eoin, *The Irish political system, 1740–65: the golden age of the undertakers* (Dublin, 2000).

—, 'In search of the moral economy: food scarcity in 1756–7 and the crowd' in P.J. Jupp and E. Magennis (eds), *Crowds in Ireland, c. 1720–1920* (Basingstoke, 2000), pp 189–211.

—, 'Coal, corn and canals: the dispersal of public moneys, 1695–1772' in D.W. Hayton (ed.), *The Irish parliament in the eighteenth century: the long apprenticeship* (Edinburgh, 2001), pp 71–86.

McGrath, Charles Ivar, *The making of the eighteenth-century Irish constitution: government, parliament and the revenue 1692–1714* (Dublin, 2000).

—, 'Securing the Protestant interest: the origins and purpose of the penal laws of 1695', *IHS*, 30 (1996), pp 25–46.

—, 'Central aspects of the eighteenth-century constitutional framework in Ireland: the government supply bill and biennial parliamentary sessions, 1715–82', *Eighteenth-Century Ireland*, 16 (2001), 9–34.

—, 'English ministers, Irish politicians and the making of a parliamentary settlement in Ireland, 1692–5', *EHR*, 119 (2004), 585–613.

McGuire, James, 'The Irish parliament of 1692' in Thomas Bartlett and D.W. Hayton (eds), *Penal era and golden age* (Belfast, 1979), pp 1–31.

—, 'Bishop Michael Boyle' (unpublished paper, 2004).

McNally, Patrick, *Parties, patriots and undertakers: parliamentary politics in early Hanoverian Ireland* (Dublin, 1997).

—, 'The Hanoverian accession and the Tory party in Ireland', *Parliamentary History*, 14 (1995), 263–83.

McParland, Edward, 'Strategy in the planning of Dublin 1750–1800' in L.M. Cullen and P. Butel (eds), *Cities and merchants* (Dublin, 1986), pp 97–108.

Malcomson, A.P.W., 'The Newtown act of 1748: revision and reconstruction', *IHS*, 18 (1972–3), pp 313–44.

—, *Archbishop Charles Agar: churchmanship and politics in Ireland, 1760–1800* (Dublin, 2002).

Melikan, R.A., 'Mr Attorney General and the politicians', *Historical Journal*, 40 (1997), 41–69.

Middleton, Richard, *Colonial America* (Oxford, 1992).

Miller, John, 'William III: the English view' in Bernadette Whelan (ed.), *Essays on the war of the three kings in Ireland* (Limerick, 1995), pp 17–38.

Morley, Vincent, *Irish opinion and the American Revolution, 1760–83* (Cambridge, 2002).

Munter, Robert, *The history of the Irish newspaper 1685–1760* (Cambridge, 1966).

O'Brien, Gerard, *Anglo-Irish politics in the age of Grattan and Pitt* (Dublin, 1987).

O'Malley, Liam, 'Patrick Darcy, Galway lawyer and politician, 1598–1668' in Diarmuid Ó Cearbhaill (ed.), *Galway: town and gown, 1484–1984* (Dublin, 1984), pp 90–109.

O'Regan, Philip, *Archbishop William King of Dublin (1650–1729) and the constitution in church and state* (Dublin, 2000).

Ó Siochrú, Mícheál, *Confederate Ireland 1642–1649: a constitutional and political analysis* (Dublin, 1999).

—, 'Catholic Confederates and the constitutional relationship between Ireland and England, 1641–49' in Ciaran Brady and Jane Ohlmeyer (eds), *British interventions in early modern Ireland* (Cambridge, 2005), pp 207–29.

Otway-Ruthven, Jocelyn, *A history of medieval Ireland* (London, 1968).

Pole, J.R., *Political representation in England and the origins of the American Republic* (New York, 1966).

Powell, M.J., 'The reform of the undertaker system: Anglo-Irish politics 1750–67', *IHS*, 31 (1998–9), 19–36.
—, *Britain and Ireland in the eighteenth-century crisis of empire* (Basingstoke, 2002).
Quinn, D.B., 'The early interpretation of Poynings' Law, 1494–1534', *IHS*, 2 (1940–41), 241–54.
Reid, John Philip, *Constitutional history of the American revolution* (3 vols, Madison, 1986–91).
Richardson H.G. and G.O. Sayles, *The Irish parliament in the middle ages* (Philadelphia, 1952).
Roberts, Clayton, 'The constitutional significance of the financial settlement of 1690', *Historical Journal*, 20 (1977), 59–76.
Russell, Conrad, 'The British background to the Irish rebellion of 1641', *Bulletin of the Institute of Historical Research*, 61 (1988), 166–82.
Russell, E.B., *The review of American colonial legislation by the King in Council* (New York, 1915).
Simms, J.G., *The Williamite confiscation in Ireland, 1690–1703* (London, 1956).
—, 'The making of a penal law (2 Anne, c. 6), 1703–04', *IHS*, 12 (1960), 105–18.
—, *Jacobite Ireland, 1685–91* (London, 1969).
—, 'The Bishops' Banishment act of 1697 (9 Will. III, c.1)', *IHS*, 17 (1970), 185–99.
—, *Colonial nationalism* (Cork, 1976).
—, *The Jacobite parliament of 1689* (Dundalk, 1974).
—et al. (eds), *War and politics in Ireland, 1649–1730* (London, 1986).
—, 'The Irish parliament of 1713' in J.G. Simms et al. (eds), *War and politics in Ireland, 1649–1730* (London, 1986), pp 277–88.
Small, Stephen, *Political thought in Ireland, 1776–1800* (Oxford, 2002).
Tierney, Mark, *Murroe and Boher: the history of an Irish country parish* (Dublin, 1966).
Turner, Edward Raymond, *The Privy Council of England in the seventeenth and eighteenth centuries, 1603–1784* (2 vols, Baltimore, 1927).
Troost, Wouter, 'William III and religious tolerance' in Bernadette Whelan (ed.), *Essays in the war of the three kings* (Limerick, 1995), pp 39–54.
—, *William III and the treaty of Limerick, 1690–97* (Leiden, 1983).
Victory, Isolde, 'The making of the Declaratory' in Gerard O'Brien, *Parliament, politics and people: essays in eighteenth-century Irish history* (Dublin, 1989), pp 9–29.
Wall, Maureen, *The Penal Laws, 1691–1760* (Dundalk, 1976)
Wauchope, Piers, *Patrick Sarsfield and the Williamite war* (Dublin, 1992).
Wilkinson, 'How did they pass the union? Secret service expenditure', *History*, 82 (1997), 223–51.
York, Neil Longly, *Neither kingdom nor nation: the Irish quest for constitutional rights* (Washington, 1994).

UNPUBLISHED THESES

Aydelotte, James E., 'The duke of Ormonde and the English government of Ireland, 1678–85' (PhD, University of Iowa, 1975).
Cummins, Seamus, 'Opposition and the Irish parliament 1759–71' (MA, St Patrick's College, Maynooth, 1978).
Dennehy, Coleman, 'Parliament in Ireland, 1661–6' (MLitt, UCD, 2002).
Donaldson, A.G., 'The application in Ireland of English and British legislation made before 1801' (PhD, QUB, 1952).
Doyle, Thomas G., 'The politics of Protestant ascendancy: politics, religion and society in Protestant Ireland, 1700–10' (PhD, UCD, 1996).
Fitzgerald, P.D., 'Poverty and vagrancy in early modern Ireland 1540–1770' (PhD, QUB, 1994).
Hayton, David, 'Ireland and the English ministers, 1707–16' (DPhil, Oxford University, 1975).
Lammey, David, 'A study of Anglo-Irish relations between 1772 and 1782 with particular reference to the "free trade" movement' (PhD, QUB, 1984).

McCoy, Gerald, 'Local political culture in the Hanoverian empire: the case of Ireland, 1714–1760' (DPhil, Oxford University, 1994).

McGeehin, Maureen, 'The activities and personnel of the General Committee of the Catholics of Ireland, 1767–84' (MA, UCD, 1952).

McGrath, C.I., 'Securing the Protestant interest: policy, politics and parliament in Ireland in the aftermath of the Glorious Revolution, 1690–95' (MA, UCD, 1991).

McNally, Patrick, 'Patronage and politics in Ireland, 1714 to 1727' (PhD, QUB, 1993).

O'Donoghue, Fergus, 'Parliament in Ireland under Charles II' (MA, UCD, 1970).

WORKS OF REFERENCE

Corish, P.J. and David Sheehy, *Records of the Irish Catholic Church* (Dublin, 2001).

Hayes, R.J., *Manuscript sources for the history of Irish civilisation* (11 vols, Boston, 1965).

Johnston-Liik, E.M., *History of the Irish parliament, 1692–1800* (6 vols, Belfast, 2002).

List and Index Society, *Privy Council office: list of unbound papers preserved in the Public Record Office* (3 vols, London, 1967–8).

Namier, Lewis and John Brooke (eds), *History of parliament: the House of Commons, 1754–90* (3 vols, London, 1964).

Moody, T.W., et al. (eds), *A new history of Ireland: ix* (Oxford, 1984).

Index

compiled by Julitta Clancy, Fellow of the Society of Indexers

The Irish Legal History Society

(www.irishlegalhistorysociety.com)

Established in 1988 to encourage the study and advance the knowledge of the history of Irish law, especially by the publication of original documents and of works relating to the history of Irish law, including its institutions, doctrines and personalities, and the reprinting or editing of works of sufficient rarity or importance.